Milk Street is changing how we cook by
searching the world for bold, simple recipes.
Adapted for home cooks everywhere,
this is what we call the *new* home cooking.

CHRISTOPHER KIMBALL'S

MILK STREET

CHRISTOPHER KIMBALL

THE
MILK STREET
COOKBOOK

The Definitive Guide to the New Home Cooking
With Every Recipe from Every Episode of the TV Show
2017 to 2022

Christopher Kimball

WRITING AND EDITING BY
J. M. Hirsch and Michelle Locke

RECIPES BY
Matthew Card, Diane Unger and the Cooks at Milk Street

ART DIRECTION BY
Jennifer Baldino Cox and Brianna Coleman

VORACIOUS
LITTLE, BROWN AND COMPANY
NEW YORK   BOSTON   LONDON

Little, Brown and Company
Hachette Book Group
1290 Avenue of the Americas, New York, NY 10104
littlebrown.com

Revised and Expanded Edition: September 2021

Voracious is an imprint of Little, Brown and Company, a division of Hachette Book Group, Inc.
The Voracious name and logo are trademarks of Hachette Book Group, Inc.

The publisher is not responsible for websites (or their content) that are not owned by the publisher.

The Hachette Speakers Bureau provides a wide range of authors for speaking events. To find out more, go to hachettespeakersbureau.com or call (866) 376-6591.

Photography Credits: Connie Miller of CB Creatives except as noted by page: Channing Johnson, pages V-XIII, 658, 679; Christopher Kimball, pages XIV, XVII (bottom right), XIX (top and bottom left), XX; Christopher Ward-Jones, pages XVII (top and bottom left), XVIII, XIX (bottom right), XXI; Albert Stumm, page XIX (top right); Kristin Teig, pages 2, 182, 650, 657; Brian Samuels, pages 28, 80, 149, 287, 347, 348, 359, 485, 508, 527, 624; Heidi Murphy of White Loft Studios, page 41; Michael Piazza, pages 54, 105, 480, 597; Joyelle West, pages 133, 139, 657; Jennifer Baldino Cox, page 681.

Food Styling Credits: Christine Tobin except as noted by page: Catrine Kelty, pages 2, 41, 46, 50, 56, 102, 105, 109, 134, 176, 182, 253, 328, 336, 471, 472, 478, 480, 481, 483, 594, 597, 618; Molly Shuster, pages 11, 49, 184, 227, 383, 504, 616; Catherine Smart, pages 51, 111, 116, 117, 142, 158, 161, 165, 199, 292, 338, 384-385, 404, 406, 515; Monica Mariano, pages 246, 249, 487; Sally Staub, page 553.

ISBN 978-0-316-25980-4
LCCN 2021936259
10 9 8 7 6 5 4 3 2 1

IM

Print book interior design by Gary Tooth / Empire Design Studio
Printed in China

*This book is dedicated to the
notion that cooking is the universal language
of the human spirit.*

Contents

Vegetables / 103

Savory Bakes / 433

Desserts / 469

Small Sweets / 583

In the Italian hilltop village of Monteveglio, we met Paolo Parmeggiani of Trattoria del Borgo who prepared passatelli in brodo.

THE NEW HOME COOKING

Monteveglio is a small village on top of a mountain 12 miles west of Bologna. There are cobblestone streets and stone houses, and it's closed to traffic. It could easily double as a movie set; the one that offers the "authentic" rural Italian experience. Remains of Roman villas date back to the 1st century, though the area has been inhabited since the Neolithic period. There are two main attractions: the pieve, or rural church that has a baptistery, and our main destination, a small restaurant/hotel called Trattoria del Borgo. The church sits at the very top of the summit, a monk in classic Hollywood garb (brown robe; rope belt) is mowing the lawn, smiling to the occasional tourist, but oblivious to their coming and going.

The trattoria's owner, Paolo Parmeggiani, is thoroughly modern in the Italian style: affable, charming and the consummate host. On his stone patio overlooking the valley, he explained some of the culinary history of the region. After the wheat was harvested, fields would be burned and any remaining wheat berries would be gathered by the poor (hence the term, farina dei poveri). A related term, cucina povera, is an important concept in Italy. It combines a style of cooking that is authentic, local and from the land. Other common culinary terms are cucina espressa and cucina immediata, which also describe passatelli, the quick homemade pasta dish we are about to make, a mixture of breadcrumbs, eggs and grated cheese, passed through a potato ricer into boiling water and served with chicken broth.

Paolo had three bowls prepared, one filled with breadcrumbs, one with eggs, and the other with finely grated Parmesan. (Parmigiano-Reggiano is made in Emilia-Romagna and so it works itself into almost every dish.) I asked about the recipe and was told that one used six handfuls each of breadcrumbs and cheese plus eggs as binder. He mixed by hand, which took just minutes, until he had a soft dough which was placed into a metal potato ricer, extruded over boiling water, cut into short lengths with a knife, and cooked for a few minutes, like spaetzle. The only other ingredient besides salt was nutmeg which, oddly enough, made all the difference, adding just enough interest to provide character. Passatelli is served in a bowl with chicken stock and, if you are in Emilia-Romagna in the fall, copious shavings of modestly-priced white truffles. It was one of the best dishes of my life. Also the fastest.

This was just one of the lessons learned from Milk Street Television, but perhaps the most important. Simplicity of preparation is something to be honored since it reflects an understanding of ingredients and technique and a true appreciation for the culinary arts. What you put into a recipe—familiarity rather than extravagant technique—is the measure of what you get out of it. And, in the case of passatelli, the reward is great indeed.

This lesson was repeated in Mexico City with Eduardo García, who cooked a pot of beans on a chinampa (a floating island) in the canals of southern Mexico City, only accessible by boat. A sofrito of onions, chilies, tomatoes and garlic was added at the end of cooking to preserve the fresh flavor. A chili salsa was thrown together using the bottom of a beer glass as the pestle. And since we had no spoons, we used rolled-up blue corn tortillas and drank beer out of caguamas (large bottles). Thousands of miles traveled for a pot of beans. And it was worth every mile of the journey.

Other travels took us to northern Israel. We learned Palestinian cooking with Reem Kassis, author of "The Palestinian Table." She invited us into her parents' home for a feast of maqlubeh (a spiced rice and meat casserole with fried vegetables) with as many dishes as there were friends and relatives at the table. On a tour of the Galilee Valley, we also tasted maftool, an Arab pasta, similar to couscous, that was cooked with onions and chicken; ka'ak asfar, a sweet turmeric-colored bread with ground nigella and sesame seeds; smeediyeh, fine bulgur mixed with caramelized onions and greens, including dandelion, mallow, and purslane; hashweh (the word means stuffing), a mix of rice and meat with allspice, cinnamon and nutmeg; freekeh, smoked wheat berries, cracked and dried, often served as a pilaf; and a fragrant rose petal jam that her mother makes and serves over a simple cornstarch pudding.

Travel changes one's perception of what food is. It's not exotic or something to be worshipped; it's simply what others around the world are making for dinner. And what joins all of us together around the table is a universal love of hospitality and a familiarity with our ingredients, our techniques and our recipes. This transforms the kitchen into a place of generational continuity and comity as opposed to the professional kitchen, which too often is bathed in tears and sweat.

At long last, cooking does not come from a book or a television show. It comes from the very hearts of our being, stretched out through our arms, connected to the past, into the warm, earth-plucked ingredients and then into skillets and ovens.

We are preparing food from the past and into our future, and that is the greatest cooking lesson of all.

Christopher Kimball
Founder, Christopher Kimball's Milk Street

Clockwise from top: On Đương Nguyen Hue, the highway leading out of Ho Chi Minh City, informal shops brewing and selling potent ruou đe rice wine are common; Milk Street visited Reem Kassis and her family in the Galilee Valley to get a first-hand cooking lesson in Palestinian food; The Aceto family has farmed lemons on the hills of Amalfi for six generations.

Facing page: Antonio Fiore's grandfather opened Paneficio Fiore focaccia shop in Bari, Italy, in 1940. Clockwise from top left: Eduardo García of Mexico City's Máximo Bistrot prepares beans on one of the city's chinampas; Roberto Góis spears cubes of beef onto the branch of a laurel tree for espetada, a specialty of the Portuguese island of Madeira that perfumes the meat as it grills over smoldering charcoal; Tigist Chane prepared doro wat, Ethiopia's national dish; Pilar Cabrera on the rooftop of her restaurant, La Olla in Oaxaca.

Facing page: Minerva Daoud prepares maftool at the Ezba Restaurant she runs with her husband, Habib, in Israel's Galilee Valley.
Above: In Ho Chi Minh City, Nguyên Thị Thúy prepares bò kho, a fragrant, brothy beef stew.

Eggs

1

Fluffy Olive Oil Scrambled Eggs

Start to finish: **10 minutes** / Servings: 4

We'd never questioned the French rule that butter is best for cooking eggs. But then we noticed that chefs at hotel breakfast stations use oil to make omelets in carbon-steel pans. Likewise, the Chinese cook their well-seasoned, well-browned omelets in oil, as do the Japanese. But scrambled eggs? As a test, we heated olive oil until just smoking and poured in whisked eggs. Whoosh! In a quick puff of steam, we had light, fluffy eggs. The oil needed a full 3 minutes at medium heat to get hot enough. Higher temperatures cooked the eggs too fast, toughening them. Two tablespoons of oil was enough to coat the bottom of the skillet and flavor the eggs without making them greasy. We like our scrambled eggs particularly wet and not entirely cooked through, which takes just 30 seconds. Leave them a little longer for drier eggs. Either way, take them off the heat before they are fully cooked and let them rest on a warm plate for 30 seconds. They finish cooking off the heat. Mixing the salt into the eggs before cooking is the best way to season them.

Don't warm your plates too much. It sounds minor, but hot plates will continue to cook the eggs, making them tough and dry. Cold plates will cool the eggs too fast. The plates should be warm to the touch, but not so hot that you can't comfortably hold them.

2 tablespoons extra-virgin olive oil

8 large eggs

Kosher salt and ground black pepper

1. In a 12-inch nonstick or seasoned carbon-steel skillet over medium, heat the oil until just starting to smoke, about 3 minutes. While the oil heats, in a bowl, use a fork to whisk the eggs and ¾ teaspoon salt until blended and foamy. Pour the eggs into the center of the pan.

2. Using a silicone spatula, continuously stir the eggs, pushing them toward the middle as they set at the edges and folding the cooked egg over on itself. Cook until just set, 60 to 90 seconds. The curds should be shiny, wet and soft, but not translucent or runny. Immediately transfer to warmed plates. Season with salt and pepper.

SUNNY-SIDE UP FRIED EGGS

Start to finish: **8 minutes** / Makes 4 eggs

Hot oil gave us the best scrambled eggs, but fried eggs turned out to be a different game. Here, butter truly was better; oil produced tough, greasy fried eggs. Every stovetop has a different low setting, and skillets vary in thickness and heat conductivity. It may take a few attempts to determine the best timing for your equipment. For us, 3 minutes was perfect for completely set whites and thick but runny yolks. If you like very loose yolks, shave off a minute; for lightly browned whites and firm yolks, add a minute. To make 2 eggs, use an 8-inch skillet and 2 teaspoons of butter.

Don't break the yolks when cracking the eggs into the bowl.
If you're not confident in your egg-cracking skills, break the eggs one at a time into a small bowl before combining them.

4 large eggs

1 tablespoon salted butter

Kosher salt and ground black pepper

Heat a 10-inch nonstick skillet over low for 3 minutes. Crack the eggs into a bowl. Add the butter to the hot pan and swirl until melted. When the butter stops foaming, slowly pour the eggs into the skillet. If necessary, gently nudge the yolks with a wooden spoon to space them evenly in the pan.

Working quickly, season the eggs with salt and pepper, then cover the skillet and cook until the whites are completely set and the yolks are bright yellow, about 3 minutes. Slide out of the pan and onto plates.

Turkish Scrambled Eggs with Spicy Tomato and Capers (Menemen)

Start to finish: **20 minutes** / Servings: 4

___

4 tablespoons extra-virgin olive oil, divided, plus more to serve

2 poblano chilies, stemmed, seeded and finely chopped

1 bunch scallions, thinly sliced

3 medium garlic cloves, minced

1 tablespoon Aleppo pepper or ½ teaspoon red pepper flakes (see headnote)

Kosher salt and ground white pepper

1 plum tomato, cored and finely chopped

2 tablespoons drained capers

8 large eggs

⅓ cup crumbled feta cheese

3 tablespoons chopped fresh dill

Poblano chilies are Mexican in heritage, but their earthy flavor and mild heat make them ideal for this version of Turkish-style scrambled eggs. Using Aleppo pepper nudges the dish closer to the traditional flavor profile, but if you don't have any, regular red pepper flakes work, too. Serve on warmed plates to prevent the eggs from cooling too quickly. Round out the meal with crisp slices of toast.

Don't wait until the eggs are firm and fully set before removing the pan from the heat; the eggs continue to cook in the time it takes to portion and serve.

___

1. In a 12-inch nonstick skillet over medium, heat 2 tablespoons of oil until shimmering. Add the poblanos, scallions, garlic, Aleppo pepper and ½ teaspoon each salt and white pepper. Cover and cook, stirring, until the chilies are softened but not browned, 6 to 8 minutes. Transfer to a medium bowl and stir in the tomato and capers; set aside. Wipe out the skillet.

2. In a medium bowl, whisk the eggs and ¾ teaspoon salt. Return the skillet to medium and heat the remaining 2 tablespoons oil until shimmering. Pour the eggs into the center of the pan.

3. Using a silicone spatula, continuously stir the eggs, pushing them toward the middle as they set at the edges and folding the cooked egg over on itself. Cook until just set, about 1½ minutes. The curds should be shiny, wet and soft. Taste and season with salt and pepper, then divide among warmed serving plates.

4. Top each serving with a portion of the poblano mixture. Sprinkle with feta and dill, then drizzle with oil.

Deep-Dish Quiche with Mushrooms, Bacon and Gruyère

Start to finish: 1½ hours (40 minutes active),
plus cooling / Servings: 8 to 10

2 tablespoons salted butter

1 medium yellow onion, finely chopped

12 ounces cremini mushrooms, trimmed, halved and thinly sliced

Kosher salt and ground black pepper

½ cup dry white wine

6 large eggs

1 cup crème fraîche

1½ cups heavy cream

⅛ teaspoon cayenne pepper

⅛ teaspoon grated nutmeg

All-purpose flour, for dusting

Pastry for deep-dish quiche, shaped into a disk and chilled (recipe follows; see headnote for using purchased dough)

6 ounces sliced Canadian bacon, cut into ¼-inch pieces

2 tablespoons finely chopped fresh tarragon

6 ounces Gruyère cheese, shredded (1½ cups)

At Le Pichet, a French brasserie in Seattle, Washington, we rekindled our love for quiche. This recipe is based on the restaurant's formula for creating a quiche that's tall and creamy, yet light and richly flavored. The key is crème fraîche in addition to the heavy cream, along with just the right number of eggs. Baking the quiche on a hot baking steel (or baking stone) obviates the need to prebake the crust (a hassle with most quiche recipes), as the heat from the steel helps brown the bottom crust, thereby staving off sogginess. We're fond of buttery homemade pastry, but if you wish to take a shortcut, stack two refrigerated pie crusts on top of each other, then fold into quarters. Press the dough layers together, shape into a 6-inch disk, wrap tightly in plastic and refrigerate for at least 1 hour. Roll out the dough and line the tart pan or pie plate following the recipe below for pastry for deep-dish quiche.

Don't slice the quiche while it's warm. Allow it to cool to room temperature or, better yet, refrigerate it, covered, for at least six hours or up to two days before slicing. If refrigerated, slice it while chilled, then bring to room temperature before serving. If you prefer to serve it warm, place individual slices on a parchment-lined rimmed baking sheet and heat in a 450°F oven for 8 to 10 minutes.

1. About 1 hour before baking, heat the oven to 450°F with a baking steel or stone on the middle rack. In a nonstick 12-inch skillet over medium-high, melt the butter. Add the onion, mushrooms and ½ teaspoon salt, then cook, stirring occasionally, until the liquid released by the mushrooms has evaporated, the onions are softened and the mixture browns, 12 to 15 minutes. Add the wine and cook, stirring, until fully evaporated, about 3 minutes. Transfer to a medium bowl and cool completely.

2. Meanwhile, in a large bowl, whisk the eggs. Add the crème fraîche and whisk until thoroughly combined. Add the cream, cayenne, nutmeg, ¼ teaspoon salt and ½ teaspoon black pepper, then whisk until well blended. Cover and refrigerate until ready to use.

3. Lightly flour the counter. Mist a 9-inch-round by 2-inch-deep tart pan with a removable bottom or a deep-dish glass pie plate with cooking spray. Unwrap the pastry disk and set it on the floured surface. If the dough is too firm to roll, let it stand for 10 to 20 minutes. Dust the surface of the dough with flour and, using a rolling pin, roll it to a 14-inch round about ⅛ inch thick, rotating often and dusting with flour as needed to prevent sticking.

4. Fold the dough round in half, then in half again, forming a wedge. Transfer the dough to the tart pan or pie plate, positioning the tip of the wedge at the center. Unfold the dough, then carefully ease it into the corners and up the sides of the pan or plate, allowing the excess to extend past the edge. If using a tart pan, roll the rolling pin across the top of the pan to trim off the excess dough, then set the pan on a large plate (so the pan is easier to handle); if using a pie plate, fold and crimp the edges of the dough. Refrigerate uncovered for at least 1 hour or cover and refrigerate up to 1 day.

5. Stir the bacon and tarragon into the cooled mushroom mixture. Distribute the mixture evenly in the chilled pastry, then top with the cheese. Set the tart pan or pie plate on a rimmed baking sheet. Slowly pour in the egg-cream mixture, allowing it to seep in; the pan will be very full. Carefully slide the baking sheet onto the hot baking steel, then immediately reduce the oven to 350°F. Bake until the quiche jiggles slightly at only the center, 55 to 65 minutes (the center should reach 165°F to 170°F); lay a sheet of foil over the quiche if the surface browns too much.

6. Transfer the quiche from the baking sheet directly to a wire rack and cool until barely warm to the touch, about 2 hours. If you've used a tart pan, carefully remove the outer ring, then return the quiche (still on the pan bottom) to the rack. Cool completely.

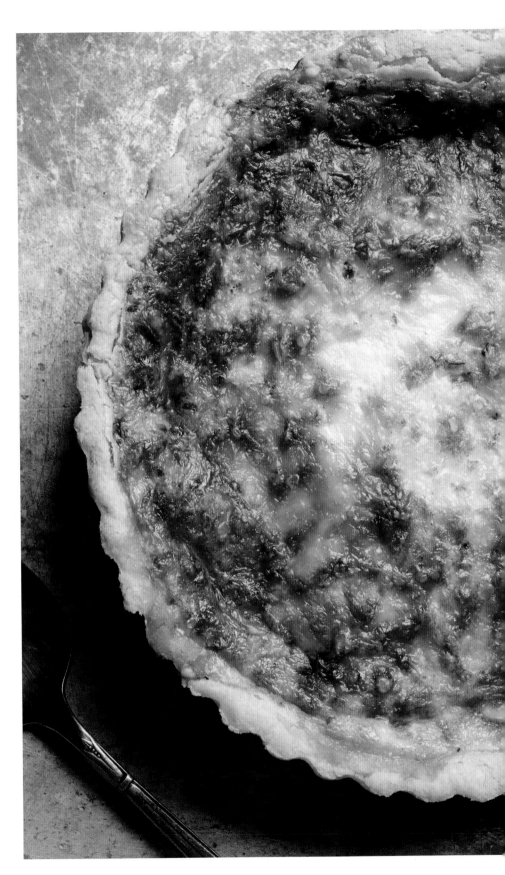

PASTRY FOR DEEP-DISH QUICHE

Start to finish: 2½ hours (25 minutes active)
Makes **one 9-inch-round deep-dish pastry**

We highly recommend using a 9-inch-round and 2-inch-deep metal tart pan with fluted sides and a removable bottom. The metal is a good conductor of heat so the crust browns nicely, even without prebaking. A deep-dish glass pie plate (such as Pyrex) will get the job done, but the crust will not brown as well.

Don't forget to freeze the flour-butter mixture for 10 minutes before processing. This helps the ingredients remain cold as they're mixed so the dough is easier to handle and the crust bakes up tender. If the flour-butter mixture is in the freezer for longer than 10 minutes, the butter will be extra-firm, so the processing time will likely need to be extended.

245 grams (1¾ cups plus 2 tablespoons) all-purpose flour, plus more for dusting

¾ teaspoon table salt

12 tablespoons (1½ sticks) cold salted butter, cut into ½-inch cubes

5 tablespoons ice water

1. In a medium bowl, whisk together the flour and salt. Add the butter and toss, separating any stuck-together cubes, until evenly coated. Freeze uncovered for 10 minutes.

2. Transfer the chilled flour-butter mixture to a food processor. Pulse until the butter chunks are about the size of peas, 10 to 12 pulses. Add the water and process until the mixture forms clumps but does not come together in a ball, 20 to 25 seconds.

3. Turn the dough out onto the counter and press it into a disk about 6 inches wide. Wrap tightly in plastic, smoothing out any ragged edges. Refrigerate for at least 1 hour or up to 2 days.

DEEP-DISH QUICHE WITH SWISS CHARD, ROASTED PEPPERS AND CHEDDAR

Follow the recipe to heat the oven and baking steel. In a 12-inch nonstick skillet over medium, melt **1 tablespoon salted butter**. Add **1 bunch Swiss chard** (both stems and leaves, chopped) and cook, stirring occasionally, until the liquid released has evaporated, about 5 minutes. Transfer to a plate and cool, then wrap in a kitchen towel and squeeze to remove excess moisture. In the same pan over medium, melt **2 tablespoons salted butter**. Add **1 medium yellow onion** (finely chopped) and **½ teaspoon kosher salt**, then cook, stirring occasionally, until translucent, about 5 minutes. Stir in **½ cup roasted red peppers** (patted dry and chopped), **2 tablespoons chopped fresh oregano** and the chard. Cook, stirring, until the oregano is fragrant, about 2 minutes. Transfer to a plate and cool completely. Meanwhile, follow the recipe to mix the egg-cream mixture and prepare the pastry. Distribute the chard mixture evenly in the chilled pastry, then top with **6 ounces shredded extra-sharp cheddar cheese** (1½ cups) and set the pan on a rimmed baking sheet. Continue with the recipe to pour in the egg-cream mixture and bake and cool the quiche.

DEEP-DISH QUICHE WITH SAUSAGE, FENNEL AND ASIAGO

Follow the recipe to heat the oven and baking steel. In a 12-inch nonstick skillet over medium, melt **1 tablespoon salted butter**. Add **8 ounces sweet Italian sausage** (casing removed) and cook, stirring to break up the meat, until no longer pink, about 5 minutes. Add **1 medium red onion** (halved and thinly sliced), **1 large fennel bulb** (trimmed, halved and thinly sliced) and **½ teaspoon kosher salt**. Cook, stirring occasionally, until the vegetables are softened, about 7 minutes. Off heat, stir in **¼ cup chopped fresh basil**. Transfer to a plate and let cool completely. Meanwhile, follow the recipe to mix the egg-cream mixture. Distribute the sausage mixture evenly in the chilled pastry, then top with **6 ounces shredded Asiago cheese** (1½ cups) and set the pan on a rimmed baking sheet. Continue with the recipe to pour in the egg-cream mixture and bake and cool the quiche.

HOW TO ROLL PASTRY FOR A DEEP-DISH QUICHE

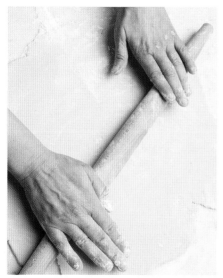

Dust the surface of the dough with flour and, using a rolling pin, roll it to a 14-inch round about ⅛ inch thick, rotating often and dusting with flour as needed to prevent sticking.

Fold the dough round in half, then in half again, forming a wedge.

Transfer the dough to the oiled tart pan or pie plate, positioning the tip of the wedge at the center.

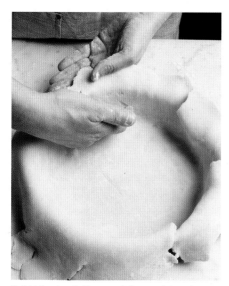

Unfold the dough, then carefully ease it into the edges and up the sides of the pan or plate, allowing the excess to extend over the edge.

Roll the rolling pin across the top of the pan to trim off the excess dough,

Curry Braised Eggs

Start to finish: 1 hour 15 minutes (50 minutes active)
Servings: 4

3 tablespoons grapeseed or other neutral oil

1 large yellow onion, halved and thinly sliced lengthwise

Kosher salt and ground black pepper

2 tablespoons finely grated fresh ginger

4 teaspoons garam masala

1 teaspoon ground turmeric

¼ teaspoon cayenne pepper

Three 14½-ounce cans diced tomatoes, drained

13½-ounce can coconut milk

1 tablespoon packed brown sugar

1 tablespoon lime juice, plus lime wedges to serve

8 large eggs

⅓ cup chopped fresh cilantro

Steamed basmati rice, naan or boiled potatoes, to serve (optional)

Eggs are bit players in Western dinners. We eat them for breakfast and brunch, but come evening they rarely appear except as accessories for the put-an-egg-on-it crowd. The rest of the world knows better. Portugal, for example, has ervilhas com ovos escalfados, braised eggs with spicy or sweet Portuguese chouriço sausage and/or bacon and peas. In India, there is muttai kuzhambu, a type of egg curry. Both dishes are built on layers of seasoning that balance the richness of the eggs. We liked the way garam masala—a warmly flavored Indian seasoning blend—added complex flavor. For our vegetables, we started with onions and found that sliced worked better than diced, adding texture and helping the sauce hold its shape. We let the sauce cool a bit in the dish before adding the eggs to ensure even cooking. While we like runny yolks, feel free to leave the dish in the oven a bit longer for firm yolks.

Don't forget that every oven is different, not to mention every egg. Cooking times will depend on oven temperature, as well as the size and temperature of the eggs.

1. **Heat the oven to 375°F** with a rack in the lower-middle position. In a 6- to 8-quart Dutch oven over medium, heat the oil. Add the onion and ¼ teaspoon salt. Cook, stirring, until browned, 7 to 9 minutes. Add the ginger, garam masala, turmeric and cayenne. Cook for 30 seconds, stirring constantly. Add the tomatoes, coconut milk, sugar, ½ teaspoon salt and ½ teaspoon pepper. Bring to a boil, scraping up any browned bits. Reduce heat to medium and simmer, stirring and scraping the pan, until thickened, 20 to 25 minutes.

2. **Remove the pan from the heat** and let sit for 10 minutes, stirring occasionally. Stir in the lime juice, then taste and season with salt and pepper. Use the back of a spoon to make 8 evenly spaced wells in the sauce. Crack 1 egg into each well, then season the eggs with salt and pepper.

3. **Bake until the sauce is bubbling** and the egg whites are opaque but still jiggle slightly, 13 to 18 minutes, rotating the pot halfway through. Remove from the oven and let sit for 5 minutes. Sprinkle with cilantro and serve with lime wedges and rice, naan or potatoes, if desired.

Spanish-Style Eggs with Garlicky Crumbs and Chorizo (Migas)

Start to finish: **30 minutes** / Servings: 4

8 large eggs

Kosher salt

3 ounces Spanish chorizo, halved lengthwise and thinly sliced crosswise

3 tablespoons extra-virgin olive oil, divided

2½ cups ½-inch chewy bread cubes

1 medium red onion, diced (about 1 cup)

2 medium garlic cloves, thinly sliced

¼ teaspoon sweet paprika

¼ teaspoon cayenne pepper (optional)

4 cups lightly packed coarsely chopped lacinato kale (about 3 ounces)

Ground black pepper

Migas evolved as a Spanish-Portuguese dish intended to use up stale bread. In fact, the word is Spanish for crumbs. Traditionally, the bread is torn into cubes, sprinkled with water and left overnight. Since most Americans don't have stale bread sitting around, we used ½-inch cubes of rustic bread. The best way to flavor them was to toss them in garlicky oil before toasting them in a skillet. We used Spanish-style chorizo, which is cured, and added a diced red onion along with chopped fresh kale. Lacinato (dinosaur) kale gave the dish heft, color and flavor. Be sure to stem the kale before measuring or weighing it, or substitute baby kale, which requires no stemming. For a variation, reduce or omit the kale and add 1 cup of chopped roasted red peppers or frozen peas (thawed). We found the bread cubes worked best when stirred in at the end of cooking, which gave them a chance to reheat and just begin to soften at the edges without losing their crunch. Their salty, garlicky flavor came through beautifully.

Don't walk away while browning the chorizo. Chorizo brands vary widely in fat content—not to mention flavor—and can go from golden brown to burnt in seconds.

1. In a medium bowl, whisk the eggs and ½ teaspoon salt. In a 12-inch nonstick skillet over medium, cook the chorizo, stirring frequently, until browned and crisp, 2 to 5 minutes. Use a slotted spoon to transfer the chorizo to a medium bowl, leaving any fat in the pan.

2. Add 2 tablespoons of the olive oil to the skillet and return to medium-high. Add the bread and a pinch of salt, then cook, stirring and tossing frequently, until browned and crisp, 3 to 5 minutes. Transfer to the bowl with the chorizo.

3. Return the skillet to medium heat and add the remaining 1 tablespoon oil, the onion, garlic, paprika, cayenne, if using, and ¼ teaspoon salt. Cook, stirring frequently, until the onion and garlic are softened and lightly browned, 3 to 5 minutes. If the garlic darkens too fast, reduce the heat. Add the kale and cook until wilted but still bright green, 1 to 2 minutes.

4. Whisk the eggs to recombine, then pour into the skillet and immediately reduce the heat to low. Cook, stirring and scraping the edges of the pan constantly, until barely set, about 1 minute. Stir in the bread and chorizo. Cook to desired consistency, 30 to 90 seconds. Transfer to a platter and season with salt and pepper.

Chinese Stir-Fried Eggs with Tomatoes

Start to finish: **15 minutes** / Servings: 4

---

3 plum tomatoes (about
12 ounces), halved, cored
and seeded

4 tablespoons unseasoned
rice vinegar, divided

Kosher salt and ground
white pepper

1 tablespoon ketchup

2 teaspoons finely grated
fresh ginger

1 medium garlic clove,
finely grated

½ teaspoon red pepper
flakes

1 teaspoon toasted
sesame oil

3 teaspoons soy sauce,
divided

8 large eggs

3 tablespoons grapeseed or
other neutral oil, divided

Stir-fried eggs with tomatoes is quick Chinese comfort food, and there are endless variations. Our version has more flavor than most since we season the ingredients from the start, rather than relying on condiments. We began by giving our tomatoes a toss in vinegar and white pepper. We didn't add sugar (a classic ingredient), but did add a dollop of sweet tomato flavor via a tablespoon of ketchup. We found the best method was to cook the eggs and tomatoes separately, starting with the eggs. We then added tomatoes to the empty skillet, cooked them until just beginning to blister, then arranged them on the eggs. Finally, our sauce went into the skillet to heat and thicken. This recipe comes together quickly, so have all ingredients assembled and prepared before you begin cooking. We liked the eggs with thinly sliced scallions, toasted sesame seeds and a drizzle of chili oil. Serve it over rice and you have a quick dinner.

Don't forget to seed the tomatoes. *The pulp made the dish watery.*

1. **Cut each tomato half** into thirds. In a medium bowl, toss the tomatoes with 1 tablespoon of the vinegar and ½ teaspoon white pepper. In a small bowl, combine the remaining 3 tablespoons vinegar, ¼ cup water, ketchup, ginger, garlic, pepper flakes, sesame oil, 2 teaspoons of the soy sauce and ½ teaspoon white pepper. Set aside. In a second medium bowl, whisk the eggs, the remaining 1 teaspoon soy sauce and ½ teaspoon white pepper.

2. **Drain the tomatoes** and set aside. In a 12-inch nonstick skillet over medium-high, heat 2 tablespoons of the grapeseed oil until barely smoking. Pour the eggs into the center of the pan, letting the eggs puff up along the edges. Use a spatula to stir the eggs, pushing them toward the middle as they begin to set at the edges and folding the cooked egg onto itself. Cook until just set, 45 to 60 seconds. Transfer to a plate.

3. **In the empty skillet,** heat the remaining 1 tablespoon of oil over medium-high until barely smoking. Add the drained tomatoes and cook undisturbed until just beginning to blister, 30 to 60 seconds. Arrange the tomatoes on top of the eggs.

4. **Return the skillet** to high heat and pour the sauce mixture into the skillet. Cook, stirring constantly, until thickened, about 30 seconds. Taste and season with salt and white pepper. Pour over the tomatoes.

Baked Persian Herb Omelet (Kuku Sabzi)

Start to finish: 1 hour (20 minutes active) / Servings: 6

5 tablespoons extra-virgin olive oil, divided

2 cups lightly packed fresh flat-leaf parsley

2 cups lightly packed fresh cilantro leaves and tender stems

1 cup coarsely chopped fresh dill

6 scallions, trimmed and roughly chopped

1½ teaspoons baking powder

¾ teaspoon ground cardamom

¾ teaspoon ground cinnamon

½ teaspoon ground cumin

Kosher salt and ground black pepper

6 large eggs

½ cup walnuts, toasted and chopped (optional)

⅓ cup dried cranberries, coarsely chopped (optional)

Whole-milk Greek-style yogurt, to serve (optional)

As France claims the omelet, Italy the frittata and Spain the tortilla, Iran has kuku, a baked egg dish. The kuku sabzi variation gets its flavor—and a deep green color—from tons of fresh herbs. Kuku sabzi—which is served at Persian New Year's feasts—remains light despite six eggs and a handful of walnuts (for texture and richness) thanks to five cups of parsley, cilantro and dill. Also helping is baking powder, which forms tiny air bubbles as the eggs cook, causing the dish to rise. While some recipes for kuku sabzi opt for stovetop cooking (with copious oil), we preferred the ease of baking. Pulsing the herbs and scallions in the food processor was easier and faster than hand chopping, and the texture was better. Dried cranberries were a good stand-in for traditional Persian barberries—lending a sweet-and-savory balance—but the recipe works without them.

Don't use less than *2 tablespoons of oil to grease the pan; the oil should pool at the bottom and generously coat the sides. This crisps the edges and boosts the omelet's flavor.*

1. **Heat the oven to 375°F** with a rack in the upper-middle position. Coat the bottom and sides of an 8-inch square or 9-inch round cake pan with 2 tablespoons of the oil. Line the bottom of the pan with a square or round of kitchen parchment, then turn the parchment to coat both sides with oil.

2. **In a food processor,** combine the parsley, cilantro, dill, scallions and the remaining 3 tablespoons oil. Process until finely chopped. In a large bowl, whisk together the baking powder, cardamom, cinnamon, cumin, 1 teaspoon salt and ¼ teaspoon pepper. Add 2 of the eggs and whisk until blended. Add the remaining 4 eggs and whisk until just combined. Fold in the herb-scallion mixture and the walnuts and cranberries, if using. Pour into the prepared pan and smooth the top. Bake until the center is firm, 20 to 25 minutes.

3. **Let the kuku cool** in the pan on a rack for 10 minutes. Run a knife around the edges, then invert onto a plate and remove the parchment. Reinvert onto a cutting board or serving platter. Cut into wedges and serve warm, cold or room temperature with a dollop of yogurt, if desired. The kuku can be refrigerated for up to 3 days, tightly wrapped.

Salads

2

Kale Salad with Smoked Almonds and Picada Crumbs

Start to finish: **15 minutes** / Servings: 6

Flavorful and seasonal, kale is a prime candidate for a winter salad. But when eaten raw, the hardy leaves can be unpleasantly tough. We started with lacinato kale, also known as dinosaur or Tuscan kale, as its long blue-green leaves are sweeter and more tender than curly kale. Thinly slicing the greens was the first step to making them more salad-friendly. Then we massaged the leaves with chopped smoked almonds that acted as an abrasive to further soften their structure. An acidic shallot-sherry vinaigrette also helped soften and brighten the kale (look for a sherry vinegar aged at least three years). Intensely flavorful paprika breadcrumbs, inspired by picada, a Catalan sauce, tied everything together.

Don't slice the kale until you're ready to make the salad; it will wilt. You can, however, stem, wash and dry it ahead of time.

2 medium shallots, halved and thinly sliced

5 tablespoons sherry vinegar

Kosher salt and ground black pepper

2 tablespoons honey

8 tablespoons extra-virgin olive oil, divided

1 cup smoked almonds

4 ounces chewy white bread, cut into 1-inch cubes

2 teaspoons fresh thyme

1 tablespoon sweet paprika

2 bunches lacinato kale, stemmed, washed, spun dry and thinly sliced crosswise (10 cups)

1 cup lightly packed fresh mint, chopped

1. In a small bowl, whisk together the shallots, vinegar and ½ teaspoon salt. Let sit for 10 minutes. Whisk in the honey, 5 tablespoons of the oil and ½ teaspoon pepper; set aside.

2. In a food processor, process the almonds until roughly chopped, about 8 pulses; transfer to a large bowl. Add the bread to the processor and process to rough crumbs, about 20 seconds. Add the thyme, the remaining 3 tablespoons oil, the paprika, ½ teaspoon salt and ½ teaspoon pepper. Process until incorporated, about 10 seconds.

3. Transfer the crumb mixture to a 12-inch skillet over medium and cook, stirring frequently, until crisp and browned, 8 to 10 minutes. Transfer to a plate and let cool.

4. Add the kale and mint to the bowl with the almonds and massage the greens until the kale softens and darkens, 10 to 20 seconds. Add the dressing and crumbs and toss to combine. Taste, then season with salt and pepper.

Japanese Potato Salad

Start to finish: 1 hour (35 minutes active) / Servings: 4

Getting potato salad right is no picnic. Too often the salad lacks the acidity or piquancy needed to cut through the richness of the mayonnaise. Our search for a better option led us to Japan, where potato salads are partially mashed to create a creamier texture. And they balance that texture with crumbled hard-cooked eggs and the crisp bite of vegetables, such as cucumber and carrots. Tying everything together is Kewpie, a Japanese mayonnaise made with rice vinegar that is smoother and richer than American mayonnaise. We started by looking for the right potatoes, which turned out to be Yukon Gold. Salting the cooking water ensured even seasoning, as did sprinkling them with vinegar and black pepper as they cooled. Waiting until the potatoes were at room temperature before adding mayonnaise was important to avoid oiliness. We used American mayonnaise but approximated the Kewpie flavor by increasing the vinegar and adding an extra hard-cooked egg yolk and 1 teaspoon of sugar. For a savory touch, we added diced ham and finished with scallions.

Don't substitute starchy russet or waxy new potatoes. The smooth texture of partly mashed Yukon Golds gave us the creamy consistency we wanted.

1 Persian cucumber, halved lengthwise and thinly sliced crosswise

1 medium carrot, peeled and shredded on the large holes of a box grater

¼ cup minced red onion

Kosher salt and ground black pepper

1½ pounds Yukon Gold potatoes, peeled and cut into ¾-inch cubes

3 tablespoons unseasoned rice vinegar

½ cup mayonnaise

2 ounces thick-cut smoked deli ham, diced (about ⅓ cup)

1 hard-cooked egg plus 1 hard-cooked egg yolk, diced

1 teaspoon white sugar

2 scallions, thinly sliced

1. In a medium bowl, stir together the cucumber, carrot, onion and 2 teaspoons salt. Set aside. In a large saucepan over high, combine the potatoes with enough water to cover by 1 inch. Add 1 teaspoon of salt and bring to a boil. Reduce heat to medium-high and simmer until a skewer inserted into the potatoes meets no resistance, 12 to 15 minutes.

2. Drain the potatoes, then transfer to a large bowl. Using a fork, coarsely mash half of the potatoes. Sprinkle with the vinegar and ¾ teaspoon pepper. Stir to combine, then spread in an even layer along the bottom and sides of the bowl. Let cool for at least 20 minutes.

3. Transfer the vegetable mixture to a fine-mesh strainer and rinse well. Working in batches, use your hands to squeeze the vegetables, removing as much liquid as possible, then add to the potatoes. Add the mayonnaise, ham, diced egg and yolk and sugar. Fold until thoroughly combined. Taste and season with salt and pepper, if necessary. Sprinkle with scallions, then serve chilled or at room temperature.

Fattoush

Start to finish: **30 minutes** / Servings: **6**

Fattoush is a Levantine chopped salad that makes tasty use of old pita. The bread may simply be left out to stale or it may be toasted before it is broken into pieces and tossed with vegetables and dressing. In this recipe, we brush the rounds with oil and bake them until nicely browned—we think the crunchy pita combined with the different textures of the other ingredients is a large part of the salad's appeal. Pickled grapes are not a common fattoush ingredient; we tried them in a fattoush at chef Ana Sortun's Oleana restaurant in Cambridge, Massachusetts, and loved their sweet-tart flavor and succulent texture. Both the pita and the grapes can be prepared a day in advance; store the pita in an airtight container. Sumac has earthy, citrusy notes, and pomegranate molasses is tangy and lightly fruity in taste. The sumac is optional, but it gives the fattoush complexity and a distinct Middle Eastern character.

Don't combine the salad ingredients until just before serving or the pita chips will get soggy.

1 pound seedless
red grapes, halved

¼ cup cider vinegar

Kosher salt and ground
black pepper

½ cup extra-virgin olive oil,
divided

3 medium garlic cloves,
finely grated

2 teaspoons ground cumin

½ to ¾ teaspoon red
pepper flakes

Two 8-inch pita bread rounds,
each split into 2 rounds

½ cup plain whole-milk
yogurt

½ cup finely chopped
fresh dill

1 tablespoon pomegranate
molasses

2 teaspoons ground sumac
(optional)

1 English cucumber,
quartered lengthwise,
thinly sliced

6- to 7-ounce romaine heart,
chopped into bite-size pieces

1 cup lightly packed fresh
mint, finely chopped

1. Heat the oven to 400°F with a rack in the middle position. In a medium bowl, stir together the grapes, vinegar and ½ teaspoon salt. Cover and refrigerate.

2. In a small bowl, stir together ¼ cup of oil, the garlic, cumin and pepper flakes. Arrange the pita rounds rough side up on a rimmed baking sheet, then brush each with the flavored oil, using all of it. Sprinkle with salt and black pepper. Bake until browned and crisp, 10 to 12 minutes. Set aside to cool. When cool enough to handle, break into bite-size pieces.

3. Drain the grapes, reserving the pickling liquid. In a large bowl, combine the remaining ¼ cup oil, the yogurt, dill, molasses and sumac, if using, and 1 teaspoon each of salt and pepper. Add the reserved pickling liquid and whisk well. Add the cucumber, romaine, mint, pickled grapes and pita pieces. Toss until evenly coated.

Shaved Zucchini and Herb Salad with Parmesan

Start to finish: **20 minutes** / Servings: 4

We adopt the Italian technique of slicing raw zucchini into thin ribbons for this vibrant salad. Inspiration for our bright lemon dressing came from The River Cafe in London and its spare, lemony, arugula-studded zucchini carpaccio. And we also took note of the hazelnut accents in zucchini salad recipes from Francis Mallmann and Yotam Ottolenghi. The hazelnuts—or almonds, if that's what you have on hand—gave the salad crunch and a slightly buttery note. A Y-style peeler makes it easy to shave zucchini into ribbons. Don't worry if the ribbons vary in width; this adds to the visual appeal of the dish. Toasted sliced, slivered or chopped whole almonds can be used in place of the hazelnuts.

Don't dress the salad *until you are ready to serve. The zucchini and herbs are delicate and quickly wilt.*

1. In a large bowl, whisk together the lemon zest and juice, oil, honey, ½ teaspoon salt and ¼ teaspoon pepper. Set aside.

2. Use a Y-style peeler or mandoline to shave the zucchini from top to bottom, rotating as you go. Stop shaving when you reach the seedy core. Discard the cores.

3. To the dressing, add the shaved zucchini, grated cheese, mint and basil. Gently toss until evenly coated. Transfer to a serving plate and sprinkle with shaved Parmesan and hazelnuts.

1 teaspoon grated lemon zest, plus 3 tablespoons lemon juice

3 tablespoons extra-virgin olive oil

¼ teaspoon honey

Kosher salt and ground black pepper

1 pound zucchini (2 medium), trimmed

1 ounce Parmesan cheese, finely grated (about ½ cup), plus extra, shaved, to serve

½ cup lightly packed fresh mint, torn

½ cup lightly packed fresh basil, torn

¼ cup hazelnuts, toasted, skinned and roughly chopped

Sichuan Chicken Salad

Start to finish: 1 hour 20 minutes (20 minutes active)
Servings: 4

___

Two 10- to 12-ounce bone-in, skin-on split chicken breasts

6 scallions, white parts roughly chopped, green parts thinly sliced on the diagonal, reserved separately

1-inch piece fresh ginger, cut into 4 pieces and smashed

2 medium garlic cloves, smashed and peeled

Kosher salt

¼ cup dry sherry (optional)

2 tablespoons chili oil

2 tablespoons tahini

1½ tablespoons white sugar

1½ tablespoons toasted sesame oil

1 tablespoon soy sauce

2 tablespoons unseasoned rice vinegar

⅛ to ¼ teaspoon cayenne pepper

1 teaspoon Sichuan peppercorns, toasted and finely ground

1 large English cucumber, halved lengthwise, seeded and thinly sliced crosswise on diagonal

⅓ cup dry-roasted peanuts, chopped

For the traditional Sichuan dish bang bang ji si, cooked chicken is pounded to shreds so the meat better absorbs the flavorful dressing. We got similar results by mashing it with a sturdy wooden spoon in a bowl; make sure the bowl you use is not fragile. We loved the tongue-tingling, piney notes of Sichuan peppercorns in the dressing. Toast them in a dry skillet over medium heat until aromatic, about 2 minutes, then grind them to a fine powder with a spice grinder or mortar and pestle.

Don't boil the chicken; keep the liquid at a bare simmer so the meat stays moist and tender.

1. **In a large saucepan,** place the chicken skin side down, then add the scallion whites, ginger, garlic and 1½ teaspoons salt. Add 4 cups water and the sherry, if using. Bring to a boil over medium-high, then cover, reduce to low and cook at a bare simmer until a skewer inserted into the thickest part of the chicken meets no resistance, or the thickest part of the chicken reaches 160°F, 20 to 25 minutes. Uncover the pan and let the chicken cool in the liquid for 15 minutes.

2. **Meanwhile, in a small bowl,** whisk together the chili oil, tahini, sugar, sesame oil, soy sauce, vinegar, cayenne, Sichuan pepper and 1½ teaspoons salt.

3. **Using tongs,** remove the chicken from the cooking liquid. Remove and discard the skin and bones, then transfer the meat to a large bowl. Add 2 tablespoons of the tahini dressing, then use a wooden spoon to smash the meat, shredding it and working in the dressing. Use your fingers to pull the shreds into bite-size pieces.

4. **Add the cucumber** and ¾ each of the peanuts and scallion greens. Drizzle with the remaining dressing and toss until evenly coated. Transfer to a serving bowl and sprinkle with the remaining peanuts and scallions.

Senegalese Avocado and Mango Salad with Rof

Start to finish: **30 minutes** / Servings: 4

This spicy yet refreshing salad—adapted from a recipe in Pierre Thiam's cookbook "Yolele!"—is a refreshing combination of sweet, sour, spicy and herbal flavors. We learned this while traveling to Dakar with Thiam. Rof is a Senegalese mixture of parsley, scallions, chilies and garlic. It's worth seeking out roasted peanut oil for the dressing, as it adds deep, nutty notes and a rich aroma, but regular peanut oil or extra-virgin olive oil worked, too. If you have flaky sea salt, use instead of kosher salt for sprinkling on the mangoes and avocados; the crunch adds dimension to the dish.

Don't prep the avocados until you're ready to assemble the salad so that the flesh remains vibrant green for serving.

1. In a food processor, combine the parsley, scallions, garlic, habanero, 1 teaspoon salt and ½ teaspoon pepper. Process until finely chopped, about 1 minute, scraping the sides of the bowl as needed. Add the lime zest and juice and peanut oil and process until smooth, about 30 seconds.

2. In a medium bowl, combine the mango slices with 3 tablespoons of the dressing and gently toss. Marinate at room temperature for 30 minutes.

3. Lay the mango slices on a serving platter; do not wash the bowl. Halve, pit, peel and thinly slice the avocados. Arrange the avocados on top of the mangoes. Sprinkle lightly with salt and drizzle with 3 tablespoons of the remaining dressing.

4. In the same bowl used for the mangoes, toss together the tomatoes and 1 tablespoon of the remaining dressing. Scatter the mixture over the mangoes and avocados. Serve with the remaining dressing on the side.

2 cups lightly packed fresh flat-leaf parsley

4 scallions, roughly chopped

2 medium garlic cloves, smashed and peeled

1 habanero chili, stemmed and seeded

Kosher salt and ground black pepper

1 teaspoon grated lime zest, plus ¼ cup lime juice

¼ cup roasted peanut oil

Two 14- to 16-ounce ripe mangoes, peeled, pitted and thinly sliced

2 ripe avocados

1 cup grape tomatoes, chopped

Pita and Chickpea Salad with Yogurt and Mint (Fatteh)

Start to finish: **25 minutes** / Servings: **4**

This dish is known as fatteh in the Levant, where it often is eaten for breakfast. It's a way to turn stale pita bread into a hearty meal. We, however, start with fresh pita, brush it with butter, crisp it in the oven, then break it into bite-size pieces before topping the pieces with warmed chickpeas. Yogurt spiked with garlic, tahini and lemon ties everything together. Za'atar, a Middle Eastern spice blend that usually includes sesame seeds, sumac, thyme and oregano, adds complex flavor. But the za'atar is optional; even without it, the salad is delicious and satisfying. If you like, instead of mint, use flat-leaf parsley or a combination.

Don't cut back on the butter that's tossed with the toasted pine nuts. It may seem like a lot, but the butter adds a sweetness that balances the tang of the yogurt and makes the dish taste full and deep.

1 cup plain whole-milk yogurt

¼ cup tahini

2 medium garlic cloves, finely grated

1 teaspoon grated lemon zest, plus 1 tablespoon lemon juice

Kosher salt and ground black pepper

Two 8-inch pita breads, each split into 2 rounds

5 tablespoons salted butter, melted, divided

2½ teaspoons ground cumin, divided

¼ cup pine nuts

⅛ to ¼ teaspoon cayenne pepper (optional)

Two 15½-ounce cans chickpeas, rinsed and drained

1½ teaspoons za'atar, plus more to serve (optional)

1½ cups lightly packed fresh mint, torn if large

1. Heat the oven to 400°F with a rack in the middle position. In a small bowl, whisk together the yogurt, tahini, garlic, lemon zest and juice, ½ teaspoon salt and ¼ teaspoon black pepper. Set aside.

2. Arrange the pita on a rimmed baking sheet. Use 2 tablespoons of the butter to brush both sides of each round, then sprinkle evenly with 2 teaspoons of the cumin. Bake for 5 minutes, then flip each round and continue to bake until browned and crisp, 5 to 6 minutes. Transfer to a wire rack and let cool; reserve the baking sheet.

3. While the pita cools, distribute the pine nuts on the reserved baking sheet and toast until golden brown, 3 to 5 minutes, stirring once about halfway through. Immediately transfer to a small bowl and toss with the remaining 3 tablespoons butter, the remaining ½ teaspoon cumin, cayenne (if using) and ¼ teaspoon each salt and black pepper. Set aside.

4. In a medium microwave-safe bowl, toss the chickpeas with the za'atar (if using), 1 teaspoon salt and 3 tablespoons water. Cover and microwave on high until hot, 3 to 3½ minutes, stirring once halfway through. Meanwhile, break the pita into bite-size pieces and place in a wide, shallow serving bowl or divide among 4 individual bowls.

5. Using a slotted spoon, scoop the warmed chickpeas onto the pita. Spoon on the yogurt mixture, top with mint and spoon on the pine nut–butter mixture. Sprinkle with additional za'atar (if using).

Eventide Green Salad with Nori Vinaigrette

Start to finish: 30 minutes, plus cooling and chilling
Servings: 6

This is our adaptation of a salad created by Eventide Oyster Co. in Portland, Maine. Roasted seaweed (also called nori) is pulverized to a coarse powder and added to the dressing, lending the dish deep, umami-rich flavor reinforced with soy sauce and mirin. Instead of using full-sized sheets of plain nori (the variety used for sushi), we opted for the convenience of an individual package of seasoned seaweed snacks that are available in most grocery stores. Quick-pickled vegetables give the salad texture and bright flavor, but keep in mind that they need to pickle for at least two hours before they're ready to use. To shave the carrot, run a sharp vegetable peeler down the length of the vegetable.

Don't use a reactive bowl *to make the pickles or the vegetables and liquid may take on an "off" metallic flavor. It's best to use glass, ceramic or stainless steel. Don't dress the salad until you're ready to serve so that the greens stay fresh and crisp (if left to stand after dressing, they'll wilt from the pickles' acidity and weight).*

4 ounces red radishes, sliced into thin rounds

1 medium carrot, peeled and shaved into long, thin strips (see headnote)

½ small red onion, thinly sliced

1½ cups plus 2 tablespoons unseasoned rice vinegar, divided

⅓ cup white sugar

¼-ounce (7-gram) package roasted seaweed snacks, torn into small pieces (about 1 cup packed)

2 tablespoons soy sauce

2 tablespoons mirin

2 tablespoons grapeseed or other neutral oil

10 ounces spring mix or other delicate greens

Kosher salt

1. In a medium heatproof bowl, combine the radishes, carrot and onion. In a small saucepan over medium-high, combine 1½ cups vinegar, the sugar and ¾ cup water. Bring to a rapid boil, stirring to dissolve the sugar, then pour over the vegetables. Cool to room temperature, then cover and refrigerate for at least 2 hours or for up to 1 week.

2. In a spice grinder, process the seaweed until finely chopped, gently shaking the grinder, about 30 seconds; check under the blade for clumps and break up any. You should have about 2 tablespoons pulverized seaweed. In a large bowl, whisk together the seaweed, soy sauce, mirin, oil and the remaining 2 tablespoons vinegar; the dressing will thicken slightly.

3. Drain the pickles in a fine mesh strainer. Add half of the drained pickles to the bowl with the dressing along with the salad greens. Toss to combine, then taste and season with salt. Transfer to a platter or bowl and top with the remaining drained pickles.

Greens with Walnuts, Parmesan and Pancetta Vinaigrette

Start to finish: **15 minutes** / Servings: **6**

Bitter greens pair with a rich dressing for this take on salade frisée aux lardons, typically made with frisée lettuce, a poached egg and meaty salt pork for the lardons. For our take, we use pancetta and a combination of bitter greens such as frisée, endive, radicchio, escarole or arugula. To toast the walnuts, spread them evenly on a rimmed baking sheet and bake at 350°F until lightly browned and fragrant, 5 to 7 minutes. A sharp Y-shaped vegetable peeler is the perfect tool for shaving the Parmesan cheese. Top with a fried egg for a heartier meal evocative of this salad's bistro roots.

Don't allow the dressing to cool down before adding it to the greens. Its consistency is best when warm, and its heat slightly softens the sturdy greens. By the same token, make sure the greens are not cold when dressed so the dressing doesn't congeal on contact.

1. Place the greens in a large bowl and set aside. In a separate bowl, whisk together the vinegar, mustard and ½ teaspoon salt.

2. In a medium skillet over medium, cook the pancetta, stirring occasionally, until crisp, about 7 minutes. Using a slotted spoon, transfer the pancetta to a paper towel–lined plate. Pour off all but 1 tablespoon pancetta fat from the skillet, then return it to medium heat. Add the shallot and cook, stirring, until light golden brown, about 2 minutes. Add the oil and the vinegar mixture, then remove from the heat and whisk until combined. Let stand for 30 seconds to warm through.

3. Add the warm dressing, walnuts and 1 teaspoon pepper to the greens and toss well. Taste and season with salt. Divide the salad among plates and top each portion with pancetta and Parmesan.

12 ounces (12 cups) mixed bitter greens, torn

2 tablespoons sherry vinegar

1 tablespoon Dijon mustard

Kosher salt and ground black pepper

6 ounces thinly sliced pancetta, chopped

1 medium shallot, finely chopped

3 tablespoons extra-virgin olive oil

1 cup walnuts, toasted and roughly chopped

1 ounce Parmesan cheese, shaved (about ½ cup)

Austrian Potato Salad (Erdäpfelsalat)

Start to finish: 30 minutes / Servings: 4

2 pounds Yukon Gold potatoes, peeled, halved and sliced ¼-inch thick

2 cups low-sodium chicken broth

Kosher salt and ground black pepper

¼ cup finely chopped cornichons, plus 1 tablespoon brine

2 tablespoons red wine vinegar, divided

½ medium red onion, finely chopped (about ½ cup)

½ teaspoon caraway seeds

¼ cup grapeseed or other neutral oil

1 tablespoon Dijon mustard

2 medium celery stalks, finely chopped (about ½ cup)

2 hard-cooked eggs, peeled and chopped (optional)

¼ cup chopped fresh dill

Austrian cooks add flavor and creaminess to their potato salad without mayonnaise by using chicken broth to cook the potatoes, then using the starchy cooking liquid as the base for the dressing. That means you can skip the mayonnaise. Cornichon brine, red wine vinegar and Dijon mustard provide sharp notes; celery and fresh dill add crunch and bright flavor. Many recipes call for waxy potatoes, but we chose Yukon Golds for their rich flavor and creamy texture. If your potatoes are quite large, quarter them instead of halving before slicing.

Don't overcook—or undercook—the potatoes. They should be firm but not grainy, creamy in the center and just starting to fall apart at the edges. This texture is important, as some of the potatoes will break down into the salad. But if they're too soft, they will turn into mashed potatoes.

1. **In a large saucepan,** combine the potatoes, broth and 2 teaspoons salt. Add enough water to just cover the potatoes. Bring to a boil over medium-high, then reduce to medium-low and cook until a skewer inserted into the potatoes meets no resistance, 8 to 10 minutes. Drain, reserving ½ cup of the cooking liquid, and transfer to a large bowl. Sprinkle with the cornichon brine, 1 tablespoon of the vinegar and ½ teaspoon pepper.

2. **In the same saucepan,** combine the reserved cooking liquid with the onion and caraway seeds and bring to a simmer over medium-high. Pour the mixture over the potatoes and stir well. Let stand, stirring occasionally, until the liquid is absorbed and thickened, about 10 minutes.

3. **Meanwhile,** in a liquid measuring cup, whisk together the oil, mustard, the remaining 1 tablespoon of vinegar, ¾ teaspoon salt and ½ teaspoon pepper until emulsified. To the potatoes, add the dressing, celery, eggs, if using, cornichons and dill, then fold until evenly coated. Taste and season with salt and pepper. Serve at room temperature.

Persian Tomato and Cucumber Salad (Shirazi Salad)

Start to finish: 30 minutes (15 minutes active) / Servings: 4

1 English cucumber, halved lengthwise, seeded and cut into ½-inch pieces (see headnote)

1½ pounds ripe tomatoes, cored and cut into 1-inch pieces

Kosher salt and ground black pepper

3 scallions, thinly sliced on the diagonal, white and green parts reserved separately

1 medium garlic clove, finely grated

1 tablespoon dried mint

1 teaspoon grated lime zest, plus ¼ cup lime juice

¼ cup chopped fresh cilantro

2 tablespoons extra-virgin olive oil (optional)

Ripe summer tomatoes shine in this simple salad inspired by a recipe from Najmieh Batmanglij's book "Cooking in Iran." To make the dish out of season, try Campari tomatoes (sometimes called cocktail tomatoes), which have a better texture than other varieties in the off seasons. English cucumbers have fewer seeds and thinner skins than the typical garden variety. Even better are smaller Persian cucumbers. If you find them, you'll need 12 ounces. And simply slice them into ½-inch rounds; no need for seeding. The dressing is bracingly fresh and sharp; if you prefer a mellower, slightly richer salad, drizzle in the optional olive oil just before serving.

Don't bypass the step of salting the cucumber and tomatoes. They will release about ½ cup of liquid, moisture that otherwise would make the salad watery and dilute.

1. **In a large colander,** combine the cucumber and tomatoes, then set in the sink. Sprinkle the chopped vegetables with 2 teaspoons salt and gently toss to combine. Let stand for 20 minutes, tossing once or twice to encourage the liquid to drain.

2. **Meanwhile, in a medium bowl,** combine the scallion whites and ½ teaspoon salt, then use your hands to gently rub the salt into the scallions until slightly softened and wilted. Stir in the garlic, mint and lime zest and juice; set aside until the cucumbers and tomatoes are ready.

3. **Transfer the cucumbers and tomatoes** to the bowl with the scallion whites. Add ½ teaspoon pepper, the scallion greens and cilantro and toss. Taste and season with salt and pepper, then drizzle with the oil (if using).

Shaved Carrot Salad with Poppy Seeds and Parsley (Zanahorias Dulces)

Start to finish: **30 minutes** (15 minutes active) / Servings: **4**

4 or 5 large carrots
(about 1½ pounds), peeled

Kosher salt

1 tablespoon poppy seeds

¼ cup extra-virgin olive oil

2 medium garlic cloves,
smashed and peeled

2 star anise pods

¼ cup lemon juice, plus
more as needed

1 teaspoon white sugar,
plus more as needed

½ cup lightly packed fresh
flat-leaf parsley, torn if large

This colorful salad is our version of one we sampled in Buenos Aires at a tapas stall that reflects Spain's lingering influence in Argentina. Chef Diego Fernandez of De Lucía Tapas at the Mercado San Telmo showed us how the dressing ingredients are heated briefly in a skillet, then the carrot shavings added and cooked just until barely tender. We further simplified by microwaving the carrots. A Y-style vegetable peeler works well for shaving the carrots into ribbons, but you also can use a mandoline. Either way, choose large, thick carrots—not the slender variety sold in bunches—because they're easier to shave. And stop shaving once you reach the fibrous cores. Carrots vary in sweetness, so you may need to add a little extra sugar, lemon juice and/or salt at the end.

Don't overcook the carrots in the microwave. The ribbons should be wilted but still have texture; they shouldn't be completely tender and limp.

1. Use a Y-style peeler or a mandoline to shave the carrots from top to bottom into long, wide ribbons, rotating as you go. Stop shaving when you reach the core; discard the cores. Put the ribbons in a large, microwave-safe bowl and toss with ¾ teaspoon salt. Cover and microwave on high until wilted but still crisp-tender, 3 to 5 minutes, stirring once halfway through; set aside, uncovered, leaving any liquid in the bowl.

2. In a small saucepan over medium, toast the poppy seeds, stirring often, until fragrant and slightly darker in color, about 2 minutes. Transfer to a small bowl. In the same saucepan over medium, heat the oil, garlic and star anise, stirring occasionally, until the garlic begins to brown at the edges, 1 to 2 minutes. Reduce to low, add the lemon juice and sugar, then whisk until the sugar dissolves. Bring to a simmer and cook, whisking occasionally, for 3 minutes. Remove and discard the garlic and star anise.

3. Pour the warm dressing over the carrots and toss. Let stand for 15 minutes. Add the poppy seeds and parsley, then toss again. Taste and season with salt, lemon juice and/or sugar, then transfer to a serving dish.

German Cucumber-Dill Salad (Gurkensalat)

Start to finish: **35 minutes** / Servings: 4

---

2 English cucumbers, peeled and sliced into ⅛-inch-thick rounds

Kosher salt and ground black pepper

½ cup sour cream

1 tablespoon Champagne vinegar (see headnote)

½ teaspoon white sugar, plus more if needed

1 medium carrot, peeled and shredded on the large holes of a box grater

2 tablespoons finely chopped fresh chives

1 cup lightly packed fresh dill, chopped

Cucumber salad is the traditional accompaniment to German Schnitzel. This recipe is based on the salad we tasted at Restaurant Lohninger in Frankfurt. Instead of tart and vinegary, like Gurkensalat from other areas of Germany, ours is creamy but not overly rich. We salt the cucumbers after slicing. This step not only seasons the slices, it draws out moisture to prevent the salad from becoming too watery and leaves the cucumbers with a pleasant crispness. Champagne vinegar lends the dressing subtle acidity and brightness; if you can't find Champagne vinegar, unseasoned rice vinegar is an acceptable substitute.

Don't forget to toss the cucumbers *once or twice while they are salting. This helps the moisture drain out of the colander. Don't rinse the cucumbers after salting. A good amount of salt drains off with the water that the cucumbers release, so the salad won't taste overseasoned.*

---

1. In a large colander set over a bowl, toss the cucumbers with 1½ teaspoons salt. Let stand for 30 minutes, tossing once or twice to encourage liquid to drain. Meanwhile, in a large bowl, stir together the sour cream, vinegar, sugar and ½ teaspoon pepper; set aside. In a small bowl, toss the carrot with the chives and ¼ teaspoon each salt and pepper; set aside.

2. Using your hands, firmly squeeze the cucumbers to remove as much water as possible; discard the liquid. Add the cucumbers to the sour cream mixture, then gently toss to combine. Stir in the dill. Taste and season with salt, pepper and sugar. Transfer to a serving dish, then top with the carrot mixture.

Turkish Tomato and Onion Salad with Olive Oil and Pomegranate Molasses

Start to finish: 45 minutes (20 minutes active) / Servings: 4

½ medium white onion,
thinly sliced

3 tablespoons pomegranate
molasses

2 tablespoons lemon juice

Kosher salt and ground
black pepper

⅓ cup extra-virgin olive oil

1½ pounds cocktail tomatoes,
cored, each cut into 6 wedges

2 teaspoons dried mint (optional)

1 cup lightly packed fresh
flat-leaf parsley, torn

½ cup lightly packed fresh
dill, minced

This is our version of the bright, bracing salad that we had in Manzara Restaurant in Söğüt, Turkey. The dish often is part of a Turkish meze spread, but we think it also is an ideal accompaniment to just about any type of grilled meat or kebabs. The salad comes together easily, but it's important to use ripe, flavorful tomatoes. We find cocktail tomatoes (sometimes sold as Campari tomatoes) to be dependably sweet and tasty no matter the season. Also, look for pomegranate molasses made without sugar (check the label), as its flavor is fruitier and more nuanced than brands containing added sweetener.

Don't bypass the step of allowing the onion to marinate in the pomegranate molasses-lemon mixture. The acidity mellows the allium's pungency. It's also important to allow the salad to stand at room temperature for about 15 minutes before serving to allow the tomatoes to soften slightly and to give the flavors a chance to meld.

1. **In a large bowl,** combine the onion, pomegranate molasses, lemon juice and 1 teaspoon each salt and pepper; let stand for 10 minutes.

2. **To the onion mixture,** add the oil and whisk to combine. Add the tomatoes, mint (if using), parsley and dill, then toss. Let stand at room temperature for about 15 minutes. Taste and season with salt and pepper, then transfer to a serving bowl.

Lebanese-Style Tabbouleh

Start to finish: **15 minutes** / Servings: **4**

Israeli-born British chef Yotam Ottolenghi is clear about tabbouleh. It should be "all about the parsley." But in the U.S., the Middle Eastern salad often goes heavy on the bulgur, a wheat that has been cooked, dried and cracked. The result is a salad that is mealy, bland and stubbornly soggy. That's because the bulgur sponges up all the juices from the tomatoes. Our solution was to barely cook the bulgur—essentially underhydrating it—allowing it to soak up those juices without becoming waterlogged. We added generous helpings of herbs, livening up the parsley with some mint. Wet herbs will dilute the dressing and make the bulgur gummy. Be sure to dry them thoroughly with a spinner and paper towels before mincing. Some type of onion is traditional; we used shallots, preferring their gentler bite, and soaked them in lemon juice to soften their flavor and texture. While the sumac is optional, we loved its fruity complexity and light acidity.

Don't use coarse-grain bulgur; it won't hydrate evenly. If you can't find fine-grain bulgur, process medium- or coarse-grain in short pulses until fine, light and fluffy, five to 10 pulses.

½ cup boiling water

⅓ cup fine-grain bulgur

1 teaspoon ground sumac (optional)

½ teaspoon ground allspice

Kosher salt and ground black pepper

3 tablespoons lemon juice

1 small shallot, minced

¼ teaspoon white sugar

¼ cup extra-virgin olive oil

2 to 3 small vine-ripened tomatoes, diced

4 cups lightly packed fresh flat-leaf parsley, well dried then minced

1 cup lightly packed fresh mint, well dried then minced

1. In a medium bowl, combine the water, bulgur, sumac (if using) allspice and ½ teaspoon of salt. Cover with plastic wrap and let sit for 10 minutes. In a large bowl, stir together the lemon juice, shallot, sugar and ¾ teaspoon of salt; let sit for 10 minutes.

2. Whisk the oil into the lemon juice mixture. Fluff the bulgur with a fork and add to the dressing along with the tomatoes; mix well. Fold the parsley and mint into the tabbouleh, then taste and season with salt, pepper and additional sumac, if needed.

Thai-Style Napa Coleslaw with Mint and Cilantro

Start to finish: **25 minutes** / Servings: **6**

Looking for a brighter, fresher cabbage slaw than the mayonnaise-rich American version, we were inspired by a recipe from San Antonio chef Quealy Watson that featured Southeast Asian flavors. Coconut milk in the dressing—instead of mayonnaise—has just the right amount of richness and body. Fish sauce adds savory pungency, while sugar balances with sweetness. For heat, we like fresh chili "cooked" in lime juice, which mellows the bite and helps disperse the heat more evenly. For vegetables, we use tender yet crunchy napa cabbage along with sliced red radishes and snap peas for vivid color and even more texture.

Don't use "light" coconut milk or sweetened "cream of coconut" for this recipe. The former is too thin, and the latter is too sweet (think pina coladas). And don't forget to vigorously shake the can before opening to ensure the fat and liquid are fully emulsified.

In a liquid measuring cup, or small bowl, mix together the lime juice, sugar, fish sauce and chili. Let sit for 10 minutes. Whisk in the coconut milk until combined, then adjust seasoning with additional fish sauce, if desired. In a large bowl, combine the cabbage, radishes, peas, cilantro and mint. Add the dressing and toss until evenly coated. Stir in the cashews.

3 tablespoons lime juice

4 teaspoons white sugar

1 tablespoon fish sauce, plus more as needed

1 medium serrano chili, seeded and minced

⅓ cup coconut milk

1 pound napa cabbage (1 small head), thinly sliced crosswise (about 8 cups)

6 radishes, trimmed, halved and thinly sliced

4 ounces sugar snap peas, strings removed, thinly sliced on the diagonal

½ cup roughly chopped fresh cilantro

½ cup roughly chopped fresh mint

½ cup roasted, salted cashews, coarsely chopped

Panzanella with Fresh Mozzarella

Start to finish: 40 minutes / Servings: 4

1½ pounds ripe tomatoes, cored and cut into 1-inch chunks

Kosher salt and ground black pepper

½ small red onion, thinly sliced

3 tablespoons sherry vinegar

8 ounces crusty white bread, sliced ½ inch thick and torn into bite-size pieces (about 8 cups)

3 tablespoons extra-virgin olive oil, plus more to serve

8 ounces fresh mozzarella cheese

2 tablespoons heavy cream

2 teaspoons grated lemon zest

1 cup lightly packed fresh basil

½ cup lightly packed fresh flat-leaf parsley

This version of the classic Italian bread salad known as panzanella was inspired by a version from "Ruffage" author Abra Berens. We tear the bread into pieces to create more texture. We also quick-pickle red onion in sherry vinegar to add sharp bites of acidity. Finally, we soak pieces of fresh mozzarella in cream to add richness and mimic the butteriness of burrata cheese. Fresh basil and parsley, left whole rather than chopped, are tossed into the salad just before serving to add vibrant color and summery fragrance as well as fresh herbal flavor.

Don't forget to salt the tomatoes as the first step. This ensures they are seasoned throughout, which is especially important if they aren't at the peak of ripeness. It also softens their texture. Don't use regular mozzarella cheese. It's important to use fresh mozzarella, often sold packed in water.

1. In a large bowl, toss the tomatoes with ½ teaspoon salt; set aside. In a small bowl, stir together the red onion, vinegar and ¼ teaspoon salt; set aside.

2. In a 12-inch skillet over medium, toss the bread with the oil and ¼ teaspoon salt. Cook, stirring occasionally, until crisp and light golden brown, 4 to 8 minutes. Immediately transfer to the bowl with the tomatoes and toss. Let stand for 10 minutes.

3. Meanwhile, using your hands, tear the mozzarella into bite-size chunks and add to a small bowl. Stir in the cream, lemon zest, a pinch of salt and ¼ teaspoon pepper.

4. Using a slotted spoon or tongs, transfer the onion to the tomato-bread mixture, reserving the vinegar. Add the parsley and basil, then toss. Taste and season with salt, pepper and some of the reserved vinegar, if needed. Transfer to a serving dish, then top with the cheese and a generous drizzle of oil.

Daikon-Carrot Salad with Sesame and Lemon

Start to finish: 30 minutes, plus marinating
Makes about 3 cups

---

1 pound daikon radish, peeled and cut into 2-inch matchsticks

1 medium carrot, peeled and cut into 2-inch matchsticks

Table salt

¾ cup unseasoned rice vinegar

¼ cup white sugar

¼ cup dried apricots, cut into thin strips

1 tablespoon sesame seeds, toasted and coarsely ground (see headnote)

1 teaspoon grated lemon zest

¼ teaspoon red pepper flakes

As Sonoko Sakai, author of "Japanese Home Cooking" explains, many vinegared Japanese salads fall somewhere between a pickle and a conventional salad, and this namasu is a good example. Meant to be served in small portions, as most Japanese pickles are, this daikon and carrot salad is traditional at New Year's, but there's no reason the refreshingly crunchy, tangy-sweet tangle of textures can't be served year-round. For our adaptation of Sakai's recipe, we skipped the harder-to-source ingredients (such as dried persimmon and yuzu) for the more widely available substitutes that she suggests (dried apricots and lemon). We also use water instead of dashi (Japanese stock) for the marinade, but if you have dashi, use an equal amount; it will add umami to make the vegetables taste fuller and richer. Though the salad is simple to make, it requires a two-step process: first, the vegetables are rubbed with salt and squeezed of moisture. Then they are dressed and marinated for at least four hours (or up to one week). A mortar and pestle works well for grinding the sesame seeds, or give them two or three pulses in an electric spice grinder.

Don't be shy about massaging the daikon and carrots with the salt. Use your hands to work the salt into the vegetables until they begin to wilt. A technique used in many types of Japanese pickles, this step forces the vegetables to release some of their water and renders their texture crunchy-crisp. Table salt has a fine texture that works best for this, so don't use kosher salt.

---

1. In a large bowl, toss together the daikon, carrots and 1 teaspoon salt. Using your hands, massage the salt into the vegetables until they begin to wilt, about 2 minutes. Set aside for about 5 minutes.

2. Meanwhile, in a small bowl, combine the vinegar, sugar and ¾ teaspoon salt and ¾ cup water. Whisk until the sugar and salt dissolve.

3. A handful at a time, squeeze the water from the vegetables. Discard any liquid accumulated in the bowl, then return the vegetables to it. Pour the vinegar mixture over the daikon and carrots, then toss to combine. Cover and refrigerate for at least 4 hours or up to 1 week.

4. When ready to serve, add the apricots, sesame seeds, lemon zest and pepper flakes, then toss to combine. Serve chilled or at room temperature.

Avocado Salad with Pickled Mustard Seeds and Marjoram Vinaigrette

Start to finish: 1 hour / Servings: 6

For the pickled mustard seeds:

¼ cup yellow mustard seeds

½ cup cider vinegar

¼ cup white sugar

¼ cup water

1½ teaspoons black peppercorns

½ teaspoon coriander seeds

3 allspice berries

1 bay leaf

⅛ teaspoon red pepper flakes

For the dressing:

2 tablespoons pickled mustard seeds and brine

1 tablespoon minced shallot

2 teaspoons whole-grain mustard

1 teaspoon honey

Kosher salt and ground black pepper

¼ cup chopped fresh marjoram

3 tablespoons canola oil

3 tablespoons extra-virgin olive oil

For the salad:

3 firm but ripe avocados

Kosher salt

6 teaspoons lemon juice

Thinly sliced ricotta salata cheese, to serve

Fresh marjoram, to serve

We discovered this dish at Stephen Oxaal's Branch Line restaurant in Watertown, Massachusetts, where mustard seeds took an avocado salad from simple to stunning. The pickling process takes just a few minutes and the result adds a tang and crunch that balance the lushness of the other ingredients. Conventional vinaigrettes—blends of fat and acid—tended to slide off the avocados. Instead, we eliminated the lemon juice from the dressing and drizzled it directly over the avocado slices, where it mingled with the dressing. We liked ricotta salata cheese best, but Parmesan cheese was a fine substitute.

1. To make the pickled mustard seeds, in a small saucepan over high, combine the mustard seeds and enough water to cover by 2 inches. Bring to a boil, then reduce the heat to medium-low and simmer until the seeds are tender, about 8 minutes. Strain the seeds through a mesh strainer and transfer to a bowl. Wipe out and reserve the pan.

2. To the pan, add the remaining pickling ingredients. Place over high heat. Bring to a boil, then reduce to medium-low and simmer until fragrant and the sugar has dissolved, 3 to 5 minutes. Strain over the mustard seeds, discarding the solids. Let the mixture cool to room temperature. Use immediately or cover and refrigerate for up to 4 weeks.

3. To make the dressing, in a small bowl, mix together 2 table-spoons of the pickled mustard seeds and brine, the shallot, mustard, honey and ¼ teaspoon each salt and pepper. Let sit for 10 minutes. Add the marjoram and both oils and whisk until emulsified.

4. To assemble and serve, halve the avocados lengthwise, remove the pits and peel away the skins. Cut each half into slices, leaving the halves intact, and fan onto serving plates, cut sides down. Sprinkle a pinch of salt and 1 teaspoon of lemon juice over each half. Spoon the dressing over the avocados and garnish with ricotta salata and marjoram.

Apple, Celery Root and Fennel Salad with Hazelnuts

Start to finish: **20 minutes** / Servings: **6**

A winter salad needs to stand up to hearty stews and roasts, and that calls for bold, bright flavors. We started with tart apples and thin slices of fennel bulb, the latter adding a pleasant anise flavor. Celery root added a fresh crispness while grated fresh horseradish gave the dish kick. Grating the horseradish triggers a chemical reaction that enhances the root's bite. Tossing it with vinegar and salt helps preserve that heat, which otherwise dissipates quickly. Make sure you grate horseradish in an open and well-ventilated space.

Don't use prepared horseradish in this recipe. It's bottled with vinegar and salt that would alter the balance of flavors.

In a large bowl, combine the shallot and vinegar. Let stand for 10 minutes. Whisk in the horseradish, oil, honey, 1 teaspoon salt and ½ teaspoon pepper. Add the apple, celery root and fennel, then toss to combine. Stir in the parsley and mint, then taste and season with salt and pepper. Transfer to a serving dish and sprinkle with hazelnuts.

1 small shallot, grated

1½ tablespoons cider vinegar

3 tablespoons lightly packed grated fresh horseradish

3 tablespoons extra-virgin olive oil

1 teaspoon honey

Kosher salt and ground black pepper

1 Granny Smith apple, cored and cut into matchsticks

½ small celery root (about 8 ounces), peeled and cut into matchsticks

1 medium fennel bulb, trimmed and thinly sliced

½ cup chopped fresh parsley leaves

¼ cup chopped fresh mint leaves

½ cup hazelnuts, toasted and roughly chopped

Smashed Cucumber Salad

Start to finish: **40 minutes (15 minutes active)** / Servings: 6

Seasoning watery vegetables such as sliced cucumbers can be a challenge; dressings won't adhere to the slick surfaces. Yet across Asia there is a whole class of boldly flavored salads made entirely of cucumber. What do they know that we don't? Our answer came from China's pai huang gua, or smashed cucumber salad. Smashing the cucumbers ruptures more cell walls than slicing and dicing, making it easier to remove the seeds, the main culprit in watery cucumbers. And, it creates craggy, porous surfaces that absorb more dressing. The easiest way to smash cucumbers is to place a rolling pin or the flat side of a chef's knife over them and smack it sharply with your hand.

Don't substitute conventional, *thick-skinned cucumbers for English. The ratio of seeds to flesh is higher and the skins are too tough.*

2 pounds English cucumbers
(about 2 large)

4 teaspoons white sugar

Kosher salt

4 teaspoons unseasoned
rice vinegar

1 medium garlic clove,
smashed and peeled

2 tablespoons grapeseed
or other neutral oil

½ teaspoon red pepper
flakes

1½ tablespoons soy sauce

1 tablespoon toasted
sesame oil

1 tablespoon grated
fresh ginger

Cilantro leaves, sliced
scallions and toasted sesame
seeds, to serve (optional)

1. Trim the ends off the cucumbers, then halve lengthwise. Place each half cut side down, then press a rolling pin or the flat side of a broad knife against the cucumber and press firmly with the heel of your hand. Repeat along the length of the cucumbers until they crack. Pull the sections apart, scraping and discarding the seeds. Cut into rough ¾-inch pieces and set in a large bowl.

2. In a small bowl, combine the sugar and 1 tablespoon salt; toss the cucumbers with 5 teaspoons of the mixture. Transfer to a colander set over a bowl. Refrigerate for 30 to 60 minutes, tossing occasionally. Meanwhile, stir the vinegar and garlic into the remaining sugar-salt mixture. Set aside.

3. In a small skillet over medium-low, combine the grapeseed oil and pepper flakes. Cook, stirring, until sizzling and the pepper flakes begin to darken, 2 to 4 minutes. Strain the oil, discarding the solids.

4. Remove and discard the garlic from the vinegar mixture. Stir in the soy sauce, sesame oil and ginger. Transfer the drained cucumbers to a kitchen towel and pat dry. In a bowl, stir together the cucumbers and dressing, then stir in half of the chili oil. Serve drizzled with more chili oil and sprinkled with cilantro, scallions and sesame seeds, if desired.

French Carrot Salad

Start to finish: **20 minutes** / Servings: **6**

Carrots tend to be a woody afterthought on U.S. salad bars. Here, we transform them into a lively side dish by taking a tip from France, where grated carrots stand alone as an iconic side dish—salade de carottes râpées. Shredding fresh carrots releases their sugars and aromas, creating an earthy sweetness that just needs a bit of acid for balance. Using relatively mild white balsamic vinegar allowed us to up the vinegar-to-oil ratio (1:2) for a punchy but not overwhelming flavor. White balsamic also paired well with a touch of honey, which heightened the carrots' natural sweetness. No tarragon? Use 1½ teaspoons chopped fresh thyme instead.

Don't use old bagged carrots. *This salad is all about the earthy, sweet carrot flavor. Large carrots can be woody, dry and bitter; small baby carrots are too juicy. Look for bunches of medium carrots with the greens still attached.*

In a large bowl, whisk together the vinegar, tarragon, shallot, honey, cayenne and 1 teaspoon salt. Let stand for 10 minutes. Add the oil and whisk to combine. Add the carrots and parsley, then stir until well combined. Taste and season with salt and cayenne pepper. Serve right away or cover and refrigerate for up to 24 hours.

2 tablespoons white balsamic vinegar

2 tablespoons chopped fresh tarragon

1 tablespoon minced shallot

1 teaspoon honey

⅛ teaspoon cayenne pepper, plus more as needed

Kosher salt

¼ cup extra-virgin olive oil

1¼ pounds carrots, peeled and shredded on the large holes of a box grater

1 cup chopped fresh flat-leaf parsley

Hot-Smoked Salmon Salad with Arugula, Avocado and Pepitas

Start to finish: **15 minutes** / Servings: **4**

Ingredients with contrasting flavors and textures are an easy way to elevate everyday meals. And it's key to one of Nigella Lawson's go-to Tuesday night dinners, which upsells basic poached salmon by pairing it with crunchy and tangy ingredients. Lawson simply flakes the salmon into a salad with some watercress, avocado, pumpkin seeds and tangy vinegar. The lush avocado complements the rich salmon, both of which are balanced by the vinegar and pepitas. Our version saves time by using hot-smoked salmon, which has a texture similar to cooked salmon, but with an intensely smoky flavor and sweet and salty overtones. We made our dressing with lemon juice and whole-grain mustard.

Don't assemble the salad *until just before serving. Otherwise, the avocado will brown and the greens will begin to wilt.*

¼ cup lemon juice

2 tablespoons whole-grain mustard

1 tablespoon honey

Kosher salt and ground black pepper

6 tablespoons extra-virgin olive oil

8 ounces hot-smoked salmon, plain or black pepper, skin removed

½ cup toasted, salted pepitas, roughly chopped

2 avocados

10 ounces baby arugula or stemmed watercress (about 10 cups)

1. In a large bowl, whisk together the lemon juice, mustard, honey and ½ teaspoon each salt and pepper. Whisking constantly, add the oil in a stream until emulsified. Into another large bowl, flake the salmon into large chunks. Add half of the chopped pepitas and 2 tablespoons of the dressing. Toss lightly.

2. Halve the avocado lengthwise and discard the pit. Using a paring knife, cut the flesh into ½-inch pieces while still in the skin. Scoop the avocado chunks into the bowl with the salmon. Stir gently to combine. Taste, then season with salt and pepper.

3. Add the greens to the bowl with the remaining dressing and toss. Transfer the arugula to a serving dish and top with the salmon mixture and remaining pepitas.

Soups and Stews

3

Georgian Chicken Soup (Chikhirtma)

Start to finish: 1 hour 45 minutes (45 minutes active)
Servings: 6

We wanted a chicken soup that tastes fresh and light, yet also robust and satisfying. We found our answer in chikhirtma, a traditional soup from Georgia, the Eurasian country that bridges Turkey and Russia. Georgian cuisine often marries Western techniques with Eastern flavors. We used a recipe from Darra Goldstein, author of "The Georgian Feast," as our starting point. Her chikhirtma calls for a whole chicken, but that much meat made the soup feel heavy, so we used just chicken legs. We built flavor with bunches of dill and cilantro stems and a head of garlic, as well as coriander, cinnamon and bay leaves.

Don't simmer the soup after adding the eggs. Heat it gently just until warm, otherwise the eggs will curdle.

For the broth and chicken:

1 bunch fresh cilantro

1 bunch fresh dill

1 garlic head

2½ to 3 pounds bone-in skin-on chicken legs

10 cups water

1 large yellow onion, quartered

2 teaspoons kosher salt

1 teaspoon black peppercorns

½ teaspoon coriander seeds

½ teaspoon red pepper flakes (optional)

3-inch cinnamon stick

2 bay leaves

For the soup:

1 pound carrots (about 5 medium), peeled, halved lengthwise and cut crosswise into ½-inch pieces

1 large yellow onion, coarsely chopped

3 tablespoons salted butter

½ teaspoon kosher salt

½ cup dry vermouth

1 tablespoon all-purpose flour

6 large egg yolks

¼ cup lemon juice

Ground black pepper

1. To make the broth, tie the stems of the cilantro and dill into bundles, then trim off the leaves, reserving ¼ cup of each for garnish. Cut off and discard the top third of the garlic head, leaving the head intact. In a large pot, combine both sets of stems, the garlic, the chicken and the remaining broth ingredients. Bring to a boil, then reduce heat to medium-low. Simmer until the chicken is tender, about 45 minutes. Remove and set aside the garlic head. Transfer the chicken to a plate and cool until easily handled. Shred the chicken into bite-size pieces, discarding the skin, bones and cartilage. Set aside.

2. To make the soup, strain the broth into another pot or bowl, discarding the solids. Using tongs, squeeze the garlic head into the broth; the tender cloves should easily pop out of their skins. Whisk into the broth. Wipe out the empty pot, then add the carrots, onion, butter and salt. Set over medium-high and cook, stirring occasionally, until the onion is browned, 10 to 12 minutes. Add the vermouth, scraping up any browned bits, and cook until evaporated, 1 to 2 minutes. Add the flour and cook, stirring constantly, for 1 minute. Add 2 cups of the broth and stir until smooth, then add the remaining broth and bring to a simmer.

3. In a medium bowl, whisk the yolks. Continue whisking while slowly adding 1 cup of hot broth from the pot. Whisk in the lemon juice, then return the mixture to the pot and whisk to combine. Add the chicken and any accumulated juices and cook until just heated through (do not simmer). Taste and season with salt and pepper. Serve with the reserved chopped cilantro and dill leaves.

Spanish Garlic Soup

Start to finish: **45 minutes** / Servings: **4**

José Andrés taught us this "end of month" recipe—the sort of meal to make quickly with whatever is on hand and when money is tight. His approach: garlic cooked in copious amounts of olive oil with handfuls of thinly sliced stale bread and several tablespoons of smoked paprika. Add some water and simmer, then, off heat, stir in four or five whisked eggs. For our version, we realized the leftover bread, garlic and smoked paprika we had in our cupboards weren't up to Andrés' standards. We boosted flavor by using broth instead of water, and we sautéed both sweet and smoked paprika with garlic and scallions. We didn't have stale bread, so we turned a loaf of rustic sourdough (a baguette or any crusty loaf will do) into croutons, and added a bit of bread directly to the broth to thicken it. To serve, the soup and croutons are married in the serving bowls, allowing each person to adjust the ratio of soup to bread, as well as how long they soak.

Don't skip tempering the egg yolks *with some of the hot broth before adding to the soup. This prevents them from curdling in the hot broth.*

6 scallions, trimmed and thinly sliced, whites and greens divided

6 medium garlic cloves, thinly sliced

6 tablespoons extra-virgin olive oil, divided, plus extra

4 teaspoons sweet paprika

1½ teaspoons smoked paprika

6 ounces sourdough or other rustic bread, cut into ½-inch cubes (about 4 cups), divided

1½ quarts low-sodium chicken broth

Kosher salt and ground black pepper

4 large egg yolks

Sherry vinegar, to taste

1. In a medium saucepan over medium-low, combine the scallion whites, garlic and 3 tablespoons of the oil. Cook, stirring occasionally, until beginning to color, 8 to 10 minutes. Add both paprikas and cook, stirring, until fragrant and darkened, 30 seconds.

2. Add 1 cup of the bread cubes and stir well. Whisk in the broth, increase heat to medium-high and bring to a simmer. Reduce heat to medium-low and simmer, whisking occasionally, for 15 minutes. Whisk vigorously to ensure the bread is thoroughly broken up.

3. Meanwhile, in a 12-inch skillet over medium, combine the remaining 3 tablespoons of oil, the remaining 3 cups of bread, the scallion greens and ½ teaspoon each salt and pepper. Cook, stirring occasionally, until browned and crisp, 8 to 10 minutes.

4. In a medium bowl, whisk the egg yolks. Slowly whisk in 1 cup of the hot broth. Remove the soup from the heat. Off heat, vigorously whisk the egg yolks into the soup, then whisk in the vinegar. Taste and season with salt and pepper. To serve, fill individual bowls with the crouton mixture, then ladle the soup over them. Drizzle with additional oil, if desired.

No-Sear Lamb or Beef and Chickpea Stew

Start to finish: 2 hours 15 minutes (40 minutes active)
Servings: 4

1 tablespoon sweet paprika

2 teaspoons ground cumin

1 teaspoon ground cardamom

¼ teaspoon ground cinnamon

Kosher salt and ground black pepper

1¼ pounds boneless lamb shoulder, trimmed of fat and cut into ¾-inch pieces

1 head garlic

2 tablespoons salted butter

1 large yellow onion, diced (about 2 cups)

2 tablespoons tomato paste

½ pound carrots (2 to 3 medium), peeled, halved lengthwise and cut crosswise into ½-inch pieces

15½-ounce can chickpeas, drained

3 ounces baby spinach (about 3 cups)

1 cup chopped fresh cilantro, plus more to garnish

3 tablespoons lemon juice

Plain whole-milk yogurt, to serve (optional)

The mess, time and trouble required to brown meat for a stew left us longing for a better way. Did we really need that step to get big flavor? Then we discovered a world of alternatives from cultures where cooks skip the browning and instead build layers of flavor with spices and condiments. For our no-sear, no-stock stew, based on the Yemeni dish known as maraq, we started with a dry seasoning mix—paprika, cumin, cardamom, cinnamon, salt and pepper. It did double duty, with half the mixture rubbed onto the meat and the rest briefly cooked in the pot with onion, butter and tomato paste. Cooking the seasonings with the fat and tomato paste bloomed their flavors and lightly browned the tomato paste. We wanted the savory sweetness of roasted whole garlic cloves (mincing releases aggressive sulfurous compounds) but not the trouble of roasting a head separately. So, we sliced off the top of the head, then added it whole to the stew to cook alongside the meat. We liked the flavor and texture of lamb shoulder. Boneless beef chuck worked, too (but needs an extra cup of water and must cook longer, 90 minutes total, before adding the carrots).

Don't use old spices. The backbone of the dish is the bold, vibrant spice mixture. Make sure yours are no more than a year old.

1. In a bowl, stir together the paprika, cumin, cardamom, cinnamon, 2 teaspoons salt and ½ teaspoon pepper. Reserve half of the spice mixture, then toss the lamb with the rest until well coated. Set aside. Cut off and discard the top third of the garlic head, leaving the head intact.

2. In a large Dutch oven over medium-high, melt the butter. Add the onion and cook, stirring often, until softened and just beginning to brown around the edges, 5 to 8 minutes. Add the tomato paste and the reserved spice mixture, then cook, stirring constantly, for 1 minute. Add 6 cups water and bring to a boil over high, then add the lamb and garlic head, cut side down. Cover, leaving the lid slightly ajar, and reduce heat to low.

3. Simmer for 1 hour, adjusting the heat as necessary to maintain a gentle bubble. Add the carrots and continue to simmer, partially covered, for another 30 minutes. Using tongs, remove the garlic head and squeeze over the stew to release the cloves. Stir in the chickpeas and spinach and cook until the spinach is wilted, about 5 minutes.

4. Stir in the cilantro and lemon juice, then season the stew with salt and pepper. Serve topped with yogurt (if using) and sprinkled with cilantro.

Taiwanese Beef Noodle Soup

Start to finish: 2 hours 45 minutes (45 minutes active)
Servings: 6

---

1 tablespoon grapeseed or other neutral oil

6 medium garlic cloves, smashed and peeled

4-inch piece fresh ginger, peeled, cut into 6 to 8 pieces and smashed

6 scallions, white parts roughly chopped, green parts thinly sliced, reserved separately

3 star anise pods

1 tablespoon Sichuan peppercorns

3 tablespoons chili-bean sauce (toban djan, see headnote)

2 tablespoons tomato paste

2 tablespoons packed dark brown sugar

⅓ cup soy sauce

⅓ cup sake

2 to 2½ pounds beef shanks (about 1 inch thick), trimmed

Kosher salt

1 pound baby bok choy, trimmed and cut crosswise into 1-inch pieces

8 ounces dried wheat noodles

Niu rou mian, or beef noodle soup, is one of Taiwan's signature dishes. Chuang Pao-hua, founder of the Chung-Hua Culinary Teaching Center, located in Taipei's Datong District, taught us how to make the hearty meal in a bowl the slow, labor-intensive traditional way. For our much-simplified and streamlined version, we use beef shanks, as the combination of bones and meat yield a richly flavored, full-bodied broth and tender, shreddable beef with a couple hours of simmering. Fragrant star anise and Sichuan peppercorns flavor this meaty broth, along with toban djan, a spicy, fermented chili-bean paste. It's sold in most Asian markets, but if you can't find it, substitute with 2 tablespoons white miso mixed with 4 teaspoons chili-garlic sauce and 2 teaspoons soy sauce. The soup is lightly spicy; you can add more toban djan and/or some ground Sichuan pepper at the table for more heat and spice. Chinese wheat noodles of any thickness worked well, as did Japanese udon and long, thin Italian pastas, such as spaghetti.

Don't forget to skim the fat off the strained cooking liquid. *This prevents the soup from tasting greasy. And don't rinse the drained noodles under cold water. Lukewarm water will keep them from cooling down completely.*

1. In a large Dutch oven over medium, combine the oil, garlic, ginger and scallion whites. Cook, stirring, until sizzling, about 3 minutes. Stir in the star anise and peppercorns, then cook until fragrant, about 30 seconds. Stir in the chili-bean sauce, tomato paste, brown sugar, soy sauce, sake and 2½ quarts water. Bring to a boil over high.

2. Add the beef shanks and return to a simmer. Cover, reduce to low and cook, adjusting as needed to maintain a gentle simmer, until the beef is tender and beginning to fall apart, about 2 hours.

3. Use a slotted spoon to transfer the beef shanks to a bowl and set aside. Pour the cooking liquid through a fine-mesh strainer set over a large bowl; discard the solids. Reserve the pot. Skim off and discard the fat from the surface of the liquid, then return to the pot. When cool enough to handle, shred the meat into bite-size pieces, discarding the bones, fat and gristle. Add the meat to the pot and bring to a simmer over medium-high, then reduce to low and cover to keep warm.

4. In a large pot, bring 4 quarts water to a boil. Add 2 tablespoons salt and the bok choy. Cook until the stems are crisp-tender, about 3 minutes. Use a slotted spoon to transfer the bok choy to a large plate and set aside. Add the noodles to the water and cook until tender. Drain, rinse under lukewarm water, then drain again.

5. Divide the noodles and bok choy among serving bowls, then ladle in the soup and sprinkle with scallion greens.

Pork and Vegetable Miso Soup (Ton-Jiru)

Start to finish: **40 minutes** / Servings: 4

6 to 8 ounces pork tenderloin, trimmed of silver skin, halved lengthwise, cut into ¼-inch slices

¼ cup soy sauce

14-ounce container firm tofu, drained

One 4-by-6-inch piece kombu seaweed

4 medium dried shiitake mushrooms

5 tablespoons white miso

3 small carrots, peeled and cut into ½-inch pieces

2-inch chunk daikon (about 5 ounces), peeled, cut into ½-inch pieces

3 scallions, thinly sliced on the diagonal, white and green parts reserved separately

3 tablespoons sake

Miso gives this simple soup—inspired by a recipe from Japanese cooking expert Elizabeth Andoh—great depth of flavor and a unique savoriness. Of the various types of miso, we liked the mild, subtle sweetness of white (shiro) miso best in this dish, but use any variety you like. For more complexity, you can even blend several different ones.

Don't allow the kombu-shiitake broth to reach a full boil. High heat damages the kombu's delicate flavors and will result in a pungent, overpowering broth.

1. **In a small bowl,** stir together the pork and soy sauce. Cover and refrigerate for at least 20 minutes or up to 1 hour. Meanwhile, line a baking dish with a triple layer of paper towels. Set the tofu in it and cover with additional paper towels. Place a second baking dish or plate on top, then weigh it down with several cans. Let stand for 10 minutes, then discard any accumulated liquid. Pat the tofu dry, cut it into ½-inch cubes and set aside.

2. **Meanwhile,** in a large saucepan over medium-high, bring 5 cups water, the kombu and mushrooms to a simmer; do not boil. Reduce to medium-low and cook, adjusting the heat to maintain a gentle simmer, for about 15 minutes, skimming off any small particles or foam.

3. **Remove** and discard the kombu and mushrooms. Add the tofu, carrots, daikon, scallion whites and sake. Bring to a gentle simmer over medium and cook until the vegetables are tender, 5 to 9 minutes.

4. **Pour off and discard** the excess pork marinade, then stir the pork into the soup. Cook until the pork is no longer pink, about 2 minutes. In a small bowl, whisk the miso and ¼ cup of the hot broth until dissolved, then stir into the soup. Ladle into bowls and sprinkle with scallion greens.

Thai Rice Soup (Khao Tom)

Start to finish: **35 minutes** / Servings: 4

8 ounces ground pork

3 tablespoons fish sauce, divided, plus extra to serve

2 tablespoons chili-garlic sauce, divided, plus extra to serve

Kosher salt and ground white pepper

3 tablespoons lard or refined coconut oil

5 large shallots, peeled, halved lengthwise and thinly sliced (2 cups)

8 medium garlic cloves, thinly sliced

3 lemon grass stalks, trimmed to bottom 6 inches, dry outer leaves removed, smashed

2 tablespoons finely grated fresh ginger

2½ quarts low-sodium chicken broth

4 cups cooked and chilled jasmine rice (see headnote)

1 cup chopped fresh cilantro

3 tablespoons lime juice, plus lime wedges, to serve

Fried shallots, to serve (see recipe p. 63)

Soft- or hard-cooked eggs, peeled and halved, to serve

Savory pork meatballs and jasmine rice give this Thai soup heft, but its aromatic broth—made with plenty of shallots, garlic, lemon grass and ginger—has excellent flavor on its own. The soup is a sort of blank canvas for garnishes; the recipe calls for our favorites, but feel free to offer only those that appeal to you.

Don't use freshly cooked rice, as the grains will turn mushy. Rice that was cooked at least a day in advance, then chilled, held its shape better than rice that was cooked the same day. To chill just-cooked rice, mist a parchment-lined baking sheet with cooking spray and spread the hot rice on it evenly. Let cool to room temperature, cover and refrigerate for at least four hours or up to three days.

1. In a medium bowl, combine the pork, 1 tablespoon of fish sauce, 1 tablespoon of chili-garlic sauce and ¾ teaspoon white pepper. Mix with your hands. Form the mixture into 20 meatballs (about 2 teaspoons each), rolling each between the palms of your hands. Place on a large plate.

2. In a large Dutch oven over medium-high, heat the lard until shimmering. Add the shallots and ½ teaspoon salt and cook, stirring occasionally, until browned, about 5 minutes. Stir in the garlic and cook until fragrant, about 30 seconds. Stir in the lemon grass and ginger and cook until fragrant, about 30 seconds. Add the broth and bring to a boil, scraping up any browned bits, then reduce to medium and simmer, uncovered, for about 15 minutes.

3. Remove and discard the lemon grass. Add the meatballs, stir gently to combine and simmer over medium until the meatballs are just cooked through, 3 to 4 minutes. Stir in the rice and cook until heated through, about 1 minute. Off heat, stir in the remaining 2 tablespoons fish sauce, the remaining 1 tablespoon chili-garlic sauce, 1 teaspoon white pepper, the cilantro and lime juice. Ladle into bowls and serve with fried shallots, egg halves, chili-garlic sauce and lime wedges.

FRIED SHALLOTS

Start to finish: 20 minutes
Makes about 1½ cups

A mandoline works well for slicing the shallots, but a sharp knife does the job, too. Fried shallots are a great garnish on soups, salads, fried rice and noodle dishes. The oil left over from frying the shallots is infused with flavor; use it for stir-frying, sautéing and in salad dressings.

Don't be tempted to turn the heat up once the shallots are added to the oil. Moderate heat and frequent stirring ensure the shallots brown evenly and without scorching.

1 cup grapeseed or other neutral oil

12 ounces shallots, thinly sliced

1. Line a large plate with a triple layer of paper towels. Place a mesh strainer over a heat-safe medium bowl and set near the stove.

2. In a large saucepan over medium-high, heat the oil to about 275°F; a slice of shallot dropped in the oil should sizzle immediately. Add the shallots and reduce to medium. Cook, stirring, until golden brown, 8 to 10 minutes. Drain immediately in the strainer and shake the strainer to remove excess oil.

3. Using tongs, transfer the shallots to the prepared plate, spreading them in an even layer. Let cool completely. Store the shallots and oil separately in airtight containers. The shallots will keep for up to 1 week at room temperature; the oil will keep for up to 1 month in the refrigerator.

Chickpea and Harissa Soup (Lablabi)

Start to finish: 1 hour, plus soaking the chickpeas
Servings: 8

For the soup:

2 cups dried chickpeas

Kosher salt and ground black pepper

5 tablespoons extra-virgin olive oil, divided

1 large yellow onion, chopped

6 medium garlic cloves, minced

2 tablespoons tomato paste

2 tablespoons ground cumin, toasted (see headnote)

6 tablespoons harissa paste

3 quarts low-sodium chicken broth or water

8 ounces crusty white bread, sliced ½-inch-thick and torn into bite-size pieces

2 tablespoons lemon juice

For serving:

8 soft-cooked eggs, peeled and halved (see headnote)

½ cup drained capers

½ cup chopped pitted green olives

½ cup chopped fresh flat-leaf parsley

½ cup chopped fresh cilantro

Extra-virgin olive oil

Harissa paste

2 tablespoons ground cumin, toasted

Lemon wedges

This brothy-bready Tunisian chickpea soup gets punches of flavor from garlic, tomato paste and cumin. For the harissa, use our recipe (p. 618) or buy it ready-made; we like the DEA brand. And instead of using stale bread—as is common in Tunisia—we got better texture by toasting chunks of crusty bread in olive oil to make croutons. Toasted ground cumin is used in the soup as well as on it as a garnish; to be efficient, toast it all at once. In a small, dry skillet over medium, toast 5 tablespoons ground cumin, stirring constantly, until fragrant, about 1 minute, then transfer to a small bowl. To make soft-cooked eggs for serving, bring 2 cups water to a simmer in a large saucepan fitted with a steamer basket. Add the desired number of eggs, cover and steam over medium for 7 minutes. Immediately transfer to ice water to stop the cooking.

Don't forget to soak *the dried chickpeas. They need to soak for at least 12 hours before cooking.*

1. First, soak the chickpeas. In a large bowl, combine 2 quarts water, the chickpeas and 2 tablespoons salt. Let soak at room temperature for at least 12 hours or up to 24 hours. Drain the chickpeas and set aside.

2. To make the soup, in a large Dutch oven, heat 2 tablespoons of oil until shimmering. Add the onion and cook, stirring occasionally, until lightly golden, about 5 minutes. Stir in the garlic and cook until fragrant, about 30 seconds. Add the tomato paste and cook, stirring, until it browns, about 2 minutes. Stir in the cumin and harissa, then cook until fragrant, about 1 minute. Add the chickpeas and broth, then bring to a boil over high. Reduce to medium and simmer, uncovered, stirring occasionally, until the chickpeas are tender, about 1 hour.

3. Meanwhile, in a 12-inch nonstick skillet over medium, combine the bread, the remaining 3 tablespoons oil and 1 teaspoon salt. Cook, stirring occasionally, until crisp and light golden brown, 4 to 6 minutes. Remove from the heat and let the croutons cool in the pan. Transfer to a bowl.

4. When the chickpeas are tender, remove the pot from the heat and stir in the lemon juice. Taste and season with salt and pepper.

5. To serve, place 2 to 3 tablespoons of croutons in each serving bowl. Ladle chickpeas and broth around them, then top each portion with soft-cooked egg halves and 1 tablespoon each capers, olives, parsley and cilantro, or as desired. Drizzle with oil and garnish to taste with harissa and cumin. Serve with lemon wedges.

Mexican Chicken Soup with Tomatillos and Hominy

Start to finish: 2 hours (1 hour active) / Servings: 6

---

2 large white onions,
1 quartered and 1 chopped

1 bunch fresh cilantro, stems
and leaves separated

2 ancho or pasilla chilies,
stemmed, seeded and torn
into rough pieces

2 tablespoons coriander
seeds, toasted, plus 1
tablespoon ground coriander

2 tablespoons cumin seeds,
toasted, plus 1 tablespoon
ground cumin

Kosher salt

1 head of garlic

2½ to 3 pounds bone-in
skin-on chicken legs

2 fresh poblano chilies

2 fresh jalapeño chilies

1 pound fresh tomatillos,
husked and quartered

2 tablespoons grapeseed
or other neutral oil

2 teaspoons dried oregano,
preferably Mexican

15-ounce can hominy, drained

Toasted pepitas, lime wedges
and sour cream or Mexican
crema (optional), to serve

For a fresh take on chicken soup we looked to Mexico for inspiration. We used charred fresh jalapeño and poblano peppers, a flavor-boosting technique common to Mexican cooking. We added depth with relatively little effort by using toasted whole as well as ground coriander and cumin. For more spice, use serranos instead of jalapeños, or include the chilies' seeds. If you can't find fresh tomatillos, substitute canned tomatillos, drained. The broth and chicken can be made a day ahead and refrigerated separately before proceeding. However, shred the chicken while it's still warm. We liked garnishing the soup with chopped avocado, sliced jalapeños, crumbled queso fresco and fried tortilla strips.

Don't leave out the tomatillos. They provide acidity and texture.

1. **In a large pot,** combine 10 cups water, the quartered onion, cilantro stems, dried chilies, coriander seeds, cumin seeds and 1 teaspoon salt. Cut off and discard the top third of the garlic head, leaving the head intact, and add to the pot. Cover and bring to a boil, then simmer for 10 minutes. Add the chicken and return to a boil. Reduce heat to medium-low and cook partially covered for 30 minutes, maintaining a gentle simmer.

2. **Meanwhile,** heat the broiler to high with an oven rack 6 inches from the element. Arrange the poblanos and jalapeños on a rimmed baking sheet and broil, turning frequently, until evenly blackened and blistered, 10 to 12 minutes. Transfer to a bowl, cover tightly and set aside. Chop the cilantro leaves and set aside.

3. **Peel, stem and seed** the charred chilies, then roughly chop and add to a food processor along with the tomatillos. Pulse until coarsely chopped, 6 to 8 pulses.

4. **Transfer the chicken** and garlic head to a plate and let cool. Strain the broth, discarding the solids. Wipe out the pot. Add the oil, chopped onion and ½ teaspoon salt. Cook over medium-high, stirring occasionally, until softened and beginning to brown, 7 to 9 minutes. Add the ground coriander, ground cumin and oregano and cook, stirring constantly, for 1 minute. Add the tomatillo-chili mixture and cook, stirring frequently and scraping up any browned bits, until most of the moisture has evaporated, about 5 minutes. Add the broth and bring to a boil.

5. **Shred the chicken** into bite-size pieces, discarding the skin, bones and cartilage. Using tongs, squeeze the garlic head into the soup. The tender cloves should easily pop out of their skins. Add the chicken and hominy. Return to a simmer and cook until heated through, about 5 minutes. Stir in ½ cup of the chopped cilantro, then taste and season with salt. Top the soup with toasted pepitas, lime juice, more chopped cilantro and sour cream, if desired.

Somali Chicken Soup

Start to finish: **50 minutes** / Servings: 6

---

1 tablespoon grapeseed or other neutral oil

2 large yellow onions, chopped

Kosher salt and ground white pepper

2 serrano chilies, stemmed and sliced into thin rounds

4 medium garlic cloves, smashed and peeled

4 teaspoons ground coriander

2 teaspoons ground cardamom

1 bunch fresh cilantro, stems chopped, leaves finely chopped, reserved separately

4 plum tomatoes, cored, seeded and chopped, divided

1½ quarts low-sodium chicken broth or water

Four 12-ounce bone-in, skin-on chicken breasts

1½ cups jasmine or basmati rice, rinsed and drained

2 tablespoons lime juice, plus lime wedges, to serve

Thinly sliced radishes and/or chopped red cabbage, to serve (optional)

Green chili sauce, berbere sauce or other hot sauce, to serve (see recipes p. 69)

This is our take on maraq cad, the Somali soup known for its finishing touches, which are added at the last moment so they retain bright bold flavor and texture. We were taught how to make it by Somalia native and Massachusetts independent food consultant Nimco De Waal. Serve this soup family style: Bring the pot to the table along with the radishes, cabbage and lime wedges, then have diners fill and garnish their bowls as they like. Offer a simple homemade or storebought hot sauce alongside. Hot steamed rice, added to bowls before the soup is ladled in, is a satisfying addition.

Don't use boneless, skinless chicken breasts. *Both the bones and skin contribute flavor to the broth.*

---

1. In a large Dutch oven over medium, heat the oil until shimmering. Add the onions and ½ teaspoon salt and cook, stirring, until beginning to brown, about 5 minutes. Add the chilies, garlic, coriander, cardamom, cilantro stems and half of the tomatoes. Cook, stirring constantly, until fragrant, about 30 seconds.

2. Add the broth and bring to a simmer over high. Submerge the chicken breasts in the broth, cover and cook over low until a skewer inserted in the thickest part of the chicken meets no resistance or the chicken reaches 160°F, about 30 minutes.

3. Meanwhile, in a medium saucepan, combine the rice, 2 cups water and 1 teaspoon salt. Bring to a simmer over medium-high, then reduce to low and cook, covered, until the liquid is absorbed and the rice is tender, 15 to 20 minutes. Off heat, remove the lid, lay a clean dish towel over the pot, replace the cover and let stand for about 10 minutes or until ready to serve.

4. Using tongs, transfer the chicken to a large plate and set aside to cool. Pour the broth through a fine-mesh strainer set over a large heatproof bowl; discard the solids. Return the broth to the pot. When the chicken is cool enough to handle, shred the meat into bite-size pieces, discarding the skin and bones.

5. Add the chicken to the broth and bring to a simmer over medium-high. Remove from the heat and stir in the remaining tomatoes, the cilantro leaves and lime juice. Taste and season with salt and pepper.

6. To serve, fluff the rice with a fork, then mound a portion into each serving bowl. Ladle the soup over the rice, then top each portion with radishes and/or cabbage (if using) and the hot sauces. Serve with lime wedges.

BERBERE SAUCE

Start to finish: **15 minutes** / Makes about **¼ cup**

For this bold, paste-like sauce, macerating the onion in lime juice tempers its harsh bite. For a brighter flavor, substitute sweet paprika instead of smoked. This sauce is best used the day it is made.

3 tablespoons lime juice

1 tablespoon minced red onion

¼ teaspoon kosher salt

1 tablespoon smoked paprika

1 teaspoon ground coriander

1 teaspoon ground ginger

½ teaspoon cayenne pepper

¼ teaspoon ground cardamom

1. In a small bowl, stir together the lime juice, onion and salt. Let stand for 10 minutes.

2. Meanwhile, in a small skillet over medium-low, toast the paprika, coriander, ginger, cayenne and cardamom, stirring constantly, until fragrant, 1 to 2 minutes. Remove from the heat and let cool for 10 minutes. Stir the spices into the lime juice-onion mixture.

GREEN CHILI SAUCE

Start to finish: **5 minutes** / Makes about **1 cup**

This sauce is spicy and sharp on its own, but a spoonful stirred into a serving of soup provides the perfect flavor accent. Refrigerate leftovers in an airtight container for up to a week.

1 plum tomato, cored and quartered

5 serrano chilies, stemmed

3 tablespoons lime juice

2 medium garlic cloves, smashed and peeled

¾ teaspoons kosher salt

In a blender, combine all ingredients and process until smooth, 1 to 2 minutes, scraping the sides as needed.

Black-Eyed Pea and Sweet Potato Stew (Ndambe)

Start to finish: 40 minutes / Servings: 6

Both sweet potatoes and black-eyed peas are staples of West African cooking. In this recipe for Senegalese ndambe (pronounced NAM-bay), they're simmered together to make a hearty vegetarian stew. Our version is based on a recipe from Pierre Thiam's "Yolele!" cookbook. Canned black-eyed peas keep this dish fast and simple.

Don't use neutral-flavored oil in place of the coconut oil. Coconut oil—particularly unrefined—infuses the stew with a sweet flavor while adding richness.

1. In a large Dutch oven over medium, heat the coconut oil until shimmering. Add the onion, 2 teaspoons salt and ½ teaspoon pepper, then cook, stirring, until the onion is light golden brown and softened, 7 to 10 minutes.

2. Stir in the garlic and chilies, then cook until fragrant, about 30 seconds. Add the black-eyed peas, bay leaves and 5 cups water. Bring to a simmer over medium-high, then reduce to medium and cook, uncovered, stirring occasionally, for about 15 minutes.

3. Stir in the sweet potatoes and 2 teaspoons salt. Cover, reduce to medium-low and cook until the potatoes are tender, 10 to 15 minutes. Off heat, stir in the tomatoes, parsley and lemon juice. Taste and season with salt and pepper. Serve with lemon wedges.

2 tablespoons coconut oil, preferably unrefined

1 large yellow onion, finely chopped

Kosher salt and ground black pepper

8 medium garlic cloves, minced

2 Fresno chilies, stemmed and sliced into thin rings

Three 14½-ounce cans black-eyed peas, rinsed and drained

2 bay leaves

1 pound sweet potatoes, peeled and cut into ½-inch cubes

1 pound plum tomatoes, cored and chopped

1 cup finely chopped fresh flat-leaf parsley

2 tablespoons lemon juice, plus lemon wedges, to serve

Turkish Red Lentil Soup

Start to finish: **45 minutes** / Servings: 4

Kırmızı mercimek çorbası is a traditional Turkish soup made with red lentils, which soften and break down during cooking, adding a rustic texture that's creamy but not starchy or heavy. Some versions include vegetables such as potatoes, carrots or fresh tomatoes, but ours lets the lentils take the lead. The Aleppo pepper brings gentle heat to the dish. If you can't find it locally, order online or substitute with an additional teaspoon of paprika and ½ teaspoon red pepper flakes. The soup can be made vegan by substituting olive oil for the butter.

Don't omit the rice. *The grains help thicken the soup.*

1. In a large saucepan over medium, melt the butter. Add the onion and cook, stirring occasionally, until softened and translucent, about 5 minutes. Stir in the garlic and cook until fragrant, about 30 seconds. Stir in the tomato paste, paprika and cumin, then cook for about 1 minute.

2. Add the lentils, rice, 5 cups water and 2 teaspoons salt. Stir to combine and bring to a boil over medium-high. Reduce the heat to maintain a steady simmer, cover and cook, stirring occasionally, until the lentils and rice are tender and broken down, about 30 minutes. Season to taste.

3. Meanwhile, in a small skillet over medium, heat the olive oil, swirling to coat the pan. Add the Aleppo pepper and cook until a few bubbles appear and the oil is bright red, 1 to 2 minutes. Remove from the heat and set aside.

4. Serve the soup with Aleppo pepper oil drizzled over each serving and sprinkled with mint, if using, and lemon wedges on the side.

3 tablespoons salted butter

1 medium yellow onion, chopped

1 medium garlic clove, finely grated

1 tablespoon tomato paste

1 tablespoon sweet paprika

½ teaspoon ground cumin

1 cup red lentils

2 tablespoons long-grain white rice

Kosher salt

3 tablespoons extra-virgin olive oil

2 teaspoons Aleppo pepper (see headnote)

Chopped fresh mint, to serve (optional)

Lemon wedges, to serve

Vietnamese Meatball and Watercress Soup (Canh)

Start to finish: **40 minutes** / Servings: 4

---

1 pound ground pork

6 scallions, white parts finely chopped, green parts thinly sliced, reserved separately

1 large egg white, lightly beaten

3 tablespoons fish sauce, divided

4 teaspoons finely grated fresh ginger, divided

Kosher salt and ground white pepper

2 tablespoons grapeseed or other neutral oil

1 medium yellow onion, chopped

4 medium garlic cloves, thinly sliced

2 quarts low-sodium chicken broth or water

1 bunch watercress, cut into 1½-inch lengths (4 cups lightly packed)

2 tablespoons lime juice

This refreshing supper is a take on canh, a type of quick, brothy Vietnamese soup. The soups can be sour, rich with vegetables, or loaded with seafood. But whatever variety, the unifying factor is simplicity. Our version stays true to the simplicity, but scales up the ingredients so it can serve as a satisfying meal on its own. Watercress adds a peppery note; look for "live" watercress, which is packaged with its roots attached. It stays fresher longer and is easier to clean. To prep it, trim off and discard the roots, rinse and drain the greens, then cut them into 1½-inch lengths, discarding any stems that are thick or tough. If you prefer, substitute an equal amount of baby spinach for the watercress, but roughly chop the leaves before using. We also liked this soup made with chicken bouillon paste instead of chicken broth; use 2 tablespoons of paste dissolved in 2 quarts of water.

Don't leave the meatballs at room temperature after shaping them. Chilling firms them so they hold together in the simmering broth.

---

1. Line a rimmed baking sheet with kitchen parchment and mist with cooking spray. In a medium bowl, combine the pork, scallion whites, egg white, 1 tablespoon of fish sauce, 2 teaspoons of ginger, 1¼ teaspoons salt and 1 teaspoon white pepper. Mix with your hands. Lightly moisten your hands with water and form into 20 balls, each about a generous tablespoon. Set on the prepared baking sheet, cover and refrigerate.

2. In a large Dutch oven over medium, heat the oil until shimmering. Add the onion and cook, stirring, until beginning to soften, about 5 minutes. Stir in the remaining 2 teaspoons ginger and the garlic, then cook until fragrant, about 30 seconds. Add the broth and bring to a boil over high. Reduce to medium-low and simmer, uncovered, until the onion is fully softened, about 10 minutes.

3. Add the meatballs, then bring to a simmer over medium-high. Reduce the heat to maintain a gentle simmer and cook without stirring until the meatballs are cooked through, 8 to 10 minutes; they should reach 160°F at the center.

4. Off heat, stir in the watercress and the remaining 2 tablespoons fish sauce. Let stand until the greens are wilted and tender, about 1 minute. Stir in the lime juice. Taste and season with salt and pepper, then stir in the scallion greens.

Singapore Shrimp and Chicken Noodle Soup (Laksa)

Start to finish: 1 hour 20 minutes / Servings: 6

6 medium shallots, peeled and halved

6 medium garlic cloves, peeled

3 tablespoons Thai red curry paste

2 lemon grass stalks, trimmed to the bottom 6 inches, dry outer layers discarded, chopped

2-inch piece fresh ginger, peeled and sliced into coins

2 teaspoons ground turmeric

1 bunch fresh cilantro, tender stems and leaves chopped, reserved separately, plus cilantro leaves, to serve

2 tablespoons grapeseed or other neutral oil

1 pound jumbo (16/20 per pound) shrimp, peeled (shells reserved) and deveined

1 pound boneless, skinless chicken thighs, trimmed

14-ounce container firm tofu, drained, patted dry and cut into ½-inch cubes

6 tablespoons fish sauce, divided

3 tablespoons chili-garlic sauce, divided, plus more to serve

6 ounces wide (¼ inch) rice stick noodles

13½-ounce can coconut milk

Kosher salt and ground white pepper

3 tablespoons lime juice, plus lime wedges, to serve

Laksa is a vibrant seafood and chicken noodle soup eaten any time of day in Singapore. We use the shrimp shells to give maximum flavor to a broth that is seasoned with shallots, lemon grass and Thai red curry paste. You can boost the spiciness of the soup with extra chili-garlic sauce. If you like, garnish with chopped cucumber, halved hard-cooked eggs and chopped roasted peanuts.

Don't discard the shrimp shells; you'll need them to make the broth. If you purchased already peeled shrimp, use just the tails for the broth.

1. **In a food processor,** combine the shallots, garlic, curry paste, lemon grass, ginger, turmeric and cilantro stems. Process until finely chopped, about 20 seconds.

2. **In a large Dutch oven** over medium-high, heat the oil until barely smoking. Add the shrimp shells and cook, stirring frequently, until they begin to char, 2 to 3 minutes. Stir in the shallot mixture and cook, stirring constantly, until fragrant and the paste begins to stick to the pot, about 2 minutes. Add 2 quarts water and bring to a boil over high, then reduce to medium-low, cover and simmer for 30 minutes.

3. **Strain the broth** through a fine-mesh strainer set over a large heat-safe bowl, pressing on the solids to extract as much liquid as possible. Discard the solids. Return the broth to the pot and bring to a simmer over medium-high. Stir in the chicken, tofu, 1 tablespoon of fish sauce and 1 tablespoon of chili-garlic sauce. Return to a simmer, cover and reduce to low. Cook until a skewer inserted into the chicken meets no resistance, about 30 minutes.

4. **Meanwhile,** in a small bowl, toss the shrimp with 1 tablespoon of the remaining fish sauce and 1 tablespoon of the remaining chili-garlic sauce. Cover and refrigerate until needed.

5. **Bring a large pot** of water to a boil, then remove from the heat. Stir in the noodles and let soak until softened but still chewy, about 10 minutes. Drain in a colander, rinse under cold water and drain again. Divide the noodles evenly among 6 serving bowls.

6. **When the chicken is cooked,** transfer to a bowl, then use 2 forks to shred it into bite-size pieces. Return the chicken to the pot and stir in the coconut milk. Bring to a simmer over medium, then reduce to low. Add the shrimp and cook, stirring occasionally, until the shrimp are cooked through and opaque, 1 to 2 minutes.

7. **Off heat,** stir in the cilantro leaves, the remaining 4 tablespoons fish sauce, the remaining 1 tablespoon chili-garlic sauce and the lime juice. Taste and season with salt and white pepper. Ladle the soup over the noodles. Sprinkle with cilantro leaves and serve with lime wedges and chili-garlic sauce.

Greek White Bean Soup (Fasolada)

Start to finish: 1½ hours, plus soaking time for beans
Servings: 6

---

6 tablespoons extra-virgin olive oil, divided, plus more to serve

1 large red onion, chopped

3 medium celery stalks, chopped

3 medium carrots, peeled and chopped, divided

Kosher salt and ground black pepper

4 medium garlic cloves, minced

½ teaspoon red pepper flakes

3 tablespoons tomato paste

1 pound dried cannellini beans, soaked and drained (see headnote)

2½ quarts low-sodium chicken broth

4 teaspoons red wine vinegar

½ cup finely chopped fresh flat-leaf parsley

½ cup pitted Kalamata olives, chopped

2 ounces feta cheese, crumbled (½ cup)

Carrots lend sweetness to this soup that's balanced by briny olives and salty feta cheese. Dried cannellini beans that are soaked before cooking yield a full-flavored soup. To soak the beans, in a large bowl, stir together 2 quarts water and 1 tablespoon kosher salt. Add the beans, soak at room temperature for at least 12 hours or up to 24 hours, then drain well. Canned beans work in a pinch; see instructions below. We use extra-virgin olive oil to give the soup a little body and fruity, peppery richness throughout, as we were shown by Argiro Barbarigou, one of Greece's leading voices on classic cooking. We vigorously whisk in a few tablespoons just before serving. Refrigerate leftovers in an airtight container for up to two days; reheat in a saucepan over low, adding water as needed to thin the consistency.

Don't skip the step of mashing 1 cup of the cooked beans to stir back into the soup. The mashed beans give the soup a creamy, slightly thickened consistency.

---

1. In a large pot over medium, heat 3 tablespoons of oil until shimmering. Add the onion, celery, half the carrots and ½ teaspoon salt, then cook, stirring occasionally, until the vegetables begin to brown, about 5 minutes. Add the garlic and red pepper flakes, then cook, stirring, until fragrant, about 30 seconds. Add the tomato paste and cook, stirring, until the paste begins to brown, about 2 minutes. Stir in the beans and the broth, then bring to a simmer over medium-high. Cover partially, reduce to low and simmer, stirring occasionally, until the beans are tender, about 1 hour.

2. Using a slotted spoon, transfer 1 cup of the beans to a medium bowl. Using a potato masher or fork, mash the beans to a paste, then whisk the mixture back into the soup. Add the remaining carrots, bring to a simmer over medium and cook, stirring occasionally, until the carrots are just tender, about 10 minutes.

3. Off heat, stir in the vinegar, then vigorously whisk in the remaining 3 tablespoons oil. Taste and season with salt and pepper. Ladle into bowls and top with the parsley, olives and cheese.

GREEK WHITE BEAN SOUP (FASOLADA) WITH CANNED BEANS:

Rinse and drain four 15½-ounce cans cannellini beans; measure 1 cup of the beans into a medium bowl, then use a potato masher or fork to mash to a paste. Follow the recipe as written, making the following changes: Add all of the carrots with the onion and celery; reduce the broth to 1½ quarts; and add both the whole and mashed beans at once. After bringing to a simmer over medium-high, reduce to medium-low, cover and cook, stirring occasionally and maintaining a gentle simmer, until the carrots are just tender,

Tortilla Soup

Start to finish: **40 minutes** / Servings: **4 to 6**

Our take on sopa de tortilla is a simple, homestyle tortilla soup like the one made for us by home cook Jazmín Martínez in Mexico City. It is pureed for smoothness; contrasting colors, flavors and textures are added with garnishes. For the best results, ripe tomatoes are key. In non-summer months, we find Campari tomatoes to be a good option, as well as cherry or grape tomatoes. The tomatoes need only to be cored before they're tossed into the pot (cherry or grape tomatoes can be used whole). Tortilla chips, called totopos in Mexico, are used in two ways: They're cooked and pureed with the base to thicken the soup, then fresh chips are added to the serving bowls before the soup is ladled in.

Don't blend all of the soup mixture at once. If the blender jar is too full with hot liquid, when the machine is turned on the rapid burst of steam may loosen the lid and cause splattering.

2 tablespoons lard or neutral oil

1 large white onion, halved and thinly sliced

6 medium garlic cloves, smashed and peeled

2 jalapeño chilies, stemmed, seeded and sliced

1 teaspoon cumin seeds

1 bunch cilantro, stems roughly chopped, leaves chopped, reserved separately

2 pounds ripe tomatoes (see headnote), cored

2 cups yellow or white tortilla chips, plus more to serve

1½ quarts low-sodium chicken broth

1 teaspoon white sugar

Kosher salt and ground black pepper

Sour cream or crumbled cotija cheese, plus finely chopped onion, to serve

Diced avocado, to serve (optional)

1. In a large pot over medium-high, heat the lard until shimmering. Add the onion and cook, stirring, until softened, about 5 minutes. Add the garlic, jalapeños, cumin and cilantro stems, then cook, stirring, until fragrant, about 30 seconds. Stir in the tomatoes, tortilla chips, broth and sugar. Bring to a boil, then cover, reduce to medium and cook, stirring, at a simmer, until the tomatoes have softened and their skins begin to peel away, about 10 minutes.

2. Remove the pot from the heat and cool, uncovered, for 5 minutes. Using a blender and working in batches so the jar is never more than half full, puree the mixture until smooth; transfer each batch to a large bowl.

3. Wipe out the pot, then pour in the puree. Cook over medium, stirring often, until heated, about 5 minutes. Taste and season with salt and pepper, then stir in half of the chopped cilantro leaves. To serve, add tortilla chips to individual bowls, then ladle in soup. Sprinkle with the remaining chopped cilantro leaves and top with sour cream, finely chopped onion, and avocado (if using).

Andalusian Tomato and Bread Soup (Salmorejo)

Start to finish: **15 minutes, plus chilling** / Servings: 4

If peak-season, perfectly ripe tomatoes are available, use them in this simple but richly flavored, no-cook chilled soup, a spin on gazpacho from Andalucia, in southern Spain. Campari or cocktail tomatoes also are a good choice, as they are dependably sweet year-round. Excellent results also require high-quality extra-virgin olive oil, so make sure the oil you use does not have bitter or harsh notes. Bread helps thicken the soup and gives it creamy consistency. Choose a crusty, country-style loaf with a relatively soft interior so the bread blends easily into the soup, but remember to remove the crust. To keep the soup chilled for as long as possible at the table, we like to refrigerate the serving bowls.

Don't forget to taste the soup for seasoning after chilling, just before serving. Chilling blunts flavor, so though the soup may have initially tasted fine, after chilling it likely will need additional salt and pepper.

2 pounds ripe tomatoes (see headnote), cored

2½ ounces country-style white bread (see headnote), crust removed, torn into small pieces (about 1½ cups)

½ medium red bell pepper, stemmed, seeded and chopped

1 medium garlic clove, smashed and peeled

1 teaspoon white sugar

3 tablespoons sherry vinegar, plus more to serve

Kosher salt and ground black pepper

¾ cup plus 1 tablespoon extra-virgin olive oil, plus more to serve

4 thin slices prosciutto (2 ounces), torn into pieces

4 hard-cooked eggs, peeled and quartered (optional)

¼ cup finely chopped fresh flat-leaf parsley

1. In a blender, combine the tomatoes, bread, bell pepper, garlic, sugar, vinegar, 2 teaspoons salt and 1 teaspoon pepper. Blend on high until completely smooth and no bits of tomato skins remain, about 1 minute. With the blender running, gradually add ¾ cup oil. Transfer to a large bowl, then taste and season with salt and pepper. Cover and refrigerate until well chilled, 2 to 4 hours.

2. While the soup chills, in a 12-inch nonstick skillet over medium, heat the remaining 1 tablespoon oil until shimmering. Add the prosciutto and cook, stirring occasionally, until crisp, about 2 minutes. Transfer the prosciutto to a paper towel–lined plate and let cool completely, then roughly chop; set aside.

3. Taste the soup and season again with salt and pepper. Ladle it into chilled bowls. Top with the prosciutto, hard-cooked egg (if using) and parsley. Drizzle with additional oil and vinegar as desired.

Gonzalo Guzmán's Pozole Rojo

Start to finish: 2¼ hours (50 minutes active) / Servings: 6

4 large ancho chilies, stemmed and seeded

Boiling water

2 medium garlic cloves, divided

½ large white onion, roughly chopped

¾ teaspoon dried Mexican oregano

½ teaspoon cumin seeds

Kosher salt

¼ medium yellow onion

4 cilantro stems

1 bay leaf

2 pounds boneless pork shoulder, trimmed and cut into 1-inch cubes

4 cups rinsed and drained canned hominy (from two 29-ounce cans)

For serving:

Shredded green cabbage

Thinly sliced radishes

Thinly sliced red onion

Chili powder

Chopped fresh oregano or dried oregano

Cilantro leaves

Tortilla chips

Lime halves

Chef Gonzalo Guzmán's pozole rojo (pork, red chili and hominy stew), from his book "Nopalito," is boldly flavored with ancho chilies, herbs, cumin and aromatics. He blends some of the hominy (dried corn kernels treated with alkali then cooked until tender) with some of the braising liquid, then adds the puree back into the soup to give the broth body. Guzmán says garnishes are a key component of pozole and encourages piling them high onto individual servings. A long list is included here, but you can offer as many or as few as you like. The pozole can be made a few days in advance, then reheated for serving.

Don't discard the chili soaking water after removing the chilies. You will need some of it to thin the chili mixture in the blender so it breaks down into a smooth puree.

1. **Place the chilies** in a medium heatproof bowl and add boiling water to cover. Let stand until the chilies are softened, about 20 minutes. Remove the chilies from the water and transfer to a blender; reserve the water. Add 1 garlic clove, the white onion, oregano, cumin and a generous pinch of salt to the blender, then puree until smooth, about 2 minutes, scraping down the jar as needed and adding just enough of the soaking water to form a thick, smooth paste.

2. **In a piece of cheesecloth,** wrap the remaining garlic clove, yellow onion, cilantro stems and bay; secure with kitchen twine to form a small bundle. Set aside.

3. **Season the pork with salt.** In a large pot, combine the pork, chili puree and cheesecloth bundle, then stir in 3 quarts water. Season generously with salt and bring to a boil. Reduce to a simmer and cook, uncovered, until a skewer inserted into the pork meets no resistance, about 1 hour. Remove from the heat.

4. **In the blender,** puree ½ cup of hominy with about ½ cup of the braising liquid from the pork until smooth, about 20 seconds. Stir the puree and the remaining 3½ cups hominy into the pot and bring to a simmer over medium-high. Remove from the heat and let stand for 5 minutes. Using a wide, shallow spoon, skim off and discard the fat on the surface.

5. **Bring the pozole** back to a simmer over medium-high. Taste and adjust the seasoning with salt. Ladle into bowls and serve with cabbage, radishes, red onion, oregano, chili powder, cilantro, tortilla chips and limes.

Passatelli in Brodo

Start to finish: 1¼ hours (30 minutes active)
Servings: 4 to 6

---

4 large eggs, plus 2 large
egg yolks

3 tablespoons extra-virgin
olive oil, divided, plus more to
serve

8 ounces Parmesan cheese
without rind, cut into rough
1-inch chunks, plus finely
grated Parmesan to serve

2½ cups (6½ ounces) panko
breadcrumbs

¼ teaspoon grated nutmeg,
plus more to serve

Kosher salt and ground
black pepper

2 quarts low-sodium chicken
broth or homemade chicken
broth (p. 85)

In the tiny village of Monteveglio, about 12 miles west of Bologna, Italy, we tasted delicious home-cooked passatelli in brodo. Paolo Parmeggiani, owner of the small restaurant/hotel Trattoria del Borgo, demonstrated the dish—made with stale bread, cheese, eggs, broth and little else. It exemplifies cucina povera, or peasant cooking. Passatelli are cylindrical dumplings—like fat, short spaghetti—made by extruding dough through smallish holes; the dumplings are simply poached and served in chicken broth. We found that in lieu of a traditional passatelli maker, a potato ricer with $^3/_{16}$-inch perforations works well for extruding the dough. Another alternative is to use a cooling rack with a $^3/_8$-inch wire grid (instructions are included in the recipe). To make passatelli dough, Italian cooks use stale bread processed into breadcrumbs. But since we rarely have leftover bread and in order to consistently produce a dough with the proper texture, we use Japanese-style panko breadcrumbs. We highly recommend using homemade chicken broth. We came up with a simple Instant Pot version (p. 85). If using purchased broth, consider upping its flavor by adding a chunk of Parmesan rind and/or ½ teaspoon red pepper flakes.

Don't use pre-grated Parmesan or domestic Parmesan-like cheese. Since there are so few ingredients in the passatelli, true Parmigiano-Reggiano is essential for flavor. Purchase it in a chunk, not pre-grated, as the cheese loses freshness once it's grated. Plus, if you buy a chunk, you will have a piece of rind to simmer in the broth as a flavor booster.

1. In a 2-cup liquid measuring cup or medium bowl, whisk the eggs and yolks, ¾ cup water and 1 tablespoon of the oil. In a food processor, process the Parmesan chunks until finely ground, about 20 seconds. Add the panko, ¼ teaspoon of nutmeg, 1 teaspoon salt and ½ teaspoon pepper. Process until the mixture is powdery, about 30 seconds. With the machine running, add the egg mixture, then process until smooth, about 1 minute. Let rest in the food processor for 5 minutes; the mixture will thicken as it stands.

2. Process for another 10 seconds. The mixture will be thick but smooth and resemble mashed potatoes. Scrape it into a medium bowl, cover with plastic wrap and let rest at room temperature for 15 minutes or refrigerate for up to 1 hour; the mixture will thicken further as it stands.

3. Line a rimmed baking sheet with kitchen parchment and brush the parchment with the remaining 2 tablespoons oil; set aside. In a large pot over medium-high, bring the broth to a boil. Transfer one-third of the dough to the hopper of a ricer with 3/16-inch perforations. Press the dough directly over the pot of simmering broth until it forms rough 3-inch lengths, then shake the ricer to release the dough into the broth. Repeat with the dough remaining in the ricer. (Alternatively, place a rack with a 3/8-inch wire grid across the pot of simmering broth. Scoop one-third of the dough onto the center of the rack, then use a silicone spatula to press the dough through the wires, allowing the dumplings to fall into the broth; rap the rack to release the last bits of dough into the pot.) Cook the passatelli until it floats to the surface, then continue to cook for 1 minute. Using a slotted spoon, scoop out the passatelli, letting it drain, then transfer to the prepared baking sheet. Cook the remaining dough in two more batches in the same way, then remove the pot from the heat. Let the passatelli rest for 15 minutes, stirring occasionally to help it cool; it will firm up as it cools.

4. Return the broth to a simmer over medium-high, then taste and season with salt and pepper. Divide the passatelli among individual bowls and ladle in the broth. Top each serving with shaved Parmesan and grated nutmeg, then drizzle with oil.

Instant Pot Chicken Broth

Start to finish: 1½ hours, plus cooling (10 minutes active)
Makes about 10 cups

3½ to 4 pounds chicken wings

1 large yellow onion,
halved and thinly sliced

2 bay leaves

Kosher salt

The Instant Pot takes the effort out of homemade broth; our version takes just 10 minutes hands-on time. Chicken wings, which contain ample collagen, yield a rich, full-bodied broth. Use this as a base for passatelli en brodo (p. 82), or in any recipe that calls for store-bought or homemade chicken broth. Store in an airtight container in the refrigerator for up to five days or freeze for up to a month.

Don't forget to allow a 20-minute natural pressure release after cooking is complete. If the steam is released any sooner, the pressure remaining in the pot may cause liquid to spout out of the vent.

---

1. **In a 6-quart Instant Pot,** combine the chicken, onion, bay, 1 teaspoon salt and 2 quarts water.

2. **Lock the lid** in place and move the pressure valve to Sealing. Select Pressure Cook or Manual; make sure the pressure level is set to High. Set the cooking time for 1 hour. When pressure cooking is complete, let the pressure release naturally for 20 minutes, then release any remaining steam by moving the pressure valve to Venting. Press Cancel, then carefully open the pot.

3. **Cool for about 30 minutes.** Strain the broth through a fine mesh strainer set over a large bowl. Cool to room temperature, then use a wide spoon to skim off and discard any fat on the surface. (Alternatively, once the broth has cooled, cover and refrigerate until cold, then scrape the congealed fat off the surface.)

Italian Bean Soup with Fresh Pasta

Start to finish: **40 minutes** / Servings: 4

2 tablespoons extra-virgin olive oil, plus more to serve

1 medium yellow onion, chopped

Kosher salt and ground black pepper

2 tablespoons tomato paste

2 medium garlic cloves, smashed and peeled

Two 15½-ounce cans Roman beans (see headnote), rinsed and drained

2 teaspoons chopped fresh rosemary or sage

1 piece Parmesan rind (optional), plus finely grated Parmesan, to serve

8- to 9-ounce package fresh pappardelle, tagliatelle or fettuccine (see headnote), cut into 2-inch lengths

This is not your typical Italian bean and pasta soup. It's a simplified version of a hearty, rustic zuppa we tasted at Trattoria dai Mugnai in Monteveglio, a village some miles from Bologna. Short, wide ribbons of fresh pasta float dumpling-like in a creamy bean puree subtly flavored with garlic and fresh herbs. If you have a piece of Parmesan rind, simmer it with the beans; it releases savory flavors into the broth. For weeknight ease, we use canned Roman beans (also known as borlotti beans or cranberry beans). If you cannot find canned Roman beans, pintos, which have a similar color and texture, are a fine substitute. If you own an immersion blender, you can use it to puree the beans directly in the saucepan without first cooling the mixture for 10 minutes. Whichever type of blender you use, if you added a piece of Parmesan rind to the pot, remember to remove it before pureeing.

Don't use dried pasta for this soup, as it will not cook properly. Fresh pasta is key. Look for wide, ribbon-like noodles such as pappardelle, tagliatelle or fettuccine and cut them into 2-inch lengths before use. If you can find sheets of fresh pasta, they work nicely, too—simply cut them into rough 2-inch squares. Don't puree the beans until completely smooth; leave them with some texture.

1. In a large saucepan over medium, heat the oil until shimmering. Add the onion and ¼ teaspoon salt, then cook, stirring occasionally, until translucent, about 4 minutes. Add the tomato paste and garlic. Cook, stirring often, until the tomato paste darkens slightly and begins to stick to the pan, about 3 minutes.

2. Add the beans, rosemary, Parmesan rind (if using), 5 cups water, ¾ teaspoon salt and ½ teaspoon pepper. Bring to a simmer over medium-high, then reduce to medium-low and cook, uncovered and stirring occasionally, until the beans are soft enough to be easily mashed with a fork, about 10 minutes.

3. Off heat, remove and discard the Parmesan rind (if used); let cool for about 10 minutes. Using a blender and working in 2 batches to avoid overfilling the jar, pulse the bean mixture until creamy but not completely smooth. Return the puree to the pot and bring to a simmer over medium.

4. Add the pasta and cook uncovered, stirring occasionally, until the pasta is al dente (refer to the package for cooking times, but begin checking for doneness a minute or two sooner than the directions indicate). Taste and season with salt and pepper. Ladle the soup into bowls, drizzle with oil and top with grated Parmesan.

Garlic and Cilantro Soup with Chickpeas (Açorda Alentejana)

Start to finish: **20 minutes** / Servings: 4

2 cups lightly packed fresh cilantro leaves and tender stems, roughly chopped

½ ounce Parmesan cheese, finely grated (¼ cup), plus more to serve

1 jalapeño chili, stemmed and roughly chopped

1 tablespoon grated lemon zest, plus 1 tablespoon lemon juice

1 teaspoon sweet smoked paprika, divided, plus more to serve

Kosher salt and ground black pepper

¾ cup extra-virgin olive oil, divided

5 ounces rustic bread (such as ciabatta), sliced ½ inch thick and torn into bite-size pieces (about 2 cups)

8 medium garlic cloves, roughly chopped

1½ quarts low-sodium chicken broth

Two 15½-ounce cans chickpeas, rinsed and drained

4 soft-cooked eggs, peeled (see headnote)

This soup, with its fragrant, bright green broth, is our take on Portuguese açorda alentejana. Soft-cooked eggs are a perfect garnish that also turn the soup into a complete meal. To soft-cook eggs, bring 2 cups water to a simmer in a large saucepan fitted with a steamer basket. Add the eggs, cover and steam over medium for 7 minutes. Immediately transfer to ice water to stop the cooking.

Don't skimp on the olive oil in this soup. The croutons absorb oil as they toast and the broth takes on a rich, creamy texture when the pesto is stirred in.

1. In a food processor, combine the cilantro, Parmesan, jalapeño, lemon zest and juice, ½ teaspoon of the paprika, and ½ teaspoon each salt and pepper. Process until finely chopped, about 20 seconds, scraping the sides as needed. With the machine running, add ½ cup of the oil and process to a pesto-like consistency, 30 to 45 seconds. Set aside.

2. In a small bowl, toss the bread with the remaining ¼ cup oil and the remaining ½ teaspoon paprika. Toast in a large Dutch oven over medium, stirring occasionally, until golden brown and crisp, 6 to 8 minutes. Using a slotted spoon, return the bread to the bowl, leaving excess oil in the pot; set the croutons aside.

3. Set the Dutch oven over medium and add the garlic. Cook, stirring constantly, until fragrant, about 1 minute. Add the broth and chickpeas and bring to a simmer over medium-high. Cook, stirring, until heated through, about 3 minutes. Off heat, stir in the pureed cilantro mixture, then taste and season with salt and pepper.

4. Divide the croutons among 4 serving bowls. Ladle in the soup and top each with 1 egg. Sprinkle with additional paprika and Parmesan.

Borsch with Duck and Prunes

Start to finish: 2¾ hours / Servings: 4 to 6

¼ cup red wine vinegar

1 medium (about 6 ounces) red beet, peeled and shredded on the large holes of a box grater (1½ cups)

2 pounds duck leg quarters, trimmed, or 2½-pound rack pork baby back ribs, cut into 3 pieces

3 medium carrots, 2 roughly chopped, 1 shredded on the large holes of a box grater

2 medium yellow onions, 1 roughly chopped, 1 finely chopped

2 medium celery stalks, roughly chopped

2 bay leaves

Kosher salt and ground black pepper

2 tablespoons grapeseed or other neutral oil

¾ cup canned crushed tomatoes

8 ounces russet potatoes, peeled and cut into ¾-inch cubes

6 pitted prunes

4 ounces Savoy cabbage or green cabbage, thinly sliced (2 cups)

2 medium garlic cloves, chopped

Sour cream, to serve

Chopped fresh dill, to serve

In "Summer Kitchens," Olia Hercules writes about the history of borsch, its importance in Ukranian cuisine, seasonal and regional influences on the soup, and her own family's recipes. For our adaptation of her resplendent borsch with duck and smoked pears, we opt to use prunes, a substitution she suggests. You also can replace the duck with a small rack of pork baby back ribs, if you're so inclined. The borsch is made by simmering duck legs (or pork ribs) with aromatics to make a flavorful broth; the meat then is shredded off the bones and added to the soup at the end. As the broth simmers, aromatics for the borsch are sautéed in a separate pot so they are ready to receive the broth, which is strained directly into the aromatics. The broth requires at least 1½ hours of simmering, so that's a good time to prep the ingredients—the aromatics, potato, cabbage—for the borsch. But wait to chop the dill garnish until later, while the finished soup stands off heat for 5 minutes, so the herbal flavor and fragrance remain fresh and strong. Serve with rye bread.

Don't be timid about trimming the duck, *if using, of excess fat, as this will prevent the soup from becoming too greasy. Also, don't cover the Dutch oven when simmering the broth. Allowing some of the moisture to evaporate produces a broth with greater flavor concentration and a richer body.*

1. **In a small bowl,** stir together the vinegar and beet; set aside. In a large pot, combine the duck legs or pork ribs, the roughly chopped carrots, the roughly chopped onion, the celery, bay, ½ teaspoon salt and ¼ teaspoon pepper. Add 10 cups water and bring to a boil over medium-high. Cook, uncovered, over medium-low, adjusting heat to maintain a simmer, until a skewer inserted into the meat meets no resistance, 1½ to 2 hours; occasionally skim off and discard the foam that rises to the surface.

2. **While the broth simmers,** in a large Dutch oven over medium, heat the oil until shimmering. Add the finely chopped onion and ½ teaspoon salt, then cook, stirring occasionally, until softened and lightly browned, 5 to 7 minutes. Add the shredded carrot and cook, stirring, until lightly browned, about 5 minutes. Add the beet-vinegar mixture and scrape up any browned bits. Stir in the crushed tomatoes and cook, stirring occasionally, until slightly thickened, about 3 minutes. Remove from the heat and set aside.

3. When the duck or pork is tender, remove the pot from the heat and transfer to a plate. Set a fine-mesh strainer over the Dutch oven containing the vegetable mixture, then pour the broth through the strainer; discard the solids in the strainer. When cool enough to handle, shred the meat into bite-size pieces, discarding the skin and bones; set the meat aside.

4. Add the potatoes and prunes to the broth and bring to a boil over medium-high. Cook, stirring occasionally, for 5 minutes. Add the cabbage and cook, stirring occasionally, until the potatoes are tender, about another 5 minutes. Stir in the garlic, along with the shredded meat; remove from the heat and let stand for about 5 minutes. Taste and season with salt and pepper. Ladle into individual bowls and garnish with sour cream and dill.

Spicy Red Lentil Stew with Coconut Milk and Spinach

Start to finish: 1 hour (10 minutes active) / Servings: 4 to 6

Located on the southwestern coast of India, Goa is known for its use of chilies, spices, coconut and bright acid (an influence from Portuguese colonization). Our spicy red lentil soup is a simplified take on a Goan staple that delivers a complete vegetarian meal in about an hour. Split red lentils, the foundation of the dish, cook in minutes. Blending turmeric, coriander and fennel created complex flavor. Fresh ginger brought welcome brightness, and adding a portion of it at the end kept the flavor vibrant. Both virgin and refined coconut oil worked, but virgin had a slightly stronger flavor. Mustard seeds added a peppery pop to the dish.

Don't substitute brown or green lentils for the split red lentils. Red lentils break down as they cook, thickening the cooking liquid and providing the ideal texture for the soup. Other lentil varieties remain intact even when fully cooked.

1. In a large saucepan over medium-high, combine the onion, oil, garlic and 1½ teaspoons of salt. Cook, stirring occasionally, until the onions have softened and are just beginning to color, 7 to 9 minutes. Stir in 2 teaspoons of ginger, the mustard seeds, turmeric, coriander, fennel and pepper flakes. Cook, stirring frequently, until fragrant, about 1 minute. Add 3½ cups water, coconut milk and lentils, then bring to a boil. Reduce heat to low, cover and cook until the lentils have broken down, 30 to 40 minutes.

2. Stir in the spinach and return to a simmer. Off the heat, add the remaining 1 teaspoon of ginger and the lime juice. Season with salt. Serve garnished with coconut flakes and tomato, if using.

1 medium yellow onion, chopped

2 tablespoons coconut or peanut oil

4 garlic cloves, smashed and peeled

Kosher salt

3 teaspoons finely grated fresh ginger, divided

2 teaspoons mustard seeds

2 teaspoons ground turmeric

1 teaspoon ground coriander

1 teaspoon ground fennel seeds

¾ teaspoon red pepper flakes

13½-ounce can coconut milk

1 cup red lentils, rinsed and drained

6 ounces (about 6 cups) baby spinach, roughly chopped

2 tablespoons lime juice

Unsweetened coconut flakes and chopped tomato, to garnish (optional)

Miso-Shiitake Soup with Napa Cabbage

Start to finish: **30 minutes** / Servings: 6

In Japan, where soup has evolved into high art, nabe (NAH-beh) is shorthand for nabemono, a broad category of soups that may be more recognizable by its Westernized name—hot pot. One such soup, yosenabe, loosely translates to "anything goes hot pot" and relies on layering flavors, adding them to the pot one at a time. Dense or long-cooking items go in first; more delicate ingredients follow. For our simplified yosenabe, we leaned heavily on vegetables. Most Japanese soups begin with dashi, a broth made from kombu seaweed and bonito, or shaved shreds of smoked tuna. We used more common but equally flavorful fresh shiitake mushrooms and dried wakame seaweed. (Wakame tastes slightly sweet and oceanic; look for it in the Asian foods aisle.) Timing was simple: Each ingredient cooked through in the time it took for the pot to return to a simmer. Yosenabe is typically flavored with a blend of soy sauce, sesame oil or scallions. We added all of them.

Don't use firm or extra-firm tofu in this recipe. Soft tofu had the best texture. Silken and medium tofu were decent substitutes.

½ pound carrots (2 to 3 medium), peeled, halved lengthwise and cut crosswise into ½-inch pieces

2 tablespoons dried wakame seaweed

8 ounces soft tofu, drained and cut into ½-inch cubes

5 ounces fresh shiitake mushrooms, stems discarded, caps thinly sliced

4 cups chopped napa cabbage (½ small head)

6 tablespoons (3½ ounces) white miso paste

1-inch chunk fresh ginger, grated

1 tablespoon soy sauce, plus more to serve

2 teaspoons toasted sesame oil, plus more to serve

4 ounces (about 4 cups) baby spinach

6 scallions, trimmed and cut into 1-inch lengths

Hot chili oil, to serve (optional)

1. In a medium Dutch oven over medium, combine 7 cups water, the carrots and wakame. Bring to a simmer and cook for 5 minutes. Add the tofu and mushrooms, then return to a simmer. Add the cabbage, then return to a simmer.

2. Place the miso in a 2-cup liquid measuring cup. Ladle out a bit of the cooking water and add to the miso, stirring until smooth. Pour the miso mixture back into the soup, then stir well.

3. As the soup returns to a simmer, stir in the ginger, soy sauce and sesame oil. Once the soup reaches a simmer, remove it from the heat and stir in the spinach and scallions. When the spinach is wilted, ladle the soup into serving bowls. Serve with soy sauce, sesame oil and chili oil, if using.

Ethiopian Chicken Stew (Doro Wat)

Start to finish: 1 hour 10 minutes (30 minutes active)
Servings: 4 to 6

___

5 tablespoons ghee, divided

2 pounds (3 large) red onions, finely chopped (see headnote)

Kosher salt and ground black pepper

⅓ to ½ cup berbere (see headnote)

10 medium garlic cloves, minced

2 pounds boneless, skinless chicken thighs, trimmed and halved

3 scallions, thinly sliced on the diagonal

1 jalapeño or Fresno chili, stemmed, seeded (if desired) and finely chopped (optional)

2 or 3 hard-cooked eggs, peeled and sliced (optional)

Lemon wedges, to serve

Doro wat, a succulent chicken stew fragrant with spices and savory-sweet with a preponderance of onions, is the national dish of Ethiopia. We were taught how to make it by home cook Tigist Chane in Addis Ababa. A generous measure of berbere, Ethiopia's signature spice blend, gives the dish its deep reddish-brown hue. Berbere is sold in spice shops and most well-stocked supermarkets; because its chili heat varies brand to brand, we call for a range in the amount. Alternatively, you can easily mix your own berbere (see following recipe). If you wish to hone your knife skills, feel free to chop the 2 pounds of onions by hand, but a food processor gets the job done quickly. Trim, peel and quarter the onions, then pulse about 10 times until finely chopped; it's fine if the pieces are a bit uneven. As a cooking fat, we use Indian ghee to mimic the flavor of Ethiopian fermented butter. Look for ghee in the dairy case next to the butter or in the grocery aisle near the coconut oil. If it's not available, butter is a fine substitute. Whole hard-cooked eggs are traditionally simmered into doro wat at the end, but we prefer sliced hard-cooked eggs as an optional garnish, along with chopped fresh chilies. Injera, a spongy, slightly sour Ethiopian flatbread, is the typical accompaniment, but rice or warmed naan are good, too.

Don't worry if the onion and spice mixture looks dry after the chicken is stirred in. As it cooks, the chicken gradually releases moisture—so much so that the stew will require uncovered simmering at the end to reduce and thicken the liquid.

___

1. In a large Dutch oven over medium-high, heat 2 tablespoons of the ghee until shimmering. Add the onions and ½ teaspoon salt, then cook, stirring occasionally and reducing the heat if the onions begin to brown before they soften, until lightly browned and completely softened, 10 to 15 minutes.

2. Stir in the remaining 3 tablespoons ghee, the berbere and ¾ cup water. Stir in the garlic, followed by the chicken. Reduce to medium-low, cover and cook at a simmer, stirring occasionally, until a skewer inserted into the chicken meets no resistance, about 30 minutes.

3. Uncover, increase to medium-high and cook, stirring and scraping along the bottom of the pot, until the stew is thickened and a wooden spoon leaves a brief trail when drawn through the sauce, 5 to 8 minutes. Taste and season with salt and pepper. Serve topped with the scallions, chilies (if using) and sliced eggs (if using); serve with lemon wedges on the side.

HOW TO MAKE YOUR OWN BERBERE

Vibrant in both color and taste, berbere is a bold spice blend that is the backbone of numerous Ethiopian dishes. Its primary ingredient is dried red chilies—also called berbere—which are finely ground with numerous dried herbs and spices. Though blends vary, most include coriander, garlic, black cumin, ginger, basil, ajwain, nigella, fenugreek and Ethiopian cardamom (which resembles dried figs). Though berbere is available at well-stocked supermarkets and online spice shops, it's easy to make a simpler homemade version using readily available spices. In a small bowl, stir together **¼ cup smoked sweet paprika, 2 tablespoons sweet paprika, 2 teaspoons cayenne pepper, 2 teaspoons ground ginger, 2 teaspoons onion powder, 2 teaspoons ground coriander, 1½ teaspoons granulated garlic or garlic powder, 1¼ teaspoons ground cardamom, 1 teaspoon dried basil** (ground or crushed to a powder in an spice mill or mortar and pestle) and **½ teaspoon ground cumin.** Keep in an airtight container in a cool, dry spot for up to two months.

Sardinian Herb Soup with Fregola and White Beans (S'erbuzzu)

Start to finish: 45 minutes / Servings: 4

2 tablespoons extra-virgin olive oil, plus more to serve

3 to 4 ounces pancetta, chopped

1 bunch flat-leaf parsley, stems minced, leaves roughly chopped, reserved separately

1½ teaspoons fennel seeds

½ cup dry white wine

Kosher salt and ground black pepper

2 quarts low-sodium chicken broth

¾ cup fregola (see headnote)

15½-ounce can large white beans, such as butter beans, rinsed and drained

3 medium garlic cloves, minced

4 ounces ricotta salata cheese (see headnote), crumbled (¾ cup), divided

4 ounces baby arugula (about 6 cups lightly packed), roughly chopped

½ cup lightly packed fresh tarragon, chopped

Traditionally, the Sardinian soup called s'erbuzzu is jammed with wild herbs and greens—sometimes more than 17 varieties. And with both fregola (a pea-shaped Sardinian pasta) and white beans in the mix, the soup—which we learned from chef Luigi Crisponi at Santa Rughe restaurant in Gavoi—is as hearty and starchy as it is herbal. For our version, we narrowed the list of herbs and greens to those we felt had the most impact: parsley for grassiness, tarragon for sweet anise notes and arugula for pepperiness. We also used pancetta to build a savory backbone and ricotta salata cheese, as Sardinians do, for complexity. If you can't find fregola, substitute an equal amount of pearl couscous, but cook it for only 5 minutes before adding the beans, parsley and garlic. And if ricotta salata is not available, finely grated pecorino Romano is a reasonable swap, but halve the amount.

Don't forget to reserve the minced parsley stems separately from the chopped leaves. The stems go into the pot early on so they soften and infuse the broth with their herbal, minerally flavor; the leaves are added near the end so they retain their freshness and color.

1. In a large pot over medium, heat the oil and pancetta. Cook, stirring occasionally, until the pancetta is browned, 6 to 8 minutes. Stir in the parsley stems and fennel seeds, then add the wine and 1 teaspoon pepper, scraping up any browned bits. Bring to a simmer over medium-high and cook, stirring, until most of the moisture has evaporated, 2 to 3 minutes.

2. Add the broth and bring to a boil over high. Stir in the fregola and cook, stirring occasionally and adjusting the heat to maintain a simmer, until the fregola is just shy of tender, about 10 minutes. Add the beans, garlic, parsley leaves and half of the ricotta salata, then continue to cook, stirring occasionally and adjusting the heat to maintain a bare simmer, until the fregola is fully tender, about another 10 minutes.

3. Off heat, stir in the arugula and tarragon, then taste and season with salt and pepper. Serve sprinkled with the remaining ricotta salata and drizzled with additional oil.

Spanish Shrimp and Chickpea Stew

Start to finish: **35 minutes** / Servings: 4

2 tablespoons smoked paprika

1 tablespoon sweet paprika

Kosher salt and ground black pepper

1 pound extra-large (21/ 25 per pound) shrimp, peeled (tails left on), deveined and patted dry

2 tablespoons extra-virgin olive oil, plus more to serve

2 tablespoons salted butter

1 medium leek, white and light green parts halved lengthwise, thinly sliced, rinsed and dried

4 medium garlic cloves, minced

15½-ounce can chickpeas, ½ cup liquid reserved, drained

8-ounce bottle clam juice

Chopped fresh flat-leaf parsley, to serve

At Palacio Carvajal Girón, in the Extremadura region of Spain, we tasted a delicious shellfish and chickpea stew. Requiring a ham- and langoustine-infused broth and made with dried chickpeas, the dish was a time- and labor-intensive preparation. Our much-simplified version captures the essence of the stew in a fraction of the time. A combination of Spanish smoked paprika and standard sweet paprika gives the stew deep color and earthy complexity without overwhelming the shrimp.

Don't forget to reserve ½ cup of the liquid before draining the can of chickpeas. The liquid adds both body and flavor to the broth. When peeling the shrimp, don't remove the tails because they also flavor the broth. But do remove the tails when halving the seared shrimp so that the pieces are easier to eat in the finished stew.

1. In a medium bowl, stir together both paprikas and ¾ teaspoon pepper; measure 2 tablespoons into a small bowl and set aside. Add the shrimp to the paprika mixture in the medium bowl and toss to coat; set aside.

2. In a large Dutch oven over medium-high, heat the oil until shimmering. Add the shrimp in an even layer; reserve the bowl. Cook without stirring until browned on the bottom, about 2 minutes. Using a slotted spoon, return the shrimp to the bowl.

3. In the same pot over medium, melt the butter. Add the leek and cook, stirring occasionally, until softened, 4 to 5 minutes. Add the garlic and the reserved paprika mixture, then cook, stirring, until fragrant, about 1 minute. Stir in the chickpeas, the reserved chickpea liquid and the clam juice. Bring to a simmer, then reduce to low, cover and cook for 10 minutes, stirring once or twice. Meanwhile, remove and discard the tails from the shrimp and cut each shrimp in half crosswise.

4. Remove the pot from the heat and stir in the shrimp along with accumulated juices. Cover and let stand until the shrimp are opaque throughout, 2 to 3 minutes. Taste and season with salt and pepper. Serve sprinkled with parsley and drizzled with additional oil.

Korean Pork and Kimchi Stew (Kimchi Jjigae)

Start to finish: 1¼ hours (25 minutes active)
Servings: 6

1 cup boiling water	4 teaspoons gochujang
½ ounce dried shiitake mushrooms	1 pound pork baby back ribs, separated into individual ribs
6 scallions, white parts finely chopped, green parts thinly sliced on the diagonal, reserved separately	12 ounces firm tofu, drained and cut into ¾-inch cubes
3 medium garlic cloves, smashed and peeled	2 teaspoons white sugar
1 tablespoon toasted sesame oil	
1 tablespoon soy sauce	
16-ounce container napa cabbage kimchi, drained (¼ cup liquid reserved) and coarsely chopped	

Bone-in baby back ribs provide meaty flavor and, when cut into individual ribs, tenderize quickly in the simmering broth. We gave the stew layers of heat by combining the Korean chili paste gochujang with the juice from the drained kimchi. If you can find sliced dried shiitake mushrooms, use them in place of whole to skip knife work. We liked this soup as a starter, but with a bowl of steamed white rice it becomes a complete meal.

Don't forget to reserve some of the kimchi liquid when you drain it. It's used to add another layer of flavor to the soup.

1. **In a bowl,** combine the boiling water and mushrooms. Let stand for 30 minutes.

2. **Drain the mushrooms,** reserving the soaking liquid. Discard the stems and thinly slice the caps. In a large Dutch oven over medium-high, combine the scallion whites, garlic, sesame oil and soy sauce. Cook, stirring occasionally, until the scallions have softened, 3 to 4 minutes. Stir in half of the kimchi, the sliced mushrooms and the gochujang. Add 5 cups cold water, the mushrooms' soaking liquid, the ribs and ¼ cup kimchi liquid and bring to a boil. Cover, leaving the lid slightly ajar, reduce the heat to medium-low and cook for 50 minutes, adjusting the heat as necessary to maintain a lively simmer.

3. **Remove the pot from the heat.** Using tongs, transfer the ribs to a plate and let rest until cool enough to handle, about 15 minutes.

4. **Shred the meat** into bite-size pieces, discarding the bones and cartilage. Add the meat to the stew along with the tofu, scallion greens, sugar and remaining kimchi. Bring to a simmer over medium and cook for 5 minutes.

Vegetables

4

Hot Oil–Flashed Chard with Ginger, Scallions and Chili

Start to finish: **20 minutes** / Servings: **4**

Most hearty greens are naturally tough and bitter, requiring extended cooking. So we tamed and tenderized Swiss chard with sizzling oil, a technique we learned from cookbook author Fuchsia Dunlop. Her recipe is modeled on a classic Cantonese method in which hot oil is poured over lightly blanched greens. We scattered fresh ginger, scallions and serrano chilies over our greens and found the hot oil bloomed the flavors beautifully. Instead of julienning the ginger, as is traditional, we used a wand-style grater to finely grate it, which distributed it better, was faster and released more of the aromatics. Bonus: No fibrous pieces in the finished dish. For the oil, we found the clean flavor and light texture of grapeseed oil was ideal, but vegetable oil worked well, too. We added toasted sesame oil for a savory touch. To finish the dish, soy sauce alone is fine, but even better was a blend of soy sauce and unseasoned rice vinegar, which added a gentle acidity and light sweetness.

Don't use the chard stems, *but also don't throw them away. The stems are tougher than the leaves and won't cook through in the short time it takes to wilt the leaves. Chard stems do have good flavor, however, and can be sautéed, pickled or added to soups and stews.*

Kosher salt

2 large bunches Swiss chard (1½ to 2 pounds), stems removed, leaves sliced crosswise into 3-inch pieces

2 scallions, thinly sliced on the diagonal

1 tablespoon finely grated fresh ginger

1 serrano chili, thinly sliced

2 tablespoons grapeseed or other neutral oil

1 tablespoon toasted sesame oil

1 tablespoon unseasoned rice vinegar

1 tablespoon soy sauce

2 teaspoons toasted sesame seeds (optional)

1. In a large skillet over medium-high, bring ¼ cup water and ¼ teaspoon salt to a boil. Pile the chard into the pan and cover (the lid may not close completely). Cook until the chard is wilted, about 5 minutes, stirring halfway through. Remove the lid and cook, stirring occasionally, until most of the liquid has evaporated, 1 to 3 minutes. Transfer the chard to a serving platter and wipe out the skillet.

2. Distribute the scallions, ginger and chili evenly over the chard. Add both oils to the skillet and return to medium-high heat until very hot, 1 to 2 minutes. Pour the oils directly over the greens and aromatics (you should hear them sizzle) and toss to distribute. Drizzle the vinegar and soy sauce over the chard and toss again. Sprinkle with the sesame seeds, if using.

Cracked Potatoes with Vermouth, Coriander and Fennel

Start to finish: **35 minutes (10 minutes active)** / Servings: 4

As much as we like them, crispy, smashed potatoes are a bother. First you boil, then flatten, then crisp in fat. And half the time our potatoes fall apart. We wanted a one-stroke solution, which we found in potatoes afelia, a Cypriot dish that calls for cracking the potatoes when raw, then braising them. Our starting point was a recipe from London chefs Sam and Sam Clark of Moro. They whack raw potatoes, causing them to split and fracture slightly, but not break apart. Next, they cook them in a covered pan with oil and coriander seeds, a traditional afelia flavoring. Red wine, added at the end, simmers into a flavorful sauce. For our version, we preferred the clean herbal flavor of dry vermouth to red wine.

Don't use a skillet with an ill-fitting lid. If the moisture evaporates too quickly, the bottom of the pan can scorch. If the pan looks dry after 10 minutes, add water 2 tablespoons at a time.

1. Using a meat mallet or the bottom of a heavy skillet, whack the potatoes one at a time to crack them until slightly flattened but still intact. In a bowl, toss the potatoes with 1 tablespoon of the oil, 1 teaspoon salt and ¼ teaspoon pepper.

2. In a 12-inch skillet over medium-high, heat the remaining oil and butter. Add the potatoes in a single layer, reduce heat to medium, then cook without moving until well browned, 6 to 8 minutes. Flip and cook until well browned on the other side, about 5 minutes.

3. Add the coriander and fennel. Cook, shaking the pan constantly, until fragrant, about 1 minute. Add the vermouth. Cover and reduce heat to medium-low. Cook until the potatoes are just tender and the liquid has nearly evaporated, 12 to 14 minutes, flipping the potatoes halfway through. Transfer to a serving bowl, scraping the sauce and seeds on top.

1½ pounds small Yukon Gold potatoes (1½ to 2 inches in diameter)

2 tablespoons extra-virgin olive oil, divided

Kosher salt and ground black pepper

1 tablespoon salted butter

2 teaspoons coriander seeds, cracked

1 teaspoon fennel seeds, cracked

1 cup dry vermouth

Potato and Green Pea Curry (Aloo Matar)

Start to finish: 1 hour / Servings: 4

¼ cup coconut oil

1 tablespoon cumin seeds

1 medium red onion, finely chopped

1 tablespoon finely grated fresh ginger

4 medium garlic cloves, finely grated

1 tablespoon sweet paprika

1 tablespoon ground turmeric

1 tablespoon garam masala

¼ teaspoon cayenne pepper

14½-ounce can diced tomatoes

1 teaspoon packed brown sugar

2½ pounds russet potatoes, peeled and cut into 1-inch chunks

Kosher salt and ground black pepper

1½ cups frozen peas, thawed

¼ cup finely chopped fresh cilantro

This classic curry balances the sweetness of tomatoes and green peas with pungent aromatics and warm spices, all tempered by the mild flavor and starchiness of potatoes. The peas in aloo matar usually are drab army green from the acidity of the tomatoes; we add them at the end so they retain their bright color. Serve with cooling plain whole-milk yogurt, if desired.

Don't forget to thaw the peas before use. They are added off heat, when cooking is complete, so if they are still frozen, they will cool the curry. Also, don't be shy about stirring the potatoes as they cook; stirring helps release potato starch that thickens the curry.

1. In a large Dutch oven over medium, heat the oil until shimmering. Add the cumin seeds and cook, stirring, until fragrant, 30 to 45 seconds. Stir in the onion, cover and cook, stirring occasionally, until beginning to brown, 3 to 5 minutes.

2. Add the ginger and garlic, then cook, stirring, until fragrant, about 30 seconds. Stir in the paprika, turmeric, garam masala and cayenne, then cook until fragrant, about 30 seconds. Add the tomatoes with their juice, sugar and 2 cups water, then bring to a simmer, stirring occasionally. Stir in the potatoes and 1½ teaspoons salt. Return to a simmer, then cover, reduce to medium-low and cook, stirring occasionally, until a skewer inserted into a potato meets just a little resistance, about 20 minutes.

3. Uncover and continue to cook, stirring often, until the potatoes are completely tender and the sauce clings lightly, another 5 to 7 minutes. Remove from the heat, stir in the peas and let stand, uncovered, until heated through, about 5 minutes. Stir in the cilantro, then taste and season with salt and pepper.

Sweet-and-Spicy Ginger Green Beans

Start to finish: **10 minutes** / Servings: 4

The challenge of stir-frying green beans is that, more often than not, the flavorings slide off and you're left biting into a bland bean. The key is cooking them in a sauce that actually sticks. Chef Charles Phan, owner of The Slanted Door, a popular Vietnamese restaurant in San Francisco, caramelizes sugar, then stir-fries string beans in the blistering heat of a wok. A final toss with sake and fish sauce coats the charred beans with a dark, bittersweet sauce. We adjusted the recipe to work without a wok. Phan's recipe calls for blanching the beans first. We simplified by adding the beans to a very hot pan with a small amount of oil, then making a sauce around them as they cooked. We found a Dutch oven worked best to control splattering—drying the beans thoroughly also helped (though a large skillet works in a pinch). Cutting the beans on the diagonal gave us more surface area for better browning. To re-create Phan's flavorful sauce—itself a take on nuoc mau, or Vietnamese caramel sauce—we used brown sugar instead of taking the time to caramelize white sugar. It gave us comparable depth and flavor.

Don't use an ill-fitting lid. A proper seal is key to this recipe, whether you cook the beans in a Dutch oven or a skillet. Have the lid ready as soon as you add the water.

2 tablespoons packed light brown sugar

1 tablespoon fish sauce

1 tablespoon soy sauce

3 tablespoons grapeseed or other neutral oil, divided

1 pound green beans, stemmed and halved crosswise on diagonal

1 tablespoon finely grated fresh ginger

½ teaspoon red pepper flakes

2 tablespoons unseasoned rice vinegar

Ground white pepper

1. In a small bowl, stir together the sugar, fish and soy sauces. Set aside.

2. In a large Dutch oven or 12-inch skillet over medium-high, heat 2 tablespoons of the oil until barely smoking. Add the beans and cook, without stirring, until beginning to color, about 3 minutes. Add ¼ cup water and immediately cover the pan. Cook until the beans are bright green and barely tender, about 2 minutes.

3. Clear a space in the center of the pan, then add the remaining 1 tablespoon of oil to the clearing. Stir in the ginger and pepper flakes, then cook until fragrant, about 30 seconds. Stir the sugar-fish sauce mixture then pour it into the skillet and cook, stirring occasionally, until the liquid has thickened and coats the beans, about 1 minute. Off heat, stir in the vinegar. Taste and season with pepper.

Skillet-Charred Brussels Sprouts with Garlic, Anchovy and Chili

Start to finish: **25 minutes** / Servings: 4

We loved the Brussels sprouts at Gjelina, a Los Angeles restaurant. Chef Travis Lett served them with chili-lime vinaigrette, and they were both wonderfully charred and tender. We assumed they'd been roasted in a very hot oven. In fact, Lett had used a cast-iron skillet, a quicker and more efficient way to transfer heat. We tried it and loved the way the searing-hot skillet gave the sprouts a delicious char we'd never achieved in the oven. For the sauce, we were inspired by bagna càuda, the warm garlic-and-anchovy-infused dip from Northern Italy, with red pepper flakes and a splash of lemon juice. A drizzle of honey in the dressing added a note of sweetness.

Don't use a stainless steel skillet. A well-seasoned cast-iron pan was key to this recipe. Stainless steel didn't hold the heat well enough to properly char. To comfortably accommodate the recipe, the pan needed to be at least 12 inches. And stick to small or medium sprouts; large ones didn't taste as good, containing a higher concentration of the compounds that lead to bitterness. Even smaller sprouts were best when cut in half, creating more surface area and contact with the skillet and therefore more charring.

1 pound small to medium Brussels sprouts, trimmed and halved

4 tablespoons extra-virgin olive oil, divided

4 teaspoons honey, divided

Kosher salt

4 medium garlic cloves, minced

4 oil-packed anchovy fillets, minced

Red pepper flakes

2 teaspoons lemon juice

1. In a large bowl, toss the sprouts with 1 tablespoon of the oil, 2 teaspoons of the honey and ½ teaspoon of salt. Set aside.

2. In a 12- to 14-inch cast-iron skillet over high, combine the remaining 3 tablespoons of oil, the garlic, anchovies and ¼ teaspoon pepper flakes. Cook, stirring, until the garlic begins to color, 3 to 4 minutes. Scrape the mixture, including the oil, into a bowl and set aside.

3. Return the skillet to high heat. Add the sprouts (reserve the bowl) and use tongs to arrange them cut side down in a single layer. Cook, without moving, until deeply browned and blackened in spots, 3 to 7 minutes, depending on your skillet. Use the tongs to flip the sprouts cut-side up and cook until charred and just tender, another 3 to 5 minutes.

4. As they finish, return the sprouts to the bowl and toss with the garlic mixture, the remaining 2 teaspoons of honey and the lemon juice. Season with salt and additional pepper flakes.

Spanish Ratatouille (Pisto Manchego)

Start to finish: **40 minutes** / Servings: **4**

Pisto manchego, Spain's colorful combination of sautéed summer vegetables, is similar to France's ratatouille. We liked the effect of using one each of red and yellow bell peppers, but you could use just one color. If you can't find Japanese or Chinese eggplant, 1 pound of globe eggplant will do, but you may need to increase the covered cooking time by a few minutes.

Don't use the seedy core of the zucchini; *it turns soft and mushy with cooking.*

1. Slice the zucchini lengthwise into planks, leaving behind and discarding the seedy core. Cut the zucchini planks into ½-inch cubes and set aside. In a medium bowl, toss the eggplant with 1 teaspoon salt and ½ teaspoon pepper.

2. In a large Dutch oven over medium-high, heat 6 tablespoons of oil until shimmering. Add the eggplant in an even layer and cook without stirring until golden brown, 3 to 5 minutes. Stir, cover and reduce to medium. Continue to cook, stirring occasionally, until tender but not falling apart, another 3 to 5 minutes. Using a slotted spoon, transfer to a paper towel–lined medium bowl and set aside.

3. To the same pot, add 1 tablespoon of the remaining oil and heat over medium-high until shimmering. Add the zucchini in an even layer and cook without stirring until well-browned, about 4 minutes. Continue to cook, stirring occasionally, until browned on all sides and tender when pierced with a fork, another 1 to 2 minutes. Using the slotted spoon, transfer to the bowl with the eggplant.

4. To the same pot, add the remaining 1 tablespoon oil and heat over medium-high until shimmering. Add the onion and ½ teaspoon salt. Cook, stirring occasionally, until golden brown, 3 to 5 minutes. Stir in the bell peppers, 1 teaspoon salt and ½ teaspoon pepper. Cover and cook, stirring, until the peppers soften, 3 to 5 minutes. Stir in the garlic, oregano and cumin, then cook until fragrant, about 30 seconds. Stir in the tomatoes with their juice, then cover and simmer over medium for 5 to 7 minutes.

5. Reduce to low and stir in the eggplant-zucchini mixture. Cook until heated through, 1 to 2 minutes. Stir in the parsley, then taste and season with salt and pepper. Transfer to a platter and top with the manchego.

One 12-ounce zucchini, trimmed

Two 8-ounce Chinese or Japanese eggplants, peeled and cut into 1-inch cubes

Kosher salt and ground black pepper

8 tablespoons extra-virgin olive oil, divided

1 large yellow onion, quartered lengthwise and thinly sliced

2 medium bell peppers, stemmed, seeded and cut into ½-inch pieces

8 medium garlic cloves, thinly sliced

1½ teaspoons dried oregano

¾ teaspoon ground cumin

14½-ounce can diced tomatoes

¼ cup chopped fresh flat-leaf parsley

2 ounces manchego cheese, shaved

Mashed Potatoes with Caraway-Mustard Butter

Start to finish: **40 minutes (10 minutes active)** / Servings: **8**

These mashed potatoes are classically creamy, but get a kick of sweet heat from horseradish. Infusing browned butter with caraway and mustard seeds and drizzling the mixture onto the mashed potatoes is a technique we picked up from Indian cooking. The spices add a complexity that balances the richness of the dish. We preferred buttery Yukon Gold potatoes; use potatoes of approximately the same size to ensure even cooking. Any brand of refrigerated prepared horseradish worked well.

Don't rush browning the butter. *It needs to cook slowly over medium heat to properly brown (you'll see brown spots on the bottom of the saucepan).*

4 pounds Yukon Gold potatoes, peeled and quartered

Kosher salt

5 bay leaves

4 medium garlic cloves, smashed and peeled

10 tablespoons (1¼ sticks) salted butter, divided

1¾ cups half-and-half, warmed

½ cup drained prepared white horseradish, liquid reserved

1 tablespoon caraway seeds, lightly crushed

1 tablespoon yellow mustard seeds

2 tablespoons finely chopped chives

1. **In a large pot,** combine the potatoes, 1 tablespoon salt, the bay leaves and garlic. Add enough water to cover by 2 inches and bring to a boil over high. Reduce to medium, then cook until a skewer inserted into the potatoes meets no resistance, 20 to 25 minutes. Drain the potatoes in a colander set in the sink. Discard the bay leaves, then return the potatoes to the pot.

2. **In a small saucepan** over medium-low, melt 6 tablespoons of the butter. Add the melted butter to the potatoes. Using a potato masher, mash until smooth. Stir in the half-and-half, horseradish and 3 tablespoons of the reserved horseradish liquid. Taste and season with salt. Cover and set over low heat to keep warm.

3. **Return the saucepan to medium** and add the remaining 4 tablespoons butter and the caraway and mustard seeds. Cook, gently swirling the pan, until the butter is browned and the seeds are fragrant and toasted, 2 to 3 minutes. Pour the mixture into a fine-mesh strainer set over a small liquid measuring cup.

4. **Transfer the potatoes** to a serving bowl, then drizzle with the flavored butter and sprinkle with chives.

Cauliflower with Spiced Tahini and Garlic-Chili Oil

Start to finish: 1 hour 10 minutes (30 minutes active), plus cooling / Servings: 4 to 6

¼ cup extra-virgin olive oil, plus more for brushing

2-pound head cauliflower, trimmed

½ to 1 teaspoon red pepper flakes

2 medium garlic cloves, finely grated

Kosher salt and ground black pepper

2 ripe but firm tomatoes, halved and cored

¼ cup tahini

1 tablespoon lemon juice, plus wedges to serve

2 teaspoons ground cumin

2 teaspoons ground sumac

¾ teaspoon ground cardamom

½ teaspoon ground cinnamon

½ cup lightly packed fresh flat-leaf parsley, roughly chopped

¼ cup pine nuts, toasted

This recipe melds the best qualities of two Middle Eastern–style cauliflower dishes we tasted at two restaurants in London—Berber & Q Shawarma and The Barbary. We start by steam-roasting a whole head of cauliflower until tender, then slather it with a mixture of tahini and spices that caramelizes under a hot broiler. Grated fresh tomatoes and a pungent garlic-chili oil finish the dish, along with parsley and toasted pine nuts. To serve, cut into wedges as if serving a cake.

Don't bother opening the foil packet to test the cauliflower for doneness; insert the skewer through the foil. When making the garlic-chili oil, be careful not to overcook the garlic and pepper flakes or the flavors will turn acrid. When the mixture sizzles gently, transfer it to a small bowl; it can scorch if left in the skillet.

1. **Heat the oven to 475°F** with a rack in the middle position. Line a broiler-safe rimmed baking sheet with foil and lightly brush the foil with oil. Place the cauliflower in the center, then draw up the edges of the foil; drizzle 2 tablespoons water onto the cauliflower, then enclose the head, folding and crimping the edges of the foil to seal. Bake until a skewer inserted into the cauliflower meets no resistance, 40 to 50 minutes.

2. **Remove the baking sheet** from the oven and let the wrapped cauliflower cool for 10 minutes. Carefully open the foil but leave it in place under the cauliflower; set aside to cool.

3. **While the cauliflower cools,** in a 10-inch skillet over medium-low, cook the oil, pepper flakes and garlic, stirring, until the mixture sizzles lightly, 2 to 3 minutes. Transfer to a small bowl, stir in ¼ teaspoon salt; set aside. Grate the tomatoes on the large holes of a box grater set in a medium bowl, pressing the cut sides against the grater, until only the skin remains; discard the skins. Stir a pinch of salt into the tomato pulp and set aside. In a small bowl, stir together the tahini and lemon juice. Then stir in 2 table-spoons water, adding more as necessary 1 tablespoon at a time until the mixture is a smooth, spreadable paste. Stir in the cumin, sumac, cardamom, cinnamon and ¼ teaspoon each salt and black pepper; set aside.

4. **Heat the broiler.** Spread the tahini mixture onto the entire surface of the cauliflower, then broil until deeply browned, 3 to 4 minutes. Transfer to a serving platter and cool for about 5 minutes. Spoon the tomato pulp over the top, drizzle with the chili-garlic oil and sprinkle with the parsley and pine nuts. Serve with lemon wedges.

Thai Stir-Fried Spinach

Start to finish: 20 minutes / Servings: 4

This simple, bold stir-fry, based on a recipe from "Pok Pok" by Andy Ricker, uses regular bunch spinach rather than the water spinach common in Thai cooking. The wilted leaves and crisp-tender stems combine for a pleasing contrast of textures. Be sure to dry the spinach well after washing; excess water will cause splattering and popping when the spinach is added to the hot oil. A salad spinner works well, or roll the spinach in kitchen towels and squeeze dry. We like to serve this with steamed jasmine rice to soak up the sauce.

Don't use baby spinach, which can't handle high-heat cooking and doesn't have stems to offer textural contrast. And don't allow the spinach leaves to fully wilt in the pan; some leaves should still look fairly fresh, but will continue to cook after being transferred to the bowl.

1 tablespoon fish sauce

1 tablespoon oyster sauce

2 teaspoons white sugar

¾ teaspoon red pepper flakes

3 tablespoons grapeseed or other neutral oil, divided

3 tablespoons roughly chopped garlic

1½ pounds bunch spinach, trimmed of bottom 1½ inches, washed and dried

1. In a small bowl, whisk together the fish sauce, oyster sauce, sugar and pepper flakes until the sugar dissolves. Set aside.

2. In a 14-inch wok over medium-high, heat 2 tablespoons of the oil until barely smoking. Remove the wok from the heat, add the garlic and cook, stirring, until just beginning to color, 20 to 30 seconds. Return the wok to high and immediately add ½ of the spinach. Using tongs, turn the spinach to coat with the oil and garlic. When the spinach is nearly wilted and the garlic has turned golden brown, after 30 seconds or less, transfer to a large bowl. The leaves will continue to wilt but the stems should remain crisp-tender.

3. Return the wok to high heat. Add the remaining 1 tablespoon oil, swirl to coat the wok and heat until barely smoking. Add the remaining spinach and cook as before, for 20 to 30 seconds. Transfer to the bowl with the first batch of spinach.

4. Pour the fish sauce mixture over the spinach and toss. Transfer to a platter and drizzle with any accumulated liquid.

Stir-Fried Broccoli with Sichuan Peppercorns

Start to finish: **30 minutes** / Servings: **4**

Sichuan peppercorns don't provide heat so much as an intriguing, slightly resinous flavor and tingling sensation on your lips and tongue. The spice in this stir-fry instead comes from red pepper flakes. Use a spice grinder to grind the Sichuan peppercorns to as fine a powder as possible; if using an electric grinder, it helps to shake the grinder as it whirs. Pouring the vinegar-soy mixture down the sides of the wok rather than directly over the broccoli quickly heats and concentrates the mixture so the liquid doesn't cause the broccoli to overcook.

Don't be slow to cover the wok after adding the water or too much moisture may evaporate and the broccoli won't cook through properly. If your wok doesn't have a lid, improvise with a baking sheet or a lid from a large pot, such as a Dutch oven (the lid does not need to sit on the rim of the wok—it can sit slightly inside).

2 tablespoons unseasoned rice vinegar, divided

1½ tablespoons soy sauce

1 teaspoon white sugar

3 medium garlic cloves, finely grated

1½ teaspoons finely grated fresh ginger

1 teaspoon Sichuan peppercorns, finely ground

¼ to ½ teaspoon red pepper flakes

2 scallions, white and pale green parts minced, dark green parts thinly sliced on the diagonal

3 tablespoons peanut or grapeseed oil

1¼ pounds broccoli, florets cut into 1-inch pieces, stems peeled and sliced ¼-inch thick

Kosher salt

2 teaspoons toasted sesame oil

1. In a small bowl, stir together 1 tablespoon of vinegar, the soy sauce and sugar. In another small bowl, stir together the garlic, ginger, Sichuan pepper, pepper flakes and minced scallions.

2. Heat a 12- to 14-inch wok over medium-high for 1 to 2 minutes; a drop of water should evaporate within 1 to 2 seconds. Add the peanut oil and swirl to coat the wok. Add the garlic-ginger mixture and stir-fry until fragrant, about 30 seconds. Add the broccoli and stir-fry for 30 seconds, then add ¼ teaspoon salt and 3 tablespoons water. Cover and cook for 1 minute. Uncover and cook, stirring, until the broccoli is crisp-tender, 3 to 5 minutes.

3. Drizzle the vinegar-soy mixture around the wok, down its sides. Cook, stirring and scraping up any browned bits, until the liquid is slightly reduced, about 1 minute. Off heat, stir in the sesame oil and remaining 1 tablespoon vinegar. Transfer to a platter and sprinkle with the sliced scallions.

Spicy Egyptian Eggplant with Fresh Herbs

Start to finish: **40 minutes** / Servings: 4

The inspiration for this recipe was btingan mekhalel, a spicy, vinegary deep-fried eggplant dish sold by street vendors in Cairo. We made a lighter, easier and oven-friendly version of the dish. But because broilers vary in heat output, check the eggplant for doneness after 10 minutes. For the same reason, it also may need longer than called for. The pieces should be tender and lightly charred, but not falling apart. Harissa is a North African red pepper paste seasoned with spices and other ingredients; our favorite brand is DEA, which is sold in a yellow tube. Or, see our recipe for homemade harissa (p. 618). Serve warm or at room temperature.

Don't allow the eggplant to cool before tossing it with the harissa mixture. As they cool, the chunks absorb the flavorings. Allow the mixture to stand for at least 10 minutes before serving.

1 tablespoon coriander seeds

1 tablespoon cumin seeds

2 pounds globe or Italian eggplant, trimmed

6 tablespoons extra-virgin olive oil

¼ cup harissa paste

¼ cup cider vinegar

3 tablespoons honey

1 medium garlic clove, finely grated

¼ cup finely chopped fresh mint

3 tablespoons finely chopped fresh dill, divided

Kosher salt and ground black pepper

1. In a small skillet over medium, toast the coriander and cumin, shaking the pan, until fragrant, about 2 minutes. Transfer to a spice grinder and let cool slightly, then pulse until coarsely ground; set aside.

2. Heat the oven to broil with a rack 6 inches from the element. Line a rimmed baking sheet with foil and mist with cooking spray. Cut each eggplant crosswise into 1½-inch-thick rounds, then cut each round into 1½-inch cubes. In a large bowl, toss the eggplant with the oil to coat. Distribute in an even layer on the prepared baking sheet; reserve the bowl. Broil without stirring until tender and lightly charred on top, 10 to 12 minutes.

3. Meanwhile, in the reserved bowl, whisk together the harissa, vinegar, honey, garlic, mint, 2 tablespoons of dill and the coriander and cumin. When the eggplant is done, immediately add it to the bowl, then gently toss to combine. Taste and season with salt and pepper. Let stand for 10 minutes. Transfer to a serving platter and sprinkle with the remaining 1 tablespoon dill.

Cumin-Coriander Potatoes with Cilantro (Patates Mekhalel)

Start to finish: **20 minutes (10 minutes active)** / Servings: 4

In Cairo, patates mekhalel are served by street vendors as a side to liver sandwiches, their gentle acidity and crunchy spices balancing the richness of the liver. For our version, we peel, cut and cook the potatoes in water seasoned with both salt and vinegar, then dress the hot, just-drained potatoes with additional vinegar. To lightly crush the cumin and coriander seeds, use a mortar and pestle or the back of a heavy pan, or pulse them several times in a spice grinder. If you can't find hot paprika, use 2 teaspoons sweet paprika plus ¼ teaspoon cayenne pepper.

Don't overcook the potatoes; the chunks should be tender but not fall apart. Also, don't allow the garlic to brown in the oil or its flavor may be acrid and bitter. Remove the pan from the heat as soon as the garlic begins to turn golden and immediately add the paprika and honey, which lower the oil's temperature.

1. **In a large saucepan** over high, combine the potatoes, ¼ cup of vinegar, 2 tablespoons salt and 6 cups water. Bring to a boil and cook, stirring occasionally, until a skewer inserted into the potatoes meets no resistance, 6 to 8 minutes. Drain, then transfer to a large bowl. Drizzle with the remaining ¼ cup vinegar and toss; set aside.

2. **In a small saucepan** over medium-high, combine the oil, cumin and coriander, then cook, frequently swirling the pan, until sizzling, 45 to 90 seconds. Add the garlic and cook, stirring, until it just begins to turn golden, about 30 seconds. Off heat, stir in the paprika and honey, then pour the mixture over the potatoes. Add the cilantro, 1 teaspoon salt and ½ teaspoon pepper and toss. Let stand at room temperature for at least 10 minutes or up to 45 minutes. Serve warm or at room temperature.

2½ pounds Yukon Gold potatoes, peeled and cut into 1-inch chunks

½ cup white vinegar, divided

Kosher salt and ground black pepper

¼ cup grapeseed or other neutral oil

4 teaspoons cumin seeds, lightly crushed

4 teaspoons coriander seeds, lightly crushed

4 medium garlic cloves, minced

2 teaspoons hot paprika (see headnote)

2 teaspoons honey

1½ cups lightly packed fresh cilantro, roughly chopped

Croatian Mashed Potatoes

Start to finish: 1 hour / Servings: 4 to 6

___

2 tablespoons grapeseed
or other neutral oil

1 large yellow onion, chopped

Kosher salt and ground
black pepper

2 pounds Yukon Gold potatoes,
unpeeled, halved lengthwise
and sliced about ¼ inch thick

4 tablespoons (½ stick) salted
butter, cut into 4 pieces

¼ teaspoon sweet paprika,
plus more to serve

2 tablespoons finely chopped
fresh chives, divided

Croatian restani krumpir is a hearty, rustic dish of mashed potatoes studded with onions that are sautéed until soft and sweet, oftentimes seasoned with paprika and brightened with fresh herbs. Our version, modeled after the potatoes we tasted at Samoborska Klet restaurant in Zagreb, is a one-pot recipe. The onion is caramelized, removed and set aside while the potatoes cook. Rather than boiling whole or chunked potatoes in copious water, we instead slice them unpeeled and steam them in the covered pot with only enough water to facilitate even cooking and prevent scorching. This keeps the potatoes from absorbing lots of moisture so the finished dish tastes rich and earthy instead of thin and washed-out. This dish is a perfect side to sausages, braises or stews.

Don't forget to rinse the sliced potatoes before cooking. Rinsing washes off excess starch so the finished dish has a creamy consistency and isn't dense and gluey. Also, don't undercook the potatoes—they should almost fall apart when poked with a skewer so they can be easily mashed with a wooden spoon.

1. In a large Dutch oven over medium, heat the oil until shimmering. Add the onion and ¼ teaspoon salt, then cook, stirring occasionally, until softened and well browned, 22 to 25 minutes. Remove the pot from the heat. Transfer the onion to a small bowl and set aside; reserve the pot.

2. In a colander under cold running water, rinse the potatoes. Drain well, then add to the pot. Stir in ¾ cup water and ½ teaspoon salt, then distribute the potatoes in an even layer. Cover and bring to a boil over medium-high. Reduce to medium and cook at a simmer, stirring occasionally, until the slices almost fall apart when poked with a skewer, 18 to 20 minutes.

3. If there is water remaining in the pot, increase to medium-high and cook, uncovered and stirring often, until no moisture remains. Reduce to low, add the butter and cook, stirring and mashing the potatoes with a spoon, until the butter is melted and incorporated, about 1 minute. Stir in the onion, paprika and ¼ teaspoon each salt and pepper. Stir in 1 tablespoon of the chives, then taste and season with salt and pepper. Transfer to a serving dish. Sprinkle with additional paprika and the remaining 1 tablespoon chives.

Roasted Cauliflower with Miso Glaze

Start to finish: **30 minutes** / Servings: 4

This recipe—inspired by a dish at Fujisaki, a Japanese restaurant along the Sydney waterfront—coats chunks of cauliflower with a thick, miso-based glaze that is sweet and savory. We roast the cauliflower before tossing the richly browned florets with miso blended with vinegar and ginger, then top it with toasted pistachios, scallions and cilantro. The result is fresh, warm and rich.

Don't forget to heat the baking sheet while preparing the cauliflower. A heated baking sheet—along with allowing the cauliflower to roast without stirring—ensures flavor-building caramelization.

1. Heat the oven to 500°F with a rack in the lowest position. Line a rimmed baking sheet with foil and place the baking sheet in the oven.

2. Place the cauliflower in a large bowl. Add the oil and ¼ teaspoon pepper, then toss to coat. When the oven is at temperature, quickly remove the baking sheet and distribute the cauliflower in an even layer; reserve the bowl. Roast until the cauliflower is just tender and browned in spots, 15 to 18 minutes; do not stir.

3. Meanwhile, in the reserved bowl, whisk together the miso, vinegar, sake, honey, ginger and 2 tablespoons water. As soon as the cauliflower is done, transfer to the bowl with the miso mixture and gently toss. Carefully stir in the pistachios, scallions and cilantro. Transfer to a serving platter.

2-pound head cauliflower, trimmed, cored and cut into 1½- to 2-inch florets

3 tablespoons peanut oil

Ground white pepper

⅓ cup red or white miso

4 teaspoons unseasoned rice vinegar

2 teaspoons sake

1 teaspoon honey

1 teaspoon finely grated fresh ginger

¼ cup shelled roasted pistachios, chopped

1 bunch scallions, thinly sliced

¼ cup chopped fresh cilantro

Roasted Acorn Squash with Browned Butter–Orange Vinaigrette

Start to finish: **40 minutes** / Servings: 4

This elegant, wintry side dish was inspired by a recipe from chef Travis Lett's "Gjelina" cookbook. Caramelized roasted squash is finished with a sauce of browned butter, orange juice and white wine vinegar, the brightness of the acids balancing the richness of the butter. Roasted pistachios lend both texture and vivid color, and their flavor echoes the nuttiness of the browned milk solids in the butter. To double the recipe, place the oven racks in the upper- and lower-middle positions and roast the squash on two baking sheets. Halfway through cooking, when flipping the squash slices, also switch the position of the baking sheets. The sauce is easily doubled.

Don't add the parsley *or the final 1 tablespoon of cold butter to the sauce until ready to serve. The parsley will darken if added in advance and the last bit of butter ensures the sauce is emulsified.*

1½- to 2-pound acorn squash, halved lengthwise, seeded and sliced into 1-inch-thick half rings

5 tablespoons salted butter, cut into 1-tablespoon pieces, 1 tablespoon chilled

Kosher salt

⅓ cup orange juice

⅓ cup white wine vinegar

⅓ cup salted roasted pistachios, chopped

2 tablespoons finely chopped fresh flat-leaf parsley

1. Heat the oven to 475°F with a rack in the middle position. Line a rimmed baking sheet with kitchen parchment. Place the squash in a large bowl. In a small saucepan over medium, melt 4 tablespoons of the butter. Drizzle 1 tablespoon over the squash; set the pan with the remaining melted butter aside. Season the squash with salt, then toss to coat. Arrange the slices in a single layer on the prepared baking sheet, then roast until browned on both sides and a skewer inserted into a piece meets no resistance, 25 to 30 minutes, flipping the slices once halfway through.

2. Meanwhile, set the pan with the melted butter over medium and cook the butter, swirling occasionally, until golden brown with a nutty aroma, about 3 minutes. Add the orange juice and vinegar, then bring to a boil over medium-high. Cook until reduced by about half, 5 to 6 minutes; adjust the heat as needed to maintain a steady simmer. Taste and season with salt, then set aside until ready to serve.

3. When the squash is done, use a wide metal spatula to transfer the slices to a platter, then sprinkle with pistachios. If the sauce has cooled, rewarm over low, then remove from the heat. Whisk in the 1 tablespoon chilled butter and the parsley until the butter is incorporated. Drizzle the sauce over the squash.

Smashed Potatoes with Chili-Lemon Vinaigrette

Start to finish: 1 hour 20 minutes (25 minutes active) / Servings: 4

To make these creamy-inside, crisp-outside potatoes, we first boil whole fingerlings or small Yukon Golds, then flatten and roast them in a very hot oven. We took a cue from Mokonuts, a popular Parisian café, and dressed the smashed potatoes with a tangy-spicy vinaigrette that nicely accents the potatoes' starchy, mildly sweet flavor. When boiling the potatoes, begin timing as soon as they're added to the water. To make ahead, the potatoes can be boiled, smashed, cooled and refrigerated a day in advance; to finish, brush with oil and roast as directed. The vinaigrette can be made in advance except for the chilies, then covered and refrigerated until ready. To use, bring to room temperature and add the chilies.

Don't let the potatoes cool completely before smashing. They are easier to flatten and they hold their shape better when warm.

2½ pounds fingerling potatoes or small (1- to 1½-inch) Yukon Gold potatoes

4 medium garlic cloves, peeled

3 rosemary sprigs

Kosher salt

¼ cup lemon juice

6 tablespoons extra-virgin olive oil, divided

1 small jalapeño or Fresno chili, stemmed and sliced into thin rings

¼ cup lightly packed fresh flat-leaf parsley, chopped

1. Heat the oven to 500°F with a rack in the middle position. In a large pot over high, bring 2 quarts water to boil. Add the potatoes, garlic, rosemary and 1 cup salt, then cook, uncovered and stirring occasionally, until a skewer inserted into the largest potato meets no resistance, 18 to 22 minutes.

2. Using a slotted spoon, transfer the potatoes to a wire rack set in a rimmed baking sheet (leaving the rosemary behind); place the garlic in a small bowl. Let the potatoes cool for about 10 minutes. Meanwhile, using a fork, mash the garlic to a paste, then stir in the lemon juice and 2 tablespoons of oil, followed by the chilies; set aside.

3. After the potatoes have cooled slightly, carefully remove the rack from the baking sheet. Wipe away any moisture on the baking sheet and place the potatoes in an even layer directly on the sheet. Using the bottom of a dry measuring cup or ramekin, press down on each potato so it is slightly flattened and splits open but remains intact. Brush the tops of the potatoes with the remaining 4 tablespoons oil.

4. Roast the potatoes without turning them until browned and crisp, 35 to 40 minutes. Using a wide metal spatula, transfer to a serving platter, then sprinkle with the parsley and drizzle with the vinaigrette.

Roasted Cauliflower with Tahini and Lemon

Start to finish: **40 minutes** / Servings: 4

In the Levant, cauliflower often is deep-fried and paired with tahini. We ditch the deep-fryer and opt for high-heat roasting. But first we coat the cauliflower with a little cornstarch mixed with oil, tomato paste and tahini. The starch helps the florets develop crisp, nicely browned exteriors. Hot sauce in the coating adds some piquancy; we preferred brands that aren't too vinegary, such as Cholula and Tapatío. Cilantro and lemon, added just before serving, brighten the colors and flavors.

Don't forget to line the baking sheet with foil, then coat it liberally with cooking spray. This helps prevent sticking and scorching. Also, don't stir the cauliflower as it roasts; undisturbed cooking allows the florets to crisp well and brown deeply.

1. **Heat the oven to 500°F** with a rack in the middle position. Line a rimmed baking sheet with foil and spray generously with cooking spray.

2. **In a large bowl,** whisk together the oil, tomato paste, tahini, hot sauce, cornstarch, 2 tablespoons water, 2 teaspoons salt and 1 teaspoon pepper. Add the cauliflower and toss with your hands, rubbing the mixture into the florets. Transfer the cauliflower to the prepared baking sheet and turn the florets cut side down as much as possible. Roast without stirring until tender and lightly charred, 25 to 30 minutes.

3. **Meanwhile, in a small bowl,** stir together the cilantro and lemon zest. When the cauliflower is done, transfer to a platter, then sprinkle with the cilantro-zest mixture. Serve with lemon wedges and additional tahini for drizzling.

3 tablespoons extra-virgin olive oil

3 tablespoons tomato paste

2 tablespoons tahini, plus more to serve

1 tablespoon hot sauce (see headnote)

2 teaspoons cornstarch

Kosher salt and ground black pepper

2- to 2½-pound head cauliflower, trimmed, cored and cut into 1½- to 2-inch florets

¼ cup finely chopped fresh cilantro

1 tablespoon grated lemon zest, plus lemon wedges to serve

Ethiopian Stewed Collard Greens (Gomen Wat)

Start to finish: 1 hour (20 minutes active) / Servings: 4

---

3 tablespoons ghee
(see headnote)

1 medium yellow onion,
halved and thinly sliced

6 medium garlic cloves,
minced

3 tablespoons minced fresh
ginger, divided

¾ teaspoon ground
cardamom

½ teaspoon ground turmeric

1 bunch (about 1 pound)
collard greens, stemmed and
roughly chopped

1½ cups low-sodium beef,
chicken or vegetable broth

Kosher salt and ground
black pepper

1 or 2 Fresno or serrano
chilies, stemmed, seeded and
thinly sliced

1 tablespoon lemon juice

Gomen wat translates as "collard greens stew." In Ethiopia, we tasted multiple versions of the hardy greens braised with beef (in which case, the dish is called gomen besiga), but we prefer the lighter, brighter, more flavorful version in which the greens are cooked without meat. Ethiopian butter, made from fermented milk, infuses dishes to which it's added—including the gomen wat we sampled—with a unique depth of flavor and appealing funkiness, not unlike a fragrant cheese. Indian ghee, which is easier to find, is a reasonably good substitute. Look for ghee in either the refrigerator section near the butter or in the grocery aisle near the coconut oil. If you cannot find it, use salted butter in its place but also add 1 teaspoon white miso along with the broth to subtly boost flavor. If for some reason collard greens are not available, curly kale will work, but reduce the greens' cooking time to 15 to 20 minutes.

Don't forget to reserve 1 tablespoon of the minced ginger to stir in at the end. It adds a bright zing to the rich, stewed greens.

---

1. In a large pot over medium, melt the ghee. Add the onion and cook, stirring occasionally, until lightly browned, 5 to 10 minutes. Stir in the garlic, 2 tablespoons of ginger, the cardamom and turmeric. Cook, stirring occasionally, until fragrant and lightly toasted, about 1 minute.

2. Add about half of the collards and cook, stirring, until slightly wilted, then add the remaining collards. Stir in the broth and ½ teaspoon pepper. Cover and cook, stirring occasionally, until the collards are tender, 20 to 30 minutes.

3. Off heat, stir in the chili(es), lemon juice and remaining 1 tablespoon ginger. Taste and season with salt and pepper, then transfer to a serving dish.

Cauliflower Steaks with Pickled Peppers, Capers and Parmesan

Start to finish: 45 minutes / Servings: 4

Two 2- to 2½-pound
cauliflower heads, trimmed

6 tablespoons extra-virgin
olive oil, divided

Kosher salt and ground
black pepper

½ cup Peppadew peppers
or seeded pickled sweet cherry
peppers, patted dry and finely
chopped

½ cup lightly packed fresh
flat-leaf parsley, chopped

1 ounce Parmesan cheese,
finely grated (½ cup)

¼ cup drained capers, patted
dry and roughly chopped

To make a satisfying vegetarian main, we cut thick cauliflower "steaks" from the center section of a whole head; you'll get two steaks per head. The ends that are left over tend to fall apart because they're detached from the core, but don't discard them—use them to make cauliflower rice, roast them separately or make them into soup. The savory-sweet topping for these cauliflower steaks riffs on a recipe in "Six Seasons" by Joshua McFadden.

Don't forget to pat dry the pickled peppers and capers. *Removing excess moisture will help the topping brown better in the oven.*

1. **Heat the oven to 500°F** with a rack in the middle position. Mist a rimmed baking sheet with cooking spray. Halve each cauliflower top to bottom. From the cut side of each half, slice off a 1½-inch-thick slab to make a total of 4 "steaks"; reserve the ends for another use. Brush the steaks on all sides with 4 tablespoons of oil and season with salt and pepper. Roast on the prepared baking sheet until browned on the bottoms, about 20 minutes. Meanwhile, in a small bowl, stir together the Peppadews, parsley, Parmesan, capers and the remaining 2 tablespoons oil.

2. **After the cauliflower has roasted** for 20 minutes, spread the Peppadew mixture onto the steaks. Continue to roast until the topping is well browned and the steaks are tender, another 8 to 10 minutes.

Tuscan Braised Potatoes
(Patate in Umido)

Start to finish: **1 hour** / Servings: **4**

This hearty vegetable stew is based on a recipe in "Auten-tico" by Rolando Beramendi. The potatoes are cooked using a technique that's often employed with risotto: the liquid is incorporated in multiple additions. This concentrates flavors while using the potatoes' natural starch to create a sauce that clings lightly to the chunks. We like the flavor backbone of chicken broth, but you could make this dish vegetarian by substituting vegetable broth. Patate in umido is an excellent accompaniment to roasted chicken, pork or seafood.

Don't use a narrow pot; the wide diameter of a Dutch oven allows for more rapid evaporation of liquid. Also, don't use lower-starch potatoes, such as red, white or Yukon Gold potatoes. Russets are the best choice, as their starchiness gives them a light, tender texture when cooked and lends the sauce a velvety quality.

¼ cup extra-virgin olive oil, plus more to serve

2 small red onions, quartered lengthwise and thinly sliced crosswise

3 medium garlic cloves, smashed and peeled

2 pounds russet potatoes, peeled and cut into 1-inch chunks

14½-ounce can whole peeled tomatoes, crushed by hand

2½ cups low-sodium chicken broth, divided

½ teaspoon red pepper flakes

8-inch sprig fresh rosemary

Kosher salt and ground black pepper

½ cup lightly packed fresh basil leaves, roughly chopped

1. In a large Dutch oven over medium, combine the oil, onions and garlic. Cook, stirring occasionally, until the onions just begin to brown, 8 to 10 minutes. Add the potatoes and stir to coat with the oil. Cook, stirring occasionally, until the potato starch that coats the bottom of the pot starts to brown, about 5 minutes.

2. Stir in the tomatoes, 1 cup of broth, the pepper flakes, rosemary and ½ teaspoon salt. Bring to a simmer over medium-high, then distribute the potatoes in an even layer. Cook, occasionally scraping along the bottom of the pot with a silicone spatula and gently folding the mixture, for 10 minutes; adjust the heat as needed to maintain a steady simmer.

3. Add ½ cup of the remaining broth and cook, occasionally scraping and folding, for another 10 minutes. Add the remaining 1 cup broth in 2 additions in the same way, cooking for only 5 minutes after the final addition and stirring gently so the potatoes don't break up. Cover the pot, remove from the heat and let stand for 5 minutes.

4. Stir in half the basil, then season to taste. Remove and discard the rosemary, then transfer the potatoes to a bowl, drizzle with additional oil and sprinkle with the remaining basil.

Roasted Whole Cauliflower with Feta

Start to finish: **1 hour 10 minutes (20 minutes active)**
Servings: **4**

This is our adaptation of a recipe from Diane Kochilas' book "My Greek Table." A mixture of olive oil, mustard, balsamic vinegar, honey and garlic is slathered onto a head of cauliflower before roasting. The cauliflower then gets a finishing swipe of mustard and an herb-feta coating before roasting for a few minutes more.

Don't forget to line the baking sheet with foil or kitchen parchment. This will help prevent any drips of the oil-mustard mixture from scorching and smoking during roasting. Also, don't worry if the cauliflower browns very deeply—chars, even—in the oven. This caramelization adds sweet, nutty flavor to the dish.

1. **Heat the oven to 450°F** with a rack in the middle position. Line a rimmed baking sheet with foil or kitchen parchment. In a small bowl, whisk the oil, 2½ tablespoons of the mustard, the vinegar, honey, garlic, 1 teaspoon salt and ¼ teaspoon pepper until creamy. Measure ¼ cup of the mixture into a small bowl and set aside.

2. **Place the cauliflower** on the prepared baking sheet and brush the surface with the remaining oil-mustard mixture. Roast the cauliflower until deeply browned and a skewer inserted all the way through the head and into the core meets just a little resistance, 40 to 55 minutes.

3. **While the cauliflower roasts,** in a small bowl, toss together the crumbled feta and the chopped parsley. When the cauliflower is ready, remove the baking sheet from the oven. Brush the remaining 1½ tablespoons mustard over the surface of the cauliflower, then pat on the feta-parsley mixture, pressing so that it adheres. Return to the oven and continue to roast until the feta begins to melt, 5 to 8 minutes.

4. **Using a wide metal spatula,** transfer the cauliflower to a cutting board, then cut the head into 4 wedges. Serve with lemon wedges and the reserved oil-mustard mixture.

½ cup extra-virgin olive oil

4 tablespoons Dijon mustard, divided

1 tablespoon balsamic vinegar

2 teaspoons honey

2 medium garlic cloves, finely grated

Kosher salt and ground black pepper

2-pound head cauliflower, trimmed

2 ounces feta cheese, crumbled (½ cup)

¼ cup finely chopped fresh flat-leaf parsley

Lemon wedges, to serve

Mushroom and Cheese Quesadillas

Start to finish: 30 minutes / Servings: 4 to 6

4 tablespoons lard, divided
(see headnote)

1 medium white onion,
chopped

1 pound mixed mushrooms,
such as cremini, oyster,
portobello or shiitakes
(stemmed), roughly chopped

Kosher salt and ground
black pepper

2 medium garlic cloves,
minced

1 chipotle chili in adobo
sauce, finely chopped

3 ounces queso Oaxaca,
shredded (¾ cup) (see
headnote)

⅓ cup lightly packed fresh
cilantro, chopped

Eight 4- to 5-inch flour
tortillas

You'll find quesadillas of all types in Mexico. In Mexico City, they're often made from fresh masa and without cheese; in other parts of the country, they're made with flour tortillas, with lots of melty Oaxaca cheese. Fillings vary from stewed or griddled meat to squash blossoms to nopales (cactus paddles). In this recipe, we stuff tortillas with a mixture of sautéed mushrooms and cheese, with a little smoky and spicy heat from a chipotle chili. Made with 4- to 5-inch flour tortillas, the quesadillas are perfect for a lunch or snack. If you can't find queso Oaxaca, any mild melting cheese, such as mozzarella or muenster, will work. Lard is traditional for cooking these quesadillas, but for a vegetarian version, use grapeseed or another neutral oil. For best browning, cook these in a nonstick skillet.

Don't use a conventional (i.e., not nonstick) skillet. The quesadillas brown best in a nonstick pan.

1. **In a 12-inch nonstick skillet** over medium-high, heat 2 tablespoons of lard until shimmering. Add the onion and cook, stirring occasionally, until softened and beginning to brown, 4 to 5 minutes. Add the mushrooms and ½ teaspoon each salt and pepper, then cook, stirring occasionally, until tender and well browned, 7 to 8 minutes. Add the garlic and chipotle; cook, stirring, until fragrant, 30 to 60 seconds. Transfer to a medium bowl, then stir in the cheese and cilantro. Taste and season with salt and pepper. Wipe out the skillet with paper towels; set aside.

2. **Divide the mushroom** mixture evenly among the tortillas, spreading it over half of each. Fold the unfilled sides over and press to seal.

3. **In the same skillet** over medium-high, heat 1 tablespoon of the remaining lard until shimmering. Add 4 of the quesadillas and cook until the tortillas are golden brown on the bottom, about 2 minutes. Flip and cook, adjusting the heat as needed, until the second sides are browned, another 2 to 3 minutes. Transfer to a platter and repeat with the remaining quesadillas using the remaining 1 tablespoon lard.

Cauliflower with Tahini and Egyptian Nut-and-Seed Seasoning (Dukkah)

Start to finish: 35 minutes / Servings: 4

½ cup tahini

1 teaspoon grated lemon zest, plus 2 tablespoons lemon juice, divided

2 tablespoons extra-virgin olive oil, plus more to serve

2 medium garlic cloves, grated

Kosher salt

1 teaspoon sweet paprika

¼ to ½ teaspoon cayenne pepper

1 large head cauliflower (about 2½ pounds), cut into 1½- to 2-inch florets

⅓ cup roasted, salted cashews, chopped

⅓ cup chopped fresh cilantro

This recipe dresses roasted cauliflower florets with a tahini sauce brightened with lemon juice and cayenne. We used cilantro in our sauce, but flat-leaf parsley is a good substitute. When buying cauliflower, look for a head with densely packed florets. Medium florets, about 1½ to 2 inches, were best in this dish; smaller pieces became mushy. And a hot oven and heated baking sheet were key to browning the cauliflower before it overcooked. For a crunchy, nutty alternative topping, substitute ⅓ cup dukkah (see sidebar) for the cashews.

Don't forget to line the baking sheet with foil before heating. *The tahini mixture makes a mess of an unlined pan.*

1. **Heat the oven to 500°F** with a rack in the lowest position. Line a rimmed baking sheet with foil and set on the rack to heat. In a large bowl, whisk together the tahini, lemon zest, 1 tablespoon of the lemon juice, the oil, garlic, 1½ teaspoons salt, paprika and cayenne. Add the cauliflower and toss, massaging the dressing into the florets.

2. **Working quickly,** remove the baking sheet from the oven and carefully spread the cauliflower on it in an even layer, scraping any remaining tahini onto the florets. Reserve the bowl. Roast until well browned in spots and just tender, 15 to 18 minutes, stirring and turning the florets and rotating the pan halfway through.

3. **Transfer the roasted florets** to the reserved bowl. Add the remaining 1 tablespoon of lemon juice and toss. Add half of the nuts and the cilantro and toss. Sprinkle with the remaining cashews and serve drizzled with more oil, if desired.

EGYPTIAN NUT-AND-SEED SEASONING (DUKKAH)

Start to finish: 15 minutes
Makes about 1 cup

The Egyptian seasoning mixture known as dukkah—a rich blend of seeds, nuts and spices—adds welcome texture and complexity to dips and salads, and even can be used as a rub for meat or fish. For our version, we use cashews instead of traditional hazelnuts; it saves us from peeling the nuts after toasting. Store in an airtight container at room temperature for up to a week. Freeze for longer use.

½ cup raw cashews

2 tablespoons sesame seeds

2 tablespoons coriander seeds

2 tablespoons cumin seeds

1 tablespoon caraway seeds

1 teaspoon dried oregano

½ teaspoon kosher salt

½ teaspoon ground black pepper

In a large skillet over medium, toast the cashews, stirring, until beginning to brown, 3 to 4 minutes. Add the sesame seeds and toast, stirring, until golden, 1 to 2 minutes. Add the coriander, cumin and caraway, and toast, stirring, until fragrant, about 1 minute. Transfer to a food processor and let cool for 5 minutes. Add the oregano, salt and pepper. Pulse until coarsely ground, 12 to 15 pulses.

Sweet Potato Gratin with Vanilla Bean and Bay Leaves

Start to finish: 3 hours (50 minutes active), plus cooling
Servings: 8

Sweet potato casserole is a Thanksgiving staple, but our version is good year-round. We ditch the marshmallows and boost flavor with a dash of spice. For ease, we roast the sweet potatoes, which can be done a day ahead and produces cleaner, deeper flavors and better texture. In lieu of marshmallows we infuse cream with vanilla bean and bay leaves and add a dusting of black pepper. A crunchy topping of dark brown and white sugar with a touch of cayenne keeps the dish appropriate for the adults' table.

Don't get distracted *while the gratin is broiling; all broilers are different, and the difference between browned and burnt can be a matter of seconds.*

5 pounds sweet potatoes

1 cup heavy cream

4 bay leaves

1 vanilla bean

⅓ cup plus 1 tablespoon packed dark brown sugar, divided

Kosher salt and ground black pepper

⅓ cup white sugar

Pinch cayenne pepper

1. Heat the oven to 400°F with one rack in the middle and another 6 inches from the broiler. Pierce the sweet potatoes with a fork and arrange on a rimmed baking sheet. Bake on the middle rack, turning once, until tender, 1 to 1½ hours. Let cool. Increase oven to 425°F.

2. Meanwhile, in a medium saucepan, combine the cream and bay leaves. With a paring knife, split the vanilla bean lengthwise, then scrape out the seeds. Add the seeds and pod to the cream and bring to a simmer over medium-high. Set aside, covered, for 30 minutes. Strain out and discard the solids.

3. Once the potatoes have cooled, scrape the flesh from the skins; discard the skins. In a food processor, combine half the flesh and half the infused cream. Add 1 tablespoon of the brown sugar, 1¼ teaspoons salt and ¾ teaspoon pepper. Process until smooth, about 1 minute, scraping the bowl halfway through; transfer to a large bowl. Repeat with the remaining potatoes and cream, then add to the first batch. Mix well, then transfer to a 13-by-9-inch broiler safe baking dish. Smooth the top.

4. In a bowl, stir together the remaining ⅓ cup of brown sugar, the white sugar and the cayenne. Transfer to a medium-mesh strainer, then evenly sift the mixture over the surface of the potatoes (or do by hand). Brush any sugar off the rim of the baking dish.

5. Bake on the middle rack until bubbling at the edges, about 20 minutes. Remove from the oven, then heat the broiler. When ready, place the dish on the upper rack and broil until deeply browned and crisp, 2 to 7 minutes. Let sit for 20 minutes before serving.

Harissa Roasted Potatoes

Start to finish: 1 hour (10 minutes active)
Servings: 4

Harissa (pronounced ha-REE-sah) may well be one of the original hot sauces. It's generally believed to have originated in Tunisia, where it's often served with couscous and brik, a tuna-and-egg turnover. This recipe uses our homemade harissa sauce (p. 618) to give potatoes a sweet-spicy kick, but harissa also can be found online and in the supermarket's international aisle. Tossing the raw potatoes with harissa before roasting muted the chili paste's flavor, so we crisped "naked" potatoes on the bottom rack first, then tossed them with a portion of the harissa and returned them to the oven. That gave the potatoes the right texture and a spicy crust. A final hit of the remaining harissa, along with parsley and lemon juice, kept the flavors bright.

Don't forget to taste your harissa for heat and pungency before tossing the potatoes. A harissa with gentle heat and smooth texture, like Milk Street's recipe, worked best here. If your variety is particularly spicy, you may want to reduce the total amount to ¼ cup, reserving 1 tablespoon to finish the dish.

2 pounds Yukon Gold potatoes, peeled and cut into 1½-inch pieces

4 ounces shallots (about 4 small), peeled and quartered

2 tablespoons extra-virgin olive oil

Kosher salt and ground black pepper

6 tablespoons harissa paste, divided (recipe p. 618)

⅓ cup chopped flat-leaf fresh parsley

1 tablespoon lemon juice, plus lemon wedges to serve

1. Heat the oven to 400°F with racks in the middle and lowest positions and a rimmed baking sheet on the bottom rack. In a large bowl, toss the potatoes and shallots with the oil, 1 teaspoon salt and ½ teaspoon pepper.

2. Working quickly, remove the baking sheet from the oven, add the potato-shallot mixture and spread in an even layer; reserve the bowl. Roast on the bottom rack until the potatoes are well browned on the bottoms, about 20 minutes, rotating the sheet halfway through.

3. Use a thin metal spatula to transfer the potatoes to the reserved bowl, scraping up any browned bits. Add 4 tablespoons of the harissa and toss until evenly coated. Return the potatoes to the sheet, spreading in an even layer and reserving the bowl. Roast on the middle rack until tender, 18 to 22 minutes, rotating the sheet halfway through.

4. Return the potatoes to the reserved bowl, scraping up any browned bits from the pan. Add the parsley, the remaining 2 tablespoons of harissa and the lemon juice. Toss to coat. Serve with lemon wedges.

Beans

5

Israeli Hummus with Spiced Beef Topping (Kawarma)

Start to finish: 1 hour (15 minutes active), plus soaking
Makes 4 cups

---

8 ounces (227 grams) dried chickpeas	1 to 2 tablespoons extra-virgin olive oil
Kosher salt	1 tablespoon chopped fresh parsley
½ teaspoon baking soda	
¾ cup tahini, room temperature	½ teaspoon ground cumin
	½ teaspoon sweet paprika
3½ tablespoons lemon juice	

In Israel, hummus is breakfast, not a party dip. Our education began in Tel Aviv at Abu Hassan, the country's premier hummus shop, where customers get wide, shallow bowls of hummus topped with whole chickpeas, a sprinkle of parsley, pops of red paprika and amber cumin. The hummus is light, almost sour cream smooth—and warm. When re-creating the hummus, we found we needed to start with dried chickpeas, not canned, and simmer them with baking soda to ensure they completely softened. Small chickpeas like Whole Foods Market 365 Everyday Value brand worked well. Make sure to soak the chickpeas for at least 12 hours before cooking, and if your chickpeas are on the large side, you'll need to cook them for an additional 10 to 15 minutes, or until starting to break down. And for the smoothest, lightest hummus, process the chickpeas while they're still warm, and give them a full three minutes during the first stage. As for tahini, we liked the Kevala brand, but Soom and Aleppo were good, too. Hummus traditionally is served warm and garnished with paprika, cumin, chopped fresh parsley and a drizzle of extra-virgin olive oil. Sometimes a sliced hard-boiled egg is added. Leftover hummus can be refrigerated for up to five days. To reheat, transfer to a microwave-safe bowl, cover and gently heat, adding a few tablespoons of tap water as needed to reach the proper consistency, one to two minutes.

Don't forget to stir the tahini very well. Some brands separate and can become quite thick at the bottom of the container.

1. In a large bowl, combine 8 cups water, the chickpeas and 2 tablespoons salt. Soak for at least 12 hours.

2. In a stockpot over high, bring another 10 cups water and the baking soda to a boil. Drain the soaked chickpeas, discarding the soaking water, and add to the pot. Return to a simmer, then reduce heat to medium and cook until the skins are falling off and the chickpeas are very tender, 40 to 50 minutes.

3. Set a mesh strainer over a large bowl and drain the chickpeas into it; reserve ¾ cup of the chickpea cooking water. Let sit for 1 minute to let all liquid drain. Set aside about 2 tablespoons of the chickpeas, then transfer the rest to the food processor. Add 1 teaspoon salt, then process for 3 minutes.

4. Add the tahini. Continue to process until the mixture has lightened and is very smooth, about 1 minute. Use a silicone spatula to scrape the sides and bottom of the processor bowl. With the machine running, add the reserved cooking liquid and the lemon juice. Process until combined. Taste and season with salt.

5. Transfer the hummus to a shallow serving bowl and use a large spoon to make a swirled well in the center. Drizzle with olive oil, then top with the reserved chickpeas, the parsley, cumin and paprika.

SPICED BEEF TOPPING (KAWARMA)

Start to finish: 25 minutes
Makes about 2 cups

Warm ground meat toppings lend rich, savory notes to hummus, and make it a more robust meal.

½ pound lean ground beef

2 teaspoons sweet paprika

¾ teaspoon kosher salt

½ teaspoon cinnamon

½ teaspoon ground cumin

½ teaspoon dried oregano

½ teaspoon cayenne pepper

2 garlic cloves, grated

¾ cup water

½ small yellow onion, chopped

1 tablespoon extra-virgin olive oil

2 tablespoons tomato paste

2 tablespoons chopped fresh parsley or mint

1½ teaspoons lemon juice

Tahini, to serve

1. In a medium bowl, mix together the beef, paprika, salt, cinnamon, cumin, oregano, cayenne, garlic and 2 tablespoons of the water.

2. In a 10-inch skillet over medium-high, add the ground beef mixture, the onion and oil. Cook until the onion is softened and the beef is no longer pink, 6 to 8 minutes. Stir in the tomato paste and cook until fragrant, about 30 seconds.

3. Add the remaining water and cook, scraping the pan, until the water has evaporated and the mixture sizzles, about 5 minutes. Off heat, stir in the parsley and lemon juice. salt. Spoon over hummus, then drizzle with tahini.

Turkish Beans with Pickled Tomatoes

Start to finish: 3 hours (15 minutes active)
Servings: 6

---

1 pound dried cannellini beans, soaked overnight and drained

12- to 16-ounce beef or lamb shank

1 large yellow onion, chopped (about 2 cups)

4 tablespoons (½ stick) salted butter

8 medium garlic cloves, smashed and peeled

4 sprigs fresh thyme

2 bay leaves

1 teaspoon sweet paprika

1 teaspoon red pepper flakes

14½-ounce can diced tomatoes, drained

Kosher salt

½ cup chopped fresh parsley

2 tablespoons chopped fresh dill, plus more to serve

2 tablespoons pomegranate molasses, plus more to serve

Ground black pepper

Whole-milk yogurt and extra-virgin olive oil, to serve

Pickled tomatoes (see recipe p. 141), to serve

This hearty white bean stew was inspired by the Turkish dish kuru fasulye, basically beans stewed in a spicy tomato sauce. We also borrowed a bit of flavor from the Middle Eastern pantry, using pomegranate molasses, a syrup of boiled pomegranate juice, to add a unique and fruity sweetness. You'll find it in the grocer's international section or near the honey, maple syrup and molasses. This dish calls for dried beans, which means an overnight soak for evenly cooked beans. We found the creamy texture of dried cannellini beans was best, but Great Northern beans worked, too. We maximized meaty flavor—without using a lot of meat—by using a collagen-rich beef or lamb shank. Serve these beans as is or with a drizzle of extra-virgin olive oil and a spoonful of whole-milk yogurt. We also loved the bright contrast provided by pickled tomatoes (see recipe p. 141). The beans can be made up to two days ahead. Reheat over low, adding water to reach your desired consistency.

Don't forget to salt *the beans' soaking water. The salt tenderizes and seasons the beans. We liked a ratio of 1½ tablespoons kosher salt to 3 quarts water.*

1. Heat the oven to 325°F with a rack in the lower middle position. In a large oven-safe pot or Dutch oven over high, combine 5½ cups water, the beans, shank, onion, butter, garlic, thyme, bay leaves, paprika and red pepper flakes. Bring to a boil, then cover and transfer to the oven. Bake for 1 hour 15 minutes.

2. Remove the pot from the oven. Stir in the tomatoes and 2 teaspoons salt. Return, uncovered, to the oven and bake until the beans are fully tender and creamy and the liquid is slightly thickened, another 1 hour 15 minutes. Transfer the pot to a rack. Remove the shank and set aside. Discard the thyme sprigs and bay leaves.

3. When cool enough to handle, remove the meat from the bone, discarding fat, gristle and bone. Finely chop the meat and stir into the beans. Stir in the parsley, dill and molasses. Taste and season with salt and pepper. Serve with yogurt, oil, pickled tomatoes and additional pomegranate molasses and dill.

PICKLED TOMATOES

Start to finish: 5 minutes,
plus chilling / Servings: 1½ cups

These pickled tomatoes are delicious with our Turkish beans, but also can be used on sandwiches or in hearty soups. Make them up to two days ahead. If you can't find Aleppo pepper, substitute with a slightly smaller amount of red pepper flakes. Be sure to seed the tomatoes. Seeds gave the final product an unpleasant texture.

3 plum tomatoes (12 ounces),
cored, seeded and diced

3 tablespoons cider vinegar

1 tablespoon chopped fresh dill

1 teaspoon crushed Aleppo pepper
(see headnote)

1 teaspoon white sugar

½ teaspoon kosher salt

In a medium bowl, stir together all ingredients. Refrigerate for at least 1 hour. Will keep, refrigerated, for 3 days.

Lebanese Lentils and Rice with Crisped Onions (Mujaddara)

Start to finish: **50 minutes** / Servings: 4

___

4 medium garlic cloves, smashed and peeled

4 bay leaves

2½ teaspoons ground cumin

½ teaspoon ground allspice

Kosher salt and ground black pepper

1 cup brown lentils, rinsed and drained

1 cup basmati rice, rinsed and drained

⅓ cup extra-virgin olive oil

2 medium yellow onions, halved and thinly sliced

1 bunch scallions, thinly sliced

Plain whole-milk yogurt, to serve

Rice and lentils with caramelized onions is a much-loved food in the Middle East. This is our take on the version we tasted in Lebanon. The rice and lentils are simmered together in the same pot, with the lentils getting a 10-minute head start so both finish at the same time. Meanwhile, the onions are fried until crisp and deeply caramelized—almost burnt, really—to coax out a savory bittersweet flavor. Serve mujaddara hot, warm or at room temperature with a dollop of plain yogurt. It's a delicious accompaniment to grilled or roasted meats, but it's also hearty enough to be the center of a vegetarian meal.

Don't use French green lentils (lentils du Puy) *in place of the brown lentils called for. Even when fully cooked, green lentils retain a firm, almost al dente texture, while brown lentils take on a softness that combines well with the rice. Don't worry if the onions turn quite dark at the edge of the skillet; deep browning is desirable. But do stir the browned bits into the mix to ensure the onions color evenly. However, if the onions brown deeply before they soften, lower the heat a notch or two and keep stirring until the pan cools slightly.*

___

1. In a large Dutch oven over medium-high, combine 5 cups water, the garlic, bay, cumin, allspice, 1 tablespoon salt and 1 teaspoon pepper. Bring to a boil, then stir in the lentils and reduce to medium. Cover and cook, stirring occasionally and adjusting the heat to maintain a simmer, until the lentils are softened but still quite firm at the center, about 10 minutes.

2. Stir in the rice and return to a simmer. Cover, reduce to medium-low and cook until the liquid is absorbed and the lentils and rice are tender, about 25 minutes.

3. Meanwhile, in a 12-inch skillet over medium-high, heat the oil until shimmering. Add the onions and cook, stirring only occasionally at the start then more frequently once browning begins at the edges of the pan, until the onions are deeply caramelized and crisped, 10 to 15 minutes; adjust the heat if the onions brown too quickly. Using a slotted spoon, transfer the onions to a paper towel–lined plate and spread evenly. Sprinkle with ¼ teaspoon salt and set aside; the onions will crisp as they cool.

4. When the lentils and rice are tender, remove the pot from the heat. Uncover and lay a kitchen towel across the pan, then replace the lid and let stand for 10 minutes.

5. Using a fork, fluff the lentils and rice, removing and discarding the bay. Taste and season with salt and pepper. Stir in half the scallions, then transfer to a serving bowl. Top with the fried onions and remaining scallions. Serve hot, warm or at room temperature with yogurt on the side.

Lentil Salad with Gorgonzola

Start to finish: 1½ hours (30 minutes active)
Servings: 6

½ cup white balsamic vinegar	2 bay leaves
2 medium shallots, thinly sliced	1½ cups French green lentils, sorted, rinsed and drained
Kosher salt and ground black pepper	1 tablespoon extra-virgin olive oil
1 garlic head, outer papery skins removed	2 ounces Gorgonzola cheese, crumbled (about ¾ cup)
2 medium carrots, halved crosswise	½ cup chopped fresh flat-leaf parsley leaves
1 celery stalk, halved crosswise	½ cup walnuts, toasted and chopped
1 tablespoon yellow mustard seeds	
6 sprigs thyme, tied together	

Green lentils du Puy, also known as French lentils, cook quickly, hold their shape well and do a great job at soaking up flavors in a rich broth or stew. But it can be a bit of a race to develop that flavor before the lentils overcook and become mushy. Our solution: Simmer vegetables and aromatics in advance, then add lentils. To really punch up the flavor we turned to one of our favorite seasoning shortcuts and simmered a whole head of garlic with the herbs until it was mellow and tender; the cloves became soft enough to be mashed and formed the basis of a richly savory dressing. Pungent Gorgonzola cheese gave the salad sharp contrast, while toasted walnuts added crunch.

Don't use brown lentils here. *They are larger and have a different cooking time from green lentils.*

1. **In a liquid measuring cup,** combine the vinegar, shallots and 1 teaspoon salt. Let stand for 10 minutes. Meanwhile, cut off and discard the top third of the garlic head, leaving the head intact. In a 2-quart saucepan over medium-high, combine the garlic, 6 cups water, carrots, celery, mustard seeds, thyme, bay leaves and 1 teaspoon salt. Bring to a boil, then cover, reduce heat to low and simmer for 30 minutes. Remove and discard the carrots, celery, thyme and bay leaves.

2. **Return the pot to medium-high** and stir in the lentils. Return to a boil, then cover and reduce heat to low. Simmer until the lentils are tender but still hold their shape, 30 to 35 minutes. Remove the garlic and set aside. Drain the lentils, reserving the liquid, and transfer to a large bowl. Stir in the vinegar-shallot mixture and let cool to room temperature.

3. **Squeeze the pulp from the garlic** into a bowl and mash with a fork. Stir in ¼ cup of the reserved cooking water, the oil and ½ teaspoon salt. Stir the garlic mixture, half of the cheese, the parsley and half of the walnuts into the lentils. Taste and season with salt and pepper. Transfer to a platter and top with the remaining cheese and walnuts.

Oaxacan Refried Black Beans

Start to finish: 2¾ hours (35 minutes active)
Servings: 6

---

4 tablespoons lard or refined coconut oil, divided

1 large white onion, chopped

1 pint grape or cherry tomatoes

5 guajillo chilies, stemmed and seeded

1 pound dried black beans, rinsed and drained

10 medium garlic cloves, peeled and kept whole, plus 5 medium garlic cloves, minced

3 bay leaves

1 teaspoon aniseed

Kosher salt and ground black pepper

4 teaspoons ground cumin

4 teaspoons ground coriander

1 tablespoon ancho chili powder

1 teaspoon dried oregano

In Oaxaca, black beans are part of almost every meal. Though they sometimes are served whole, we especially liked the balanced, complex flavor and smooth, velvety consistency of refried black beans. We got a lesson in the importance of the daily basic from Rodolfo Castellanos, Oaxaca native and winner of Top Chef Mexico, and his mother, restaurant owner Doña Fuensanta. Lard gives these beans a rich meatiness, but coconut oil is a good vegetarian substitute. The beans can be stored in an airtight container in the refrigerator for up to a week. We liked these topped with crumbled cotija cheese and fresh cilantro.

Don't soak the beans before cooking. *Unlike other types of dried beans, black beans soften readily without soaking. And don't forget to reserve the bean cooking liquid; you'll need 2 cups when pureeing the beans in the food processor. And if you'll be making black bean soup (see recipe p. 147), you'll need 3 cups to thin the beans. The liquid also is useful for thinning the beans when reheating (they thicken as they stand).*

1. In a large pot over medium-high, heat 1 tablespoon of the lard until barely smoking. Add the onion, tomatoes and guajillo chilies, then cook, stirring occasionally, until the onion is well browned, 5 to 7 minutes. Add the beans, whole garlic cloves, bay and aniseed, then stir in 10 cups water. Bring to a boil, then cover partially and reduce to low. Cook, stirring occasionally, until the beans are completely tender, 1½ hours to 2 hours.

2. Stir in 2 teaspoons salt. Set a colander in a large bowl and drain the beans, reserving the cooking liquid. Remove and discard the bay leaves from the beans. Transfer the drained beans to a food processor and pulse a few times to break them up. With the machine running, add 1½ cups of the reserved cooking liquid and process until smooth, 2 to 3 minutes, scraping the bowl as needed. Taste and season with salt, then set aside.

3. In a 12-inch nonstick skillet over medium, heat 2 tablespoons of the remaining lard until shimmering. Add the minced garlic, cumin, coriander, chili powder and oregano, then cook, stirring, until fragrant, about 30 seconds.

4. Stir in the pureed beans and cook, stirring frequently, until beginning to brown on the bottom, 8 to 10 minutes. Continue to cook and stir, adding reserved cooking water as needed, until the mixture has the consistency of mashed potatoes, 5 to 7 minutes. Off heat, stir in the remaining 1 tablespoon lard, then taste and season with salt and pepper.

MORE WAYS WITH REFRIED BEANS

Our recipe for Oaxacan refried black beans makes about 5 cups of beans, enough for one meal, plus leftovers that easily can be turned into lunch or a light dinner. In Oaxaca, the beans are spread onto tortillas, then folded into half-rounds and triangles to make tlayudas and tetelas, respectively. Here are a couple more of our favorite ways to use them. Be sure to save your bean cooking liquid, which you'll need for the soup, but which also is perfect for using to reheat the refried beans.

BLACK BEAN SOUP: In a large saucepan over medium, heat 3 cups cooking liquid from refried beans, stirring occasionally, until hot. Add 3 cups refried beans and cook, whisking frequently, until the mixture is well combined and heated through, about 5 minutes. Off heat, stir in ½ cup finely chopped fresh cilantro and ¼ cup lime juice. Taste and season with salt and pepper. Serve with lime wedges, diced avocado, sour cream, sliced scallions and tortilla chips.

HONDURAN BALEADAS: Heat the oven to 450°F with racks in the upper- and lower-middle positions. In a medium microwave-safe bowl, microwave 2 cups refried beans, covered, until hot, about 2 minutes. Stir in 2 tablespoons finely chopped fresh cilantro and 1 tablespoon lime juice, then taste and season with salt and pepper. Place three 8-inch flour tortillas in a single layer on each of 2 baking sheets lined with kitchen parchment. Spread ⅓ cup of the bean mixture onto each tortilla. Use ½ cup shredded cheddar cheese to sprinkle over the tortillas, dividing it evenly. Bake until the cheese melts, 6 to 8 minutes, switching and rotating the baking sheets halfway through. Sprinkle with ½ cup crumbled cotija cheese, dividing it evenly, then top with diced avocado, pickled jalapeños and thinly sliced scallions. Fold each tortilla in half and serve.

Molletes with Pico de Gallo

Start to finish: **15 minutes** / Servings: 4

Eight ½-inch-thick slices
crusty bread (see headnote)

¼ cup extra-virgin olive oil

Kosher salt and ground
black pepper

2 cups black bean puree
(see recipe p. 349)

1 pound whole-milk
mozzarella cheese, shredded

½ cup finely chopped
fresh cilantro

Pico de gallo (see recipe p. 149),
to serve

Sliced avocado, to serve
(optional)

Pickled sliced jalapeños,
to serve (optional)

Mexican molletes are not unlike Italian bruschetti, but the bread is topped with pureed beans and cheese, then toasted until the cheese is melted and browned. They make a great breakfast, light lunch or midday snack. We had molletes in Oaxaca, Mexico, where the bread of choice typically is soft-crumbed, thin-crusted rolls called bolillos that are split open before they're topped. We opted for ½-inch-thick slices of supermarket bakery bread with a soft crumb; look for a loaf that measures about 10-by-5 inches and weighs about 1 pound. Pico de gallo (fresh tomato salsa) adds color and fresh flavor to the molletes, so we consider it a necessary embellishment; sliced avocado and pickled jalapeños are delicious, but optional.

Don't walk away from the bread as it broils. Broilers vary in heat output, so keep a close eye on the slices to make sure they don't scorch.

1. **Heat the broiler** with a rack about 6 inches from the element. Line a rimmed baking sheet with foil and mist with cooking spray. Arrange the bread in a single layer on the baking sheet and brush the tops with the oil. Season with salt and pepper. Broil until the bread is golden brown, 3 to 5 minutes. Flip each slice and broil until the second sides are golden brown, 1 to 2 minutes. Remove from the broiler.

2. **Flip each slice once again.** Spread ¼ cup bean puree on each slice, then top each with some of the cheese, dividing it evenly (½ cup each). Broil until the cheese is melted and begins to brown, 4 to 6 minutes. Transfer the baking sheet to a wire rack and cool for 5 minutes. Sprinkle with cilantro, then transfer to a platter. Serve with pico de gallo, sliced avocado (if using) and pickled jalapeños (if using).

PICO DE GALLO

Start to finish: 30 minutes
Makes about 2 cups

Pico de gallo is a bright, fresh tomato salsa. We use grape or cherry tomatoes because they tend to be dependably sweet and flavorful even when regular tomatoes are dull, mealy and out of season. For a spicier salsa, leave the seeds in the jalapeño.

Don't make the pico de gallo too far ahead. Even after the tomatoes are transferred to a serving bowl with a slotted spoon, they will continue to release liquid and their texture will soften.

1 pint grape or cherry tomatoes, roughly chopped

¼ small red onion, finely chopped (about 3 tablespoons)

¼ cup lightly packed fresh cilantro, chopped

½ jalapeño chili, stemmed, seeded and minced

2 teaspoons white vinegar

1½ teaspoons extra-virgin olive oil

Kosher salt

In a medium bowl, stir together the tomatoes, onion, cilantro, chili, vinegar, oil and 1 teaspoon salt. Cover and let stand at room temperature for 15 minutes. Using a slotted spoon, transfer to a serving bowl, letting the liquid drip away. Taste and season with salt.

Mexican Stewed Beans with Salsa Fresca

Start to finish: 1¾ hours, plus overnight soak and resting
Servings: 6 to 8

For the beans

1 pound dried cranberry beans (see headnote), picked over and rinsed

Kosher salt and ground black pepper

2 tablespoons lard or neutral oil

1 medium white onion, chopped

2 medium garlic cloves, thinly sliced

1 bunch cilantro, stems finely chopped, leaves roughly chopped, reserved separately

1½ quarts low-sodium chicken broth, pork broth (recipe follows; optional) or water

For the sofrito

2 tablespoons lard or neutral oil

1 large white onion, chopped

Kosher salt and ground black pepper

4 medium garlic cloves, minced

2 pounds ripe tomatoes, cored and roughly chopped

2 jalapeño chilies, stemmed, seeded and finely chopped

To serve

3 cups shredded pork (see recipe p. 151, optional)

Salsa fresca (see recipe p. 151)

In Mexico City, we we were taught how to prepare traditional stewed beans by chef Eduardo García of Máximo Bistrot. Sofrito—a sauté of aromatics cooked separately from the dish's central ingredient(s)—is a key flavoring for the beans. Our sofrito consists of onion, garlic, tomatoes and jalapeños cooked down to concentrate their essences and is added only after the beans are fully cooked. Instead of the pinto beans so common in Mexican cooking, we opted to use cranberry beans (also called Roman or borlotti beans). We found that the pinto beans available in the U.S. do not cook up with the same plumpness and velvety texture as the ones we tasted in Mexico; cranberry beans were a closer approximation. Though tan with speckles of red, cooked cranberry beans resemble pinkish beige pinto beans. If you wish to make this dish with pork, see recipe p. 151; it yields a meaty broth for cooking the beans and shredded pork for stirring in at the end. A fresh tomato salsa served on the side brightens and lightens the earthiness of the beans. The most efficient way to approach this multi-component recipe is to prep and cook the sofrito during the 1 hour that the beans simmer and make the salsa while the cooked beans rest for 30 minutes. Note that the pork and broth need to be made before you begin cooking the beans, but can be made up to three days in advance.

Don't forget to soak the beans overnight. Soaked beans cook more evenly and quickly than unsoaked ones. A couple tablespoons of salt in the soaking water produces a creamier, more velvety texture in the cooked beans.

---

1. To prepare the beans, in a large bowl, combine the beans with 2 quarts water and 2 tablespoons salt; stir to dissolve the salt. Cover and soak overnight at room temperature.

2. Drain the beans. In a large Dutch oven, heat the oil over medium heat until shimmering. Add the onion and 1 teaspoon salt, then cook, stirring occasionally, until it begins to brown, about 5 minutes. Stir in the garlic and cilantro stems. Cook, stirring, until fragrant, about 30 seconds. Stir in the beans and broth, then bring to a boil over medium-high. Cover, reduce to low and cook, stirring occasionally, until the beans are tender, about 1 hour.

3. While the beans cook, make the sofrito. In a 12-inch nonstick skillet over medium, heat the lard until shimmering. Add the onion and ½ teaspoon salt, then cook, stirring occasionally, until well browned, 5 to 7 minutes. Stir the garlic and cook until fragrant, about 30 seconds. Add the tomatoes and jalapeños and cook,

SHREDDED PORK AND PORK BROTH FOR STEWED BEANS

Start to finish: 1 hour 20 minutes
Makes 3 cups shredded meat and 1½ quarts broth

2 pounds boneless pork shoulder, trimmed
and cut into 1½-inch cubes

2 jalapeño chilies, stemmed

Kosher salt

In a large pot, combine the pork, jalapeños, 1 teaspoon salt
and 7 cups water. Bring to a boil over high, then reduce to low,
cover and cook until a skewer inserted into the pork meets no
resistance, 60 to 75 minutes.

Using a slotted spoon, transfer the pork to a medium bowl;
set aside to cool slightly. Meanwhile, pour the broth through a
fine-mesh strainer set over a large bowl and let cool.

When the pork is cool enough to handle, shred into bite-size
pieces, discarding any fat and gristle. Cover both the broth and
shredded meat and refrigerate until ready to use or up to 3 days.

SALSA FRESCA

Start to finish: 30 minutes
Makes 2 cups

1 pound ripe tomatoes, cored and finely chopped

3 tablespoons finely chopped red onion

¼ cup lightly packed fresh cilantro, chopped

½ jalapeño chili, stemmed, seeded and minced

2 teaspoons white vinegar

2 teaspoons extra-virgin olive oil

Kosher salt

In a medium bowl, stir together the tomatoes, onion, cilantro,
jalapeño, vinegar, oil and 1 teaspoon salt. Let stand at room
temperature for 15 minutes. Using a slotted spoon, transfer
the salsa to a serving bowl, leaving behind the liquid. Taste and
season with salt.

stirring often, until the tomatoes have broken down, the liquid
they released has cooked off and the mixture begins to sizzle,
10 to 15 minutes. Remove from the heat and set aside.

4. When the beans are done, remove the pot from the heat and
let stand uncovered for 30 minutes to allow the liquid to thicken
slightly. Return the beans to a simmer over medium, stirring
occasionally. Add the sofrito and shredded pork (if using). Cook,
stirring occasionally, until heated through, about 5 minutes. Taste
and season with salt and pepper, then stir in the cilantro leaves.
Serve with salsa fresca on the side.

Hummus with Chipotle Black Beans and Tomato Salsa

Start to finish: 45 minutes / Servings: 4 to 6

Three 15½-ounce cans chickpeas, 2 cups liquid reserved, drained

¼ teaspoon baking soda

Kosher salt and ground black pepper

15½-ounce can black beans, 2 tablespoons liquid reserved, drained

8 tablespoons lime juice, divided

1 tablespoon ground cumin

1 chipotle chili in adobo sauce, plus 1 teaspoon adobo sauce

½ cup finely chopped fresh cilantro, divided

½ cup tahini

1 cup cherry or grape tomatoes, finely chopped

½ small red onion, finely chopped

1 jalapeño chili, stemmed, seeded and minced

2 cups tortilla chips, roughly crushed

Family-owned Shlomo & Doron in Tel Aviv's Yemenite Quarter is famous for its hummus, both classic and unconventional. The eatery's Mexican-inspired hummus—complete with toppings of black beans, salsa and tortilla chips—inspired us to make our own version at home. For ease, we use canned chickpeas to make the hummus base, but first we simmer them with a little baking soda, which softens the legumes along with their skins so they break down into a perfectly smooth puree. Processing the chickpeas while warm for a full three minutes also helps achieve the finest, silkiest consistency. The hummus is topped with a black bean puree made subtly smoky and spicy by the addition of chipotle chili in adobo sauce, followed by a fresh pico de gallo salsa and crushed tortilla chips for texture. Serve with warmed flatbread and, if you like, with additional tortilla chips.

Don't forget to reserve some of the liquid from the chickpeas and black beans before draining. You'll need 2 cups and 2 tablespoons, respectively. Also, don't rinse the chickpeas and black beans after draining. The residual liquid gives the purees a smoother, silkier consistency.

1. In a large saucepan over high, combine the chickpeas and their 2 cups reserved liquid, the baking soda, ½ teaspoon salt and 3 cups water. Bring to a boil, then reduce to medium and cook, uncovered and stirring occasionally, until very tender and the chickpea skins begin to fall off, 15 to 20 minutes.

2. Meanwhile, in a food processor, combine the black beans and their 2 tablespoons reserved liquid, 2 tablespoons of the lime juice, the cumin, chipotle chili and adobo sauce, and ¼ teaspoon each salt and pepper. Process until smooth, scraping the bowl as needed, 20 to 30 seconds. Add ¼ cup of the cilantro and pulse 2 or 3 times to combine. Transfer to a medium bowl, then taste and season with salt and pepper; set aside. Wipe out the food processor.

3. When the chickpeas are done, drain them in a colander set in a large bowl. Reserve ¾ cup of the chickpea cooking liquid; discard the remainder. Let the chickpeas drain for about 1 minute, shaking the colander to drain as much liquid as possible. Add the warm chickpeas to the processor along with ½ teaspoon salt. Process until completely smooth, about 3 minutes. Add the tahini and continue to process until the mixture is lightened and very smooth, about 1 minute. Scrape the sides and bottom of the processor bowl. With the machine running, add the reserved cooking liquid and 4 tablespoons (¼ cup) of the remaining lime juice, then process until well combined, about 1 minute. Taste and season with salt.

4. Transfer the hummus to a shallow serving bowl. Spread the black bean mixture on top in an even layer. Wipe out the bowl used for the black beans, then add to it the tomatoes, onion, jalapeño, the remaining 2 tablespoons lime juice and ¼ teaspoon salt; stir to combine.

5. Distribute the tortilla chips over the black-bean layer and spoon the tomato salsa on top. Sprinkle with the remaining ¼ cup cilantro and serve immediately.

Punjabi Chickpeas with Potato (Chole)

Start to finish: **45 minutes** / Servings: 4

1 large red onion

4 tablespoons grapeseed or other neutral oil, divided

1½ teaspoons ground coriander

1 teaspoon ground cardamom

1 teaspoon sweet paprika

½ teaspoon ground cinnamon

¼ teaspoon ground cloves

¼ teaspoon nutmeg

⅛ teaspoon cayenne pepper

Kosher salt and ground black pepper

1 teaspoon cumin seeds

¾ pound russet potatoes (about 2 medium potatoes), peeled and cut into ½-inch cubes

1 tablespoon finely grated fresh ginger

3 medium garlic cloves, finely grated

1 tablespoon tomato paste

Two 15½-ounce cans chickpeas, drained

1 tablespoon lime juice, plus lime wedges, to serve

¼ cup coarsely chopped cilantro leaves, plus more to garnish

Chopped fresh tomato, thinly sliced bird's eye or serrano chilies and whole-milk Greek-style yogurt, to serve (optional)

Seasoning blends known as masalas are the backbone of much of Indian cooking. But they often involve intimidatingly long lists of spices, each requiring toasting and grinding. Buying prepared blends is easier, but they can taste faded and stale. For our chole (pronounced CHO-lay)—a chickpea curry popular in India and Pakistan—we mix our own garam masala, a warm seasoning blend that features cayenne pepper and cinnamon. To make the sauce, we started with onion cooked until it practically melted. Grating the onion before browning helped it cook faster and gave it a better texture. Amchoor powder made from dried green mangoes gives traditional chole its characteristic tang, but we found lime juice was a good—and more convenient—substitute. When preparing this dish, make sure your potato pieces are no larger than ½ inch thick so they cook quickly. Chole typically is eaten with flatbread, such as roti or naan.

Don't use a nonstick skillet for this recipe; the fond (browned bits on the bottom of the pan) won't form, which will alter the chole's flavor. And don't be deterred by the lengthy list of spices here. Most are pantry staples and are key to producing the dish's complex flavor.

1. Using the large holes of a box grater, grate the onion, then transfer to a mesh strainer and drain. In a small bowl, stir together 1 tablespoon of the oil with the coriander, cardamom, paprika, cinnamon, cloves, nutmeg, cayenne, 1¼ teaspoons salt and ½ teaspoon pepper.

2. In a 12-inch skillet over medium-high, heat the remaining 3 tablespoons of oil. Add the cumin seeds and cook, shaking the pan, until the seeds are fragrant and darken, 30 to 60 seconds. Add the drained onion and cook, stirring frequently, until the moisture has evaporated, 1 to 3 minutes. Add the potatoes, reduce heat to medium and cook, stirring frequently, until the onions begin to brown and a fond forms on the bottom of the pan, 6 to 8 minutes. Add the ginger, garlic and tomato paste, then cook for 1 minute, stirring constantly.

3. Clear the center of the pan, then add the spice paste to the clearing and cook, mashing and stirring until fragrant, about 15 seconds. Stir into the potatoes. Add 1½ cups water and bring to a boil, scraping up all the browned bits. Add the chickpeas and return to a boil, then cover, reduce heat to low and cook until the potatoes are tender and the oil separates from the sauce at the edges of the pan, 13 to 15 minutes.

4. Off the heat, stir in the lime juice and cilantro. Taste and season with salt and pepper. Serve with lime wedges, chopped tomato, chilies and yogurt, if desired.

Quick Refried Beans

Start to finish: **25 minutes** / Servings: **4**

Two 15½-ounce cans pinto
or black beans, drained

4 tablespoons lard, olive oil
or neutral oil, divided

1 large yellow onion,
quartered and thinly sliced

2 medium garlic cloves,
thinly sliced

Kosher salt

1 teaspoon ground cumin

1 teaspoon ground coriander

¾ teaspoon dried oregano

2 chipotle chilies in adobo sauce,
plus 1 tablespoon adobo sauce

½ cup chopped fresh cilantro

1 tablespoon lime juice

Pinto beans are slightly sweeter and creamier than black beans, but either work in this recipe. Though we love the rich flavor lard gives to the beans, olive or vegetable oil are fine, too. We prefer our refried beans on the chunkier side, but if you prefer yours smoother, process the bean-onion mixture for a little longer after adding the water. And you can adjust the consistency of the finished beans by stirring in more water at the end. Serve these as a side with shredded cheese, sliced scallions or chopped onion, or spread them on a torta, fold them into a quesadilla or spoon them over nachos.

Don't remove the remaining beans from the food processor after measuring out 1 cup. Set aside until needed later.

1. In a food processor, pulse the beans until coarsely chopped, about 7 pulses. Transfer 1 cup of the beans to a bowl and set aside, leave the remainder in the food processor.

2. In a 12-inch nonstick skillet over medium, heat 2 tablespoons of lard until shimmering. Add the onion, garlic and 1 teaspoon salt. Cook, stirring occasionally, until the onion is lightly browned, about 5 minutes. Stir in the cumin, coriander and oregano; cook until fragrant, about 30 seconds. Stir in the chipotles and adobo sauce and cook, breaking up the chilies with a spatula, until fragrant, about 30 seconds.

3. Transfer the onion mixture to the processor with the beans, reserving the skillet; pulse until coarsely chopped, about 7 pulses. Add ⅓ cup water and continue to pulse until the onions and beans are coarsely pureed, another 7 to 12 pulses.

4. In the same skillet over medium, heat the remaining 2 tablespoons lard until barely smoking. Add the reserved chopped beans and cook until they begin to brown and most of the lard has been absorbed, 1 to 2 minutes. Stir in the bean-onion puree, then spread the mixture to the edges of the skillet. Cook, without stirring, until the beans begin to brown at the edges, 1 to 2 minutes. Stir the beans well and repeat the process twice more.

5. Off heat, stir in the cilantro and lime juice. Taste and season with salt. Adjust the consistency with additional water, if desired.

Grains

6

Thai Fried Rice

Start to finish: **20 minutes** / Servings: 4

---

1 tablespoon fish sauce

1 teaspoon soy sauce

1 teaspoon white sugar

4 cups cooked and chilled jasmine rice

1 tablespoon peanut or vegetable oil

2 large eggs, lightly beaten

4 ounces thinly sliced pancetta, chopped

4 scallions, white and green parts thinly sliced, reserved separately

1 large shallot, minced

1 medium garlic clove, minced

¼ cup chopped fresh cilantro

Sliced cucumber and lime wedges, to serve

Cooked in under five minutes in the open-air kitchen of his home in Thailand, chef Andy Ricker's fried rice was speedy, simple—and delicious. Pork belly, shallot and garlic added bold flavors. Soy and fish sauces added savory depth. Fresh herbs kept everything bright and light. Ricker prefers to use a wok because it allows him to move food away from the hot oil at the center to the cooler sides of the pan. In a nod to the Western kitchen, we began with a large nonstick skillet, though you can use a wok if you have one. Pork belly can be hard to find in the U.S. Looking for a substitute we found ground pork too greasy and bacon too smoky. Pancetta—if culturally odd—was just right, which makes sense since it's cured pork belly. In a skillet, we had to reverse-engineer the process and move foods in and out, starting with the eggs, then the pancetta. We liked the aromatic flavor of jasmine rice, but long-grain white or basmati work, too. If you have no leftover rice, follow our recipe (see recipe, p. 161). Thai restaurants offer condiments for fried rice, including sliced green chilies in white vinegar. We came up with our own (see recipe p. 612). Use it with the fried rice or any dish that needs a hit of gentle heat and acid.

Don't use hot or warm rice. The fried rice will be clumpy and gummy (see sidebar).

1. In a bowl, stir together the fish sauce, soy sauce, 1 teaspoon water and sugar. Set aside. Use your hands to break up the rice so no clumps remain. Set aside.

2. In a 12-inch nonstick skillet over medium-high, heat the oil until barely smoking. Pour in the eggs and cook, stirring, until just set. Transfer the eggs to a plate. Add the pancetta to the skillet and cook over medium until crisp. Using a slotted spoon, transfer to the plate with the eggs.

3. Pour off all but 1 tablespoon of the fat from the skillet and return to medium-high. Add the scallion whites, shallot and garlic and cook until softened, about 1 minute. Add the rice and cook, stirring occasionally, until heated through, about 2 minutes.

4. Stir the fish sauce mixture, then pour over the rice. Cook, stirring, until well mixed. Stir in the egg and pancetta, breaking up the eggs. Transfer to a large platter and sprinkle with cilantro and scallion greens. Serve with cucumber, lime wedges and fish sauce–pickled chilies (see recipe p. 612), if desired.

RICE AT THE READY

While our Thai fried rice takes just minutes to prepare, it does require cooked-and-cooled plain rice. Warm, freshly cooked rice won't work; it sticks to the pan and turns gummy. For rice to fry, its starches must first cool and recrystallize. Fresh rice needed two hours minimum to chill adequately, but it can be prepared up to three days in advance and kept refrigerated. For real make-ahead convenience, cooked rice also can be frozen. Make a batch or two, then freeze in zip-close plastic bags.

Rice for Thai Fried Rice

Start to finish: 20 minutes, plus cooling / Makes 4 cups

2 cups water

1½ cups jasmine rice, rinsed

½ teaspoon kosher salt

Line a rimmed baking sheet with kitchen parchment and lightly coat it with vegetable oil. In a large saucepan, combine the water, rice and salt. Bring to a simmer, then reduce to low, cover and cook until tender and fluffy, 15 to 18 minutes. Fluff with a fork, then spread on the prepared baking sheet. Let cool, then cover and refrigerate until cold.

Japanese-Style Rice with Flaked Salmon and Shiitake Mushrooms (Sake to Kinoko Takikomi Gohan)

Start to finish: **50 minutes (20 minutes active)** / Servings: **4**

This recipe is our version of a dish we learned from Elizabeth Andoh. The salmon here is thinly sliced and marinated in a mixture of soy sauce, sake and mirin, and it serves more as a flavoring for the rice than as a feature protein. After the fish marinates, the soy mixture is repurposed as a seasoning for the rice as it steams. Layering the salmon slices onto the rice after cooking and giving the rice a final quick burst of medium-high heat ensures the fish doesn't dry out. If you like, serve the rice with lemon wedges and additional soy sauce.

Don't use a saucepan with a loose-fitting lid. For the rice to cook properly, the lid must fit securely. If the lid has a vent hole, plug it with a bit of foil to prevent steam from escaping.

1. In a small bowl, stir together the soy sauce, sake and mirin. Holding your knife at a 45-degree angle to the cutting board, cut the salmon crosswise into ⅛-inch-thick slices. Add to the soy sauce mixture and gently toss. Cover and refrigerate for at least 20 minutes or up to 1 hour.

2. In a medium saucepan, combine the rice, mushrooms, scallion whites, 1 teaspoon salt and 1¾ cups water. Drain the salmon marinade into the rice and stir to combine; return the salmon to the refrigerator. Cover the pan and bring to a boil over high; this should take about 5 minutes. Reduce to low and cook for another 5 minutes.

3. Without lifting the lid, remove the pot from the heat and let stand for at least 10 minutes or up to 30 minutes. Uncover and arrange the salmon slices in an even layer on the surface of the rice. Cover and cook over medium-high until the salmon begins to turn opaque at the edges, about 1 minute. Remove from the heat and let stand, covered, until the salmon is fully opaque, another 1 to 2 minutes.

4. Run a silicone spatula around the edge of the pan to loosen the rice. Gently lift and fluff the grains, flaking the fish and mixing it into the rice. Make sure to scrape along the bottom of the pan. Spoon into bowls, sprinkle with the scallion greens and serve with lemon wedges.

¼ cup soy sauce

3 tablespoons sake

1 tablespoon mirin

One 6-ounce skinless salmon fillet

2 cups Japanese-style short-grain white rice, rinsed well and drained

4 ounces fresh shiitake mushrooms, stemmed and thinly sliced

3 scallions, thinly sliced on the diagonal, whites and greens reserved separately

Kosher salt

Lemon wedges, to serve

Coconut-Ginger Rice

Start to finish: **30 minutes** / Servings: 4

Jasmine rice steamed with shallots, ginger, lemon grass and coconut yields a richly aromatic side dish that's perfect with Southeast Asian mains, such as seafood curries. Rice cooked with all coconut milk was too rich and heavy. A combination of water and coconut milk made for fluffy grains that were light yet robustly flavored. Using unrefined coconut oil reinforced the coconut flavor.

Don't use the rice without first rinsing and draining. Rinsing removes excess starch that would otherwise make the cooked grains heavy and gluey.

1. In a large saucepan over medium-high, heat the oil until barely smoking. Add the shallots and cook, stirring frequently, until lightly browned, 3 to 5 minutes. Stir in the ginger and lemon grass and cook until fragrant, about 30 seconds.

2. Stir in the rice, 1½ cups water, the coconut milk and 1 teaspoon salt, then bring to a simmer. Cover, reduce to low and cook until the rice absorbs the liquid, 15 to 20 minutes.

3. Remove and discard the ginger and lemon grass, then fluff the rice with a fork. Taste and season with salt.

1 tablespoon coconut oil (preferably unrefined)

2 medium shallots, halved and thinly sliced

1-inch piece fresh ginger, peeled, sliced into thirds and lightly bruised

1 stalk lemon grass, trimmed to the lower 6 inches, dry outer leaves discarded, lightly bruised

1½ cups jasmine rice, rinsed and drained

½ cup coconut milk

Kosher salt

Bulgur-Tomato Salad with Herbs and Pomegranate Molasses (Eetch)

Start to finish: **30 minutes** / Servings: 4

This Armenian salad, known as eetch, is reminiscent of tabbouleh, but because it's grain-centric rather than herb-focused, it's heartier and more substantial. Instead of soaking the bulgur in water—as is done for tabbouleh—the bulgur is hydrated in a mixture of tomato paste and water, so the grains take on a red-orange hue. We like Aleppo pepper in this salad, but red pepper flakes work, too. If you want to make the salad more tart and tangy, mix in a splash of lemon juice. For a more substantial meal, add blanched green beans and crumbled feta cheese.

Don't use fine or medium bulgur. These varieties have different liquid-absorption rates than coarse bulgur, the type called for in this recipe. They also don't have the same hearty chew.

1. In a small bowl, whisk together 1⅓ cups water and the tomato paste. Set aside. In a 10-inch skillet over medium, heat the oil until shimmering. Add the bell pepper, chopped scallions and ½ teaspoon salt. Cover and cook, stirring occasionally, until the bell pepper is tender, about 5 minutes. Stir in the garlic, cumin and Aleppo pepper, then cook until fragrant, about 1 minute.

2. Stir in the bulgur, the tomato paste mixture and 1¼ teaspoons salt. Bring to a boil over medium-high. Cover, reduce to low and cook until the bulgur has absorbed the liquid, 12 to 15 minutes. Remove from the heat and let stand, covered, for 5 minutes.

3. Transfer to a wide, shallow bowl and let cool until just warm, about 5 minutes. Drizzle the pomegranate molasses over the bulgur, then fold until combined. Fold in the tomatoes, mint and sliced scallions. Taste and season with salt, black pepper and additional pomegranate molasses.

3 tablespoons tomato paste

2 tablespoons extra-virgin olive oil

1 medium red bell pepper, stemmed, seeded and finely chopped

6 scallions (4 finely chopped, 2 thinly sliced, reserved separately)

Kosher salt and ground black pepper

3 medium garlic cloves, finely chopped

1½ teaspoons ground cumin

1 teaspoon Aleppo pepper or ¼ teaspoon red pepper flakes (see headnote)

1 cup coarse bulgur

1 tablespoon pomegranate molasses, plus more if needed

1 pint grape tomatoes, halved

¾ cup chopped fresh mint or flat-leaf parsley

Middle Eastern Rice with Toasted Pasta and Herbs

Start to finish: **25 minutes** / Servings: 4

The combination of rice and pasta, introduced to the U.S. in the mid-20th century as Rice-A-Roni, is based on a classic Middle Eastern pilaf often served as a side dish with meat. Toasting the dry pasta in butter is key; it caramelizes some of the starch molecules, adding color and forming nutty flavors. We prefer thin vermicelli pasta, but thin spaghetti or angel hair (capellini) work well, too. We add the vermicelli halfway through the cooking to make sure the noodles don't overcook. We finish the dish with herbs and toasted sliced almonds. Toast the almonds in a small skillet over medium, stirring often, until browned and fragrant, 3 to 5 minutes.

Don't forget to rinse and drain the rice. Rinsing removes excess starch that can make the cooked grains sticky instead of light and fluffy.

1. In a large saucepan over medium, melt 2 tablespoons of butter. Add the pasta and cook, stirring frequently, until the noodles are deeply browned, about 5 minutes. Transfer to a small bowl and set aside.

2. In the same pan, combine the rice and broth, then set over medium-high. Bring to a boil, then reduce to low, cover and cook for 8 minutes. Stir in the toasted pasta. Cover and continue to cook until all of the liquid has been absorbed, about another 7 minutes.

3. Off heat, stir in the remaining 2 tablespoons butter and 2 tablespoons each of dill and parsley. Taste and season with salt and pepper. Transfer to a bowl and sprinkle with the remaining herbs and the almonds.

4 tablespoons (½ stick) salted butter, divided

1 ounce vermicelli pasta, broken into 1-inch pieces (generous ⅓ cup)

1 cup basmati rice, rinsed and drained

1⅔ cups low-sodium chicken broth

4 tablespoons lightly packed fresh dill, chopped, divided

4 tablespoons lightly packed fresh parsley, chopped, divided

Kosher salt and ground black pepper

¼ cup toasted sliced almonds

Risotto with Fresh Herbs

Start to finish: 25 minutes / Servings: 4

3½ cups vegetable broth
(see recipe p. 167)

6 tablespoons (¾ stick) salted
butter, cut into 1-tablespoon
pieces, divided

1 cup carnaroli or
Arborio rice

1 ounce Parmesan cheese,
finely grated (½ cup)

2 teaspoons minced fresh
thyme

⅓ cup thinly sliced scallions

¼ cup finely chopped parsley

½ teaspoon grated
lemon zest

Kosher salt

4 teaspoons white
balsamic vinegar

We learned the principals of risotto from chefs in Milan. Max Masuelli (and his son, Andrea) at Trattoria Masuelli San Marco used vegetable, not chicken, broth, and no onion for cleaner flavor. And Diego Rossi, of Trippa, skipped the traditional wine and added a splash of sherry vinegar at the end (we use white balsamic vinegar). Cooks in Milan—and at Milk Street—preferred carnaroli rice, but, with careful cooking, the more common Arborio also will yield delicious results. Homemade vegetable broth is best for this risotto; its fresh, clean flavor won't compete with the delicate herbs. Serve in warmed, shallow bowls. To try Milan's signature saffron version see the following variation.

Don't cook the rice to the ideal al dente texture before removing the pan from the burner. The grains will continue to cook with residual heat as the cheese and butter are stirred in.

1. In a small saucepan over medium, bring the broth, covered, to a simmer. Reduce to low to keep warm.

2. In a large saucepan over medium-high, melt 2 tablespoons of butter. Add the rice and cook, stirring constantly, until translucent at the edges, 1 to 2 minutes. Add 2½ cups of the hot broth and bring to a boil, then reduce to medium and cook, stirring frequently and briskly, until the grains are almost tender but still quite firm at the core (it will be quite soupy), 8 to 10 minutes; adjust the heat as needed to maintain a vigorous simmer.

3. Add ½ cup broth and cook, stirring frequently and briskly, until the rice is just shy of al dente but still soupy, 3 to 5 minutes. If the rice is thick and dry but the grains are still too firm, add the remaining hot broth in ¼-cup increments and continue to cook, stirring, until the rice is just shy of al dente.

4. Off heat, stir in the Parmesan, thyme, scallions, parsley, lemon zest, ½ teaspoon salt and the remaining 4 tablespoons butter, 1 piece at a time. Taste and season with salt, then stir in the vinegar. Serve immediately.

SAFFRON VARIATION (RISOTTO MILANESE):

Prepare the broth, substituting 2 medium carrots (peeled and chopped) for the Parmesan rind, decreasing the garlic to 1 clove and omitting the parsley. In a small saucepan over medium, bring the broth, covered, to a simmer. Reduce to low to keep warm. In a small bowl or measuring cup, combine ½ cup of the hot broth and 1 teaspoon saffron threads; set aside. Follow the risotto recipe to cook the rice, adding the saffron broth in place of the ½ cup plain broth. When adding the Parmesan at the end, omit the thyme, scallions and chopped parsley.

EASY VEGETABLE-PARMESAN BROTH

This simple vegetarian broth can be made in about 30 minutes. Use immediately after straining or cool to room temperature, cover and refrigerate for up to five days.

Don't simmer the broth uncovered. Partially covering the pan prevents excessive evaporation, but allows for some concentration of flavors.

Start to finish: 30 minutes
Makes about 1 quart

One 1-ounce chunk of Parmesan rind

2 large celery stalks, chopped

1 medium yellow onion, chopped

1 medium tomato, roughly chopped

3 large garlic cloves, smashed and peeled

1 cup lightly packed fresh flat-leaf parsley

In a large saucepan over high, combine all ingredients with 5 cups water and bring to a boil. Partially cover, then reduce to medium and cook for 20 minutes, adjusting the heat to maintain a lively simmer.

Pour the broth through a fine-mesh stainer into a large bowl; discard the solids. You should have about 1 quart of broth.

Soft Polenta

Start to finish: 1¾ hours (10 minutes active) / Servings: 6

Polenta, a savory cornmeal porridge, can be a disappointment in the U.S., tasting mostly of the cheese and fat that
weigh it down. Not to mention it requires near-constant
whisking. But in Cossano Belbo, Italy, we learned a better
way from Maria Teresa Marino, whose family has run a
grain mill for centuries: No cheese, no butter, not much
stirring. The porridge was light and fresh and the taste
of the corn shined through. We followed that lead, using
more water than called for in conventional recipes—
11 cups. Combining the cornmeal with cold, not boiling,
water, then bringing the entire pot to a simmer, prevented
clumping. We finished cooking the polenta in the oven
rather than the stovetop, for more consistent, gentle heat.
For the best flavor and texture, use coarse stone-ground
cornmeal; fine cornmeal produced gluey polenta, while
steel-ground cornmeal had less flavor. We liked Bob's
Red Mill coarse-grind cornmeal and its polenta corn grits,
but found that different brands can cook up with slightly
different consistencies. The finished polenta should be
pourable; if it's too thick, thin it with water as needed.

*Don't use white cornmeal. Its flavor is milder than yellow
cornmeal. And don't skip the whisk for stirring the polenta
as it cooks; its wires are more effective than a wooden spoon.*

2 cups coarse stoneground
yellow cornmeal (see
headnote)

Kosher salt and ground
black pepper

1. Heat the oven to 375°F with a rack in the lower-middle position.
In a large Dutch oven, whisk together the cornmeal, 1 tablespoon
salt and 11 cups water. Bring to a gentle simmer over medium-
high, stirring frequently. Transfer the pot, uncovered, to the oven
and bake for 1 hour.

2. **Remove the pot from the oven.** Carefully whisk until smooth
and use a wooden spoon to scrape along the bottom and into the
corners of the pot. Return the pot, uncovered, to the oven and
cook until the cornmeal is thick and creamy and the granules
are tender, another 10 to 30 minutes.

3. **Remove the pot from the oven.** Vigorously whisk the polenta
until smooth and use the spoon to scrape the bottom, sides and
corners of the pot. Let stand for 5 minutes. The polenta should
thicken just enough for a spoon to leave a brief trail when drawn
through; whisk in water, if needed, to thin the consistency. Taste
and season with salt and pepper. Serve immediately.

Persian Jeweled Rice (Javaher Polow)

Start to finish: **55 minutes (20 minutes active)** / Servings: 4

This rice pilaf is named for the colorful dried fruits and nuts that embellish the saffron-tinted basmati rice. Traditionally, jeweled rice is a labor-intensive dish; we've created a simplified version that's visually stunning as well as richly flavorful. We almost always toast nuts to enhance their flavor and texture, but here raw pistachios are best, as they are more vivid in color and subtler in flavor than toasted or roasted.

Don't forget to rinse and drain the rice. Rinsing removes excess starch so the grains cook up fluffy and light.

1. In a microwave-safe bowl, combine the saffron with 2⅔ cups water. Microwave on high until the water has a yellow hue, about 1 minute; set aside.

2. In a 12-inch skillet over medium, melt the butter. Add the onions and 2 teaspoons salt, then cook, stirring occasionally, until softened and light golden brown, 10 to 12 minutes. Stir in the rice, cumin, cardamom, 1 teaspoon salt and ½ teaspoon pepper. Cook, stirring, until the grains are lightly browned and no longer translucent, 4 to 7 minutes. Stir in the saffron water, carrots and cranberries. Bring to a boil over medium-high, then cover, reduce to low, and cook until the rice has absorbed the liquid and the carrots are tender, 25 to 30 minutes.

3. Fluff the rice with a fork, then stir in the orange zest and ¼ cup of pistachios. Taste and season with salt and pepper. Transfer to a shallow bowl and sprinkle with the remaining ¼ cup pistachios.

1 teaspoon saffron threads

4 tablespoons (½ stick) salted butter

2 medium yellow onions, halved and thinly sliced

Kosher salt and ground black pepper

2 cups basmati rice, rinsed and drained

2 teaspoons ground cumin

1¾ teaspoons ground cardamom

2 medium carrots, peeled and shredded on the large holes of a box grater (about 1 cup)

1 cup dried cranberries

1 teaspoon finely grated orange zest

½ cup shelled pistachios, chopped, divided

Tomato Rice with Oregano and Feta

Start to finish: **25 minutes** / Servings: **4**

On the Greek island of Ikaria, Diane Kochilas, authority on the cuisine of her native Greece, taught us to make a risotto-esque tomato rice in which the grains are cooked until al dente (the centers are still slightly firm) and the consistency is a little soupy. Instead of the regular round tomatoes that Kochilas grated to a pulp before use, we opt for grape or cherry tomatoes, halved, because they tend to be dependably good no matter the season. She used ouzo, the Greek anise-flavored liqueur, as seasoning in the rice, and we do so as well. However, if you prefer, substitute an equal amount of white wine plus 1 teaspoon fennel seeds. To avoid a flare-up, take the skillet off the heat when adding the ouzo (this step is not necessary if using wine instead of ouzo).

Don't use long-grain rice. *It lacks the starchiness of Arborio rice and won't yield a creamy, risotto-like consistency.*

3 tablespoons extra-virgin olive oil, plus more to serve

1 tablespoon salted butter

1 small red onion, finely chopped

1 pint grape or cherry tomatoes, halved

Kosher salt and ground black pepper

1 tablespoon tomato paste

3 medium garlic cloves, finely grated

1 cup Arborio rice

⅓ cup ouzo (see headnote)

4 cups hot water, divided

¼ cup minced fresh oregano

2 tablespoons lemon juice

2 ounces feta cheese, crumbled (½ cup)

1. In a 12-inch skillet over medium-high, heat the oil and butter until the butter melts. Add the onion, tomatoes and 1 teaspoon salt, then cook, stirring occasionally, until the onion has softened and the tomatoes begin to release their juice, about 5 minutes.

2. Add the tomato paste and cook, stirring, until the tomato paste begins to brown, about 1 minute. Stir in the garlic and cook until fragrant, about 30 seconds. Add the rice and cook, stirring constantly, until the grains are translucent at the edges, 1 to 2 minutes. Remove the pan from the heat and stir in the ouzo. Return to medium-high and bring to a simmer, then cook, stirring, until most of the moisture has been absorbed, about 1 minute.

3. Stir in 3 cups of the hot water and 1½ teaspoons salt. Bring to a boil, then reduce to medium and cook uncovered, stirring often and briskly, until the rice is al dente (tender but with some firmness at the center) and the consistency is creamy but still rather loose, 8 to 10 minutes; adjust the heat as needed to maintain a vigorous simmer. If the rice is thick and dry but the grains are still too firm, add the remaining 1 cup hot water and continue to cook, stirring, until the rice is al dente.

4. Off heat, stir in the oregano and lemon juice, then taste and season with salt and pepper. Transfer to a serving bowl and sprinkle with the feta. Serve with oil for drizzling.

Quinoa Pilaf with Dates, Almonds and Carrot Juice

Start to finish: **40 minutes (15 minutes active)** / Servings: 4

We like the nutty, earthy flavor and gentle crunch of quinoa, but too often salads made with this seed—it's technically not a grain—end up mushy and flavorless. For a better way, we looked to Deborah Madison, author of "Vegetarian Cooking for Everyone." She cooks her quinoa in carrot juice, a winning combination that perked up its natural sweetness and tempered its tendency to muddiness. We also liked a quinoa by Erik Ramirez of Brooklyn's Llama Inn. His famously madcap quinoa pilaf studded with bananas, bacon, cashews and avocado showed us that texture and contrast can make quinoa exciting. We liked a simple combo of chewy-sweet dates and crunchy almonds. We took a three-step approach to keeping our pilaf light and fluffy: first toasting the quinoa, then cooking it with less liquid than typically called for, and finally letting the cooked quinoa rest before fluffing. For texture, we added dates and almonds or cashews; both worked. Finishing with scallions, lemon and fresh dill brightened the final dish. Eat this as is or pair it with sautéed shrimp, broiled salmon or fried tofu.

Don't worry about rinsing the quinoa. *Most varieties sold in the U.S. are pre-rinsed. Just check the packaging.*

2 tablespoons salted butter

1 medium carrot, peeled and diced (about ½ cup)

1 small yellow onion, diced (about ½ cup)

Kosher salt

1 cup white quinoa

1 tablespoon finely grated fresh ginger

1 teaspoon ground cumin

½ cup carrot juice

4 medjool dates, pitted and diced

⅓ cup chopped almonds or cashews, toasted

2 scallions, trimmed and chopped

3 tablespoons chopped fresh dill, plus more to garnish

1 teaspoon grated lemon zest, plus 1 tablespoon lemon juice

Ground black pepper

Extra-virgin olive oil, for drizzling (optional)

1. In a medium saucepan over medium, melt the butter. Add the carrot, onion and ¼ teaspoon salt. Cook, stirring, until softened, 3 to 5 minutes. Add the quinoa and cook, stirring, until fragrant and beginning to pop, about 5 minutes. Stir in the ginger and cumin. Cook, stirring, for 1 minute. Add the carrot juice, ¾ cup water and ½ teaspoon salt. Bring to a boil. Cover, reduce to medium-low and cook until the liquid is absorbed, 11 to 13 minutes.

2. Remove the pan from the heat and uncover. Sprinkle in the dates, cover the pan with a kitchen towel and replace the lid. Let sit for 10 minutes. Fluff the quinoa with a fork, then add the almonds or cashews, scallions, dill, lemon zest and juice. Stir gently to combine, season with salt and pepper, then garnish with dill and a drizzle of olive oil, if desired.

Polenta with Shrimp and Tomatoes

Start to finish: 1¼ hours / Servings: 6

___

1 cup coarse stoneground yellow cornmeal

Kosher salt and ground black pepper

4 tablespoons extra-virgin olive oil, divided

1½ pounds extra-large (21/25 per pound) shrimp, peeled (tails removed) and deveined

4 large garlic cloves, 2 finely grated, 2 smashed and peeled, reserved separately

1½ pounds ripe tomatoes (see headnote), cored and cut into 1-inch chunks

½ teaspoon red pepper flakes

½ cup chopped fresh basil or flat-leaf parsley

Polenta e schie, a specialty of Venice, Italy, is polenta topped with tiny local shrimp called schie. The dish typically is a minimalist, sauce-free marriage of corn and crustacean, but Michela Tasca, owner of Ca' de Memi farm and bed and breakfast in Piombino Dese, just north of Venice, taught us a version in which the schie are poached in a simple tomato sauce accented with garlic and fresh herbs. Our version uses the large shrimp available in the U.S. in place of the schie. We simmer the polenta in the oven; the gentle, even heat obviates the need for frequent stirring. This means that while the polenta cooks, you're free to prep the other ingredients. Be sure to use coarse stoneground cornmeal; fine cornmeal produces gluey polenta, and steel-ground cornmeal lacks flavor. If juicy, ripe tomatoes are not available, look for cocktail or Campari tomatoes, as we find them to be dependably good no matter the season.

Don't begin cooking the shrimp until the polenta is done. In the covered pan or pot, the polenta will remain hot for the short amount of time it takes to cook the shrimp and tomatoes. Don't worry if the shrimp are only parcooked after their quick sear. They'll finish cooking when they simmer with the tomatoes for a couple of minutes.

___

1. **Heat the oven to 375°F** with a rack in the lower-middle position. In a large oven-safe saucepan or small (4- to 5-quart) Dutch oven, combine the cornmeal, 1 teaspoon salt and 5½ cups water, then whisk to combine. Bring to a gentle simmer over medium, stirring often, then place uncovered in the oven and cook for 45 minutes.

2. **Remove from the oven,** whisk the polenta, then return, still uncovered, to the oven. Cook until the polenta is thick and creamy, another 15 to 30 minutes. Remove from the oven, whisk until smooth, cover and let stand for 5 minutes. Taste and season with salt and black pepper, then cover and set aside while you cook the shrimp.

3. **In a medium bowl,** stir together 1 tablespoon of oil, the grated garlic and ½ teaspoon salt. Add the shrimp and toss to coat. In a 12-inch skillet over medium-high, heat the remaining 3 tablespoons oil until shimmering. Add half of the shrimp in a single layer and cook until browned on the bottom, 1 to 2 minutes. Using tongs or a slotted spoon, transfer to a large plate. Cook the remaining shrimp in the same way using the residual oil in the pan.

4. **Set the now-empty skillet** over medium, add the smashed garlic and cook, stirring, until fragrant and lightly browned, about 2 minutes. Add the tomatoes, pepper flakes and ½ teaspoon each salt and black pepper. Cook, stirring occasionally, until the tomatoes begin to soften and release their juices, 2 to 3 minutes. Stir in the shrimp with accumulated juices and cook, stirring occasionally, until the shrimp are opaque throughout, about 2 minutes. Off heat, remove and discard the whole garlic cloves and stir in the basil, then taste and season with salt and pepper.

5. **Whisk the polenta** to smooth it out, adding water as needed to thin. Divide the polenta among individual bowls, then spoon on the shrimp-tomato mixture.

Venetian Rice and Peas (Risi e Bisi)

Start to finish: 1¼ hours / Servings: 4 to 6

1 medium carrot, peeled and thinly sliced

1 large white onion, half thinly sliced, half finely chopped

1 medium celery stalk, thinly sliced

2 teaspoons fennel seeds

1 quart low-sodium chicken broth

2 cups frozen peas, divided (1 cup still frozen, 1 cup thawed and at room temperature)

2 cups lightly packed fresh flat-leaf parsley

3 to 4 ounces pancetta, finely chopped

4 tablespoons salted butter, cut into 1-tablespoon pieces, divided

1 cup vialone nano or Arborio rice

Ground black pepper

2 ounces Parmesan cheese, finely grated (1 cup), plus more to serve

Rice and peas, or risi e bisi, is a classic Venetian dish, traditionally eaten on April 25, St. Mark's Day. Much like risotto, the rice is rich and creamy because of the starchiness of the grains and how they are cooked. But risi e bisi typically is a bit soupier. Sweet peas stud the dish, and in the version taught to us by Michela Tasca, owner of Ca' de Memi farm and bed and breakfast in Piombino Dese outside of Venice, the al dente grains were bathed in beautiful pale green broth, a result of peas pureed into the cooking liquid. For our version, we puree peas plus fresh parsley with a small amount of a broth infused with aromatics. To keep the flavors and color vibrant, we hold off on adding the puree, along with additional whole peas, until the rice has finished cooking. Pancetta provides salty, meaty backbone and fennel seeds, with their notes of licorice, complement the grassy, sweetness of the peas. Vialone nano is the preferred variety of Italian medium-grain rice for risi e bisi, but easier to find Arborio works just as well.

Don't thaw all of the peas. The 1 cup of peas that's blended with hot broth and parsley should be kept frozen so that the puree remains a brilliant green; the 1 cup stirred in at the end should be fully thawed and at room temperature so the peas don't cool the rice.

1. In a large pot, combine the carrot, the sliced onion, celery, fennel seeds, broth and 2 cups water. Bring to a boil over medium-high, then cover, reduce to medium-low and simmer until the vegetables have softened, 10 to 12 minutes.

2. Remove the pot from the heat and, using a slotted spoon, transfer the solids to a blender, draining off as much liquid as possible. Add 1 cup of the broth to the blender along with the still-frozen peas and the parsley; leave the remaining broth in the pot so it remains warm. Blend until the mixture is smooth, 1½ to 2 minutes; you should have about 3 cups puree. Set aside in the blender jar.

3. In a large saucepan over medium, combine the chopped onion, pancetta and 2 tablespoons butter. Cook, stirring occasionally, until the onion is lightly browned and the pancetta is rendered and lightly browned, 6 to 8 minutes. Add the rice and stir until the grains are coated with fat, then stir in 1 cup of the broth. Cook, stirring, until the liquid is mostly absorbed, about 5 minutes. Ladle in additional broth to barely cover the rice and simmer, stirring often, until the broth is mostly absorbed. Repeat the addition of broth and simmering until mostly absorbed 4 or 5 times, until the rice is al dente and most of the broth has been used; this process should take 25 to 30 minutes.

4. Remove the pan from the heat and let stand uncovered for 5 minutes. Add the thawed peas and the puree, then stir until heated through, about 1 minute. Add the remaining 2 tablespoons butter and stir until melted. Stir in the Parmesan, then taste and season with salt and pepper. Serve sprinkled with additional Parmesan.

Herb-and-Pistachio Couscous

Start to finish: **30 minutes** / Servings: 6

Couscous may be fast and convenient to prepare, but it's also pretty dull. We found a way to up the flavor by under-cooking—technically underhydrating—the couscous by preparing it with less water than typically called for. We then combine the couscous with a flavorful paste made from oil and pureed fresh herbs. The "thirsty" couscous absorbs tons of flavor as it finishes hydrating. Inspired by a recipe from Yotam Ottolenghi, we piled on the herbs— 2 cups each of cilantro and flat-leaf parsley—plus another 2 cups of arugula. We also added currants as we doused the couscous with boiling water, giving them time to plump. Jalapeños brought a spicy kick; we used pickled peppers, which have more consistent heat and contributed welcome piquancy. Toasted pistachios and thinly sliced scallions added a finishing crunch. The couscous pairs well with most any meat, though it is particularly good with salmon.

Don't use pearl couscous, also known as Israeli couscous or ptitim. The larger "grains" won't hydrate sufficiently in this recipe.

1 cup couscous

3 tablespoons dried currants

½ teaspoon ground cumin

Kosher salt and ground black pepper

¾ cup boiling water

6 tablespoons extra-virgin olive oil, divided, plus more for serving

2 cups lightly packed fresh cilantro leaves and tender stems

2 cups lightly packed fresh flat-leaf parsley leaves

2 tablespoons finely chopped pickled jalapeños, plus 2 teaspoons brine

2 ounces baby arugula, coarsely chopped (about 2 cups)

½ cup shelled pistachios, toasted and chopped

2 scallions, trimmed and thinly sliced

1. In a large bowl, combine the couscous, currants, cumin and ¼ teaspoon each salt and black pepper. Stir in the boiling water and 1 tablespoon of the oil, then cover and let sit for 10 minutes.

2. Meanwhile, in a food processor, combine the cilantro, parsley, the remaining 5 tablespoons of oil, the jalapeño brine and ¼ teaspoon salt. Process until a smooth paste forms, about 1 minute, scraping down the bowl 2 or 3 times.

3. Fluff the couscous with a fork, breaking up any large clumps, then stir in the herb paste until thoroughly combined. Fold in the jalapeños, arugula, pistachios and scallions, then let sit for 10 minutes. Season with salt and pepper. Serve at room temperature, drizzled with oil.

Indian Tomato Rice

Start to finish: **35 minutes (15 minutes active)** / Servings: 4

Robust tomato flavor is key to this popular southern Indian dish, typically prepared when there is an abundance of ripe, red tomatoes and leftover basmati rice. It can be eaten as a light meal with a dollop of yogurt or pairs well with seafood, poultry or even a simple fried egg. We needed a year-round recipe, so we concentrated on finding the best way to impart deep tomato flavor. A combination of cherry or grape tomatoes and tomato paste was best. We also focused on making sure the rice was cooked properly, fluffy and tender with each grain separate. We were inspired by Madhur Jaffrey's tomato rice recipe in "Vegetarian India," though we upped the intensity of both the spices and tomato flavor. We preferred brown or black mustard seeds for their pungency; if you substitute yellow mustard seeds, increase the volume to 1½ teaspoons. Serrano chilies can be used in place of bird's eye chilies, also called Thai bird or Thai chilies. Or you can leave them out entirely. If your pan does not have a tight-fitting lid, cover it with foil before putting the lid in place.

Don't skip soaking the rice. This traditional approach to cooking the rice gives it time to expand gently and cook up in tender, separate grains.

1 cup white basmati rice, rinsed and drained

2 tablespoons tomato paste

2 tablespoons grapeseed or other neutral oil

1 teaspoon cumin seeds

1 teaspoon coriander seeds

1 teaspoon brown or black mustard seeds

2 bird's eye chilies, stemmed and halved lengthwise (optional)

1 medium garlic clove, finely grated

1 teaspoon finely grated fresh ginger

Kosher salt

½ pound cherry or grape tomatoes, quartered

¼ cup chopped fresh cilantro leaves

1. In a bowl, combine the rinsed rice with enough cold water to cover by 1 inch. Let soak for 15 minutes. Drain the rice very well. In a 2-cup liquid measuring cup, combine 1¼ cups water and the tomato paste and whisk until dissolved. Set aside.

2. In a large saucepan over medium, combine the oil, cumin, coriander, mustard seeds, chilies, garlic and ginger. Cook until the seeds begin to pop and the mixture is fragrant, about 1 minute.

3. Stir in the rice and 1½ teaspoons salt and cook, stirring, until coated with oil, about 30 seconds. Stir in the water-tomato paste mixture and bring to a simmer. Cover, reduce heat to low and cook until the water has been absorbed, about 15 minutes. Remove from the heat, add the tomatoes and let stand, covered, for 5 minutes. Stir in the cilantro, fluffing the rice with a fork.

Lemon and Shrimp Risotto with Fresh Basil

Start to finish: 45 minutes / Servings: 4

---

2 lemons

2 teaspoons plus 2 tablespoons extra-virgin olive oil, divided, plus more to serve

12 ounces extra-large (21/25 per pound) shrimp, peeled (shells reserved), deveined and patted dry

Kosher salt

1 small yellow onion, finely chopped

1 cup carnaroli or Arborio rice

½ cup dry white wine

1 large egg yolk

2 tablespoons heavy cream

½ cup loosely packed fresh basil, roughly chopped

This is our version of the rich, intensely flavored risotto di limone that Giovanna Aceto taught us to make in Amalfi, Italy. In an unusual twist, the risotto is finished with an egg yolk and a couple tablespoons of cream, giving the rice a lush, velvety taste and texture. To create a flavorful broth for simmering the risotto, we steep the shrimp shells and strips of lemon zest in water, and for citrus notes that register at every level, we stir in bright, puckery lemon juice and floral, fragrant grated zest just before serving. If you purchase shrimp that are already shelled, bottled clam juice is a fine substitute. Bring two 8-ounce bottles clam juice, 3 cups water, ½ teaspoon salt and the zest strips to a simmer in the saucepan and cook, covered, for 10 minutes to infuse, then strain as directed.

Don't uncover the pot for at least 5 minutes after adding the shrimp. Lifting the lid releases some of the residual heat that's needed to cook the shrimp.

---

1. Using a vegetable peeler (preferably a Y-style peeler), remove the zest from 1 of the lemons in long, wide strips; try to remove only the colored portion of the peel, not the bitter white pith just underneath. Using a rasp-style grater, grate the zest from the remaining lemon; set aside separately. Halve the lemons and squeeze ¼ cup juice; set the juice aside.

2. In a medium saucepan over medium, heat 2 teaspoons oil until shimmering. Add the shrimp shells and cook, stirring constantly, until pink, 1 to 2 minutes. Add 5 cups water, the zest strips and ½ teaspoon salt, then bring to a simmer. Cover, reduce to low and cook for 10 minutes. Pour the broth through a strainer set over a medium bowl; rinse out the pan. Press on the solids to extract as much liquid as possible, then discard. Return the broth to the pan, cover and set over low to keep warm.

3. In a large Dutch oven over medium-high, heat 1 tablespoon of oil until shimmering. Add the onion and ¼ teaspoon salt, then cook, stirring occasionally, until softened, 6 to 7 minutes. Add the rice and cook, stirring, until the grains are translucent at the edges, 1 to 2 minutes. Add the wine and cook, stirring occasionally, until the pan is almost dry, about 3 minutes. Add 3 cups of the hot broth and cook, stirring often and briskly, until a spoon drawn through the mixture leaves a trail, 10 to 12 minutes.

4. Add the remaining broth and cook, stirring, until the rice is tender, 8 to 10 minutes. Remove the pot from the heat and stir in the shrimp. Cover and let stand until the shrimp are opaque throughout, 5 to 7 minutes.

5. Stir in the remaining 1 tablespoon oil, the lemon juice, egg yolk, cream, basil, and the grated zest. The risotto should be loose but not soupy; if needed, stir in water 1 tablespoon at a time to achieve the proper consistency. Taste and season with salt. Serve drizzled with additional oil.

Noodles

7

Gemelli Pasta with Chèvre, Arugula and Walnuts

Start to finish: **45 minutes** / Servings: **4**

Creamy pasta sauces pose two problems: They are finicky to make and they quickly decompose into a stringy or grainy mess. So when we came across a recipe that suggested using fresh goat cheese instead of the Parmesan called for in classic Alfredo and carbonara, we were intrigued. The notion was simple. The heat of freshly cooked pasta and a splash of its cooking water would dissolve the soft chèvre into a rich, smooth sauce in no time. Except it didn't work. The ingredients quickly broke down into a chalky mess. Then we discovered a technique by Marcella Hazan in which you first mix the cheese with oil. It worked wonderfully, but why? Goat's milk has more fat than cow's milk, so turning it into cheese requires the addition of acid. The acid forms the cheese curds but also creates strong water-insoluble bonds between the proteins. Hence our clumpy mess. But add oil to the chevre and those bonds slip apart, and the cheese melts easily. The same trick works for any acid-set cheese, such as ricotta, cottage and feta.

12 ounces gemelli or
casarecce pasta

Kosher salt

4 ounces chèvre
(fresh goat cheese)

5 tablespoons
extra-virgin olive oil

Red pepper flakes

4 ounces baby arugula
(about 4 cups)

¾ cup walnuts, toasted
and chopped

⅓ cup finely chopped
fresh chives

1. In a large pot, bring 4 quarts of water to a boil. Add the pasta and 1 tablespoon salt, then cook until al dente. Meanwhile, in a medium bowl, combine the cheese, oil and ¼ teaspoon each salt and red pepper flakes, stirring and mashing with a fork until smooth. Drain the pasta, reserving ¾ cup of the cooking water, then return the pasta to the pot.

2. Add the arugula, the goat cheese mixture and the reserved pasta cooking water, then toss until the cheese mixture is evenly distributed and the arugula begins to wilt.

3. Stir in the walnuts and chives, reserving a tablespoon of each for garnish, if desired, then season with additional salt and red pepper flakes. Transfer the pasta to a warmed serving bowl, then garnish with the remaining walnuts and chives.

Soba Noodles with Asparagus, Miso Butter and Egg

Start to finish: **25 minutes** / Servings: **4**

To cook asparagus evenly, we cut the spears into stalks and tips, toss the stalks into the noodle cooking water first, and a minute later add the tips. Stalks that measured about ½ inch at the thickest end were best. To flavor our asparagus and noodles, we liked savory-sweet miso, but we needed a fat to draw out the flavors. We turned to Momofuku's David Chang, who blends miso and butter. We liked that combination, particularly when balanced with grated fresh ginger. For the noodles, we preferred those made from a blend of whole-wheat and buckwheat flours; 100 percent buckwheat noodles were fragile and expensive. A sunny-side up egg proved the perfect topper. Most soba noodles cook in 4 minutes. For noodles that need longer, adjust the timing for adding the asparagus. Assembling and preparing all the ingredients before cooking the noodles was essential for proper timing. While the soba cooks, heat the skillet, then fry the eggs while tossing the noodles with the miso butter. To finish, we liked a sprinkle of shichimi togarashi, the Asian rice seasoning.

Don't add salt to the soba cooking water. *We don't usually salt the water when cooking Asian noodles, and miso can be quite salty.*

1 pound medium asparagus, tough ends trimmed

5 tablespoons white miso

4 tablespoons (½ stick) salted butter, room temperature

1½ tablespoons finely grated fresh ginger

12 ounces soba noodles

3 scallions, chopped, plus thinly sliced scallions to garnish

4 fried eggs (see recipe p. 3)

Shichimi togarashi rice seasoning, to serve (optional)

Lemon wedges, to serve

1. Bring a large pot of water to a boil. Meanwhile, snap or cut off the tender tips of the asparagus. Set aside. Slice the stalks on the diagonal into ½-inch pieces. Set aside separately. In a large bowl, combine the miso, butter and ginger, stirring and mashing.

2. Add the noodles to the boiling water. Cook for about 1 minute. Add the asparagus stalks and cook for another minute. Add the tips, then cook for 2 minutes. Drain the noodles and asparagus, reserving ½ of the cup cooking water. The noodles should be just tender. Add the noodles, asparagus and chopped scallions to the miso butter. Add enough reserved cooking water to reach a creamy consistency, using tongs to toss until the butter melts and coats the noodles.

3. Divide the noodles among 4 serving bowls and top each with a fried egg. Sprinkle with sliced scallions and shichimi togarashi, if using. Serve with lemon wedges.

Pasta with Peruvian Pesto (Tallarines Verdes)

Start to finish: **45 minutes** / Servings: 4

---

12 ounces linguine or fettuccine

Kosher salt and ground black pepper

1 yellow onion chopped (1 cup)

½ cup extra-virgin olive oil

3 medium garlic cloves, smashed and peeled

12 ounces baby spinach (about 12 cups)

¼ cup heavy cream

2 ounces Parmesan cheese, grated (about 1 cup)

4 ounces queso fresco, crumbled (about 1 cup)

Lime wedges, to serve

The origin of Peruvian pesto, or tallarines verdes, dates to the 19th century, when a wave of Italian immigrants settled in Peru. Many came from Genoa—the birthplace of pesto—and they adapted the recipe to the available ingredients. A shocking amount of spinach replaces the basil, and crumbled queso fresco supplements (and sometimes entirely replaces) salty Parmesan cheese. "It became a kind of dialogue or maybe a love story" between two worlds, says Gastón Acurio, Peruvian culinary star, founder of the La Mar restaurants, and champion of his country's food. For bright color and fresh flavor, we pureed ¾ pound of spinach for this pesto, along with onion and garlic. A quick simmer in a skillet took the raw edge off the onion and spinach, giving a depth and complexity lacking in traditional raw Italian pestos. Once the sauce thickened, we added reserved pasta cooking water, followed by undercooked pasta. The starch-infused water gave the pesto body, and the pasta finished cooking in the sauce, absorbing more of its flavor.

Don't be alarmed if the skillet seems very full after adding the pasta. Use tongs to gently lift and stir the noodles, and a silicone spatula to scrape the edges of the pan.

---

1. In a large pot, bring 4 quarts of water to a boil. Add the pasta and 1 tablespoon salt, then cook until just tender but not fully cooked, about 2 minutes less than package directions. Drain the pasta, reserving 1½ cups of the cooking water.

2. Meanwhile, in a food processor, combine the onion, oil, ¼ cup water, garlic and 1 teaspoon each salt and pepper. Add a third of the spinach and process until smooth, about 30 seconds. Add the remaining spinach in 2 batches, processing until smooth after each.

3. Transfer the spinach mixture to a 12-inch nonstick skillet over medium-high. Bring to a boil and cook, stirring occasionally, until it begins to thicken, 3 to 5 minutes. Add the reserved pasta water and return to a simmer, then add the pasta and stir to coat. Simmer, stirring occasionally, until the pasta is al dente and the pesto no longer appears watery, 3 to 5 minutes. Stir in the cream. Off the heat, stir in the Parmesan, then taste and season with salt and pepper. Transfer to a serving dish, sprinkle with the queso fresco and serve with lime wedges.

Pasta with Trapanese Pesto

Start to finish: **30 minutes** / Servings: 4

We hear "pesto" and see shades of green, but the word refers to prep, not pigment. It stems from pestare, to pound—this Italian sauce traditionally was made with a mortar and pestle. The basil-heavy, and therefore green, version we know best comes from northwestern Italy. In Sicily, you'll find pesto Trapanese (named for the town of Trapani), a sauce also known as mataroccu. It has less basil than the northern version and adds tomatoes, garlic and almonds, the latter a nod to Sicily's Arabic heritage. To make this a truly year-round recipe we ruled out standard winter tomatoes and instead settled on cherry tomatoes, though grape or small plum tomatoes worked, too. For ease, we used a food processor, though we found it was best to incorporate the olive oil and cheese (pecorino) by hand at the end. Raw almonds are common, but we found them a little dull. When we toasted them they brought out the sweetness of the tomato, added a crispier crunch and improved the balance of the dish. We preferred blanched, slivered almonds, which were easiest to toast and grind, but any variety is fine.

Don't add the cooking water to the sauce right away. While we always reserve some starchy cooking water before draining pasta, this sauce has so much moisture from the tomatoes that it wasn't always necessary.

4 ounces slivered almonds (about 1 cup), toasted

1 small garlic clove

¼ teaspoon red pepper flakes

1 pound cherry tomatoes

¾ ounce fresh basil leaves (1 cup lightly packed)

Kosher salt

½ cup extra-virgin olive oil

1 ounce grated pecorino Romano cheese (½ cup), plus more to serve

12 ounces short, sturdy pasta, such as gemelli, casarecce or rigatoni

Ground black pepper

1. In a large pot, bring 4 quarts water to a boil. Meanwhile, in a food processor, combine the almonds, garlic and pepper flakes. Process until coarsely ground, 20 to 30 seconds. Add the tomatoes, basil and ¾ teaspoon salt. Pulse until uniformly ground but still chunky, 10 to 12 pulses. Transfer to a large bowl and stir in the oil and cheese.

2. To the boiling water, add the pasta and 1 tablespoon salt. Cook until al dente. Drain, reserving 1 cup of the cooking water. Add the pasta to the bowl with the pesto and toss. If the sauce is too thick, add a bit of the reserved pasta water. Taste and season with salt, pepper, red pepper flakes and more cheese.

Cacio e Pepe

Start to finish: **20 minutes** / Servings: **4**

Made of just pasta, cheese and plenty of freshly ground black pepper, cacio e pepe (literally, "cheese and pepper") is a study in the power of letting a few ingredients shine. We were introduced to it by Lucia Ziroli at her family trattoria, Sora Margherita, in Rome. The origins of the dish are debated, but it's widely accepted as the mother of classic Roman pastas. Add pancetta and you have pasta alla gricia (see recipe p. 228). Add eggs and it becomes carbonara (see recipe p. 229). The pepper in cacio e pepe is key, cutting through the richness of the cheese and bringing balance to the dish. Pecorino Romano, a salty hard sheep's milk cheese, is traditional. The addition of cornstarch allowed us to overcome the tendency of pecorino cheese in the U.S. to clump (even imported varieties). But for best flavor, we still recommend using cheese imported from Italy.

Don't use pre-grated cheese, even if it's true pecorino Romano. Grate the cheese on a wand-style grater; larger shreds won't melt. Don't pour the pecorino mixture onto the hot, just-drained pasta; letting the pasta cool ensures the mixture won't break from overheating.

2 teaspoons cornstarch

6 ounces pecorino Romano cheese, finely grated (3 cups), plus more to serve

12 ounces linguine or spaghetti

Kosher salt and ground black pepper

1. In a large pot, bring 4 quarts water to a boil. Meanwhile, in a large saucepan, whisk 1½ cups water and the cornstarch until smooth. Add the pecorino and stir until evenly moistened. Set the pan over medium-low and cook, whisking constantly, until the cheese melts and the mixture comes to a gentle simmer and thickens slightly, about 5 minutes. Remove from heat and set aside.

2. Stir the pasta and 1 tablespoon salt into the boiling water and cook until al dente. Reserve about ½ cup of the cooking water, then drain the pasta very well. Return the pasta to the pot and let cool for about 1 minute.

3. Pour the pecorino mixture over the pasta and toss with tongs until combined, then toss in 2 teaspoons pepper. Let stand, tossing 2 or 3 times, until most of the liquid has been absorbed, about 3 minutes. The pasta should be creamy but not loose. If needed, toss in reserved pasta water 1 tablespoon at a time to adjust the consistency. Transfer to a warmed serving bowl and serve with additional pecorino and pepper on the side.

Yakiudon with Pickled Ginger

Start to finish: 45 minutes / Servings: 4

12 ounces dried udon noodles

2 tablespoons plus
2 teaspoons grapeseed or
other neutral oil, divided

¼ cup soy sauce

2 tablespoons mirin

1 teaspoon white sugar

3 small dried shiitake
mushrooms, broken in half

8 ounces fresh shiitake
mushrooms, stemmed,
halved if large, thinly sliced

1 small yellow onion, halved
and thinly sliced

2 medium garlic cloves,
minced

12 ounces baby bok choy,
trimmed and sliced
crosswise ½ inch thick

Ground white pepper

2 scallions, thinly sliced on
diagonal

1 tablespoon sesame seeds,
toasted

Shichimi togarashi, to serve
(optional)

Pickled ginger, to serve
(see recipe p. 189)

This Japanese stir-fried noodle dish is largely about the chew, which comes from hearty wheat udon noodles. We got the dense chewiness we wanted by using the Italian technique of cooking until al dente—still quite firm. Japanese noodles often are rinsed after cooking, and chilling helps prevent them from turning soggy. We streamlined the process by adding ice to the strainer as we rinsed the udon under cold running water. Fresh udon is sold frozen, refrigerated and in shelf-stable packages, but for this recipe we used dried noodles, which are more widely available. The sharp bite of pickled ginger complements the salty, savory noodles. If you're not up to making your own, look for jars of it in the grocery store's Asian section. Also in that section: shichimi togarashi, a Japanese spice blend for sprinkling on at the table to add a little heat.

Don't fully cook the udon. Check for doneness well before the cooking time suggested on the package.

1. In a large pot, bring 4 quarts of water to a boil. Add the udon, stir well and cook until al dente. Drain in a colander, then add 2 cups ice to the noodles. Run under cool water, tossing, until chilled. Drain well, then transfer to a large bowl. Toss with 2 teaspoons of oil; set aside.

2. In a small saucepan over medium, combine the soy sauce, ¼ cup water, the mirin and sugar. Bring to a simmer, stirring, then add the dried mushrooms, pushing them into the liquid. Remove from the heat, cover and set aside until the mushrooms have softened and cooled, 20 to 30 minutes.

3. Remove the mushrooms from the soy sauce mixture, squeezing them to allow any liquid to drip back into the pan. Remove and discard the stems, then finely chop. Transfer to a medium bowl and set aside.

4. In a large nonstick skillet over medium-high, heat 1 tablespoon of the remaining oil. Add the fresh mushrooms and cook, stirring occasionally, until lightly browned and slightly shrunken, about 3 minutes. Add the onion, drizzle with the remaining 1 tablespoon oil and cook, stirring occasionally, until softened, about 3 minutes. Stir in the garlic and cook until fragrant, about 30 seconds. Add the bok choy and cook, stirring, until the leaves are wilted and the stem pieces are crisp-tender, about 2 minutes. Transfer to the bowl with the chopped dried shiitakes.

5. Set the now-empty skillet over medium and add the udon, gently tossing with tongs. Add the vegetable mixture, gently toss, then add the soy sauce mixture and ½ teaspoon pepper. Cook, tossing constantly, until the noodles are heated and have absorbed most of the liquid, about 2 minutes. Transfer to serving bowls and sprinkle with scallions and sesame seeds. Serve with shichimi togarashi, if using, and pickled ginger.

PICKLED GINGER

Start to finish: 40 minutes
(10 minutes active)
Makes 1⅓ cups

Look for large, plump, chunky pieces of fresh ginger without many nubs; they will be easier to peel and slice. A mandoline works well for slicing, but a Y-style peeler works, too.

Don't cut thick slices of ginger. They can be tough and chewy.

¾ cup unseasoned rice vinegar

¼ cup water

2 tablespoons white sugar

1 teaspoon kosher salt

4 ounces fresh ginger, peeled and sliced paper thin

In a small bowl, stir together the vinegar, water, sugar and salt. Stir in the ginger. Cover and refrigerate for 30 minutes or for up to 1 week.

Pasta all'Amatriciana

Start to finish: **30 minutes** / Servings: 4

3 tablespoons extra-virgin
olive oil, divided

3 ounces thinly sliced pancetta,
finely chopped

10 medium garlic cloves,
thinly sliced

½ teaspoon red pepper flakes

¾ cup dry white wine

14½-ounce can whole peeled
tomatoes, drained, juices
reserved, tomatoes crushed
by hand into small pieces

1-ounce chunk pecorino
Romano cheese, plus more
finely grated, to serve

Kosher salt and ground
black pepper

12 ounces spaghetti

Amatriciana is a minimalist equation of pasta, tomatoes, guanciale and pecorino Romano cheese, and in Rome it's served with barely any sauce, as we learned from Mario Ive, retired artillery colonel in the Italian army and cookbook author. The cooking method—using as little liquid as possible when cooking the sauce—concentrates flavors in the sauce, which coats the pasta nicely. We apply that principle for the pasta in this recipe, as well, cooking spaghetti in half the amount of water (2 quarts) we usually use. To that we add a chunk of pecorino Romano, which infuses the noodles with rich, savory flavor. We also undercook the pasta, allowing it to finish cooking in the sauce. One 14½-ounce can of whole tomatoes, drained and cooked down, is plenty to dress four servings. Likewise, just 3 ounces of pancetta—more widely available than guanciale—provides ample flavor. Be sure to purchase thinly sliced pancetta and chop it finely to ensure the pieces crisp well.

Don't boil the pasta until it's done. Drain it a minute or two shy of al dente; it will continue to cook when added to the sauce in the skillet.

1. In a 12-inch skillet over medium, heat 1 tablespoon of the oil until shimmering. Add the pancetta and cook, stirring, until well browned and crisp, 5 to 7 minutes. Using a slotted spoon, transfer to a paper towel–lined plate and set aside.

2. Return the skillet to medium and add the garlic; cook, stirring, until light golden brown, about 2 minutes. Stir in the pepper flakes and cook until fragrant, about 30 seconds. Add the wine, increase to medium-high and cook, stirring, until most of the liquid has evaporated, 5 to 7 minutes. Add the drained tomatoes and cook, stirring, until heated, about 2 minutes. Stir in 3 tablespoons of the reserved tomato juice, then remove from the heat.

3. Meanwhile, in a large pot, bring 2 quarts of water and the pecorino chunk to a boil, stirring occasionally to prevent the cheese from sticking to the pot. Stir in the pasta and 1 teaspoon salt. Cook, stirring often, until the pasta is just shy of al dente. Discard the pecorino, then drain the pasta in a colander set in a large heat-safe bowl; reserve the cooking water.

4. Set the skillet over medium-high, stir in 1½ cups of the reserved pasta water and bring to a simmer. Add the drained pasta, tossing with tongs. Cook, stirring occasionally, until most of the liquid has been absorbed, 3 to 6 minutes.

5. Off heat, stir in the remaining 2 tablespoons oil, 2 teaspoons black pepper and the pancetta. Transfer to a serving bowl and serve with grated pecorino on the side.

Spaghetti al Limone

Start to finish: **35 minutes** / Servings: **4**

This simple dish may have few ingredients, but it boasts bold, bright flavors. Many versions include cream, but we preferred to use a little butter and some of the starchy spaghetti-cooking water; this gave the pasta a saucy consistency and light creaminess that didn't mute the freshness of the lemon. Feel free to switch out linguine for the spaghetti and adjust the lemon zest and juice to your taste.

Don't cook the pasta until al dente. *Drain it when it's a minute or two shy of al dente; it will continue to cook in the skillet.*

1. In a 12-inch skillet over medium, melt 3 tablespoons of the butter. Add the garlic and cook, stirring constantly, until fragrant, about 30 seconds. Add the pepper flakes and cook, stirring constantly, until the garlic begins to turn golden, about 1 minute. Pour in the wine and cook until reduced to about ½ cup, about 3 minutes. Remove from the heat and set aside.

2. In a large pot, bring 2 quarts of water to a boil. Stir in 1½ teaspoons salt and the pasta; cook until just shy of al dente. Reserve 2 cups of the cooking water, then drain and set aside.

3. Set the skillet with the garlic mixture over medium-high, stir in 1½ cups of the reserved pasta water and bring to a simmer. Add the drained pasta and toss. Cook, stirring, until most of the liquid has been absorbed, 2 to 3 minutes.

4. Off heat, stir in the remaining 2 tablespoons butter, 1 teaspoon black pepper, the lemon juice and zest, and the parsley. Taste and season with salt and, if needed, adjust the consistency by adding additional pasta water a few tablespoons at a time. Transfer to a serving bowl and serve with grated Parmesan.

5 tablespoons salted butter, divided

8 medium garlic cloves, minced

1 teaspoon red pepper flakes

¾ cup dry white wine

12 ounces spaghetti

Kosher salt and ground black pepper

2 tablespoons grated lemon zest, plus 3 tablespoons lemon juice

¾ cup finely chopped fresh flat-leaf parsley or basil

Grated Parmesan cheese, to serve

Pasta con Fagioli

Start to finish: **35 minutes** / Servings: **6**

We thought this rustic pasta and bean dish from Sicily would feel heavy, but the starches are lightened by tomatoes, rosemary and lemon. We were taught how to make it by two Sicilian cooks, Piera Ferruzza, winery cook at Cantina della Val di Suro, and Maria Enza Arena, a shopkeeper in the hilltop town of Castelbuono. In Italy, dried borlotti beans (often called cranberry beans in the U.S.) are used. For weeknight ease, we opted for canned beans. Some producers label canned borlotti beans as "Roman beans." If you cannot find them, use pink or kidney beans, which have a similar creaminess and mildly sweet flavor. Don't use cannellini beans, which are too tender. The pasta is boiled only until very slightly softened, then drained and rinsed to stop the cooking. It finishes cooking when combined with the beans and vegetables.

Don't rinse the canned beans after draining them; the starchy liquid clinging to them adds body to the sauce.

8 ounces campanelle or other short pasta

Kosher salt and ground black pepper

5 tablespoons extra-virgin olive oil, divided, plus more to serve

2 pints grape or cherry tomatoes

1 large red onion, chopped

1 large fennel bulb, halved, cored and thinly sliced

4 medium garlic cloves, minced

1 tablespoon minced fresh rosemary

1 teaspoon fennel seeds

¾ teaspoon red pepper flakes

Two 15½-ounce cans Roman (borlotti) beans, drained but not rinsed (see headnote)

2 cups low-sodium chicken broth

2 teaspoons grated lemon zest, plus 2 tablespoons lemon juice

2 ounces Pecorino romano cheese, grated (1 cup)

1. In a large Dutch oven over medium-high, bring 2 quarts water to a boil. Add the pasta and 1½ teaspoons salt. Cook, stirring occasionally, until just shy of al dente. Reserve 2 cups of cooking water, then drain and rinse with cold water until cool; set aside.

2. In the same pot over medium-high, heat 3 tablespoons of oil until barely smoking. Add the tomatoes, cover, reduce to medium and cook, stirring occasionally, until lightly charred, about 5 minutes. Add the onion, sliced fennel and ½ teaspoon salt, then cook on medium-high, stirring occasionally, until the vegetables begin to soften, about 5 minutes.

3. Add the garlic, rosemary, fennel seeds and pepper flakes, then cook, stirring, until fragrant, about 30 seconds. Add the beans, broth and ½ cup of the reserved cooking water. Bring to a simmer over medium-high. Cover, reduce to medium and cook, stirring once or twice, until the vegetables are tender, about 10 minutes.

4. Add the pasta and cook, stirring frequently, until the pasta is al dente and the sauce is creamy, 3 to 5 minutes. If needed, add additional cooking water, 1 tablespoon at a time, to reach the proper consistency. Off heat, stir in the lemon zest and juice and the remaining 2 tablespoons oil. Taste and season with salt and pepper. Serve with the cheese and additional oil for drizzling.

Campanelle Pasta with Sweet Corn, Tomatoes and Basil

Start to finish: **30 minutes** / Servings: **4**

This recipe was inspired by a pasta dish served at Al Forno restaurant in Providence, Rhode Island. There, ears of corn are blanched, then the kernels are sliced off and mixed with chopped tomatoes, minced habanero chilies and fresh herbs, then tossed with olive oil and hot pappardelle. We instead grate the corn off the cobs, which yields a coarse puree of kernels and starchy corn "milk." We then simmer the cobs to make a corn-infused broth to use as the base of the sauce as well for cooking the pasta. Fresh corn and ripe tomatoes are key. Yellow corn gives a golden hue, but white corn works, too. Whichever you use, remove as much of the silk as possible before grating. Short, sauce-catching pasta shapes are best—if you can't find campanelle, look for penne rigate, fusilli or farfalle.

Don't fear the habanero in this dish. It does add a little heat, but seeding the chili removes much of its burn.

1 pint grape or cherry tomatoes, halved

Kosher salt and ground black pepper

4 ears corn, husked

4 tablespoons (½ stick) salted butter, cut in 1-tablespoon pieces, divided

2 medium shallots, minced

1 habanero chili, stemmed, seeded and minced

12 ounces campanelle or other short pasta

1 cup lightly packed fresh basil, sliced

1. In a small bowl, stir together the tomatoes and ½ teaspoon salt; set aside. Set a box grater in a large bowl or pie plate. Using the grater's large holes, grate the corn down to the cobs; reserve the cobs.

2. In a large pot, bring 2½ quarts water to a boil. Add the corn cobs and 1 tablespoon salt, reduce to medium and cook, covered, for 10 minutes. Using tongs, remove and discard the cobs, then remove the pot from the heat.

3. In a 12-inch nonstick skillet over medium, melt 2 tablespoons of butter. Add the grated corn, shallots, habanero and 1 teaspoon salt. Cook, stirring, until the shallots have softened, about 5 minutes. Stir in 1½ cups of the cooking liquid. Cook over medium-low, stirring occasionally, until slightly thickened, 10 to 15 minutes.

4. Meanwhile, return the remaining corn-infused water to a boil. Add the pasta and cook, stirring occasionally, until al dente. Reserve 1 cup of the cooking water, then drain the pasta. Add the pasta to the skillet and cook over medium, stirring constantly, until the pasta is coated and the sauce is creamy, about 2 minutes; if needed, add the reserved cooking water 2 tablespoons at a time to reach proper consistency.

5. Off heat, add the remaining 2 tablespoons butter, basil and tomatoes with their juice, then toss until the butter has melted. Taste and season with salt and pepper.

Pasta with Pistachios, Tomatoes and Mint

Start to finish: **20 minutes** / Servings: 4

Sicily is known for its pistachios, so it's no surprise that the colorful, subtly sweet nuts feature heavily in the region's cuisine. This recipe is our take on a pistachio- and tomato-dressed pasta taught to us by Doriana Gesualdi, owner of Sicilia in Tavola, a stone-arched trattoria in Siracusa. With lemon zest and mint as accent ingredients, the flavors are fresh and bright. Just about any pasta shape worked well, but we particularly liked long strands, such as linguine and spaghetti.

Don't use raw pistachios; opt for roasted, as they don't require toasting before chopping. Either salted or unsalted worked well.

1. In a large pot, bring 4 quarts water to a boil. Add the pasta and 1 tablespoon salt, then cook, stirring occasionally, until just shy of al dente. Reserve about 2 cups of the cooking water, then drain the pasta.

2. In a 12-inch skillet over medium, combine the oil and tomatoes. Cook, stirring only once or twice, until the tomatoes have softened and the oil has taken on a reddish hue, 4 to 6 minutes. Stir in half the pistachios, 1½ cups of the reserved cooking water, ½ tea-spoon salt and ¼ teaspoon pepper. Bring to a simmer and cook, stirring occasionally, until the mixture is slightly reduced and the tomatoes are completely softened, about 2 minutes.

3. Add the pasta and lemon zest, then cook, stirring frequently, until the pasta is al dente and has absorbed most of the liquid but is still quite saucy, 2 to 4 minutes. Off heat, stir in the mint, then taste and season with salt and pepper. If the pasta is dry, add more cooking water, 1 tablespoon at a time. Transfer to a serving bowl, then sprinkle with the remaining pistachios and drizzle with additional oil. Serve with cheese.

12 ounces long pasta
(see headnote)

Kosher salt and ground
black pepper

¼ cup extra-virgin olive oil,
plus more to serve

1 pint grape or cherry
tomatoes, halved

½ cup shelled roasted
pistachios, finely chopped

1 tablespoon grated
lemon zest

2 tablespoons roughly
chopped fresh mint

Grated Parmesan or pecorino
Romano cheese, to serve

Pasta with Pesto alla Genovese

Start to finish: 30 minutes / Servings: 4

1¾ ounces Parmesan cheese (without rind), chopped into rough 1-inch pieces

1 ounce pecorino Sardo cheese (without rind), chopped into rough 1-inch pieces (see headnote)

¼ cup pine nuts

2 medium garlic cloves, smashed and peeled

Kosher salt

⅓ cup extra-virgin olive oil

2½ ounces fresh basil leaves (about 5 cups lightly packed)

12 ounces dried pasta

We were taught to make pesto alla Genovese in its birthplace—Genoa, Italy—by chef Roberto Panizza. It traditionally is made in a mortar and pestle of nothing more than basil, pine nuts, cheese, garlic, salt and olive oil, emphasis on the basil. We use a food processor for convenience but follow the tradition of processing ingredients separately to ensure we preserve the appropriate texture of each. Good-quality cheese is essential for a rich, full-flavored pesto. Seek out true Italian Parmesan cheese, as well as pecorino Sardo, a sheep's milk cheese from Sardinia. If you can't find pecorino Sardo, don't use pecorino Romano, which is too strong. The best substitute is Manchego, a Spanish sheep's milk cheese. To store pesto, press a piece of plastic wrap against its surface and refrigerate for up to three days.

Don't toast the pine nuts. In Italy, the pine nuts for pesto are used raw. Don't be tempted to add all the ingredients at once to the food processor. Adding them in stages ensures the pesto has the correct consistency and texture, and that it won't end up thin and watery, the result of over-processing.

1. In a food processor, process both cheeses until broken into rough marble-sized pieces, about 10 seconds, then pulse until they have the texture of coarse sand, 5 to 10 pulses, scraping the bowl as needed. Transfer to a small bowl and set aside.

2. In the food processor, combine the pine nuts, garlic and ¾ teaspoon salt. Process until a smooth, peanut butter–like paste forms, about 1 minute, scraping the bowl as needed. Add the cheeses and about ½ of the oil, then process until mostly smooth, 10 to 20 seconds, scraping the bowl as needed; the mixture should hold together when pressed against the bowl with a silicone spatula.

3. Using a chef's knife, roughly chop the basil, then add to the food processor. Pulse about 10 times, scraping the bowl several times, until the basil is finely chopped and well combined with the cheese mixture. Add the remaining oil and pulse just until incorporated, about 2 pulses. The pesto should be thick, creamy and spreadable. Set the pesto aside.

4. In a large pot, bring 4 quarts water to a boil. Add the pasta and 1 tablespoon salt, then cook, stirring occasionally, until just shy of al dente. Reserve about ½ cup of the cooking water, then drain the pasta. Transfer the pasta to a large warmed bowl and top with the pesto. Pour in ⅓ cup of the reserved cooking water for long pasta shapes (such as spaghetti and linguine) or ¼ cup cooking water for short pasta shapes (such as penne and fusilli).
Toss to combine.

HOW TO PROPERLY
SAUCE PASTA WITH PESTO

Cook 12 ounces dried pasta in 4 quarts boiling water seasoned with 1 tablespoon kosher salt until al dente. Reserve ½ cup of the pasta cooking water, then drain the pasta. Transfer to a warmed large bowl and add ⅓ cup of the reserved cooking water for long pasta shapes (such as linguine and spaghetti) or ¼ cup water for short pasta shapes (such as fusilli and penne). Top with 1 recipe (1 cup) pesto alla Genovese. Toss to combine at the table.

Potato Gnocchi with Butter, Sage and Chives

Start to finish: 1¾ hours, plus cooling / Servings: 4 to 6

2¾ to 3 pounds russet potatoes, peeled and cut into 1-inch chunks

Kosher salt

146 grams (1 cup plus 2 tablespoons) all-purpose flour, plus more for shaping

½ teaspoon baking powder

3 tablespoons extra-virgin olive oil, divided

1 large egg, lightly beaten

Our take on classic potato gnocchi was inspired by a cooking lesson we got in Paris from chef Peter Orr at his Robert restaurant in the 11th arrondissement. To process the cooked potatoes, a ricer or food mill works best for obtaining the smooth texture needed for light, fine gnocchi. A potato masher works, too, but the gnocchi will be slightly denser (but still delicious). The gnocchi can be cooked, cooled completely, covered with plastic wrap and refrigerated for up to a day. For longer storage, after covering with plastic, freeze the gnocchi until solid, about 2 hours, then transfer to a zip-close bag and freeze for up to a month. To thaw, spread the gnocchi in an even layer on a lightly oiled baking sheet and let stand at room temperature until soft to the touch, about 1 hour. Heat the chilled or thawed gnocchi by adding them to a skilletful of hot sauce, tossing with a silicone spatula until warmed.

Don't use Yukon Gold potatoes. *The high starch content of russets is needed for light, tender gnocchi. Also, don't mash the potatoes without first drying them in the pot on the stovetop, then letting them cool on the rack-lined baking sheet. The drier the potatoes, the lighter the gnocchi. Finally, don't sauce the gnocchi immediately after removing them from the water. Give them 15 minutes to cool and firm up a bit.*

1. In a large pot, combine the potatoes and 4 quarts water. Bring to a boil over high, then stir in 1 tablespoon salt. Reduce to medium-high and cook, stirring occasionally, until the potatoes break apart when pierced with a knife, 15 to 20 minutes. Meanwhile, set a wire rack in a rimmed baking sheet and line the rack with kitchen parchment.

2. Drain the potatoes in a colander, shaking the colander to remove excess water. Return the potatoes to the pot and cook over low, gently folding with a silicone spatula, until the potatoes look dry and slightly powdery and the bottom of the pot is coated with a thin film of potato starch, 3 to 4 minutes. Transfer the potatoes to the prepared cooling rack in an even layer. Cool to room temperature. Meanwhile, in a small bowl, whisk together the flour, baking powder and 1 teaspoon salt.

3. Weigh out 1¼ pounds (about 4 cups) of the cooked potatoes into a large bowl; save the remainder for another use. Discard the parchment from the baking sheet, then line with fresh parchment and coat with 1 tablespoon of oil; set aside. Add 1 teaspoon salt to the potatoes and pass the potatoes through a ricer or a food mill fitted with the fine disk back into the bowl, or mash with a potato masher until smooth.

4. Sprinkle the flour mixture evenly over the potatoes. Using your hands, lightly toss the potatoes to distribute the flour mixture. Add the egg and gently mix with your hands until incorporated. Turn the dough out onto a lightly floured counter and gently knead just until smooth; do not overknead. Using a bench scraper or knife, divide the dough into 4 pieces.

5. Roll 1 piece of dough into a rope about 16 inches long, then use the dough scraper to cut it into 16 pieces. Place the pieces in a single layer on the prepared baking sheet. Dip the back of the tines of a fork into flour, then gently press into each piece to create a ridged surface. Repeat with the remaining pieces of dough.

6. Set a wire rack in another rimmed baking sheet and line the rack with kitchen parchment. Coat the parchment evenly with the remaining 2 tablespoons oil. In a large pot, bring 4 quarts water to a boil and stir in 1½ tablespoons salt. Add half of the gnocchi, return to a boil and cook, stirring gently and occasionally, until the gnocchi float to the surface. Cook for 1 minute, then use a slotted spoon to transfer the gnocchi, letting excess water drain, to the prepared rack. Return the water to a boil and repeat with the remaining gnocchi. Let the gnocchi cool for at least 15 minutes before using.

BUTTER, SAGE AND CHIVES SAUCE

Start to finish: 20 minutes
Servings: 4 to 6

A combination of lightly browned butter and fresh herbs creates a simple sauce that pairs perfectly with the delicate gnocchi.

4 tablespoons (½ stick) salted butter, cut into 4 pieces, divided

⅓ cup chopped fresh sage

1 recipe potato gnocchi

¼ cup finely chopped fresh chives

2 tablespoons lemon juice

Kosher salt and ground black pepper

In a nonstick 12-inch skillet over medium, melt 2 tablespoons of butter. Add the sage and cook, stirring, until fragrant and the butter just begins to brown, about 1 minute. Add the gnocchi and ½ cup water and bring to a simmer over medium-high, gently tossing with a silicone spatula.

Add the remaining 2 tablespoons butter and cook, swirling the pan to melt the butter, until the sauce has thickened slightly, about 1 minute. Off heat, stir in the lemon juice and chives. Taste and season with salt and pepper.

Pasta with Zucchini, Pancetta and Saffron

Start to finish: **40 minutes** / Servings: **4 to 6**

This is our version of a fantastic pasta offering from Trattoria Bertozzi in Bologna, Italy. In lieu of guanciale (cured pork jowl), we opted for easier-to-find but equally meaty pancetta, and we lightened up the dish's richness by swapping half-and-half for the cream. The restaurant uses gramigna pasta, a tubular, curled shape from the Emilio-Romagna region. We found that more widely available cavatappi or gemelli works just as well combining with the zucchini and catching the lightly creamy sauce in its crevices.

Don't boil the pasta until al dente. Drain it when it has a little more bite than is desirable in the finished dish; the noodles will cook a bit more in the sauce. Also, don't forget to reserve 2 cups of the cooking water before draining the pasta.

1. Halve the zucchini lengthwise, then use a spoon to scrape out the seeds. Slice each half lengthwise about ¼ inch thick, then cut the strips crosswise into 1-inch sections. In a large pot, boil 4 quarts of water. Add the pasta and 1 tablespoon salt, then cook, stirring occasionally, until just shy of al dente. Reserve 2 cups of the cooking water, then drain. In a small bowl, combine 1½ cups of the reserved water and the saffron; set aside the remaining ½ cup water.

2. While the pasta cooks, in a 12-inch skillet over medium, cook the pancetta and garlic, stirring occasionally, until the pancetta has rendered some of its fat and begins to crisp, about 3 minutes. Remove and discard the garlic, then stir in the zucchini and ½ teaspoon pepper. Cook, stirring occasionally, until the pancetta is fully crisped and the zucchini is lightly browned, 4 to 6 minutes.

3. Add the pasta and the saffron water to the skillet. Bring to a simmer over medium-high and cook, stirring often, until the pasta is al dente, 4 to 5 minutes. Add the half-and-half and cook, stirring, until the sauce is lightly thickened and clings to the pasta, about 1 minute. Off heat, taste and season with salt and pepper. If needed, stir in additional reserved pasta water 1 tablespoon at a time to create a lightly creamy sauce. Transfer to a serving bowl and top with Parmesan.

1 pound zucchini

12 ounces short, curly pasta, such as cavatappi or gemelli

Kosher salt and ground black pepper

½ teaspoon saffron threads

3 ounces pancetta, finely chopped

1 medium garlic clove, smashed and peeled

½ cup half-and-half

1 ounce Parmesan cheese, shaved with a vegetable peeler

Bucatini with Cherry Tomato Sauce and Fresh Sage

Start to finish: **45 minutes** / Servings: **4 to 6**

This Instant Pot pasta takes inspiration from a recipe in "Simple" by Yotam Ottolenghi. But instead of conventional stovetop simmering, we pressure-cook cherry or grape tomatoes, which tend to be dependably good no matter the season, into a tangy-sweet sauce. The pasta cooks in the pot at the same time, so there's no need to boil a separate pot of water. Fresh sage, smoked paprika and pecorino Romano cheese ratchet up the flavors. We especially liked this dish made with bucatini pasta, which is a thick, tubular spaghetti; linguine is a good alternative, but reduce the pressure-cooking time to 4 minutes.

Don't forget to break the pasta in half so the strands lay flat in the pot. And when adding the pasta, make sure no pieces poke above the surface of the liquid. All of the pasta must be fully submerged to cook properly.

⅓ cup extra-virgin olive oil, plus more to serve

4 medium garlic cloves, thinly sliced

¼ teaspoon red pepper flakes

2 bay leaves

2 pints (1 pound) cherry or grape tomatoes, halved

½ teaspoon white sugar

Kosher salt

1 pound bucatini pasta, broken in half

2 tablespoons chopped fresh sage, divided

¾ teaspoon smoked paprika

Pecorino Romano cheese, shaved or finely grated, to serve

1. On a 6-quart Instant Pot, select More/High Sauté. Add the oil and heat until shimmering. Add the garlic, pepper flakes and bay, then cook, stirring, until the garlic is light golden brown, about 2 minutes. Stir in the tomatoes, sugar, 1 tablespoon salt and 3 cups water. Add the pasta, placing the strands horizontally so they lay flat, then press them into the liquid until submerged.

2. Press Cancel, lock the lid in place and move the pressure valve to Sealing. Select Pressure Cook or Manual; make sure the pressure level is set to High. Set the cooking time for 5 minutes. When pressure cooking is complete, quick-release the steam by moving the pressure valve to Venting. Press Cancel, then carefully open the pot.

3. Using tongs, toss and stir the mixture to separate the strands of pasta, then stir in 1 tablespoon of sage and the paprika. Re-cover without locking the lid in place and let stand until the pasta is al dente, 3 to 5 minutes. Remove and discard the bay, then transfer to a serving dish and top with pecorino and the remaining 1 tablespoon sage.

Lasagna Bolognese

Start to finish: 1 hour 20 minutes (20 minutes active), plus cooling / Servings: 8 to 10

___

12 no-boil 6½-by-3½-inch lasagna noodles (see headnote)

1 tablespoon extra-virgin olive oil

Kosher salt

6 cups ragù Bolognese, warmed (see recipe p. 205)

3 cups Parmesan besciamella, warmed (see recipe p. 203)

Finely grated Parmesan cheese, to serve

In Bologna, ragù Bolognese is a silky, rich meat sauce to serve over pasta or polenta. Married to creamy besciamella (the Italian version of French béchamel sauce), it makes a terrific lasagna. We also pair it with tagliatelle (see recipe p. 206). Our take on lasagna Bolognese was inspired by a dish we ate at Osteria Broccaindosso in Bologna. We liked Barilla oven-ready lasagna noodles, preferring them even over fresh sheet pasta. Both the ragù and the besciamella should be warm for lasagna assembly; the ragù reheats well in a large saucepan over medium and the besciamella can be microwaved in a covered 1-quart liquid measuring cup or medium microwave-safe bowl. A serrated knife is best for cutting the lasagna for serving.

Don't use the noodles without first soaking them. Unsoaked noodles absorb moisture from both the ragù and besciamella, leaving the lasagna too dry. But don't soak them for longer than 10 minutes.

1. Heat the oven to 350°F with a rack in the middle position. Place the noodles in a 9-by-13-inch baking dish, then add hot water (about 140°F) to cover, along with the oil and 1 tablespoon salt; swish the noodles around to dissolve the salt. Let stand for 10 minutes, moving the noodles around halfway through to ensure they do not stick together.

2. Remove the noodles from the water and arrange in a single layer on a kitchen towel; pat dry with paper towels. Discard the water in the baking dish, then wipe it dry. Distribute 2 cups ragù evenly in the baking dish, then place 3 noodles in a single layer on top. Spread ¼ cup besciamella onto each noodle, all the way to the edges. Pour 1 cup ragù on top and spread evenly. Repeat the layering 3 more times, using the remaining noodles, besciamella and ragù, then cover the baking dish tightly with foil.

3. Bake until the edges of the lasagna are bubbling, 45 minutes to 1 hour. Transfer to a wire rack, uncover and cool for about 30 minutes. Cut into pieces and serve sprinkled with Parmesan.

PARMESAN BESCIAMELLA

Start to finish: 40 minutes
Makes about 3 cups

This white sauce is packed with flavor from bay, basil and Parmesan, and gets a hint of heat from red pepper flakes. The finished besciamella can be refrigerated in an airtight container for up to two days.

Don't allow the sauce to cool completely *before straining. It flows more easily through the mesh of the strainer when warm and fluid.*

6 tablespoons (¾ stick) salted butter, cut into 6 pieces

¼ cup all-purpose flour

1 quart half-and-half

3 bay leaves

½ teaspoon red pepper flakes

3 ounces Parmesan cheese, finely grated (1½ cups)

6 large fresh basil leaves

Kosher salt and ground black pepper

In a large saucepan over medium, melt the butter. Whisk in the flour, then cook, whisking constantly, for 2 minutes. While whisking, gradually add the half-and-half and bring to a simmer. Add the bay and pepper flakes, then reduce to low. Cook, whisking often, until the sauce thickens and reduces slightly and no longer tastes of raw starch, 10 to 15 minutes.

Off heat, whisk in the Parmesan and basil. Cool for 5 minutes, then set a fine-mesh strainer over a medium bowl, pour the sauce into the strainer and press on the solids with a silicone spatula; discard the solids. Taste and season with salt and pepper.

RAGÙ BOLOGNESE

Start to finish: 3¼ hours (40 minutes active)
Makes about 8 cups

---

4 tablespoons (½ stick) salted butter

3 tablespoons extra-virgin olive oil

1 large yellow onion, cut into rough 1-inch pieces

1 medium celery stalk, cut into rough 1-inch pieces

1 medium carrot, peeled and cut into rough 1-inch pieces

Two 28-ounce cans whole tomatoes

1½ pounds boneless beef short ribs, cut into rough 1-inch chunks

1 pound boneless pork shoulder, cut into rough 1-inch chunks

8-ounce piece pancetta, cut into rough 1-inch chunks (see headnote)

¼ cup tomato paste

½ cup dry white wine

2 cups low-sodium beef broth

4 bay leaves

½ teaspoon red pepper flakes

2 tablespoons unflavored powdered gelatin

Kosher salt and ground black pepper

This recipe makes enough ragù for lasagna Bolognese with sufficient leftovers for another night's pasta dinner. We were taught how to make it at chef Alberto Bettini's Michelin-starred Amerigo restaurant outside Bologna. Try to purchase pancetta in a large chunk from the deli counter. And if it comes in casing-like plastic, make sure to remove and discard the wrap before use. The next best option is packaged already diced pancetta. If pre-sliced is the only option, it will work, but will cost a lot more and requires less time in the food processor. We add a bit of powdered gelatin to give the ragù a rich, velvety body that otherwise would require a lengthy simmer to achieve. The finished ragù can be cooled to room temperature and refrigerated for up to three days.

Don't trim the fat from the beef and pork. *The fat makes the ragù rich and supple, and carries the flavors of the other ingredients.*

---

1. In a large Dutch oven, combine the butter and oil. In a food processor, pulse the onion, celery and carrot until roughly chopped, about 5 pulses. Transfer to the Dutch oven. One can at a time, add the tomatoes with juices to the food processor and puree until smooth; transfer to a medium bowl. Add half the beef to the food processor and pulse until coarsely ground, 5 to 10 pulses, then transfer to another medium bowl; repeat with the remaining beef. Repeat with the pork, in batches, adding it to the beef. Finally, process the pancetta to a coarse paste, about 30 seconds; add to the other meats.

2. Set the pot over medium-high and cook, stirring occasionally, until the vegetables are lightly browned, about 5 minutes. Stir in the tomato paste and cook, stirring, until the paste begins to brown, about 5 minutes. Add the wine and cook, scraping up any browned bits, until the pot is almost dry, about 1 minute. Stir in the ground meats, then stir in the broth, tomatoes, bay and pepper flakes. Bring to a simmer, then partially cover, reduce to medium-low and cook, stirring occasionally, until the meat is tender, the sauce is thick and the volume has reduced to about 8 cups, 2½ to 3 hours. Remove the pot from the heat.

3. Pour ¼ cup cold water into a small bowl and sprinkle the gelatin evenly over the top; let stand for 5 minutes to soften. Meanwhile, taste and season the ragù with salt and pepper, then remove and discard the bay. Stir in the softened gelatin until fully dissolved.

Tagliatelle alla Bolognese

Start to finish: **20 minutes** / Servings: 4

Tagliatelle resembles fettuccine, but typically is made with eggs, so the noodles have a yellow hue, a richer flavor and a more delicate texture than eggless pasta. It's not uncommon to find tagliatelle wound into small nests for packaging; other times, the noodles are in straight strands, like fettuccine.

Don't boil the pasta until al dente. Drain it when it's just shy of al dente. It will finish cooking in the ragù. This technique yields better integration of pasta and sauce.

1. In a large pot, bring 3 quarts water to a boil. Add 1 tablespoon salt and the pasta, then cook, stirring occasionally, until just shy of al dente. Reserve ½ cup of the cooking water, then drain.

2. In the same pot over medium, bring the ragù to a simmer, stirring occasionally. Add the tagliatelle and cook, stirring occasionally, until the pasta is al dente, about 2 minutes; add cooking water as needed to thin. Off heat, taste and season with salt and pepper. Serve drizzled with oil (if using) and sprinkled with Parmesan.

8.8-ounce package dried tagliatelle

Kosher salt and ground black pepper

2 cups ragù Bolognese (p. 205)

Extra-virgin olive oil, to serve (optional)

Finely grated Parmesan cheese, to serve

Orecchiette with Broccolini

Start to finish: 40 minutes / Servings: 4

Orecchiette with broccoli rabe (orecchiette con cime di rapa) is a signature pasta dish from the Puglia region of southern Italy. We were taught how to make it by Nunzia da Scalo, a cook in Bari, Italy. The bitterness of rabe is challenging for some palates, so we use sweeter, milder broccolini. However, if you like the assertiveness of rabe, it can easily be used in place of the broccolini, though rabe will cook a little more quickly. We boil the pasta in a minimal amount of water, then the starchy liquid that remains becomes the base for the sauce that marries the orecchiette and broccolini. A finishing sprinkle of toasted seasoned breadcrumbs adds a crisp texture.

Don't use fine dried breadcrumbs *instead of panko bread-crumbs. Their sandy, powdery texture doesn't offer the light, delicate crispness of panko.*

6 tablespoons extra-virgin olive oil, divided

8 medium garlic cloves, 4 minced, 4 thinly sliced

8 oil-packed anchovy fillets, minced

¾ cup panko breadcrumbs

1½ pounds broccolini, trimmed and cut crosswise into ¼-inch pieces

½ to 1 teaspoon red pepper flakes

Kosher salt and ground black pepper

12 ounces orecchiette pasta

1. In a large Dutch oven over medium-high, heat 2 tablespoons of oil until shimmering. Add the minced garlic and half the ancho-vies, then cook, stirring, until fragrant, about 45 seconds. Add the panko and cook, stirring, until golden brown, about 3 minutes. Transfer to a bowl and set aside; wipe out the pot.

2. In the same pot over medium-high, heat 2 tablespoons of the remaining oil until shimmering. Add the broccolini, pepper flakes, sliced garlic, 1½ teaspoons salt and ½ teaspoon black pepper. Cook, stirring occasionally, until the broccolini is crisp-tender and the garlic is golden brown, 6 to 7 minutes. Add ½ cup water and continue to cook, stirring, until most of the moisture has evaporated and the broccolini is fully tender, about 2 minutes. Transfer to a medium bowl and set aside.

3. In the same pot over medium-high, boil 5 cups water. Add 2 teaspoons salt and the pasta, then cook, stirring occasionally, until the pasta is al dente. Stir in the broccolini mixture, the remaining 2 tablespoons oil and the remaining anchovies. Continue to cook over medium-high, stirring constantly, until the liquid has thickened enough to cling lightly to the pasta and broccolini, about 1 minute. Remove from the heat, then taste and season with salt and pepper. Transfer to a serving bowl and sprinkle with the breadcrumbs.

Fregola with Shrimp and Tomatoes

Start to finish: 1 hour 10 minutes / Servings: 4

1½ pounds extra-large (21/25 per pound) shrimp, peeled (shells reserved), deveined and patted dry

Two 8-ounce bottles clam juice

3 cups low-sodium chicken broth

4 bay leaves

1 sprig fresh thyme

1 tablespoon black peppercorns

Kosher salt and ground black pepper

4 tablespoons extra-virgin olive oil, divided

1 pint cherry or grape tomatoes, halved

1 medium yellow onion, finely chopped

1 medium carrot, peeled, halved lengthwise and thinly sliced

2 medium garlic cloves, finely grated

1 cup fregola (see note)

2 tablespoons lemon juice

½ cup finely chopped fresh flat-leaf parsley

This is our simplified version of the fregola with seafood and tomato sauce taught to us by chef Francesco Pinna at Trattoria Lillicu in Sardinia. Cooking the pasta in chicken broth and bottled clam juice that were first simmered with shrimp shells adds deep complexity without calling for a lengthy ingredient list. If your shrimp already are shelled, remove the tails and use those to infuse the liquid. And if you have trouble finding fregola, an equal amount of toasted pearl couscous is a good stand-in; see sidebar for toasting instructions. You'll also need to reduce the chicken broth to only 2 cups. After cooking the fregola for 8 to 10 minutes following the second addition of shrimp-infused broth, remove the pot from the heat before adding the shrimp.

Don't fully cook the shrimp when browning them. They'll be only parcooked when they come out of the pot, but will finish in the residual heat of the fregola.

---

1. In a medium microwave-safe bowl, combine the shrimp shells, clam juice, chicken broth, bay, thyme and peppercorns. Microwave on high until the shrimp tails are pink and the mixture is hot, 4 to 5 minutes. Pour through a fine-mesh strainer set over another medium bowl; discard the solids in the strainer.

2. Season the shrimp with salt and pepper. In a large pot over medium-high, heat 1 tablespoon of oil until barely smoking. Add half the shrimp and cook without stirring until well browned on one side, 2 to 3 minutes. Transfer to a large plate. Repeat with another 1 tablespoon oil and the remaining shrimp.

3. Return the pot to medium-high. Add 1 tablespoon of the remaining oil. Add the tomatoes, onion, carrot and ½ teaspoon salt, then cook, stirring, until the tomatoes are spotty brown and the onion has softened, 3 to 5 minutes.

4. Add the garlic and fregola, then cook, stirring, until the garlic is fragrant, about 30 seconds. Stir in 2 cups of the shrimp broth, then bring to a simmer. Reduce to medium and cook, stirring occasionally, until most of the liquid is absorbed, 8 to 10 minutes. Stir in another 2 cups broth, return to a simmer and cook, stirring, until most of the liquid is absorbed, 8 to 10 minutes. Stir in the remaining 1 cup broth and cook, stirring constantly, until the fregola is tender and the mixture is creamy but not soupy, 6 to 8 minutes.

5. Off heat, stir in the shrimp and accumulated juices, remaining 1 tablespoon oil, lemon juice and parsley. Cover and let stand until the shrimp are opaque throughout, 5 to 7 minutes. Taste and season with salt and pepper.

FAUX FREGOLA

Pearl couscous, sometimes called Israeli couscous, makes a good substitute for fregola, but it must be toasted. To toast, put the couscous in a large, dry pot (the same one you'll later use to cook the dish). Cook over medium, stirring often, until golden brown, about 5 minutes. Even after toasting, the couscous will absorb liquid differently than true fregola, so be sure to adjust the broth as directed in the recipe notes.

Couscous "Risotto"

Start to finish: 45 minutes / Servings: 4

4 tablespoons (½ stick) salted butter, cut into 1-tablespoon pieces

1 medium yellow onion, chopped

Kosher salt and ground black pepper

3 medium garlic cloves, thinly sliced

1 cup pearl couscous (see headnote)

⅓ cup dry white wine

1 ounce Parmesan cheese, finely grated (½ cup), plus more to serve

½ cup lightly packed fresh flat-leaf parsley, finely chopped, plus more to serve

Traditional risotto is made with starchy medium-grain Italian rice. This "risotto," modeled on a dish we had at restaurant Igra Rama in Tel Aviv, uses pearl couscous (which actually is a pasta) and a cooking technique similar to the classic risotto method to produce "grains" with a rich, creamy consistency. The wheaty flavor of pearl couscous (sometimes called Israeli couscous) is nicely complemented by the salty, nutty notes of Parmesan cheese and the grassiness of fresh parsley.

Don't allow the onion to brown. The assertive bittersweet flavor of caramelized onion will easily overwhelm the other flavors in the dish.

1. **In a 12-inch skillet** over medium-high, melt 3 tablespoons butter. Add the onion, 1 teaspoon salt and ½ teaspoon pepper, then cook, stirring, until it begins to soften, 3 to 5 minutes. Add the garlic and cook, stirring, until fragrant, 1 to 2 minutes. Add the couscous and cook, stirring often, until it begins to brown, 2 to 3 minutes.

2. **Add the wine and cook,** stirring, until the pan is almost dry, about 1 minute. Add 3 cups water and 1 teaspoon salt, then cook, stirring occasionally, until almost all the liquid has been absorbed, 9 to 10 minutes.

3. **Off heat, add the Parmesan,** parsley and remaining 1 tablespoon butter, then stir until the butter melts. Taste and season with salt and pepper. Serve sprinkled with additional Parmesan and parsley.

COUSCOUS "RISOTTO" WITH ASPARAGUS

Trim **1 pound pencil-thin asparagus,** then cut the spears on the diagonal into ½-inch pieces; reserve the stalks and tips separately. Follow the recipe to add the **3 cups water** and **1 teaspoon kosher salt** to the pan; after the couscous has simmered for 5 minutes, stir in the asparagus stalks. Cook, stirring, for another 3 minutes, then add the asparagus tips. Cook, stirring, until almost all the liquid has been absorbed and the asparagus is tender, another 2 minutes. Continue the recipe as directed.

Two-Cheese Pasta with Cauliflower

Start to finish: **40 minutes** / Servings: **4**

Kosher salt and ground
black pepper

2-pound head cauliflower,
halved and trimmed of leaves

3 tablespoons extra-virgin
olive oil, plus more to serve

1 medium garlic clove,
smashed and peeled

½ teaspoon red pepper flakes,
plus more to serve

8 ounces short, curly pasta,
such as campanelle, cavatappi
or fusilli

1½ ounces pecorino Romano
cheese, finely grated (¾ cup),
plus more to serve

1½ ounces aged provolone
cheese (see headnote), finely grated
(¾ cup), plus more to serve

We learned this recipe from home cook Antonella Scala in Naples. We loved how it uses the same water to both parcook the cauliflower and to cook the pasta. Parcooking means the cauliflower browns quickly when it is later added to the skillet. It also enriches the water, infusing the pasta with some of the vegetable's flavor. To contrast the cauliflower's subtle sweetness, we like equal amounts of salty, savory pecorino Romano cheese and aged provolone (also called provolone picante, or sharp provolone). If you can't find aged provolone, regular provolone is an acceptable, though milder, substitute. Short, twisty pasta shapes such as campanelle, cavatappi or fusilli combine perfectly with the cauliflower florets. We boil the pasta for only 5 minutes (it will be well shy of al dente), then finish cooking it directly in the skillet with the cauliflower.

Don't forget to reserve 2½ cups of the cooking water before you drain the pasta. You'll need it for simmering the cauliflower and for creating the sauce. Also, don't add the grated cheeses all at once. Sprinkling each one over the surface of the pasta and stirring before sprinkling on more prevents the cheese from clumping.

1. **In a large pot,** bring 4 quarts water to a boil. Add 1 tablespoon salt and the cauliflower halves, then cook for 5 minutes; begin timing from the moment the cauliflower is added to the pot. Using tongs, transfer the cauliflower to a cutting board; reserve the pot and the water. When the cauliflower is cool enough to handle, chop the florets and stems into pieces slightly smaller than the pasta, discarding the thick, tough core. You should have about 4 cups. Return the water to a boil.

2. **In a nonstick 12-inch skillet** over medium, cook the oil and garlic, stirring often, until the garlic is golden brown, 2 to 3 minutes. Remove and discard the garlic, then add the cauliflower, pepper flakes and ½ teaspoon salt. Increase the heat to medium-high and cook, stirring occasionally, until the cauliflower is well browned, 7 to 9 minutes.

3. **Meanwhile, add the pasta** to the boiling water and cook, stirring occasionally, for 5 minutes. Reserve about 2½ cups cooking water, then drain. Add the pasta and ¼ teaspoon black pepper to the skillet with the cauliflower, then stir in 1 cup of the reserved cooking water. Cook over medium-high, stirring often, until the pasta is al dente, 3 to 5 minutes. If the pan becomes dry before the pasta is done, add another ¼ cup cooking water and continue to cook.

4. **When the pasta is al dente,** with the skillet still over medium-high, stir in another ¼ cup cooking water. Sprinkle on the pecorino, then stir until the cheese is evenly distributed and melted. Sprinkle on the provolone, then stir until the pasta is glossy and lightly coated with melted cheese. Remove the pan from the heat. If the mixture looks sticky and dry, stir in additional cooking water a few tablespoons at a time until the proper consistency is reached. Taste and season with salt and black pepper. Serve drizzled with additional oil and sprinkled with additional cheese and pepper flakes.

Spaghetti Aglio e Olio with Tomatoes and Basil

Start to finish: 25 minutes / Servings: 4 to 6

1 pound spaghetti

Kosher salt and ground
black pepper

⅓ cup extra-virgin olive oil

4 medium garlic cloves,
thinly sliced

½ teaspoon red pepper
flakes

1 pint grape tomatoes, halved

½ cup chopped fresh basil
or flat-leaf parsley

Finely grated Parmesan or
pecorino Romano cheese,
to serve

Classic Italian pasta aglio e olio, or pasta with garlic and oil, is made with those ingredients and little else. This version gets an infusion of bright color and fresh flavor from halved grape tomatoes and chopped basil (or parsley). We boil the pasta until just shy of al dente, then reserve about ¾ cup of the cooking water and drain. The noodles will finish cooking when returned to the pot along with the tomatoes and some of the cooking water. This technique allows the pasta to absorb the flavors of the sauce and become better integrated with it.

Don't forget to halve the tomatoes. It's a bit time consuming, but worthwhile, so that the tomatoes soften slightly and relinquish some of their juice during the brief cooking time.

1. **In a large pot,** bring 4 quarts water to a boil. Stir in the pasta and 1 tablespoon salt, then cook, stirring occasionally, until just shy of al dente. Reserve about ¾ cup of the cooking water, then drain.

2. **In the same pot over medium-low,** combine the oil, garlic and pepper flakes. Cook, stirring, until the garlic is light golden brown, 1 to 2 minutes. Add the pasta, tomatoes, ½ cup reserved pasta water and ½ teaspoon each salt and black pepper. Cook, tossing, until the pasta is al dente, 1 to 2 minutes; add more reserved water as needed so the noodles are lightly sauced. Off heat, toss in the basil, then taste and season with salt and pepper. Serve sprinkled with cheese.

Spaghetti Puttanesca

Start to finish: **25 minutes** / Servings: 4

We think of puttanesca as a saucy dish built on anchovies. But in Naples, where it originates, two varieties of briny olives and pungent capers, not anchovies, give the dish bold savoriness that balances the sweetness of the tomatoes. We got a lesson in how to make it from Antonella Scala, who hosted pop-up dinners in her rooftop kitchen on the outskirts of modern Pompeii. We call for a generous amount of capers, which often are sold in small bottles or jars. When shopping, you will need to buy two 4-ounce bottles to get the ½ cup drained capers needed for this recipe. So that the spaghetti is extra-flavorful and each noodle is seasoned throughout, we boil it in water for just 5 minutes—it will be underdone at the center—then finish cooking it directly in the sauce.

Don't use more than 2 quarts of water to boil the pasta; the idea is to concentrate the starches in the cooking water, which later is used to thicken the sauce.

12 ounces spaghetti

2 tablespoons extra-virgin olive oil, divided

3 medium garlic cloves, smashed and peeled

1 teaspoon red pepper flakes

½ cup pitted Kalamata olives, roughly chopped

½ cup pitted green olives, roughly chopped

½ cup (two 4-ounce bottles) drained capers, rinsed, patted dry and chopped

28-ounce can whole peeled tomatoes, drained, 1 cup juices reserved, tomatoes crushed by hand into small pieces

½ cup lightly packed fresh basil, chopped

1 ounce Parmesan or pecorino Romano cheese, grated (½ cup), plus more to serve

1. In a large pot, bring 2 quarts water to a boil. Add 1½ teaspoons salt and the spaghetti, then cook, stirring occasionally, for 5 minutes. Reserve 2 cups of cooking water, then drain and set aside.

2. In a 12-inch skillet over medium, heat 1 tablespoon of oil and the garlic cloves, then cook, stirring often, until the garlic is light golden brown, about 1 minute. Off heat, remove and discard the garlic. Add the pepper flakes, both types of olives and the capers, then cook over medium-high, stirring, until the capers begin to brown, about 1 minute. Add the tomatoes and cook, stirring occasionally, until most of the liquid has evaporated, 5 to 7 minutes.

3. Add the reserved tomato juice and 1 cup of the reserved cooking water; bring to a simmer. Add the pasta and toss to coat. Cover and cook, tossing occasionally, until the pasta is al dente and the sauce clings lightly to the noodles; add more cooking water if needed.

4. Remove from the heat, cover and let stand for 3 minutes. Stir in the basil, cheese and remaining 1 tablespoon olive oil. Taste and season with salt and black pepper. Serve topped with additional cheese.

Pasta with Parmesan Cream

Start to finish: **25 minutes** / Servings: 4 to 6

The key to this simple, ultra-rich sauce, our adaptation of the Parmesan cream perfection we discovered at Trattoria Bertozzi in Bologna, is using good-quality true Parmesan cheese (Parmigiano-Reggiano). We simmer a piece of Parmesan rind into the cream for added flavor and umami; some supermarkets and cheese shops sell just rinds, or simply cut the rind off your chunk of Parmesan.

Don't use domestic Parmesan or even true Parmesan that's pre-grated. Neither will yield the correct flavor and consistency.

1. In a medium saucepan over medium, combine the cream, Parmesan rind and bay. Bring to a simmer and cook, stirring occasionally and adjusting the heat as needed, until slightly thickened and reduced to 2 cups, 10 to 15 minutes.

2. Remove the pan from the heat, then remove and discard the cheese rind and bay. Whisk in the lemon juice; the mixture will thicken slightly. Whisk in the cheese a handful at a time, then continue to whisk until completely smooth. Taste and season with pepper, then set aside uncovered.

3. In a large pot, bring 4 quarts water to a boil. Add 1 tablespoon salt and the pasta, then cook, stirring occasionally, until al dente. Reserve ½ cup of the cooking water, then drain. Return the pasta to the pot.

4. Pour the sauce over the pasta and toss until well coated, adding cooking water as needed to thin. Taste and season with salt and pepper. Serve sprinkled with additional black pepper.

2½ cups heavy cream

2-inch Parmesan rind, plus
6 ounces Parmesan cheese,
finely grated (3 cups)

2 bay leaves

2 tablespoons lemon juice

Kosher salt and ground
black pepper

1 pound linguine
or spaghetti

Spaghetti with Lemon Pesto

Start to finish: 25 minutes / Servings: 4

4 lemons

Kosher salt and ground
black pepper

1½ teaspoons white sugar,
divided

1 pound spaghetti

½ cup slivered almonds

1 ounce (without rind) Parmesan
cheese, cut into rough 1-inch
pieces, plus finely grated
Parmesan to serve

⅓ cup extra-virgin olive oil,
plus more to serve

2 tablespoons finely chopped
fresh chives

This pasta dish is modeled on the spaghetti al pesto di lim-one that Giovanna Aceto made for us on her family's farm in Amalfi, Italy. The lemons commonly available in the U.S. are more acidic than Amalfi's lemons, so to make a lemon pesto that approximates the original, we use a little sugar to temper the flavor. For extra citrus complexity, we add lemon zest to the pasta cooking water; the oils from the zest lightly perfume the spaghetti, reinforcing the lemony notes of the pesto.

Don't forget to remove the lemon zest from the boiling water before dropping in the pasta. If left in as the spaghetti cooks, the zest may turn the water bitter, and the strips are a nuisance to remove from the strands of cooked noodles.

1. Using a vegetable peeler (preferably a Y-style peeler), remove the zest from the lemons in long, wide strips; try to remove only the colored portion of the peel, not the bitter white pith just underneath. You should have about ⅔ cup zest strips.

2. In a large pot, combine 2 quarts water, 1½ teaspoons salt, 1 teaspoon of sugar and half of the zest strips. Bring to a boil and cook for 2 minutes, then remove and discard the zest. Add the spaghetti and cook until al dente. Reserve 1½ cups of the cooking water, then drain the pasta and return it to the pot.

3. Meanwhile, in a food processor, combine the remaining zest strips, the almonds, Parmesan, the remaining ½ teaspoon sugar and ¼ teaspoon each salt and pepper. Process until the mixture resembles coarse sand, 10 to 20 seconds. Add the oil and process just until the oil is incorporated (the mixture will not be smooth), about another 10 seconds; set aside until the pasta is ready.

4. To the spaghetti in the pot, add the pesto and ¾ cup of the reserved pasta water, then toss to combine; add more reserved pasta water as needed so the pesto coats the noodles. Toss in the chives. Taste and season with salt and pepper. Serve drizzled with additional oil and with additional grated Parmesan on the side.

Spaghetti with Anchovies, Pine Nuts and Raisins

Start to finish: **30 minutes** / Servings: 4

This pasta dish features the classic Sicilian flavor combination of savory, sweet and sour. Our version was inspired by a recipe from Vecchia Trattoria da Totò run by Giuseppe and Piera di Noto in Palermo. Toasted breadcrumbs, sprinkled on just before serving, provide pleasant crispness. We preferred fluffy panko breadcrumbs over regular powder-fine breadcrumbs, but crushing or chopping the panko before toasting ensured better blending with the pasta. Crush the panko in a zip-close plastic bag with a meat pounder or rolling pin, or simply chop with a chef's knife on a cutting board. To be efficient, pile the pine nuts, raisins and garlic together on the cutting board and chop them all at once.

Don't overcook the pasta after adding it to the sauce. The noodles should be al dente and slippery. If needed, loosen them by tossing with additional reserved pasta water.

12 ounces spaghetti

Kosher salt and ground black pepper

6 tablespoons extra-virgin olive oil, divided, plus more to serve

⅓ cup panko breadcrumbs, finely crushed or chopped (see headnote)

¼ cup pine nuts, finely chopped

3 tablespoons golden raisins, finely chopped

10 oil-packed anchovy fillets, patted dry

8 medium garlic cloves, finely chopped

2 tablespoons white wine vinegar

½ cup lightly packed fresh flat-leaf parsley, chopped

1. In a large pot, bring 4 quarts water to a boil. Add the spaghetti and 1 tablespoon salt, then cook, stirring occasionally, until just shy of al dente. Reserve about 1½ cups of the cooking water, then drain the pasta.

2. While the pasta cooks, in a 12-inch skillet over medium, combine 2 tablespoons of oil and the panko. Cook, stirring frequently, until golden brown, 3 to 5 minutes. Transfer to a small bowl and set aside; wipe out the skillet.

3. Set the skillet over medium-high and add the remaining 4 tablespoons oil, the pine nuts, raisins, anchovies and garlic. Cook, stirring frequently, until the anchovies have broken up and the garlic is golden brown, about 2 minutes. Stir in the vinegar and cook until syrupy, 30 to 60 seconds. Add 1 cup of the reserved pasta water, ½ teaspoon salt and ¼ teaspoon pepper and bring to a simmer.

4. Add the pasta, reduce to medium, and cook, occasionally tossing to combine, until the pasta is al dente and has absorbed most of the moisture but is still a little saucy, about 2 minutes. Remove from the heat. If the pasta is dry, add more cooking water, 1 tablespoon at a time. Stir in the parsley, then taste and season with salt and pepper. Transfer to a serving bowl. Sprinkle with the panko and top with additional oil and pepper.

Spaghetti with Lemon, Anchovies and Capers

Start to finish: **30 minutes (15 minutes active)** / Servings: 4

Lidia Bastianich reminded us that the water we cook our pasta in is worth saving. The starchy liquid can be used to thicken quick, flavorful sauces made from potent pantry staples, such as anchovies and capers. Our quick pasta dish, inspired by Bastianich, draws its intense flavor from anchovies, capers, garlic, lemon and red pepper flakes. We intentionally undercooked the pasta to leave it under-hydrated and ready to absorb more flavor when cooking in the sauce.

Don't salt the pasta water *as much as usual; the other ingredients provide plenty of salt. One tablespoon kosher salt for 4 quarts of water worked for this recipe.*

1. In a large pot, bring 4 quarts water to a boil. Add the pasta and 1 tablespoon salt, then cook until just tender but not fully cooked, about 2 minutes less than package directions. Reserve 2 cups of the cooking water, then drain.

2. In a large skillet over medium, combine the oil, garlic, pepper flakes, anchovies and capers. Cook, stirring occasionally, until fragrant and the garlic is golden, about 5 minutes. Add the reserved pasta water and bring to a simmer. Add the pasta and stir. Cook, stirring occasionally, until the pasta is al dente, 3 to 5 minutes.

3. Off heat, stir in the lemon zest and juice, the caper brine, parsley and half of the cheese. Taste, then season with salt and pepper. Serve topped with the remaining cheese.

12 ounces spaghetti

Kosher salt and ground black pepper

¼ cup extra-virgin olive oil

6 medium garlic cloves, thinly sliced

¾ teaspoon red pepper flakes

12 anchovies, minced (2-ounce can)

3 tablespoons drained capers, chopped, plus 2 tablespoons caper brine

2 teaspoons lemon zest, plus 3 tablespoons lemon juice

¾ cup chopped fresh parsley leaves

2 ounces finely grated Parmesan cheese (about 1 cup)

Homemade Udon Noodles

Start to finish: 4 hours (1½ hours active)

Makes about 1¾ pounds uncooked noodles
(about 3 pounds cooked noodles)

___

25 grams (1½ tablespoons)
table salt

1 cup warm water
(about 100°F)

520 grams (4 cups)
all-purpose flour

Cornstarch, for dusting

Udon is a type of Japanese wheat noodle. The thick, chewy strands can be served in hot soup, eaten cold with dipping sauce, stir-fried or simply sauced. When adapting Sonoko Sakai's udon formula from her book, "Japanese Home Cooking," we found that the type of flour used and relative humidity can impact how much water is needed to make the noodle dough. For best results, the dough should be on the dry side, but should contain just enough moisture so it holds together when first mixed; if needed, work in more water 1 tablespoon at a time, but err on the side of dry rather than wet. With resting and kneading, the dough will hydrate and become smooth, silky and very elastic. And as for kneading, the classic homestyle way is to stomp on the dough by foot, a good—and fun!—way to develop strong gluten structure; we put the dough into a doubled heavy-duty plastic bag before stepping on it to ensure everything stays clean. If this method isn't for you, we also include instructions for kneading the dough by rolling it with a rolling pin, a technique that also develops strength in the dough. Unlike most types of fresh noodles, this udon requires lengthy cooking—about 15 minutes of boiling—in order to attain the correct texture.

Don't salt the cooking water for the udon. The noodles themselves contain a good amount of sodium (it helps develop structure and chewiness), so if the water is also salted, the noodles may end up overseasoned. After draining the noodles, it's important to rinse them under running cold water to wash off excess starch and to stop the cooking.

1. In a small bowl, mix together the salt and warm water until the salt dissolves. Put the flour in a large bowl, add half of the saltwater and mix with a wooden spoon until the water is absorbed. Add the remaining saltwater and mix, using your hands once the water has been absorbed, until a shaggy but cohesive dough forms. If the mixture is very dry and won't come together, mix in additional water 1 tablespoon at a time, but it's best to err on the side of too little water than too much. Transfer to a 1-gallon heavy-duty zip-close bag, press out the air and seal the bag; let rest for 30 minutes.

2. If kneading by foot, place the bag with the dough inside another 1-gallon zip-close bag, press out the air and seal; set the bag on the floor and repeatedly step on the dough with your feet, being careful not to tear or puncture the plastic, until the dough fills the bag. If kneading with a rolling pin, lay the bag on the counter and, using a rolling pin, press down on the dough to flatten it, then roll it out until it fills the bag. Remove the dough

from the bag, fold it into thirds like a business letter, return it to the (inner) bag and seal both bags, pressing out the air. Repeat the process 4 more times, until the dough is very smooth and elastic; after the fifth pressing or rolling, leave the dough flat (do not fold the dough into thirds). Make sure the bags are well sealed and let rest at room temperature for 2 hours or refrigerate for up to 1 day (if refrigerated, let the dough stand at room temperature for 45 to 60 minutes before proceeding).

3. Lightly dust a rimmed baking sheet with cornstarch. Remove the dough from the bag(s) and set it on the counter. Using a chef's knife, cut the dough in half. Set one piece aside and cover with a clean kitchen towel. Using a rolling pin, roll the second piece into a 12-inch square ⅛ inch thick. It's fine if the square isn't perfect; it's more important that the dough be of an even thickness. Evenly dust the surface of the dough with cornstarch, then accordi-on-fold it in thirds. Using a chef's knife and a decisive cutting motion (do not use a sawing action), cut the dough crosswise into ⅛-inch-wide noodles. Unfold the noodles, transfer to the prepared baking sheet and cover with another kitchen towel. Repeat with the remaining dough.

4. In a large pot, bring 5 quarts water to a boil. Using your hands, add the noodles to the pot, shaking them over the baking sheet to remove excess starch. Cook, stirring occasionally, until a noodle rinsed under cold water is tender, 15 to 17 minutes. Drain in a colander, rinse the noodles under running cold water and drain again.

UDON NOODLES WITH SPICY MEAT AND MUSHROOM SAUCE

Start to finish: 50 minutes / Servings: 6

This meaty, umami-rich sauce adapted from "Japanese Home Cooking" by Sonoko Sakai is a perfect match for thick, hearty udon noodles, whether you use homemade or store-bought. A salty fermented chili-bean paste called toban djan provides the spiciness; use the smaller dose if you're sensitive to chili heat. If you've used the larger amount and still want more heat in the sauced noodles, offer a bottle of chili oil at the table.

Don't forget to stir the cornstarch-water slurry before adding it to the sauce. Upon standing, the starch settles to the bottom of the bowl, so stirring is necessary to recombine. After adding the slurry to the sauce, make sure to return to a simmer while stirring so the sauce thickens properly and doesn't form starchy lumps.

2 tablespoons toasted sesame oil

8 ounces 80 percent lean ground beef

8 ounces ground pork

4 shiitake mushrooms, stemmed and finely chopped

8-ounce can bamboo shoots, rinsed, drained and finely chopped (optional)

2 medium garlic cloves, minced

2 tablespoons minced fresh ginger

2 cups low-sodium chicken broth

¼ cup sake

1 to 2 tablespoons chili-bean sauce (toban djan)

2 tablespoons miso, preferably red

2 tablespoons soy sauce

1 tablespoon mirin

2 tablespoons cornstarch

1 recipe (about 1¾ pounds) homemade udon noodles (see recipe p. 222), cooked, drained and rinsed

4 scallions, thinly sliced on the diagonal

½ English cucumber, cut into matchsticks

1. In a large Dutch oven over medium-high, heat the sesame oil until shimmering. Add the ground beef and pork, then cook, stirring and breaking the meat into small pieces with a wooden spoon, until browned, 4 to 5 minutes. Add the mushrooms, bamboo shoots (if using), garlic and ginger; cook, stirring, until fragrant, 1 to 2 minutes. Stir in the broth, sake, chili-bean sauce, miso, soy sauce and mirin. Bring to a simmer and cook, stirring occasionally and adjusting the heat to maintain a simmer, until the liquid has reduced by half, 6 to 7 minutes. Meanwhile, in a small bowl, stir together the cornstarch and 2 tablespoons water; set aside.

2. When the liquid is properly reduced, stir the cornstarch slurry to recombine, then stir it into the meat-mushroom mixture. Cook, stirring constantly, until the sauce returns to a simmer and has thickened, about 1 minute. Add the noodles to the pot, toss to combine with the sauce and cook, stirring, just until the noodles are heated through, 2 to 3 minutes. Divide among individual bowls and top with the scallions and cucumber.

UDON NOODLES IN SOY BROTH

Start to finish: **30 minutes** / Servings: 4

A simple broth of dashi (Japanese stock) and soy sauce is a great way to appreciate the chewy texture and wheaty flavor of homemade udon noodles. This broth is based on Sonoko Sakai's kombu and bonito dashi formula in "Japanese Home Cooking." To make this with dried udon, use 6 ounces, cook them according to package instructions, but rinse them after draining under warm water rather than cool water so they aren't completely cold when divided among the serving bowls.

4-inch square (about ½ ounce) kombu

3½ to 4 cups (about 1 ounce)
lightly packed bonito flakes (katsuobushi)

⅓ cup soy sauce

1½ tablespoons mirin

2 teaspoons white sugar

½ recipe (about 14 ounces) homemade udon
noodles (p. 222), uncooked

4 scallions, thinly sliced on the diagonal

Shichimi togarashi, to serve (optional)

1. In a large saucepan over medium, heat the kombu and 6 cups water to just below a simmer. Remove the kombu (discard it or reserve it for another use) and bring the liquid to a boil over medium-high. Turn off the heat, add the bonito flakes and let steep for about 2 minutes. Pour the broth through a fine-mesh strainer set over a medium bowl. Discard the bonito and return the broth to the pan. Stir in the soy sauce, mirin and sugar; set aside.

2. In a large pot, bring 3 quarts water to a boil. Using your hands, add the noodles to the pot, shaking them over the baking sheet to remove excess starch. Cook, stirring occasionally, until a noodle rinsed under cold water is tender, 15 to 17 minutes. Meanwhile, bring the broth to a simmer over medium, then remove from the heat and cover to keep warm.

3. When the noodles are done, drain in a colander, rinse under running warm water and drain again. Divide the noodles among individual bowls. Ladle in the hot broth and sprinkle with the scallions. If desired, serve with shichimi togarashi.

Chinese Chili-and-Scallion Noodles

Start to finish: 40 minutes (20 minutes active) / Servings: 4

Every cook needs a few back-pocket recipes that can be thrown together quickly from pantry staples. Think spaghetti carbonara, the Italian pasta dish of bacon and eggs. Or Fuchsia Dunlop's game-changing "midnight noodles," a fresh spin on a Chinese staple. The simple sauce comes together in the time it takes the noodles to cook. Our version swaps out some of the hard-to-find Chinese ingredients and creates a simple chili oil that can be adjusted to taste. We cooked scallion whites in the hot oil to soften their bite and used the milder green parts to add brightness at the end. While we preferred udon noodles, chewy Chinese wheat noodles such as lo mein were a fine substitute. Even spaghetti worked in a pinch. These noodles also are great topped with a fried egg, see our recipe (p. 3).

Don't walk away while heating the oil. The sesame seeds can burn in an instant, and the red pepper flakes will blacken and become bitter. The seeds should be just turning golden, and the pepper flakes should be pleasantly fragrant.

12 ounces udon noodles, lo mein or spaghetti

5 tablespoons soy sauce

3 tablespoons unseasoned rice vinegar

3 tablespoons packed dark brown sugar

1 tablespoon toasted sesame oil

¼ cup grapeseed or other neutral oil

5 teaspoons sesame seeds

1¼ teaspoons red pepper flakes

2 bunches scallions, thinly sliced on the diagonal, white and green parts reserved separately

4 fried eggs, to serve (optional)

1. Bring a large pot of water to a boil. Add the noodles and cook until al dente, then drain. Meanwhile, in a large bowl whisk together the soy sauce, vinegar, sugar and sesame oil.

2. In a 10-inch nonstick skillet over medium, heat the grapeseed oil, sesame seeds and pepper flakes until fragrant and the sesame seeds begin to brown, 3 to 5 minutes. Off heat, stir in the scallion whites, then transfer the oil mixture to the bowl with the soy sauce mixture.

3. Add the cooked noodles to the sauce and toss. Add the scallion greens, reserving some for garnish, and toss. Divide among 4 individual bowls and top each with reserved scallion greens and a fried egg (if using).

Whole-Wheat Pasta with Yogurt and Tahini

Start to finish: **25 minutes** / Servings: **4**

With its earthy flavor and dense chew, whole-wheat pasta often gets passed over. But with the right ingredients it can be a star. Take our Greek-inspired pasta tossed with a simple, creamy sauce of thick yogurt and nutty tahini. While we recommend whole-grain, the dish also is delicious with traditional pasta. Chunky pastas such as orecchiette, farfalle and penne worked as well as long noodles, such as fettuccine and tagliatelle. To add interest to our sauce we toasted cumin seeds and finely chopped walnuts—they also provided the basis for a garnish. The ratio of tahini to yogurt—1:3—was key to a full-flavored, creamy sauce; a bit of olive oil helped with emulsification. For a tangy touch, we added lemon zest to both the toasted walnuts and the tahini sauce, giving us a double layer of flavor.

Don't substitute traditional yogurt for Greek-style or the sauce will be too thin.

1. In a large pot bring 4 quarts water to a boil. Meanwhile, in a medium bowl combine the garlic and lemon juice and let sit for 10 minutes. In a small skillet over medium-low, toast the walnuts and cumin seeds, stirring frequently, until golden brown and fragrant, 3 to 5 minutes. Transfer to a small bowl and stir in the scallions, ½ teaspoon of the lemon zest and ¼ teaspoon salt.

2. Stir in the pasta and 1 tablespoon salt and cook until al dente. Drain, reserving 1 cup of the cooking water, then return the pasta to the pot. Into the lemon juice–garlic mixture, whisk in the yogurt, tahini, oil, the remaining ½ teaspoon of lemon zest, ½ teaspoon salt and ½ cup of the reserved pasta water. Add the sauce to the pasta and toss until evenly coated. Stir in half of the walnut mixture. Transfer the pasta to a platter or individual bowls, then garnish with the remaining walnut mixture.

2 medium garlic cloves, finely grated

1 teaspoon grated lemon zest, plus 3 tablespoons lemon juice

½ cup walnuts, finely chopped

1½ teaspoons cumin seeds

2 scallions, trimmed and finely chopped

Kosher salt

12 ounces whole-wheat pasta

1 cup plain whole-milk Greek-style yogurt

⅓ cup tahini

2 tablespoons extra-virgin olive oil

Spaghetti with Pancetta (Pasta alla Gricia)

Start to finish: **20 minutes** / Servings: **4**

This classic Roman pasta dish, taught to us by Roman cookbook author Mario Ive, depends on the quality of the pecorino Romano, a salty, hard sheep's milk cheese. The addition of cornstarch allowed us to overcome the tendency of this cheese to clump. For best flavor we recommend seeking out pecorino imported from Italy. Guanciale (cured pork cheek) is traditional for gricia, but we used more widely available pancetta.

Don't use pre-grated cheese, even if it's true pecorino Romano. Make sure to grate it on a wand-style grater; larger shreds won't melt. Don't pour the pecorino mixture onto the piping-hot, just-drained pasta; letting the pasta cool for a minute or so ensures the mixture won't break from overheating.

1. In a large pot, bring 4 quarts water to a boil. Meanwhile, in a 10-inch skillet over medium, cook the pancetta, stirring occasionally, until crisp, about 5 minutes. Using a slotted spoon, transfer the pancetta to a paper towel-lined plate; reserve 2 tablespoons of the rendered fat.

2. In a large saucepan, whisk 1½ cups cold water and the cornstarch until smooth. Add the pecorino and stir until evenly moistened. Set the pan over medium-low and cook, whisking constantly, until the cheese melts and the mixture comes to a gentle simmer and thickens slightly, about 5 minutes. Off heat, whisk in the reserved pancetta fat and set aside.

3. Stir the pasta and 1 tablespoon salt into the boiling water and cook until al dente. Reserve about ½ cup of the cooking water, then drain the pasta very well. Return the pasta to the pot and let cool for about 1 minute.

4. Pour the pecorino mixture over the pasta and toss with tongs until combined, then toss in 2 teaspoons pepper and the crisped pancetta. Let stand, tossing 2 or 3 times, until most of the liquid has been absorbed, about 3 minutes. The pasta should be creamy but not loose. If needed, toss in reserved pasta water 1 tablespoon at a time to adjust the consistency. Transfer to a warmed serving bowl and serve, offering additional pecorino and pepper on the side.

3 ounces pancetta, finely chopped

2 teaspoons cornstarch

6 ounces pecorino Romano cheese, finely grated (3 cups), plus extra to serve

12 ounces linguine or spaghetti

Kosher salt and ground black pepper

Roman Spaghetti Carbonara

Start to finish: **25 minutes** / Servings: 4

This brighter take on carbonara came from Pipero Roma in Rome. Chef David Puleio whisked the egg yolks until cooked and slightly foamy, creating a sauce that is much lighter in texture than most carbonara recipes. Mixing the yolks with water and cornstarch ensures the cheese won't clump when tossed with the pasta.

Don't substitute bacon for the pancetta. *The smokiness of the bacon will overwhelm the cleaner flavors of the egg-based sauce.*

1. In a 10-inch skillet over medium, cook the pancetta, stirring, until crisp, about 5 minutes. Using a slotted spoon, transfer to a paper towel-lined plate. Measure out and reserve 3 tablespoons of the rendered fat; if needed, supplement with olive oil. Set the pancetta and fat aside.

2. In a large pot, bring 4 quarts water to a boil. Meanwhile, in a large saucepan, whisk 1¾ cups water, the egg yolks and cornstarch until smooth. Add the cheese and stir until evenly moistened. Set the pan over medium-low and cook, whisking constantly, until the mixture comes to a gentle simmer and is airy and thickened, 5 to 7 minutes; use a silicone spatula to occasionally get into the corners of the pan. Off heat, whisk in the reserved pancetta fat. Set aside.

3. Stir the pasta and 1 tablespoon salt into the boiling water and cook until al dente. Reserve about ½ cup of the cooking water, then drain the pasta very well. Return the pasta to the pot and let cool for about 1 minute.

4. Pour the pecorino-egg mixture over the pasta and toss with tongs until well combined, then toss in 2 teaspoons pepper. Let stand, tossing 2 or 3 times, until most of the liquid has been absorbed, about 3 minutes. Crumble in the pancetta, then toss again. The pasta should be creamy but not loose. If needed, toss in up to 2 tablespoons reserved pasta water to adjust the consistency. Transfer to a warmed serving bowl and serve with additional pecorino and pepper on the side.

3 ounces thinly sliced
pancetta, chopped

6 large egg yolks

2 teaspoons cornstarch

6 ounces pecorino Romano
cheese, finely grated (3 cups),
plus more to serve

12 ounces spaghetti

Kosher salt and ground
black pepper

Seafood

Shrimp in Chipotle Sauce (Camarones Enchipotlados)

Start to finish: **25 minutes** / Servings: 4

A perfectly cooked shrimp—pink, firm but not tough, curved but not coiled—stymies most of us. The window between done and overdone is narrow. We solved that problem by giving the shrimp very little time over direct heat. Instead, we let the residual heat of a flavorful sauce cook them more gently. For the sauce, we used canned chipotle chilies and the adobo sauce in which they are packed, which give the dish pleasant, lingering heat and deep smoky flavor. The shrimp got a brief sear to start, then finished cooking off the burner in the warm sauce. Perfect results, effortlessly, every time. These shrimp made wonderful tacos when paired with diced avocado, fresh cilantro, lime wedges and sour cream. This dish also is delicious served alongside rice or cold as an appetizer.

Don't worry if your chipotles vary in size. *Despite appearances, most weigh about half an ounce.*

4 vine-ripened tomatoes (1¼ pounds), quartered

4 chipotle chilies in adobo sauce and the sauce clinging to them

Kosher salt and ground black pepper

4 tablespoons extra-virgin olive oil, divided

1½ pounds extra-large raw shrimp, peeled, deveined, tails removed and patted dry

4 tablespoons lime juice, divided

1 medium yellow onion, chopped

3 medium garlic cloves, thinly sliced

½ teaspoon dried oregano

¼ cup dry white wine

½ cup chopped fresh cilantro, plus more to serve

Eight 6-inch corn tortillas, warmed

Avocado, sour cream and lime wedges, to serve

1. In a food processor, pulse the tomatoes, chilies and any sauce coating them and ¾ teaspoon salt until mostly smooth, 1 minute. Set aside.

2. In a 12-inch nonstick skillet over medium-high, heat 2 tablespoons of the oil until barely smoking. Add half the shrimp and cook, stirring, until golden, about 45 seconds. Transfer to a bowl. Repeat with the remaining shrimp, adding them to the bowl. Toss with 2 tablespoons of the lime juice. Set aside.

3. Return the skillet to medium-high and add the remaining 2 tablespoons of oil. Add the onion and cook for 3 to 4 minutes. Add the garlic and oregano and cook until just beginning to brown, 1 minute. Stir in the wine and any accumulated shrimp juice from the bowl. Cook until the liquid is nearly evaporated. Add the chipotle mixture and simmer, stirring, until thick enough to coat a spoon, 10 to 12 minutes.

4. Remove the skillet from the heat. Stir in the shrimp, cover and let sit until the shrimp are opaque and cooked through, 2 to 4 minutes. Stir in the cilantro and remaining lime juice. Taste, then season with salt and pepper. Serve with warmed tortillas, avocado, sour cream, lime wedges and cilantro.

Salmon Chraimeh

Start to finish: **20 minutes** / Servings: 4

Center-cut salmon fillets deliver weeknight ease with vibrant flavor in this recipe inspired by the Sephardic dish chraimeh, or fish braised in a mildly spicy tomato sauce. The name comes from the word for thief and refers to the way the spice comes at the end of the sauce, sneaking up on the diner. We tailored ours to work with pantry staples and scaled down the amount of garlic typically used. Whole cumin and coriander, paprika, jalapeño and scallions rounded out the aromatics. Look for salmon pieces that are evenly thick, about 1 to 1½ inches. We liked our salmon cooked between 115°F and 120°F, which leaves the thickest part with some translucency. If you like yours more thoroughly cooked, after simmering remove the skillet from the heat and leave the fillets in the covered pan until cooked to desired doneness.

Don't use fillets of widely varying thickness; they will require different cooking times. If unavoidable, begin checking the thinner fillets ahead of the thicker ones.

Four 6-ounce center-cut salmon fillets, 1 to 1½ inches thick

Kosher salt and ground black pepper

1 tablespoon extra-virgin olive oil, plus more to serve

4 scallions, thinly sliced, dark green parts reserved separately

3 medium garlic cloves, thinly sliced

1 jalapeño chili, stemmed, halved, seeded and thinly sliced crosswise

1 teaspoon coriander seeds

1 teaspoon cumin seeds

¾ teaspoon smoked paprika

14½-ounce can diced tomatoes, with juices

2 tablespoons finely chopped fresh mint

¼ cup lightly packed fresh cilantro, chopped

Lemon wedges, to serve

1. Season the salmon fillets on both sides with salt and pepper. In a 10-inch skillet over medium-high, heat the oil until shimmering. Add the white and light green scallion parts, the garlic and jalapeño. Cook, stirring occasionally, until lightly browned, about 2 minutes. Stir in the coriander, cumin and paprika, then cook until fragrant, about 30 seconds.

2. Stir in the tomatoes, ½ teaspoon salt and ¼ teaspoon pepper. Bring to a simmer, then nestle the fillets skin side up in the sauce. Reduce to medium, cover and simmer for 6 to 8 minutes, until only the center of the thickest parts of the fillets are translucent or until they reach 115°F to 120°F.

3. Using tongs, carefully peel off and discard the skin from each fillet, then use a spatula to transfer to serving plates flesh side up. If the sauce is watery, continue to simmer over medium-high until slightly thickened, 1 to 2 minutes.

4. Off heat, stir in the mint and cilantro. Taste and season with salt and pepper. Spoon the sauce over the salmon, sprinkle with the scallion greens, drizzle with oil and serve with lemon wedges.

Ginger-Scallion Steamed Cod

Start to finish: 45 minutes / Servings: 4

3 tablespoons chopped fresh cilantro, plus ¼ cup whole leaves, divided

6 scallions, 3 minced and 3 thinly sliced on diagonal, reserved separately

2 tablespoons finely grated fresh ginger

6 tablespoons soy sauce, divided

3 tablespoons grapeseed or other neutral oil, divided

6 large green cabbage leaves, plus 2 cups thinly sliced green cabbage

Four 6-ounce skinless cod, haddock or halibut fillets

2 tablespoons unseasoned rice vinegar

2 teaspoons white sugar

1 teaspoon ground white pepper

1 serrano chili, stemmed and sliced into thin rings

1 tablespoon toasted sesame oil

In southern China, cooks have a worry-free method for cooking delicate, flaky white fish to perfection: steaming the fish whole with aromatic-spiked water. The mild heat slowly firms the protein, allowing it to stay moist. We adapted the technique, using skinless cod fillets for convenience and lining our steamer basket with cabbage leaves to mimic the skin of the whole fish. Rubbing the fillets with a seasoning paste of ginger, cilantro, scallions and soy sauce produced deep flavor in the mild-tasting fish. We drew on another classic Chinese technique for a flavorful finish—topping the fillets with raw chopped scallions and serrano chilies, then pouring sizzling-hot oil over them to bring out the flavors and aromas. Though this recipe calls for cod, haddock and halibut—or any firm, thick white fish fillets—also work. Because fillets vary in thickness, a general guide is to steam them for about 8 minutes per 1-inch thickness.

Don't let the steaming water reach a full boil. A gentle heat cooks the fish slowly and evenly, helping it stay moist.

1. In a wide, shallow bowl, stir together the chopped cilantro, the minced scallions, ginger, 2 tablespoons of soy sauce and 1 tablespoon of grapeseed oil. Add the fish and coat well. Let stand at room temperature for 10 minutes.

2. Place a steamer basket in a large pot. Add enough water to fill without reaching the basket. Remove the basket. Cover the pot and bring to a simmer over medium-high. Line the basket with 4 of the cabbage leaves. Place the fish fillets on the leaves, then cover with the remaining 2 leaves. Turn off the heat under the pot, then set the basket in the pot. Cover and return to a simmer over medium. Steam until the fish flakes easily, 8 to 12 minutes.

3. Meanwhile, in a small bowl, whisk the remaining 4 tablespoons soy sauce, the rice vinegar, sugar and pepper. Transfer 3 tablespoons to a medium bowl, add the sliced cabbage and toss. Arrange on a serving platter. Reserve the remaining dressing.

4. When the fish is ready, discard the cabbage leaves covering it. Use a spatula to transfer the fillets to the platter, placing them on the sliced cabbage. Sprinkle with the sliced scallions and the chili.

5. In a small skillet over medium-high, heat the remaining 2 tablespoons grapeseed oil until barely smoking. Carefully pour the oil over the fillets. Drizzle with the sesame oil and sprinkle with the cilantro leaves. Serve with the reserved dressing on the side.

Shrimp with Feta Cheese (Garides Saganaki)

Start to finish: **30 minutes** / Servings: 4

3 tablespoons extra-virgin olive oil, divided

1¼ pounds jumbo shrimp (16/20 per pound), peeled, deveined, tails removed, patted dry

4 large garlic cloves, finely chopped

4 teaspoons fennel seeds, finely ground

¼ teaspoon red pepper flakes

⅓ cup dry white wine

1½ pounds small tomatoes, such as Campari, chopped, plus ¼ cup finely diced

⅓ cup pitted Kalamata olives, chopped

2 tablespoons plus 2 teaspoons chopped fresh oregano

Kosher salt and ground black pepper

4 ounces feta cheese, coarsely crumbled (1 cup)

¼ cup chopped Peppadew peppers (optional)

This classic Greek dish pairs plump, sweet shrimp with briny feta cheese. We added chopped Kalamata olives for added savory flavor, as well as ground fennel seed for a hint of licorice. Our preferred tomatoes for this recipe are Campari (or cocktail) tomatoes, as they tend to be sweet and flavorful year-round; they're larger than cherry tomatoes but smaller than standard round tomatoes and usually are sold on the vine in plastic containers. We tried cherry and grape tomatoes but found their skins to be tough and unpleasant in the finished sauce. Chopped Peppadew peppers are an unconventional ingredient, but their mild, sweet heat makes them a welcome addition. Serve with crusty bread to sop up the sauce.

Don't use pre-crumbled feta. The cheese plays a prominent role in this dish, so good-quality feta sold in blocks is important.

1. In a 12-inch nonstick skillet over medium-high, heat 1 tablespoon of the oil until shimmering. Add half the shrimp in an even layer and cook without disturbing until deep golden brown on the bottoms, 1 to 2 minutes. Stir and cook until the shrimp are pink and opaque on all sides, another 20 to 30 seconds. Transfer to a medium bowl. Repeat with 1 tablespoon of the remaining oil and the remaining shrimp. Set aside.

2. Add the remaining 1 tablespoon oil to the pan and heat over medium-high until shimmering. Add the garlic, fennel and red pepper flakes and cook, stirring constantly, until the garlic is light golden brown, about 20 seconds. Add the wine and cook, stirring, until the liquid is almost evaporated, 30 to 60 seconds. Add the chopped tomatoes, olives and 1½ teaspoons salt. Cook, stirring, until the tomatoes have broken down into a sauce, 6 to 7 minutes.

3. Remove the pan from the heat. Stir in 2 tablespoons of the oregano, then taste and season with salt and pepper. Return the shrimp to the skillet, along with the accumulated juices. Cover the pan and let stand until the shrimp are heated through, about 1 minute.

4. Transfer to a serving dish. Sprinkle with the feta, finely diced tomatoes, the Peppadews (if using) and the remaining 2 teaspoons oregano.

Baked Salted Salmon with Dill

Start to finish: 1¾ hours (15 minutes active)
Servings: 4 to 6

___

3 tablespoons finely chopped
fresh dill, plus more to serve

Kosher salt and ground
black pepper

2-pound skin-on center-cut
side of salmon (see
headnote), pin bones
removed

2 tablespoons grapeseed
or other neutral oil

Lemon wedges, to serve

Quick-pickled cucumbers
(see sidebar), to serve

We were taught how to make this salmon by chef Nikolas Paulsson of the Lanternen restaurant on the Oslo fjord in Norway. For our take, we use a 2-pound skin-on center-cut side of salmon and salt it for about an hour before baking in a moderate oven. When shopping, look for a salmon side about 1 inch thick at its thickest part; pieces that are thicker or thinner will require timing adjustments when baking. The salmon will be slightly underdone when removed from the oven; a tented 5- to 10-minute rest will finish the cooking and bring the internal temperature up to 120°F at the thickest part. At this temperature, the fish should be just opaque, not translucent.

Don't delay tenting the salmon with foil after removing it from the oven. If not tented immediately, the salmon may lose too much heat to finish cooking through.

1. Line a rimmed baking sheet with kitchen parchment. In a small bowl, combine the dill and 2 tablespoons salt, then rub the mixture with your fingers to break down the dill. Place the salmon flesh side up on the prepared baking sheet. Rub the dill-salt mixture into the surface and sides. Refrigerate, uncovered, for 45 to 60 minutes.

2. Heat the oven to 350°F with a rack in the middle position. Line a second rimmed baking sheet with kitchen parchment, then mist with cooking spray. Rinse the salmon under cold water, rubbing to remove the salt. Pat completely dry with paper towels, then place flesh side up on the second baking sheet. Coat the surface of the fish with the oil and season with pepper. Bake until the edges are opaque and firm to the touch and the center of the thickest part reaches 112°F to 115°F, 12 to 15 minutes.

3. Remove the baking sheet from the oven and tent the salmon with foil; let rest 5 to 10 minutes (the temperature of the fish will climb to about 120°F). Using 2 large spatulas, carefully transfer to a serving platter. Sprinkle with chopped dill and serve with lemon wedges and pickled cucumbers.

QUICK-PICKLED CUCUMBERS

Start to finish: 15 minutes,
plus chilling / Makes about 2 cups

½ cup white vinegar

¼ cup white sugar

2 teaspoons kosher salt

1 tablespoon finely chopped
fresh dill

1 English cucumber, trimmed,
quartered lengthwise and thinly
sliced on the diagonal

In a large bowl, stir together 1 cup
water, the vinegar, sugar, salt and
dill. Stir in the cucumber, then cover
and refrigerate for at least 1 hour or
up to 24 hours.

Shrimp, Orzo and Zucchini with Ouzo and Mint

Start to finish: 1 hour 25 minutes (30 minutes active)
Servings: 4

___

3 tablespoons extra-virgin olive oil, divided

1 pound extra-large (21/25 per pound) shrimp, peeled (tails removed) and deveined, shells reserved

3 medium celery stalks, roughly chopped

1 medium red bell pepper, stemmed, seeded and roughly chopped

1 medium yellow onion, roughly chopped

3 bay leaves

Kosher salt and ground black pepper

¼ cup brandy

1 cup orzo

2 medium zucchini (about 1 pound total), trimmed, halved lengthwise, seeded and thinly sliced crosswise

1 pound ripe plum or cocktail tomatoes, cored and roughly chopped

1 teaspoon fennel seeds, lightly crushed

1 tablespoon plus 1 teaspoon ouzo

1½ teaspoons grated lemon zest

½ cup lightly packed fresh mint, chopped

In her acclaimed cookbook "Aegean," Crete-born London chef Marianna Leivaditaki coaxes orzo pasta to a rich, creamy texture, as if making risotto. A fragrant broth of brandy, aromatic vegetables and shrimp shells is the cooking liquid for the orzo, infusing the dish with richness and subtle sweetness. The shrimp themselves are added only after the orzo is al dente so they remain plump and tender. Our adaptation of her recipe takes a simpler approach to the cooking and calls for fewer ingredients but retains the delicious, bracing flavors of Leivaditaki's creation. Ouzo is a Greek anise-flavored spirit; it's added at the very end of cooking to accentuate the licorice notes of the fennel seed.

Don't choose large zucchini for this recipe. Look for small to medium squash (ones that weigh 6 to 8 ounces each), as they have fewer seeds to remove. To seed the zucchini, use a small spoon to scrape along the center of each half. Also, when simmering the shrimp broth, don't allow it to boil or simmer vigorously or the liquid will evaporate too quickly and the finished volume will be too slight.

___

1. In a large pot over medium-high, heat 1 tablespoon of oil until shimmering. Add the shrimp shells and cook, stirring just once or twice, until bright pink and dry, 3 to 4 minutes. Add the celery, bell pepper, onion, bay and ¼ teaspoon salt, then cook, stirring occasionally, until the vegetables begin to release moisture, 2 to 4 minutes. Add the brandy and scrape up any browned bits. Add 4 cups water, bring to a boil, then reduce to medium and simmer, uncovered, for 30 minutes.

2. Cool for about 10 minutes, then strain through a fine-mesh sieve set over a 1-quart liquid measuring cup or medium bowl; press on the solids to extract as much liquid as possible (discard the solids). You should have about 3 cups strained broth.

3. Season the shrimp with salt and pepper; set aside. In a 12-inch skillet over medium, heat the remaining 2 tablespoons oil until shimmering. Add the orzo and stir to coat. Add the zucchini, tomatoes, fennel seeds, ½ teaspoon salt and ¼ teaspoon pepper. Cook, stirring often, until the tomatoes begin to release their liquid, 3 to 5 minutes. Add 1½ cups shrimp broth and bring to a simmer over medium-high. Cook, uncovered and stirring often, until most of the liquid has been absorbed, about 6 minutes; reduce the heat as the mixture thickens.

4. Add another 1 cup broth and cook, stirring vigorously and adjusting the heat to maintain a simmer, until the orzo is tender and the consistency is slightly soupy, 3 to 6 minutes. Add the shrimp and another ¼ cup broth, then cook over medium, stirring occasionally, until the shrimp are opaque throughout, about 3 minutes.

5. Remove the pot from the heat. Remove and discard the bay, then stir in the ouzo and lemon zest. If desired, thin the consistency by stirring in additional broth, then taste and season with salt and pepper. Transfer to a serving dish and sprinkle with the mint.

Curry-Coconut Braised Fish

Start to finish: 30 minutes / Servings: 4

14-ounce can coconut milk

2 medium carrots, peeled,
halved lengthwise and cut into
½-inch pieces

1 medium yellow onion,
halved and thinly sliced

6 medium garlic cloves,
finely grated

2 teaspoons turmeric

2 teaspoons curry powder

½ teaspoon red pepper flakes

1 cup low-sodium chicken broth

1½ pounds firm white fish,
cut into 2-inch chunks

Kosher salt and ground
white pepper

Steamed white rice, to serve

Lime wedges, to serve

Comfortingly creamy with a little hit of heat, this easy weeknight dish was inspired by chef Edward Lee, author of "Smoke & Pickles," which explores his philosophy of finding innovative ways to blend Southern cuisine and Asian flavors. The coconut milk curry evokes traditional Thai flavors as well as fish amok, the Cambodian classic fish curry often served steamed in a banana leaf. And assembly couldn't be simpler—dump everything but the fish into a pot for about 10 minutes, then add the fish to gently cook for another 10. Any thick, firm whitefish, such as cod, hake or Chilean sea bass, will work. Avoid a thin fillet such as sole or tilapia, which will break down in the braising liquid. Using full-fat coconut milk was important, as it will not break as the vegetables cook. Low-sodium chicken broth gave us better control over the dish's final seasoning.

Don't cook the fish too long *or it will fall apart.*

1. In a large Dutch oven over medium-high, combine the coconut milk, carrots, onion, garlic, turmeric, curry powder and pepper flakes. Cook over medium heat, uncovered and stirring occasionally, until thickened and the vegetables are softened, about 10 minutes.

2. Stir in the broth and bring to a simmer. Season the fish with salt and white pepper, then stir into the pot. Cover and cook over low until the fish flakes easily when poked with a fork but remains intact, 7 to 10 minutes. Taste and season with salt and pepper. Serve over steamed white rice with lime wedges.

Mussels with Chorizo and Slow-Roasted Tomatoes

Start to finish: 45 minutes / Servings: 4

---

4 ounces Spanish chorizo, halved lengthwise and sliced into ½-inch pieces

3 tablespoons extra-virgin olive oil

1 small red onion, halved and thinly sliced

1 small fennel bulb, halved, cored and thinly sliced crosswise

8 medium garlic cloves, smashed and peeled

2 bay leaves

1 teaspoon fennel seeds

16 slow-roasted tomato halves, chopped (see headnote)

1½ cups dry vermouth

3 pounds blue mussels, scrubbed

4 tablespoons (½ stick) salted butter, chilled

½ cup chopped fresh flat-leaf parsley

1 tablespoon lemon juice

Kosher salt and ground black pepper

Mussels have a reputation as being tricky, but actually are quick and easy to cook. And they generate their own broth, producing maximum taste in minutes. Our take on mussels turns up the taste with Spanish chorizo, giving this dish smoky, savory flavor. Then we add our slow-roasted tomatoes (see recipe p. 634). If you don't want to make your own, substitute a 14½-ounce can of fire-roasted tomatoes with juice. Buy mussels from a reliable fishmonger and refrigerate them in a loosely covered colander set over a bowl. You may need to remove the "beard" from the mussels if they aren't cleaned already. Be sure to discard any mussels that are partially opened or broken. Larger mussels will take a bit longer to cook than smaller ones. Keep a close eye on the mussels; once they start to open, take them off the burner to finish cooking in the residual heat. When buying chorizo for this recipe look for Spanish style, which is cured, smoked and quite firm. Mexican chorizo is soft and crumbles easily. Our favorite brand is Palacios, which is available at many grocers or online. We liked the mussels served with crusty bread and extra-virgin olive oil.

Don't fully cook the mussels on the stove. They continue to cook as they sit off the heat.

1. **In a large pot over medium,** cook the chorizo in the olive oil until the chorizo begins to brown, about 3 minutes. Stir in the onion, fennel, garlic, bay leaves and fennel seeds. Cover and cook until the onion softens, about 5 minutes. Stir in the tomatoes, vermouth and ½ cup water, then bring to a simmer. Cover and cook, stirring occasionally, until the fennel is tender, about 7 minutes.

2. **Add the mussels and stir.** Cover and cook until the mussels just begin to open, about 3 minutes. Remove the pot from the heat and let the mussels continue to cook, covered, until all mussels open, another 3 to 5 minutes, quickly stirring once halfway through.

3. **Using a kitchen spider or slotted spoon,** transfer the mussels to a serving platter, leaving the sauce in the pot. Discard any unopened mussels. Return the sauce to a simmer over low, then remove from the heat. Whisk in the butter until melted. Stir in the parsley and lemon juice. Taste and season with salt and pepper. Pour the sauce over the mussels.

Oven-Poached Salmon with Thyme, Dill and Vermouth

Start to finish: 1½ hours / Servings: 8

½ cup soy sauce

3½- to 4-pound salmon fillet, skin on, pin bones removed

2 medium carrots, finely chopped

1 celery stalk, finely chopped

1 shallot, thinly sliced

8 sprigs fresh thyme

8 sprigs fresh dill, plus 3 teaspoons minced, divided

Kosher salt and ground black pepper

1 cup dry vermouth

2 tablespoons salted butter

1 tablespoon lemon juice

Lemon wedges, to serve

Ideal for a crowd, a side of salmon is an impressive main course that's as good at room temperature as it is hot from the oven. Trouble is, it can be difficult to cook without drying out and often is flavorless. Our inspiration for a better way came from an oven-poaching method we learned from French chef Michel Bras. He slow cooks smaller cuts of salmon in a 250°F oven over a water-filled baking pan. To adapt the technique for a larger side of salmon, we ratcheted up the heat; surrounded the fish with carrots, celery, shallot and a bit of vermouth; and covered it all tightly with foil. This allowed the salmon to steam and infuse with flavor while cooking faster and staying tender. And for even more flavor, we start by soaking the salmon briefly in soy sauce. A fillet between 1½ and 1¾ inches thick worked best. We found temperature was a better indicator for doneness than cooking time. To test the salmon's temperature, carefully peel back the foil just enough to insert a digital thermometer at the thickest end. The best way to perfectly cook this dish was to remove it from the oven a little before the salmon was fully cooked. The residual heat gently finished the cooking.

Don't marinate the salmon longer than 20 minutes. The soy sauce adds an earthy dimension to the salmon's flavor, but if left too long its saltiness will become overpowering.

---

1. **Heat the oven to 500°F** with a rack in the middle position. Pour the soy sauce into a baking dish large enough to fit the salmon. Add the fish, flesh side down. Marinate for 15 to 20 minutes.

2. **Meanwhile, in a bowl** toss the carrots, celery, shallot, thyme, 8 dill sprigs and 1 teaspoon salt. Set aside. Fold an 18-inch-long sheet of foil lengthwise into a strip wide enough for the salmon to fit on. Lightly coat the foil with oil, then place it, oiled side up, in the center of a rimmed baking sheet. Arrange the carrot-celery mixture around the outside edges of the foil. Drizzle the vegetables with the vermouth. Place the salmon on the foil, flesh side up. Season with pepper.

3. **Cover the entire pan tightly with foil,** allowing it to dome over the salmon. Roast until the salmon registers 120°F, 20 to 25 minutes. Remove the pan from the oven, keeping the foil in place, and let the salmon rest until it is between 125°F and 130°F, another 5 to 8 minutes. Remove the top foil, then use the foil under the salmon to lift and transfer it to a serving platter. Let cool for 5 minutes.

4. **Meanwhile, strain the liquid** and solids on the baking sheet into a saucepan. Discard the solids and all but ¾ cup of the liquid. Over medium heat, bring the liquid to a simmer. Off the heat, stir in the butter, lemon juice and 1 teaspoon of the minced dill. Season with salt and pepper. Pour 3 tablespoons of the sauce over the salmon. Sprinkle the remaining 2 teaspoons dill over the salmon. Serve with lemon wedges and the remaining sauce.

Salmon Packets with Chermoula

Start to finish: 50 minutes (15 minutes active) / Servings: 4

Four 6-ounce center-cut
skinless salmon fillets
(1 to 1¼ inches thick)

Kosher salt and ground
black pepper

1 teaspoon extra-virgin olive oil

Chermoula sauce, to serve
(see sidebar)

Lemon wedges, to serve

Cooking salmon can be a conundrum. Cook it long enough to brown the skin and the inside becomes dry and over-cooked. Take it off the heat sooner and the flesh is tender but wanly unappetizing. To get our salmon both browned and delectably moist we use the classic French method of cooking food in a sealed packet. The packet traps the natural moisture of the food inside, puffing impressively and steaming the dish in its own juices. Known as cooking en papillote, variations of the technique, such as cooking food wrapped in leaves, husks or even paper bags, exist around the world. But there's one drawback: The results can be bland because browning—the source of rich caramelized flavors—occurs only above 300°F. But steaming (which is the cooking that occurs inside a packet) never gets above 212°F. So we borrowed a varia-tion we'd seen French chef and restaurateur Jean-Georges Vongerichten use—foil. Encasing a salmon fillet in a foil packet that is cooked on the stovetop allowed us to both brown (because of the direct heat beneath the fish) and steam (because of the trapped moisture) the fish. Six-ounce fillets were the perfect size; if the fillets were thinner than 1 inch or thicker than 1¼ inches, we needed to adjust the cooking time.

Don't hesitate to remove the packet from the skillet a little early if you think it's cooking too quickly. It's easy to return it to the skillet.

1. Remove the salmon from the refrigerator and let sit at room temperature for 20 to 30 minutes.

2. Pat the salmon dry with paper towels and season with salt and pepper. Place a 12-by-24-inch sheet of foil on the counter, shiny side down. Fold in half to form a 12-inch square. Unfold the foil and spread oil evenly over half of it (one 12-inch square), leaving a 3-inch border.

3. Arrange the salmon fillets over the oiled area, leaving at least ½ inch between them. Fold the top square of foil over the salmon and, without pressing down on the fillets, roll and crimp the open sides to create an airtight packet. Fold in the corners of the packet to help it fit in the pan.

4. Heat a 12-inch skillet over high heat for 5 minutes. Carefully place the packet in the skillet and cook 5 minutes for medium and 6 minutes for medium-well, rotating the pan frequently to ensure even cooking. The packet should begin puffing after 2 minutes and be fully inflated after 4 minutes. If the bottom edges of the packet start lifting up, reduce the heat slightly.

5. Using tongs, slide the packet onto a platter and let sit for 1 min-ute. Carefully open the packet. Spoon the accumulated juices over the salmon and serve topped with chermoula and lemon wedges.

CHERMOULA SAUCE

Start to finish: 10 minutes
Makes enough to top 4 salmon fillets

1 cup lightly packed fresh flat-leaf parsley

2 tablespoons pine nuts, toasted

2 teaspoons grated lemon zest

1 large garlic clove

1 teaspoon ground coriander

1 teaspoon sweet paprika

½ teaspoon kosher salt

½ teaspoon ground cardamom

¼ teaspoon red pepper flakes (optional)

3 tablespoons extra-virgin olive oil

In a food processor, combine all ingredients but the oil. Process until finely ground, about 20 seconds. Scrape down the bowl, add the oil, then process until incorporated, about 10 seconds.

Chicken

9

Chinese White-Cooked Chicken with Ginger-Soy Dressing

Start to finish: 2 hours (30 minutes active) / Servings: 4

For the chicken and poaching broth:

3½- to 4-pound chicken, giblets discarded

1 bunch fresh cilantro

6 scallions, trimmed and halved crosswise

4½ quarts water

2 cups dry sherry or mirin

4-inch piece fresh ginger, cut into 4 pieces and smashed

2 tablespoons kosher salt

For the dressing:

4 scallions, thinly sliced on diagonal

3 tablespoons soy sauce

2 tablespoons grapeseed or other neutral oil

4 teaspoons finely grated fresh ginger

1 tablespoon unseasoned rice vinegar

1 tablespoon toasted sesame oil

½ teaspoon white sugar

½ pound (½ small head) napa or savoy cabbage, thinly sliced (4 cups)

Cooked white rice, to serve (optional)

It's easy to take a skin-deep approach to chicken, paying lots of attention to getting a golden brown crust only to end up with dull, bland—and too often overcooked—meat. We avoid that trap by adopting the Chinese technique of whole-bird poaching to create a chicken with simple, clean flavors and a silky, tender-but-firm meat primed for a variety of vibrant sauces. Simmered without soy sauce (and therefore white), the classic Cantonese dish is known as white-cooked or white-cut chicken. Poaching—in which the chicken is slowly cooked in liquid just below a simmer—delivers heat evenly, so no worries about dry breasts or pink thighs. The whole process takes about the same amount of time as roasting, most of it hands-off. In fact, the last 30 minutes of cooking occurs off the heat entirely. Poaching results in blond skin that you may wish to discard (though Chinese cooks leave it on and consider it perfectly tasty). The bright aromatics of raw scallions and ginger worked best in a soy sauce–based dressing, which we thinned with some of the poaching liquid.

Don't use cooking sherry for this recipe; it usually has added sodium and little, if any, actual sherry flavor. Look for a good-quality (but affordable) dry sherry.

---

1. Remove the chicken from the refrigerator and let sit at room temperature while making the broth. Reserving a few sprigs for garnish, cut the cilantro bunch in half crosswise, separating the stems and leaves. Use kitchen twine to tie the stems and scallions into a bundle. Chop enough of the cilantro leaves to measure ½ cup and set aside. (The remaining cilantro leaves are not needed; save for another use.)

2. In a large pot (at least 8 quarts) over high, combine the cilantro-scallion bundle with the remaining broth ingredients and bring to a boil. Using tongs, lower the chicken into the broth breast side up, letting the liquid flow into the cavity. If the chicken isn't fully submerged in the broth after flooding the cavity, weigh it down with a plate.

3. Allow the broth to return to a boil, then reduce heat to medium and cook for 25 minutes, adjusting the heat to maintain a bare simmer; flip the chicken to be breast side down after 15 minutes. Turn off the heat, remove the pot from the burner and let the chicken sit in the hot broth for 30 minutes. Transfer the chicken to a carving board and let rest for 15 minutes.

4. While the chicken rests, prepare the dressing. In a small bowl, stir together ¼ cup of the poaching broth, the scallions, soy sauce, grapeseed oil, ginger, vinegar, sesame oil and sugar.

5. Using a sharp knife, remove the legs from the chicken by cutting through the thigh joints, then separate the thighs from the drumsticks. Carve the breast meat from the bone and slice each breast crosswise into 4 pieces. Discard the chicken skin, if desired. Spread the cabbage on a serving platter, then arrange the chicken pieces on top. Pour the dressing over the chicken and sprinkle with the reserved ½ cup chopped cilantro. Garnish with cilantro sprigs.

DON'T TOSS YOUR POACHING BROTH

While the poached chicken cools before carving, use the hot, seasoned broth to cook rice to round out the meal. Use the broth 1:1 for any water called for by the variety of rice you use. For long-grain white rice, for example, combine 1½ cups rinsed rice with 2 cups of the broth. Bring to a simmer, then reduce heat to low, cover and cook until the rice is fluffy and tender, 15 to 18 minutes. And be sure to save any remaining broth for use in rice, soup, sauces and braises. We freeze it in 2-cup portions in zip-close freezer bags.

Chiang Mai Chicken (Gai Yang)

Start to finish: 3 hours (20 minutes active) / Servings: 4

1 cup lightly packed fresh cilantro leaves and tender stems

½ cup fish sauce

½ cup soy sauce

¼ cup packed light brown sugar

1 stalk lemon grass, trimmed to lower 6 inches, dry outer layers discarded, chopped

4 medium garlic cloves, smashed and peeled

1 tablespoon coriander seeds

1 tablespoon black peppercorns

1 teaspoon white peppercorns

Two 10- to 12-ounce whole chicken legs

Two 10- to 12-ounce bone-in, skin-on chicken breasts, ribs trimmed

1 cup kosher salt

Lime wedges, to serve (optional)

We first tried this chicken at a sidewalk restaurant in Chiang Mai in northern Thailand. The spatchcocked birds were stuck with two bamboo skewers set in a V shape that were used first to turn the chicken, then to elevate it above the heat. The chicken had started the day before with a marinade of fish sauce, coconut milk, lemon grass, crushed coriander and peppercorns, garlic, cilantro root and palm sugar. The marinade had actually flavored the chicken, a rare event. The barbecue sauce was another surprise, a tamarind-based concoction that included dried chilies, galangal (a relative of ginger), salt and more fish sauce. Our version uses brown sugar in place of harder-to-find palm sugar. We opted for the ease of chicken parts; you can buy leg quarters and breasts. Use four whole legs or four split breasts, or break down a whole chicken. Lemon grass added bright, citrusy flavor that's characteristic of Thai food. The lemon grass paste sold in tubes near the fresh herbs worked in a pinch; substitute 2 tablespoons of paste for the fresh lemon grass. Cooking the chicken over a bed of salt prevented the marinade from burning as it dripped off the chicken. While a simple squeeze of lime was enough to dress the meat, we also liked dipping it in tangy tamarind (p. 613) or chili-lime sauce (see sidebar).

Don't marinate the chicken longer than two hours. The salt in the marinade can toughen the meat and overwhelm its flavor.

1. In a blender, combine the cilantro, fish sauce, soy sauce, sugar, lemon grass, garlic, coriander and both peppercorns. Blend until smooth, about 1 minute. Reserve ¼ cup of the marinade for the glaze.

2. Place the chicken in a large zip-close plastic bag. Pour in the remaining marinade and seal. Set in a bowl and refrigerate for 2 hours.

3. Heat the oven to 400°F with a rack in the middle position. Line a rimmed baking sheet with foil and spread the salt over it. Mist a wire rack with cooking spray, then set over the salt. Arrange the chicken on the rack. Bake for 30 minutes.

4. Brush the chicken with the reserved marinade and continue to bake until the thighs register 175°F and the breasts register 160°F, another 10 to 15 minutes. Transfer the chicken to a carving board and let rest for 15 minutes. Serve with lime wedges or dipping sauce, if desired.

CHILI-LIME DIPPING SAUCE

Start to finish: 5 minutes
Makes about ¾ cup

Chili-garlic sauce has a coarser texture, fuller body and more pronounced garlic flavor than Sriracha. Look for it in the grocer's Asian foods aisle.

½ cup lime juice (4 to 6 limes)

3 tablespoons fish sauce

2 tablespoons packed light brown sugar

2 teaspoons chili-garlic sauce

In a bowl, stir together all ingredients until the sugar dissolves. Use immediately or refrigerate for up to 3 days.

Japanese Fried Chicken (Karaage)

Start to finish: 1 hour 45 minutes (15 minutes active), plus resting / Servings: 4

For the chicken:

3-ounce piece unpeeled fresh ginger, coarsely grated

¼ cup sake

¼ cup tamari

1 tablespoon grated lemon zest

2 pounds boneless, skinless chicken thighs, trimmed and cut into thirds

2 cups cornstarch

1 tablespoon shichimi togarashi (or 1 teaspoon red pepper flakes)

1 teaspoon ground black pepper

2 quarts peanut or vegetable oil

For the dipping sauce:

¼ cup tamari

¼ cup unseasoned rice vinegar

1 teaspoon finely grated peeled fresh ginger

¼ teaspoon toasted sesame oil

We found a better way to make fried chicken in karaage (kah-rah-ah-gay), the Japanese bite-sized fried chicken that starts with a zesty marinade and is coated with potato starch or potato flour, which creates a thin, crispy crust. We chose boneless, skinless chicken thighs and soaked them briefly in a slurry featuring fresh ginger. We also used tamari, a Japanese soy sauce. Tamari has a bolder flavor and darker color than Chinese-style soy sauces, but if you can't find it any soy sauce will work. For our coating, we tried potato starch, which was good but tricky to work with. Cornstarch proved easier to handle—and find at the store—and produced good results. A large Dutch oven, at least 7 quarts, was essential for frying. We finished with a dipping sauce that mirrored the marinade with tamari, unseasoned rice vinegar, grated fresh ginger and toasted sesame oil.

Don't let the chicken sit for longer than an hour after coating it before frying. It will get gummy.

1. To make the chicken, gather the ginger in your hands and squeeze as much juice as possible into a large bowl. Add the ginger solids to the bowl and stir in the sake, tamari and lemon zest. Add the chicken and stir to coat. Refrigerate for at least 30 minutes or up to 1 hour.

2. Set a wire rack in a rimmed baking sheet. In a large bowl, combine the cornstarch, shichimi togarashi and pepper. Working 1 piece at a time, remove the chicken from the marinade, letting excess drip off, then dredge in the cornstarch mixture, pressing evenly to adhere on all sides. Transfer to the rack and refrigerate, uncovered, for at least 30 minutes and up to 1 hour.

3. In a 7-quart Dutch oven, heat the oil to 375°F. Add a third of the chicken to the hot oil and fry, stirring to prevent sticking, until the chicken is deep golden brown, 5 to 7 minutes. Transfer the chicken to a clean wire rack, return the oil to 375°F and repeat twice with the remaining chicken.

4. For the dipping sauce, whisk together all ingredients.

Three-Cup Chicken

Start to finish: **35 minutes (15 minutes active)** / Servings: 4

Taiwanese three-cup chicken is named for the formula once used to prepare the dish: one cup each of sesame oil, soy sauce and rice wine. Not surprisingly, recipes no longer adhere to that ratio, but the name has stuck. Bone-in chicken legs that have been hacked into pieces are traditional for this one-pan dish; we opted for boneless, skinless chicken thighs for easier prep and eating. Though we prefer to use a wok, this recipe also works in a 12-inch skillet. Serve with rice and steamed or stir-fried vegetables.

Don't begin cooking until all ingredients are prepared; the dish comes together quickly. Don't stir the chicken for about 5 minutes after adding it to the skillet. This helps the chicken brown and develop flavor.

1. In a small bowl, stir together the cornstarch and soy sauce, then stir in the sake and sugar until the sugar has dissolved. Set aside. Heat a 14-inch wok over medium-high for about 3 minutes, or until a drop of water evaporates within 1 to 2 seconds of contact. Add the grapeseed oil and swirl to coat. Add the chicken in an even layer and cook without stirring until browned, about 5 minutes.

2. Add the garlic and cook, stirring occasionally, until the garlic is well-browned and softened, about 4 minutes. Add the scallions, chili, ginger and sesame oil, then cook, stirring constantly, until the scallions begin to wilt, about 1 minute.

3. Stir the sake-cornstarch mixture to recombine, then add to the wok. Cook, stirring constantly, until the sauce has thickened, about 3 minutes. Off heat, add the basil and stir until it begins to wilt, about 30 seconds. Sprinkle with sesame seeds.

2 teaspoons cornstarch

3 tablespoons soy sauce

¾ cup sake

2 tablespoons packed brown sugar

1 tablespoon grapeseed or other neutral oil

2 pounds boneless, skinless chicken thighs, trimmed, patted dry and cut into 1-inch-wide strips

12 medium garlic cloves, halved lengthwise

1 bunch scallions, cut into 1-inch lengths

1 serrano chili, stemmed and sliced into thin rounds

¼ cup minced fresh ginger

2 tablespoons toasted sesame oil

3 cups lightly packed fresh basil, torn if large

Sesame seeds, to serve

Sumac-Spiced Chicken (Musakhan)

Start to finish: 1 hour 15 minutes / Servings: 4

Sumac is the secret to this dish, a lesson we learned from a young Palestinian named Nadir, who showed us how to make musakhan in a kitchen in downtown West Ramullah. He used a generous amount of the deep-red spice, as do we; its tart, citrusy flavor balances the sweetness of the sautéed onion and the rich pine nuts. Look for sumac in well-stocked grocery stores, spice shops and Middle Eastern markets; it also can be ordered online.

Don't skip the tahini for drizzling at the table. Its nutty flavor and richness perfectly complement the chicken. And don't forget to stir the tahini well before serving.

2 pounds boneless, skinless chicken thighs, trimmed

Kosher salt and ground black pepper

6 tablespoons extra-virgin olive oil, divided

½ cup pine nuts, toasted, divided

1 large yellow onion, halved lengthwise and thinly sliced

4 medium garlic cloves, thinly sliced

4 tablespoons ground sumac, divided

2 teaspoons sweet paprika

Four 8-inch pita bread rounds

½ cup lightly packed flat-leaf parsley, chopped

Tahini, to serve

1. **Pat the chicken dry,** then season with salt and pepper. In a large Dutch oven over medium-high, heat 1 tablespoon of oil until barely smoking. Add half the chicken in a single layer and cook until well browned, 5 to 7 minutes. Transfer to a bowl. Repeat with 1 tablespoon of the remaining oil and the remaining chicken. Set aside.

2. **Chop ¼ cup of the pine nuts and set aside.** In the Dutch oven over medium, heat 2 tablespoons of the remaining oil. Add the onion and cook, stirring, until softened slightly, about 5 minutes. Add the garlic, chopped pine nuts, 3 tablespoons of sumac and the paprika. Cook, stirring, until fragrant, 30 to 60 seconds. Add 3 cups water, stir and bring to a simmer. Return the chicken to the pot. Cover, reduce to medium-low and simmer until a skewer inserted into the chicken meets no resistance, 25 to 30 minutes.

3. **Meanwhile, heat the oven to 450°F** with a rack in the middle position. Use a slotted spoon to transfer the chicken to a bowl, then use 2 forks to shred the meat. Bring the liquid in the pot to a simmer over medium-high. Cook, stirring, until most of the liquid has evaporated, 10 to 15 minutes. Return the chicken to the pot and stir in the remaining ¼ cup whole pine nuts. Taste and season with salt and pepper. Cover and set aside.

4. **Brush the pita on both sides** with the remaining 2 tablespoons oil and arrange the rounds on a rimmed baking sheet. Bake until warm and soft, 5 to 7 minutes. Sprinkle the pita with the remaining 1 tablespoon sumac, cut each in half and transfer to a platter. Stir the parsley into the chicken. Drizzle with tahini and serve with the pita.

Za'atar-Roasted Chicken

Start to finish: **50 minutes** / Servings: 4

Za'atar is a Middle Eastern blend of herbs and sesame seeds; look for it in well-stocked markets, Middle Eastern grocery stores or online. We mix za'atar with dried oregano to boost its herbal flavor. Use chicken breasts, legs, thighs or a combination.

Don't use a roasting pan. The low sides of a sturdy rimmed baking sheet allow the chicken to cook quickly and brown evenly.

1. Heat the oven to 450°F with a rack in the middle position. In a small bowl, combine the za'atar, dried oregano, sugar, 1 tablespoon salt and 2 teaspoons pepper.

2. Place the chicken parts on a rimmed baking sheet and evenly season both sides with the za'atar mixture. Place the garlic cloves in a single layer down the center of the baking sheet, then arrange the chicken parts, skin up, around the garlic; this prevents the garlic from scorching during roasting.

3. Roast the chicken until the thickest part of the breast (if using) reaches 160°F and the thickest part of the largest thigh/leg (if using) reaches 175°F, 30 to 40 minutes. Transfer the chicken to a platter; leave the garlic on the baking sheet.

4. Using a fork, mash the garlic to a paste on the baking sheet. Carefully pour ⅓ cup water onto the baking sheet and use a wooden spoon to scrape up any browned bits. Pour the mixture into a small bowl and whisk in the lemon zest and juice, oil and fresh oregano. Taste and season with salt and pepper. Serve the sauce with the chicken.

3 tablespoons za'atar seasoning

2 teaspoons dried oregano

1¼ teaspoons white sugar

Kosher salt and ground black pepper

3 pounds bone-in, skin-on chicken parts, trimmed and patted dry

10 medium garlic cloves, peeled

1 tablespoon finely grated lemon zest, plus ¼ cup lemon juice

2 tablespoons extra-virgin olive oil

2 tablespoons minced fresh oregano

Chicken Teriyaki Rice Bowls (Teriyaki Donburi)

Start to finish: **40 minutes** / Servings: 4

Contrary to popular belief, "teriyaki" refers not to a sauce, but a technique. Meat is seared or broiled, then given a lustrous shine with a glaze of soy, mirin and sugar. In this recipe, our adaptation of one taught to us by Japanese cooking expert Elizabeth Andoh, chicken thighs are briefly marinated and tossed with a little cornstarch before they're cooked in a skillet. "Donburi" refers to deep, usually ceramic, bowls, as well as to the food typically served in those bowls—rice with various toppings. To complement the chicken and add texture and freshness to the donburi we also throw together a simple cabbage slaw.

Don't forget to drain the chicken before coating it with corn-starch. Excess liquid will cause splattering during cooking.

4 tablespoons sake, divided

4 tablespoons plus
1 teaspoon soy sauce, divided

1½ pounds boneless, skinless chicken thighs, trimmed and cut into 1-inch pieces

¼ cup mirin

2 teaspoons white sugar

1 tablespoon finely grated fresh ginger

1½ cups finely shredded green cabbage

3 medium scallions, thinly sliced on the diagonal

2 teaspoons unseasoned rice vinegar

¼ teaspoon toasted sesame oil

2 tablespoons cornstarch

4 teaspoons grapeseed or other neutral oil, divided

3 cups cooked Japanese-style short-grain rice, hot

1. In a medium bowl, whisk together 3 tablespoons of sake and 1 teaspoon of soy sauce. Add the chicken and toss. Let stand at room temperature for 20 minutes or cover and refrigerate for up to 2 hours. Meanwhile, in a small saucepan over medium, combine the remaining 1 tablespoon sake, 3 tablespoons of the remaining soy sauce, the mirin and sugar. Cook, stirring, until the sugar is dissolved, about 1 minute. Off heat, stir in the ginger; set aside.

2. In a medium bowl, toss the cabbage and scallions with the remaining 1 tablespoon soy sauce, the rice vinegar and sesame oil. Set aside. Drain the chicken in a fine-mesh strainer. Wipe out the bowl, then return the chicken to it. Sprinkle with the cornstarch and toss to coat.

3. In a 12-inch nonstick skillet over medium-high, heat 2 tea-spoons of grapeseed oil until barely smoking. Add half the chicken in an even layer and cook without stirring until well browned on the bottom and the edges turn opaque, 3 to 4 minutes. Flip and cook without stirring until well browned on the second side, about another 3 minutes. Transfer to a clean bowl and repeat with the remaining 2 teaspoons oil and remaining chicken.

4. Wipe out the skillet, then return the chicken to the pan. Pour in the soy sauce–ginger mixture and stir to coat. Cook over medium-high, stirring, until the liquid is syrupy and the chicken is glazed, about 2 minutes. Remove from the heat. Divide the rice among 4 bowls. Top with the cabbage mixture and chicken.

North African Chicken Couscous

Start to finish: 1 hour 15 minutes (30 minutes active)
Servings: 6

2 cups couscous

4 tablespoons extra-virgin olive oil, divided, plus extra to serve

Kosher salt and ground black pepper

1½ tablespoons ground turmeric

2 pounds boneless, skinless chicken thighs, trimmed and halved crosswise

1 pound Yukon Gold potatoes, cut into 1½-inch chunks

6 medium carrots, peeled, halved lengthwise and cut into 2-inch pieces

1 large red onion, root end intact, peeled and cut into 8 wedges

2 jalapeño chilies, stemmed and sliced into thin rounds

6 medium garlic cloves, minced

2 tablespoons tomato paste

½ cup harissa paste, divided (see headnote)

Lemon wedges, to serve

We got an education in couscous in Tunisia, including a lesson from Amel Cherif, a home cook, who showed us the basics of making couscous light and flavorful at her apartment on the outskirts of Tunis. For our version, we use an 8-quart pot fitted with a stackable steamer insert that sits on top. If you don't own one, a large pot and a folding steamer basket worked well, too. Whisking the liquid from the stew into the steamed couscous is a key step, deeply flavoring the grain-like pasta and helping it stay light, fluffy and distinct. We especially liked this dish made with our homemade harissa (see recipe p. 618). Among store-bought brands, we preferred DEA, which is sold in a tube and in cans. We start the recipe using ¼ cup of harissa to flavor the stew, then finish by mixing another ¼ cup into the stew liquid just before whisking it with the steamed couscous. If your harissa is particularly spicy or you prefer less heat, reduce the second addition of harissa.

Don't worry about the couscous falling through the steamer basket holes. The lightly oiled, partially hydrated specks hold together enough that they won't fall through. Also, don't stir the stew during simmering. The vegetables better retain their shape and flavor when cooked on top of the chicken, rather than submerged in liquid.

1. In a medium bowl, combine the couscous and 2 tablespoons of oil, rubbing with your fingers until the couscous is evenly coated. Stir in 1¼ cups water and ¾ teaspoon salt. Let stand for 15 minutes.

2. Meanwhile, in a medium bowl, stir together the turmeric and 1 teaspoon each salt and pepper. Add the chicken and toss. Set aside for 15 minutes. In a large bowl, combine the potatoes, carrots, onion, 1 tablespoon of the remaining oil and 1 teaspoon each salt and pepper. Toss, then set aside.

3. Stir the couscous to separate the granules, then mound it in a steamer insert or basket that fits onto or into an 8-quart pot. Set aside. Set the pot over medium-high, then heat the remaining 1 tablespoon oil until barely smoking. Add the jalapeños and cook, stirring, until slightly softened, about 1 minute. Add the garlic, tomato paste and ¼ cup of the harissa and cook, stirring, until beginning to brown, 1 to 2 minutes.

4. Add 2 cups water and bring to a simmer. Place the chicken in the pot in an even layer, then top with the vegetables and any liquid in the bowl; do not stir. Bring to a simmer, then set the steamer insert with the couscous on the pot; if using a folding steamer basket, set it directly on the vegetables. Cover, reduce to low and cook at a gentle simmer until the chicken and vegetables are tender, about 45 minutes; do not stir the couscous or the stew.

5. Remove the steamer basket and transfer the couscous to a large bowl; cover with foil. Stir the vegetables and chicken, cover and let stand 5 minutes.

6. Use a slotted spoon to transfer the chicken and vegetables to a large bowl; taste and season with salt and pepper. Measure out 2 cups of the cooking liquid from the pot, add the remaining ¼ cup harissa to it and stir to combine.

7. Whisk the couscous until no clumps remain, then whisk in the cooking liquid-harissa mixture. Taste and season with salt and pepper. Transfer to a large, deep platter and make a well in the center. Spoon the chicken and vegetables into the well. Drizzle with oil and serve with lemon wedges.

Piri Piri Chicken

Start to finish: 2½ hours (30 minutes active) / Servings: 4

3 tablespoons New Mexico or California chili powder

1 tablespoon ground cumin

1 tablespoon ground coriander

1 tablespoon sweet paprika

Kosher salt

4- to 4½-pound whole chicken, spatchcocked (see instructions pp. 282-283)

2 tablespoons white sugar

8 medium Fresno chilies, stemmed and quartered (see headnote)

3 medium garlic cloves, peeled

⅓ cup lemon juice

¼ cup red wine vinegar

1 cup lightly packed fresh cilantro, finely chopped

Piri piri can refer to a finger-staining chili pepper sauce—usually spiked with garlic, sugar and plenty of cayenne, lemon and paprika—or to whatever the sauce douses. Its origins are Portuguese, but today it is found in South Africa, Mozambique and Namibia. Ancho, chipotle and regular chili powders tasted off in this recipe, but New Mexico or California chili powders worked well. If you can't find either, purchase whole chilies, toast and seed them, then finely grind them. Or simply leave out the chili powder and increase the paprika to ¼ cup. Fresno chilies are fresh red chilies similar in size and shape to jalapeños, but with pointy tips; if they are unavailable, fresh cherry peppers work well, too.

Don't reduce the number of fresh chilies in the sauce; all eight were needed for flavor and color. For milder heat, remove some or all of the seeds and ribs before processing.

ON THE GRILL:

1. In a medium bowl, mix together the chili powder, cumin, coriander, paprika and 1½ tablespoons salt. Transfer 2 tablespoons of the mixture to a small bowl, setting the rest aside. Loosen the skin over the chicken's breast and thighs by gently working your fingers between the skin and flesh. Using a small spoon, evenly distribute the 2 tablespoons of spice mixture under the skin, then rub it into the flesh. Set the chicken on a baking sheet.

2. In a food processor, combine the reserved spice mixture, the sugar, chilies and garlic. Pulse until finely chopped, scraping the bowl as needed. With the machine running, add the lemon juice and vinegar; process until smooth, scraping the bowl once or twice. Measure out ¼ cup of the sauce, reserving the rest for later, and brush evenly over the chicken, including the bone side. Let stand at room temperature for 45 minutes to 1 hour.

3. Meanwhile, prepare a grill for indirect, high-heat cooking. For a charcoal grill, spread a large chimney of hot coals evenly over one side of the grill bed; open the bottom grill vents. For a gas grill, set half of the burners to high. Heat the grill, covered, for 5 to 10 minutes, then clean and oil the cooking grate.

4. Set the chicken skin side up on the cooler side of the grill. Cover and cook for 25 minutes. Using tongs, rotate the chicken 180 degrees to bring the far side of the chicken closest to the heat. Cover and continue to cook until a skewer inserted into the thickest part of the breast meets no resistance or until the thickest part of the breast reaches 160°F and the thighs reach 175°F, another 25 to 35 minutes.

5. Brush the chicken with 2 tablespoons of the reserved sauce, then use tongs to flip it skin side down onto the hot side of the grill. Cook until the skin is lightly charred, 1 to 2 minutes. Transfer skin side up to a cutting board and let rest for 10 minutes. Stir the cilantro into the remaining sauce, then baste the chicken once more. Serve with the sauce on the side.

OVEN-COOKING METHOD:

Heat the oven to 425°F with a rack in the middle position. Line a rimmed baking sheet with foil and spread 1 cup kosher salt over it. Mist a wire rack with cooking spray, then set over the salt. Arrange the seasoned, sauce-brushed chicken skin side up on the rack and let stand at room temperature for 45 minutes to 1 hour. Roast the chicken until well browned, 45 to 50 minutes. Brush with 2 tablespoons of the reserved sauce, then continue to roast until a skewer inserted into the thickest part of the breast meets no resistance or the thickest part of the breast reaches 160°F and the thighs reach 175°F, another 10 to 15 minutes. Remove from the oven and let rest for 10 minutes. Stir the cilantro into the remaining sauce, then baste the chicken once more. Serve with the sauce on the side.

Cape Malay Chicken Curry

Start to finish: 1 hour / Servings: 6

___

1 tablespoon fennel seeds

1 tablespoon cumin seeds

1 teaspoon ground turmeric

Kosher salt and ground black pepper

2 pounds boneless, skinless chicken thighs, trimmed

2 tablespoons grapeseed or other neutral oil

2 medium yellow onions, chopped

4-ounce piece fresh ginger, peeled and cut into 5 pieces

4 medium garlic cloves, minced

2 serrano chilies, stemmed and halved lengthwise

2 cups low-sodium chicken broth or water

1 pint grape or cherry tomatoes

Two 3-inch cinnamon sticks

2 bay leaves

1 pound Yukon Gold potatoes, cut into 1-inch cubes

2 tablespoons lemon juice, plus lemon wedges, to serve

½ cup lightly packed fresh mint, torn

Cooked basmati or jasmine rice, to serve

Lemony and richly savory, Cape Malay curry is a chicken and vegetable one-pot dish from South Africa. Its ingredients are similar to those in Indian curries, but the techniques are different, creating a refreshingly light curry. Spices aren't ground but are dropped whole into the broth and often discarded just before serving. We learned to make it from Faldela Tolker, who teaches Cape Malay cuisine in her home in Cape Town's Bo-Kaap neighborhood. Like Tolker, we built the flavor base of our Cape Malay curry on lightly browned onions. We also used whole fennel seeds and cumin seeds, allowing them to add both texture and flavor. Tolker broke down a whole chicken for her dish, but we liked the ease of boneless, skinless thighs, which stay moist and taste richer than chicken breasts.

Don't forget to remove the ginger, cinnamon sticks, bay leaves and chili halves from the cooking liquid after removing the chicken. Also, don't cut the potatoes smaller than 1-inch chunks; smaller pieces will overcook and break apart. Finally, don't pull the chicken into fine shreds after simmering—the pieces should be bite-size.

1. **In a bowl,** mix the fennel, cumin, turmeric, 2 teaspoons salt and 1 teaspoon pepper. Using 1 tablespoon of this mixture, season the chicken on all sides.

2. **In a large Dutch oven** over medium-high, heat the oil until barely smoking. Add the onions and cook, stirring occasionally, until lightly browned, 8 to 10 minutes. Stir in the ginger, garlic and chilies, then cook, stirring, until fragrant, about 30 seconds. Stir in the broth or water, tomatoes, cinnamon sticks, bay leaves and remaining spice mixture, then add the chicken thighs, submerging them in the cooking liquid.

3. **Bring to a simmer,** then cover and cook for 25 minutes, adjusting the heat to maintain a steady but gentle simmer. Stir in the potatoes, cover and return to a simmer. Cook until the chicken and potatoes are tender, another 12 to 15 minutes.

4. **Using tongs,** transfer the chicken to a large plate. Remove and discard the ginger, cinnamon sticks, bay leaves and chili halves, then continue to simmer over medium until the liquid is slightly reduced, about 5 minutes.

5. **Meanwhile, using 2 forks,** pull the chicken into bite-size pieces. Return the chicken to the pot and stir to combine, taking care not to break up the potatoes. Stir in the lemon juice, then taste and season with salt and pepper. Transfer to a serving bowl and sprinkle with the mint. Serve with rice and lemon wedges.

Chicken en Cocotte

Start to finish: 1 hour 35 minutes (15 minutes active)
Servings: 4

___

4- to 4½-pound whole chicken, wings tucked and legs tied

Kosher salt and ground black pepper

5 tablespoons salted butter, divided

1 large yellow onion, peeled and cut into 8 wedges

8 medium garlic cloves, peeled and halved

1½ cups dry white wine

10 thyme sprigs

3 tablespoons lemon juice

2 tablespoons Dijon mustard

½ cup finely chopped fresh tarragon

There is little prep involved in this chicken en cocotte—or chicken in a pot—and most of the cooking is hands-off. Chicken en cocotte is a French classic; a cocotte is simply a covered oven-safe dish or casserole similar to a Dutch oven. We found that cooking the chicken breast side down in the pot allows the delicate white meat to gently poach in the wine while the legs cook up above, a technique that helps equalize the cooking of the white meat (done at 160°F) and dark meat (done between 175°F to 180°F). Allowing the chicken to rest breast side up after prevents the white meat from overcooking.

Don't use a Dutch oven smaller than 7 quarts or a chicken larger than 4½ pounds. If the bird fits too snugly, there won't be enough space for heat to circulate, hindering even cooking.

___

1. Heat the oven to 400°F with a rack in the lower-middle position. Using paper towels, pat the chicken dry then season with salt and pepper.

2. In a large Dutch oven over medium, melt 1 tablespoon of butter. Add the onion and garlic and cook until lightly browned, about 5 minutes. Add the wine and bring to a simmer. Lay the thyme sprigs on the onion mixture. Set the chicken, breast down, on the thyme and onions.

3. Cover and bake until a skewer inserted into the thickest part of the breast meets no resistance or the thickest part of the breast reaches 160°F and the thighs reach 175°F to 180°F, 55 to 65 minutes. Using tongs inserted into the cavity of the chicken, carefully transfer it to a large baking dish, turning it breast up. Let rest for at least 15 minutes.

4. Meanwhile, remove and discard the thyme sprigs. Tilt the pot to pool the liquid to one side and use a wide spoon to skim off and discard the fat. Bring to a simmer over medium and cook until thickened and reduced to about 1 cup (with solids), about 5 minutes. Off heat, whisk in the remaining 4 tablespoons butter, the lemon juice and mustard. Taste and season with salt and pepper.

5. Remove the legs from the chicken by cutting through the hip joints. Remove and discard the skin from the legs, then separate the thighs from the drumsticks. Remove the breast meat from the bone, remove and discard the skin, then cut each breast crosswise into thin slices. Arrange the chicken on a platter. Transfer the sauce to a bowl, stir in the tarragon and serve with the chicken.

Crispy Sichuan-Chili Chicken

Start to finish: 1 hour / Servings: 4

⅓ cup soy sauce

3 tablespoons unseasoned rice vinegar

4 tablespoons white sugar, divided

2 large egg whites, lightly beaten

2 pounds boneless, skinless chicken thighs, trimmed and cut into 1-inch pieces

2 cups cornstarch

¼ cup Sichuan peppercorns, toasted and finely ground

Kosher salt

2 quarts peanut oil

6 tablespoons Sichuan chili oil, plus extra to serve (see recipe p. 271)

8 scallions, thinly sliced

1 tablespoon Sichuan seasoning salt, plus extra to serve (see recipe p. 271)

1 cup lightly packed fresh cilantro

La zi ji (which translates from the Mandarin as chicken with chilies) is a traditional Sichuan dish that gets some of its kick from Sichuan peppercorns, which lend a citrusy, floral note followed by tingling—but not eye-watering—heat. To toast the peppercorns, heat them in a small skillet over medium. Cook, shaking the pan, until fragrant, about 2 minutes. Transfer to a bowl and let cool, then finely grind. We used the peppercorns in a light, cornstarch-based coating that added crunch and flavor to briefly marinated chicken thighs. For additional heat, we made our own chili oil from Sichuan chili flakes, more peppercorns and whole dried red Sichuan chilies. Tailor the heat of this dish by using more or less of the chili oil.

Don't marinate the chicken longer than 30 minutes or it will be too salty.

1. **In a large bowl,** combine the soy sauce, vinegar, 2 tablespoons of sugar and the egg whites. Stir until the sugar dissolves. Stir in the chicken, cover and marinate at room temperature, 20 to 30 minutes. Meanwhile, set a wire rack in a rimmed baking sheet. In a large bowl, mix the remaining 2 tablespoons sugar, the cornstarch, Sichuan pepper and 2 teaspoons salt.

2. **Drain the chicken in a colander.** Add ⅓ of the chicken to the cornstarch mixture and toss to coat, pressing the pieces into the cornstarch. Transfer to a mesh strainer and shake to remove excess cornstarch. Transfer to the prepared rack in a single layer. Repeat with the remaining chicken and cornstarch mixture.

3. **Set another wire rack** in a rimmed baking sheet. In a large Dutch oven over medium-high, heat the peanut oil to 350°F. Add half of the coated chicken and cook, stirring occasionally, until well browned, about 5 minutes. Using a slotted spoon, transfer to the second rack. Allow the oil to return to 350°F, then repeat with the remaining chicken.

4. **In a small microwave-safe bowl** or glass measuring cup, microwave the Sichuan chili oil on high until just warm, about 30 seconds. Combine the chicken and scallions in a large bowl, sprinkle with the seasoning salt and drizzle with the warm chili oil, then toss to coat. Add the cilantro and toss again, then transfer to a platter. Serve with additional chili oil and seasoning salt at the table.

SICHUAN CHILI OIL

Start to finish: 5 minutes,
plus cooling / Makes about 1 cup

1 cup peanut oil

1 ounce whole dried red Sichuan
chilies (1 cup)

3 tablespoons Sichuan chili flakes

2 tablespoons Sichuan peppercorns

1. **In a small saucepan** over medium-
low, combine all ingredients. Heat
until the oil reaches 275°F, 3 to 4
minutes. Remove from the heat and
let cool to room temperature.

2. **Pour the oil** into a fine mesh
strainer set over a bowl or liquid
measuring cup; discard the solids.
Store in a tightly sealed jar in a cool,
dark place for up to 1 month.

SICHUAN SEASONING

Start to finish: 5 minutes
Makes about ¼ cup

3 tablespoons Sichuan peppercorns,
toasted and ground

2 teaspoons white sugar

1 teaspoon kosher salt

In a small bowl, stir together all
ingredients. Store in an airtight
container for up to 1 month.

Stir-Fried Chicken with Snap Peas and Basil

Start to finish: **30 minutes** / Servings: **4**

1 pound boneless, skinless chicken breasts, cut into 1-inch chunks

3 tablespoons fish sauce, divided

1 tablespoon soy sauce

Ground white pepper

2 tablespoons peanut oil, divided

¼ cup chopped fresh basil, plus 3 cups torn and lightly packed

2 tablespoons white vinegar

4 ounces sugar snap peas, strings removed, halved on the diagonal

8 scallions, white and light green parts finely chopped, dark green parts cut into 1-inch pieces, reserved separately

2 or 3 serrano chilies, stemmed and sliced into thin rings

4 medium garlic cloves, thinly sliced

1 tablespoon white sugar

A double dose of basil adds herbal flavor and fragrance to this stir-fry. Inspired by Thailand's popular chicken-and-basil dish known as gai pad krapow, we follow the Thai approach of using herbs by the fistful. Using both chopped basil (mixed with the cooked chicken) and torn basil leaves (stirred in at the end) provided the full herbal flavor and fragrance we were looking for. Serve with steamed white or brown jasmine rice.

Don't begin cooking until all ingredients are prepared. The stir-fry comes together quickly, so make sure everything is ready and close at hand.

1. In a medium bowl, stir together the chicken, 1 tablespoon of fish sauce, the soy sauce and ½ teaspoon white pepper. Let stand at room temperature for 15 minutes, then drain and pat dry with paper towels.

2. Heat a 14-inch wok over medium-high for about 3 minutes, or until a drop of water evaporates within 1 to 2 seconds of contact. Add 1 tablespoon of oil and swirl to coat. Add the chicken in an even layer and cook without stirring until it begins to brown, about 1 minute. Stir and continue to cook, stirring occasionally, until well browned and cooked through, about 4 minutes. Transfer to a clean bowl, then stir in the chopped basil and vinegar.

3. Return the wok to medium-high and add the remaining 1 tablespoon oil. Swirl to coat and heat until barely smoking. Add the snap peas, the finely chopped scallion parts and the chilies. Cook, stirring, until the peas are lightly browned, about 2 minutes. Add the garlic and stir-fry until fragrant, about 30 seconds. Stir in the sugar, the scallion greens and chicken, along with any accumulated juices. Stir-fry until most of the juices have evaporated, about 1 minute.

4. Off heat, add the remaining 2 tablespoons fish sauce and the torn basil. Stir until the basil is wilted, about 30 seconds. Taste and season with white pepper.

Singapore Chicken Satay

Start to finish: 35 minutes, plus marinating
Servings: 4

For the chicken:

2 tablespoons grated
fresh ginger

6 medium garlic cloves,
finely grated

¼ cup white sugar

3 tablespoons toasted
peanut oil

2 tablespoons ground
turmeric

4 teaspoons ground cumin

Kosher salt

2 pounds boneless, skinless
chicken thighs, trimmed and
cut lengthwise into 1-inch-
wide strips

For the sauce:

¼ cup boiling water

1 tablespoon creamy
peanut butter

¼ cup soy sauce

¼ cup unseasoned
rice vinegar

2 tablespoons white sugar

2 tablespoons toasted
peanut oil

2 teaspoons grated
fresh ginger

1 medium garlic clove,
finely grated

2 teaspoons chili-garlic sauce

½ teaspoon ground turmeric

¼ cup finely chopped salted
dry-roasted peanuts

In Singapore, satay—thin strips of boldly seasoned and skewered meat—is cooked quickly over long beds of hot coals. The skewers are flipped frequently to ensure even cooking and plenty of delicious charred bits at the edges. It typically is served with a thin vinegar-based sauce that includes a scant amount of peanut butter and chopped peanuts for flavor and texture. In our recipe, the skewers are broiled on a wire rack set over a baking sheet lined with foil and sprinkled with 1 cup of kosher salt. The salt absorbs the fat when drips hit the pan, preventing the fat from smoking.

Don't marinate the chicken for more than three hours or it will be too salty. And don't substitute chicken breasts. Under the high heat of the broiler, they easily overcook and dry out.

1. **To prepare the chicken,** in a large bowl, combine the ginger, garlic, sugar, oil, turmeric, cumin, 1 tablespoon salt and ½ cup water. Stir until the sugar dissolves, then stir in the chicken. Cover and refrigerate for 2 to 3 hours.

2. **To make the sauce,** in a medium bowl, whisk the boiling water and peanut butter until smooth. Whisk in the soy sauce, vinegar and sugar, then set aside. In a small skillet over medium, heat the oil, ginger and garlic. Cook, stirring constantly, until fragrant, about 1 minute. Stir in the chili-garlic sauce and turmeric, then cook until fragrant, about 30 seconds. Whisk the garlic mixture into the soy sauce mixture. Reserve ¼ cup for basting the chicken. Cover and refrigerate the remaining sauce for serving.

3. **About 30 minutes** before skewering and cooking the chicken, remove the sauce from the refrigerator. Stir in the chopped peanuts. Heat the broiler with a rack about 4 inches from the element. Line a rimmed baking sheet with foil and spread 1 cup salt in an even layer over it. Set a wire rack in the baking sheet over the salt and mist with cooking spray.

4. **Drain the chicken** in a colander. Thread 2 or 3 pieces of chicken onto each of eight 8-inch metal skewers, evenly dividing the meat and pushing the pieces together, but not tightly packing them. Evenly space the skewers on the wire rack.

5. **Broil the chicken** until beginning to brown, 5 to 7 minutes. Flip the skewers and continue to broil until the second sides begin to brown, another 4 to 6 minutes. Remove from the oven and brush the surface of each skewer with 1 to 2 tablespoons of the re-served sauce. Continue to broil until well-charred, 2 to 4 minutes. Remove from the oven once again, flip the skewers and brush with another 1 to 2 tablespoons of the reserved sauce. Continue to broil until the second sides begin to char and the chicken is cooked through, another 2 to 4 minutes. Serve with the dipping sauce.

Senegalese Braised Chicken with Onions and Lime (Yassa Ginaar)

Start to finish: 1 hour 15 minutes, plus marinating
Servings: 4

---

4 tablespoons peanut oil, divided

3 tablespoons grated lime zest, plus 6 tablespoons lime juice

1 habanero chili, seeded and minced

Kosher salt and ground black pepper

2 teaspoons chicken bouillon concentrate (see headnote)

2 pounds bone-in, skin-on chicken breasts, thighs or drumsticks, trimmed

3 medium yellow onions, halved and thinly sliced

Finely chopped fresh chives, to serve

With just a few ingredients, yassa ginaar delivers multiple layers of flavor—savory yet sweet with lightly caramelized onions, citrusy with lime zest and juice, meaty from deeply browned chicken, and spicy from the heat of a habanero chili. Our version is based on a recipe in "Yolele!" by Pierre Thiam, who marinates and sears the chicken, then uses the marinade as a base for the flavorful sauce. Bouillon concentrate adds to the savoriness of the dish; our preferred brand is Better than Bouillon. Serve with steamed rice.

Don't marinate the chicken for longer than two hours; the acidity of the lime juice will soften the meat. Don't use an uncoated cast-iron pot to cook this dish. The lime's acidity will react with the metal, causing the sauce to taste metallic.

1. **In a large bowl,** stir together 3 tablespoons of oil, the lime zest, habanero, 1 tablespoon salt and 1 teaspoon pepper. Transfer 2 teaspoons of the mixture to a small bowl and set aside. To the remaining oil-zest mixture, whisk in the lime juice, bouillon concentrate and ¼ cup water. Add the chicken and onions and toss. Cover and marinate at room temperature for 1 hour or refrigerate up to 2 hours, stirring once.

2. **Remove the chicken** from the marinade and pat dry with paper towels. Set a colander over a large bowl and drain the onions, reserving both the marinade and the onions.

3. **In a large Dutch oven** over medium-high, heat the remaining 1 tablespoon oil until barely smoking. Add the chicken, skin side down, and cook until well browned, about 4 minutes. Transfer to a plate and pour off and discard all but 1 tablespoon of the fat. Set the pot over medium heat and stir in the onions and ¼ cup water, scraping up any browned bits. Cover and cook, stirring frequently, until the onions are softened and lightly browned, 15 to 20 minutes.

4. **Stir the reserved marinade** into the onions. Return the chicken, skin side up, to the pot, nestling the pieces in the onions, then pour in any accumulated juices. Reduce to medium-low, cover and cook, stirring occasionally, until a skewer inserted into the thickest part of the meat meets no resistance, about 25 minutes.

5. **Using a slotted spoon,** transfer the chicken to a serving platter or shallow bowl. Off heat, stir the reserved oil-zest mixture into the onions, then taste and season with salt and pepper. Spoon the onions and sauce around the chicken and sprinkle with chives.

Chicken Traybake with Roasted Poblano and Tomato Salsa

Start to finish: **50 minutes** / Servings: **4**

1 tablespoon chili powder

Kosher salt and ground black pepper

2 poblano chilies, stemmed, seeded and roughly chopped

1 medium yellow onion, root end intact, cut into 8 wedges

1 pint cherry or grape tomatoes

1 habanero chili, stemmed halved and seeded (optional)

¼ cup extra-virgin olive oil

1 tablespoon firmly packed light or dark brown sugar

1 tablespoon dried oregano

3 pounds bone-in, skin-on chicken parts, trimmed and patted dry

10 medium garlic cloves, peeled

¼ cup lightly packed fresh cilantro, roughly chopped

1 tablespoon white vinegar

In Oaxaca, in southeastern Mexico, salsas start with charring chilies, tomatoes, onions and garlic on a steel or clay comal (a flat griddle used to make tortillas) to soften and deepen their flavors. We adapt that concept in this traybake, roasting chilies alongside chicken parts. Glossy, dark green poblano chilies have an earthy, minerally flavor and moderate heat level. Habanero adds a burst of bright, fruity heat that sharpens the tomatoes' flavor. If you want a lot of heat in your salsa, include the optional habanero chili. The tomatoes release their juice during cooking, so deglazing the baking sheet with water after roasting isn't necessary.

Don't forget to leave the root end of the onion intact so the wedges don't separate into layers. If the layers separate, they tend to scorch during roasting.

1. **Heat the oven to 450°F** with a rack in the middle position. In a small bowl, stir together the chili powder and 2 teaspoons salt. In a large bowl, toss together the poblanos, onion wedges, tomatoes, habanero (if using), 1 tablespoon of the chili powder mixture and the oil. Into the remaining chili powder mixture, stir the sugar, oregano, 1 tablespoon salt and 2 teaspoons pepper.

2. **On a rimmed baking sheet,** evenly season both sides of the chicken parts with the chili powder mixture. Place the garlic cloves in the center of the baking sheet, then arrange the chicken parts, skin up, around the garlic; this prevents the garlic from scorching during roasting. Arrange the vegetables evenly around the chicken.

3. **Roast until the thickest part** of the breast (if using) reaches about 160°F and the thickest part of the largest thigh/leg (if using) reaches about 175°F, 30 to 40 minutes.

4. **Using tongs,** transfer the chicken to a platter and transfer the onion wedges and habanero to a cutting board. Pour the garlic, the remaining vegetables and any liquid on the baking sheet into a medium bowl. Roughly chop the onion and habanero, then add to the bowl. Using a fork or potato masher, mash the mixture until broken down but slightly chunky, then stir in half of the cilantro and the vinegar. Serve the salsa with the chicken and sprinkle with the remaining cilantro.

Crispy Chicken Under a Brick (Tsitsila Tabaka)

Start to finish: 2 hours (50 minutes active) / Servings: 4

1½ teaspoons ground coriander

½ teaspoon granulated garlic

Kosher salt and ground black pepper

3½- to 4-pound whole chicken, spatchcocked (see instructions, pp. 282-283)

1 tablespoon grapeseed or other neutral oil

2 tablespoons salted butter

8 medium garlic cloves, peeled and chopped

2 cups low-sodium chicken broth

⅛ to ¼ teaspoon cayenne pepper

2 tablespoons lemon juice

¼ cup lightly packed fresh cilantro, chopped

For this recipe, we find inspiration in Georgia, set at the crossroads of Eastern Europe and Western Asia and known for dishes that benefit from both cuisines. The chicken is spatchcocked, which puts thighs and breasts on the same plane for even cooking. Georgian cooks use a brick to keep their chickens truly flat (you'll find the same technique in Italy's pollo al mattone). The weight presses the chicken down, ensuring the bird makes good contact with the pan's hot surface, which renders the fat and ensures even browning. If crisp skin is what you're after, this is the way to get it. For the "brick," we use a second heavy skillet or a large, sturdy pot (such as a Dutch oven); it's easier and works just as well. However, if you have them on hand, you instead could use one or two clean bricks wrapped in heavy-duty foil. An easy pan sauce with garlic, lemon and cilantro perfectly complements the chicken.

Don't use a chicken much larger than 4 pounds, as it may not fit comfortably in the skillet. Don't forget to pat the chicken dry before searing (after it has stood for 45 minutes). The drier the skin, the better it crisps. After searing, drain off the fat in the pan before putting the bird in the oven; this helps reduce splatter. Finally, don't forget that the skillet's handle will be hot when taken out of the oven.

1. **In a small bowl,** stir together the coriander, granulated garlic, 1 tablespoon salt and ½ teaspoon black pepper. Place the spatchcocked chicken, skin-side up, on a cutting board. Season the chicken all over with the spice mixture, rubbing it into the skin. Let stand uncovered at room temperature for 30 to 45 minutes.

2. **Heat the oven to 450°F** with a rack in the lowest position. Thoroughly pat the chicken dry with paper towels.

3. **In a 12-inch oven-safe skillet** over medium-high, heat the oil until barely smoking. Place the chicken breast down in the pan. Lay a small sheet of foil over the chicken, then place a second heavy skillet or pot on top. Reduce to medium and cook until the skin is golden brown, 10 to 15 minutes, removing the weight and foil and checking every 4 to 5 minutes to ensure even browning.

4. **Using tongs,** carefully transfer the chicken to a large plate, turning it breast up. Pour off and discard the fat in the skillet. Slide the chicken breast up back into the pan and place in the oven. Roast until the thickest part of the breast reaches 160°F, 25 to 35 minutes. Carefully transfer the chicken to a cutting board and let rest while you make the sauce.

5. **Set the skillet (the handle will be hot)** over medium-high and cook the butter and garlic, stirring occasionally, until the garlic is lightly browned, about 2 minutes. Add the broth and bring to a simmer, scraping up any browned bits, then cook until the garlic is softened and the mixture is lightly thickened and reduced to about ¾ cup, 10 to 15 minutes. Using a silicone spatula, mash the garlic until almost smooth and mix it into the sauce. Off heat, stir in the cayenne, lemon juice and cilantro, then transfer to a serving bowl. Carve, then serve with the sauce.

HOW TO SPATCHCOCK A CHICKEN

1. Set the chicken breast down on a cutting board. Using sturdy kitchen shears, cut along one side of the backbone from top to bottom.

2. Repeat the cut on the other side of the backbone, then remove and discard the backbone.

3. Spread the sides of the chicken, opening it like a book and flattening it as much as possible.

4. Flip the chicken breast up, then use your hands to press firmly on the highest point of the breast to flatten the bird. The breast bone may crack.

5. If desired, the skin of the thighs and breasts can be loosened from the edges to allow seasonings to be rubbed under the skin.

Filipino Chicken Adobo with Coconut Broth

Start to finish: 1¾ hours (30 minutes active)
Servings: 4

1½ cups unseasoned
rice vinegar

¾ cup low-sodium soy sauce

6 medium garlic cloves,
smashed

3 serrano chilies, halved
lengthwise

4 bay leaves

1 teaspoon black
peppercorns

3 pounds bone-in, skin-on
chicken thighs, trimmed

1 cup coconut milk

⅓ cup chopped fresh cilantro

Steamed white rice, to serve

Thousands of islands make up the Philippines. And there probably are as many recipes for chicken adobo, the classic Filipino dish that turns a handful of ingredients— loads of garlic, black pepper and vinegar—into a bright and tangy meal. We tailored our recipe for weeknight ease, using a hefty dose of rice vinegar blended with soy sauce and aromatics to create a potent marinade for bone-in thighs. For heat we used serrano chilies. Look for chicken thighs that are uniform in size; if some are smaller than others, begin to check them early and remove them as they come up to temperature.

Don't use regular soy sauce. As the chicken braises, the cooking liquid reduces, concentrating the flavor—and salt. Low-sodium soy sauce produced a broth that was well-seasoned.

1. In a large Dutch oven, combine the vinegar, soy sauce, garlic, chilies, bay leaves and peppercorns. Add the chicken thighs, submerging them. Cover and refrigerate for 30 to 60 minutes.

2. Bring the mixture to a boil over medium-high. Reduce to medium-low and cook, turning the thighs occasionally, until the chicken registers 170°F, 25 to 30 minutes, adjusting the heat as necessary to maintain a medium simmer.

3. Heat the broiler with an oven rack 6 inches from the element. Line a rimmed baking sheet with foil. Remove the chicken thighs from the pot and arrange skin side up on the baking sheet. Pat dry with paper towels and set aside.

4. Strain the cooking liquid, discarding the solids, then skim off the fat. Return 1 cup of the defatted liquid to the pot, stir in the coconut milk and bring to a simmer over medium. Take the pan off the heat, stir in the cilantro, then cover and set aside.

5. Broil the chicken until the skin is deeply browned and blackened in spots, 3 to 8 minutes. Serve in shallow bowls with steamed white rice, ladling the broth over the rice.

Green Enchiladas with Chicken and Cheese (Enchiladas Verdes)

Start to finish: 45 minutes / Servings: 4

---

3 tablespoons extra-virgin olive oil, divided

3 medium poblano chilies (about 12 ounces), stemmed, seeded and chopped

1 pound tomatillos, husked, cored and chopped

1 medium white onion, chopped

6 medium garlic cloves, peeled

1 tablespoon ground cumin

½ cup low-sodium chicken broth or water

1 cup lightly packed cilantro leaves and stems

Kosher salt and ground black pepper

1½ cups finely chopped cooked chicken (see headnote)

6 ounces whole-milk mozzarella cheese, shredded (1½ cups)

2 tablespoons hot sauce (see headnote)

Eight 6-inch corn tortillas

Lime wedges, to serve

To make the filling for these enchiladas, use leftover roasted or grilled chicken or meat from a store-bought rotisserie bird. You also can poach your own chicken. To do so, place 1 pound boneless, skinless chicken breasts in a medium saucepan, cover with water or chicken broth, bring to a simmer over medium-high, then reduce to low, cover and cook until the thickest part of the meat registers 160°F, about 20 minutes. Let the chicken cool in the liquid until just warm to the touch, then finely chop the meat. Our homemade green chili and tomatillo hot sauce (see recipe p. 349) is especially good here, but any bottled hot sauce that's not too vinegary (such as Tapatío or Cholula) will work. Chopped white onion and sour cream or Mexican crema are great garnishes.

Don't skip the step of brushing the tortillas with oil and briefly warming them in the oven. If the tortillas are filled and rolled straight from the package, they will crack and tear. But take care not to overheat them, which will dry them out and make them too brittle to roll.

---

1. Heat the oven to 475°F with a rack in the middle position. In a large pot over medium-high, combine 1 tablespoon of the oil, the poblanos, tomatillos, onion and garlic. Cook, stirring occasionally, until the vegetables are well-browned and beginning to soften, 5 to 8 minutes. Stir in the cumin and cook until fragrant, about 30 seconds. Add the broth and cook, stirring occasionally, until the vegetables have softened, about 5 minutes. Remove from the heat and let cool for 5 minutes.

2. Transfer the mixture to a food processor and process until smooth, about 1 minute. Add the cilantro and continue to process until smooth, about 1 minute. Taste and season with salt and pepper. Spread 1 cup of the sauce in the bottom of a 13-by-9-inch baking dish; set aside.

3. In a medium bowl, toss together the chicken, cheese, hot sauce, 1½ teaspoons salt and 1 teaspoon pepper; set aside.

4. Brush both sides of the tortillas with the remaining 2 tablespoons oil, then arrange them on a rimmed baking sheet (it's fine to overlap them slightly). Cover tightly with foil and warm in the oven just until soft and pliable, about 3 minutes.

5. Uncover the tortillas; reserve the foil. Lay the tortillas out on a large cutting board or clean counter. Divide the chicken mixture evenly among the tortillas (about 3 heaping tablespoons each), arranging and pressing the filling in a line along the bottom edge of each tortilla.

6. Working one at a time, roll up the tortillas to enclose the filling and place seam side down in a tight row down the center of the prepared baking dish. Spoon ½ cup of the sauce over the enchiladas. Cover tightly with the reserved foil and bake until the cheese begins to melt out of the ends, about 15 minutes.

7. Uncover and spread ½ cup of the remaining sauce over the enchiladas. Re-cover and let stand for 5 minutes. Serve with lime wedges and the remaining sauce.

Orange–Guajillo Chili Pulled Chicken

Start to finish: **45 minutes** / Servings: **4**

Chilorio, a pulled pork from the Mexican state of Sinaloa, inspired this dish, but instead of pork shoulder, we used faster-cooking chicken thighs. Fresh orange juice amplified the fruity notes of the guajillo chilies while giving the sauce a natural sweetness; a little vinegar and honey helped the balance. Serve with Mexican rice or tortillas, or use it as a filling for tacos. Diced white onion, sliced radishes and/or crumbled queso fresco are excellent garnishes.

Don't forget to trim any excess fat *from the chicken thighs before cooking to prevent the dish from being greasy.*

1. In a 12-inch skillet over medium-high, toast the chilies, pressing with a wide metal spatula and flipping halfway through, until fragrant, about 1 minute. Transfer to a small bowl and pour in the juice; press on the chilies to submerge. Let stand until the chilies have softened, about 10 minutes. Set the skillet aside.

2. In a blender, combine the chilies and juice, garlic, vinegar, coriander, honey, oregano and 1 teaspoon salt. Puree until smooth, about 30 seconds. Pour the puree into the same skillet and bring to a boil over medium-high. Nestle the chicken into the sauce, cover and cook over medium-low, stirring and flipping the chicken halfway through, until a skewer inserted into the chicken meets no resistance, about 20 minutes.

3. Using tongs, transfer the chicken to a large plate and set aside until cool enough to handle, 10 to 15 minutes. Using 2 forks, shred into bite-size pieces. While the chicken cools, bring the sauce to a simmer over medium-high and cook, stirring, until thickened and reduced to 1 cup, about 10 minutes. Stir the shredded chicken into the sauce, then taste and season with salt.

1 ounce dried guajillo chilies (5 medium), stemmed, seeded and torn into 1-inch pieces

1½ cups orange juice

5 medium garlic cloves, smashed and peeled

2 tablespoons white vinegar

2 teaspoons ground coriander

2 teaspoons honey

1 teaspoon dried oregano

Kosher salt

2 pounds boneless, skinless chicken thighs, trimmed

Lemon-Saffron Chicken (Tangia)

Start to finish: **1 hour** / Servings: 4

Tangia—which originates in Marrakech and often is slow-cooked in the community wood-fired ovens that heat bathhouses—is a stew-like dish of fall-apart tender hunks of lamb bathed in a thick, but spare broth rich with saffron, turmeric, cumin, ginger, garlic and lemon. We got a lesson in cooking tangia the traditional way from taxi driver Youssef Boufelja. Lamb is typical, but we use boneless, skinless chicken thighs. In Morocco, preserved lemons lend a gentle acidity, lightening the richness. For an easier version, we get similar flavor from lemon zest and juice—as well as chopped green olives for brininess—added at the end of cooking. Serve with warmed, halved pita bread for scooping up the meat and thickened sauce.

Don't reduce the amount of lemon zest or juice. *The zest provides both flavor and fragrance, and the juice adds tang and acidity. You'll need 3 to 4 lemons to get 3 tablespoons grated zest; a wand-style grater works best.*

5 teaspoons ground cumin, divided

Kosher salt and ground black pepper

3 pounds boneless, skinless chicken thighs, trimmed and patted dry

2 tablespoons extra-virgin olive oil

2 medium yellow onions, finely chopped

12 medium garlic cloves, chopped

2 teaspoons ground turmeric

2 teaspoons ground ginger

2 teaspoons ground coriander

1 teaspoon saffron threads, crumbled

3 tablespoons salted butter, cut into 3 pieces

½ cup pimento-stuffed green olives, chopped

3 tablespoons grated lemon zest, plus ¼ cup lemon juice

1. In a small bowl, stir together 2 teaspoons of cumin and 2 teaspoons salt. Set aside. Season the chicken on both sides with salt and pepper.

2. In a large Dutch oven over medium-high, heat the oil until shimmering. Add the onions and garlic and cook, stirring occasionally, until softened, about 5 minutes. Add the remaining 3 teaspoons cumin, the turmeric, ginger and coriander, then cook, stirring, until fragrant, about 30 seconds. Stir in 1½ cups water and the saffron, scraping up any browned bits. Nestle the chicken in the liquid, turning to coat. Cover, reduce to medium-low and cook for 20 minutes at a gentle simmer.

3. Using tongs, turn the chicken. Cover and continue cooking until tender, another 25 minutes. Using tongs, transfer the chicken to a plate. Bring the liquid to a simmer over medium-high and cook, stirring, until thickened, 10 to 14 minutes.

4. Return the chicken to the pot and stir. The chicken will break up a bit. Off heat, add the butter, stirring until melted, then stir in the olives and lemon zest and juice. Taste and season with salt and pepper. Transfer to a platter and serve, sprinkling with the cumin-salt mixture to taste.

Southern Thai-Style Fried Chicken

Start to finish: 40 minutes, plus marinating / Servings: 4

3 tablespoons ground cumin

3 tablespoons ground coriander

3 tablespoons ground white pepper, divided

1 large egg white

¼ cup fish sauce

1 bunch fresh cilantro, finely chopped

2 serrano chilies, stemmed and finely chopped

2 pounds boneless, skinless chicken thighs, trimmed, each cut crosswise into 3 strips

2 cups cornstarch

Kosher salt

2 quarts peanut oil, plus more if needed

Lime wedges, to serve

Sweet chili sauce, to serve (see headnote; optional)

Gai tod hat yai, fried chicken from the southern region of Thailand, inspired this recipe, but for ease, we use boneless, skinless thighs cut into strips instead of the typical bone-in, skin-on parts. Toasted spices are added to the marinade so they infuse the chicken with flavor; they're also dusted onto the pieces after frying for additional seasoning. The chicken is customarily sprinkled with crisp fried shallots after cooking, but we opted out of this garnish, as the spices themselves provide plenty of bold flavor. If you like, you can purchase fried shallots in most Asian grocery stores; scatter them over the chicken just before serving. Serve this with our extra-easy version of Thai sweet chili sauce, see recipe p. 291, or with store-bought sweet chili sauce, or simply offer lime wedges for squeezing.

Don't marinate the chicken for longer than an hour or it will be too salty. Don't crowd the pot when frying. Cook only a third of the chicken at a time so the temperature of the oil won't drop drastically, which results in greasy chicken.

1. In a 10-inch skillet over medium, toast the cumin and coriander until fragrant and just beginning to color, 2 to 3 minutes. Transfer to a small bowl and stir in 1 tablespoon of white pepper; set aside.

2. In a large bowl, whisk together the egg white, fish sauce and ¼ cup water. Stir in the cilantro, chilies and 3 tablespoons of the spice mixture. Add the chicken and stir to thoroughly coat, then cover and refrigerate for 30 to 60 minutes.

3. Set a wire rack in a rimmed baking sheet. In a large bowl, whisk together the cornstarch, the remaining 2 tablespoons white pepper and 2 teaspoons salt.

4. Drain the chicken in a colander. Scraping off excess marinade, add ⅓ of the chicken to the cornstarch mixture and toss to coat completely, then firmly press the pieces into the cornstarch. Transfer the pieces to the prepared rack in a single layer, shaking to remove excess coating. Repeat with the remaining chicken and cornstarch mixture, working in two more batches.

5. Set another wire rack in a rimmed baking sheet. In a large Dutch oven over medium-high, heat the oil to 350°F (the oil should be at least 2 inches deep; add more if needed). Add ⅓ of the chicken pieces and cook, stirring occasionally to prevent sticking, until golden brown, about 5 minutes. Using a slotted spoon or wire skimmer, transfer the chicken to the second rack and season on all sides with about ⅓ of the reserved spice mixture. Allow the oil to return to 350°F, then repeat with the remaining chicken and spice mixture, working in two more batches. Serve with lime wedges and sweet chili sauce (if using).

TANGY-SWEET CHILI SAUCE

Start to finish: 10 minutes
Makes about ¾ cup

1 cup white vinegar

½ cup white sugar

Kosher salt

3 tablespoons chili-garlic sauce

In a small saucepan over medium-high, bring the vinegar, sugar and ¼ teaspoon salt to a boil, stirring to dissolve the sugar. Cook until the mixture thickens and is reduced to about ¾ cup, 10 to 12 minutes. Off heat, stir in the chili-garlic sauce. Cool to room temperature.

Oaxacan Green Mole with Chicken

Start to finish: **1 hour 10 minutes** / Servings: 4

2 pounds boneless, skinless chicken thighs, trimmed and halved

Kosher salt and ground black pepper

Seven 6-inch corn tortillas

1 quart low-sodium chicken broth

4 medium garlic cloves, peeled

2 medium tomatillos, husked and halved

1 medium poblano chili (about 4 ounces), stemmed, seeded and quartered lengthwise

1 small white onion, root end intact, quartered lengthwise

1 bunch cilantro, leaves and tender stems

1 cup lightly packed fresh flat-leaf parsley

½ cup lightly packed fresh mint

1 teaspoon fennel seeds

1 teaspoon cumin seeds

8 ounces small Yukon Gold potatoes (1 to 1½ inches in diameter), halved

6 ounces green beans, trimmed and cut into 1-inch pieces

1 medium yellow zucchini, cut into 1-inch pieces (about 2 cups)

When we think of mole, we most often think of mole negro, mahogany in color and flavored with chocolate, dried chilies and nuts. But as we learned from Oaxaca chef Olga Cabrera Oropeza, there is a wide variety of moles, each with a unique character. Mole verde—or green mole—traditionally is made with pork and gets its bright, fresh flavor from a blend of fresh chilies, tomatillos and herbs. We opted for quicker-cooking but equally tasty chicken thighs, and we sought out supermarket substitutes for hard-to-find epazote and hoja santa, two herbs that are standard ingredients in Mexico (we mimicked their flavors with mint and fennel seeds). Oaxacans thicken this stew-like soup with masa, the corn dough used to make tortillas and tamales. For ease, we opted to use what Oropeza showed us was the second-best option: corn tortillas themselves softened in liquid then blended until smooth.

Don't brown the vegetables too darkly under the broiler. Light charring provides complexity, but too much will muddle the fresh herbal notes.

1. **Season the chicken thighs** with salt and pepper. In a large pot over medium-high, combine the tortillas and broth, then bring to a boil. Using a slotted spoon, transfer the tortillas (they will have softened) to a blender, add ¼ cup water and blend until smooth, about 1 minute.

2. **Pour the puree into the boiling broth** and stir to combine; rinse out the blender and reserve. Add the chicken to the pot, cover and reduce to low. Cook, stirring occasionally and adjusting the heat as needed to maintain a gentle simmer, until a skewer inserted into the chicken meets just a little resistance, 30 to 35 minutes.

3. **Meanwhile, heat the broiler** with a rack about 4 inches from the element. Line a rimmed baking sheet with foil. Arrange the garlic, tomatillos, poblano chili and onion in an even layer on the baking sheet. Broil until the vegetables are lightly charred, about 4 minutes, then flip them and continue to broil until the second sides are lightly charred, 3 to 5 minutes. Let cool for about 5 minutes, then transfer to the blender.

4. **Add ½ cup water to the blender,** then puree until smooth, about 30 seconds. Add the cilantro, parsley, mint, fennel, cumin, 2 teaspoons salt and ¾ teaspoon pepper. Blend until smooth and bright green, about 2 minutes, scraping the sides as needed. You should have about 2 cups of puree; set aside.

5. **When the chicken is ready,** stir the potatoes, green beans and zucchini into the pot. Bring to a simmer over medium and cook, uncovered and stirring occasionally, until the skewer inserted into a potato meets no resistance, about 15 minutes. Stir in the puree, then taste and season with salt and pepper.

Chicken and Bean Paella

Start to finish: 1½ hours / Servings: 4

2 teaspoons sweet paprika

1½ teaspoons smoked paprika, divided

Kosher salt and ground black pepper

1 pound boneless, skinless chicken thighs, trimmed, cut into 1-inch pieces and patted dry

4 tablespoons extra-virgin olive oil, divided

15½-ounce can cannellini beans, rinsed and drained

1 pint grape or cherry tomatoes, halved

1 tablespoon tomato paste

6 medium garlic cloves, minced

½ cup dry sherry

3 cups low-sodium chicken broth

4 bay leaves

2 teaspoons minced fresh rosemary

½ teaspoon saffron threads (optional)

1 cup Valencian rice (see headnote)

8 ounces green beans, trimmed and cut into 1-inch pieces

Lemon wedges, to serve

Outside of Spain, paella is considered a luxurious dish, loaded with seafood, scented with pricy saffron and served as an event in and of itself. Its beginnings, however, are more humble. The one-pan dish was prepared by Valencian farm workers as a midday meal. This type of paella, called paella Valenciana, still is made today. For our version—adapted for a nonstick 12-inch skillet with a lid—we opted for chicken thighs, canned white beans, fresh green beans and grape or cherry tomatoes; saffron is a nice addition, but entirely optional. Using the right rice is key to getting the proper subtly creamy but not overly starchy consistency. Look for Bomba rice, sometimes labeled simply as "Valencian rice." Calasparra rice from Murcia, Spain, is another good option. If neither is available, substitute an equal amount of Arborio rice, but before cooking, rinse it well and drain, and also reduce the amount of broth to 2½ cups. To be efficient, during the 30 minutes that the chicken marinates, prepare the remaining ingredients.

Don't forget to stir in the rice after sprinkling it into the pan. Distributing the grains in an even layer and making sure they're submerged ensures even cooking. But after that, resist the urge to stir. Undisturbed cooking allows the paella to form a nicely browned bottom crust called socarrat. Finally, don't cover the pan as the paella cooks or the rice will wind up soggy and overdone.

1. **In a medium bowl,** combine the sweet paprika, ½ teaspoon of smoked paprika, 1 teaspoon each salt and pepper. Add the chicken and toss until coated. Cover and refrigerate for at least 30 minutes.

2. **In a nonstick 12-inch skillet** over medium-high, heat 2 tablespoons of oil until barely smoking. Add the chicken in an even layer and cook without stirring until well-browned, about 3 minutes. Using tongs, flip the pieces and cook until the second sides are well-browned, another 1 to 2 minutes. Using the tongs, return the chicken to the bowl, leaving the fat in the pan.

3. **To the same skillet over medium,** add the beans and cook, stirring, until the beans are fragrant and coated with oil, about 30 seconds. Transfer to the bowl with the chicken.

4. **Set the skillet over medium-high,** then stir in the tomatoes and 1 teaspoon salt. Cover and cook, stirring occasionally, until the tomatoes are browned, the liquid they released has evaporated and the mixture begins to sizzle, 5 to 7 minutes. Stir in the remaining 2 tablespoons oil and the tomato paste and cook,

stirring, until the mixture is beginning to brown, about 2 minutes. Stir in the garlic and the remaining 1 teaspoon smoked paprika, then cook until fragrant, about 30 seconds. Add the sherry and cook, stirring occasionally, until most of the liquid has evaporated and the mixture begins to sizzle, 2 to 4 minutes.

5. Stir in the broth, bay, rosemary and saffron (if using), then bring to a boil over medium-high. Stir in the green beans and the cannellini bean-chicken mixture along with any accumulated juices. Sprinkle the rice into the skillet, then stir to combine and evenly distribute the grains, pressing down to ensure they are fully submerged. Return to a boil, then reduce to medium and cook, uncovered, until most of the liquid is absorbed and craters appear in the rice, 16 to 18 minutes. Increase to medium-high and continue to cook, without stirring but rotating the pan every 10 seconds or so, until you hear sizzling and smell a toasty aroma, 1 to 2 minutes.

6. Remove the pan from the heat. Drape a clean kitchen towel across the top, then cover with a lid and let rest for 10 minutes. Use a wooden spoon or silicone spatula to scoop the paella onto individual plates, scraping along the pan to loosen the bottom crust (socarrat). Serve with lemon wedges.

Palestinian Upside-Down Chicken and Rice (Maqlubeh)

Start to finish: 2 hours (30 minutes active), plus resting
Servings: 8

---

2 cups basmati rice

Kosher salt and ground black pepper

1½ pounds bone-in, skin-on chicken thighs, trimmed

4 tablespoons extra-virgin olive oil, divided

⅓ cup slivered almonds

8 ounces cauliflower florets (1-inch pieces)

8 medium garlic cloves, chopped

4 tablespoons (½ stick) salted butter, melted

4 teaspoons ground cumin

1 tablespoon ground allspice

2 teaspoons ground turmeric

1 teaspoon grated nutmeg

8 ounces eggplant (½ medium), sliced into ¼-inch-thick rounds

1 quart low-sodium chicken broth

Maqlubeh translates from the Arabic as "upside down," which describes how this traditional multilayered rice dish is served. Reem Kassis, author of "The Palestinian Table," showed us how to make the dish on a trip to Galilee. Our streamlined recipe still requires a small investment in ingredients and prep, but the work mostly is front-loaded and produces a one-pot dish impressive enough for a special occasion. For proper cooking, it's important to use a pot 9½ to 11 inches in diameter and 4 to 6 inches deep. After searing and removing the chicken, we line the bottom of the pot with a parchment round to guarantee that the rice, which forms a crisp, browned bottom layer, does not stick when the pot is inverted for serving. If you prefer, you can serve directly from the pot, but we still recommend lining the bottom of the pot with parchment. The classic accompaniment for maqlubeh is a tomato, cucumber and yogurt salad.

Don't forget to soak and rinse the rice. *This helps the grains cook up light and separate.*

---

1. In a large bowl, combine the rice and 2 tablespoons salt. Add water to cover by 1 inch, then set aside. Have ready a lidded pot that measures 9½ to 11 inches in diameter and 4 to 6 inches deep. Cut 2 rounds of kitchen parchment the same diameter as the pot.

2. Season the chicken all over with salt and pepper. Set the pot over medium and heat 1 tablespoon of the oil until shimmering. Add the chicken skin down and cook until browned, about 10 minutes. Transfer to a plate and set aside. Remove the pot from the heat. Place 1 parchment round on the bottom, then turn to coat it with fat.

3. Add the remaining 3 tablespoons oil to the parchment-lined pot, then sprinkle evenly with the almonds. Drain the rice in a fine-mesh strainer, then rinse under cool running water and drain again. Scatter 1 cup of the rice in a thin, even layer over the almonds. In a medium bowl, mix the remaining rice with the cauliflower, garlic, butter, cumin, allspice, turmeric, nutmeg and 1¾ teaspoons each salt and pepper. Reserve ½ cup of this mixture, then distribute the remainder in an even layer in the pot.

4. Place the chicken in the pot, slightly nestling the pieces into the rice-cauliflower layer; discard any accumulated juices. Shingle the eggplant slices over the chicken in an even layer. Sprinkle with the reserved ½ cup rice.

5. Pour the broth into the pot (it will not fully cover the eggplant), then bring to a boil over medium-high. Lay the second parchment round against the surface of the pot's contents, then cover with the lid. Cook for 5 minutes, reduce to low and cook, undisturbed, for 35 minutes.

6. Remove the pot from the heat, uncover and let stand for 15 minutes. Remove the parchment, then invert a serving platter onto the pot. Holding the platter against the pot, carefully invert the two together; leave the pot overturned on the platter and let rest for about 10 minutes. Slowly lift off the pot and, if needed, remove and discard the parchment.

Chicken Tinga
(Tinga Poblana de Pollo)

Start to finish: 1 hour 10 minutes (40 minutes active)
Servings: 4

1½ pounds bone-in, skin-on chicken breasts

1 large white onion, halved and thinly sliced, divided

6 medium garlic cloves, minced, divided

2 medium carrots, peeled and thinly sliced

2 bay leaves

Kosher salt and ground black pepper

2 tablespoons grapeseed or other neutral oil

1 teaspoon dried Mexican oregano (see headnote)

½ teaspoon ground cumin

1 bunch cilantro, chopped, stems and leaves reserved separately

2 chipotle chilies in adobo sauce, chopped, plus 2 teaspoons adobo sauce

1 pound ripe tomatoes, cored and roughly chopped

½ teaspoon packed light brown sugar

Tinga poblana de pollo is a stewy dish of shredded chicken in a light, fresh tomato sauce that's spicy and smoky with chipotle chilies. It's an excellent filling for tacos or topping for tostadas. For our version, based on the recipe we learned in Mexico, we poach chicken breasts, shred the meat into bite-size pieces, then add the chicken to the tomato-chipotle sauce that has been simmered separately. Mexican oregano, which has earthy, citrus notes, is more closely related to verbena than to Mediterranean oregano, which is in the mint family. Many supermarkets sell Mexican oregano; if it's not shelved with the jarred herbs and spices, check the international aisle or where dried Mexican chilies are sold. If you can't find it, substitute an equal amount of dried marjoram.

Don't allow the chicken breasts to boil in the poaching liquid, and make sure to remove them promptly when cooked through. White meat is lean and delicate and becomes dry and tough if boiled vigorously or cooked past 160°F.

1. **In a large saucepan,** combine 7 cups water, the chicken, a quarter of the onion, half the garlic, the carrots, bay and 1 tablespoon salt. Bring to a simmer over medium-high then reduce to low, cover and cook at a bare simmer. Cook until the chicken is opaque throughout and the thickest part registers 160°F, 20 to 30 minutes; flip the breasts once about halfway through.

2. **Using tongs,** transfer the chicken to a large plate and and set aside to cool. Strain enough of the cooking liquid through a fine-mesh strainer to yield 1 cup; discard the remainder. Using 2 forks or your hands, shred the chicken into bite-size pieces, discarding the skin and bones.

3. **In a 12-inch skillet over medium,** heat the oil until shimmering. Add the remaining onion, the remaining garlic and 2 teaspoons salt. Cook, stirring, until the onion has wilted, 2 to 4 minutes. Add the oregano, cumin and cilantro stems, then cook, stirring, until fragrant, about 30 seconds. Stir in the chipotle chilies and adobo sauce, tomatoes and sugar. Increase to medium-high and cook, stirring often, until the tomatoes begin to release their liquid, 2 to 3 minutes. Add the reserved cooking liquid, scraping up any browned bits. Bring to a boil and cook, stirring often, until the sauce is slightly thickened and clings to the skillet, 5 to 8 minutes.

4. **Stir in the shredded chicken,** reduce to medium-low and cook, stirring occasionally, until the sauce clings to the meat, about 2 minutes. Taste and season with salt and pepper, then stir in the cilantro leaves.

Garlicky Spiced Chicken and Potato Traybake with Pomegranate Molasses

Start to finish: 1 hour 10 minutes (20 minutes active) /
Servings: 4

¼ cup extra-virgin olive oil

2 teaspoons pomegranate molasses (see headnote), plus more to serve

1 tablespoon ground allspice

1 teaspoon ground coriander

¾ teaspoon ground cinnamon

⅛ teaspoon ground cardamom

Kosher salt and ground black pepper

3 pounds bone-in, skin-on chicken parts, trimmed and patted dry

1½ pounds medium to large red potatoes, unpeeled, cut into 1½-inch-thick wedges

8 medium garlic cloves, peeled

Fresh flat-leaf parsley, to serve

This meal-in-one is our adaptation of a recipe in "The Palestinian Table" by Reem Kassis, which she prepared for us on a recent trip to Galilee. In lieu of seasoning the chicken and potatoes with the Kassis family's nine-spice blend, we make a simpler mixture from a few select ground spices. If you want to use the blend, see recipe p. 301; use 2 tablespoons of it in place of the allspice, cinnamon, coriander and cardamom. To make a simple but flavorful sauce, we roast a handful of garlic cloves with the chicken and potatoes, then mash the softened cloves directly on the pan before deglazing with water. Dark, syrupy pomegranate molasses has a fruity, floral, tart-sweet taste that complements the fragrant spices as well as the caramelization that results from roasting. Look for it in the international aisle of the supermarket or in Middle Eastern grocery stores. If not available, substitute with 1 teaspoon each lemon juice and honey in the seasoning mixture and serve with lemon wedges.

Don't use boneless, skinless chicken parts, as they will overcook. Also, make sure to put the garlic cloves at the center of the baking sheet, where they're protected from the oven's high heat, so they don't wind up scorched.

1. In a large bowl, stir together the oil, molasses, allspice, coriander, cinnamon, cardamom, 4 teaspoons salt and ¼ teaspoon pepper. Add the chicken and potatoes, then toss to coat. Set aside at room temperature while the oven heats.

2. Heat the oven to 450°F with a rack in the middle position. Place the garlic cloves in the center of a rimmed baking sheet. Arrange the chicken parts, skin up, around the garlic; this prevents the garlic from scorching during roasting. Arrange the potatoes evenly around the chicken.

3. Roast until the thickest part of the breast (if using) reaches about 160°F and the thickest part of the largest thigh/leg (if using) reaches about 175°F, 30 to 40 minutes.

4. Using tongs, transfer the chicken and potatoes to a platter, leaving the garlic on the baking sheet. With a fork, mash the garlic until relatively smooth. Carefully pour ¼ cup water onto the baking sheet, then use a wooden spoon to scrape up the browned bits. Taste the sauce and season with salt and pepper, then pour over the chicken and potatoes. Drizzle with additional pomegranate molasses and sprinkle with parsley.

REEM KASSIS SPICE BLEND

Reem Kassis says every household in Galilee has its own spice blend, a mix that is used daily. To make her family's recipe, Kassis calls for **6 tablespoons whole allspice, 6 cinnamon sticks** (broken in half), **3 tablespoons coriander seed, 1 tablespoon black peppercorns, 10 whole cloves, ½ whole nutmeg** (crushed), **1 teaspoon cardamom seeds, ½ teaspoon cumin seeds** and **2 blades mace.** Toast all ingredients in a skillet until aromatic, stirring frequently. Cool, then use a spice grinder to grind to a powder. Makes about 1 cup. Keeps for three months in an airtight container. If you don't have blades of mace, stir in **½ teaspoon ground mace** after grinding.

Pearl Couscous with Chicken and Chickpeas

Start to finish: **1 hour** / Servings: 4 to 6

2 pounds bone-in, skin-on chicken breasts, leg quarters or thighs

2 large or 3 medium yellow onions, chopped

2 bay leaves

Kosher salt and ground black pepper

2 tablespoons extra-virgin olive oil

4 medium garlic cloves, chopped

1 tablespoon ground cumin

½ teaspoon ground cinnamon

½ teaspoon grated nutmeg

1 cup pearl couscous

15½-ounce can chickpeas, rinsed and drained

1 teaspoon pomegranate molasses, plus more to serve

1 cup lightly packed fresh flat-leaf parsley, roughly chopped

This is our version of the fragrantly spiced, stew-like maftoul with chicken and chickpeas that we tasted in Galilee. Maftoul, sometimes referred to as Palestinian couscous, resembles pearl couscous in shape and size but is made with bulgur. It is difficult to source in the U.S., but pearl couscous is a good substitute. For this dish, we first simmer bone-in chicken parts in water with aromatics, then remove and chop the meat, reserving it to add at the end. The broth that results from poaching the chicken is used to cook the couscous, so that its rich, full flavor permeates the dish. Cumin, cinnamon and nutmeg add earthy, warm, spicy notes, and a spoonful of pomegranate molasses brightens with its fruity tang.

Don't use boneless, skinless chicken parts. Bones and skin give flavor and body to the poaching liquid, and since the liquid is used to cook the couscous, the added richness is good. And don't worry if browned bits form on the bottom of the pot as you cook the garlic and onion. These bits build flavor.

1. **In a large saucepan,** combine 5 cups water, the chicken, 1 cup of the chopped onions, the bay and 1 tablespoon salt. Bring to a simmer over medium-high, then reduce to low, cover and cook at a bare simmer until the thickest part of the chicken reaches 160°F for breasts or 175°F for legs/thighs, 20 to 30 minutes; flip the pieces once about halfway through.

2. **Using tongs,** transfer the chicken to a large plate and let cool. Strain enough of the cooking liquid through a fine-mesh strainer to yield 4 cups; discard the remainder or reserve for another use. Remove the meat from the bones, discarding the skin and bones; chop the meat into bite-size pieces.

3. **In the same pan** over medium-high, heat the oil until shimmering. Add the remaining onions and cook, stirring, until lightly browned, 7 to 10 minutes. Add the garlic, cumin, cinnamon, nutmeg and 1 teaspoon each salt and pepper, then cook, stirring, until fragrant, about 30 seconds. Add the 4 cups chicken-cooking liquid and bring to a boil. Stir in the couscous, then cover, reduce to medium-low and cook until tender, 5 to 8 minutes.

4. **Remove the pan from the heat,** then stir in the chopped chicken, chickpeas, pomegranate molasses and half the parsley. Taste and season with salt and pepper. Transfer to a serving bowl, drizzle with additional pomegranate molasses and sprinkle with the remaining parsley.

Vietnamese Caramel Chicken

Start to finish: **40 minutes** / Servings: **4 to 6**

¼ cup white sugar

4 tablespoons coconut water or water, divided

3 tablespoons fish sauce

2 Fresno or serrano chilies, stemmed and sliced into thin rings

1 stalk lemon grass, trimmed to the lower 5 or 6 inches, bruised

2 teaspoons finely chopped fresh ginger

1 teaspoon ground black pepper

2 pounds boneless, skinless chicken thighs, trimmed and cut into 1½-inch pieces

1 tablespoon lime juice

2 scallions, thinly sliced on the diagonal

The classic Vietnamese technique of simmering meat or fish in dark, bittersweet caramel mixed with fish sauce and a few aromatics yields rich, wonderfully complex savory-sweet flavors. And the technique could hardly be simpler. Instead of a traditional clay pot, we use a 12-inch skillet to make our version of gà kho, or caramel-simmered chicken, and we cook the chicken until the sauce forms a glaze, as we were taught in Vietnam by Peter Franklin, owner of the Anan Saigon restaurant. Bruising the lemon grass releases its flavor and fragrance but since the stalk is still whole, it is easy to remove and discard before serving; the simplest way to bruise it is with the blunt side of the blade of a chef's knife or the butt end of the handle. Serve with steamed jasmine rice.

Don't be shy when cooking the caramel. Allow it to darken deeply—a smoky, bitter caramel is what gives this dish depth of flavor. It should reach a mahogany hue and will smoke lightly when ready.

1. In a 12-inch skillet, combine the sugar and 2 tablespoons of the coconut water. Cook over medium-high, occasionally swirling the pan to help the sugar dissolve and to encourage even browning, until the caramel is mahogany in color and smokes lightly, 4 to 6 minutes.

2. Remove the pan from the heat and add the fish sauce along with the remaining 2 tablespoons coconut water; the mixture will bubble vigorously and the caramel will harden in spots. Bring to a simmer over medium and cook, stirring, until the hardened bits have dissolved. Add the chilies, lemon grass, ginger and pepper, then cook, stirring, until fragrant, about 30 seconds. Increase to medium-high and stir in the chicken. Bring to a simmer and cook, stirring occasionally, until the sauce reduces and clings to the chicken, 10 to 14 minutes.

3. Remove from the heat, then discard the lemon grass. Stir in the lime juice. Transfer to a serving dish and sprinkle with the scallions.

VIETNAMESE CARAMEL PORK TENDERLOIN

Cut **two 1¼-pound pork tenderloins** (trimmed of silver skin) in half lengthwise, then crosswise into ½-inch-thick pieces. Follow the recipe to make the caramel and cook the chilies, lemon grass, ginger and pepper. Add the pork and cook, stirring often, until just cooked through, 2 to 3 minutes. Using a slotted spoon, transfer the pork to a medium bowl, then continue to cook the caramel mixture, stirring occasionally, until thickened to the consistency of honey, about 2 minutes. Off heat, return the pork to the skillet and stir to coat. Discard the lemon grass, then stir in the lime juice. Transfer to a serving dish and sprinkle with the scallions.

VIETNAMESE CARAMEL SALMON

Cut **2 pounds 1-inch-thick skinless salmon fillets** into 1½-inch cubes. Follow the recipe to make the caramel and cook the chilies, lemon grass, ginger and pepper. Add the salmon and cook, stirring often, until the salmon is just opaque throughout, 5 to 6 minutes. Remove and discard the lemon grass, then stir in the lime juice. Transfer to a serving dish and sprinkle with the scallions.

Vietnamese Chicken Curry

Start to finish: 35 minutes, plus marinating / Servings: 4

¼ cup grapeseed or other neutral oil

4 medium garlic cloves, smashed and peeled

3-inch piece fresh ginger, peeled and roughly chopped

1 medium yellow onion, roughly chopped

3 stalks lemon grass, trimmed to the lower 5 or 6 inches, dry outer layers discarded, thinly sliced

2 tablespoons coriander seeds

2 teaspoons ground turmeric

1 teaspoon ground cinnamon

Kosher salt and ground black pepper

2 pounds boneless, skinless chicken thighs, trimmed and cut crosswise into 1- to 1½-inch pieces

5 star anise pods

2 medium carrots, peeled, halved and sliced ¼ inch thick

2 tablespoons fish sauce

¼ cup lime juice

Chopped fresh cilantro, to serve

The category of complexly spiced dishes we know collectively as "curry" was brought to Vietnam by Indian immigrants who arrived in the country in the 19th century, while both Indochina and the port of Pondicherry, India, were under French rule. Lemon grass, fish sauce and star anise were incorporated as curry ingredients to adapt the flavors to local palates. As a result, Vietnamese curry has a uniquely bright, yet deeply savory taste and aroma. Though many versions of cà ri gà, or chicken curry, call for store-bought curry powder, we prefer to mix our own spices so we can control the seasoning. Serve with steamed jasmine rice.

Don't underblend the spice mixture. Make sure it's perfectly smooth, without any fibrousness or tough bits from the lemon grass and ginger. Also, don't use chicken breasts in place of the chicken thighs. Breast meat is delicate and mild; it will wind up overcooked and the curry will lack flavor.

1. **In a blender,** combine the oil, garlic, ginger, onion, lemon grass, coriander, turmeric, cinnamon, ½ cup water and 1 teaspoon each salt and pepper. Blend until smooth, 1 to 2 minutes, scraping the blender jar as needed. Transfer the puree to a medium bowl, add the chicken and stir until evenly coated. Cover and refrigerate for at least 30 minutes or up to 1 hour.

2. **In a 12-inch skillet,** combine the chicken and all of the marinade, the star anise and carrots. Bring to a simmer over medium-high and cook, stirring occasionally, until the marinade begins to brown, 6 to 7 minutes. Stir in ⅓ cup water and the fish sauce. Return to a simmer, then cover, reduce to medium-low and cook, stirring occasionally and adjusting the heat as needed to maintain a simmer, until the carrots are crisp-tender, about 5 minutes. Uncover and continue to cook, stirring, until the sauce thickens enough to cling to the chicken, about another 5 minutes.

3. **Remove from the heat** and stir in the lime juice. Remove and discard the star anise, then taste and season with salt and pepper. Transfer to a serving dish and sprinkle with cilantro.

Butter Chicken

Start to finish: 1 hour 25 minutes (45 minutes active), plus marinating / Servings: 4 to 6

1 cup plain whole-milk yogurt

2 tablespoons honey

1 tablespoon sweet paprika

½ teaspoon cayenne pepper

4 tablespoons garam masala, divided

2 tablespoons ground cumin, divided

2 tablespoons finely grated fresh ginger, divided

Kosher salt and ground black pepper

2½ pounds boneless, skinless chicken thighs, cut crosswise into 3 strips

1 cup roasted salted cashews

4 tablespoons (½ stick) salted butter, divided

1 large yellow onion, finely chopped

6 medium garlic cloves, finely grated

28-ounce can crushed tomatoes

¼ cup finely chopped fresh cilantro

2 tablespoons lime juice

In our take on the butter chicken made for us in Mumbai by home cook Rumya Misquitta, boneless chicken thighs are briefly marinated in yogurt and spices, then broiled until lightly charred. We make a separate sauce into which the chicken then is stirred. In many recipes for butter chicken, copious amounts of butter and heavy cream supply richness. But we do as we were taught in India and use cashews pureed with a small amount of water until smooth. The nut puree adds creaminess without making the dish heavy. Serve this with steamed basmati rice for soaking up the sauce.

Don't scrape the marinade off the chicken before broiling. The yogurt and honey help the chicken brown and char under the broiler.

1. **In a large bowl,** whisk together the yogurt, honey, paprika, cayenne, 3 tablespoons of the garam masala, 1 tablespoon of the cumin, 1 tablespoon of the ginger and 2 teaspoons salt. Add the chicken and stir until evenly coated. Cover and refrigerate for at least 30 minutes or up to 1 hour.

2. **Heat the broiler** with a rack about 6 inches from the broiler element. Line a rimmed baking sheet with foil, set a wire rack in the baking sheet and mist it with cooking spray. In a blender, puree the cashews with ¾ cup water until smooth, about 1 minute; set aside.

3. **In a large Dutch oven** over medium, melt 2 tablespoons of the butter. Add the onion and cook, stirring occasionally, until beginning to brown, about 5 minutes. Stir in the remaining 1 tablespoon ginger and the garlic, then cook until fragrant, about 30 seconds. Stir in the remaining 1 tablespoon garam masala and the remaining 1 tablespoon cumin. Add the cashew puree and cook, stirring constantly, until the mixture begins to brown, about 3 minutes. Stir in the tomatoes and 2 cups water, scraping up any browned bits. Add the remaining 2 tablespoons butter and bring to a simmer, stirring to combine. Reduce to medium and cook, stirring often, until the sauce is thick enough to heavily coat a spoon, 12 to 14 minutes. Taste and season with salt and pepper. Remove from the heat and cover to keep warm.

4. **Arrange the chicken** with its marinade still clinging to it in an even layer on the prepared rack. Broil until well browned and lightly charred on both sides, 15 to 20 minutes, flipping the pieces once about halfway through. Transfer to the sauce, bring to a simmer over medium and cook, stirring occasionally, until a skewer inserted into the chicken meets no resistance, about 10 minutes. Off heat, stir in the cilantro and lime juice, then let stand for 5 minutes. Taste and season with salt and pepper.

Chicken Vindaloo

Start to finish: 1 hour 20 minutes / Servings: 4

¼ cup plus 2 tablespoons white vinegar, divided

12 medium garlic cloves, smashed and peeled

1-inch piece fresh ginger, peeled and roughly chopped

2 tablespoons sweet paprika

2 tablespoons packed brown sugar

4 whole cloves or ⅛ teaspoon ground cloves

2½ teaspoons ground turmeric

2 teaspoons cumin seeds

½ to 1 teaspoon cayenne pepper

¼ teaspoon ground cinnamon

Kosher salt and ground black pepper

2 pounds boneless, skinless chicken thighs, trimmed and halved

2 tablespoons grapeseed or other neutral oil

Fresno or jalapeño chilies, stemmed and sliced into thin rings, to serve

Fresh cilantro leaves, to serve

Vindaloo, an Indian dish of Portuguese influence, typically is associated with the state of Goa on India's southwestern coast, but the curry is popular in other areas of the country and the world over. It is made with pork, lamb or chicken, and is notable for its vinegary tang, a generous dose of garlic and the spiciness of dried chilies. The Kashmiri chilies used in India are vibrantly colored with moderate heat; we found a mixture of sweet paprika and cayenne to be a good substitute. If you purchase Kashmiri chili powder, substitute 4 teaspoons for the paprika and cayenne. Serve with basmati rice.

Don't worry if the chicken sticks to the pot immediately after it is added. Allow it to cook undisturbed and it eventually will release with ease. And don't be afraid to allow the chicken and puree to brown as they cook. This brings out the flavors in the spices and tames the pungency of the aromatics, yielding a sauce that tastes full and round.

1. **In a blender,** combine ¼ cup vinegar, garlic, ginger, paprika, sugar, cloves, turmeric, cumin, cayenne, cinnamon, 1¼ teaspoons each salt and pepper, and 3 tablespoons water. Puree until smooth, scraping the blender as needed. Pour into a medium bowl, add the chicken and toss to coat. Let stand at room temperature for 15 minutes.

2. **In a large Dutch oven** over medium, heat the oil until shimmering. Add the chicken and marinade, distributing in an even layer, then cook without stirring until the marinade has browned and the chicken releases easily from the pot, 5 to 9 minutes. Stir, then add ⅓ cup water and bring to a simmer. Cover, then reduce to medium-low and cook, stirring occasionally, until a skewer inserted into the chicken meets no resistance, 35 to 45 minutes.

3. **Stir in the remaining** 2 tablespoons vinegar, increase to medium and cook, stirring often, until the sauce is thick enough that a spoon drawn through leaves a trail, about 8 minutes. Taste and season with salt and pepper. Transfer to a serving dish and sprinkle with sliced chilies and cilantro.

Japanese-Style Chicken and Vegetable Curry

Start to finish: 1 hour / Servings: 4

---

1 pound boneless, skinless chicken thighs, trimmed and cut into 1-inch pieces

Kosher salt and ground black pepper

5 tablespoons salted butter, cut into 1-tablespoon pieces, divided

1 medium yellow onion, halved and thinly sliced

2 medium garlic cloves, finely grated

1½ teaspoons finely grated fresh ginger

3 tablespoons all-purpose flour

1 tablespoon Japanese-style curry powder (recipe follows)

8 ounces Yukon Gold potatoes, peeled and cut into ½-inch chunks

1 medium carrot, peeled and sliced into ½-inch rounds

1 small red bell pepper, stemmed, seeded and cut into ½-inch pieces

2 tablespoons soy sauce

1 tablespoon mirin

Japanese curry is wildly popular, including outside Japan. Some restaurants specialize in the dish, offering dozens of iterations, from basic beef curry to fried cutlets and croquettes with curry, hamburger curry, even curried omelets. At home, Japanese curry typically is made using commercially produced "bricks," which are seasonings mixed with a roux and packaged much like bars of chocolate. Added near the end of cooking, a curry brick, broken into pieces, melts into the mix, seasoning the dish as well as thickening it. Sonoko Sakai, a cooking instructor based in Los Angeles and author of "Japanese Home Cooking," blends her own curry powder, which she uses to create all-natural, additive-free homemade curry bricks. This recipe is our adaptation of Sakai's chicken curry. We simplified her curry powder and skipped the brick-making process in favor of a built-in roux for thickening. Serve with steamed short-grain rice and, if you can find it, fukujinzuke, a crunchy savory-sweet pickle-like condiment that's commonly offered alongside Japanese curry. Lemon wedges for squeezing are a nice touch, too.

Don't worry if the flour sticks to the bottom of the pot and begins to brown. This is normal, and the browning helps build flavor in the curry. But stir constantly and lower the heat if the flour is coloring too quickly. Also, when adding the first 1 cup water, do so in two additions and be sure to scrape the bottom of the pot to loosen any stuck bits of flour. A rigid wooden spoon is better suited to the task than a flexible silicone spatula.

1. In a medium bowl, toss the chicken with ½ teaspoon each salt and pepper; set aside. In a large Dutch oven over medium-high, melt 2 tablespoons of butter. Add the onion and cook, stirring occasionally, until golden brown, about 9 minutes. Push the onion to the edges of the pot, add the chicken to the center and cook, stirring just once or twice, until the chicken is no longer pink on the exterior, 2 to 3 minutes. Reduce to medium, then stir the onion into the chicken. Add the garlic, ginger and the remaining 3 tablespoons butter, then cook, stirring, until the butter melts. Add the flour and cook, stirring constantly, until lightly browned, 2 to 3 minutes; some of the flour will stick to the bottom of the pot. Add the curry powder and continue to cook, stirring constantly, until fragrant and toasted, 2 to 3 minutes.

2. Working in two additions, add 1 cup water while stirring and scraping the bottom of the pot to loosen the browned bits, then cook, stirring, until the mixture is smooth and thick, about 2 minutes. Stir in another 1¼ cups water and bring to a simmer. Add the potatoes, carrot and bell pepper, then cook, uncovered and stirring occasionally and scraping the bottom of the pot, until a skewer inserted into the potatoes and carrots meets no resistance, about 20 minutes; adjust the heat as needed to maintain a simmer.

3. Stir in the soy sauce, mirin and ½ teaspoon pepper. Cook, stirring often, until the curry is thick enough to lightly coat the chicken and vegetables, 2 to 4 minutes. Remove from the heat, then taste and season with salt and pepper.

JAPANESE-STYLE CURRY POWDER

Start to finish: 15 minutes
Makes about ⅓ cup

1 small dried shiitake mushroom (about 1 inch in diameter), stemmed and broken in small pieces

1½ teaspoons brown or black mustard seeds

1½ teaspoons coriander seeds

1½ teaspoons fennel seeds

1½ teaspoons cumin seeds

1½ teaspoons ground ginger

1 teaspoon ground turmeric

½ teaspoon sweet paprika

½ teaspoon ground black pepper

¼ teaspoon ground cloves

¼ teaspoon ground cinnamon

1. In an 8-inch skillet over medium, toast the shiitake, mustard seeds, coriander, fennel and cumin, stirring often, until fragrant, 2 to 4 minutes. Transfer to a small bowl and cool for about 5 minutes.

2. In a spice grinder, process the toasted spice mixture to a fine powder, 1 to 2 minutes, periodically shaking the grinder. Return to the bowl and stir in the ground ginger, turmeric, paprika, pepper, cloves and cinnamon. Store in an airtight container for up to 2 months.

Chicken, Salsa Verde and Tortilla Casserole (Pastel Azteca)

Start to finish: 2 hours (1¼ hours active), plus resting
Servings: 8

---

1 pound poblano chilies

1½ pounds tomatillos, husked and halved

3 medium garlic cloves, smashed and peeled

2 tablespoons white vinegar

1 cup lightly packed fresh cilantro, plus ½ cup chopped fresh cilantro, divided

3 teaspoons ground cumin, divided

Kosher salt and ground black pepper

1 tablespoon grapeseed or other neutral oil

1 pound boneless, skinless chicken thighs

1 large white onion, chopped

1 cup corn kernels, thawed if frozen

Eight 6-inch corn tortillas

1 cup Mexican crema or one 8-ounce container crème fraîche, room temperature

12 ounces pepper Jack cheese, shredded (4 cups)

4 ounces cotija cheese grated (1 cup)

2 tablespoons pumpkin seeds, finely chopped (optional)

Though pastel azteca translates from the Spanish as "Aztec cake," the dish often is referred to in English as Mexican lasagna, enchilada casserole or tortilla pie—and understandably so. It is made up of corn tortillas layered with sauce, meat, cheeses, crema (a cultured cream similar to crème fraîche) and vegetables; a stint in the oven brings together all the elements. Our recipe is an adaptation of the pastel azteca taught to us in Mexico City by chef Esmeralda Brinn Bolaños. We swapped chicken thighs for the dark-meat turkey that she used and found readily available substitutes for the locally made Mexican cheeses. We opted for pepper Jack because of its melting qualities and mild spiciness; if you prefer, use regular Jack cheese or even mozzarella. To assemble and bake the casserole, we use a 9-inch springform pan for a presentation that reveals the impressive layers and allows for slicing into wedges for serving.

Don't use sour cream in place of Mexican crema. Sour cream has a lower fat content and will curdle during baking. If crema is not available, crème fraîche is the next best option, but it's much thicker than crema, so allow it to come to room temperature before use so it's easier to spread. Don't slice the pastel until it has rested for at least 30 minutes to allow the layers to set up for easier slicing and serving.

---

1. **Heat the broiler** with a rack about 6 inches from the element. Place the poblanos on a rimmed baking sheet and broil until charred, about 10 minutes. Flip the chilies and broil until charred on the second sides, 3 to 5 minutes. Transfer to a medium bowl, cover with plastic wrap and let steam to loosen the skins while you make the puree and cook the chicken. Turn the oven to 375°F.

2. **In a blender,** combine the tomatillos, garlic, vinegar, 1 cup of cilantro, 2 teaspoons of cumin and 1 teaspoon salt. Blend until smooth, about 1 minute, scraping the blender jar as needed.

3. **In a large Dutch oven** over medium-high, heat the oil until shimmering. Carefully add the puree (it may splatter) and cook, stirring occasionally, until slightly reduced and a spoon drawn through leaves a brief trail, about 6 minutes. Remove ½ cup of the sauce and set aside. To the remaining sauce in the pot, add the chicken, onion, remaining 1 teaspoon cumin, ¼ teaspoon salt and ½ teaspoon pepper. Bring to a simmer, then cover, reduce to medium-low and cook, stirring occasionally, until a skewer inserted into the chicken meets no resistance, 15 to 20 minutes.

4. While the chicken cooks, peel the skins off the chilies and remove and discard the stems and seeds. Chop the chilies and set aside. When the chicken is done, remove the pot from the heat. Using 2 forks, shred the chicken; you should have about 3½ cups chicken in sauce. If you have more, return the pot to medium heat and cook, stirring occasionally, until reduced. Stir in the corn, ¼ cup of the chopped cilantro and the chopped chilies. Taste and season with salt and pepper.

5. Wrap the exterior of a 9-inch springform pan with a sheet of foil and set on a rimmed baking sheet. Add half of the reserved sauce to the pan and spread in an even layer. Line the bottom of the pan with 2⅔ tortillas, tearing them as needed to fit; it's fine if the tortillas overlap slightly and if a few small spots are uncovered. Spoon in half of the chicken mixture and distribute in an even layer. Dollop with half of the crema, then spread evenly. Sprinkle with a third of the pepper Jack cheese. Repeat the layering using another 2⅔ tortillas, the remaining chicken mixture, the remaining crema and half of the remaining pepper Jack. Layer in the remaining tortillas, then spread evenly with the remaining reserved sauce. Sprinkle on the remaining pepper Jack followed by the cotija. Bake the pastel on the baking sheet until browned on top and bubbling at the edges, about 35 minutes.

6. Set the baking sheet on a wire rack. Sprinkle the pastel with the remaining ¼ cup chopped cilantro and the pumpkin seeds (if using). Let rest for at least 30 minutes or up to 1 hour.

7. To serve, run a knife around the inside of the springform pan to loosen. Remove the foil, set the pan on a large, flat platter and remove the sides. Cut into wedges and serve.

Chicken Roasted with Garlic-Herb Crème Fraîche

Start to finish: 1¾ hours (45 minutes active), plus refrigeration and standing time / Servings: 4

1 bunch dill, leaves and stems, roughly chopped (about 2 cups)

1 bunch flat-leaf parsley or cilantro, leaves and stems, roughly chopped (about 2 cups)

6 medium garlic cloves, smashed and peeled

Kosher salt and ground black pepper

1 cup crème fraîche

3½- to 4-pound whole chicken, patted dry inside and out

2 tablespoons lemon juice

In "Summer Kitchens," Ukraine-born Londoner and cookbook author Olia Hercules writes, "Chicken smothered and baked in cultured cream is an old classic, but sometimes I like to go one step further." So she packs bold flavor into crème fraîche by mixing it with fresh herbs and garlic before slathering it onto a whole bird. In this recipe, our adaptation of her simple yet succulent pot-roasted chicken, we coat the bird inside and out with garlicky, herby crème fraîche and refrigerate it for at least two hours or up to 24 hours before roasting. The crème fraîche not only adheres the garlic and herbs to the bird, its high fat content helps with browning and adds flavor. (Sour cream, which is much leaner, is not a suitable substitute.) Hercules shreds the meat off the bones after cooking, but we like to serve the chicken carved, its richly browned skin adding to the flavor and overall allure. We also make a simple sauce to serve alongside.

Don't leave the herbs damp after washing them. Be sure to dry them well or the moisture may cause them to become watery when processed. Don't use a glass or ceramic baking dish. A metal baking pan is best because it's a good conductor of heat and is guaranteed not to crack when water is poured in midway through roasting. A 9-by-13-inch pan is perfectly sized for the chicken; in a larger pan, the drippings are apt to scorch because of the greater surface area. Finally, make sure to remove the chicken from the refrigerator about 1 hour before roasting. This will help it cook more evenly.

1. **In a food processor,** combine the dill, parsley or cilantro, garlic and 1 teaspoon each salt and pepper. Process until the herbs are finely chopped, about 1 minute. Add the crème fraîche and process just until combined, 20 to 30 seconds, scraping the bowl as needed; do not overprocess. Transfer ½ cup of the mixture to a small bowl, cover and refrigerate for making the sauce. Scrape the remainder into another small bowl and refrigerate until chilled and slightly thicker, about 30 minutes; this portion will be used directly on the chicken.

2. **Place the chicken** in a 9-by-13-inch metal baking pan. Using a spoon, spread ¼ cup of the crème fraîche mixture for the chicken in the cavity of the bird. Tie the legs together with kitchen twine. Slather the remaining crème fraîche mixture all over the exterior of the chicken (it's fine if some of it falls into the pan). Cover loosely with plastic wrap and refrigerate for at least 2 hours or up to 24 hours.

3. About 1 hour before roasting, remove the chicken from the refrigerator and let stand, still covered, at room temperature. Heat the oven to 425°F with a rack in the lower-middle position.

4. After the chicken has stood for about 1 hour, remove the plastic wrap and tent the pan with a large sheet of extra-wide foil; try to keep the foil from touching the chicken. Roast for 40 minutes. Remove the reserved crème fraîche mixture for the sauce from the refrigerator and let stand at room temperature.

5. Working quickly, remove the foil from the chicken, pour ¾ cup water into the pan and continue to roast, uncovered, until the thickest part of the breast registers 160°F and the thighs reach 175°F, another 20 to 30 minutes; if at any point the pan is close to dry, add water to prevent scorching. Carefully tip the juices from the cavity of the bird into the pan, then transfer the chicken to a cutting board. Let rest while you make the sauce.

6. Scrape up any browned bits in the bottom of the pan, then pour the liquid into a fine-mesh strainer set over a liquid measuring cup. Let the liquid settle for a few minutes, then use a spoon to skim off and discard the fat from the surface. You should have ½ to ¾ cup defatted liquid; if you have more, you will need to reduce it to that amount. Either way, pour the liquid into a small saucepan and bring to a simmer over medium-high; if needed cook, stirring occasionally, until reduced to ½ to ¾ cup. Remove the pan from the heat, whisk in the reserved ½ cup crème fraîche mixture and the lemon juice. Taste and season with salt and pepper.

7. Carve the chicken and transfer to a platter. Pour about ¼ cup of the sauce over the chicken, then serve with the remaining sauce on the side.

Jerusalem-Style Mixed-Grill Chicken

Start to finish: 35 minutes / Servings: 4 to 6

¼ cup white vinegar

½ teaspoon white sugar

Kosher salt and ground black pepper

1 large red onion, halved and thinly sliced

⅓ cup tahini

4 tablespoons lemon juice, divided

3 tablespoons extra-virgin olive oil, divided

1½ teaspoons ground coriander

1 teaspoon ground allspice

1 teaspoon ground turmeric

¾ teaspoon ground cinnamon

2 pounds boneless, skinless chicken thighs, trimmed and cut into 1½-inch chunks

Jerusalem mixed grill, or meorav yerushalmi, is a popular Israeli street food, one that is said to originate in Jerusalem's Mahane Yehuda market. The term "mixed" refers to the sundry ingredients that go into the dish—chicken meat, hearts, spleen and liver, along with bits of lamb, plus onions and spices. To re-create a simplified mixed grill at home, we borrowed from chef Daniel Alt's version at The Barbary and Omri McNabb's take on it at The Palomar, two London restaurants that serve up modern Levantine and Middle Eastern cuisine. We limited the meat to boneless, skinless chicken thighs and seasoned them assertively with select spices. Our "grill" is a nonstick skillet on the stovetop. Amba, a pickled mango condiment, is commonly served with mixed grill to offset the richness of the meat; we, however, quick-pickle sliced red onion to offer a similar acidity and brightness. Nutty, creamy tahini sauce is, of course, a requirement. Serve the chicken with warmed pita.

Don't stir the chicken-onion mixture too often while cooking; doing so disrupts browning. Intermittent stirring—no more than every 2 to 3 minutes—allows the chicken to develop nice, deep, flavor-building char.

1. **In a small bowl,** stir together the vinegar, sugar and ¼ teaspoon salt until the sugar and salt dissolve. Stir in 1 cup of sliced onion; set aside. In another small bowl, mix together the tahini and 2 tablespoons of lemon juice, then whisk in 6 tablespoons water. Season to taste with salt and pepper; set aside.

2. **In a medium bowl,** stir together 2 tablespoons of oil, the coriander, allspice, turmeric, cinnamon and ½ teaspoon each salt and pepper. Add the chicken and the remaining sliced onion, then stir until evenly coated.

3. **In a 12-inch nonstick skillet** over medium-high, heat the remaining 1 tablespoon oil until barely smoking. Add the chicken mixture in an even layer and cook, uncovered and stirring only every 2 to 3 minutes, until the chicken is well browned all over and no longer is pink when cut into, 10 to 12 minutes.

4. **Off heat,** stir in the remaining 2 tablespoons lemon juice, then taste and season with salt and pepper. Transfer to a serving dish, drizzle lightly with some of the tahini sauce and top with the pickled onion. Serve the remaining tahini sauce on the side.

Provençal Braised Chicken

Start to finish: 45 minutes / Servings: 4

1½ pounds boneless, skinless chicken thighs, trimmed, patted dry and cut crosswise into 1-inch pieces

Kosher salt and ground black pepper

¼ cup extra-virgin olive oil

1 medium red onion, halved and thinly sliced

1 medium fennel bulb, trimmed, cored and thinly sliced

2 tablespoons tomato paste

3 medium garlic cloves, minced

¼ teaspoon red pepper flakes

2 wide strips orange zest (each about 2 inches long), plus 2 tablespoons orange juice

½ cup dry white wine

¼ teaspoon saffron threads

1 cup lightly packed fresh basil, torn

Think of this dish as bouillabaisse made with chicken instead of seafood. Fresh fennel, garlic, white wine, orange zest and saffron give the braise rich, heady perfume and an unmistakably Mediterranean flavor. Any unoaked dry white wine works well here, but ideally look for one produced in southern France, such as white Côtes du Rhône or marsanne. We use strips of orange zest instead of grated zest to lend citrusy notes to the braise. A sharp Y-style vegetable peeler is the best tool for peeling away zest strips, but try to remove only the colored peel, not the bitter white pith just underneath. Serve the chicken with toasted crusty bread drizzled with olive oil.

Don't be shy about cooking the tomato paste. Allowing it to brown not only adds color, it also helps develop flavor in the braising liquid.

1. **In a medium bowl,** toss the chicken with ½ teaspoon each salt and black pepper; set aside. In a large Dutch oven over medium-high, heat the oil until shimmering. Add the onion, fennel and ½ teaspoon salt, then cook, stirring occasionally, until the vegetables begin to brown, about 10 minutes.

2. **Add the tomato paste,** garlic, pepper flakes and orange zest. Cook, stirring often, until the tomato paste begins to darken and stick to the pot, about 4 minutes. Reduce to medium and add the wine. Bring to a simmer and cook, scraping up any browned bits, until the liquid is almost evaporated, about 3 minutes.

3. **Add the chicken,** 3 cups water and the saffron, then stir to combine. Bring to a simmer, then reduce to medium-low and cook, uncovered and stirring occasionally, until a skewer inserted into the chicken meets no resistance, about 15 minutes.

4. **Off heat,** remove and discard the zest strips. Stir in the orange juice and about half the basil, then taste and season with salt and black pepper. Transfer to a serving dish and sprinkle with the remaining basil.

Vietnamese Braised Lemon Grass Chicken

Start to finish: 1 hour (30 minutes active) / Servings: 4

1 tablespoon grapeseed or other neutral oil

6 medium garlic cloves, minced

2 Fresno or jalapeño chilies, stemmed, seeded and thinly sliced

1 tablespoon ground turmeric

3 stalks fresh lemon grass, trimmed to the bottom 6 inches, dry outer layers discarded, bruised

1 cup low-sodium chicken broth

2 tablespoons soy sauce

2 tablespoons packed brown sugar

2½ pounds bone-in, skin-on chicken thighs, skin removed and discarded, patted dry

1 teaspoon cornstarch

2 tablespoons lime juice

1 tablespoon fish sauce

Ground black pepper

Cilantro or sliced scallions, to serve

In Ho Chi Minh City, Vietnam, home cook Pham Thi Thanh Tâm taught us to make her version of braised chicken with lemon grass. Seasoned with turmeric, garlic, chilies and fish sauce—staple ingredients in the Vietnamese kitchen—the dish was remarkably simple, yet wonderfully aromatic and full of flavor. Instead of mincing fresh lemon grass, which requires a good amount of time and effort, we simply bruise the stalks so they split open and release their essential oils into the braising liquid; we remove and discard the stalks when cooking is complete. The soy sauce in the recipe is our own addition, a stand-in for the MSG and pork bouillon that Pham used, and we opt to thicken the braising liquid with a little cornstarch to give the sauce just a little body. Serve the chicken with steamed jasmine rice.

Don't leave the skin on the chicken. We want the bone, which adds flavor to the braise, but not the skin, which turns soggy with simmering and releases fat into the liquid. But bone-in thighs are almost always sold with skin, so we simply pull it off before cooking.

1. In a large Dutch oven over medium, heat the oil until shimmering. Add the garlic, chilies and turmeric, then cook, stirring, until fragrant, about 30 seconds. Add the lemon grass, broth, soy sauce, sugar and 1 cup water, then bring to a simmer. Add the chicken skin side down in an even layer and return to a simmer. Cover, reduce to medium-low and cook until a skewer inserted into the chicken meets no resistance, 30 to 40 minutes.

2. Using tongs, transfer the chicken skinned side up to a serving bowl. Cook the braising liquid over medium until reduced by about half, about 12 minutes. Remove and discard the lemon grass. In a small bowl, stir together the cornstarch and 1 tablespoon water. Whisk the mixture into the braising liquid, return to a simmer and cook, stirring constantly, until lightly thickened, about 1 minute.

3. Off heat, stir the lime juice and fish sauce into the braising liquid, then taste and season with pepper. Return the chicken and any accumulated juices to the pot, cover and let stand until heated through, about 5 minutes. Return the braise to the serving bowl and sprinkle with cilantro.

Za'atar Chicken Cutlets and Lemon-Parsley Salad

Start to finish: **30 minutes** / Servings: 4

1½ pounds boneless, skinless chicken breast cutlets (4 cutlets), pounded to ¼-inch thickness

Kosher salt

¼ cup plus 1 teaspoon za'atar, divided

3 tablespoons all-purpose flour

¾ teaspoon Aleppo pepper (see headnote)

2 tablespoons plus 1 teaspoon extra-virgin olive oil, divided

¾ cup lightly packed fresh flat-leaf parsley

2 scallions, trimmed and thinly sliced on diagonal

½ teaspoon lemon zest, plus 1 tablespoon lemon juice

2 tablespoons pomegranate molasses

3 tablespoons finely chopped walnuts

Our search for ways to spice up weeknight chicken took us to the Middle East where za'atar is a popular seasoning blend that often includes sesame seeds, sumac, thyme, oregano, marjoram and salt. We were influenced by Ana Sortun, who often uses za'atar at her Oleana restaurant in Cambridge, Massachusetts. She calls za'atar "craveable" and jokes, "I can imagine it as the next Doritos flavor." Her recipe for crispy lemon chicken with za'atar calls for making a lemon confit and stuffing it under the skin of whole halves of deboned chicken along with cubes of butter. We took a simpler tack and coated chicken cutlets in a flour-za'atar mixture. We also used lemon zest and juice in our sauce along with tart and smoky Aleppo pepper, which has a fruity, moderate heat. If you can't find Aleppo pepper, sweet paprika makes a decent substitute, but add a pinch of cayenne for a touch of heat.

Don't substitute chicken breasts here without pounding the meat first. Boneless, skinless chicken cutlets were ideal for fast cooking and are widely available at grocers. If you have only chicken breasts, use a meat mallet or heavy skillet to flatten them to an even ¼ inch.

1. Season the chicken all over with salt. In a wide, shallow dish, combine ¼ cup of the za'atar, the flour and pepper. In a 12-inch stainless steel skillet over medium-high, heat 2 tablespoons of the oil until shimmering. One cutlet at a time, transfer the chicken to the za'atar mixture, coating and pressing onto all sides. Add the cutlets to the pan and cook until well browned, about 3 minutes per side. Transfer to a platter.

2. In a medium bowl, mix together the parsley, scallions, lemon zest and juice, the remaining 1 teaspoon of oil and a pinch of salt. Drizzle the molasses evenly over the chicken, then mound the greens over the cutlets. Sprinkle with walnuts and the remaining za'atar.

MAKING CHICKEN CUTLETS

1. Start with boneless, skinless chicken breasts that weigh 6½ to 7 ounces each. (If breasts are larger than 8 ounces, halve horizontally after removing the tenderloin. Cutlets will require less pounding but will be smaller.)

2. Remove the tenderloin from the breast using kitchen shears and save for another use, such as chicken fingers.

3. Use a sharp knife or kitchen shears to trim away any fat, then, if necessary, trim the breasts to 6 ounces each.

4. Working with 1 breast at a time, place on a cutting board and lay a sheet of plastic wrap on top. Use a meat mallet or small, heavy skillet to gently but firmly pound the breast to an even, ¼-inch thickness.

Brown Ale Turkey with Gravy

Start to finish: 3½ hours (30 minutes active), plus cooling
Servings: 10

2 medium yellow onions
(1 to 1¼ pounds), cut into
8 wedges each

4 large sprigs fresh thyme

2 large sprigs fresh
rosemary

2 large sprigs fresh sage

2 bay leaves

2 medium garlic cloves,
crushed

Two 12-ounce bottles brown
ale, such as Newcastle
Brown Ale

4 tablespoons (½ stick)
salted butter, cut into 4 pieces

¼ cup fish sauce

Kosher salt and ground
black pepper

12- to 14-pound turkey, neck
and giblets discarded

2 stalks celery, quartered

Low-sodium chicken broth,
as needed

¼ cup instant flour, such
as Wondra

Roasting a turkey, whether for Thanksgiving, Christmas or just because, can be an ordeal. The debate over brining alone is enough to make one consider going vegetarian. And, of course, there is the finicky business of how to get the thigh and breast meat to cook to perfect—yet different— temperatures simultaneously. We skipped the culinary gymnastics in favor of a tried-and-true method—basting. Then we made it better with beer. We doused our turkey— but only twice, so no worries about having to babysit the bird–with a reduction of brown ale, onions, garlic and fresh herbs, which combined to form a rich, malty base. Avoid hoppy beers, which turned unpleasantly bitter when reduced. We also used a secret ingredient: fish sauce. It adds savory depth to the baste that is reflected in the umami-rich gravy made from pan drippings. Relax, it doesn't taste at all fishy.

1. Heat the oven to 350°F with a rack in the lower middle position. In a 12-inch skillet, combine the onions, thyme, rosemary, sage, bay leaves, garlic and beer. Bring to a boil, then reduce heat to medium and simmer until reduced to ⅔ cup, about 20 minutes.

2. Strain the mixture into a large bowl, pressing on the solids. Reserve the solids. The liquid should measure ⅔ cup. If not, either reduce further or add water. Return the reduction to the skillet, add the butter, and whisk until melted. Stir in the fish sauce and ½ teaspoon each salt and pepper.

3. Pat the turkey dry inside and out with paper towels. Tuck the wings underneath. Spread the reserved solids and celery in a large roasting pan and place the turkey breast side up over the mix- ture. Pour half of the beer reduction over the turkey; use your hands to coat it evenly. Cover loosely with foil, then roast for 1½ hours.

4. Remove the foil. Whisk the remaining beer reduction, then pour over the turkey. Roast until the breast registers 160°F and the thigh registers 175°F, 1 to 1 hour 45 minutes. If the turkey gets too dark, cover with foil.

5. Transfer the turkey to a platter or carving board, letting the juices run into the pan, then tent with foil and let rest for 30 minutes. Strain the pan drippings into a 4-cup liquid measuring cup, pressing on the solids; discard the solids.

6. Skim the fat from the drippings. If you have less than 3 cups of defatted drippings, add stock to measure 3 cups, then return to the roasting pan. Whisk in the flour, then set the pan on the stove- top and bring to a boil over medium. Simmer, whisking constantly and scraping the bottom, until thickened, 1 to 3 minutes. Season with salt and pepper. Carve the turkey, adding any accumulated juices to the gravy, then serve with gravy.

Easy-Bake Herbed Dressing

Start to finish: 2 hours 15 minutes (30 minutes active), plus cooling / Servings: 8

Let's face it, stuffing is basically a flavorful sponge to soak up gravy and any stray melting butter that escapes a vegetable. But mincing and sauteing the aromatics that help turn bland bread tasty is a chore. We sped things up—and maximized flavor—by giving butter, fresh herbs and raw shallots a whiz in the food processor, then using the resulting paste to season bread cubes as they toast in the oven. We found that any sturdy, high-quality sliced sandwich bread worked well. As the bread bakes, the raw bite of the shallots cooks off, leaving behind a mellow tang. Chopped celery was tossed with melted butter and mixed into the bread, softening as the cubes toast. The mixture then was moistened with chicken broth and a touch of cream before being baked to create a relatively carefree stuffing that will satisfy even the strictest traditionalists.

Don't use regular chicken broth. *Make sure to use low-sodium, otherwise you'll end up with an oversalted stuffing.*

1 cup finely chopped celery

8 tablespoons (1 stick) salted butter, melted

8 ounces shallots, peeled

⅓ cup lightly packed fresh sage leaves

2 tablespoons fresh thyme leaves

Kosher salt and ground black pepper

1½ pounds sturdy white sandwich bread, cut into ¾-inch cubes

3 cups low-sodium chicken broth

½ cup heavy cream

½ cup chopped fresh flat-leaf parsley leaves

1. Heat the oven to 325°F with racks in the upper- and lower-middle positions. In a bowl, toss the celery with 1 tablespoon of the butter; set aside. In a food processor, combine the shallots, sage, thyme, 1½ teaspoons salt, 1 teaspoon pepper and the remaining butter. Process to form a smooth paste, about 30 seconds.

2. In a large bowl, combine the bread and shallot-herb paste, tossing gently. Fold in the celery, then divide the mixture between 2 rimmed baking sheets. Bake until the celery is tender and the bread is crisp and golden, 50 to 60 minutes, stirring the bread and switching and rotating the pans halfway through. Let cool slightly. At this stage the bread mixture can be cooled, bagged and stored for a day.

3. When ready to proceed, increase the oven temperature to 400°F. Transfer the bread mixture to a large bowl, scraping any browned bits off the sheet pans. Fold in the broth, cream and parsley; let sit for 10 minutes, stirring occasionally. Transfer to a 9-by-13-inch baking dish and spread evenly. Bake on the upper-middle rack until well browned on top, 40 to 45 minutes, rotating the dish halfway through. Let sit for 20 minutes before serving.

Burmese Chicken

Start to finish: **30 minutes** / Servings: 4

Food writer and photographer Naomi Duguid's stunning books provide keen insight into the people and foods of the countries she visits. One of our favorites, "Burma," includes a terrific recipe called Aromatic Chicken from the Shan Hills. It's simple, yet has deep flavor. We wanted to finesse things to make this even faster and easier for the home cook. We swapped in boneless thighs for Duguid's bone-in chicken and switched to a Dutch oven instead of a wok. She suggests a mortar and pestle, but we used a blender to make a paste of lemon grass, garlic, ginger and shallots. This meant we could skip a marinade and let the chicken season as it cooked. A dose of red pepper flakes added moderate heat, but traditional Burmese food can be fairly spicy; if you want more heat, increase the red pepper flakes or stir in a slivered jalapeño, serrano or bird's eye chili with the cilantro. We liked the chicken over steamed rice or thin rice noodles.

Don't use *the fibrous outer layers of the lemon grass. You want only the white, slightly tender (but still firm) inner bulb. Trim the root and all but the bottom 6 inches of the stalk, then peel off the first few layers. If you buy lemon grass in a plastic clamshell container, it likely already has been trimmed.*

8 ounces plum tomatoes (2 large), quartered

4 tablespoons grapeseed or other neutral oil, divided

Kosher salt

2 teaspoons ground turmeric

¼ teaspoon red pepper flakes

2 stalks lemon grass, trimmed to the lower 6 inches, dry outer layers discarded, chopped

2 large shallots, quartered

2 ounces fresh ginger, peeled and thinly sliced (about ¼ cup)

8 medium garlic cloves, peeled

1½ pounds boneless, skinless chicken thighs, trimmed and cut into 1½-inch pieces

½ cup chopped fresh cilantro

2 tablespoons lime juice, plus lime wedges, to serve

1. In a blender, combine the tomatoes, 1 tablespoon of the oil, 1 teaspoon salt, the turmeric, pepper flakes, lemon grass, shallots, ginger and garlic. Blend until a thick paste forms, about 1 minute, scraping down the blender as needed.

2. In a large Dutch oven over medium-high, add the remaining 3 tablespoons of oil, the chicken and 2 teaspoons of salt. Cook, stirring occasionally, until the chicken is no longer pink, about 5 minutes. Add the spice paste and cook, stirring occasionally, until fragrant and the paste coats the chicken, 2 to 3 minutes.

3. Cover, reduce heat to medium-low and cook, stirring occasionally, for 10 minutes. Uncover, increase heat to medium-high and simmer until the chicken is cooked through and the sauce is thickened, 7 to 9 minutes. Off heat, stir in the cilantro and lime juice. Serve with lime wedges.

Red Chili Spatchcocked Roast Chicken

Start to finish: 1 hour 45 minutes (30 minutes active)
Servings: 4

¼ cup grapeseed
or other neutral oil

2 ounces ancho
chilies, stemmed and seeded

1 tablespoon dried oregano,
Mexican if available

2 medium garlic cloves,
smashed and peeled

2 tablespoons packed light
brown sugar

1 tablespoon cider vinegar

Kosher salt and ground
black pepper

½ teaspoon ground cumin

¼ teaspoon ground cinnamon

3½- to 4-pound whole
chicken, backbone cut out
(see instructions pp. 282-283)

¼ cup lime juice, plus lime
wedges to serve

Warmed corn tortillas, to
serve (optional)

How to cook a whole chicken quickly and evenly? Remove its backbone and flatten the bird—a technique called spatchcocking or butterflying. The next challenge is adding flavor that doesn't stop at the skin. Our solution is to slide a chili-herb-spice mixture between the skin and meat. Our flavoring rub is based on a classic adobado, a seasoning common in Mexican cooking, revamped for indoor cooking without a long marination. Roasting and coarsely grinding the dried chilies before rehydrating them means we can use less water, giving the resulting chili paste deeper flavor.

1. Heat the oven to 375°F with a rack in the middle position. In a 12-inch oven-safe heavy skillet over medium-high, heat the oil until shimmering. Add the chilies and toast until lightly browned, about 20 seconds per side. Transfer to a food processor, reserving the pan and oil. Process until coarsely chopped, about 30 seconds. In a small saucepan, bring ⅔ cup water to a boil. Add the chilies, oregano and garlic, then cover, remove from heat and let sit for 15 minutes.

2. In the food processor, combine the sugar, vinegar, 2½ teaspoons salt, ¼ teaspoon pepper, cumin, cinnamon and 2 tablespoons of the reserved chili oil from the skillet. Add the chili-water mixture and process until smooth, about 1 minute, scraping the bowl as needed. Reserve a third of the mixture, about 5 tablespoons.

3. With the breast side up, flatten the chicken by pressing on the center of the breast with your palms. Carefully lift the skin from the meat of the breasts and legs, avoiding tears. Spoon the remaining chili paste under the skin, massaging the skin to evenly distribute. Rub the skin of the chicken with the remaining reserved chili oil, then season with salt and pepper. Tuck the wing tips under the breasts, then place the chicken breast side up in the empty skillet. Transfer to the oven and roast until the breast registers 160°F, 45 to 50 minutes.

4. Transfer the chicken to a carving board, tent with foil and let rest for 15 minutes. Meanwhile, place the empty skillet over medium heat on the stovetop, then add the reserved chili paste and lime juice. Cook until warmed through. Taste and season with salt and pepper. Carve the chicken, adding any juices to the sauce, and serve with the sauce, lime wedges and warmed tortillas, if desired.

Chicken Tagine with Apricots, Butternut Squash and Spinach

Start to finish: 1 hour (30 minutes active) / Servings: 4

4 tablespoons extra-virgin olive oil, divided

Kosher salt and ground black pepper

2 teaspoons ground cinnamon

2 teaspoons ground cumin

2 teaspoons sweet paprika

1 teaspoon ground coriander

¼ teaspoon cayenne pepper

1½ pounds boneless, skinless chicken thighs, trimmed and cut into 1½-inch pieces

1 large yellow onion, thinly sliced lengthwise

4 medium garlic cloves, smashed and peeled

4 teaspoons grated fresh ginger

2½ cups low-sodium chicken broth

14½-ounce can diced tomatoes

¾ cup dried apricots, quartered

8 ounces peeled butternut squash, cut into ¾-inch cubes (about 2 cups)

1 cup Greek green olives, pitted and halved

1 cup chopped fresh cilantro, divided

¼ cup pistachios, toasted and chopped

2 teaspoons grated lemon zest, plus 3 tablespoons lemon juice

4 ounces baby spinach (about 4 cups)

This spicy, fruity chicken stew is based on tagine, a classic North African dish that cooks meat, vegetables and fruit mostly in their natural juices. We love it because the richness of the dish comes from layers of flavor, not laborious browning. The word tagine refers to both the dish and the clay pot it typically is cooked in. The pot has a shallow pan and a conical top designed to collect condensation from the steam of the cooking food and return the moisture to it. We used a more commonly available Dutch oven, but kept to the spirit of the tagine, using a fragrant spice paste to season the chicken and act as a base for the stew. Apricots added sweetness (we preferred sulfured for their vibrant color) that was balanced by briny green olives. An equal amount of carrots can be substituted for the butternut squash. Serve the tagine with couscous, rice or warmed pita bread.

Don't drain the diced tomatoes. *Their liquid adds sweetness and acidity to the stew.*

1. **In a small bowl,** stir together 2 tablespoons of the oil, 2½ teaspoons salt, ½ teaspoon black pepper, the cinnamon, cumin, paprika, coriander and cayenne. In a medium bowl, toss the chicken with half the spice paste, rubbing the meat to coat evenly; set aside.

2. **In a large Dutch oven** over medium-high, combine the onion, garlic, the remaining 2 tablespoons of oil and ¼ teaspoon salt. Cook until the onion is browned and softened, 7 to 9 minutes. Add the ginger and remaining spice paste and cook, stirring constantly, for 1 minute. Add the broth, tomatoes and apricots and bring to a boil, scraping up any browned bits. Add the chicken, return to a boil, then reduce heat to medium-low and simmer for 10 minutes.

3. **Add the squash and olives,** return to a simmer and cook, partially covered, until the liquid has thickened and the squash is tender, 20 to 25 minutes, stirring occasionally and adjusting the heat to maintain a medium simmer.

4. **Meanwhile, in a medium bowl,** stir together ½ cup of the cilantro, the pistachios and lemon zest. Stir the spinach into the stew and cook until wilted, 1 to 2 minutes. Stir in the remaining ½ cup of cilantro and the lemon juice, then taste and season with salt and pepper. Serve topped with the cilantro-pistachio mixture.

Pork

10

Spice-Crusted
Pork Tenderloin Bites
(Pinchos Morunos)

Start to finish: **50 minutes (25 minutes active)** / Servings: **4**

1½ teaspoons ground
coriander

1½ teaspoons ground cumin

1½ teaspoons smoked
paprika

Kosher salt and ground
black pepper

1-pound pork tenderloin,
trimmed of silver skin and cut
into 1- to 1½-inch pieces

1 tablespoon lemon juice,
plus lemon wedges for
serving

1 tablespoon honey

1 medium garlic clove,
finely grated

2 tablespoons extra-virgin
olive oil, divided

1 tablespoon chopped
fresh oregano

Loosely translated as "Moorish bites impaled on thorns or small pointed sticks," pinchos morunos is a Basque dish of seared pork tenderloin rubbed with a blend of spices, garlic, herbs and olive oil. The recipe dates back generations, boasting influences from Spain and North Africa. Classic versions skewer the meat, which is seasoned with ras el hanout, a Moroccan spice blend, among other flavorings. We streamlined, nixing the skewers. And since ras al hanout can be hard to find, we went with a blend of cumin, coriander and black pepper. A bit of smoked paprika added the requisite Basque touch. We finished with a drizzle of honey, which heightened the flavor of the pork and seasonings.

Don't cut the tenderloin too small. Cutting it into 1- to 1½-inch pieces produced more surface area, allowing the spice rub to quickly penetrate and season the meat. Any smaller and the meat cooked too quickly.

1. In a medium bowl, combine the coriander, cumin, paprika and ¾ teaspoon each salt and pepper. Add the pork and toss to coat evenly, massaging the spices into the meat until no dry rub remains. Let the pork sit at room temperature for at least 30 minutes and up to 1 hour. Meanwhile, in another bowl, combine the lemon juice, honey and garlic. Set aside.

2. In a large skillet over high, heat 1 tablespoon of the oil until barely smoking. Add the meat in a single layer and cook without moving until deeply browned on one side, about 3 minutes. Using tongs, flip the pork and cook, turning occasionally, until cooked through and browned all over, another 2 to 3 minutes. Off the heat, pour the lemon juice-garlic mixture over the meat and toss to evenly coat, then transfer to a serving platter. Sprinkle the oregano over the pork and drizzle with the remaining 1 tablespoon of oil. Serve with lemon wedges.

Pork and Chorizo with Piquillo Peppers (Carcamusa)

Start to finish: 1 hour (35 minutes active) / Servings: 4

6 ounces Spanish chorizo, halved lengthwise and thinly sliced

8 medium garlic cloves, peeled

2½ teaspoons dried oregano

2½ teaspoons ground cumin

Kosher salt and ground black pepper

28-ounce can whole peeled tomatoes, drained, juices reserved

1¼-pound pork tenderloin, trimmed of silver skin and cut into ½-inch pieces

3 tablespoons grapeseed or other neutral oil, divided

1 large yellow onion, finely chopped

½ cup dry sherry

10.4-ounce jar piquillo peppers (see headnote), drained and cut into ½-inch pieces (1 cup)

1 cup roughly chopped flat-leaf parsley

Carcamusa, a Spanish tapas dish, traditionally calls for three different types of pork—fresh pork, cured ham and chorizo—all simmered with seasonal vegetables in tomato sauce. To simplify, we skipped the ham and opted for jarred roasted piquillo peppers, which are heat-free, meaty red peppers from Spain. If you can't find them, jarred roasted red bell peppers are a fine substitute. Serve the dish with slices of toasted rustic bread.

Don't use Mexican chorizo, which is a fresh sausage, in place of the Spanish chorizo called for here. Spanish chorizo is dry-cured and has a firm, sliceable texture similar to salami. If the chorizo you purchased has a tough casing, peel it off before cooking.

1. **In a food processor,** combine half the chorizo, the garlic, oregano, cumin, 1 teaspoon pepper and 3 tablespoons of the tomato juices. Process until smooth, about 2 minutes, scraping down the bowl as needed. Transfer 3 tablespoons of the chorizo paste to a medium bowl and stir in 1 teaspoon salt and another 1 tablespoon of the tomato juices. Add the pork and toss, then marinate at room temperature for 15 minutes. Meanwhile, add the drained tomatoes to the chorizo paste in the processor and process until smooth, about 1 minute; set aside.

2. **In a 12-inch skillet** over medium-high, heat 1 tablespoon of the oil until barely smoking. Add the pork in a single layer and cook without stirring until well-browned, 4 to 6 minutes. Return the pork to the bowl. Add the remaining 2 tablespoons oil to the skillet and heat over medium until shimmering. Add the onion, cover and cook, stirring occasionally, until softened, about 8 minutes.

3. **Add the sherry and cook,** scraping up any browned bits, until most of the liquid evaporates, 2 to 4 minutes. Stir in the tomato-chorizo mixture and the remaining tomato juice. Bring to a simmer, then reduce to medium-low. Cover and cook for 10 minutes.

4. **Uncover and continue to cook,** stirring occasionally, until the mixture is slightly thickened, another 5 minutes. Return the pork and any accumulated juices to the skillet and add the remaining chorizo and the piquillo peppers. Cook, stirring occasionally, until the pork is heated through, about 5 minutes. Stir in the parsley, then taste and season with salt and pepper.

Taiwanese Five-Spice Pork with Rice (Lu Rou Fan)

Start to finish: **40 minutes** / Servings: **6**

1½ pounds ground pork

1 cup low-sodium soy sauce, divided, plus more, as needed

¼ cup grapeseed or other neutral oil

12 ounces shallots, halved and thinly sliced

10 medium garlic cloves, minced

1¼ cups dry sherry

⅓ cup packed dark brown sugar

2 tablespoons five-spice powder

1 tablespoon unseasoned rice vinegar

Steamed rice, to serve

3 scallions, thinly sliced on diagonal

This Taiwanese dish is a one-bowl meal consisting of richly flavored, soy-simmered pork served over steamed rice. Pork belly is traditional, but we found ground pork faster to cook and just as delicious. Hard-cooked eggs are a common garnish, but we preferred soft-cooked eggs for their runny yolks. To make soft-cooked eggs, bring 2 cups of water to a simmer in a large saucepan fitted with a steamer basket. Add the eggs, cover and steam over medium for 7 minutes. Transfer the eggs to ice water to stop the cooking, then shell and halve the eggs before serving. We liked serving steamed or stir-fried bok choy or broccoli alongside, a nice balance to the richness of the pork.

Don't use regular soy sauce; it will become too salty because the sauce is reduced during cooking. And don't use cooking sherry, which contains added salt; use an inexpensive dry sherry.

1. In a medium bowl, mix the pork with ¼ cup of the soy sauce. Cover and refrigerate until needed. In a large Dutch oven over medium, heat the oil until barely smoking. Add the shallots and cook, stirring, until deeply browned, 15 to 20 minutes. Add the garlic and cook, stirring constantly, until the garlic is fragrant and just beginning to brown, about 1 minute.

2. Add the sherry, sugar, five-spice and remaining ¾ cup soy sauce. Stir until the sugar has dissolved, then increase to high and bring to a boil. Cook, stirring, until reduced and syrupy and a spoon leaves a clear trail, about 5 minutes.

3. Reduce to low and allow the simmering to subside. Add the pork, breaking it into small pieces. Cook, stirring, until the meat is no longer pink, 5 to 7 minutes. Stir in the vinegar, then taste and add more soy sauce, if needed. Spoon steamed rice into 6 bowls, top with the pork and sprinkle with the scallions.

Fennel-Rosemary Porchetta

Start to finish: 1½ days (30 minutes active) / Servings: 8

For the roast:

7- to 8-pound boneless pork butt

8 ounces pancetta, cut into ½-inch cubes

4 tablespoons salted butter, room temperature

1 cup (1½ ounces) lightly packed fresh rosemary

1 cup (1 ounce) lightly packed fresh oregano

20 medium garlic cloves, peeled

1 tablespoon red pepper flakes

½ cup plus 2 tablespoons ground fennel seed, divided

Kosher salt and ground black pepper

2 tablespoons packed light brown sugar

For the sauce:

¾ cup defatted pan juices

⅓ cup lemon juice

2 tablespoons extra-virgin olive oil

1 teaspoon ground fennel

Ground black pepper

Porchetta is a roasted whole hog tradition from the Italian region of Umbria. Turning it into a home cook–friendly pork roast proved challenging. After testing recipes with pork loin (too dry) and pork belly (too fatty), we settled on a boneless pork butt roast. Traditional porchetta is succulent and complex because almost all parts of the pig are used. For our scaled-down version, we added pancetta (seasoned and cured pork belly that has not been smoked), which lent a richness to the filling and helped baste the roast from the inside out. Fennel is a key flavor of the dish. We used ground fennel seeds in a seasoning rub and, while the roasted pork rested, we used the time (and the flavorful fond in the pan) to roast wedges of fresh fennel. Be sure to buy a boneless pork butt, not a boneless picnic roast; both are cut from the shoulder, but the butt comes from higher up on the animal and has a better shape for this recipe. Porchetta leftovers make great sandwiches, thinly sliced and served on crusty bread or ciabatta rolls. Leftover roasted fennel is perfect for sandwiches, as well.

Don't cut short the porchetta's one-hour resting time. The roast is much easier to slice after it rests for the full hour.

1. **To prepare the roast,** remove any twine or netting around the pork. Locate the cut made to remove the bone, then open up the roast. Using a sharp knife, continue the cut until the roast opens like a book; do not cut all the way through, as the meat must remain in one piece. Using the tip of a paring knife, make 1-inch-deep incisions into the pork spaced about 1 inch apart; do not cut all the way through the meat. Set aside.

2. **In a food processor,** pulse the pancetta until coarsely chopped, about 15 pulses. Add the butter, rosemary, oregano, garlic, pepper flakes, ½ cup of ground fennel and 2 teaspoons salt. Process until the mixture forms a spreadable paste, about 1 minute, scraping the bowl as needed. Spread the paste evenly over the interior of the pork, pressing it into the cuts. Roll the roast into a tight cylinder, then set it seam side down.

3. **Cut 7 to 9 pieces of kitchen twine,** each 28 to 30 inches long. In a small bowl, stir together the remaining 2 tablespoons ground fennel, 1 tablespoon salt, the brown sugar and 2 teaspoons black pepper. Rub this mixture over the top and sides of the roast. Using the twine, tie the roast at 1-inch intervals, seam side down; you may not need all of the twine. Trim the ends of the twine. Wrap the roast tightly in plastic, transfer to a large baking dish and refrigerate for at least 24 hours or up to 48 hours.

4. Heat the oven to 300°F with a rack in the middle position. Set a roasting rack in a roasting pan and pour 4 cups water into the pan. Unwrap the roast and set it fat side up on the rack. Roast until the center registers 195°F, 6 to 7 hours.

5. Transfer the roast to a carving board and let rest, uncovered, for 1 hour. Reserve the liquid in the pan.

6. Meanwhile, make the sauce. Pour the liquid from the roasting pan into a fat separator; if making roasted fennel (see recipe below), do not wash the pan. Let the liquid settle for 5 minutes, then measure out ¾ cup. In a medium bowl, whisk together the pan juices, the lemon juice, ¼ cup water, the oil, ground fennel and 2 teaspoons pepper.

7. Cut the pork into thin slices, removing the twine as you slice. Serve with the sauce.

ROASTED FENNEL

Start to finish: 50 minutes
Servings: 8

This side dish makes good use of the fond left in the porchetta's roasting pan.

4 large fennel bulbs, trimmed, halved, cored and cut lengthwise into 1-inch wedges

¼ cup extra-virgin olive oil

Kosher salt

1. Heat the oven to 450°F with a rack in the middle position. In the roasting pan used for the porchetta, combine the fennel, oil and 1 teaspoon salt; stir until evenly coated.

2. Roast for 20 minutes, then stir. Roast for another 10 minutes, then add ½ cup water and scrape up the browned bits on the bottom of the pan. Continue to roast until tender and lightly browned, another 10 minutes.

Carne Adovada

Start to finish: 5 hours (50 minutes active) / Servings: 8

---

3 ounces dried New Mexico chilies, stemmed, seeded and torn into pieces

3 ounces dried guajillo chilies, stemmed, seeded and torn into pieces

4 cups boiling water

5 pounds boneless pork butt roast, trimmed of excess fat and cut into 1½-inch cubes

Kosher salt and ground black pepper

2 tablespoons lard or grapeseed oil

2 medium white onions, chopped

6 medium garlic cloves, minced

4 teaspoons cumin seed

4 teaspoons ground coriander

1 teaspoon dried oregano, preferably Mexican

¾ teaspoon cayenne pepper

1 tablespoon molasses

Lime wedges, to serve

Sour cream, to serve

Fresh cilantro leaves, to serve

We found that 3 ounces of New Mexico chilies—the widely available medium-hot chilies grown in the state—and 3 ounces of fruity, mildly smoky Mexican guajillos gave us just the right flavor. If guajillos are hard to find, another 3 ounces of New Mexico chilies can be substituted. Pork butt, which is cut from the shoulder, is a fatty cut. Trimming as much fat as possible from the meat—not just from the surface but also from between the muscles—helps prevent a greasy stew. After trimming, you should have 4 to 4½ pounds of pork. If the stew nonetheless ends up with fat on the surface, simply use a wide, shallow spoon to skim it off. This adovado is rich and robust; it pairs perfectly with Mexican rice, stewed pinto beans and/or warmed flour tortillas.

Don't use a picnic shoulder roast for this recipe. The picnic cut, taken from the lower portion of the shoulder, has more cartilage and connective tissue, which will make trimming more difficult. Also, don't use blackstrap molasses, which has a potent bittersweet flavor.

1. **Place all of the chilies** in a large bowl, add the boiling water and stir. Let stand, stirring occasionally, until the chilies have softened, about 30 minutes. Transfer half of the mixture to a blender and blend until smooth, about 1 minute. Add the remaining mixture and blend until smooth, scraping down the blender as needed. Measure ½ cup of the chili puree into a small bowl, cover and refrigerate until needed. Pour the remaining puree into a medium bowl and set aside; do not scrape out the blender jar. Pour ½ cup cool water into the blender, cover tightly and shake to release all of the puree.

2. **Place the pork in a large bowl.** Add 2 teaspoons salt and the chili-water mixture in the blender. Stir to coat, then cover and refrigerate for 1 hour.

3. **Heat the oven to 325°F** with a rack in the lower-middle position. In a large Dutch oven over medium, heat the lard until shimmering. Add the onions and cook, stirring occasionally, until softened, 8 to 10 minutes. Stir in the garlic, cumin, coriander, oregano and cayenne, then cook until fragrant, about 30 seconds. Stir in ½ cup water and the chili puree from the medium bowl. Add the pork. Stir to combine, then cover the pot, place in the oven and cook for 2 hours.

4. **Remove the pot from the oven.** Uncover, stir and return, uncovered, to the oven. Continue to cook until the pork is tender, another 1¼ to 1½ hours. Remove from the oven and set on the stove over medium heat and simmer, stirring occasionally, until the sauce has thickened slightly, 8 to 10 minutes.

5. **Stir in the reserved** ½ cup chili puree and the molasses. Taste and season with salt and pepper. Serve with lime wedges, sour cream and cilantro leaves.

Carnitas

Start to finish: 4 hours (45 minutes active) / Servings: 4 to 6

---

5 to 6 pounds boneless pork butt, not trimmed, cut into 2-inch cubes

1 large yellow onion, halved and thinly sliced

10 medium garlic cloves, smashed and peeled

2 tablespoons ground cumin

2 tablespoons ground coriander

2 teaspoons dried oregano

½ teaspoon dried thyme

1 teaspoon red pepper flakes

Kosher salt and ground black pepper

1 cup grapeseed or other neutral oil

Authentic Mexican carnitas involve slow-cooking pork in lard until fall-apart tender, then increasing the heat so the meat fries and crisps. The fried pork then is broken into smaller pieces for eating. In the U.S., however, the dish usually is made by simmering pork in liquid, then shredding the meat. The result is moist and tender, but lacks intense porkiness as well the crisping traditional to carnitas. Our method melds the two techniques. We cook cubes of pork shoulder in 1 cup each of neutral oil and water, along with spices and aromatics, until the meat is fork-tender. We then break the pork into smaller pieces, moisten it with its own juices, and fry it in a hot skillet. The pork gets to keep its flavor and develop crisp bits. If you have a fat separator, it makes quick work of removing the fat from the cooking liquid: pour the liquid into it after removing the pork from the pot, then return the defatted cooking liquid to the pot, but remember to reserve the fat. You can cook, shred and moisten the pork with the reduced cooking liquid up to three days in advance; fry the pork just before serving so it's hot and crisp. And if you like your carnitas extra-crisp, after browning the first side, use the spatula to flip the pork and cook until the second side is well-browned and crisp, another 5 to 7 minutes. You can serve carnitas simply with rice and beans or make tacos with warmed corn tortillas. Either way, pickled red onions (recipe follows) are a must—their sharp acidity perfectly balances the richness of the pork. Also offer sliced radishes and a salsa, such as our tomatillo-avocado salsa (see recipe p. 624).

Don't trim the fat from the pork shoulder. The pork should render its fat in the oven so the meat cooks slowly in it and the juices. And after cooking, don't discard the fat you skim off the cooking liquid—you'll need some of it to crisp the shredded pork in a hot skillet.

1. **Heat the oven to 325°F** with a rack in the lower-middle position. In a large (at least 7-quart) Dutch oven, stir together the pork, onion, garlic, cumin, coriander, oregano, thyme, pepper flakes and 2 teaspoons salt. Stir in the oil and 1 cup water. Cover, transfer to the oven and cook for 3 hours.

2. **Remove the pot from the oven.** Stir the pork and return the pot, uncovered, to the oven. Cook until a skewer inserted into the meat meets no resistance, another 30 minutes. Using a slotted spoon, transfer the meat to a rimmed baking sheet in an even layer to cool. Tilt the pot to pool the cooking liquid to one side, then use a wide spoon to skim off as much fat as possible;

reserve the fat. Bring the defatted cooking liquid to a simmer over medium-high and cook, stirring occasionally, until reduced to about ⅓ cup, about 5 minutes. Set aside.

3. When the meat is cool enough to handle, break the chunks into ¾- to 1-inch pieces, discarding any large pieces of fat. Add the pork back to the pot and stir until evenly moistened with the reduced cooking liquid.

4. In a 12-inch nonstick skillet over medium-high, heat 1 teaspoon of the reserved fat until barely smoking. Add the pork in an even layer and cook without stirring, pressing the meat against the skillet with a spatula, until the bottom begins to brown and the pork is heated through, 3 to 5 minutes. Taste and season with salt and pepper.

PICKLED RED ONIONS

Start to finish: 10 minutes, plus chilling

Makes about 2 cups

1 cup white vinegar

2 teaspoons white sugar

Kosher salt

2 medium red onions, halved and thinly sliced

1 jalapeño chili, stemmed, halved lengthwise and seeded

In a medium bowl, combine the vinegar, sugar and 2 teaspoons salt, then stir until the salt and sugar dissolve. Stir in the onions and jalapeño. Cover and refrigerate for at least 1 hour or up to 24 hours.

Tlayudas

Start to finish: **20 minutes** / Servings: 4

Oaxaca, Mexico, is home to the antojito (street food) known as the tlayuda, an oversized corn tortilla topped with black beans, cheese, meats and a spate of other ingredients, then toasted on a grill. Since fresh, extra-large corn tortillas are difficult to find in much of the U.S., we use flour tortillas instead. And we do as some Oaxacans do and fold them in half to enclose the fillings. For ease, we bake them in a hot oven rather than cook them over a live fire. Fill the tlayudas to your liking and cut into wedges just before serving.

Don't use Spanish chorizo, which is dry-cured and firm, like salami. Mexican chorizo, which is soft and fresh, is the variety to use here.

3 tablespoons grapeseed or other neutral oil, divided

8 ounces fresh Mexican chorizo sausage (see headnote), casing removed, crumbled

4 large jalapeño chilies, stemmed, seeded and thinly sliced

1 bunch scallions, cut into 1-inch pieces

Four 8-inch flour tortillas

1 cup black bean puree (see recipe p. 349)

4 ounces whole-milk mozzarella cheese, shredded (1 cup)

Shredded lettuce, to serve

Pickled red onions (see recipe p. 347), to serve

Sliced tomato, to serve

Green chili and tomatillo hot sauce (see recipe p. 349) to serve

1. Heat the oven to 450°F with a rack in the middle position. In a 12-inch cast-iron or other heavy skillet over medium-high, heat 1 tablespoon of oil until barely smoking. Add the chorizo and cook, stirring occasionally and breaking the meat into small bits, until well browned, about 5 minutes. Using a slotted spoon, transfer the chorizo to a paper towel–lined plate; set aside. Add the jalapeños and scallions to the pan, then cook, stirring occasionally, until the vegetables are lightly charred, 3 to 5 minutes. Transfer to the plate with the chorizo; set aside.

2. Pour the remaining 2 tablespoons oil onto a rimmed baking sheet and brush to coat the entire surface. Place 2 tortillas on the baking sheet to coat the bottoms with oil, then flip them and coat the second sides. Spread ¼ cup of the bean mixture evenly on half of each tortilla, all the way to the edges. Top the beans on each with ¼ of the cheese, then fold the unfilled half over to cover and press gently to seal. Transfer to a plate. Repeat with the remaining tortillas, beans and cheese.

3. Place the filled and folded tortillas in a single layer on the baking sheet. Bake until the cheese has melted and the bottoms of the tortillas are golden brown, about 10 minutes.

4. Using a metal spatula, transfer the tlayudas to a wire rack and cool for 5 minutes. Carefully open each and fill as desired with the chorizo-jalapeño- scallion mixture, lettuce, pickled onions, tomato and hot sauce. Re-fold, then cut into wedges. Serve warm.

BLACK BEAN PUREE

Start to finish: 15 minutes
Makes 3 cups

This bean puree is quick and simple to make. Keep some on hand for use as a filling for tacos, quesadillas or molletes; serve it warm as a side dish to any Mexican-inspired meal; or use it as a dip for tortilla chips. Leftovers can be thinned with water or broth to the desired consistency.

Don't forget to reserve ¼ cup of the bean liquid when you drain the cans. And don't rinse the beans after draining them; the liquid left clinging to them helps create a puree with a silky consistency.

1 tablespoon ground cumin

1 tablespoon ground coriander

Two 15½-ounce cans black beans, drained (do not rinse), ¼ cup liquid reserved

2 chipotle chilies in adobo sauce, plus 2 teaspoons adobo sauce

2 tablespoons lime juice

Kosher salt and ground black pepper

½ cup finely chopped fresh cilantro

In a small skillet over medium, toast the cumin and coriander, stirring often, until fragrant, about 1 minute. Transfer to a food processor and add the beans and reserved liquid, chipotle chilies and adobo sauce, lime juice and 1 teaspoon salt. Process until smooth, scraping the bowl as needed. Transfer to a medium bowl. Stir in the cilantro, then taste and season with salt and pepper.

GREEN CHILI AND TOMATILLO HOT SAUCE

Start to finish: 45 minutes (15 minutes active)
Makes 1 cup

This brightly acidic, cumin-spiked hot sauce is an excellent condiment for any Mexican-inspired meal. To give the sauce kick, we use a serrano chili with its seeds, but you could remove the seeds for less heat. For an even milder sauce, replace the serrano with a seeded jalapeño. Stored in an airtight container in the refrigerator, the sauce will keep for up to a week.

Don't worry if the vegetables broil somewhat unevenly. The chilies may brown the most and the tomatillos should be fully softened, but be careful not to scorch the garlic. And don't worry about removing the charred skins before processing— they add a subtly smoky flavor.

3 medium tomatillos (about 6 ounces), husked, cored and halved lengthwise

1 medium poblano chili (about 4 ounces), stemmed, halved lengthwise and seeded

1 serrano chili, stemmed and halved lengthwise

1 medium garlic clove, smashed and peeled

2 teaspoons white vinegar

1 teaspoon ground cumin

Kosher salt

1. Heat the broiler with a rack about 6 inches from the element. Line a rimmed baking sheet with foil. Place the tomatillos and both chilies cut sides down on the prepared baking sheet, then add the garlic. Broil until the chilies are deeply charred and the tomatillos are softened, 5 to 8 minutes, rotating the baking sheet about halfway through. Remove from the oven and cool for about 5 minutes.

2. In a food processor, combine the broiled vegetables, vinegar, cumin, 1 teaspoon salt and ¼ cup water. Process until smooth, scraping down the bowl as needed, about 1 minute. Transfer to a small bowl, then taste and season with salt. Cover and let stand at room temperature for 30 minutes before serving

Sesame Stir-Fried Pork with Shiitakes

Start to finish: 30 minutes / Servings: 6

1-pound pork tenderloin, trimmed of silver skin

2½ tablespoons soy sauce, divided

Kosher salt and ground black pepper

3 tablespoons grapeseed or other neutral oil, divided

8 ounces shiitake mushrooms, stems discarded, caps sliced ¼ inch thick

3 medium garlic cloves, thinly sliced

2½ cups well-drained napa cabbage kimchi, roughly chopped, plus 2 tablespoons kimchi juice

3 tablespoons mirin

1 tablespoon toasted sesame oil

2 tablespoons sesame seeds, toasted

1 bunch scallions, thinly sliced

Kimchi—Korea's spicy, fermented cabbage—most often is eaten raw as a small plate or as a side. But this recipe cooks kimchi, turning it into a one-ingredient way to add complex flavors and vegetables to a simple dish. Fresh shiitake mushrooms, a full bunch of scallions and sesame (both oil and seeds) add to its richness. Serve with steamed short- or medium-grain rice.

Don't finely chop the kimchi. Larger pieces retain a slightly crisp texture and have more presence in the stir-fry.

1. Cut the tenderloin in half lengthwise, then slice each half crosswise about ¼ inch thick. In a medium bowl, toss the pork with 1 tablespoon of soy sauce and ½ teaspoon pepper.

2. Heat a 12- to 14-inch wok over high until a drop of water evaporates within 1 to 2 seconds of contact, about 2 minutes. Add 1½ teaspoons of grapeseed oil and swirl to coat the wok, then distribute half the pork in an even layer. Cook without stirring until well browned, 1 to 2 minutes, then stir and continue to cook, stirring often, until no longer pink, 1 to 2 minutes. Transfer to a clean medium bowl. Repeat using another 1½ teaspoons oil and the remaining pork.

3. Set the wok over medium-high and heat 1 tablespoon grapeseed oil until barely smoking. Add the mushrooms and ½ teaspoon salt. Cook, stirring occasionally, until the moisture released by the mushrooms has mostly evaporated, about 4 minutes. Stir in the remaining 1 tablespoon oil and the garlic and cook until fragrant, about 1 minute. Return the pork and any juices to the wok and cook, stirring, until the juices evaporate, 30 to 60 seconds.

4. Add the kimchi and kimchi juice, mirin and remaining 1½ tablespoons soy sauce. Cook, stirring and scraping up any browned bits, until the kimchi is heated through, about 3 minutes. Stir in the sesame oil, half the sesame seeds and half the scallions. Transfer to a platter and sprinkle with remaining scallions and sesame seeds.

Argentinian-Style Stuffed Pork Loin with Chimichurri

Start to finish: 3 hours (1 hour active) / Servings: 8

For the Chimichurri:

3 cups lightly packed fresh flat-leaf parsley

⅓ to ½ cup lightly packed fresh oregano

7 medium garlic cloves, smashed and peeled

1½ teaspoons ground cumin

1½ teaspoons ground coriander

¾ teaspoon red pepper flakes

Kosher salt and ground black pepper

¼ cup red wine vinegar

¾ cup extra-virgin olive oil

For the Roast:

1 tablespoon ground cumin

1 tablespoon ground coriander

2 teaspoons packed light brown sugar

Kosher salt and ground black pepper

4-pound boneless center-cut pork loin

6 ounces thinly sliced capicola or mortadella

½ cup pitted green olives, roughly chopped

1½ cups drained roasted red peppers, patted dry and torn into large pieces

⅓ cup panko breadcrumbs

3 hard-cooked large eggs, peeled and halved crosswise

1½ tablespoons extra-virgin olive oil

Flaky sea salt, to serve (optional)

This holiday-worthy roast was inspired by Argentinian matambre arrollado, or beef that is stuffed with hard-cooked eggs, vegetables and sliced cured meats, then poached or roasted. We opted for a boneless pork loin roast because its uniform shape makes it easy to cut into a ½- to ¾-inch-thick slab ideal for filling and rolling. Herbal, garlicky and subtly spicy chimichurri is the perfect accompaniment to the sweet, mild pork; we use some inside the roast, too. You'll need a digital thermometer to test the roast for doneness. For convenience, the chimichurri can be made and refrigerated in an airtight container up to a day ahead. The seasonings for the roast can be combined and stored at room temperature and the pork loin can be butterflied and refrigerated a day in advance, too. Additionally, the roast rests for 30 to 60 minutes after cooking, so your oven will be free for last-minute sides.

Don't trim the fat off the pork loin. The fat cap lends richness to an otherwise lean cut and gives the roast an appealing burnished-brown appearance. Don't rush when butterflying the pork loin. Short, small cuts allow for the best control so you can maintain an even slice and adjust as you go. Don't worry if the surface of the butterflied meat is not perfectly flat or even; it won't matter in the finished dish.

1. To prepare the chimichurri, in a food processor, combine the parsley, oregano, garlic, cumin, coriander, pepper flakes, 1 teaspoon salt and ½ teaspoon black pepper. Process until finely chopped, 30 to 45 seconds. Scrape the bowl, add the vinegar and oil, then process until as smooth as possible, 45 to 60 seconds. Measure ¼ cup of the chimichurri into a small bowl and set aside; transfer the remainder to a serving bowl; cover and refrigerate until ready to serve.

2. To prepare the roast, heat the oven to 350°F with a rack in the lower-middle position. Line a rimmed baking sheet with foil, then fit with a wire rack. In a small bowl, stir together the cumin, coriander, brown sugar, 3½ teaspoons salt and 1½ teaspoons pepper. Set aside.

3. Cut eight 24-inch lengths of kitchen twine. Place the roast, fat side down, on a cutting board, positioning a short end facing you (see step-by-step photographs pp. 354-355). With a sharp boning or carving knife, cut along the length of the roast, slicing down its center, stopping about ½ inch from cutting through the roast.

4. Starting at the base of the cut and with the knife blade held as parallel as possible to the cutting board, slice along one side of the roast, unrolling the meat with your free hand as you go.

Continue cutting and opening up the meat until the half is a flat, fairly even surface ½ to ¾ inch thick. Rotate the roast 180 degrees and repeat with the second side. If there are areas that are slightly too thick, use a meat mallet to pound those spots to the same thickness.

5. Season the pork on both sides with the spice mixture. Place the meat fat side down and with a short side nearest you. Spread the reserved ¼ cup chimichurri evenly on the meat. Shingle on the capicola slices, covering the entire surface, then sprinkle evenly with the olives. Lay the red peppers on top, tearing them as needed to cover the entire surface. Sprinkle the filling evenly with the panko. Place the egg halves cut sides down in a row about 3 inches from the bottom edge.

6. Lift the bottom edge of the roast over the eggs and slowly roll the meat into a tight cylinder. Position the cylinder seam side down and tie at even intervals with the twine, then snip off excess twine. If any bits of filling fall out, simply tuck them back in at the ends. Brush the roast on all sides with the oil.

7. Transfer the roast fat side up to the prepared baking sheet. Bake until the top is nicely browned and the center of the roast reaches 135°F, 1½ to 2 hours. Let rest on the wire rack for 30 to 60 minutes.

8. Remove the chimichurri from the refrigerator about 30 minutes before serving. Cut the roast into ½-inch-thick slices, removing the twine as you go. Arrange the slices on a platter, sprinkle with flaky salt (if using) and serve with the remaining chimichurri on the side.

BUTTERFLYING, STUFFING, ROLLING, AND TYING PORK LOIN

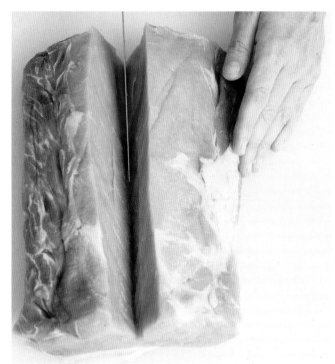

1. Position the roast on a cutting board with a short end facing you. Make a lengthwise cut, stopping about ½ inch from cutting all the way through the roast.

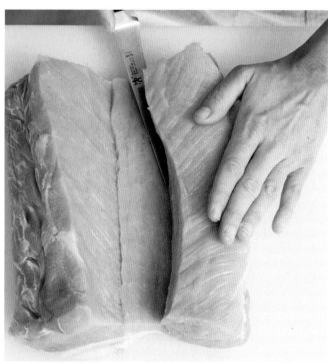

2. With the knife blade parallel to the meat surface, make small incisions into the meat, slicing lengthwise and opening the loin like a book as you slice.

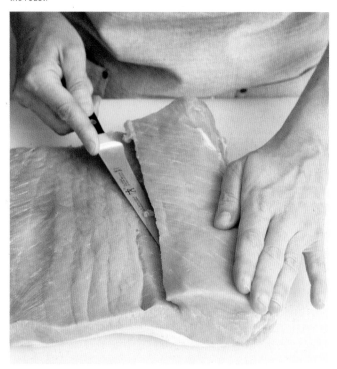

3. Rotate the roast 180 degrees to cut the second side, then repeat the cutting and opening to create a large, flat piece of meat with an even surface.

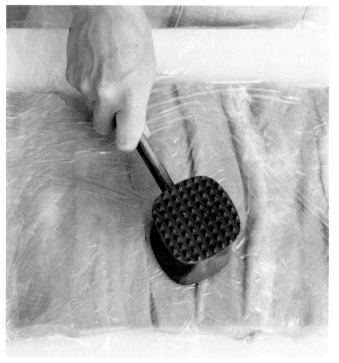

4. If there are spots in the meat that are thicker than desired, use a meat mallet to pound those spots to the same thickness—roughly ½ to ¾ inch thick.

5. With the roast positioned so the grain of the meat runs parallel to the cutting board, brush the reserved ¼ cup chimichurri sauce over the surface of the meat, then shingle the capicolla, olives, pepper and panko on the pork.

6. Using both hands, roll the edge of the meat up over the eggs, pressing down gently to keep the eggs in place. The panko will act as a binder for the filling.

7. Stabilizing the meat at either end, continue to roll the pork loin into a tight cylinder. Position the roast, seam side down, on a cutting board before tying.

8. Starting in the middle of the roast, tightly tie the roast in 1-inch intervals with kitchen twine. Tuck any filling that falls out back into the ends.

Tacos al Pastor

Start to finish: 1 hour / Servings: 4

1 medium pineapple, peeled

¼ cup grapeseed or other neutral oil, plus more for the baking sheet and pineapple

¼ cup packed dark brown sugar

8 medium garlic cloves, peeled

4 chipotle chilies in adobo, plus 1 tablespoon adobo sauce

4 teaspoons ground cumin

4 teaspoons ancho chili powder

Kosher salt and ground black pepper

2 tablespoons lime juice, divided, plus lime wedges, to serve

1¼-pound pork tenderloin, trimmed of silver skin and halved lengthwise

⅓ cup lightly packed fresh cilantro, chopped

8 corn tortillas, warmed

Finely chopped white onion, to serve

We combine tender broiled pork, spicy chilies and the subtle smokiness of charred pineapple in this take on tacos al pastor. The dish is from Mexico but has Levantine roots, stemming from the 19th century when Lebanese immigrants arrived, bringing their tradition of vertical spits for roasting lamb shawarma. Not finding much lamb, cooks switched to pork and instead of sandwiching the meat in flatbread, they used tortillas. Subsequent generations added pineapple and dried chilies. For everyday ease, we use pork tenderloin that has been pounded, briefly marinated and broiled. Chopped pineapple, also broiled, and fresh finely chopped white onion complete the tacos. For extra color and crunch, offer finely shredded red cabbage for sprinkling. To simplify prep, you can buy fresh pineapple that has already been peeled, cored and sliced.

Don't substitute regular chili powder for the ancho chili powder. If you can't find ancho chili powder, pulverize whole ancho chilies (stemmed, seeded and torn) in a spice grinder.

1. Slice the pineapple into seven ½-inch-thick rounds. Quarter 2 rounds, discarding the core. In a food processor, puree the quartered pineapple slices, oil, brown sugar, garlic, chipotles and adobo, cumin, ancho powder and 4 teaspoons salt until smooth, about 1 minute. Pour ½ cup into a baking dish; pour the rest into a medium bowl and stir in 1 tablespoon of the lime juice. Set both aside.

2. Place the tenderloin halves between 2 large sheets of plastic wrap. Using a meat mallet, pound the pork to an even ½-inch thickness. Season both sides of each piece with salt and pepper, place in the baking dish and turn to coat with the puree. Let marinate at room temperature for 15 minutes.

3. Meanwhile, heat the broiler with a rack about 4 inches from the element. Line a rimmed baking sheet with extra-wide foil and mist with cooking spray. Arrange the 5 remaining pineapple slices in a single layer on the prepared baking sheet. Brush the slices with oil and sprinkle with salt and pepper, then broil until charred in spots, 7 to 10 minutes. Transfer the pineapple to a cutting board and set aside; reserve the baking sheet.

4. Transfer the tenderloin halves to the same baking sheet and broil until charred in spots and the center reaches 140°F or is just barely pink when cut, 7 to 10 minutes. Let rest for 5 minutes.

5. While the pork rests, chop the pineapple into rough ½-inch cubes, discarding the core. Transfer to a small bowl and stir in the cilantro and the remaining 1 tablespoon lime juice, then taste and season with salt and pepper.

6. Cut the pork crosswise into thin slices on the diagonal. Transfer to a medium bowl, then stir in any accumulated pork juices along with 3 tablespoons of the reserved pineapple puree. Serve the pork, chopped pineapple and remaining pineapple puree with the tortillas, chopped onion and lime wedges.

Thai Braised Pork and Eggs with Star Anise and Cinnamon (Moo Palo)

Start to finish: 1 hour 40 minutes (30 minutes active)
Servings: 6

---

1 bunch cilantro, stems chopped, leaves roughly chopped, reserved separately

8 medium garlic cloves, smashed and peeled

1 tablespoon whole white peppercorns

3 whole cloves

6 tablespoons low-sodium soy sauce, plus more as needed

⅓ cup fish sauce

⅓ cup packed dark brown sugar, plus more as needed

5 star anise pods

Three 3-inch cinnamon sticks

4 pounds boneless pork shoulder, trimmed and cut into 1½-inch chunks

6 large eggs

Moo palo is a classic Thai braise that combines the richness of pork belly and eggs in a savory-sweet broth flavored with Chinese five-spice powder. For our version, we opted for easier-to-source pork shoulder; it's a leaner cut but it cooks up equally flavorful. Traditionally, hard-cooked eggs are simmered with the pork and take on a brown hue from the braising liquid, along with a firm texture from long cooking. We opted instead to simply garnish with hard-cooked eggs so their color is brighter and texture more tender. For seasoning, we preferred the clean, pure notes of whole cloves, star anise and cinnamon sticks. Serve the pork and eggs with steamed jasmine rice. As with most braises, this dish tastes even better the next day.

Don't use preground white pepper. Whole white peppercorns have far more flavor and aroma. Black peppercorns would be a better substitute than preground white pepper, but its flavor is sharper and more pungent and will slightly alter the flavor profile of the dish. And don't use regular soy sauce, which is too salty.

1. **In a blender,** combine the cilantro stems, garlic, peppercorns, cloves, soy sauce, fish sauce and 6 tablespoons water. Puree until almost smooth, about 20 seconds. Set aside.

2. **In a large Dutch oven** over medium-high, stir together the sugar and 1 tablespoon water. Bring to a simmer and cook, stirring often, until the sugar turns foamy, then dry and begins to smoke lightly, 3 to 4 minutes. Stir in the cilantro stem–garlic mixture, then add 7 cups water to the blender, swirl to rinse it, then add the water to the pot. Stir, scraping up any caramelized sugar from the bottom and sides of the pot.

3. **Add the star anise,** cinnamon sticks and pork, distributing the meat in an even layer. Bring to a boil, then cover and reduce to medium-low and cook, adjusting the heat as needed to maintain a gentle simmer, for 50 minutes.

4. **Meanwhile,** place a folding steamer basket in a large saucepan and add enough water to skim the bottom of the basket. Bring to a boil over medium-high. Add the eggs to the steamer basket, cover and cook for 12 minutes. While the eggs cook, fill a medium bowl with ice water. When the eggs are done, immediately transfer them to the ice water and let stand until cooled. Crack and peel the eggs, then set aside.

5. After the pork has simmered for 50 minutes, uncover, increase heat to medium and cook until a skewer inserted into the pork meets no resistance, 20 to 30 minutes. Remove and discard the star anise and cinnamon sticks, then let stand for about 5 minutes. Tilt the pot to pool the liquid to one side, then use a wide spoon to skim off and discard as much fat as possible from the surface of the liquid. Taste and season with additional soy sauce, then return to a simmer over medium.

6. Spoon the pork and broth into bowls. Cut the eggs lengthwise in halves or quarters and place 2 or 4 pieces in each bowl, then top with cilantro leaves.

Miso-Gochujang Pulled Pork

Start to finish: 4 hours (1 hour active) / Servings: 6 to 8

___

5 pound boneless pork butt, trimmed and cut into 2-inch cubes

¾ cup gochujang, divided

6 tablespoons white miso, divided

1 bunch fresh cilantro, stems minced, leaves left whole, reserved separately

¼ cup hoisin sauce

3 ounces fresh ginger, peeled and cut into 3 chunks

2 tablespoons grapeseed or other neutral oil

2 large yellow onions, thinly sliced

Kosher salt and ground black pepper

3 tablespoons unseasoned rice vinegar

Pickled jalapeños, to serve

This Asian-inflected take on barbecue pulled pork was inspired by the "Pigalicious" wrap served at Bird & Ewe in Sydney. White miso and gochujang provide deep, savory-sweet notes and lots of complex flavor to oven-braised pork butt. Miso usually is sold in the refrigerator case; gochujang, or Korean red pepper paste, does not require refrigeration until the container is opened. Both are available in well-stocked supermarkets and Asian grocery stores. The pork cooks for about three hours; use this time to prep and cook the miso-seasoned onions that are combined with the meat after shredding.

Don't forget to skim the fat off *the cooking liquid so the pulled pork doesn't end up greasy. But make sure to allow the liquid to settle before skimming so all the fat has time to rise to the surface.*

1. Heat the oven to 325°F with a rack in the lower-middle position. In a large Dutch oven, combine the pork, ½ cup of gochujang, 2 tablespoons of miso, the cilantro stems, the hoisin, ginger and 1 cup water; stir to combine. Bring to a simmer over medium-high, then cover and place in the oven. Cook until a skewer inserted into the meat meets no resistance, about 3 hours.

2. Meanwhile, in a 12-inch nonstick skillet over medium-high, heat the oil until shimmering. Add the onions and ½ teaspoon salt, then reduce to medium. Cook, stirring occasionally, until the onions are golden brown, about 15 minutes. Stir in the remaining 4 tablespoons miso and cook, stirring frequently, until the miso begins to brown, about 5 minutes. Transfer to a plate and let cool, then cover and refrigerate until ready to use.

3. Using a slotted spoon, transfer the pork to a large bowl. When cool enough to handle, shred into bite-size pieces, discarding any fat; set aside. Remove and discard the ginger chunks from the cooking liquid. Tilt the pot to pool the liquid to one side and use a wide spoon to skim off and discard as much fat as possible from the surface. Bring to a simmer over medium-high and cook, stirring occasionally, until reduced by about half and a spatula drawn through the sauce leaves a trail, 5 to 7 minutes.

4. Whisk the remaining 4 tablespoons gochujang into the sauce. Stir in the pork and onions. Reduce to medium and cook, stirring frequently, until heated through, 5 to 10 minutes. Off heat, stir in the vinegar, then taste and season with pepper. Serve with cilantro leaves, pickled carrots and pickled jalapeños.

GINGERY PICKLED CARROTS

Start to finish: 10 minutes,
plus resting
Makes about 2 cups

1 cup unseasoned rice vinegar

1 tablespoon white sugar

Kosher salt

3 medium carrots, peeled and
shredded on the large holes of
a box grater

2-inch piece fresh ginger, peeled
and sliced into thin rounds

In a large bowl, stir together the
vinegar, sugar and 1 teaspoon salt.
Stir in the carrots and ginger. Cover
and refrigerate for at least 3 hours
or up to 24 hours.

GOCHUJANG SOUR CREAM

Start to finish: 5 minutes
Makes about ¾ cup

½ cup sour cream

4 to 6 tablespoons gochujang

In a small bowl, whisk together the
sour cream and gochujang. Cover
and refrigerate for up to 1 week.

Bolognese-Style Pork Cutlets

Start to finish: 50 minutes, plus chilling / Servings: 4

2½ cups panko breadcrumbs

Ground black pepper

1 cup all-purpose flour

2 large eggs

1¼-pound pork tenderloin, trimmed of silver skin and patted dry

4 slices prosciutto (about 2 ounces total)

12 tablespoons grapeseed or other neutral oil, divided

4 ounces Parmesan cheese (without rind), grated on the small holes of a box grater (2 cups)

4 tablespoons (½ stick) salted butter, cut into 4 pieces

3 medium garlic cloves, finely grated

¾ cup low-sodium chicken broth

2 tablespoons lemon juice, plus lemon wedges to serve

Classic cotoletta alla bolognese are pan-fried breaded veal cutlets topped with salty, savory prosciutto and Parmigiano-Reggiano cheese. After frying, the crisp cutlets usually are placed in a simple pan sauce and cooked just long enough to melt the cheese. For our version, instead of veal we use pork tenderloin, which is similarly mild in flavor, and we layer the prosciutto slices onto the cutlets, under the breading, to better integrate them into the dish. For an extra-crisp crust, we use Japanese-style panko breadcrumbs, but we lightly crush them before use so the breading isn't overly light and airy. Our method for melting the cheese keeps the bottoms of the cutlets crisp, and the lemon-spiked sauce, served on the side, brightens up all the rich, salty flavors.

Don't pound the pork without using plastic wrap. The plastic wrap prevents the meat pounder from sticking to the meat, thereby helping to avoid tears. This is especially important when the meat is pounded very thin, as it is here. After pounding the cutlets, season them only with pepper, not with salt, as the prosciutto and Parmesan provide lots of salinity. Finally, when adding the water to the pan of fried cutlets, make sure to pour it around them, not on them.

1. Place the panko in a large zip-close bag and seal. Run a rolling pin over the panko until finely crushed. Empty into a pie plate or wide shallow bowl, then stir in ½ teaspoon pepper. In a second similar dish, stir the flour and 1 teaspoon pepper. In a third dish, beat the eggs with a fork.

2. Cut the pork tenderloin in half crosswise, making the tail-end slightly larger, then cut each piece in half lengthwise. Place 2 pieces between 2 large sheets of plastic wrap. Using a meat pounder, gently pound each piece to an even ⅛-inch thickness. Repeat with the remaining pieces. Season both sides of each cutlet with pepper, then lay a prosciutto slice on each cutlet. Re-cover with plastic wrap and gently pound so the prosciutto adheres.

3. One at a time, dredge the cutlets in the flour, turning to coat and shaking off any excess, then dip in the egg and, finally, coat with the panko, pressing so it adheres. Set the cutlets on a large plate. Refrigerate uncovered for 15 minutes. Set a wire rack in a rimmed baking sheet and place near the stovetop.

4. In a 12-inch nonstick skillet over medium-high, heat 6 tablespoons of oil until barely smoking. Add 2 cutlets and cook until golden, 1 to 2 minutes. Using tongs, flip and cook until the second sides are golden, about 1 minute. Transfer to the prepared rack. Repeat with the remaining 6 tablespoons oil and remaining cutlets. Wipe out the skillet and set aside.

5. Evenly sprinkle the cutlets with the Parmesan. Place 2 cutlets, cheese side up, in the same skillet, then set the pan over medium-high. Pour ¼ cup water around the cutlets, immediately cover and cook until the cheese has melted, the water has evaporated and the cutlets begin to sizzle, 1 to 2 minutes. Using a large spatula, return the cutlets to the rack and repeat with the remaining cutlets; tent with foil. Using paper towels, wipe out the skillet.

6. In the same skillet over medium, melt the butter. Add the garlic and cook, stirring, until fragrant, about 30 seconds. Add the broth, then cook over medium-high, stirring occasionally, until reduced to about ⅓ cup, about 3 minutes. Off heat, stir in the lemon juice, then taste and season with pepper. Pour into a serving bowl. Transfer the cutlets to a platter and serve with the sauce and lemon wedges on the side.

Seared Pork Tenderloin with Smoked Paprika and Oregano

Start to finish: **35 minutes** / Servings: **4**

In the Extremadura region of Spain that is home to pimentón de la Vera, or Spanish smoked paprika, we were taught that exposure to high heat blunts the spice's unique earthiness, smokiness and fruitiness. This recipe, inspired by chef Ana Lopez of Alcor del Roble restaurant in Collado de la Vera, Spain, illustrates how best to preserve pimentón's flavors when searing is involved: the paprika is mixed with olive oil, then brushed onto butterflied and pounded pork tenderloin only after the meat has been browned in a hot skillet. Spanish smoked paprika is available in different degrees of spiciness. For this dish, if you have the choice, opt for sweet (dulce) or bittersweet (agridulce).

Don't use a heavy hand when pounding the pork, which can result in tears and uneven thickness. And when pounding, work from the center of the piece outward to the edges.

3 tablespoons extra-virgin olive oil

1 tablespoon smoked paprika (see headnote)

1 teaspoon dried oregano

½ teaspoon white sugar

Two 1¼-pound pork tenderloins, trimmed of silver skin

Kosher salt

2 tablespoons grapeseed or other neutral oil

1 tablespoon fresh oregano, chopped

1. In a small bowl, stir together the olive oil, smoked paprika, dried oregano and sugar; set aside. Halve each tenderloin crosswise, then halve each piece lengthwise, stopping about ¼ inch short of cutting all the way through; open the meat like a book. Using a meat pounder or mallet, pound the pork to an even ¼-inch thickness, then season each piece all over with ½ teaspoon salt.

2. In a 12-inch skillet over medium-high, heat 1 tablespoon of the grapeseed oil until shimmering. Place 2 pieces of pork in the pan and cook undisturbed until golden brown, 2 to 3 minutes. Flip and cook until the seconds sides are browned, 1 to 2 minutes. Lightly brush some paprika oil onto each piece, then flip the pork and brush the second sides. Transfer to a platter.

3. Repeat with the remaining 1 tablespoon grapeseed oil and pork. Brush the remaining paprika oil onto the pork, then let rest for 5 minutes. Sprinkle with the fresh oregano.

Caramelized Pork with Orange and Sage

Start to finish: **25 minutes** / Servings: **6**

Looking for a way to add flavor to pork tenderloin, we drew inspiration from Francis Mallmann, the Argentine chef known for using live fire to cook vegetables, meat and fruit until they're almost burnt. Mallmann tops pork tenderloin with brown sugar, thyme and a fruity orange confit tinged by bay leaves and black peppercorns. The flavorful coating is seared onto the surface in a cast-iron griddle until the orange and thyme are crispy and charred. To simplify, we streamlined the orange confit: Orange zest and fresh sage, coarsely chopped, gave a similar texture and fragrance. Gently pounding the tenderloin ensured a flat surface for a sugar mixture to adhere. We broiled the pork instead of searing and used coarse turbinado sugar; it kept its shape and crunch better under the broiler. If the sugar gets too dark before the meat comes to temperature, turn off the oven; the pork will finish cooking in the residual heat.

Don't tent the pork with foil after removing it from the oven. It will lose its candy-like crust. For the same reason, don't spoon the sauce over it.

2 pounds pork tenderloin, silver skin trimmed, cut into 6 pieces

Kosher salt and ground black pepper

½ cup turbinado sugar

3 strips orange zest, chopped (1 tablespoon), plus ½ cup orange juice

2 tablespoons chopped fresh sage, divided

¼ teaspoon cayenne pepper

2 tablespoons extra-virgin olive oil

2 tablespoons cider vinegar

1. Heat the broiler with a rack 6 inches from the element. Pat the pork dry, then use a meat mallet or a small heavy skillet to gently flatten the pieces to an even 1-inch thickness. Season with salt and pepper. In a small bowl, rub together the sugar, orange zest, 1 tablespoon of the sage and the cayenne. Set aside.

2. In a 12-inch oven-safe skillet over medium-high, heat the oil until barely smoking. Add the pork and cook until deep golden brown on one side, about 3 minutes. Transfer the pork, browned side up, to a large plate; reserve the skillet. Press the sugar mixture onto the tops of the pork pieces in an even layer. Return the meat to the skillet, sugar side up. Set under the broiler until the meat registers 135°F at the center and the sugar mixture is golden brown, 5 to 7 minutes, rotating the pan halfway through. Transfer to a carving board and let rest.

3. Meanwhile, return the skillet to medium-high heat on the stovetop. Add the orange juice and the remaining 1 tablespoon of sage. Cook, scraping up any browned bits, until the sauce is syrupy, 2 to 3 minutes. Stir in the vinegar. Taste and season with salt and pepper. Serve the pork over the sauce.

Ikarian Braised Pork with Honey, Orange and Rosemary

Start to finish: 3¼ hours (1 hour 10 minutes active)
Servings: 6 to 8

5 to 6 pounds boneless pork shoulder, trimmed, cut into 2-inch chunks and patted dry

Kosher salt and ground black pepper

¼ cup extra-virgin olive oil

1 large red onion, halved and thinly sliced

1 cup dry white wine

2 tablespoons minced fresh rosemary, divided

3 bay leaves

2 teaspoons dried oregano

1 tablespoon fennel seeds

½ cup honey (see headnote), divided

1 tablespoon grated orange zest, plus ½ cup orange juice

3 tablespoons finely chopped fresh oregano

2 tablespoons cider vinegar

This savory-sweet pork braise is our version of the tigania, or skillet-cooked meat meze, that Diane Kochilas demonstrated for us on the Greek island of Ikaria. Instead of serving the dish in the Greek meze tradition—that is, as a small plate along with a host of others—we opted to make a larger batch to offer as a main course. We preferred the braise sweetened with a strong, dark honey, such as buckwheat, which holds its own in the mix of wine, herbs, citrus and fennel seed. But a lighter, milder variety worked, too; orange blossom honey is a good option. An orzo pilaf or rice is perfect for serving alongside.

Don't crowd the pot when browning the pork. If the meat is packed too tightly, the pieces will throw off liquid and steam rather than brown. Also, don't stir when browning the pork to ensure the pieces develop a nice, deep sear. Note that only two-thirds of the pork is browned, not the entire amount; this saves some time but still develops caramelization that builds flavor.

1. Heat the oven to 325°F with a rack in the middle position. Season the pork with salt and pepper and toss. In a large (at least 7-quart) Dutch oven over medium-high, heat the oil until barely smoking. Add a third of the pork in an even layer and cook without stirring until well browned, about 7 minutes. Using tongs, flip the pieces and cook without stirring until well browned on the second sides, about 5 minutes. Transfer to a medium bowl and brown half the remaining pork using the oil remaining in the pot, then transfer to the bowl. Add the remaining pork to the bowl; it does not need to be browned.

2. Reduce the heat to medium and add the onion and ½ teaspoon salt to the pot. Cover and cook, stirring occasionally, until softened, about 3 minutes. Add the wine and cook, scraping up any browned bits, until most of the liquid has evaporated, about 5 minutes. Add 1 tablespoon rosemary, the bay, dried oregano, fennel seeds and ¼ cup honey. Return the pork and any juices to the pot, pour in ¾ cup water and stir. Cover, transfer to the oven and cook until a skewer inserted into a piece of pork meets no resistance, 2 to 2½ hours.

3. Using a slotted spoon, transfer the pork to a large bowl and cover to keep warm. Tilt the pot to pool the cooking liquid to one side, then use a wide spoon to skim off and discard as much fat as possible. Stir in the orange juice and remaining ¼ cup honey. Bring to a boil over high, then reduce to medium and cook, stirring often, until a spatula drawn through the liquid leaves a trail, about 10 minutes.

4. Off heat, stir in the orange zest, the remaining 1 tablespoon rosemary, the fresh oregano and the vinegar. Return the pork to the pot and stir to coat with the sauce. Taste and season with salt and pepper.

Slow-Roasted Pork with Sauerkraut, Apples and Dried Fruits

Start to finish: 6 hours (30 minutes active) / Servings: 8 to 10

7- to 8-pound bone-in pork butt roast (see headnote)

7 tablespoons Dijon mustard, divided

¼ cup plus 1 tablespoon cider vinegar, divided

4 medium garlic cloves, minced

2 tablespoons caraway seeds, coarsely ground, divided

2 tablespoons fennel seeds, coarsely ground, divided

1 tablespoon ground coriander

Kosher salt and ground black pepper

3 pounds refrigerated sauerkraut (see headnote), rinsed and drained (about 6 cups)

1 large red onion, root end intact, cut into ½-inch wedges

6 ounces (1 cup) pitted prunes, halved

6 ounces (1 cup) dried apricots, halved

2 firm-textured apples, such as Honeycrisp or Fuji, cored and cut into 1-inch chunks

Rich, succulent roasted pork with a savory-sweet mix of sauerkraut and fruits. What's not to love? We adapted Olia Hercules' recipe from her book "Summer Kitchens," making the recipe a one-pan endeavor. That pan needs to be a large roasting pan to accommodate the roast. You'll also need a sturdy V-style roasting rack—the type with handles—plus extra-wide foil. When shopping for the roast, seek out a bone-in pork butt (sometimes called Boston butt), which is cut from the upper shoulder of the animal. A picnic roast, often sold skin-on, is a different cut, from an area lower down on the shoulder; a roast labeled simply as "pork shoulder" is likely a picnic roast, but it's best to check with the butcher, as nomenclature can be confusing. As for the sauerkraut, look for the "fresh" type sold in the refrigerator case near the pickles; shelf-stable jarred sauerkraut has a soft, mushy texture in comparison. Bubbies is a widely available brand that works well in this recipe. To coarsely grind the caraway and fennel seeds, use an electric spice grinder or a mortar and pestle.

Don't forget to rinse and drain the sauerkraut, otherwise its saltiness will be overwhelming. After removing the roast from the oven after the first three hours of cooking, don't forget to reduce the oven temperature to 350°F.

---

1. **Heat the oven to 450°F** with a rack in the lower-middle position. Set a V-rack in a large roasting pan. Using a sharp knife, score the fat side of the roast in a ½-inch crosshatch pattern.

2. **In a medium bowl,** whisk together 6 tablespoons of mustard, the ¼ cup vinegar, garlic, 1 tablespoon of caraway, 1 tablespoon of fennel, the coriander and ½ teaspoon each salt and pepper. Measure 2 tablespoons of the mixture into a small bowl, cover and refrigerate. Rub the remaining mustard mixture onto the pork, coating all sides.

3. **Set the pork scored side up** on the rack. Add 6 cups water to the roasting pan, then cover tightly with extra-wide foil. Roast for 3 hours, then remove from the oven. Reduce the oven temperature to 350°F. Uncover the pork and, using potholders or oven mitts, carefully transfer the V-rack with the roast to a rimmed baking sheet. Tilt the roasting pan and use a wide spoon to remove and discard the fat from the surface of the liquid; leave the liquid in the pan.

4. To the roasting pan, add the sauer-kraut, onion, prunes, apricots, apples, the remaining 1 tablespoon caraway, the remaining 1 tablespoon fennel, 1 teaspoon pepper and the reserved mustard mixture. Stir, then push the sauerkraut mixture to the edges of the roasting pan, creating a clearing in the center to allow air to circulate under the roast. Pour 1½ cups water into the pan and return the V-rack with the pork to the pan. Continue to roast until the center of the pork reaches 195°F and a skewer inserted into the thickest part meets just a little resistance, about another 2 hours.

5. Transfer the pork without the rack to a cutting board and let rest uncovered for about 30 minutes. Meanwhile, remove the rack from the roasting pan, then mix the sauerkraut mixture in the roasting pan with the juices accumulated in the pan. Stir in ½ cup water, the remaining 1 tablespoon mustard and the remaining 1 tablespoon vinegar; if needed, stir in additional water 1 tablespoon at a time until the sauerkraut mixture is slightly saucy. Taste and season with salt and pepper.

6. Remove the bone from the pork (it should slide out easily). Slice the pork against the grain about ½ inch thick. Transfer the sauerkraut mixture to a serving platter, then arrange the pork on top.

Pork in Veracruz Sauce (Puntas a la Veracruzana)

Start to finish: **50 minutes** / Servings: **4**

1 pound boneless pork loin chops (about 1 inch thick), sliced no thicker than ¼ inch on the diagonal

Kosher salt and ground black pepper

3 tablespoons grapeseed or other neutral oil

12 medium garlic cloves, peeled and chopped (about ¼ cup)

½ medium white onion, finely chopped

1½ pounds ripe tomatoes, cored and chopped

3 bay leaves

2 jalapeño chilies, stemmed, seeded and chopped

⅓ cup pimento-stuffed green olives, chopped

2 tablespoons drained capers

1 cup lightly packed fresh flat-leaf parsley, finely chopped

Adriana Luna, who runs La Cocina de Mi Mamá in Mexico City, showed us how to make puntas a la Veracruzana, a dish of sliced pork in garlicky tomato sauce that, to us, tasted both new and familiar. The term "puntas," which translates from the Spanish as "tips," refers to small pieces of meat; "a la Veracruzana" means in the style of Veracruz—that is, prepared with tomato, garlic, olives and capers. The sauce reflects the culinary influence of the Spanish, who arrived in 1519 in what is now the coastal state of Veracruz, on Mexican cuisine. Whereas "a la Veracruzana" typically is applied to fish, Luna used thin slices of pork loin to a delicious result—the mild, lean meat finds a perfect partner in the punchy, tangy-sweet sauce. We adapted her recipe, making it a simpler one-pan affair. But in the spirit of her dish, we use chopped fresh tomatoes, a healthy amount of garlic and finish the puntas with a good dose of parsley. Serve with charred tortillas or rice and beans, and if you like, offer pickled jalapeños on the side.

Don't slice the pork thicker than ¼ inch or the pieces will be quite chewy when cooked. If you like, for easier slicing, freeze the chops until partially frozen so the knife blade glides through the meat. Also, when cooking the tomato sauce, simmer it down to a very thick consistency, as the accumulated juices from the pork will thin it out.

1. Season the pork with salt and pepper. In a 12-inch skillet over high, heat the oil until barely smoking. Add the pork in an even layer and cook without stirring until well browned on the bottom, about 3 minutes. Using tongs, transfer the pork to a plate and set aside.

2. To the fat remaining in the skillet, add the garlic and stir off heat. Set the pan over medium and cook, stirring often, until the garlic is lightly browned, 1 to 2 minutes; adjust the heat as needed if the garlic sizzles too vigorously. Add the onion, ¼ teaspoon salt and ½ teaspoon pepper, then cook over medium, stirring occasionally, until the onion is translucent, 5 to 6 minutes. Stir in the tomatoes, bay and jalapeños. Increase to medium-high and bring to a boil, then cover, reduce to medium and cook, stirring occasionally, until the vegetables are fully softened, about 8 minutes.

3. Uncover, increase to medium-high and cook, stirring occasionally, until most of the moisture has evaporated and the sauce is thick, 3 to 5 minutes. Add the olives and the pork with accumulated juices. Cook, stirring often, until the pork is no longer pink at the center, 1 to 3 minutes.

4. Off heat, remove and discard the bay, then stir in the capers and parsley. Taste and season with salt and pepper, then transfer to a serving dish.

Colima-Style Shredded Braised Pork

Start to finish: 5¾ hours (40 minutes active)
Servings: 8

___

4 large (1¼ ounces) guajillo chilies, stemmed and seeded

5- to 7-pound bone-in pork butt or pork shoulder roast

2 cups coconut vinegar or unseasoned rice vinegar

1 cup coconut milk

⅓ cup roughly chopped peeled fresh ginger

9 medium garlic cloves, smashed and peeled

3 bay leaves

1 tablespoon tomato paste

½ teaspoon coriander seeds

½ teaspoon cumin seeds

½ teaspoon white sugar

Kosher salt and ground black pepper

The state of Colima on the western coast of Mexico is home to the pork dish called tatemado de Colima. Dried chilies, spices and aromatics, all blended to a smooth puree, are key flavorings, but a defining ingredient, other than the pork itself, is vinegar. In her version, recipe writer Paola Briseño González uses a generous amount of smooth-tasting, subtly sweet coconut vinegar, a common ingredient in the coconut-producing region of Colima, and after slow-cooking the pork, she shreds the meat and mixes it with the braising liquid. The flavors are rich and porky but deliciously balanced by the tangy vinegar and fresh ginger. We adapted González's recipe, and in doing so, found widely available rice vinegar to be a decent alternative to coconut vinegar. Traditionally, the pork is marinated, but we shortened this step to the time it takes the oven to heat (we braise in the oven, where the heat is steady and all-encompassing); we find that no taste is lost without a long marination, as the meat does a fine job of soaking up the seasonings after it is shredded. The meat is briefly broiled after braising to develop deep browning, so you will need a broiler-safe Dutch oven for this recipe. Serve the shredded pork with rice and beans, or make tacos with it, offering shredded cabbage, chopped onion and lime wedges alongside.

Don't use an uncoated cast-iron Dutch oven, even if it is well seasoned. The acidity of the vinegar may react with the metal, resulting in a tinny, "off" flavor. However, an enamel-coated Dutch oven is fine.

1. In a small saucepan, combine the chilies and enough water to cover by about 1 inch. Bring to a boil over medium-high, pressing on the chilies to submerge them. Remove from the heat, cover and let stand until the chilies are fully softened, 15 to 20 minutes. Meanwhile, using a sharp knife, score the fat side of the pork roast with a 1-inch crosshatch pattern. Set the pork scored side up in a large Dutch oven.

2. Using a slotted spoon, transfer the chilies to a blender; discard the soaking water. Add the vinegar, coconut milk, ginger, garlic, bay, tomato paste, coriander, cumin, sugar, 1 tablespoon salt and 1 teaspoon pepper. Blend until smooth, about 1 minute. Pour the puree over the pork and rub it into the meat, then cover the pot.

3. Heat the oven to 325°F with a rack in the lower-middle position. When the oven comes up to temperature, place the pot in the oven and cook until a skewer inserted into the center of the pork meets no resistance, 4½ to 5½ hours.

4. Remove the pot from the oven and heat the broiler. Return the pot, uncovered, to the oven and broil until the surface of the pork is deeply browned, 2 to 4 minutes. Transfer the pork to a large bowl and set aside. Tilt the pot to pool the braising liquid to one side, then use a wide spoon to skim off and discard fat from the surface, leaving just a couple tablespoons for flavor. You should have between 2 and 4 cups defatted braising liquid; if you have more than 2 cups, set the pot over medium-high, bring the liquid to a rapid simmer and cook, stirring occasionally, until reduced to about 2 cups. Meanwhile, shred the pork into large bite-size pieces, discarding the bone and excess fat.

5. Return the shredded pork to the pot and stir to combine with the braising liquid. Cover and cook over medium-low, stirring occasionally, just until heated through, 5 to 8 minutes, then taste and season with salt and pepper.

Pork Souvlaki with Tzatziki and Tomato-Onion Salad

Start to finish: 1 hour / Servings: 6 to 8

___

2 teaspoons dried oregano, divided

2 teaspoons dried thyme

1 teaspoon Aleppo pepper or ¾ teaspoon sweet paprika plus ¼ teaspoon cayenne pepper

1 teaspoon ground fenugreek (see headnote)

1 teaspoon smoked paprika, preferably hot

Kosher salt and ground black pepper

Two 1¼-pound pork tenderloins, trimmed of silver skin and halved crosswise

1 English cucumber, halved lengthwise and seeded

½ large red onion, halved and thinly sliced

2 tablespoons lemon juice

6 tablespoons extra-virgin olive oil, divided

½ cup plain whole-milk Greek yogurt

2 medium garlic cloves, finely grated

1 teaspoon red wine vinegar

2 ripe medium tomatoes, cored, halved lengthwise and sliced into thin half-moons

Yogurt and olive oil flatbreads (see recipe p. 377) or pita bread, to serve

In her book "Aegean," Crete-born London chef Marianna Leivaditaki reveals that after a recent visit to Turkey, she began incorporating fenugreek in her cooking, especially with grilled pork of all sorts. We, too, think that fenugreek, with its notes of mustard, fennel and maple, brings intriguing and unique flavor to any dish to which it's added (fenugreek is a key ingredient in curry powder). In adapting Leivaditaki's recipe for an herb and spice-rubbed pork tenderloin, we sear the seasoned meat on the stovetop and finish it in a hot oven before thinly slicing it for serving (you will need an oven-safe 12-inch skillet for this recipe). To the seasoning mix, we add a little smoked paprika to evoke the flavors of an outdoor grill. "Souvlaki" often refers to meat cooked on skewers, but Leivaditaki explains that in Crete, souvlaki is meat wrapped in pita. This recipe also makes a creamy, garlicky tzatziki and a juicy tomato-onion salad for tucking into the bread with the pork.

Don't sear the pork until it's deeply browned. Aim for a light to medium sear so the spice rub doesn't scorch and the meat does not wind up overcooked. Also, be sure to allow the pork to rest for about 10 minutes before slicing. This gives the juices time to redistribute throughout the muscle fibers so they won't all run out when the tenderloin is sliced.

1. Heat the oven to 450°F with a rack in the middle position. In a small bowl, stir together 1 teaspoon of oregano, the thyme, Aleppo pepper, fenugreek, paprika and 1 teaspoon each salt and black pepper. Sprinkle this mixture all over the pork, rubbing it into the meat; set aside at room temperature for about 15 minutes.

2. Meanwhile, set a colander in a medium bowl and set a box grater in the colander. Shred the cucumber on the grater's large holes. Sprinkle the cucumber with ½ teaspoon salt, toss to combine and set aside to drain. In another medium bowl, stir together the onion, lemon juice and ¼ teaspoon each salt and pepper; set aside.

3. In an oven-safe 12-inch skillet over medium-high, heat 2 tablespoons of oil until shimmering. Add the pork and cook, turning occasionally with tongs, until browned on all sides, about 4 minutes total. Transfer the skillet to the oven and roast until the center of the thickest tenderloin reaches 135°F or is just slightly pink when cut into, 9 to 12 minutes. Remove the skillet from the oven (the handle will be hot) and transfer the pork to a platter. Let rest for about 10 minutes.

4. While the pork rests, use your hands to squeeze the cucumber to remove excess water. In a small bowl, stir together the cucumber, yogurt, garlic, vinegar and 3 tablespoons of the remaining oil. Taste and season with salt and pepper.

5. To the onion mixture, add the tomatoes, the remaining 1 teaspoon oregano and the remaining 1 tablespoon oil. Gently toss to combine, then taste and season with salt and pepper. Transfer the pork to a cutting board. Thinly slice each piece and return to the platter. Serve the pork with the tzatziki, tomato salad and pita.

YOGURT AND OLIVE OIL FLATBREADS

Start to finish: 1 hour / Makes eight 7-inch flatbreads

---

1 cup warm water (110°F)

¼ cup whole-milk Greek yogurt, room temperature

½ cup extra-virgin olive oil, divided, plus more for the bowl

293 grams (2¼ cups) all-purpose flour, plus more for dusting

85 grams (½ cup) semolina flour

1 tablespoon instant yeast

1 teaspoon table salt, divided

1 teaspoon za'atar

½ teaspoon ground sumac

½ teaspoon dried oregano

These soft, plush flatbreads from chef Marianna Leivaditaki are simple to make. Yogurt and olive oil give them rich flavor and a little semolina flour adds a pleasing texture. The breads are cooked one at a time in a skillet on the stovetop (cast iron works best for browning, but nonstick does a decent job, too) and hot out of the pan, they're brushed with olive oil seasoned with za'atar, sumac and dried oregano. Serve them warm with Leivaditaki's pork souvlaki (see recipe p. 374), for making sandwich or kebab wraps, as an accompaniment to stews or braises, or for dipping into hummus and other spreads. The flatbreads are best when freshly made, of course, but extra can be stored in a zip-close bag at room temperature for up to three days; to rewarm, wrap the breads in foil and pop them into a 350°F oven for a few minutes.

Don't be afraid to add more all-purpose flour when rolling out the dough. The dough is quite sticky, so additional flour is needed to prevent it from sticking to the counter.

1. In a small bowl, whisk together the water, yogurt and ¼ cup oil. In a large bowl, whisk together both flours, the yeast and ¾ teaspoon salt. Make a well in the center and pour the liquids into the well. Using a silicone spatula, gradually incorporate the dry ingredients into the wet; once combined, the mixture should form a shaggy dough.

2. Dust the counter with all-purpose flour and turn the dough out onto it; reserve the bowl. Knead the dough until smooth and elastic, about 2 minutes, adding flour as needed to prevent sticking. Lightly coat the same bowl with oil, then return the dough to it. Cover with a clean kitchen towel and let rise at room temperature until the dough has doubled in bulk, 30 to 60 minutes.

3. Meanwhile, cut eight 9-inch squares of kitchen parchment; set aside. In a small bowl, stir together the remaining ¼ cup oil, the za'atar, sumac, oregano and the remaining ¼ teaspoon salt; set aside.

4. When the dough is ready, dust the counter with flour, then turn the dough onto the surface. Using a dough scraper or bench knife, divide the dough into 8 pieces, each about 87 grams (3 ounces). Form each portion into a taut ball, keeping the formed balls covered with the kitchen towel as you shape the rest. Set 1 ball on a lightly floured surface and, using a rolling pin, roll it into an 8-inch round about ⅛ inch thick, dusting with flour as needed. Lightly flour a parchment square and set the round on top. Repeat with the remaining dough balls, stacking the rounds on top of each other, with a parchment square between the layers.

5. Heat a 10- to 12-inch cast-iron skillet over medium until water flicked onto the surface immediately sizzles and evaporates. Pick up a dough round by its parchment liner, invert it into the pan and peel off and discard the parchment. Cook until large bubbles form and the bottom is spottily browned, 1 to 2 minutes. Using tongs, flip the bread and cook until the second side is golden brown, about 1 minute. Transfer to a wire rack and brush the surface with the za'atar oil. Cook the remaining dough rounds in the same way and brush them with za'atar oil. Wipe out the pan if excess flour begins to build up and smoke, and adjust the heat as needed. Serve warm or room temperature.

German Pork Schnitzel

Start to finish: 40 minutes / Servings: 4

1 cup all-purpose flour

2 large eggs

1 tablespoon plus 2 cups grapeseed or other neutral oil

1 cup plain dry breadcrumbs (see headnote)

1¼-pound pork tenderloin, trimmed of silver skin

Kosher salt and ground black pepper

2 tablespoons ghee (optional)

Lingonberry preserves, to serve (optional)

Lemon wedges, to serve

During a visit to Berlin, we learned that the coating for authentic German pork Schnitzel, or Schweineschnitzel, is dry breadcrumbs made from kaiser rolls, which are extremely fine-textured. For ease, we developed this recipe using store-bought plain dry breadcrumbs, but if you'd like to make kaiser crumbs, which are a touch sweeter, wheatier and fresher tasting than prepared breadcrumbs, see the instructions below. Indian ghee (clarified butter) is a surprising ingredient for Schnitzel, but adding just a small amount to the frying oil adds richer, fuller flavor; look for ghee in the refrigerator case near the butter or in the grocery aisle alongside the coconut oil. If you cannot find it, the Schnitzel still is tasty without. To fry the cutlets, we use a large Dutch oven instead of a skillet; the pot's high walls safely contain the hot oil and reduce splatter on the stovetop. To test if the oil is at the correct temperature, an instant or deep-fry thermometer is best. Lingonberry preserves and lemon wedges are classic Schnitzel accompaniments.

Don't use a heavy hand when pounding the tenderloin. A lighter touch works best to flatten the cutlets to a ⅛-inch thickness without inadvertent tears. After breading the cutlets, fry them right away; if left to stand, the coating won't puff properly. Finally, when frying the cutlets, don't crowd them in the pot or they will brown unevenly. Depending on the dimensions of the cutlets and the diameter of your pot, the pieces may need to be fried one at a time.

1. Set a wire rack in a rimmed baking sheet and place in the oven on the middle rack; heat the oven to 200°F. Put the flour in a wide, shallow bowl. In a second wide, shallow bowl, beat the eggs with the 1 tablespoon oil. Put the breadcrumbs in a third wide, shallow bowl.

2. Cut the pork tenderloin in 2 pieces crosswise, making the thinner end slightly larger, then cut each piece in half again. Place 2 pieces between 2 large sheets of plastic wrap. Using a meat pounder, gently pound each piece to an even ⅛-inch thickness. Repeat with the 2 remaining pieces. Season each cutlet on both sides with salt and pepper.

3. One at a time, coat the cutlets on both sides with flour, shaking off the excess, then dip into the eggs, turning to coat and allowing excess to drip off, then coat both sides with breadcrumbs, pressing to adhere. Place the cutlets on a large plate, stacking them if needed.

4. In a large Dutch oven over medium-high, heat the 2 cups oil and ghee (if using) to 350°F. Carefully place 1 or 2 cutlets in the oil—add only as many as will fit without overlapping—and cook, gently jostling the pot so oil flows over the cutlets, until light golden brown on both sides, 2 to 3 minutes total; use tongs to flip the cutlet(s) once about halfway through. Transfer to the prepared rack in the oven to keep warm.

5. Return the oil to 350°F and cook the remaining cutlets in the same way. Serve with lingonberry preserves (if using) and lemon wedges.

HOW TO MAKE KAISER ROLL BREADCRUMBS

Heat the oven to 300°F with a rack in the middle position. Tear 6 to 8 plain kaiser rolls (about 1 pound) into 1-inch pieces, then distribute in an even layer on a rimmed baking sheet. Toast until completely dry but not browned, about 45 minutes, stirring every 15 minutes or so. Cool completely, then transfer to a food processor and process to fine, even crumbs, about 2 minutes. Makes about 1 cup.

Madeiran Pork with Wine and Garlic (Carne Vinha d'Alhos)

Start to finish: 2½ hours (50 minutes active), plus marinating
Servings: 4 to 6

---

5 pounds boneless pork shoulder, trimmed and cut into 1- to 1½-inch chunks

2 cups dry white wine

1 cup cider vinegar

10 bay leaves

6 medium garlic cloves, smashed and peeled

1 tablespoon dried oregano

1 teaspoon red pepper flakes

6 whole cloves (optional)

Kosher salt and ground black pepper

1 cup Madeira

¼ cup minced fresh oregano

Carne vinha d'alhos, or pork with wine and garlic, is a traditional Christmas dish from the Portuguese island of Madeira and the precursor to the spicy Indian curry called vindaloo. To make it, chunks of pork are marinated in a heady mixture of wine, vinegar, garlic and herbs for up to a few days before they're cooked until tender. The meat is subtly tangy, lightly garlicky and fragranced with herbs, with browned bits that provide great depth of flavor. The version that we learned to make in Madeira informed this recipe, but to achieve results as delicious as those we tasted there, we opted to use pork shoulder rather than leaner loin. Shoulder is a cut that requires lengthy cooking to become tender, so rather than a quick 30-minute simmer, we oven-braise the pork for about 1½ hours. From there we stay true to what we were taught: brown the meat after simmering to develop rich, flavorful caramelization, reduce the marinade-cooking liquid to a light glaze, and finish the pork by coating it with the reduction. In Madeira, the pork typically is piled onto crusty rolls to make sandwiches, but we think it also is great with mashed or roasted potatoes alongside.

Don't use an uncoated cast-iron Dutch oven. Enamel-coated cast-iron is fine, but in an uncoated cast-iron pot—even in one that is well seasoned—the acidity of the marinade may react with the iron, producing metallic "off" flavors. A stainless steel cooking surface is fine, too, but avoid aluminum unless it has been treated to make it nonreactive. After simmering the pork, be sure to drain the pieces on a rack as directed. This helps ensure nice caramelization when the pork is browned in the skillet. Finally, when skimming the fat off the braising liquid, be sure to reserve it for browning the pork.

1. **In a large Dutch oven,** stir together the pork, wine, vinegar, bay, garlic, dried oregano, pepper flakes, cloves (if using) and 1 teaspoon each salt and pepper. Cover and refrigerate for at least 1 hour or for up to 48 hours.

2. **When you are ready to cook** the pork, heat the oven to 325°F with a rack in the lower-middle position. Set the pot, uncovered, over medium-high and bring to a simmer, stirring occasionally. Re-cover, transfer to the oven and cook until a skewer inserted into the pork meets just a little resistance, about 1½ hours, stirring once about halfway through.

3. **Set a wire rack** in a rimmed baking sheet. Using a slotted spoon, transfer the pork and garlic to the rack, removing and discarding the bay and cloves (if used); set aside. Tilt the pot to pool the cooking liquid to one side, then use a wide spoon to skim off as much fat as possible; reserve the fat.

4. **Add the Madeira** to the pot, bring to a boil over medium-high and cook, stirring occasionally, until the mixture has reduced to about 1 cup, 15 to 20 minutes; set aside. Remove and discard any large bits of fat on the exterior of the pieces of pork.

5. **In a 12-inch nonstick skillet** over medium-high, heat 2 tablespoons of the reserved pork fat until barely smoking. Add the pork and cook, stirring every 2 to 3 minutes, until well browned on all sides, 5 to 7 minutes. Remove the skillet from the heat and add the reduced cooking liquid. Return to medium-high and continue to cook, stirring occasionally, until the liquid has reduced and the pork is lightly glazed and begins to sizzle, 3 to 5 minutes. Taste and season with salt and black pepper, then stir in the fresh oregano. Transfer to a serving dish.

Cuban-Style Pork Shoulder with Mojo Sauce

Start to finish: 4½ hours, plus marinating / Servings: 6

Kosher salt and ground black pepper

1 tablespoon smoked sweet paprika

4- to 5-pound bone-in pork butt roast, fat cap trimmed to ¼ to ½ inch

1 teaspoon grated orange zest, plus ⅔ cup orange juice

1 teaspoon grated lime zest, plus ⅓ cup lime juice

⅓ cup lightly-packed fresh oregano

8 medium garlic cloves, smashed and peeled

2 tablespoons extra-virgin olive oil

1 tablespoon ground cumin

½ cup roughly chopped fresh cilantro

Lime wedges, to serve

To replicate the flavor of sour Seville oranges in traditional Cuban mojo sauce, we combine the juices and zest from regular oranges and limes. A 400°F oven cooks the pork in under 4 hours, and enclosing it completely in a packet of foil and kitchen parchment keeps the meat moist, eliminating the need to baste. (The parchment-lined packet also makes cleanup a breeze.) Before cooking, we season the pork with a mixture of salt and smoked paprika; the latter is unconventional in Cuban mojo, but the paprika's earthy, smoky notes are a nice complement to the citrus and garlic. We prefer the flavor of the pork after seasoning for at least 8 hours, but if you're pressed for time, 1 hour will suffice. A roll of 18-inch-wide heavy-duty foil is essential for sealing in the pork, and 15-inch-wide kitchen parchment is ideal. Be careful when forming the packet. Tears or openings may cause the meat to dry out. See step-by-step instructions pp. 384-385.

Don't let the pork or its juices come into contact with the foil during cooking; it can cause a metallic taste and discolor the juices. Make sure the parchment fully lines the bottom of the pan and covers the pork on top.

1. In a small bowl, mix together 3 tablespoons salt and paprika. Using a paring knife and a twisting motion, make twelve 1-inch-deep cuts all over the pork. Rub with the salt mixture, then wrap tightly in plastic wrap and refrigerate for 8 to 24 hours.

2. Heat the oven to 400°F with a rack in the lower-middle position. In a liquid measuring cup, combine both juices. In a food processor, combine both zests, the oregano, garlic, oil, cumin and 1 teaspoon pepper. Process until the garlic is finely chopped, about 1 minute. Add ¼ cup of the juice and process until combined, about 10 seconds.

3. Using 18-inch-wide heavy-duty foil, make a sling in a large roasting pan. Leaving generous overhang on either side, gently press 1 sheet of foil into the pan lengthwise. Press a second sheet over that crosswise, again leaving ample overhang. Using kitchen parchment, repeat the process, setting the parchment sling over the foil. Set a wire roasting rack over the parchment.

4. Unwrap the pork and rub all over with the herb-garlic paste. Place fat side up on the rack in the prepared pan. Pour ¼ cup of the juice into the bottom of the pan. Loosely fold the excess parchment around the pork, then fold the excess foil up over the pork. Crimp the foil to create a loose but sealed packet. Roast until the meat is tender and registers 190°F in the thickest part, about 3½ hours.

5. Transfer the pork to a carving board, tent loosely with foil and let rest for 30 minutes. Pour the accumulated juices from the pan into a medium saucepan over medium heat, then add the remaining ½ cup of citrus juice. When hot, remove from the heat and stir in the cilantro; cover and keep warm.

6. Using tongs and a knife or carving fork, cut and shred the meat into chunks, discarding the bone and any fat. Transfer to a bowl and toss with ¼ to ½ cup of the sauce. Serve with the remaining sauce and lime wedges.

STEAM COOKING WITH A FOIL-PARCHMENT PACKET

1. Leaving a generous amount of overhang on either side, gently press 1 sheet of 18-inch-wide foil lengthwise into a large roasting pan. Press a second sheet over that crosswise, again leaving ample overhang.

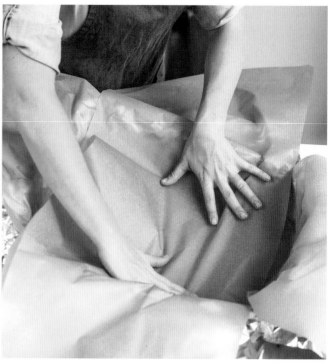

2. Using kitchen parchment, repeat this process, setting the sheets over the foil.

3. Set a wire roasting rack over the parchment.

4. Loosely fold the excess parchment around the pork.

5. Fold the excess foil up over the pork. Crimp the foil together to create a loose but sealed packet.

Beef

11

Turkish Meatballs with Lime-Yogurt Sauce

Start to finish: 20 minutes, plus cooling / Servings: 6

---

3 tablespoons extra-virgin olive oil, divided

1 medium shallot, finely chopped

1 medium garlic clove, grated

½ teaspoon ground cumin

½ teaspoon cinnamon

½ teaspoon dried oregano

One 8-inch pita bread, torn into small pieces (about 3 ounces)

¼ cup plain whole-milk yogurt

1 cup packed fresh mint leaves, finely chopped

1½ pounds 90 percent lean ground beef

Kosher salt and ground black pepper

Lime-yogurt sauce, to serve (see sidebar)

There are many variations (and spellings) of kofta across the Middle East and North Africa, but essentially they're seasoned patties, often made from ground lamb or a blend of beef and lamb. It's the rest of the world's answer to the Italian meatball. We particularly liked Turkish kofta, which sometimes are squashed flat and can be grilled, fried or even cooked on a skewer. We went with an all-beef version using 90 percent lean beef, though this recipe also works with a blend of lamb and beef. We pan-fried our patties, which gave us a deliciously crispy crust. To stop our meat mixture from getting tough in the middle we borrowed the French technique known as panade. It involves mixing a bread and dairy paste into the ground meat to bind it together and keep it moist during cooking. Since we already were serving pita bread with the patties, we used crumbled pita for our panade. We served the cooked patties in pita pockets with sliced tomato, cucumber, red onion and parsley. They also would be good over rice pilaf and served with a simple salad.

Don't use stale bread for the meatballs. *The fresh pita added a lighter texture and fresh flavor. Likewise, use plain whole-milk yogurt, not Greek-style, to get the right consistency in both the meatballs and the sauce.*

1. In a small bowl, stir together 2 tablespoons of the oil, the shallot, garlic, cumin, cinnamon and oregano. Microwave until fragrant, about 30 seconds, then set aside to cool.

2. In a large bowl, combine the pita bread, yogurt and ¼ cup water. Use your hands to mash the mixture to a smooth paste. Add the reserved oil mixture, the mint, beef, 1½ teaspoons salt and 1 teaspoon pepper. Use your hands to thoroughly mix. Divide the meat into 12 portions, then use your hands to roll each into a smooth ball. Refrigerate for 15 minutes.

3. In a 12-inch nonstick skillet, heat the remaining tablespoon of oil over medium-high until barely smoking. Add the meatballs and use a metal spatula to press them into ½-inch-thick patties. Cook over medium, adjusting the heat as necessary, until the meatballs register 160°F at the center and are cooked through and well browned on both sides, 5 to 7 minutes per side. Transfer to a platter, tent with foil and let rest for 5 minutes. Serve with lime-yogurt sauce.

LIME-YOGURT SAUCE

Start to finish: 5 minutes
Makes about 1½ cups

1 cup plain whole-milk yogurt

3 tablespoons tahini

3 tablespoons lime juice

½ teaspoon kosher salt

¼ teaspoon cayenne pepper

In a small bowl, whisk together all ingredients until smooth.

Prune, Peppercorn and Fresh Herb–Rubbed Roast Beef

Start to finish: 2 hours 45 minutes, plus 48 hours to marinate
Servings: 10

---

8 ounces pitted prunes
(about 1½ cups)

½ cup soy sauce

¼ cup ketchup

Kosher salt

2 tablespoons black
peppercorns

2 tablespoons chopped
fresh rosemary

2 tablespoons fresh
thyme leaves

3 oil-packed anchovy fillets

5- to 6-pound beef eye round
roast, trimmed

Fresh horseradish sauce,
(see sidebar) to serve
(optional)

We challenged ourselves to transform a thrifty, low-cost cut of beef into a lush, celebratory meal. The answer was eye round, a roast often deemed too lean to be tender. The cut is taken from the hind leg of a steer, so there's little marbling, the usual key to keeping meat moist. To roast this tough cut and get succulent, perfectly cooked results, we marinated the meat in ingredients that would do the work for us. We started with a sticky, sweet puree of prunes. That may sound unusual, but prunes are high in hygroscopic sorbitol and fructose, which—along with salt and soy sauce—amplify the way the meat absorbs flavor. The puree also adhered well to the roast, promoting moisture retention and a caramelized crust without the trouble of browning. Ketchup and anchovies added rich umami, while rosemary, thyme and black peppercorns brought an herbal kick. To boost the marinade's effect, we poked the roast repeatedly with a fork. The roast beef tasted best after marinating for 48 hours, but 24 will work.

Don't check the roast too frequently. A succulent roast relied on even cooking at a low temperature; opening the oven door interrupted that process.

1. **In a food processor,** blend the prunes, soy sauce, ketchup, 3 tablespoons salt, peppercorns, rosemary, thyme and anchovies until smooth, about 1 minute. Transfer to a 2-gallon zip-close bag. Poke the roast all over with a fork, then place in the bag. Turn to coat, then refrigerate for 48 hours.

2. **Heat the oven to 275°F** with a rack in the middle position. Set a wire rack in a rimmed baking sheet. Remove the roast from the bag and transfer to the rack. Discard the marinade in the bag and evenly brush any marinade sticking to the roast's surface. Roast until the meat registers 125°F, 1 hour 45 minutes to 2 hours.

3. **Transfer the roast** to a carving board, tent loosely with foil and let rest for 30 minutes. Thinly slice and serve with fresh horseradish sauce (if using).

FRESH HORSERADISH SAUCE

Start to finish: 5 minutes
Makes about 1½ cups

We preferred the brightness and intensity of fresh horseradish in this sauce, but bottled horseradish worked well, too. If you use bottled, reduce the vinegar to 1 tablespoon. Look for fresh horseradish root in the produce aisle, often near the fresh ginger. For maximum flavor, peel and finely grate the root with a wand-style grater. If you have extra horseradish, try grating it into mashed potatoes, or over a warm steak or pork chop.

1 cup sour cream

½ cup freshly grated horseradish root (3-inch piece)

2 tablespoons white wine vinegar

1 tablespoon water

2 teaspoons minced fresh rosemary

1 teaspoon kosher salt

In a bowl, stir together all the ingredients. The sauce can be refrigerated for up to 2 days.

Spicy Stir-Fried Cumin Beef

Start to finish: 1 hour (35 minutes active)
Servings: 4

---

1 pound beef sirloin tips, trimmed, cut with the grain into 2-inch pieces and sliced thinly against the grain

3½ tablespoons soy sauce, divided

Ground black pepper

4 teaspoons unseasoned rice vinegar

1 teaspoon white sugar

12 dried red chilies (such as árbol or japones), stemmed

1½ tablespoons cumin seeds, toasted

5 medium garlic cloves, minced

6 teaspoons grapeseed or other neutral oil, divided

1 large yellow onion, thinly sliced lengthwise

2 teaspoons toasted sesame oil

1½ cups roughly chopped fresh cilantro

Cumin is not thought of as a traditionally Chinese spice, but it is used in some regional cuisines, including in Hunan where an abundance of whole cumin seeds is combined with whole chilies and aromatics to great effect in Hunan beef. We also loved this dish made with boneless lamb leg or shoulder, trimmed and thinly sliced; if using lamb, start with about 1½ pounds, as more weight is lost with trimming than with beef. Toasted cumin seeds add both earthy flavor and crunchy texture to this stir-fry. Breaking some of the chilies in half releases the seeds, giving the dish an assertive spiciness; leave all of the chilies whole for a milder version. The chili pods are edible, but we advise eating around them. Serve with steamed white rice.

Don't start cooking until all ingredients are prepared, as things move along quickly at the stove. Also, make sure to turn on your hood vent or open a window or two. Toasting the chilies and searing the meat produces a fair amount of smoke and fumes.

1. In a medium bowl, combine the beef, 1 tablespoon of soy sauce and ½ teaspoon black pepper. Stir to coat, then set aside at room temperature. In a small bowl, stir together the remaining 2½ tablespoons soy sauce, the vinegar and sugar.

2. Meanwhile, break open about half of the chilies, then transfer all of them to a 14-inch wok. Toast over medium, pressing the pods against the wok, until fragrant and darkened in spots, 1 to 3 minutes. Transfer to a large bowl and add the cumin. In a small bowl, stir together the garlic and 2 teaspoons of grapeseed oil to form a paste.

3. Heat the wok over medium-high for about 3 minutes, or until a drop of water evaporates within 1 to 2 seconds of contact. Add 2 teaspoons of the remaining grapeseed oil and swirl to coat. Add the onion and cook, stirring, until charred in spots and partially softened, 3 to 5 minutes. Transfer to the bowl with the cumin seeds and chilies.

4. Return the wok to high, add 1 teaspoon of the remaining grapeseed oil and arrange half of the beef in a single layer. Cook without stirring until deeply browned, 1 to 2 minutes. Stir, scraping the bottom and sides of the wok, and continue to cook until no pink remains, 60 to 90 seconds. Transfer to the bowl with the onion. Repeat with the remaining 1 teaspoon grapeseed oil and the remaining beef.

5. Set the wok over medium-high, add the garlic paste and cook, mashing the paste against the pan, until fragrant, about 30 seconds. Add the contents of the bowl and stir to combine. Pour the soy sauce–vinegar mixture in a thin stream down the sides of the wok, then cook, scraping up any browned bits, until the liquid is slightly thickened, about 1 minute. Off heat, stir in the sesame oil and cilantro.

Thai Beef Salad (Yam Neua)

Start to finish: 40 minutes / Servings: 4

1 large shallot, sliced into very thin rings

3 tablespoons lime juice (about 2 limes)

4 teaspoons packed brown sugar, divided

Kosher salt and ground white pepper

1½ pounds skirt steak, trimmed and cut into 2 or 3 pieces

Neutral oil (if using a skillet)

1 to 2 tablespoons fish sauce

1 teaspoon red pepper flakes

1½ cups (about 7 ounces) red or yellow cherry tomatoes, halved

½ cup coarsely chopped fresh cilantro, plus cilantro sprigs to garnish (optional)

½ cup coarsely chopped fresh mint

Thai beef salad, or yam neua, is a tangle of thinly sliced grilled steak tossed with a hot, sour, salty and slightly sweet dressing, shallots and a heap of cilantro and fresh mint—and possibly some sliced cucumbers and chopped tomatoes. "Yam" refers to a style of salads that are spicy and slightly sour thanks to the classic Thai combination of fish sauce, lime juice, palm sugar and chilies. For our version, we started by choosing the right steak—skirt. The thin, well-marbled cut has big beefy flavor that can stand up to the salad's robust dressing. To season the meat, we used white pepper instead of black for its complexity. A couple teaspoons of brown sugar, balanced with salt, approximated the faint maple flavor of palm sugar. Rubbing the steak with sugar first increased the char.

Don't ignore the steak's grain. *Cutting with the grain results in tough slices. Cutting against the grain shortens the muscle fibers, producing tender, juicy meat.*

1. In a large bowl, combine the shallot and lime juice and let sit for 10 minutes, stirring occasionally. In a small bowl, combine 2 teaspoons of the sugar, 1½ teaspoons salt and ¾ teaspoon white pepper. Pat the steak dry with paper towels, then rub all over with the sugar-salt mixture. If using a cast-iron or carbon-steel skillet, cut the steak into 4 to 6 pieces if needed to fit into the pan.

2. Prepare a grill or skillet for very high heat. For a charcoal grill, spread a full chimney of hot coals evenly over half of the grill bed. For a gas grill, set all burners to a high, even flame. Heat the grill for 5 minutes, then clean and oil the cooking grate. For a cast-iron or carbon-steel pan, heat 1 teaspoon canola oil over medium-high until smoking, about 5 minutes.

3. If using a grill, grill the steak (directly over the coals, if using a charcoal grill) until charred all over, 2 to 4 minutes per side. If using a skillet, sear the steak in 2 batches until charred, 2 to 4 minutes per side. Transfer the steak to a carving board and let rest for 10 minutes.

4. Meanwhile, add 1 tablespoon of the fish sauce, the pepper flakes and the remaining 2 teaspoons of sugar to the shallot–lime juice mixture and stir until the sugar has dissolved. Taste, then add additional fish sauce, if desired. Thinly slice the steak against the grain, then transfer to the bowl along with any accumulated juices. Add the tomatoes, cilantro and mint and stir. Transfer to a platter and garnish with cilantro sprigs, if desired.

Lomo Saltado

Start to finish: 35 minutes / Servings: 4

1½ pounds beef sirloin tips, trimmed, cut with the grain into 3-inch pieces and sliced ½ inch thick against the grain

1½ teaspoons ground cumin

Kosher salt and ground black pepper

5 tablespoons soy sauce, divided

3 tablespoons grapeseed or other neutral oil, divided

1 large red onion, halved and cut into ½-inch half-rings

¼ cup red wine vinegar

2 medium garlic cloves, minced

1 jalapeño chili, stemmed and sliced into thin rounds

1½ cups grape tomatoes, halved

Peru's lomo saltado is a quick stir-fry of soy-marinated beef, tomatoes and onions. It's part of chifa cuisine—Asian-influenced dishes created by indentured Chinese workers in the late 19th century. For our take, we add earthy flavor by mixing ground cumin into the soy sauce marinade. Tenderloin is often used here, but we preferred sirloin tips (also called flap meat) for their meatier flavor as well as lower price. And we seared the meat instead of stir-frying. Readily available jalapeño peppers made a good substitute for the traditional yellow ají peppers. If you prefer little to no spiciness, halve and seed the jalapeño before slicing it into half rings. Classic lomo saltado is frequently served over french fries; your favorite, frozen or otherwise, would be a good choice here. Steamed rice is an equally good accompaniment.

Don't cook the beef without patting it dry. Marinating in soy sauce adds flavor, but also moisture. Drying the beef helps ensure that the slices sear nicely, rather than steam. Also, cook it in two batches; crowding the pan inhibits browning.

1. In a medium bowl, combine the beef, cumin, 1 teaspoon each salt and pepper, and 2 tablespoons of soy sauce. Marinate at room temperature for 10 minutes. Pat the meat dry and set aside.

2. In a 12-inch skillet over high, heat 1 tablespoon of oil until barely smoking. Add half of the meat in a single layer and cook, turning once, until well browned on both sides, 2 to 3 minutes total. Transfer to a plate. Repeat with 1 tablespoon of the remaining oil and the remaining meat.

3. In the same pan over medium-high, heat the remaining 1 tablespoon oil over medium-high until shimmering. Add the onion and cook, stirring, until just starting to soften, about 2 minutes.

4. Stir in the vinegar and the remaining 3 tablespoons soy sauce, scraping up any browned bits on the bottom of the pan. Cook for about 1 minute, or until the sauce thickens slightly. Stir in the garlic and jalapeño and cook until fragrant, about 30 seconds. Add the tomatoes and the meat, along with any accumulated juices. Cook until the meat is just warmed through, about 30 seconds. Taste and season with salt and pepper.

Colombian Braised Beef (Posta Negra)

Start to finish: 5 hours (30 minutes active) / Servings: 4

5-pound boneless beef chuck roast, trimmed and patted dry

Kosher salt and ground black pepper

2 tablespoons grapeseed or other neutral oil

1 large yellow onion, chopped

10 medium garlic cloves, peeled

2 tablespoons tomato paste

½ cup packed dark brown sugar

2 cinnamon sticks

1 tablespoon whole allspice

2 teaspoons whole black peppercorns

1 teaspoon whole cloves

1 cup dry red wine

¼ cup Worcestershire sauce

1 cup pitted prunes, roughly chopped

1 tablespoon cornstarch

3 tablespoons red wine vinegar

Named after its dark, sweet sauce, posta negra is a classic Colombian dish made by braising beef in a flavorful liquid seasoned with panela (a type of raw cane sugar) and spices. For our version, we call for a 5-pound beef chuck roast; it's a fat-rich cut, so trim it well before tying the roast. In the end, the meat will be superbly tender and succulent. In Colombia, the dish might be served with fried plantains, yucca fritters and a simple salad; we liked it with fresh pico de gallo (see recipe p. 399) and potatoes.

Don't carve the roast without first letting it rest. *Resting makes the meat easier to cut into neat slices.*

1. **Heat the oven to 300°F** with a rack in the lower-middle position. Using kitchen twine, tie the roast at 2-inch intervals. Season all over with salt and pepper.

2. **In a large Dutch oven** over medium-high, heat the oil until shimmering. Add the onion and ½ teaspoon salt, then cook, stirring occasionally, until well browned, 5 to 7 minutes. Stir in the garlic and cook until fragrant, about 30 seconds. Add the tomato paste and cook, stirring constantly, until it begins to brown, about 2 minutes. Stir in the sugar, cinnamon, allspice, peppercorns and cloves. Pour in the wine, bring to a simmer and cook until thick and syrupy, 3 to 5 minutes. Stir in the Worcestershire sauce and prunes.

3. **Place the roast in the pot,** then turn to coat with the liquid. Cover, place in the oven and cook until a paring knife inserted into the thickest part meets no resistance, 3½ to 4 hours. Transfer the roast to a shallow baking dish and tent with foil. Let rest for 30 minutes.

4. **Meanwhile,** set a fine-mesh strainer over a medium bowl. Pour the contents of the pot into the strainer and press on the solids to extract as much liquid and pulp as possible, scraping the underside to collect the pulp. Discard the solids. Let the liquid settle for about 5 minutes (you should have about 1½ cups), then skim off the fat. Return the defatted liquid with pulp to the Dutch oven and bring to a simmer over medium.

5. **In a small bowl,** stir together 3 tablespoons water and the cornstarch. Whisk into the simmering liquid and cook, stirring constantly, until lightly thickened, about 2 minutes. Stir in the vinegar. Taste and season with salt and pepper.

6. **Transfer the roast** to a cutting board. Remove and discard the twine. Cut the meat against the grain into ½-inch slices and transfer to a platter. Pour about 1 cup of the sauce over the meat. Serve with the remaining sauce on the side.

QUICK PICO DE GALLO

Start to finish: 40 minutes
(10 minutes active)
Makes about 1 cup

3 medium plum tomatoes, cored,
seeded and finely chopped

1 jalapeño chili, stemmed, seeded
and sliced into thin half rings

¾ teaspoon kosher salt

3 tablespoons red wine vinegar

2 tablespoons finely chopped
fresh cilantro

In a small bowl, stir together all
ingredients. Cover and let stand,
stirring occasionally, for at least
30 minutes or up to 2 hours.

Vietnamese Shaking Beef (Bò Lúc Lắc)

Start to finish: **30 minutes**/ Servings: 4

1½ pounds beef sirloin tips or tri-tip, trimmed, patted dry and cut into 1½-inch pieces

3 tablespoons soy sauce, divided

Kosher salt and ground black pepper

5 tablespoons lime juice, divided, plus lime wedges, to serve

3 tablespoons fish sauce

2 tablespoons white sugar

2 tablespoons grapeseed or other neutral oil, divided

8 medium garlic cloves, finely chopped

1 small red onion, halved and sliced ¼ inch thick

1 bunch watercress, stemmed

The name of this Vietnamese dish refers to the way the pan is shaken while the beef cooks. We, however, prefer to minimize the meat's movement so the pieces achieve a nice dark, flavor-building sear. Sirloin tips (also called flap meat) or tri-tip are excellent cuts for this recipe—both are meaty, tender and reasonably priced (many recipes for shaking beef call for pricier beef tenderloin). If you can find baby watercress, use a 4-ounce container in place of the regular watercress; baby cress has a particularly peppery bite that pairs well with the beef. Serve with steamed jasmine rice.

Don't cut the beef into pieces smaller than 1½ inches or they may overcook. And don't forget the lime wedges for serving. A squeeze of fresh lime juice brightens the other flavors.

1. In a medium bowl, combine the beef, 2 tablespoons of the soy sauce and ½ teaspoon pepper. Toss and set aside. In a small bowl, stir together 4 tablespoons of the lime juice, the fish sauce, sugar and remaining 1 tablespoon soy sauce.

2. In a 12-inch skillet over medium-high, heat 1 tablespoon of the oil until barely smoking. Swirl to coat the pan, then add the beef in a single layer. Cook without stirring until well browned, about 1½ minutes. Flip each piece and cook until the second sides are well browned, about another 1½ minutes. Transfer to a medium bowl.

3. To the same skillet, add the remaining 1 tablespoon oil, the garlic and 1 teaspoon pepper. Cook over low, stirring constantly, until fragrant and the garlic is no longer raw, about 30 seconds. Pour in the lime juice mixture and any accumulated meat juices (don't add the meat), increase to medium-high and cook, stirring constantly, until a spoon leaves a trail when drawn across the skillet, 2 to 4 minutes.

4. Add the beef and cook, stirring and scraping up any browned bits, until the sauce clings lightly to the meat, about 2 minutes. Add the onion and stir until slightly softened, about 1 minute. Remove from the heat.

5. In a bowl, toss the watercress with the remaining 1 tablespoon lime juice and ½ teaspoon salt. Make a bed of the watercress on a serving platter. Top with the beef mixture and its juices. Serve with lime wedges.

Tuscan Beef and Black Pepper Stew (Peposo alla Fornacina)

Start to finish: 4 hours (30 minutes active) / Servings: 6

6½- to 7-pound boneless beef chuck roast, well trimmed and cut into 2-inch chunks

Kosher salt and coarsely ground black pepper

2 tablespoons extra-virgin olive oil

1 large yellow onion, halved and thinly sliced

12 medium garlic cloves, peeled

3 tablespoons tomato paste

2 sprigs rosemary, plus 1 tablespoon minced fresh rosemary

2 cups dry red wine

The simple, generously peppered beef stew known as peposo is said to have been created by 15th century kiln (fornacina) workers in Tuscany, Italy. Chianti is the best-known wine produced in that region and is the traditional choice for peposo, but any dry, medium-bodied red wine works well. Make sure to use coarsely ground black pepper, as it has more presence and better coats the beef. This recipe makes a generous amount of stew—about 2 quarts. The stew keeps well, so it can be made up to three days ahead and reheated in the microwave or in a saucepan over low.

Don't be shy about trimming the fat from the chuck roast. Remove as much as you can, which may mean shedding about 1 pound. Pull the roast apart at the natural seams, then use a sharp knife to trim the fat and cut the meat into 2-inch chunks.

1. Heat the oven to 325°F with a rack in the lower-middle position. Place the beef in a large bowl, sprinkle with 1 tablespoon salt and 2 tablespoons pepper, then toss.

2. In a large Dutch oven over medium, heat the oil until shimmering. Add the onion and garlic and cook, stirring, until the onion is lightly browned, 7 to 9 minutes. Add the tomato paste and cook, stirring, until the paste begins to brown, 3 to 5 minutes. Nestle the beef and rosemary sprigs in the onion mixture, cover and transfer to the oven. Cook for 2 hours.

3. Remove the pot from the oven. Stir, then return to the oven uncovered. Cook until a metal skewer inserted into a piece of beef meets no resistance, another 1 to 1½ hours.

4. Using a slotted spoon, transfer the meat to a medium bowl. Set a fine-mesh strainer over a fat separator or a medium bowl. Pour the meat juices into the strainer and press on the solids to push them through the strainer; discard the solids.

5. Pour the wine into the empty pot and bring to a boil over medium-high, scraping up any browned bits. Reduce to medium and simmer until the wine is syrupy and reduced to 1 cup, 5 to 7 minutes. Meanwhile, if you strained the meat juices into a bowl, use a spoon to skim off and discard the fat from the surface.

6. Pour the defatted meat juices into the pot. Bring to a simmer over medium-high and cook, stirring occasionally, until thickened to the consistency of heavy cream, 5 to 7 minutes. Return the beef to the pot, add the minced rosemary and stir gently. Bring to a gentle simmer and cook, stirring occasionally, until the meat is heated through, 4 to 5 minutes. Stir in 2 teaspoons pepper, then taste and season with salt.

STEW TODAY, PASTA TOMORROW

If you have about 3 cups of leftover stew, you can transform it into an altogether different meal. We liked:

Pasta with beef ragu: In a large skillet, sauté 5 medium garlic cloves (minced) and 3 tablespoons tomato paste in 2 tablespoons extra-virgin olive oil for 1 to 3 minutes. Add a 28-ounce can whole peeled tomatoes (crushed) and simmer until thickened, 5 to 7 minutes. Add 3 cups of the Tuscan beef stew, cook for 5 to 7 minutes, then break up the beef into bite-size pieces. Add 12 ounces pappardelle or fettuccine (cooked just shy of al dente) and ½ cup of pasta cooking liquid, toss, then cook for 3 minutes. Off heat, stir in ½ cup fresh basil. Serve with grated Parmesan.

Beef and broccoli rabe sandwiches: Blanch 1 pound broccoli rabe (trimmed) in a large pot of well-salted water for about 40 seconds; immediately transfer to an ice bath, then pat dry and cut into 1-inch pieces. Reheat 3 cups of the Tuscan beef stew, then shred the meat into bite-size pieces. In a large skillet, sauté the broccoli rabe in 3 tablespoons extra-virgin olive oil for 2 to 3 minutes. Add 5 medium garlic cloves (thinly sliced) and ¼ teaspoon red pepper flakes and cook for 1 minute. Off heat, toss with 2 tablespoons red wine vinegar. Place slices of provolone onto the cut sides for 4 crusty rolls and broil under the cheese melts. Divide the beef and broccoli rabe among the rolls, filling the sandwiches evenly.

Beef Kibbeh

Start to finish: 50 minutes (20 minutes active) / Servings: 4

1 medium yellow onion, peeled

½ cup fine bulgur (see headnote)

Kosher salt and ground black pepper

12 ounces 85 percent lean ground beef

1 large egg, beaten

¼ cup pine nuts, toasted and chopped

¾ teaspoon ground allspice

¾ teaspoon ground cardamom

¾ teaspoon ground cinnamon

¼ teaspoon cayenne pepper

6 medium garlic cloves, finely grated

1 cup whole-milk plain yogurt

1 cup lightly packed fresh flat-leaf parsley, chopped

¼ cup tahini

4 tablespoons grapeseed or other neutral oil, divided

Lemon wedges, to serve

Kibbeh, a popular dish throughout the Levant, is a spiced mixture of bulgur and ground meat. It may be layered with stuffing in a baking dish and baked, or shaped into small portions, filled and fried, with the goal of getting a toasty, browned crust that brings out the nuttiness of the bulgur. In this version, we skip the stuffing and form the mixture into patties, then pan-fry them, rather than deep-fry, for ease. We use ground beef, but you could substitute 12 ounces of ground lamb. Pine nuts add their distinct, slightly resinous flavor to the mix. Toast them in a small skillet over medium-low, shaking the pan frequently, until light golden brown and fragrant, about 4 minutes. Serve the kibbeh, yogurt-tahini sauce and lemon wedges for squeezing with warmed flatbread.

Don't use coarse bulgur. Fine bulgur, with particles that are very small and flaky, is key for yielding a mixture that holds together when formed into patties. If you can't find fine bulgur, process coarse bulgur in a spice grinder for 10 to 30 seconds. If the bulgur-meat mixture is very sticky or wet when you attempt to shape it, refrigerate for an additional 10 minutes to allow the bulgur to soak up more moisture.

1. Grate the onion on the large holes of a box grater, catching the pulp and liquid in a medium bowl. Stir in the bulgur and 2 teaspoons salt. Set aside for 10 minutes, until the bulgur has absorbed the onion liquid and is slightly softened.

2. Add the beef, egg, pine nuts, allspice, cardamom, cinnamon, cayenne, 1 teaspoon black pepper and ⅔ of the grated garlic. Knead with your hands or mix vigorously with a wooden spoon until well combined, then cover and refrigerate for 20 minutes.

3. Meanwhile, in a small bowl, whisk together the yogurt, parsley, tahini, ½ teaspoon salt, ¼ teaspoon black pepper and the remaining garlic. Set aside until ready to serve.

4. Line a rimmed baking sheet with kitchen parchment. Using your hands, form the bulgur-beef mixture into 12 balls (about 2 heaping tablespoons each) and place on the prepared baking sheet. Using your hands, flatten the balls into ½-inch-thick patties about 2½ inches in diameter.

5. In a 12-inch skillet over medium, heat 2 tablespoons of oil until barely smoking. Add half the patties and cook undisturbed until browned and crisp on the bottoms, about 4 minutes. Flip and continue to cook until the second sides are browned and crisp, about another 4 minutes, then transfer to a plate. Wipe out the skillet with paper towels and repeat with the remaining oil and patties. Serve with the yogurt-tahini sauce and lemon wedges.

Austrian Beef Stew with Paprika and Caraway (Rindsgulasch)

Start to finish: 4 hours (30 minutes active) / Servings: 4 to 6

5 pounds boneless beef chuck roast, trimmed, cut into 1½-inch pieces, patted dry

6 tablespoons Hungarian sweet paprika, divided

Kosher salt and ground black pepper

2 cups low-sodium beef broth

¼ cup tomato paste

4 tablespoons (½ stick) salted butter

1 large yellow onion, finely chopped

2 tablespoons caraway seeds, lightly crushed

⅓ cup all-purpose flour

1 tablespoon Hungarian hot paprika

3 bay leaves

2 teaspoons dried marjoram (optional)

¼ cup finely chopped fresh dill, plus dill sprigs to serve

1 tablespoon cider vinegar

Sour cream, to serve

This simple stew, inspired in part by classic Austrian versions of goulash and in part by Kurt Gutenbrunner's recipe in "Neue Cuisine," derives much of its bold flavor and rich color from sweet and hot paprika, so make sure the paprika you use is fresh and fragrant. For the deepest, earthiest flavor, we recommend seeking out true Hungarian paprika; we use a combination of sweet and hot to achieve just the right degree of spice. Serve with egg noodles, Spätzle or mashed potatoes.

Don't be shy about trimming the chuck roast; removing as much fat as possible before cooking prevents the stew from being greasy. In our experience, the roast usually loses about 1 pound with trimming. Also, don't cut the beef into pieces smaller than 1½ inches or the meat will overcook.

1. **Heat the oven to 325°F** with a rack in the lower-middle position. Season the beef with 1 tablespoon of sweet paprika, 2 teaspoons salt and 1 teaspoon pepper; toss to coat. In a measuring cup or small bowl, whisk together the broth and tomato paste; set aside.

2. **In a large Dutch oven** over medium, melt the butter. Add the onion and 1 teaspoon salt, then cook, stirring occasionally, until the onion is lightly browned, 8 to 10 minutes. Stir in the caraway and flour, then cook, stirring frequently, until the flour begins to brown, 2 to 4 minutes. Stir in the hot paprika and the remaining 5 tablespoons sweet paprika and cook until fragrant, about 30 seconds. Slowly whisk in the broth mixture and bring to a simmer, stirring frequently. Stir in the beef, bay and marjoram (if using), then bring to a simmer over medium-high. Cover, place in the oven and cook for 2 hours.

3. **Remove the pot from the oven.** Uncover and stir, then return to the oven uncovered and continue to cook until a skewer inserted into the meat meets no resistance, another 1 to 1½ hours. Remove from the oven, stir and let stand, uncovered, at room temperature for 15 minutes. Stir in the dill and vinegar. Taste and season with salt and pepper. Ladle into bowls and garnish with dill sprigs. Serve with sour cream.

Spicy Beef Salad with Mint and Cilantro (Larb Neua)

Start to finish: 20 minutes / Servings: 4

2 tablespoons jasmine rice

3 tablespoons lime juice

2 tablespoons fish sauce

2 teaspoons white sugar, divided

Kosher salt and ground black pepper

2 medium shallots, sliced into thin rings

2 Fresno chilies, stemmed and sliced into thin rings

2 teaspoons grapeseed or other neutral oil

1 pound 85 percent lean ground beef

1 cup lightly packed fresh mint, torn

1 cup lightly packed fresh cilantro leaves

Larb is a minced-meat salad from northern Thailand. This beef version was inspired by the spicy, tangy Isaan style from the northeast that's also popular in neighboring Laos. Easy-to-make toasted rice powder, called khao kua, is an essential ingredient here—it imparts a unique flavor, absorbs a small amount of the liquid and adds a subtle crunch. Cabbage leaves and sticky rice are the traditional accompaniments, but lettuce leaves and steamed jasmine rice are equally good. If you like, for more spiciness, add another chili or two.

Don't use extra-lean ground beef. A little fat keeps the meat moist, adds flavor and balances the acidity of the dressing.

1. In a 12-inch skillet over medium-low, toast the rice, stirring often, until browned and fragrant, 6 to 7 minutes. Transfer to a small bowl and let cool, about 10 minutes; set the skillet aside.

2. Meanwhile, in a medium bowl, whisk together the lime juice, fish sauce, 1 teaspoon of sugar, 1 teaspoon salt and ½ teaspoon pepper. Stir in the shallots and chilies. Let stand for at least 10 minutes or up to 20 minutes while you prepare the rest of the dish.

3. Using a spice grinder or mortar and pestle, pulverize the toasted rice to a coarse powder. Return the powder to the bowl and set aside.

4. In the same skillet over medium-high, heat the oil until shimmering. Add the beef, the remaining 1 teaspoon sugar and ½ teaspoon salt and cook, breaking the meat into very small bits, until no longer pink, 4 to 5 minutes. Immediately add the beef and any juices to the shallot-chili mixture, along with the mint, cilantro and half of the rice powder, then toss to combine. Let stand for 5 minutes. Taste and season with salt and pepper, then transfer to a serving platter and sprinkle with the remaining rice powder.

Beef, Orange and Olive Stew (Boeuf à la Gardiane)

Start to finish: 4½ hours (1 hour active) / Servings: 6 to 8

6 to 7 pounds boneless beef chuck roast, trimmed and cut into 2-inch cubes

Kosher salt and ground black pepper

4 medium carrots, peeled and cut crosswise into ½-inch rounds, divided

3 oil-packed anchovy fillets, patted dry

2 tablespoons extra-virgin olive oil

2 medium garlic cloves, thinly sliced

1 medium yellow onion, chopped

1 cup pitted Kalamata olives, rinsed, patted dry and chopped, divided

2½ cups dry red wine

1 medium red bell pepper, stemmed, seeded and cut into 1-inch pieces

1 tablespoon grated orange zest, plus ⅓ cup orange juice

2 teaspoons red wine vinegar

1 cup lightly packed fresh flat-leaf parsley, roughly chopped

Our version of this hearty stew from Camargue, in the south of France, uses chuck roast, a well-marbled cut. The dish gets robust flavor from Provençal ingredients—red wine, olives, anchovies and garlic. Orange is traditional, too; it lends the braise a balancing touch of brightness. Wine is key to this dish, and we wait until the beef is cooked before we add it, retaining more of the flavors. A bold, full-bodied dry red wine such as Côtes du Rhône or syrah is ideal, as it holds its own against the other big flavors. Serve with rice, egg noodles or potatoes.

Don't forget to zest the orange before juicing it—it's much easier to grate the zest from a whole orange than from one that's been halved and squeezed. Don't add all of the carrots to the pot with the beef. Adding some at the beginning gives the stew a subtle sweetness, but after hours of braising, these carrots are spent. We add more carrots near the end of cooking so that they are tender but still flavorful.

1. **Heat the oven to 325°F** with a rack in the lower-middle position. In a large Dutch oven, toss the beef with 2 tablespoons salt and 2 teaspoons pepper. Add ½ the carrots, the anchovies, oil, garlic and onion, then toss. Cover, transfer to the oven and cook for 2 hours.

2. **Remove the pot** from the oven and stir in ½ cup of the olives. Return to the oven uncovered and cook until a knife inserted into a piece of beef meets no resistance, 1 to 1½ hours.

3. **Using a slotted spoon,** transfer the meat to a large bowl, leaving the vegetables in the pot. Set a fine-mesh strainer over a medium bowl. Pour the meat juices into the strainer, pressing on the solids to extract as much liquid as possible; discard the solids. You should have about 2½ cups liquid; if needed, add water.

4. **Pour the wine** into the now-empty pot and bring to a boil over medium-high, scraping up any browned bits. Reduce to medium and simmer, stirring occasionally, until the wine is reduced by half, about 8 minutes. Meanwhile, use a spoon to skim off and discard the fat from the surface of the strained cooking liquid.

5. **Pour the defatted cooking liquid** into the pot and add the remaining carrots and the bell pepper. Return to a simmer and cook, uncovered and stirring occasionally, until the vegetables are tender and the sauce is slightly thickened, 10 to 15 minutes. Stir in the orange juice and beef. Continue to cook, stirring occasionally, until the sauce begins to cling to the meat, 3 to 6 minutes.

6. **Off heat,** stir in the remaining ½ cup olives, the orange zest, vinegar and half of the parsley. Taste and season with salt and pepper. Sprinkle with the remaining parsley.

Egg-Stuffed Mexican Meatballs with Salsa Roja

Start to finish: 50 minutes / Servings: 4

1 tablespoon grapeseed or other neutral oil

1 pound plum tomatoes, whole

½ medium white onion, halved

2 medium garlic cloves, peeled

1 or 2 chipotle chilies in adobo sauce, plus the sauce clinging to them

1½ teaspoons chili powder

1 teaspoon Mexican oregano

Kosher salt and ground black pepper

⅓ cup (¾ ounce) panko breadcrumbs

1 large egg yolk

12 ounces 85 percent lean ground beef

12 ounces ground pork

3 hard-cooked large eggs, peeled, each cut into 4 wedges

Fresh cilantro, to serve

Chicharrones, crumbled, to serve (optional)

These meatballs, or albondigas, hide a sliver of hard-cooked egg at the center, like the ones we were taught to make in Mexico. For best flavor and texture, we use a combination of ground beef and pork. The tomato-onion-garlic puree that becomes the salsa roja doubles as a seasoning for the meat mixture. As you shape the meatballs, if you find the mixture is too tacky for easy handling, moisten your hands with water. These meatballs typically are garnished with crumbled chicharrones (fried pork rinds); we've made them optional, but they are delicious served this way. Serve with rice and/or warm tortillas.

Don't allow the sauce to come to a full boil when cooking the meatballs, or they will end up dry and tough. Gentle simmering will keep their texture tender and light.

1. In a 12-inch skillet over medium-high, heat the oil until barely smoking. Add the tomatoes, onion and garlic, then cook, occasionally turning the vegetables, until deeply charred in spots, about 5 minutes; if the garlic is done before the tomatoes and onion, remove the cloves from the skillet.

2. Add the charred vegetables to a blender along with the chipotle chilies, chili powder, oregano and 1 teaspoon salt; set the skillet aside. Blend until the mixture is smooth, about 1 minute, scraping the blender jar as needed. Measure ⅓ cup of the puree into a medium bowl, mix in the panko and let stand until fully softened, about 5 minutes. Pour the remaining puree into the reserved skillet and set aside.

3. Line a rimmed baking sheet with kitchen parchment. To the panko mixture, add the egg yolk, both ground meats, 1½ teaspoons salt and ¾ teaspoon pepper. Using your hands, mix until homogeneous. Divide into 12 portions (about ¼ cup each) and place on the prepared baking sheet. One portion at a time, in the palm of your hand, flatten into a 3- to 4-inch disk. Place a wedge of hard-cooked egg in the center, then enclose meat around the egg and roll between your palms to form a smooth ball. Set the meatball on the prepared baking sheet and repeat with remaining portioned meat mixture and egg wedges. Refrigerate uncovered for 10 minutes.

4. Meanwhile, set the skillet over medium and bring the sauce to a simmer. Reduce to medium-low and cook, stirring occasionally, until slightly thickened and darkened, about 10 minutes. Place the meatballs in the skillet, then cover and cook at a gentle simmer until the centers reach 160°F, 15 to 20 minutes; turn the meatballs once about halfway through. Serve sprinkled with cilantro and chicharrones (if using).

Roman Braised Beef with Tomato and Cloves

Start to finish: 4 hours (30 minutes active) / Servings: 6

---

6 to 7 pounds boneless beef chuck roast, trimmed and cut into 2-inch chunks

¾ teaspoon ground cloves

Kosher salt and ground black pepper

4 ounces pancetta, roughly chopped

6 medium garlic cloves, smashed and peeled

1 medium yellow onion, halved and thinly sliced

1 medium fennel bulb, trimmed, halved, cored and thinly sliced

28-ounce can whole peeled tomatoes, crushed

2 teaspoons fresh thyme, minced

In Rome, cloves are used to flavor the pot roast-like dish known as garofolato di manzo alla Romana. Cloves, known as chiodi di garofano, give the dish its name. The earthy, subtly smoky and slightly bitter flavor of cloves complements the natural sweetness of the onion, fennel and tomatoes used to flavor this dish. The beef typically is cooked as a large roast, similar to a pot roast. We prefer cutting a chuck roast into chunks and simmering the meat as a stew. This ensures that the pieces are succulent and flavorful throughout, while also slightly reducing the cooking time. For a cool contrast, we make a salad of fresh fennel, tomatoes and parsley (see following recipe) to serve with the stew. Polenta or crusty bread is an excellent accompaniment for absorbing the flavorful sauce.

Don't use ground cloves that have gone stale, as they won't add much flavor or fragrance to the braise. If your cloves have been in the pantry for more than a few months, uncap and take a whiff. The aroma should be sharp and strong. If not, it's time to get a new jar.

---

1. Heat the oven to 325°F with a rack in the lower-middle position. Place the beef in a large bowl and season with the cloves, 1 tablespoon salt and 2 teaspoons pepper.

2. In a large Dutch oven over low, cook the pancetta, stirring occasionally, until sizzling and the fat has begun to render, about 5 minutes. Increase the heat to medium-low and continue to cook, stirring occasionally, until the pieces begin to brown, another 7 minutes. Add the garlic, onion and fennel, then increase to medium. Cook, stirring occasionally, until the vegetables are softened and translucent, about 6 minutes. Stir in the tomatoes and bring to a simmer. Stir in the beef, then cover, transfer to the oven and cook for 2 hours.

3. Remove the pot from the oven. Stir, then return to the oven uncovered. Cook until a skewer inserted into a piece of beef meets no resistance, another 1 to 1½ hours. Using a slotted spoon, transfer the meat to a medium bowl. With a wide spoon, skim off and discard the fat from the surface of the cooking liquid, then bring to a boil over medium-high, scraping up any browned bits. Cook until the liquid has thickened to the consistency of heavy cream, 10 to 12 minutes.

4. Stir in the thyme, then return the beef to the pot. Reduce to medium and cook, stirring occasionally, until the meat is heated through, about 5 minutes. Taste and season with salt and pepper.

FENNEL, TOMATO AND PARSLEY SALAD

Start to finish: 15 minutes
Servings: 6

1 medium fennel bulb, trimmed, halved and thinly sliced

1 pint cherry or grape tomatoes, halved or quartered if large

½ cup lightly packed fresh flat-leaf parsley, chopped

1 tablespoon red wine vinegar

Kosher salt and ground black pepper

In a medium bowl, toss together the fennel, tomatoes, parsley, vinegar, 1 teaspoon salt and ¼ teaspoon pepper.

Neapolitan Meatballs with Ragù

Start to finish: **50 minutes** / Servings: 6 to 8

---

4 tablespoons extra-virgin olive oil, divided, plus more to serve

1 large yellow onion, finely chopped

Kosher salt and ground black pepper

6 medium garlic cloves, finely grated

1½ teaspoons red pepper flakes, divided

6½ ounces (2½ cups) panko breadcrumbs

3 ounces pecorino Romano cheese, 2 ounces finely grated (1 cup), 1 ounce as a chunk, plus more grated, to serve

1 large egg, plus 1 large egg yolk, beaten together

1½ pounds 90 percent lean ground beef

Two 28-ounce cans whole peeled tomatoes

6 to 8 large basil leaves

In Naples, Rosa Vittozzi, part of the family-run Trattoria La Tavernetta, showed us how to make meatballs Neapolitan style—generously sized and ultra-tender from a high ratio of bread to meat. For our version, we opted to use Japanese panko breadcrumbs. Panko, which has a neutral flavor and a light and fluffy but coarse texture, greatly streamlines the meatball-making process, eliminating the need to remove the crusts from fresh bread, cut and measure, soak in water, then squeeze out excess moisture. Panko needs only to be moistened with water and it's ready to use. Neapolitans serve their meatballs with a basic tomato sauce they refer to as "ragù." We use pecorino liberally in this recipe: a chunk simmered in the sauce, as well as grated both in and over the meatballs. Though not traditional, pasta is a fine accompaniment. Or offer warm, crusty bread alongside.

Don't be shy about mixing the panko-meat mixture with your hands. It takes a few minutes to work the mixture together until homogeneous. Your hands are the best tools for this. Don't bake the meatballs without first allowing them to chill for 15 to 20 minutes; this helps them hold their shape. And after baking, make sure to let the meatballs rest for about 10 minutes before adding them to the sauce; if the timing is off and the sauce is ready before the meatballs have rested, simply remove the pot from the heat and let it wait.

1. Heat the oven to 475°F with a rack in the middle position. Line a rimmed baking sheet with kitchen parchment and mist with cooking spray. In a large Dutch oven over medium-high, heat 2 tablespoons of the oil until shimmering. Add the onion and ½ teaspoon salt, then cook, stirring occasionally, until softened, about 5 minutes. Add the garlic and 1 teaspoon of the pepper flakes; cook, stirring, until fragrant, about 30 seconds. Remove from the heat, then transfer half of the onion mixture to a large bowl.

2. In a medium bowl, combine the panko and 1¼ cups water; press the panko into the water and let stand until fully softened, about 5 minutes. Mash with your hands to a smooth paste, then add to the bowl with the onion mixture. Using a fork, mix until well combined and smooth. Stir in the grated cheese, beaten eggs, remaining 2 tablespoons oil, 1½ teaspoons salt and 2 teaspoons black pepper. Add the meat and mix with your hands until completely homogeneous.

3. Using a ½-cup dry measuring cup, divide the mixture into 8 portions. Using your hands, shape each into a compact ball and place on the prepared baking sheet, spacing them evenly apart.

Refrigerate uncovered for 15 to 20 minutes. Reshape the meatballs if they have flattened slightly, then bake until lightly browned, about 20 minutes. Let cool on the baking sheet set on a wire rack for about 10 minutes.

4. While the meatballs cook, in a food processor or blender, puree the tomatoes with their juices one can at a time, until smooth, about 30 seconds, transferring the puree to a large bowl. Return the Dutch oven to medium and heat the remaining onion mixture, stirring, until warmed through, about 2 minutes. Stir in the tomatoes, remaining ½ teaspoon pepper flakes, the basil and the chunk of cheese. Bring to a simmer over medium-high and cook, stirring occasionally, until slightly thickened, about 15 minutes. Taste and season with salt and pepper.

5. Using a large spoon, carefully transfer the meatballs to the sauce, then, using 2 spoons, turn each to coat. Bring to a gentle simmer, then reduce to medium-low, cover and cook for 5 minutes. Remove the pot from the heat and let stand, covered, for about 5 minutes to allow the meatballs to firm up slightly. Remove and discard the pecorino chunk. Serve with additional grated cheese.

Oven-Perfect Strip Steak with Red Chimichurri

Start to finish: 1¼ hours (15 minutes active), plus refrigeration
Servings: 4 to 6

___

Kosher salt and ground black pepper

1 tablespoon freshly grated nutmeg (from 2 whole nutmegs)

2 teaspoons white sugar

Two 20-ounce strip steaks (each about 2 inches thick), patted dry

2 tablespoons grapeseed or other neutral oil

Red Chimichurri (see recipe p. 419)

This recipe uses the gentle, controlled heat of the oven to replicate the "reverse sear" technique Argentinians use when grilling beef. Rather than start the steak over high heat to brown, then finish over low heat, the steaks start in a cool oven, then finish with a quick sear in either a blistering-hot cast-iron skillet or on a grill. The result is steak with a deep, flavorful crust that's evenly cooked throughout, not overdone at the surface and just-right at only the core. We call for strip steaks (also called strip loin or New York strip), but bone-in or boneless ribeyes work well, too, as long as they're 1½ to 2 inches thick. We learned to season cuts of beef with nutmeg at La Carbrera in Buenos Aires; the spice doesn't leave a distinct flavor of its own but rather enhances the steaks' meatiness and smoky notes.

Don't use preground nutmeg. For best flavor, purchase whole nutmeg and grate it yourself. You could use a grater made specifically for nutmeg, but a fine wand-style grater also works well.

1. **Set a wire rack in a rimmed baking sheet.** In a small bowl, stir together 2 tablespoons salt, 1 tablespoon pepper, the nutmeg and sugar. Measure out and reserve 2 teaspoons of the seasoning mixture, then rub the remainder onto all sides of the steaks, pressing it into the meat. Place the steaks on the prepared rack and refrigerate uncovered for at least 1 hour or up to 24 hours.

2. **Heat the oven to 250°F** with a rack in the middle position.

3. **Place the baking sheet** with the steaks in the oven and cook until the centers reach 110°F, 45 to 55 minutes. Remove from the oven and let stand for up to 30 minutes.

4. **In a 10- or 12-inch cast-iron skillet** over medium-high, heat the oil until barely smoking. Place the steaks in the skillet and cook, without moving them, until well browned, about 3 minutes. Using tongs, flip the steaks and cook until the second sides are well browned and the centers reach 120°F (for medium-rare), 2 to 3 minutes. Alternatively, the steaks can be seared for the same time over direct heat on a very hot charcoal or gas grill with a well-oiled grate.

5. **Transfer the steaks** to a carving board and let rest for 10 minutes, then cut into thin slices. Place on a platter, pour on the accumulated juices and sprinkle with the reserved seasoning mixture. Drizzle with a few spoonfuls of chimichurri and serve with additional chimichurri on the side.

RED CHIMICHURRI

Start to finish: **15 minutes, plus cooling.**/ Makes **1½ cups**

This recipe can easily be halved, but if you're like us, you'll find uses other than steak for this delicious condiment. We also like it on grilled pork, fish and other seafood. Chimichurri can be stored in an airtight container in the refrigerator for up to a week; bring to room temperature before serving.

Don't substitute fresh oregano. The stronger flavor and texture of dried oregano are hallmarks of chimichurri.

¾ cup neutral oil

¼ cup sweet paprika

¼ cup red pepper flakes

¼ cup dried oregano

2 medium garlic cloves, finely grated

½ cup balsamic vinegar

Kosher salt

1. In a small saucepan over low, combine the oil, paprika, pepper flakes and oregano. Cook, stirring occasionally, until the mixture begins to bubble, 5 to 7 minutes. Remove from the heat and stir in the garlic. Let cool to room temperature.

2. In a medium bowl, combine the vinegar and 1 teaspoon salt, then stir until the salt dissolves. Slowly whisk in the cooled oil mixture.

Lebanese Baked Kafta with Potatoes and Tomatoes

Start to finish: 1½ hours (1 hour active), plus cooling
Servings: 4 to 6

___

1 pound Yukon Gold potatoes, unpeeled, sliced into ¼-inch rounds

2 tablespoons plus ¼ cup extra-virgin olive oil, divided

Kosher salt and ground black pepper

1 pound ground lamb or 80 percent lean ground beef

1 medium yellow onion, halved and grated on the large holes of a box grater

½ cup finely chopped fresh flat-leaf parsley

½ teaspoon ground allspice

½ teaspoon ground cinnamon

14½-ounce can crushed tomatoes

2 medium garlic cloves, minced

1 pound plum tomatoes, cored and sliced into ¼-inch rounds

1 small green bell pepper or Anaheim chili, stemmed, seeded and sliced into thin rings

It's easy to see why kafta bil sanieh, a casserole, if you will, of sliced potatoes, rounds of tomatoes and flavorful kafta (seasoned meatballs or meat patties), is Lebanese comfort food. The ingredients are shingled into a baking dish and baked until the flavors meld and the textures become deliciously succulent and tender. Our rendition, based on a recipe from "The Palestinian Table" by Reem Kassis, starts with a simple no-cook tomato sauce in the bottom of the baking dish, where juices collect during baking and form a delicious sauce. To ensure the potatoes cook evenly and thoroughly, we precook them by roasting them for about 10 minutes, enough time to begin making the kafta. We especially like the flavor of ground lamb kafta, but if you prefer, use 80 percent lean ground beef instead.

Don't overmix the meat mixture or the kafta will cook up with a firm, bouncy texture. Using a light hand when mixing and shaping will keep the kafta tender. The patties don't need to be perfectly round, but do try to keep them about ¼ inch thick, as they'll puff a little when baked. And if one or two (or a few) fall apart while you layer the ingredients into the baking dish, not to worry—gently smoosh the patties back together.

___

1. **Heat the oven to 450°F** with a rack in the middle position. On a rimmed baking sheet, toss the potatoes with 1 tablespoon of oil and ¼ teaspoon salt. Distribute in a single layer and roast without stirring just until a skewer inserted into the potatoes meets no resistance, 10 to 13 minutes. Remove from the oven and set aside to cool slightly. Leave the oven on.

2. **While the potatoes cook,** line a second baking sheet with kitchen parchment. In a medium bowl, combine the lamb, onion, parsley, allspice, cinnamon, ¾ teaspoon salt and ¼ teaspoon pepper. Using your hands, mix gently until just combined; do not overmix. Divide the mixture into about 20 golf ball-size portions (1½ to 1¾ inches in diameter) and place on the prepared baking sheet. Flatten each ball into a patty about 2½ inches wide and ¼ inch thick (it's fine if the patties are not perfectly round); set aside until ready to assemble.

3. **In a 9-by-13-inch baking dish,** combine the crushed tomatoes, garlic, the ¼ cup oil, ½ teaspoon salt and ¼ teaspoon pepper. Stir well, then distribute in an even layer. Shingle the potatoes, tomato slices, green pepper rings and meat patties in 3 or 4 rows down the length of the baking dish, alternating the ingredients. Drizzle with the remaining 1 tablespoon oil and sprinkle with pepper.

4. **Bake, uncovered,** until the kafta and potatoes are browned and the juices are bubbling, 25 to 35 minutes. Cool for about 10 minutes before serving.

Vietnamese Beef Stew with Star Anise and Lemon Grass (Bò Kho)

Start to finish: 3¼ hours (45 minutes active) / Servings: 4 to 6

2 tablespoons grapeseed or other neutral oil

1 large yellow onion, halved and thinly sliced

3 ounces fresh ginger, unpeeled, sliced

8 medium garlic cloves, finely grated

2 tablespoons tomato paste

2 tablespoons chili-garlic sauce, divided, plus more if needed

4 stalks fresh lemon grass, trimmed to the bottom 6 inches, dry outer layers discarded, bruised

6 star anise pods

1 cinnamon stick

3 pounds boneless beef chuck roast, trimmed and cut into 1½-inch chunks

4 cups or one 33-fluid ounce container unsweetened coconut water (see headnote)

2 cups low-sodium beef broth

4 medium carrots, peeled, halved lengthwise and cut on the diagonal into 1-inch pieces

2 tablespoons fish sauce

2 tablespoons lime juice, plus lime wedges to serve

Kosher salt and ground black pepper

Thinly sliced white onion, to serve

Fresh cilantro and/or basil, to serve

In Ho Chi Minh City, Vietnam, literature teacher and home cook Nguyên Thị Thúy showed us how to make bò kho, a fragrant beef stew that marries local ingredients with French culinary technique. Though recipes for bò kho vary from cook to cook, star anise and lemon grass are essential flavorings, the finished broth is always quite soupy (not thickened as Western stews are) and its color is deep red. In simplifying the formula we were taught in Vietnam, we skipped the 30-minute marination of beef with seasonings and we opted to use low-sodium beef broth instead of concentrated meat bouillon. We also chose to use beef chuck instead of brisket, as we find chuck has the right amount of fat and connective tissue to yield rich flavor and body. Coconut water, along with the beef broth, is the cooking liquid; its natural sugars and minerals enhance the flavor of the stew. Ladle the bò kho over rice stick noodles (prepared according to package directions) or serve with steamed jasmine rice or a crusty baguette.

Don't use sweetened coconut water. A small amount of natural sugar is normal but check the ingredients listed on the label for added sugar. Also, after adding the liquid to the pot and bringing it to a boil, be sure to turn down the heat and simmer without stirring to allow the scum (proteins from the meat) to rise to the surface. After a few minutes of simmering, use a spoon to skim off and discard the scum; this results in a clearer, more visually appealing broth.

1. **In a large Dutch oven** over medium-high, heat the oil until barely smoking. Add the yellow onion and cook, stirring occasionally, until lightly browned, 5 to 7 minutes. Add the ginger and garlic, then cook, stirring, until fragrant, about 1 minute. Add the tomato paste and cook, stirring, until well browned and beginning to stick to the pot, about 1 minute. Stir in the chili-garlic sauce, then add the lemon grass, star anise, cinnamon and beef; stir to coat. Add the coconut water and broth. Bring to a boil over medium-high, then reduce to medium-low and cook, uncovered and without stirring, for about 4 minutes, adjusting the heat as needed to maintain a simmer.

2. **Using a wide spoon,** skim off and discard the scum from the surface of the liquid. Reduce to medium-low, cover and cook, adjusting the heat as needed to maintain a simmer, until a skewer inserted into the beef meets no resistance, 2 to 2½ hours.

3. **Remove the pot from the heat.** Remove and discard the lemon grass, star anise, cinnamon and ginger. Tilt the pot to pool the cooking liquid to one side, then use the wide spoon to skim off and discard as much fat as possible from the surface.

4. Stir the carrots into the stew and return to a simmer over medium. Cover and cook, stirring occasionally and adjusting the heat as needed to maintain a simmer, until the carrots are tender, about 15 minutes.

5. Remove the pot from the heat. Stir in the fish sauce and lime juice. Taste and season with additional chili-garlic sauce (if desired), salt and pepper. Ladle the stew into bowls and top with sliced onion and cilantro and/or basil. Serve with lime wedges.

Rib-Eye Steaks with Rosemary and Pomegranate Molasses

Start to finish: 40 minutes, plus marinating and resting / Servings: 4

1 medium white onion, peeled and cut lengthwise into quarters

¼ cup pomegranate molasses, plus more to serve

1 teaspoon Aleppo pepper or ¾ teaspoon sweet paprika plus ¼ teaspoon cayenne pepper

3 teaspoons minced fresh rosemary, divided

Kosher salt and ground black pepper

Two 12- to 14-ounce boneless rib-eye steaks (about 1 inch thick), patted dry

Grapeseed or other neutral oil, for brushing

2 tablespoons salted butter, cut into 4 pieces

At Manzara Restaurant in Söğüt, in southeastern Turkey, we tasted a superb grilled rib-eye steak prepared by chef Naci Isik. We thought the fruity, tangy-sweet flavor of pomegranate molasses, the savoriness of onion and the resinous notes of fresh rosemary in the marinade worked together as a delicious complement for the richness and smoky char of the beef. Our adaptation hews closely to Isik's recipe, with a few modifications for cooking in a home kitchen and using ingredients available in the U.S. We recommend seeking out pomegranate molasses that does not contain added sugar; its flavor is purer and more intense than types made with sweetener.

Don't forget to scrape off the marinade and pat the steaks dry before cooking. The marinade contains moisture and sugar that inhibit browning and cause sticking. Making sure the steaks are as clean and dry as possible will help with better browning and easier release.

1. Set a box grater in a 9-by-13-inch baking dish. Grate the onion quarters on the large holes, allowing the pulp and juice to fall into the baking dish. To the grated onion, stir in the pomegranate molasses, Aleppo pepper, 1 teaspoon of rosemary, 1 teaspoon salt and ½ teaspoon black pepper. Add the steaks and turn to coat. Cover and refrigerate for at least 30 minutes or up to 24 hours; flip the steaks once or twice during marination. If refrigerated for longer than 1 hour, remove the steaks from the refrigerator about 30 minutes before cooking.

2. Brush a 12-inch cast-iron grill pan with 2 teaspoons oil and heat over medium-high until barely smoking. Meanwhile, scrape the marinade off the steaks and pat dry with paper towels. Add the steaks to the pan and cook without disturbing until well browned on the bottom, 5 to 7 minutes. Flip the steaks and cook until the second sides are well browned and the centers reach 120°F (for medium-rare), 6 to 8 minutes. Transfer to a serving platter, sprinkle with the remaining 2 teaspoons rosemary and top each with 2 pieces of butter. Tent with foil and let rest for about 10 minutes.

3. Transfer the steaks to a cutting board and cut against the grain into thin slices on the diagonal. Return to the platter and pour over the juices from the cutting board. Sprinkle with salt and black pepper and, if desired, drizzle with additional pomegranate molasses.

TO COOK ON A CHARCOAL OR GAS GRILL

Follow the recipe to marinate the steaks; if refrigerated for longer than 1 hour, remove the steaks from the refrigerator about 30 minutes before grilling. Prepare a charcoal or gas grill. For a charcoal grill, ignite three-fourths of a large chimney of coals, let burn until lightly ashed over, then distribute the coals evenly over one side of the grill bed; open the bottom grill vents. Heat the grill, covered, for 5 minutes, then clean and oil the grill grate. For a gas grill, turn all burners to high and heat the grill, covered, for 10 to 15 minutes, then clean and oil the cooking grate. Scrape the marinade off the steaks and pat dry with paper towels. Brush one side of the steaks with oil, then place oiled-side down on the grill (on the hot side if using charcoal). Cover and cook until nicely charred on the bottom, about 4 minutes. Brush the side facing up with oil, then flip the steaks. Cover and cook until the second sides are nicely charred and the centers reach 120°F (for medium-rare), another 3 to 4 minutes. Transfer the steaks to a serving platter, sprinkle with the remaining rosemary and top each with 2 pieces of butter. Tent with foil and let rest for about 10 minutes. Continue with the recipe to finish and slice.

Carne en su Jugo

Start to finish: 1¾ hours (45 minutes active) / Servings: 4 to 6

1½ pounds boneless beef short ribs, trimmed

2 tablespoons Worcestershire sauce

1 teaspoon soy sauce

Kosher salt and ground black pepper

1½ pounds tomatillos, husked

1 medium white onion, half roughly chopped, half finely chopped, reserved separately

4 cups low-sodium beef broth, divided

1 tablespoon grapeseed or other neutral oil

3 medium garlic cloves, minced

2 bay leaves

1 serrano chili, stemmed and thinly sliced, plus more to serve

Two 15½-ounce cans pinto beans, rinsed and drained

Chopped fresh cilantro, to serve

Lime wedges, to serve

Warmed tortillas, to serve

Carne en su jugo, or "meat in its own juices" translated from the Spanish, is from Jalisco state on the west coast of central Mexico. It's a stewy, brothy meal in a bowl that, as its name suggests, derives its hearty, meaty flavor from beef simmering in the juices it releases as it cooks. Just a handful of other ingredients play supporting roles. The version of carne en su jugo shown to us by Paola Briseño González includes tangy, vegetal tomatillos, and takes the unusual step of pureeing a little of the sautéed meat with the aromatics to add body to the broth. Commonly used cuts for the dish are flank and skirt steak, but we prefer boneless short ribs, as they contain the right amount of flavor-enhancing fat and pack tons of meaty richness. The beef is cut into small pieces before cooking; freezing it for a few minutes firms it up so it's easier to slice. For convenience, we used canned pinto beans instead of starting with dried beans, and we add them near the end of cooking so they spend some time in the broth turning tasty without becoming too soft. Carne en su jugo loves garnishes. In addition to the ones called for in the recipe, we like to spoon on some salsa macha (see recipe p. 630). It's a non-traditional pairing, but a delicious one.

Don't use a Dutch oven, as the surface area is too wide. A large pot with a smaller diameter is the better choice. We intentionally crowd the beef in the pot so the meat readily releases its juices and the juices remain in the pot rather than cook off.

1. Place the beef on a plate and freeze, uncovered, until firm at the edges, about 15 minutes. Remove from the freezer and slice ⅛ to ¼ inch thick against the grain. Now, cut the slices, stacking a few at a time, into small strips and bits (no need to be precise). In a medium bowl, toss the beef with the Worcestershire, soy sauce and ½ teaspoon pepper; set aside at room temperature.

2. In a medium saucepan, combine the tomatillos and enough water to cover. Cover and bring to a boil over medium-high, then reduce to medium and cook until the tomatillos are softened, about 5 minutes. Using a slotted spoon, transfer the tomatillos to a blender; discard the water. To the blender, add the roughly chopped onion and 1 cup of the broth.

3. In a large pot over medium, heat the oil until shimmering. Add the garlic and cook, stirring, until fragrant and lightly browned, about 1 minute. Add the beef with its marinade and cook, stirring occasionally, until the meat releases its juices and no longer is pink, 5 to 8 minutes. Remove the pan from the heat. Measure 2 tablespoons of the meat and add to the blender, then blend on high until the mixture is smooth, about 1 minute.

4. Add the puree to the pot along with the remaining 3 cups broth, the bay and chili. Bring to a boil over medium-high and simmer, uncovered and stirring occasionally, until the meat is tender but not completely soft, 35 to 45 minutes (the best way to test doneness is by tasting a piece of beef).

5. Add the beans to the pot and simmer, stirring occasionally, until the meat is fully softened and the broth is slightly thickened, about 15 minutes. Remove and discard the bay, then taste and season with salt and pepper. Ladle into bowls and garnish with the finely chopped onion, sliced chili and cilantro; serve with lime wedges and tortillas.

Braised Beef with Dried Figs and Quick-Pickled Cabbage

Start to finish: 3¼ hours (1¼ hours active) / Servings: 4 to 6

For the braise:

1 tablespoon extra-virgin olive oil

3 pounds beef shanks, patted dry

28-ounce can whole peeled tomatoes, crushed by hand

1 quart low-sodium beef broth or water

4 teaspoons juniper berries, finely ground

1 cup dried mission figs, finely chopped

2 medium carrots, peeled, halved lengthwise and cut crosswise into ½-inch pieces

2 teaspoons grated orange zest

Kosher salt and ground black pepper

For the quick-pickled cabbage:

1 pound green cabbage, chopped

2 medium carrots, peeled and shredded on the large holes of a box grater

¾ cup white vinegar

1 tablespoon white sugar

Kosher salt and ground black pepper

¼ cup finely chopped fresh mint

For this rich, warming beef braise, adapted from a recipe in "Aegean" by Marianna Leivaditaki, London chef and native of Crete, we use bone-in beef shanks, braise them until meltingly tender, pluck the meat off the bones and return it to the flavorful braising liquid. Dried figs and orange zest lend sweetness that balances the meatiness of the shanks and perfume the dish with the essence of the Mediterranean, while ground juniper berries add piney, resinous notes. Leivaditaki serves the braise with a quick-pickled salad that brightens the flavors and counters the beef's silkiness with a little crunch.

Don't use Calimyrna (Smyrna) figs, which are brownish-tan. The seeds have an especially crunchy, gritty texture that doesn't soften with cooking. Small black mission figs, which are widely available, are the better choice.

1. To make the braise, in a large Dutch oven over medium-high, heat the oil until barely smoking. Add the shanks and cook, occasionally turning them, until well browned on both sides, 7 to 10 minutes. Add the tomatoes with juices, the broth, juniper and figs, then bring to a simmer, scraping up any browned bits. Cover, reduce to medium-low and simmer until a skewer inserted into the meat meets no resistance, about 2 hours; stir once about halfway through.

2. While the beef is cooking, make the pickled cabbage. In a large bowl, stir together the cabbage, carrots, vinegar, sugar and ¾ teaspoon salt. Cover and refrigerate until ready to serve.

3. Transfer the shanks to a large bowl; set aside to cool. Tilt the pot to pool the cooking liquid to one side, then use a wide spoon to skim off and discard as much fat as possible from the surface. Add the carrots, bring to a simmer over medium and cook, uncovered and stirring occasionally, until the carrots are tender, about 15 minutes.

4. Meanwhile, shred the meat into bite-size pieces, discarding the fat, bone and gristle. When the carrots are tender, return the meat to the pot and cook, stirring occasionally, until heated through. Off heat, stir in the orange zest, then taste and season with salt and pepper.

5. Stir the mint into the pickled cabbage, then taste and season with salt and pepper. Serve the braise with the pickled cabbage on the side.

Skirt Steak Salad with Arugula and Peppadews

Start to finish: 30 minutes / Servings: 4

---

2 teaspoons ground fennel

Kosher salt and ground
black pepper

1 pound skirt steak, trimmed

7 tablespoons extra-virgin
olive oil, divided

3 tablespoons lemon juice

½ cup chopped Peppadew
peppers, drained

1 large garlic clove,
thinly sliced

8 ounces arugula (about
12 cups lightly packed)

1½ ounces Parmesan cheese,
shaved (¾ cup)

Our steak salad takes inspiration from classic Italian tagliata, then skips across continents with the addition of Peppadews, tangy peppers from South Africa. A popular dish in Tuscany, tagliata is a simple presentation of thinly sliced, rare steak, extra-virgin olive oil, arugula and shaved Parmesan. We made ours work with an inexpensive skirt steak seasoned with a dry rub of salt, pepper and ground fennel. We then whipped up a simple lemon juice–olive oil vinaigrette. The steak got a quick sear. Then, while it rested, we added thinly sliced garlic and chopped Peppadew peppers to the pan. In an unusual touch, we used half the vinaigrette to dress the arugula and the other half to deglaze the pan, creating a warm, sweet-and-sour garlicky sauce that blended with the steak's juices. Pay attention to how you slice the steak. Cuts like skirt steak have longer, thicker muscle fibers than sirloin and tenderloin; they are relatively tough unless cut against the grain, which results in shorter fibers. Skirt steaks can sometimes come as long pieces; if needed, cut the meat in half to fit the pan. If you can't find skirt steak, flank, flat iron and bavette steaks all work well.

Don't cook the steak beyond medium-rare or it will be tough.

1. In a small bowl, combine the fennel, 1 teaspoon salt and 2 teaspoons pepper. Coat the steak with the seasoning, then let sit for 15 minutes. Meanwhile, in a liquid measuring cup, whisk together 6 tablespoons of the oil, the lemon juice, ¾ teaspoon salt and ½ teaspoon pepper. Set aside.

2. In a large skillet over medium-high, heat the remaining tablespoon of oil until barely smoking. Add the steak and sear, without moving, until well browned, about 3 minutes. Flip and brown on the second side, about another 2 minutes for rare to medium-rare.

3. Transfer to a plate and let rest for 10 minutes. Return the skillet to medium-high. Add the Peppadews and garlic, then cook for 30 seconds. Stir the dressing, then add half of it to the skillet, along with any juices from the meat on the plate, scraping the pan to deglaze.

4. In a large bowl, toss the arugula with the remaining dressing and half of the Parmesan, then divide among serving plates. Thinly slice the steak against the grain, then arrange the slices over the arugula. Spoon some warm pan sauce over each serving. Top with the remaining Parmesan.

Savory Bakes

12

Italian Flatbread (Piadine)

Start to finish: 30 minutes / Makes four 10-inch flatbreads

Flatbread is among the quickest of quick breads. Leavened or not, folded, topped or used as a scoop, it appeals with promises of warm, fresh dough. One of our favorite variations originated in Romagna, in northern Italy. There they throw together flour, salt, water or milk, and lard or olive oil to make a quick dough. After a short rest, the flatbread—a piadina—is cooked on a griddle or skillet. The cooked piadine then are stuffed with sweet or savory fillings and folded in half to make a sandwich. We started by finding the right fat for our dough. Butter was wrong. Olive oil gave us a pleasant texture and flavor, but something still was missing. So we gave lard a shot. And what a difference. The piadine were tender with just the right chew. But we wanted yet more suppleness and found our answer in naan, a tender flatbread from India that adds a scoop of yogurt to the dough. Fat hinders gluten development, keeping bread soft. It worked well in our piadine and gave the dough more complex flavor. Though it was not as flavorful, vegetable shortening worked as a substitute for lard. If the dough doesn't ball up in the processor, gather it together and briefly knead it by hand. For a simple topping, brush the cooked piadine with our spicy garlic oil (see recipe p. 638), or try one of the fillings on the facing page.

½ cup water, divided

¼ cup plain whole-milk yogurt

274 grams (2 cups) bread flour

1 teaspoon table salt

1½ teaspoons baking powder

63 grams (⅓ cup) lard, room temperature

1. In a liquid measuring cup, whisk together ¼ cup of the water and the yogurt. In a food processor, combine the flour, salt and baking powder. Process for 5 seconds. Add the lard and process until combined, about 10 seconds. With the processor running, add the yogurt mixture. With the processor still running, add the remaining water 1 tablespoon at a time until the dough forms a smooth, moist ball, about 1 minute.

2. Divide the dough into 4 pieces. Roll each into a ball, then cover with plastic wrap. Let rest for 15 minutes. Meanwhile, prepare the toppings.

3. Roll each dough ball into a 10-inch round. Poke the surfaces all over with a fork. Heat a 12-inch cast-iron skillet over medium until a drop of water sizzles immediately, 4 to 6 minutes. One at a time, place a dough round in the skillet and cook until the bottom is charred in spots, 1 to 2 minutes. Using tongs, flip and cook for 30 seconds. Transfer to a plate and cover loosely with foil.

SPICED BEEF AND TOMATO

Start to finish: 30 minutes / Makes 4 piadine

Ground meat, tomatoes and spices is a common topping for flatbread in Armenia. If you prefer, swap in ground lamb.

8 ounces 80 percent lean ground beef

½ large yellow onion, finely chopped (about ¾ cup)

1 large red bell pepper, cored and finely chopped

2 teaspoons red pepper flakes

1 teaspoon smoked paprika

1 teaspoon ground cumin

Kosher salt and ground black pepper

14½-ounce can fire-roasted crushed tomatoes

½ cup plain whole-milk Greek-style yogurt

4 tablespoons lemon juice, divided

2 cups lightly packed fresh flat-leaf parsley

2 cups lightly packed fresh mint, torn

___

In a 12-inch nonstick skillet over medium, cook the beef, stirring and breaking up the meat, until beginning to brown, 2 to 3 minutes. Add the onion, bell pepper, pepper flakes, paprika, cumin, 1 teaspoon salt and 1 teaspoon pepper. Cook, stirring occasionally, for 5 minutes. Add the tomatoes and cook until most of the liquid has evaporated, about 8 minutes.

In a small bowl, whisk together the yogurt and 2 tablespoons of the lemon juice. In a medium bowl, combine the parsley, mint and the remaining 2 tablespoons of lemon juice. Taste and season with salt and pepper. Spread the beef mixture evenly over half of each piadina. Drizzle with the yogurt mixture, top with the herbs and fold in half.

PROSCIUTTO, ARUGULA AND RICOTTA

Start to finish: 10 minutes / Makes 4 piadine

In Romagna, piadine often are served with cured meats, greens and fresh cheeses that soften with the warmth of the freshly cooked bread. If possible, purchase fresh-cut prosciutto, sliced as thinly as possible, and allow it to come to room temperature. The flavor and texture of ricotta cheese varies widely by brand; we like Calabro.

¾ cup whole-milk ricotta cheese

½ teaspoon grated lemon zest, plus 2 tablespoons lemon juice

Kosher salt and ground black pepper

8 slices prosciutto, room temperature

4 ounces baby arugula (about 4 cups)

3 tablespoons extra-virgin olive oil

___

In a medium bowl, stir together the ricotta and lemon zest. Taste and season with salt and pepper. Spread the ricotta mixture evenly over half of each piadina, then top with 2 slices of the prosciutto. In a medium bowl, toss the arugula with the lemon juice and a pinch of salt. Mound on top of the prosciutto. Drizzle with the oil and fold.

Pita Bread

Start to finish: 4 hours (40 minutes active)
Servings: Ten 5½-inch pita rounds

---

4 tablespoons grapeseed
or other neutral oil, divided

171 grams (1¼ cups) bread
flour, plus more for dusting

175 grams (1¼ cups)
whole-wheat flour

2¼ teaspoons instant yeast

2 teaspoons white sugar

¾ cup warm water (100°F to
110°F), plus more if needed

¼ cup plain whole-milk
yogurt

1¼ teaspoons table salt

Pita bread is a yeast-leavened flatbread from the Mediterranean and Middle East. We make ours with whole-wheat flour and whole-milk yogurt for full flavor and a pleasant chew. Yogurt is common in some flatbreads but is generally not used in pita. We, however, found it helped produce a soft, elastic dough and a tender, but slightly chewy baked bread. To ensure the breads puff nicely and form pockets, they're baked two at a time on a heated baking steel or stone. We preferred a stand mixer for making the dough, but a food processor worked, too. To make the dough in a processor, combine both flours, the yeast and sugar in the work bowl and pulse until combined. Add the water, yogurt and 2 tablespoons of oil and process until a smooth, slightly sticky ball forms, about 1 minute. Add additional water, 1½ teaspoons at a time (up to 2 tablespoons total), if the dough feels too dry. Let the dough rest in the processor for 5 minutes, then add the salt and process until smooth and pliable, about 1 minute. Knead by hand on a lightly floured counter for 1 minute, then transfer to an oiled medium bowl and turn to coat. Cover with plastic wrap and let rise in a warm, draft-free spot until not quite doubled in bulk. Continue with the recipe from the third step to shape and bake. It's not unusual if one or two of the rounds don't puff during baking—the bread still will taste great. The ones that do puff will not deflate as they cool. Store leftover rounds in a zip-close bag for up to a day. To warm, wrap the pitas in foil and heat for 4 minutes at 300°F.

Don't forget to heat the baking steel or stone for a full hour before baking. And do cover the pita breads with a towel when they come out of the oven to keep them soft.

---

1. Coat a medium bowl with 1 teaspoon of oil; set aside. In the bowl of a stand mixer fitted with the dough hook, add both flours, the yeast and sugar. Mix on low until combined, about 5 seconds. Add the water, yogurt and 2 tablespoons of oil. Mix on low until a smooth ball forms, about 3 minutes. Feel the dough; it should be slightly sticky. If not, add water 1½ teaspoons at a time (no more than 2 tablespoons total), mixing after each addition, until slightly sticky. Let rest in the mixer bowl for 5 minutes.

2. Add the salt and knead on low until smooth and pliable, 10 minutes. Transfer to the prepared bowl, forming it into a ball and turning to coat with oil. Cover with plastic wrap and let rise in a warm, draft-free area until well risen but not quite doubled in volume, 1 to 1½ hours.

3. Dust a rimmed baking sheet evenly with bread flour. Transfer the dough to the counter. Using a dough scraper or bench knife, divide the dough into 10 pieces (about 2 ounces each). Form each into a tight ball and place on the prepared baking sheet. Brush each ball with ½ teaspoon of the remaining oil, then cover with a damp kitchen towel. Let rise in a warm, draft-free area until well risen but not quite doubled, 30 to 60 minutes. Meanwhile, heat the oven to 500°F with a baking steel or stone on the upper-middle rack

4. Lightly dust 2 rimmed baking sheets with bread flour and lightly dust the counter. Place a dough ball on the counter; use a lightly floured rolling pin to roll the ball into a round ⅛ inch thick and 5½ inches in diameter. Set on one of the prepared baking sheets. Repeat with the remaining dough balls, placing them in a single layer on the baking sheets. Cover with a damp kitchen towel and let rest for 10 minutes.

5. Lightly dust a baking peel with bread flour, then place 2 dough rounds on the peel without flipping them. Working quickly, open the oven and slide the rounds onto the baking steel. Immediately close the door. Bake until the breads have puffed and are very lightly browned, about 3 minutes. Using the peel, remove the breads from the oven. Transfer to a wire rack and cover with a dry kitchen towel. Repeat with the remaining dough rounds. Serve warm or at room temperature.

Roasted Mushroom Pizza with Fontina and Scallions

Start to finish: 35 minutes, plus heating the oven
Makes one 12-inch pizza

___

1 pound portobello mushroom caps

⅓ cup extra-virgin olive oil

Table salt and ground black pepper

1 tablespoon finely chopped fresh thyme

3 medium garlic cloves, minced

1 portion pizza dough (see recipe p. 440), warmed to 75°F

Bread flour, for dusting

1 tablespoon semolina flour, for dusting

1 cup fontina-Parmesan cream (see recipe p. 439)

2 scallions, thinly sliced on the diagonal

¼ teaspoon red pepper flakes

Heating the oven and pizza steel or stone for pizza-baking takes about an hour. We use this time to roast portobello mushrooms, which we combine with our fontina-Parmesan cream sauce. The mushrooms can also be prepared and refrigerated up to 24 hours beforehand. When shaping the pizza dough, make sure that the edges are thicker than the center so they will contain the sauce, which becomes runny during baking. We found that pizza bakes best at 550°F; if your oven heats only to 500°F, the pie will need to bake for an extra two minutes. If you don't have a pizza steel or stone, use an overturned rimmed baking sheet.

Don't undercook the mushrooms. *Roasting them until they are well browned removes moisture that would otherwise make the pizza crust soggy.*

___

1. One hour before baking, heat the oven to 550°F with a baking steel or stone on the upper-middle rack and a second rack in the lower-middle position.

2. Using a spoon, scrape off and discard the gills on the undersides of the mushroom caps. Halve any caps that are 5 inches or larger in diameter, then cut the caps into ¼-inch slices. In a large bowl, toss the mushrooms, olive oil and ¼ teaspoon salt.

3. Spread the mushrooms in an even layer on a rimmed baking sheet. Roast on the lower oven rack, stirring once, until they have released their moisture, the moisture evaporates and the mushrooms begin to brown, about 15 minutes. Stir in the thyme and garlic, then roast until the mushrooms have browned and the garlic is no longer raw, another 3 to 4 minutes. Let cool completely on a wire rack. Leave the oven on.

4. Turn the dough out onto a counter dusted with bread flour. Flour your hands and, using your fingers, press the dough, starting at the center and working out to the edges, into a 12-inch round, turning the dough over once. The round should be thin at the center, with slightly thicker edges. Lightly dust a baking peel, inverted baking sheet or rimless cookie sheet with the semolina. Transfer the dough to the peel and, if needed, reshape into a round.

5. Using the back of a spoon, spread the fontina-Parmesan cream evenly on the dough, leaving a ½-inch border at the edge. Scatter the mushrooms over it and season with pepper. Slide the pizza onto the baking steel or stone and bake until the crust is well browned, 7 to 9 minutes.

6. Using the peel, transfer the pizza to a wire rack. Let cool for a couple of minutes, then sprinkle with the scallions and red pepper flakes.

FONTINA-PARMESAN CREAM

Start to finish: 10 minutes
Makes 2 cups (enough for 2 pizzas)

This cream-based pizza sauce—inspired by Nancy Silverton, who in turn picked it up at Pellicano, a pizzeria in Umbria—pairs well with roasted portobello mushrooms. We also liked it with sausage and hot peppers (but make sure the peppers are cooked first so they don't leak moisture into the sauce).

¾ cup heavy cream, cold

2 ounces (1 cup) shredded fontina cheese

¼ cup grated Parmesan cheese

1 tablespoon minced fresh rosemary

½ teaspoon ground black pepper

In a stand mixer fitted with the whisk attachment, whip the cream on medium until stiff peaks form, about 2½ minutes. Using a rubber spatula, fold in the fontina, Parmesan, rosemary and pepper. Refrigerate in an airtight container for up to 3 days.

Pizza Dough

Start to finish: 1½ days (20 minutes active)
Makes four 8-ounce portions of dough

Though any brand of bread flour will work in this recipe, we liked King Arthur Flour best. It has a higher protein content, producing crusts with good flavor, nicely crisped surfaces and a satisfying chew. We found that making the dough with cool or cold water helped prolong the fermentation process, which developed better flavor. For fermenting the dough, quart-size zip-close plastic bags coated on the inside with cooking spray are easiest, but well-oiled bowls or plastic containers with lids work well, too. Following the overnight fermentation, the dough can be frozen for longer storage; to use, allow to thaw overnight in the refrigerator, then proceed with the recipe.

Don't shorten the fermentation and room-temperature warming times. The dough requires at least 24 hours in the refrigerator to ferment, then needs to come up to 75°F before shaping.

1. In a stand mixer fitted with the dough hook, combine the flour, sugar and yeast. Mix on low to combine, about 15 seconds. With the mixer running, slowly add the water, then mix on low until a slightly bumpy dough forms and clears the sides of the bowl, about 5 minutes. Cover the bowl with plastic wrap and let rest for 20 minutes.

2. Uncover the bowl, sprinkle the salt over the dough and mix on low until smooth and elastic, 5 to 7 minutes. If the dough climbs up the hook, stop the mixer, push it down and continue kneading.

3. Scrape the dough onto a well-floured counter and divide it into 4 pieces. With floured hands, form each into a taut ball and dust with flour. Mist the insides of 4 quart-size zip-close plastic bags with cooking spray, then add 1 ball to each. Seal and refrigerate for 24 to 72 hours.

4. About 1 hour before making pizza, mist 4 small bowls with cooking spray. Transfer the dough balls to the bowls. Cover with plastic wrap, then set each bowl into a larger bowl of 100°F water for 30 minutes, or until the dough reaches 75°F, changing the water as needed. Shape according to directions.

548 grams (4 cups) bread flour, plus more for dusting

1 tablespoon white sugar

¾ teaspoon instant yeast

1½ cups cool (65°F) water

1 teaspoon table salt

Portuguese Cornbread (Broa)

Start to finish: 4½ hours (15 minutes active) / Makes 1 loaf

Known as broa, Portuguese cornbread shares little but its name with the cakey, honeyed version familiar to Americans. Beneath a crackling, creviced crust, the heart of broa is dense, moist and deeply flavored. At Padaria Amadina & Neto, a 200-year-old broa bakery in Avintes, Portugal, we learned that traditionally, the bread is made with corn flour, which is dried corn that is ground finer than cornmeal. If you can't find corn flour, you can use finely ground cornmeal, but the bread will have some granularity in the crumb. This hearty loaf is delicious sliced and spread with salted butter. Stored in an airtight container or zip-close bag, leftover broa will keep for up to three days at room temperature; the flavor and texture are best if the bread is toasted before serving.

Don't let the loaf rise for longer than indicated, as the bread may bake up with an unpleasantly boozy, slightly sour flavor. Unlike most bread doughs that double in bulk during rising, this one increases only by about 50 percent.

204 grams (1⅔ cups) corn flour

2 tablespoons honey

1 cup boiling water, plus ¼ cup room-temperature (70°F) water

137 grams (1 cup) bread flour, plus more for dusting

70 grams (½ cup) rye flour

2 teaspoons instant yeast

1 teaspoon table salt

1. Line a rimmed baking sheet with kitchen parchment. In a stand mixer fitted with the paddle attachment, mix the corn flour, honey and boiling water on low until evenly moistened and a thick mash forms, 30 to 60 seconds. Turn off the mixer and let stand until just warm to the touch, about 30 minutes.

2. Add the room-temperature water, bread and rye flours, yeast and salt. Using the dough hook attachment, mix on low, scraping down the bowl as needed, until a cohesive dough forms, about 5 minutes; the dough should clear the sides of the bowl and feel tacky but not excessively sticky.

3. Turn the dough out onto the counter and use your hands to shape the dough into a ball about 5 inches in diameter. Set on the prepared baking sheet, dust the top with bread flour and cover with a kitchen towel. Let rise in a warm, draft-free spot until the volume increases by about half, 1 to 1½ hours. Meanwhile, heat the oven to 500°F with a rack in the middle position.

4. Bake the bread for 15 minutes. Reduce the oven to 300°F and continue to bake until deep golden brown, another 30 to 35 minutes. Transfer the bread from the baking sheet to a wire rack and let cool completely, about 2 hours.

Taiwanese Flaky Scallion Pancakes

Start to finish: 2 hours plus 24-hour rest / Makes 8 pancakes

1 large egg

582 grams (4¼ cups) bread flour, plus more for dusting

Table salt

2 sticks (16 tablespoons) salted butter, 1 melted and 1 at room temperature

½ cup peanut or canola oil, plus more for counter

1 cup finely chopped scallions

These flaky scallion pancakes are similar to Malaysian or Indonesian roti and are rich in flavor yet light because of the many delicate layers. You'll need a large, smooth table or countertop for working. The pancakes are best when the dough is made and refrigerated a day ahead, but they can be shaped and frozen, then thawed and cooked just before serving. To do so, once the pancakes have been pressed into 8-inch ovals, freeze them in a single layer on baking sheets lined with lightly oiled kitchen parchment. Freeze until rigid, then stack between sheets of lightly oiled parchment and place in a large zip-close bag. Seal and freeze for up to a month. When ready to cook, thaw on the parchment liners just until pliable, then cook as directed.

Don't worry *if the dough forms a few tears or holes as you stretch it; they won't matter in the finished pancakes. Make sure to oil the countertop with a thin but thorough coating.*

1. In a 2-cup liquid measuring cup or small bowl, whisk together 1¼ cups water and the egg. In a stand mixer fitted with the dough hook, combine the flour and 1 teaspoon salt; mix on medium until well combined, about 1 minute. Add the melted butter to the water-egg mixture then, with the mixer running on medium, slowly add to the flour and mix until incorporated, about 1 minute. Reduce to medium-low and knead until a smooth, elastic dough forms, about 7 minutes.

2. Transfer the dough to a very lightly floured counter and divide into 8 portions (about 4 ounces each). Shape each into a taut ball. On an unfloured area of the counter, roll each portion against the counter under a cupped hand until the surface of the ball is completely smooth. Pour the oil into a 9-by-13-inch baking dish. Place the balls in the dish and rotate to coat with oil on all sides. Cover with plastic wrap and refrigerate overnight.

3. Remove the dough from the refrigerator and let stand at room temperature for at least 1 hour or up to 2 hours. Using your hands, spread 2 to 3 tablespoons of oil in an even layer on a large area of counter (about 2 feet square). Working with 1 dough ball at a time, use your fingertips to push the dough gently out from the center until it forms an 8-inch round. Flip the round, adding more oil as needed to the counter to keep the surface slicked, and continue to push and stretch the dough until it forms a paper-thin round about 18 inches in diameter; you should be able to see through the dough. Shape the dough into an 18-inch square. If at any point the dough isn't moving easily, add more oil to the counter.

4. Grease your hands with 1 tablespoon of the room-temperature butter, then gently rub the entire surface of the dough with butter. Sprinkle with ¼ teaspoon salt. Using your fingertips, lift the far edge of the dough square and fold the top third of the dough down toward you, then fold the bottom third up as if folding a letter; align the edges as much as possible. The dough will spring back slightly as you fold, leaving you with a long strip about 4 inches wide. Scatter 2 tablespoons of the scallions over the strip and gently press them in. Fold over 4 inches of one end of the strip, then continue folding the 4-inch area until you reach the other end of the strip. Transfer to an oiled plate and cover with plastic wrap. Repeat with the remaining dough; you'll need 2 plates, each holding 4 packets. Cover and refrigerate for at least 15 minutes, or up to 24 hours.

5. Heat the oven to 350°F with a rack in the middle position. Heat a 10-inch cast-iron or nonstick skillet over medium-low until flecks of water instantly sizzle when they hit the pan, 3 to 5 minutes. Place 1 dough packet on an oiled counter and gently spread it into an 8-inch oval of even thickness; it's fine if the oval is not perfectly shaped. Transfer the oval to the skillet, reduce heat to low and cook, occasionally rotating the pancake in the pan, until the bottom is golden brown and crisp, 5 to 7 minutes. Flip the pancake and cook until the second side is golden brown and crisp, another 5 to 7 minutes. While the pancake cooks, shape another dough packet into an 8-inch oval.

6. Using a spatula, transfer the pancake to a cutting board and cover with a dry kitchen towel. Using your hands, scrunch the pancake, pushing the edges together to help the layers separate. Flatten the pancake, then rotate 90 degrees, re-cover with the towel and repeat the scrunching process. Flatten the pancake and place it on a wire rack set in a rimmed baking sheet. Repeat the entire process until all the dough squares have been cooked. Transfer the pancakes to the oven and bake until heated through, about 3 minutes.

Pumpkin Seed Rolls

Start to finish: 3½ hours (1 hour active) / Makes 15 rolls

For the sponge:

70 grams (½ cup) rye flour

½ cup warm (100°F) water

1 tablespoon honey

2 teaspoons instant yeast

For the dough:

1 cup shelled pumpkin seeds (pepitas)

½ cup sesame seeds

4 tablespoons (½ stick) salted butter, cut into 4 pieces and chilled

343 grams (2½ cups) bread flour, plus more for dusting

1 cup room-temperature (70°F) water

1¼ teaspoons table salt

1 large egg, lightly beaten

Flaky salt, such as Maldon sea salt

Rye flour brings texture to these pumpkin seed rolls that are based on a classic Bavarian bread, Kürbiskern Brötchen. We added toasted pumpkin seeds, as is traditional, and threw in some sesame seeds, as well. Then we processed the seeds with chilled butter in a food processor to create a nut butter, which we added to the sponge before kneading for a tender, moist and flavorful crumb. These rolls are best served the day they are baked. For ease, they can be made in the morning, then reheated in a 350°F oven for 10 minutes just before serving. The seed-butter mixture can be prepared up to three days ahead and refrigerated. Just be sure to pull it out an hour before using to bring it to room temperature.

Don't be tempted to add extra flour when mixing the dough; it will look and feel quite sticky, but will firm up as it rises. Otherwise, the rolls won't have enough chew.

1. To make the sponge, in the bowl of a stand mixer, whisk together the rye flour, warm water, honey and yeast. Cover and let sit until doubled and bubbly, about 1 hour.

2. Meanwhile, in a 12-inch skillet over medium, combine the pumpkin and sesame seeds and toast, stirring, until the sesame seeds are golden (some pumpkin seeds will pop), 5 to 8 minutes. Measure out ½ cup of the mixture and set aside. Transfer the rest to a food processor and process until finely ground, about 1 minute. Add the butter and process until just melted and combined, about another 20 seconds.

3. When the sponge is ready, add the bread flour, water and seed-butter mixture. Mix with the dough hook on low until just combined, about 1 minute. Let sit for 5 minutes. Add the salt, then mix on low until the dough forms a mass around the hook but still adheres to the sides, about 5 minutes. The dough should look and feel sticky but not wet. Cover the bowl and let rise until tripled in size, about 1 hour.

4. Heat the oven to 450°F with a rack in the middle position. Line a baking sheet with kitchen parchment. Turn the dough out onto a well-floured surface, being careful not to deflate it. Lightly flour the top of the dough and gently press it into a 10-by-6-inch rectangle. To create 15 equal portions of dough (about 2 ounces each), cut the rectangle into thirds lengthwise, then into fifths crosswise.

5. Gently round each portion into a ball, creating a smooth, taut surface and pinching together any seams on the bottom. Arrange the rolls evenly on the prepared baking sheet. Brush the tops generously with the egg and sprinkle the reserved seed mixture over them, pressing very gently to adhere. Top each with a small sprinkle of flaky salt. Cover and let rise until nearly doubled in size, 30 to 35 minutes.

6. Bake until deep golden brown, 20 to 25 minutes, rotating the pan once halfway through. Using tongs, immediately transfer the rolls to a wire rack. Let cool for at least 30 minutes before serving.

Easy Flatbread Dough

Start to finish: 1½ hours (30 minutes active)
Makes two 12-inch pizzas or flatbreads

---

241 grams (1¾ cups) bread
flour, plus more for dusting

1½ teaspoons instant yeast

¾ teaspoon table salt

¾ cup plain whole-milk
Greek-style yogurt

1 tablespoon honey

This versatile dough is a breeze to make in a food processor and can be used for pizzas with various toppings or Middle Eastern–style flatbreads. The addition of Greek yogurt helps create a supple dough that's easy to work with and bakes up with a chewy-soft crumb and subtle richness. For convenience, the dough can be made a day in advance. After dividing the dough in half and forming the pieces into rounds, place each portion in a quart-size zip-close bag that's been misted with cooking spray, seal well and refrigerate overnight. Allow the dough to come to room temperature before shaping.

Don't undermix the dough in the food processor; it needs a full minute of processing to build the gluten that provides structure and strength. When done, the dough may be warm to the touch; this is normal.

1. In a food processor, combine the flour, yeast and salt, then process until combined, about 5 seconds. Add the yogurt, honey and ¼ cup water. Process until the mixture forms a ball, about 30 seconds; the dough should be tacky to the touch and should stick slightly to the sides of the bowl. If it feels too dry, add more water, 1 tablespoon at a time, and process until incorporated. Continue to process until the dough is shiny and elastic, about 1 minute.

2. Transfer the dough to a lightly floured counter. Flour your hands and knead the dough a few times, until it forms a smooth ball. Divide the dough in half and form each half into a taut ball by rolling it against the counter in a circular motion under a cupped hand. Space the balls about 6 inches apart on a lightly floured counter, then cover with plastic wrap. Let rise until doubled in volume, 1 to 1½ hours.

3. About 1 hour before baking, heat the oven to 500°F with a baking steel or stone on the upper-middle rack. Working one at a time, gently stretch each ball on a lightly floured counter to an oval approximately 6 inches wide and 12 inches long. The dough is now ready to top and bake, see recipes p. 448-449.

SHAPING FLATBREAD (PIZZA) DOUGH

1. Place one ball of dough on a lightly-floured counter.

2. Using your hands, begin patting and stretching the dough into an oval.

3. A ruler helps ensure that the dough reaches the correct dimensions.

4. Continue stretching the dough, making sure it is of even thickness.

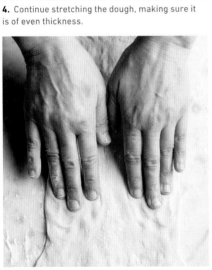

5. The dough is properly shaped when it forms a 6-by 12-inch oval.

Toppings for Easy Flatbread Dough

ZA'ATAR FLATBREADS

Start to finish: 25 minutes
Makes two 12-inch oval flatbreads

6 tablespoons extra-virgin olive oil

2 tablespoons sesame seeds, toasted

2 tablespoons za'atar

Semolina, for dusting

Easy flatbread dough (p. 446)

About 1 hour before baking, heat the oven to 500°F with a baking steel or stone on the upper-middle rack. In a small bowl, stir together the oil, sesame seeds and za'atar. Lightly dust a baking peel, inverted baking sheet or rimless cookie sheet with semolina.

Transfer one portion of the shaped dough to the peel and, if needed, reshape into a 6-by-12-inch oval. Spoon half of the oil mixture evenly over the entire surface of the dough. Slide the dough onto the baking steel and bake until the edges are golden brown, 7 to 9 minutes.

Using the peel, transfer the baked flatbread to a wire rack. Let cool for about 10 minutes. Meanwhile, top and bake the second portion of dough in the same way. Serve warm.

SPICED BEEF FLATBREADS WITH YOGURT AND TOMATOES

Start to finish: 45 minutes
Makes two 12-inch oval flatbreads

1 medium shallot, roughly chopped

1 cup lightly packed fresh flat-leaf parsley, roughly chopped, plus more to serve

¼ cup chopped drained roasted red peppers, patted dry

2 tablespoons tomato paste

1¼ teaspoons ground cumin

¾ teaspoon sweet smoked paprika

⅛ to ¼ teaspoon cayenne pepper

Kosher salt and ground black pepper

8 ounces 85 percent lean ground beef or ground lamb

Semolina, for dusting

Easy flatbread dough (p. 446)

1 large egg white, beaten

Plain whole-milk yogurt, to serve

Chopped tomato, to serve

Chopped red onion, to serve

About 1 hour before baking, heat the oven to 500°F with a baking steel or stone on the upper-middle rack. In a food processor, combine the shallot, parsley, roasted peppers, tomato paste, cumin, paprika, cayenne and ½ teaspoon each salt and black pepper. Process until finely chopped, about 30 seconds, scraping the bowl as needed. Add the beef and pulse just until incorporated, 3 or 4 pulses.

Lightly dust a baking peel, inverted baking sheet or rimless cookie sheet with semolina. Transfer one portion of the shaped dough to the peel and, if needed, reshape into a 6-by-12-inch oval. Brush the surface of the dough with a thin but even layer of egg white, then spread half of the beef mixture over the surface. Slide the dough onto the baking steel or stone and bake until the edges are golden brown, 9 to 11 minutes.

Using the peel, transfer the flatbread to a wire rack. Top and bake the second portion of dough in the same way. Serve warm with yogurt, chopped tomatoes, chopped onion and additional chopped parsley.

Tomato-Olive Focaccia

Start to finish: 7¼ hours (40 minutes active), plus cooling
Servings: 12

---

500 grams (3⅔ cups)
bread flour

5 teaspoons instant yeast

1 teaspoon white sugar

2 cups water, cool room
temperature

8 tablespoons extra-virgin
olive oil, divided

1¾ teaspoons table salt,
divided

1 cup cherry tomatoes,
halved

1 cup Castelvetrano olives,
pitted and halved (see
headnote)

1 teaspoon dried oregano

¾ teaspoon ground
black pepper

This recipe recreates the light, open-crumbed focaccia we ate at Paneficio Fiore in Bari, Italy. To achieve that texture, the dough must be wet—so wet, in fact, it verges on a thick, yet pourable batter. Resist the temptation to add more flour than is called for. Shaping such a sticky, high-hydration dough by hand is impossible. Instead, the dough is gently poured and scraped into the oiled baking pan; gravity settles it into an even layer. If you have trouble finding Castelvetrano olives, substitute any large, meaty green olive. To slice the baked focaccia for serving, use a serrated knife and a sawing motion to cut through the crust and crumb without compressing it. If desired, serve with extra-virgin olive oil for dipping. For convenience, the dough can be prepared and transferred to the baking pan a day in advance. After it has settled in the pan, cover tightly with plastic wrap and refrigerate. The next day, prepare the toppings. Uncover, top the dough with the olives and tomatoes and let stand at room temperature for 45 minutes, then finish and bake as directed.

Don't disturb the dough during its rise. And when transferring the dough to the baking pan, handle it gently. The goal is to retain as much gas in the dough as possible so the focaccia bakes up with an airy texture. Don't use a baking dish made of glass or ceramic; neither will produce a crisp, browned exterior, and glass is not safe to use in a 500°F oven.

1. **In a stand mixer with the dough hook,** mix the flour, yeast and sugar on medium until combined, about 30 seconds. With the mixer on low, drizzle in the water, then increase to medium and mix until the ingredients form a very wet, smooth dough, about 5 minutes. Turn off the mixer, cover the bowl and let stand for 10 minutes. Meanwhile, coat the bottom and sides of a large bowl with 2 tablespoons of oil; set aside.

2. **Sprinkle 1 teaspoon of salt** over the dough, then knead on medium until smooth and elastic, about 5 minutes; the dough will be wet enough to cling to the sides of the bowl. Using a silicone spatula, scrape the dough into the oiled bowl. Dip your fingers into the oil pooled at the sides of the bowl and dab the surface of the dough until completely coated with oil. Cover tightly with plastic wrap and let stand at room temperature for 5½ to 6 hours; during this time, the dough will double in volume, deflate, then rise again (but will not double in volume again).

3. **After the dough has risen** for about 4½ hours, heat the oven to 500°F with a baking steel or stone on the middle rack. Mist a 9-by-13-inch metal baking pan with cooking spray, then pour 2 tablespoons of the remaining oil in the center of the pan; set aside.

4. When the dough is ready, gently pour it into the prepared pan, scraping the sides of the bowl with a silicone spatula to loosen; try to retain as much air in the dough as possible. The dough will eventually settle into an even layer in the pan; do not spread the dough with a spatula, as this will cause it to deflate. Set aside while you prepare the tomatoes.

5. In a medium bowl, use a potato masher to lightly crush the tomatoes. Scatter the olives evenly over the dough, then do the same with the tomatoes, leaving the juice and seeds in the bowl. If the dough has not fully filled the corners of the pan, use your hands to lightly press the toppings to push the dough into the corners. Let stand uncovered at room temperature for 20 minutes.

6. Drizzle the dough with the remaining 4 tablespoons oil, making sure each tomato is coated. Sprinkle evenly with the oregano, remaining ¾ teaspoon salt and the pepper. Place the pan on the baking steel or stone and bake until golden brown and the sides of the focaccia have pulled away from the pan, 20 to 22 minutes. Cool in the pan on a wire rack for 5 minutes. Using a wide metal spatula, lift the focaccia from the pan and slide it onto the rack. Cool for at least 30 minutes before serving.

Lahmajoun

Start to finish: 2¼ hours (40 minutes active)
Makes two 12-inch flatbreads

For the dough:

241 grams (1¾ cups) bread flour, plus more for dusting

1½ teaspoons instant yeast

¾ teaspoon table salt

¾ cup plain whole-milk Greek yogurt

1 tablespoon honey

For shaping and topping:

1 small yellow onion, roughly chopped

¼ cup chopped drained roasted red peppers

2 tablespoons tomato paste

2 teaspoons smoked paprika

1½ teaspoons ground cumin

¾ teaspoon red pepper flakes

Kosher salt and ground black pepper

8 ounces 80 percent lean ground beef or ground lamb

¼ cup plain whole-milk Greek yogurt

Semolina flour, for dusting the pizza peel

2 tablespoons extra-virgin olive oil, divided

2 cups (1 ounce) lightly packed baby arugula

Lahmajoun (also spelled lahmacun) is a meat-topped flatbread common in the Levant, as well as in Turkey and Armenia. Arugula and a drizzle of yogurt are unusual finishes for lahmajoun, but they add fresh, peppery flavor and a creamy coolness that complement the spiced meat topping. For convenience, the dough can be made a day in advance. After dividing the dough in half and forming each piece into a round, place each portion in a quart-size zip-close bag that's been misted with cooking spray, seal well and refrigerate overnight. Allow the dough to come to room temperature before shaping.

Don't undermix the dough in the food processor; it needs a full minute of processing to build structure and strength. The dough may be warm to the touch when done; this is normal. But when processing the meat mixture, don't overdo it or the protein may get tough. Pulse only three or four times, just until combined.

1. To make the dough, in a food processor, combine the flour, yeast and salt; process until combined, about 5 seconds. Add the yogurt, honey and ¼ cup water. Process until the mixture forms a ball, about 30 seconds; the dough should be tacky to the touch and should stick slightly to the sides of the bowl. If it feels too dry, add more water, 1 tablespoon at a time, and process until incorporated. Continue to process until the dough is shiny and elastic, about 1 minute.

2. Transfer the dough to a lightly floured counter. Flour your hands and knead a few times to form a smooth ball. Divide the dough in half and form each half into a taut ball by rolling it against the counter in a circular motion under a cupped hand. Space the balls about 6 inches apart on a lightly floured counter, then cover with plastic wrap. Let rise until doubled in volume, 1 to 1½ hours.

3. Meanwhile, to make the topping, in a food processor, pulse the onion until finely chopped, about 5 pulses. Add the roasted peppers, tomato paste, paprika, cumin, pepper flakes, ½ teaspon salt and 1 teaspoon black pepper. Process until smooth, about 10 seconds, scraping the bowl as needed. Add the beef and pulse just until incorporated, 3 or 4 pulses. Transfer to a medium bowl. In a small bowl, stir together the yogurt and 1 tablespoon water, adding more water as needed to thin to drizzling consistency. Cover both bowls and refrigerate until needed.

4. About 1 hour before shaping the dough, heat the oven to 500°F with a baking steel or stone on the upper-middle rack. Working one at a time, gently stretch each dough ball on a lightly floured counter to an oval approximately 6 inches wide and 12 inches long.

5. Dust a baking peel, inverted baking sheet or rimless cookie sheet with semolina. Transfer one shaped dough to the peel and, if needed, reshape into an oval. Brush the entire surface with 1 tablespoon of oil. Using a spatula, spread half the meat mixture on the dough, leaving a ½-inch border around the edge. Slide the dough onto the baking steel and bake until well browned, 9 to 12 minutes.

6. Using the peel, transfer the flatbread to a wire rack. Repeat with the remaining dough, oil and meat mixture. After the second flatbread has cooled on the rack for a couple minutes, top both with the arugula. Drizzle with yogurt, then serve.

Savory Kale and Two-Cheese Scones

Start to finish: 1¼ hours (40 minutes active), plus cooling
Makes 12 large scones

___

80 grams (½ cup) dried currants

87 grams (4 cups) stemmed and finely chopped lacinato or curly kale (see headnote)

1 tablespoon lemon juice

455 grams (3½ cups) all-purpose flour, plus more for dusting

50 grams (¼ cup) white sugar

4 teaspoons baking powder

½ teaspoon baking soda

1¼ teaspoons table salt

2 teaspoons ground black pepper

16 tablespoons (2 sticks) salted butter, cut into ½-inch pieces and chilled

115 grams (4 ounces) sharp or extra-sharp cheddar cheese, cut into ¼-inch cubes (1 cup)

15 grams (½ ounce) finely grated pecorino Romano cheese (¼ cup)

1½ cups cold buttermilk

1 large egg, beaten

36 grams (¼ cup) raw shelled sunflower seeds

When standard breakfast pastries are too sugary, bake a batch of these flavorful savory scones. This recipe is our adaptation of the hearty kale and cheese scones created by Briana Holt, of Tandem Coffee + Bakery in Portland, Maine. Dried currants and a small amount of sugar in the dough complement the minerally, vegetal notes of the kale and counterbalance the saltiness of the cheddar and pecorino, while a good dose of black pepper adds an undercurrent of spiciness. Either lacinato kale (also called dinosaur or Tuscan kale) or curly kale will work; you will need an average-sized bunch to obtain the amount of chopped stemmed leaves for the recipe.

Don't allow the buttermilk and butter to lose their chill before use. Keeping them cold helps ensure that the dough will remain workable and won't become unmanageably soft during shaping. When rotating the baking sheets halfway through the baking time, work quickly so the oven doesn't lose too much heat.

___

1. Heat the oven to 375°F with racks in the upper- and lower-middle positions. Line 2 rimmed baking sheets with kitchen parchment. In a small microwave-safe bowl, stir together the currants and 2 tablespoons water. Microwave uncovered on high until warm and plump, about 30 seconds; set aside. In a medium bowl, toss the kale and lemon juice; set aside. In a large bowl, whisk together the flour, sugar, baking powder, baking soda, salt and pepper.

2. To a food processor, add about half of the flour mixture and scatter all of the butter over the top. Pulse until the butter is in pieces slightly larger than peas, 10 to 12 pulses. Transfer to the bowl with the remaining flour mixture. Add the currants and any remaining liquid, the cheddar, pecorino and kale. Toss with your hands until well combined. Add about ⅓ of the buttermilk and toss just a few times with your hands, making sure to scrape along the bottom of the bowl, until the liquid is absorbed. Add the remaining buttermilk in 2 more additions, tossing after each. After the final addition of buttermilk, toss until no dry, floury bits remain. The mixture will be quite crumbly and will not form a cohesive dough.

3. Lightly dust the counter with flour, turn the mixture out onto it, then give it a final toss. Divide it into 2 even piles, gathering each into a mound, then briefly knead each mound; it's fine if the mixture is still somewhat crumbly. Gather each mound into a ball, then press firmly into a cohesive 5-inch disk about 1½ inches thick. Using a chef's knife, cut each disk into 6 wedges. Place 6 wedges on each prepared baking sheet, spaced evenly apart. Brush the tops with the beaten egg, then sprinkle with the sunflower seeds, pressing lightly to adhere.

4. Bake until the scones are deep golden brown, 30 to 35 minutes, switching and rotating the baking sheets halfway through. Cool on the baking sheets on wire racks for 5 minutes, then transfer directly to a rack and cool for at least another 5 minutes. Serve warm or at room temperature.

Japanese Milk Bread

Start to finish: 4 hours (50 minutes active), plus cooling
Makes two 1½-pound loaves

For the water roux:

½ cup water

¼ cup plus 2 tablespoons whole milk

¼ cup (34 grams) bread flour

For the dough:

113 grams (8 tablespoons) salted butter, cut into 8 pieces, room temperature, plus 28 grams (2 tablespoons), melted, for brushing

3 large eggs, divided

1 cup whole milk, room temperature

639 grams (4⅔ cups) bread flour, plus more for dusting

60 grams (½ cup) rye flour

80 grams (¼ cup plus 2 tablespoons) white sugar

27 grams (¼ cup) nonfat or low-fat dry milk powder

1½ tablespoons instant yeast

1¾ teaspoons table salt

Japanese milk bread is a fluffy, slightly sweet, fine-textured loaf. It stays moister and softer longer than standard sandwich bread thanks to the Asian technique of mixing tangzhong into the dough. Tangzhong is a mixture of flour and liquid cooked to a gel; it's often referred to as a roux, though it does not contain any butter or oil and serves a different purpose than a classic roux. The gelatinized starch in tangzhong can hold onto more water than uncooked flour, thereby offering several benefits. The dough is easy to handle despite the high hydration level; the loaf attains a high rise and a light, airy crumb; and the baked bread keeps well. Sonoko Sakai, author of "Japanese Home Cooking," makes her milk bread with a small amount of non-wheat flour combined with bread flour. When adapting her formula, we opted to use rye flour for its nutty flavor. This recipe makes two loaves, so you will need two 8½-by-4½-inch loaf pans; metal works better than glass for heat conduction and browning. The baked and cooled bread keeps well at room temperature in an airtight container or plastic bag for several days (it can be stored in the refrigerator for slightly longer but would then be best rewarmed or toasted). Or the bread can be frozen, unsliced and wrapped in plastic then foil, for up to one month.

Don't be tempted to add more flour to the dough as it is kneaded. The dough will be sticky and gluey, but after rising, it will be workable. When shaping the dough, use minimal flour so the dough remains as moist as possible. Lastly, when inverting the loaves out of the pan and turning them upright to cool, handle them gently as they are delicate.

1. To make the water roux, in a medium saucepan, combine the water, milk and flour, then whisk until lump-free. Set over medium and cook, whisking constantly, until the mixture thickens (a silicone spatula drawn through the mixture leaves a trail) and bubbles slowly, 2 to 4 minutes. Scrape into a medium bowl, press a sheet of plastic wrap directly against the surface and cool to room temperature.

2. To make the dough, brush a large bowl with melted butter; reserve the remaining melted butter. Add two eggs to the cooled roux and whisk until well combined. Add the room-temperature milk and whisk until homogeneous and smooth.

3. In the bowl of a stand mixer, whisk together the bread and rye flours, sugar, milk powder, yeast and salt. Attach the bowl and dough hook to the mixer and, with the machine running on low, slowly add the roux-egg mixture. With the mixer still running, add the softened butter 1 tablespoon at a time. Increase the speed to medium-low and knead until the dough is very strong and elastic, 10 to 12 minutes; it will stick to the sides of the bowl. Scrape the dough into the prepared bowl, then brush the surface with melted butter. Cover the bowl with plastic wrap and let rise in a warm spot until doubled in bulk, about 1½ hours. Meanwhile, coat 2 metal 8½-by-4½-inch loaf pans with melted butter.

4. Lightly flour the counter. Gently punch down the dough, then turn it out onto the prepared counter. Using a chef's knife or bench scraper, divide the dough into 4 equal portions, each about 355 grams (about 12½ ounces). Shape each portion into a smooth ball. Using your hands, pat one ball into a 7-by-4-inch rectangle, then fold the dough into thirds like a business letter. Pinch the seam to seal. Turn the dough seam side down and place on one side of one of the prepared loaf pans so the seam is perpendicular to the length of the pan. Shape a second portion of dough, then place it in the pan alongside the first portion, positioning it the same way; there should be just a small amount of space between the 2 pieces of dough. Cover the pan with a clean kitchen towel.

5. Repeat the process with the remaining portions of dough, then place under the towel alongside the first pan. Let rise until the dough domes 1 to 1½ inches over the rim of the pan, about 1 hour. Meanwhile, heat the oven to 350°F with a rack in the middle position. In a small bowl, whisk the remaining egg until well combined; set aside.

6. When the dough is properly risen, gently brush the tops with the beaten egg. Bake until the loaves are well risen and golden brown, 30 to 35 minutes. Cool in the pans on a wire rack for 15 minutes. Gently invert the bread out of the pans, stand them upright on the rack and cool for at least 1 hour before slicing.

Yeasted Flatbreads with Za'atar Oil

Start to finish: 1¼ hours active time over the course of 1½ to 2½ days / Makes four 6-inch flatbreads

548 grams (4 cups) bread flour, plus more for dusting

1 tablespoon white sugar

2 teaspoons instant yeast

1½ cups water, cool room temperature (65°F)

3 tablespoons extra-virgin olive oil, divided

1¼ teaspoons table salt

Semolina flour or fine cornmeal, for dusting the pizza peel

Za'atar oil (see recipe p. 459)

At Magdalena restaurant in Migdal, Israel, chef Yousef "Zuzu" Hanna offers a house-baked flatbread that's a hybrid of Yemeni saluf and Moroccan frena. Soft and chewy, with a puffy, open crumb and golden brown crust, the breads, shaped like slightly flattened mini boules, have a texture somewhere between naan and ciabatta. To recreate it at home, we use a moderately wet yeasted dough and give it multiple rises, including a 24- to 48-hour rise in the refrigerator, so be sure to read the recipe before beginning so you can plan accordingly. Immediately after baking, we brush the surface of the breads with a za'atar-infused oil that also can be served alongside the bread for dipping. Za'atar is a Levantine spice, seed and herb blend; look for it in the spice aisle of the supermarket or in Middle Eastern markets. You will need a baking steel or stone for this recipe, plus a baking peel for sliding the dough onto and off it.

Don't forget to heat the oven with a baking steel or stone on the middle rack about 1 hour before baking. The best time to do this is immediately upon removing the dough balls from the refrigerator after their three-hour rise. When placing the dough rounds on the baking peel, don't position them in the center of the peel. Rather, place them as close as possible to the edge so they slide off the peel and onto the steel with minimal effort.

1. In a stand mixer with the dough hook, mix the flour, sugar and yeast on low until combined, about 15 seconds. With the mixer running, gradually add the water and 2 tablespoons of oil. Mix on low until the ingredients form a strong dough that clears the sides of the bowl, about 5 minutes. Cover the bowl with plastic wrap and let rest for 20 minutes.

2. Uncover the bowl, sprinkle the salt over the dough and mix on low until smooth and elastic, 5 to 7 minutes. Meanwhile, coat a large bowl with the remaining 1 tablespoon oil.

3. Transfer the dough to the prepared bowl. Dip your fingers into the oil pooled at the sides and dab the surface of the dough until completely coated. Using your hands, turn the dough over. Tightly cover the bowl with plastic wrap and let rise at room temperature until the dough is doubled in bulk, about 1 hour. Transfer to the refrigerator and let rise for at least 24 or up to 48 hours.

4. Line a rimmed baking sheet with kitchen parchment and mist with cooking spray. Lightly flour the counter and turn out the dough. Using a chef's knife or bench scraper, divide the dough into 4 even pieces, each about 8 ounces. Shape each into a taut, smooth ball and place seam side down, evenly spaced, on the prepared baking sheet. Mist the tops of the dough with cooking spray, cover loosely with plastic wrap and refrigerate for 3 hours.

5. Heat the oven to 500°F with a baking steel or stone on the middle rack. Remove the dough from the refrigerator. Generously flour the counter and set the dough balls on top; reserve the baking sheet. Dust the dough with flour and, using your fingertips, press each into a dimpled disk about 5½ inches wide and ½ inch thick. Return the dough to the baking sheet, evenly spacing the disks. Mist the dough with cooking spray, cover with plastic wrap and let rise at room temperature until slightly puffy, about 1 hour.

6. Generously dust a baking peel with semolina. Flour your hands, then gently slide your fingers under one round of dough, lift and transfer to the prepared peel, placing the round near the edge so it will be easier to slide onto the baking steel. Repeat with another round of dough, making sure the two don't touch. Gently shake the peel back and forth to ensure the dough is not sticking, then, working quickly, open the oven and slide the rounds onto the steel.

7. Bake until the dough is puffed and golden brown, 7 to 10 minutes. Using the peel, transfer the breads to a wire rack. Lightly brush the tops with some of the za'atar oil. Bake the 2 remaining rounds in the same way. Serve the breads warm or at room temperature with the remaining za'atar oil for dipping.

ZA'ATAR OIL

Start to finish: 5 minutes
Makes ½ cup

½ cup extra-virgin olive oil

1 tablespoon za'atar

¼ to ½ teaspoon red pepper flakes

¼ teaspoon kosher salt

In a small saucepan over medium, cook the oil, za'atar and pepper flakes, stirring, until the mixture is fragrant, about 2 minutes. Stir in the salt and let cool. Store at room temperature in an airtight container for up to 1 week.

Turkish Flatbreads (Yufka)

Start to finish: 1¾ hours (45 minutes active)
Makes six 8- to 9-inch flatbreads

½ teaspoon plus
2 tablespoons
extra-virgin olive oil

260 grams (2 cups) all-
purpose flour, plus more
for dusting

½ teaspoon table salt

⅔ cup warm water
(about 110°F)

The Turkish flatbread called yufka is fast and easy to make largely because it's unleavened (that is, yeast free). As chef Ana Sortun, whose recipe from "Soframiz" we adapted, explains, yufka is more slender than a flour tortilla but more substantial than phyllo. Yufka stuffed with filling, folded and toasted in a skillet becomes a gozleme (p. 463), or the flatbreads can be used to make sandwich wraps or for scooping up dips and spreads. This dough comes together quickly, requires only an hour of rest, is a breeze to roll out and each bread cooks in just a couple of minutes in a pan on the stovetop. A cast-iron skillet works best for getting nice browned spots on the flatbreads, but nonstick will work, too, if that's what you own. As the breads come out of the skillet, we slip them into a plastic bag to keep them soft and pliable. Once all the rounds have been cooked, let cool to room temperature, then seal the bag and store at room temperature for up to a day (the breads are best used within 24 hours of making).

Don't cook the flatbreads on both sides *or they will become too crisp and crackery for folding and wrapping. Browned on only one side, the breads will be fully cooked and ready to eat, but they will remain soft and pliable.*

1. Coat a medium bowl with ½ teaspoon oil; set aside. In a stand mixer with the dough hook, mix the flour and salt on low until combined, 10 to 15 seconds. With the mixer running, gradually add the water and 2 tablespoons oil, then mix on low until the mixture forms a ball, about 1 minute. Increase to medium and knead until the dough is smooth and elastic, about 3 minutes. Transfer to the prepared bowl, cover with plastic wrap and let rest at room temperature for about 1 hour. Meanwhile, cut six 9-inch squares of kitchen parchment; set aside.

2. Transfer the dough to the counter. Using a dough scraper or bench knife, divide the dough into 6 pieces, each about 70 grams (2½ ounces), then form each portion into a taut ball. Dust the dough balls lightly with flour and cover with a clean kitchen towel. Lightly flour the counter, set 1 ball on top and, using a rolling pin, roll it into an 8- to 9-inch round about ⅛ inch thick. Place the round on a parchment square. Repeat with the remaining dough balls and stack the rounds on top of each other, placing a square of parchment between the layers.

3. Heat a 12-inch cast-iron skillet over medium-high until water flicked onto the surface immediately sizzles and evaporates. Place 1 dough round in the pan and cook until slightly puffed and the bottom is spotty brown, 1 to 1½ minutes. Using tongs, transfer the flatbread browned side down to a 1-gallon zip-close bag (this keeps the breads soft and pliable). Cook the remaining dough rounds in the same way, stacking them in the bag (no need for parchment separators). Wipe out the pan if excess flour begins to build up and smoke, and adjust the heat as needed. Use immediately or cool, seal the bag and store at room temperature for up to 1 day.

FLATBREADS FILLED WITH PORK, GREEN OLIVES AND FETA

In a 12-inch cast-iron or nonstick skillet over medium-high, heat **1 tablespoon extra-virgin olive oil** until shimmering. Add **1½ pounds ground pork** and cook, breaking the meat into small pieces, until well-browned and crisp, 7 to 10 minutes. Stir in **2 teaspoons ground cumin, 2 teaspoons sweet paprika, 1½ teaspoons dried oregano, ¾ teaspoon Aleppo pepper** (or ¼ teaspoon red pepper flakes), **½ teaspoon ground allspice, ¾ teaspoon white sugar, 2 medium garlic cloves** (minced) and **½ teaspoon each kosher salt** and **black pepper.** Cook, stirring, until fragrant, 30 to 60 seconds. Transfer to a medium bowl, then stir in **¼ cup chopped fresh flat-leaf parsley** and **1 tablespoon grated orange zest;** taste and season with **salt** and **black pepper.** Wipe out the skillet and set aside. In a food processor, process **6 ounces feta cheese** (crumbled, 1½ cups) and **3 tablespoons salted butter** (room temperature) until smooth and spreadable, 15 to 20 seconds. In a small bowl, mix together **½ cup pitted green olives** (chopped) and **8 peperoncini** (stemmed, patted dry and chopped). Spread the feta-butter mixture onto the unbrowned sides of **6 Turkish flatbreads** (p. 460) or onto **six 8-inch flour tortillas,** dividing it evenly and leaving a 1-inch border around the edge. Divide the pork mixture among the flatbreads, placing it across the center third, then divide the olive mixture among the breads, scattering it on top the pork. Fold the filling-free ends to cover the center, like a business letter, and press to seal. In the same skillet over medium, heat **1 tablespoon of the remaining oil** until shimmering. Add 2 of the filled flatbreads seam side down, and cook, flipping them once, until golden brown on both sides, 2 to 3 minutes per side. Transfer to a wire rack. Cook the remaining flatbreads in 2 more batches in the same way, using **1 tablespoon oil** for each batch. Serve warm.

SPINACH AND CHEESE GOZLEME

In a 12-inch cast-iron or nonstick skillet over medium-high, heat **1 tablespoon extra-virgin olive oil** until shimmering. Add **1 small yellow onion** (finely chopped) and cook, stirring occasionally, until softened and beginning to brown, 3 to 5 minutes. Transfer to a medium bowl; wipe out the skillet and set aside. To the onion, stir in **1 cup whole-milk ricotta cheese, 3½ ounces feta cheese** (crumbled, ¾ cup), **2 ounces kasseri or Gruyère cheese** (shredded, ¾ cup), **⅓ cup lightly packed fresh dill** (chopped), **⅓ cup lightly packed fresh mint** (chopped), **⅓ cup lightly packed fresh parsley** (chopped) and **¼ teaspoon ground black pepper,** then taste and season with **kosher salt** and **pepper**. In another medium bowl, toss a **5-ounce container baby spinach** (chopped) with **¼ teaspoon kosher salt**. Spread the cheese mixture onto the on the unbrowned sides of **6 Turkish flatbreads** (p. 460) or onto **six 8-inch flour tortillas,** dividing it evenly and leaving a 1-inch border around the edge. Divide the spinach among the flatbreads, placing it across the center third, then fold the spinach-free ends to cover the center, like a business letter, and press to seal. In the same skillet over medium, heat **1 tablespoon extra-virgin olive oil** until shimmering. Add 2 of the filled flatbreads seam side down and cook, flipping once, until golden brown on both sides, 2 to 3 minutes per side. Transfer to a wire rack. Cook the remaining flatbreads in 2 more batches in the same way, using **1 tablespoon extra-virgin olive oil** for each batch. Serve warm.

Multigrain Soda Bread

Start to finish: 1 hour 20 minutes (10 minutes active),
plus cooling / Makes 2 small loaves

___

2 cups plain whole-milk
yogurt

161 grams (1 cup) 10-grain
hot cereal mix

315 grams (2¼ cups)
whole-wheat flour

163 grams (1¼ cups)
all-purpose flour

42 grams (3 tablespoons
packed) brown sugar

¾ teaspoon table salt

1 teaspoon baking powder

1 teaspoon baking soda

½ cup pumpkin seeds,
toasted (optional)

10 tablespoons (1¼ sticks)
salted butter, melted

Soda bread by definition already is a quick bread, but a few shortcuts helped us make it even faster. Our goal was a flavorful mixed grain soda bread—minus the chore of a long, expensive and hard to find ingredient list. Our solution was premixed multigrain porridge, which gave us 10 grains in one package. We saved even more time by soaking the cereal in yogurt—a convenient replacement for the more classic buttermilk—before mixing it into the dough. This softened the grains and meant we didn't have to cook the porridge on its own. For a little more texture and toasted flavor, we added pumpkin seeds. Some recipes call for working cold butter into the dough. We stayed in the fast lane on that step, too, borrowing a technique from scone making and stirring melted butter into our dry ingredients. It was fast, easy and less messy. If you can't find 10-grain cereal mix (Bob's Red Mill makes one), use a five- or seven-grain hot cereal or porridge mix instead.

Don't use Greek-style yogurt for this recipe; it won't mix with and hydrate the grains. We liked whole-milk yogurt, but low-fat will work, too.

___

1. Heat the oven to 350°F with a rack in the middle position. Line a baking sheet with kitchen parchment. In a medium bowl, stir together the yogurt and cereal; let stand for 15 minutes. Meanwhile, in a large bowl, whisk together both flours, the sugar, salt, baking powder, baking soda and pumpkin seeds (if using).

2. Whisk 8 tablespoons of the butter into the yogurt mixture. Add the mixture to the dry ingredients and fold until no dry flour remains; the dough will be thick and look wet and slightly sandy. Pile the dough into 2 even mounds on the prepared pan. Dampen your hands, then shape into 6-inch rounds.

3. Use a sharp serrated knife to cut a ½-inch-deep X into the top of each loaf. Bake until lightly browned and hollow-sounding when tapped, 50 to 60 minutes. Immediately brush the loaves all over with the remaining 2 tablespoons of butter. Transfer to a wire rack and let cool completely.

Potato-and-Herb Focaccia

Start to finish: 3½ hours (30 minutes active)
Makes one 9-by-13-inch loaf

---

8 ounces Yukon Gold potatoes (about 2 small or 1 large), cut into ¾-inch pieces

6 sprigs fresh rosemary or thyme, plus 2 tablespoons chopped fresh herbs

3 medium garlic cloves, smashed and peeled

1¾ teaspoons table salt, divided

457 grams (3⅓ cups) bread flour

4 tablespoons extra-virgin olive oil, divided

2 teaspoons instant yeast

2 teaspoons white sugar

½ cup Kalamata olives, pitted and slivered (optional)

1½ ounces Parmesan cheese, grated (about ¾ cup) (optional)

Ground black pepper

Common to the Puglia region of Italy, potato focaccia is a particularly moist version of the classic Italian bread. We embedded ours with deep herbal flavors by seasoning the cooking water for the potatoes with rosemary or thyme, as well as garlic. Then we made the starchy, herb-infused cooking liquid do double duty, using it in the dough, too. Yukon Gold potatoes gave the focaccia color and texture, and didn't require peeling (the soft skins disappeared into the dough). For our herbs, we liked a combination of rosemary and thyme, but oregano and bay leaves worked, too. After the dough comes together, you may need to add more cooking liquid (up to ¼ cup) to achieve the proper texture; the dough should be soft and sticky, and just barely clear the sides of the bowl. The focaccia is delicious with a sprinkling of herbs and black pepper, but Kalamata olives and Parmesan cheese were welcome additions. Flaky sea salt, such as Maldon, was a nice touch, as well.

Don't use a glass baking dish. The bread won't brown and crisp properly. If you don't have a metal baking pan, stretch the focaccia into a rough 9-by-13-inch rectangle and bake on a rimmed baking sheet.

1. **In a medium saucepan over high,** combine 3 cups water, potatoes, herb sprigs, garlic and 1 teaspoon salt. Cover and bring to a boil. Uncover, reduce heat to medium and simmer until the potatoes are tender, 12 to 14 minutes. Drain, reserving the cooking liquid. Discard the herb sprigs, then return the potatoes, garlic and any loose herb leaves to the pan. Use a potato masher or fork to mash until smooth and creamy. Transfer to the bowl of a stand mixer fitted with a dough hook attachment; let the cooking liquid cool until just barely warm, 20 to 30 minutes (it should be no more than 115°F). Meanwhile, oil a large bowl.

2. **To the stand mixer bowl,** add the flour, 2 tablespoons of the oil, the yeast, the sugar and remaining ¾ teaspoon salt. Add 1¼ cups of the reserved cooking water, then mix on low speed until the dough comes together, about 1 minute. Increase to medium-high and mix until the dough clears the sides of the bowl but sticks to the bottom, 3 to 5 minutes, adding more cooking liquid 1 tablespoon at a time as needed (dough should be very soft and sticky and just clear the sides of the bowl). Use an oiled silicone spatula to transfer the dough to the prepared bowl. Cover with plastic wrap and let sit in a warm, draft-free area until puffed but not quite doubled, 30 to 60 minutes.

3. Spread the remaining 2 tablespoons of oil over the bottom and sides of a 13-by-9-inch metal baking pan. Transfer the dough to the pan and use oiled fingers to spread in an even layer, pressing into the corners. Cover and let sit in a warm, draft-free area until puffed, 30 to 60 minutes.

4. Heat the oven to 400°F with a rack in the middle position. Use a chopstick to poke the dough all over, then sprinkle with the chopped herbs, olives and Parmesan, if using, and a few grinds of pepper. Bake until the edges are browned and crisp and the top is golden, 35 to 40 minutes. Cool in the pan on a wire rack for 10 minutes, then remove from the pan and cool on the rack. Serve warm or at room temperature.

Desserts

13

Caramel Oranges

Start to finish: 40 minutes, plus chilling / Servings: 6

8 medium navel or Cara Cara oranges (about 4½ pounds) or a combination

214 grams (1 cup) white sugar

2 cinnamon sticks or star anise pods

2 tablespoons salted butter

Oranges with caramel sauce were the hit of dessert carts across London in the 1960s. The dish never caught on in America and eventually faded overseas. But with its bright flavors and fresh-yet-familiar combination of fruit and caramel, we felt it was a classic worth reviving. Our inspiration was a recipe in Nigella Lawson's cookbook, "Forever Summer." She bathes peeled and sliced oranges in caramel spiked with cardamom, and suggests serving them with yogurt. Cardamom was good, but we preferred cinnamon sticks, as well as star anise. Cara Cara oranges are good if you can find them, but navel work fine. Be sure to remove all the bitter white pith. Substituting fresh orange juice for the water in a traditional caramel amplified the flavor of the dish tremendously.

1. **Juice 2 of the oranges** to yield ¾ cup juice. If 2 oranges don't yield enough juice, add water to measure ¾ cup total.

2. **Slice off the top and bottom** ½ inch from each of the remaining 6 oranges. Stand each orange on one of its flat ends and use a sharp knife to cut down and around the fruit, following the contours of the flesh, slicing away the skin and white pith. Turn each orange on its side and thinly slice crosswise into rounds. In a 13-by-9-inch baking dish, shingle the rounds in a single layer.

3. **In a medium saucepan,** combine the sugar, ¼ cup of the orange juice and the cinnamon or star anise and bring to a boil over medium-high, this should take 2 to 3 minutes. Cook, swirling the pan occasionally, until the sugar begins to color at the edges, another 3 to 5 minutes. The bubbles should go from thin and frothy to thick and shiny.

4. **Reduce the heat to medium-low** and cook, swirling the pan often, until the sugar is coppery-brown, 1 to 3 minutes. Remove the pan from the heat, add the butter, then whisk until melted.

5. **Add a splash** of the remaining orange juice and whisk until smooth (the mixture will steam and bubble vigorously), then add the remaining orange juice and whisk until fully incorporated. If the caramel separates and sticks to the pan, return it to the heat and simmer until the hardened caramel dissolves.

6. **Pour the caramel** evenly over the oranges, cover with plastic wrap, then refrigerate for at least 3 hours and up to 6 hours.

7. **Allowing the caramel to drip off** into the baking dish, use a slotted spoon to transfer the oranges to a serving platter or plates. Remove and discard the cinnamon or star anise from the caramel, then whisk to recombine and mix in any juices. Pour the caramel over the oranges.

ORANGE CARAMEL SAUCE

Don't think about the caramel's color for the first few minutes. The sugar mixture will melt, frothing furiously as the heat increases and moisture evaporates, then finally subside into larger, shinier bubbles before it changes color. If the sugar browns too quickly, slide the pan off the heat and whisk steadily to incorporate air, which cools it.

Chocolate, Prune and Rum Cake

Start to finish: 1 hour 20 minutes (30 minutes active), plus cooling / Servings: 12

___

9 tablespoons (1 stick plus 1 tablespoon) salted butter (1 tablespoon softened)

8 ounces pitted prunes (about 1½ cups), finely chopped

⅓ cup dark rum

1 tablespoon molasses

12 ounces bittersweet chocolate, finely chopped

6 large eggs, separated

125 grams (⅓ cup plus ¼ cup) white sugar, divided

¼ teaspoon table salt

Claire Ptak has a fairly revolutionary approach to baking—soft-whipped egg whites! undermixed batter!—that sets her apart from most bakers. We were smitten with her chocolate, prune and whiskey cake when we tasted it at her Violet bakery in East London. Ptak uses almond flour in her batter, but we preferred the lighter, more mousse-like texture we got by leaving it out. We followed her lead in under whipping the egg whites and just barely mixing them into the batter. We found dark rum was delicious warm or cool and complemented the molasses. We preferred bar chocolates with 60 to 70 percent cacao. Chocolate chips contain stabilizers that can change the cake's texture; it's best to avoid them. We liked this served with whipped cream.

___

1. **Heat the oven to 325°F** with a rack in the middle position. Coat the bottom and sides of a 9-inch springform pan evenly with the 1 tablespoon of softened butter.

2. **In a 2-cup microwave-safe liquid measuring cup,** combine the prunes, rum and molasses. Microwave until the rum is bubbling, 45 to 60 seconds. Let sit for 15 minutes, stirring occasionally.

3. **In a medium saucepan** over medium, melt the remaining 8 tablespoons of butter. Remove the pan from the heat and immediately whisk in the chocolate until melted and completely smooth. In a large bowl, whisk together the egg yolks and 71 grams (⅓ cup) of the sugar until pale and glossy, about 30 seconds. Slowly add the melted chocolate mixture and whisk until smooth. Stir in the prune mixture.

4. **Using a stand mixer** with a whisk attachment, whip the egg whites and salt on medium-high until light and foamy, about 1 minute. With the mixer running, slowly sprinkle in the remaining 54 grams (¼ cup) of sugar and continue to whip until the whites are thick and glossy and hold soft peaks, about 1 minute.

5. **Whisk a third of the whipped egg whites** into the chocolate mixture to lighten it. Gently fold in the remaining whites with a rubber spatula until the batter is marbled but not fully blended.

6. **Pour the batter into the prepared pan.** If needed, smooth the top with a spatula. Bake until the edges of the cake are firm and cracked, 35 to 40 minutes. The center will be just set, but will jiggle. Cool the cake in the pan on a wire rack for at least 1 hour before serving. The cake will settle and sink as it cools.

Austrian Plum Cake (Zwetschgenkuchen)

Start to finish: 1½ hours (10 minutes active) / Servings: 8

___

130 grams (1 cup) all-purpose flour, plus more for pan

107 grams (½ cup) white sugar, plus 2 tablespoons for sprinkling

¾ teaspoon baking powder

¼ teaspoon table salt

8 tablespoons (1 stick) salted butter, cut into 8 pieces, room temperature

1 large egg, plus 1 large egg yolk

1½ teaspoons vanilla extract

1¼ pounds ripe but firm medium plums, quartered and pitted

Powdered sugar, to serve

This simple cake showcases tangy-sweet summertime plums. Both red and black varieties work beautifully. Just make sure to choose medium plums that are ripe but still have a little firmness; soft, ultra-juicy fruits will make the center of the cake wet and soggy. Italian prune plums are great, too; use the same weight. But since they are small, cut them into halves instead of quarters. Ripe but firm pluots, a plum-apricot hybrid, are another excellent alternative. The flavor and texture of this cake are best the day of baking, but leftovers can be stored overnight in an airtight container at room temperature.

Don't forget to allow time for the butter to soften. Cold, firm butter won't blend well into the dry ingredients. And don't underbake this cake; the plums let off a lot of juice that slows down the baking, especially at the center. When testing for doneness, make sure there are no moist crumbs clinging to the toothpick.

1. **Heat the oven to 325°F** with a rack in the middle position. Mist the bottom and sides of a 9-inch springform pan with cooking spray, then dust evenly with flour; tap out the excess.

2. **In a stand mixer** with the paddle attachment, mix the flour, 107 grams (½ cup) of the sugar, the baking powder and salt on low until combined, about 5 seconds. With the mixer running, add the butter 1 piece at a time and continue mixing just until the mixture resembles moist sand, 2 to 3 minutes. Add the egg, egg yolk and vanilla. Increase to medium-high and beat until pale and fluffy, about 1 minute, scraping down the bowl as needed.

3. **Transfer the batter** to the prepared pan and spread in an even layer. Arrange the plum quarters on top of the batter in 2 concentric circles, placing the pieces on their cut sides. Sprinkle with the remaining 2 tablespoons sugar. Bake until golden brown and a skewer inserted at the center comes out clean, 1 to 1¼ hours. Let cool in the pan on a wire rack for 30 minutes, then remove the pan sides. Serve warm or at room temperature, dusted with powdered sugar.

Single-Crust Pie Dough

Start to finish: 2½ hours (30 minutes active), plus cooling
Makes one 9-inch pie shell

___

3 tablespoons water

2 teaspoons cornstarch

146 grams (1 cup plus
2 tablespoons) all-purpose
flour

2 teaspoons white sugar

⅛ teaspoon table salt

10 tablespoons (1 stick plus
2 tablespoons) salted butter,
cut into ½-inch pieces and
chilled

2 tablespoons sour cream

Finding that sweet spot in pie dough can be a challenge. Drier doughs are less likely to shrink during blind baking, but they can be stiff and difficult to roll out. Moist doughs are easier to work with, but tend to slump in the oven. We stabilize our basic but excellent pastry dough by borrowing a technique known as tangzhong that is used to make Japanese milk bread, the soft, pillowy staple of Asian bakeries. Moisture makes dough easier to work with, but it also activates gluten, which makes pie dough tough. We wanted to add moisture without activating gluten. The tangzhong technique does this by mixing a small portion of the flour with boiling water to make a paste that then gets mixed into the dough. The paste adds moisture, but also traps it, preventing it from triggering the gluten. Inspired by this, we used cornstarch blended with water for the paste, heating it briefly to create a gel. The gel trapped the water, preventing it from reacting with the proteins in the flour. We also added sour cream to the dough, which contains a small peptide called glutathione. This peptide can be a baker's secret weapon because it reduces the ability of the proteins in wheat to react and form gluten. Result: a softer, more forgiving dough that rolls out easily and resists slumping in the pan during prebaking.

Don't skimp on the pie weights. *Use enough to come three-quarters of the way up the sides. Avoid glass pie weights; they are too heavy and retain heat too long. And don't remove the foil and weights until the dough is set and dry. A moist or partially set crust can slump or shrink after the weights are removed. To check, lift up some of the foil and feel the edge of the pie or tart with your finger.*

1. In a small bowl, whisk together the water and cornstarch. Microwave until set, 30 to 40 seconds, stirring halfway through. Chill in the freezer for 10 minutes.

2. Once the cornstarch mixture has chilled, in a food processor, combine the flour, sugar and salt, then process until mixed, about 5 seconds. Add the chilled cornstarch mixture and pulse until uniformly ground, about 5 pulses. Add the butter and sour cream, then process until the dough comes together and begins to collect around the blade, 20 to 30 seconds. Pat the dough into a 4-inch disk, wrap in plastic wrap and refrigerate for at least 1 hour and up to 48 hours.

3. When ready to bake, heat the oven to 375°F with a rack in the middle position. On a well-floured counter, roll the dough into a 12-inch circle. Hang the dough over the rolling pin and transfer to a 9-inch pie pan. Gently ease the dough into the pan by lifting the edges while pressing down into the corners of the pan. Trim the edges, leaving a ½-inch overhang, then tuck the overhang under itself so the dough is flush with the rim of the pan. Crimp the dough with your fingers or the tines of a fork, then chill in the freezer for at least 15 minutes.

4. To blind bake, line the chilled crust with heavy-duty foil and fill with enough pie weights to come three-quarters up. Bake until the edges are light golden brown, about 25 minutes, rotating the pan halfway through. Remove the foil and weights and bake until the bottom of the crust just begins to color, another 5 to 7 minutes. Let cool on a wire rack for 1 hour before filling. Once baked and cooled, the crust can be wrapped in plastic wrap and kept at room temperature for up to 2 days.

Brown Sugar Tart

Start to finish: 1¾ hours (30 minutes active), plus cooling
Servings: 8

___

1 recipe single-crust pie
dough (see recipe p. 476)

100 grams (8 tablespoons
packed) dark brown sugar,
divided

1 tablespoon
all-purpose flour

Pinch table salt

4 large egg yolks

1¼ cups heavy cream

2 teaspoons vanilla extract

The inspiration for this simple yet rich tart was a French-Canadian sugar tart that originated in Waterloo, the Belgian town that was the site of Napoleon Bonaparte's 1815 defeat. Our brown sugar tart has two distinct layers: a rich, lightly sweet egg-yolk custard on top, and a thick bed of brown sugar on the bottom. Using just egg yolks in the custard resulted in a silkier, creamier texture than whole eggs, and adding flour prevented the tart from forming a skin on top. We wanted the brown sugar layer to be distinct from the custard layer, but found that adding a few tablespoons of the sugar to the custard mixture rounded out the flavor. While light brown sugar worked fine, we preferred the deep, more robust flavor of dark brown.

Don't use old, hard brown sugar. If your sugar is clumpy and dry, it will never fully incorporate into the custard mixture.

1. **Heat the oven to 375°F** with racks in the middle and lowest positions. On a well-floured counter, roll the dough into a 12-inch circle. Wrap the dough loosely around the rolling pin and transfer to a 9-inch tart pan with a removable bottom. Gently ease the dough into the corners of the pan, then trim the edges flush with the pan rim. Freeze for 15 minutes.

2. **Line the chilled tart shell** with heavy-duty foil and fill with enough pie weights to come three-quarters up, then place it on a rimmed baking sheet. Bake on the oven's lowest rack until the edges are light golden brown, 25 to 30 minutes, rotating the pan halfway through. Remove the foil and weights, then bake until the bottom of the crust just begins to color, another 5 to 7 minutes. Remove the pan from the oven and reduce the oven temperature to 325°F.

3. **In a medium bowl,** combine 25 grams (2 tablespoons) of the sugar with the flour and salt. Add the yolks and whisk until combined. Add the cream and vanilla and whisk until smooth. Sprinkle the remaining 75 grams (6 tablespoons) of sugar over the warm crust and gently press into an even layer.

4. **Slowly pour the custard over the sugar.** Bake on the oven's middle rack until the edges are set but the center jiggles slightly, about 25 minutes. Cool in the pan on a wire rack for at least 1 hour. Remove the outer metal ring and serve at room temperature.

Chocolate Tart

Start to finish: 1 hour 20 minutes (25 minutes active), plus cooling / Servings: 8

When it comes to French-style chocolate tarts, there's a fine line between elegant and unpleasant. There's much to be said for the flavor of fine bitter chocolate, but it can be overwhelming. We aimed for a balance with more richness than is common. Flour and eggs provided structure, preventing the filling from being too gooey or pudding-like, while butter and an extra egg yolk added richness.

Don't be alarmed by how soft the center is *when you remove the tart from the oven. The edges will be set, but the center still will be quite soft.*

1. Heat the oven to 375°F with racks in the middle and lowest positions. On a well-floured counter, roll the dough into a 12-inch circle. Wrap the dough loosely around the rolling pin and transfer to a 9-inch tart pan with a removable bottom. Ease the dough into the pan, then trim the edges flush with the rim. Freeze for 15 minutes.

2. Line the chilled tart shell with heavy-duty foil and fill with enough pie weights to come three-quarters up, then place it on a rimmed baking sheet. Bake on the oven's lowest rack until the edges are light golden brown, 25 to 30 minutes, rotating the pan halfway through. Remove the foil and weights, then bake until the bottom of the crust just begins to color, another 5 to 7 minutes. Set aside. Leave the oven on.

3. In a medium saucepan over medium, melt the butter. Remove from the heat and add the chocolate, whisking until smooth. Whisk in the remaining ingredients until fully incorporated; the filling should appear shiny. If the mixture separates during whisking, don't worry. Just keep whisking; it will smooth out again. Pour into the warm crust and smooth the top. Bake on the baking sheet on the middle rack until the edges are just set, 8 to 10 minutes. Cool in the pan on a wire rack for at least 15 minutes. Remove the outer ring from the pan. Serve warm or at room temperature.

1 recipe single-crust pie dough (see recipe p. 476)

6 tablespoons salted butter

6 ounces bittersweet chocolate, finely chopped

2 large eggs, plus 1 large egg yolk

40 grams (5 tablespoons) all-purpose flour

54 grams (¼ cup) white sugar

2 teaspoons vanilla extract

Pinch table salt

Lemon Tart

Start to finish: 1 hour 40 minutes (25 minutes active),
plus cooling / Servings: 8

We love the fresh, bright flavor of lemon tarts, but the classic tarte au citron is acidic enough to strip the enamel off your teeth. We wanted to tame the tartness of lemons without relying on heaps of sugar. Pairing lemon with sweeter, mellower orange worked great. Using both the juice and the zest of both citruses provided complex, well-rounded flavor. Rubbing the zest into the sugar helped release the aromatic, flavorful oils. Using a combination of whole eggs and yolks gave us the best texture. The richness of the yolks and the cream also helped balance the lemon.

Don't eat this tart warm. The flavor and texture are best when chilled, or at least at room temperature.

1. Heat the oven to 375°F with racks in the middle and lowest positions. On a well-floured counter, roll the dough into a 12-inch circle. Wrap the dough loosely around the rolling pin and transfer to a 9-inch tart pan with a removable bottom. Ease the dough into the pan, then trim the edges flush with the rim. Freeze for 15 minutes.

2. Line the chilled tart shell with heavy-duty foil and fill with enough pie weights to come three-quarters up, then place it on a rimmed baking sheet. Bake on the oven's lowest rack until the edges are light golden brown, 25 to 30 minutes, rotating the pan halfway through. Remove the foil and weights, then bake until the bottom of the crust just begins to color, another 5 to 7 minutes. Remove the pan from the oven and reduce the oven temperature to 325°F.

3. In a bowl, combine the sugar, both zests and the salt. Rub together with your fingers until fragrant and the mixture begins to clump. Add the eggs and yolks and whisk until pale and slightly thickened, about 1 minute. Whisk in the cream and both juices. Skim the foam off the top.

4. Pour the filling into the warm tart shell and bake on the baking sheet on the middle rack until set, 20 to 25 minutes. Cool in the pan on a wire rack until room temperature, at least 1 hour. Remove the outer metal ring and serve, or chill completely before serving.

1 recipe single-crust pie dough (see recipe p. 476)

107 grams (½ cup) white sugar

1 tablespoon grated lemon zest

1 teaspoon grated orange zest

Pinch table salt

2 large eggs, plus 2 large egg yolks

6 tablespoons heavy cream

5 tablespoons lemon juice

3 tablespoons orange juice

Pumpkin Tart

Start to finish: 1 hour 40 minutes (40 minutes active), plus cooling / Servings: 8

___

1 recipe single-crust pie dough (see recipe p. 476)

15-ounce can pumpkin puree

149 grams (¾ cup packed) dark brown sugar

¼ cup bourbon

8-ounce container (1 cup) crème fraîche

3 large eggs

⅛ teaspoon table salt

We love pumpkin pie, but we don't love how dense and cloying it can be. We wanted a lighter, fresher take with a pronounced pumpkin flavor. Canned pumpkin puree was a great place to start, but we intensified the flavor by giving it a quick sauté with dark brown sugar. This simmers off excess moisture and adds caramel flavors. Deglazing the pan with bourbon added a complexity we loved, but an equal amount of orange juice worked well, too. Crème fraîche gave the filling tang and richness that other dairy products couldn't match.

Don't use canned pumpkin pie filling for this recipe. Look for unsweetened canned pumpkin puree; the only ingredient listed should be pumpkin.

___

1. Heat the oven to 375°F with racks in the middle and lowest positions. On a well-floured counter, roll the dough into a 12-inch circle. Wrap the dough loosely around the rolling pin and transfer to a 9-inch tart pan with a removable bottom. Ease the dough into the pan, then trim the edges flush with the rim. Freeze for 15 minutes.

2. Line the chilled tart shell with heavy-duty foil and fill with enough pie weights to come three-quarters up, then place it on a rimmed baking sheet. Bake on the oven's lowest rack until the edges are light golden brown, 25 to 30 minutes, rotating the pan halfway through. Remove the foil and weights, then bake until the bottom of the crust just begins to color, another 5 to 7 minutes. Remove the pan from the oven and reduce the oven temperature to 325°F.

3. While the crust bakes, in a 12-inch nonstick skillet over medium-high, combine the pumpkin and sugar. Cook, stirring frequently, until the mixture is thickened, dark and leaves a film on the pan, about 10 minutes. Transfer to a 2-cup liquid measuring cup (the yield should be 1½ cups).

4. Add the bourbon to the skillet, return to medium-high heat and stir, scraping up any browned bits; add to the pumpkin mixture.

5. In a food processor, combine the pumpkin mixture and crème fraîche; process until smooth. Scrape down the bowl, add the eggs and salt, then process until smooth, about 1 minute. Pour the filling into the warm crust, smoothing the top. Bake on the baking sheet on the middle rack until the edges start to puff and crack and the center sets, 30 to 35 minutes.

6. Cool in the pan on a wire rack for at least 30 minutes. Remove the outer metal ring and serve warm or at room temperature.

HONEY-ORANGE
WHIPPED CREAM

Start to finish: 5 minutes
Makes about 3 cups

*Don't use creamed, thick or crystal-
lized honey for this recipe. For the
cream and honey to properly mix,
a thin, pourable honey is needed.*

1½ cups heavy cream

3 tablespoons honey

½ teaspoon grated orange zest

In the bowl of a stand mixer,
combine all ingredients. Using the
whisk attachment, mix on low until
frothy, about 30 seconds. Scrape the
bowl with a spatula to make sure
the honey is incorporated. Mix on
medium-high and whip until soft
peaks form, 2 to 3 minutes.

Sherry-Soaked French Toast (Torrijas)

Start to finish: **25 minutes** / Servings: 4

This is our take on torrijas, Spain's version of French toast. Cinnamon and citrus are traditional flavorings, and dry sherry infuses the bread with its subtle nuttiness and caramel undertones. Challah isn't typical for torrijas, but we liked its eggy richness and tender crumb. Torrijas are especially good warm from the oven, when the outsides are delicately crisp and the insides are soft and custardy, but they're also great at room temperature. Unlike regular French toast, the bread for torrijas is sweetened throughout, so skip syrup for serving—berries or a fresh fruit compote are the best accompaniments. You'll need a thermometer to gauge the temperature of the oil for frying.

Don't use stale challah. Stale bread will soak up too much of the sherry mixture.

1. Heat the oven to 350°F with a rack in the middle position. In a large baking dish, arrange the challah in a single layer. In a medium bowl, whisk the sherry, powdered sugar, 1 teaspoon of zest and the orange juice. Pour the mixture over the bread; do not wash the bowl. Let stand for 5 minutes, then flip each piece of bread. Let stand until the bread absorbs most of the liquid, another 5 minutes.

2. Meanwhile, in a small, shallow bowl, stir together the remaining 1 teaspoon zest, the white sugar, cinnamon and cloves. In the same bowl used for the sherry mixture, whisk together the eggs, flour and 1 tablespoon of the sugar-spice mixture. When the bread has finished soaking, one at a time, remove the slices from the baking dish and dunk in the egg mixture, coating on both sides, then return to the baking dish.

3. In a 12-inch skillet over medium, heat the oil to 350°F. Set a wire rack in a rimmed baking sheet. When the oil is ready, place half of the slices in the pan and cook until golden brown, about 1 minute. Using a thin metal spatula, flip each piece and cook until the second sides are golden brown, about 1 minute. Transfer to the prepared baking sheet. Repeat with the remaining slices of bread. Place the baking sheet in the oven and bake until the centers of the bread slices are firm and set, about 5 minutes.

4. Using tongs, dip each slice into the remaining sugar-spice mixture, turning to coat, then transfer to a serving plate. Serve warm.

Four 1-inch-thick slices challah bread, halved on diagonal

1 cup dry sherry

124 grams (1 cup) powdered sugar

2 teaspoons grated orange zest, divided, plus ¼ cup orange juice

54 grams (¼ cup) white sugar

¼ teaspoon ground cinnamon

⅛ teaspoon ground cloves

4 large eggs

65 grams (½ cup) all-purpose flour

½ cup grapeseed or other neutral oil

Salted Butter Caramel Chocolate Mousse

Start to finish: 30 minutes, plus cooling and chilling
Servings: 6

With butter-and-cream richness, bittersweet notes from the chocolate and caramel, and sea salt to cut through the sugar, this simple six-ingredient dessert from "My Paris Kitchen" by David Lebovitz is far greater than the sum of its parts. You can whip the egg whites by hand using a whisk, or use a handheld or stand mixer. Whatever method, make sure the bowl and whisk are perfectly clean and free of any residual oil, which will prevent the egg whites from achieving maximum loft. (Note that the eggs here are not cooked.) Fleur de sel is a hand-harvested, somewhat coarse-grained sea salt from France. Just about any variety of finishing sea salt can be substituted, but don't use very coarse salt (the type meant for grinding). The salt particles in the mousse don't fully dissolve; the little bursts of salinity are what makes this dessert so unique and delicious.

Don't overwhip the egg whites; stop whisking when they hold stiff peaks. Overbeaten egg whites appear dry and won't incorporate well with other ingredients.

104 grams (½ cup)
white sugar

3 tablespoons salted butter,
cut into ½-inch cubes

¾ cup heavy cream

6 ounces bittersweet or
semisweet chocolate,
chopped

4 large eggs, separated

Generous ¼ teaspoon fleur
de sel (see headnote)

1. Spread the sugar evenly over the bottom of a medium sauté pan or wide medium saucepan, then set the pan over medium. As the sugar begins to melt at the edges, use a silicone spatula to push the liquefied sugar toward the center. Continue to cook, stirring gently, until all the sugar is melted, caramelizes to a deep amber color and begins to smoke, 3 to 5 minutes. Remove the pan from the heat, quickly add the butter and stir until melted. Gradually whisk in the cream and continue to whisk to dissolve any hardened bits of caramel.

2. Once the cream mixture is smooth, add the chocolate and stir gently until melted and smooth. Transfer the mixture to a large bowl and cool to room temperature, stirring occasionally. Whisk in the egg yolks.

3. In another large bowl, whip the egg whites until they hold stiff peaks. Using a silicone spatula, fold about ⅓ of the whites into the chocolate mixture, sprinkling in the fleur de sel. Fold in the remaining whites just until no streaks of white remain.

4. Divide the mousse into serving glasses or bowls, or transfer it to a large serving bowl. Cover and refrigerate for at least 8 hours or up to 24 hours.

Sticky Toffee Pudding

Start to finish: 1½ hours (30 minutes active), plus cooling
Servings: 10

Don't chop the dates. Their texture was unpleasant in the finished dish. The food processor is the best bet. And be sure to check your dates for pits.

For the cake:

8 ounces pitted dates (about 1½ cups)

1 cup brewed coffee

130 grams (1 cup) all-purpose flour, plus more for pan

105 grams (¾ cup) rye flour

1 teaspoon baking powder

½ teaspoon table salt

½ teaspoon baking soda

199 grams (1 cup packed) dark brown sugar

4 large eggs

2 teaspoons vanilla extract

1 teaspoon ground allspice

12 tablespoons (1½ sticks) salted butter, melted and cooled slightly, plus more for pan

For the toffee sauce:

199 grams (1 cup packed) dark brown sugar

218 grams (⅔ cup) light corn syrup

2 teaspoons finely grated orange zest

⅛ teaspoon table salt

6 tablespoons rye whiskey

8 tablespoons (1 stick) salted butter, cut into 8 pieces and chilled

---

To update Britain's sticky toffee pudding—a steamed, too-often bland dessert hidden under a gluey, cloying syrup—we worked backward, starting with the sauce. Instead of the traditional cream, we gave the toffee glaze a transatlantic twist by spiking it with rye whiskey. The whiskey's spice and heat cut through the sweetness of the dark brown sugar and corn syrup; orange zest added brightness. For the cake itself, we wanted to mirror the flavor of the rye, so we used a blend of rye and all-purpose flours. Dates that are steeped in coffee, then pureed, gave body and an earthiness that boosted the rye flavor. Together, the nutty rye and bitter coffee balanced the cake's sweetness. To up the dessert's elegance, we made it in a Bundt pan. Covering the pan with foil kept the cake rich and moist. This mimicked the gentle heat of steaming in a water bath (bain marie), but was far less fussy.

FOR THE CAKE:

1. Heat the oven to 325°F with a rack in the middle position. Lightly coat a 12-cup nonstick Bundt pan with butter and flour. In a medium saucepan over medium-high, bring the dates and coffee to a boil. Remove from the heat and let sit for 15 minutes. In a large bowl, whisk together both flours, the baking powder, salt and baking soda.

2. Transfer the coffee-date mixture to a food processor, add the sugar and process until smooth, about 1 minute. Add the eggs, vanilla and allspice. Then, with the processor running, add the butter. Pour the date mixture over the flour mixture and whisk gently until combined. Transfer to the prepared pan, cover tightly with foil and bake until firm and a toothpick inserted at the center comes out clean, 55 to 65 minutes. Remove the foil and cool in the pan on a rack for 15 minutes.

FOR THE SAUCE:

3. While the cake cools, in a medium saucepan over medium-high, combine the sugar, corn syrup, orange zest and salt. Bring to a boil, then cook until the mixture registers 240°F on an instant-read thermometer, 2 to 3 minutes. Reduce heat to low and add the whiskey, 2 tablespoons at a time, allowing the bubbling to subside before adding more. Whisk in the butter 2 tablespoons at a time until melted and smooth.

4. Invert the cake onto a serving platter. Brush the top and sides generously with the warm toffee sauce. Slice and serve drizzled with additional sauce. The sauced, cooled cake can be wrapped tightly in plastic wrap and kept at room temperature for up to 3 days. Cooled sauce can be refrigerated for up to 1 week. To reheat, wrap the cake in foil and place in a 300°F oven until warmed. Microwave the sauce until bubbling.

Browned Butter and Coconut Loaf Cake

Start to finish: 5 hours (45 minutes active)
Makes one 9-inch loaf

For the cake:

10 tablespoons (1¼ sticks) salted butter

36 grams (½ cup plus 1 tablespoon) unsweetened shredded coconut

98 grams (¾ cup) all-purpose flour

135 grams (1 cup) spelt flour

1¼ teaspoons baking powder

⅛ teaspoon table salt

1 cup plus 2 tablespoons buttermilk, room temperature

1¼ teaspoons vanilla extract

214 grams (1 cup) white sugar, divided

4 large eggs, room temperature

For the syrup:

2 tablespoons coconut milk

31 grams (2 tablespoons) white sugar

For the glaze:

62 grams (½ cup) powdered sugar

1 tablespoon plus 1 teaspoon coconut milk

⅛ teaspoon table salt

This moist, dense, buttery loaf cake comes from Briana Holt of Tandem Coffee + Bakery in Portland, Maine. It's baked until the exterior is deeply browned, developing rich, toasty flavors and an amazing aroma. A coconut syrup is brushed on while the cake is still warm and, after cooling, a coconut glaze coats the surface. Holt uses spelt flour, a whole-grain flour with a subtle nuttiness. If you prefer, you can use all-purpose flour instead; if so, the total amount of all-purpose would be 228 grams (1¾ cups). Don't use whole-wheat flour in place of the spelt flour, as it changes the texture of the cake. Stored in an airtight container, the cake will keep at room temperature for up to three days.

Don't attempt to warm the buttermilk to room temperature by heating it in the microwave or in a saucepan. Buttermilk curdles if overheated, so it's best to let it stand on the counter until it reaches room temperature. If you're in a rush, warm it very gently in a warm water bath. Don't be afraid to brown the butter until the milk solids (the bits that separate out to the bottom) are deeply browned—almost black in color. They won't taste scorched in the finished cake. Rather, they will infuse it with a rich, nutty flavor and aroma.

1. To make the cake, in a medium saucepan over medium, heat the butter, occasionally swirling the pan and scraping the bottom with a wooden spoon, until dark amber and the milk solids at the bottom are almost black, 8 to 10 minutes. Transfer to the bowl of a stand mixer, making sure to scrape in all of the milk solids. Cool until the butter is opaque, spreadable and cool to the touch, about 1 hour.

2. While the butter cools, heat the oven to 350°F with a rack in the middle position. Spread the shredded coconut in a 9-by-5-inch loaf pan and toast in the oven until golden brown, 5 to 7 minutes, stirring once about halfway through. Measure 1 tablespoon of the toasted coconut into a small bowl, then transfer the remainder to a medium bowl; set both aside. Let the pan cool.

3. Mist the loaf pan with cooking spray. Line it with an 8-by-12-inch piece of kitchen parchment, fitting the parchment into the bottom and up the pan's long sides; mist the parchment with cooking spray. To the medium bowl with the coconut, whisk in both flours, the baking powder and salt. In a liquid measuring cup or small bowl, stir together the buttermilk and vanilla.

4. Add the white sugar to the cooled browned butter. In the stand mixer with the paddle attachment, mix the butter and sugar on medium until well combined, about 2 minutes, scraping the bowl about halfway through. With the mixer running on medium, add the eggs one at a time, scraping the bowl after the first 2 additions. Beat on medium until the mixture is shiny and lightened in color, about 1 minute. With the mixer running on low, add half of the flour, then the buttermilk mixture, followed by the remaining flour mixture. Mix on low for about 10 seconds, then stop the mixer. Using a silicone spatula, fold the batter just until the flour is incorporated, scraping the bottom of the bowl to ensure no pockets of butter or flour remain.

5. Transfer the batter to the prepared pan and smooth the surface. Bake until the top is deeply browned and a toothpick inserted into the center comes out with a few small crumbs attached, 75 to 80 minutes.

6. While the cake bakes, make the syrup. In a small microwave-safe bowl, stir together the coconut milk, white sugar and 2 tablespoons water. Microwave on high for 30 seconds, stirring once about halfway through to ensure the sugar is dissolved. Set aside to cool.

7. When the cake is done, cool in the pan on a wire rack for 15 minutes. Using the parchment overhang as handles, remove the cake from the pan and set on the rack. With a toothpick, poke holes in the top of the cake at 1-inch intervals. Brush all of the syrup onto the cake, allowing it to soak in. Cool to room temperature, about 2 hours. Remove and discard the parchment.

8. To make the glaze, in a medium bowl, whisk the powdered sugar, coconut milk and salt until smooth. Spoon over the cooled cake, spreading it to cover the surface and allowing it to drip down the sides slightly. Sprinkle with the reserved 1 tablespoon toasted coconut. Allow the glaze to dry for at least 5 minutes before serving.

Caprese Chocolate and Almond Torte

Start to finish: 1 hour 10 minutes (20 minutes active)
Servings: 10

___

233 grams (2⅓ cups) sliced almonds

5 large eggs

2 teaspoons vanilla extract

8 ounces bittersweet chocolate (see headnote), roughly chopped

199 grams (1 cup) packed dark brown sugar

½ teaspoon table salt

This flourless chocolate cake from Capri, Italy (where it is called torta caprese), gets its rich, almost brownie-like texture from ground almonds and a generous amount of egg. Before grinding the nuts, we toast them to intensify their flavor and accentuate the deep, roasted notes of the chocolate. We preferred the cake made with bittersweet chocolate containing 70 to 80 percent cocoa solids. You can, of course, use a lighter, sweeter bittersweet chocolate, but the cake will have less chocolate intensity. Serve slices warm or at room temperature dolloped with unsweetened whipped cream.

Don't forget to reduce the oven to 300°F after toasting the almonds. Also, don't overbake the cake or its texture will be dry and tough. Whereas most cakes are done when a toothpick inserted at the center comes out clean, a toothpick inserted into this one should come out with sticky, fudgy crumbs, similar to brownies.

___

1. Heat the oven to 350°F with a rack in the middle position. Spread the almonds in an even layer on a rimmed baking sheet and toast in the oven until golden brown, 8 to 10 minutes, stirring once about halfway through. Cool to room temperature.

2. While the almonds cool, reduce the oven to 300°F. Mist the bottom and sides of a 9-inch round cake pan with cooking spray, line the bottom with a round of kitchen parchment, then mist the parchment. Crack the eggs into a liquid measuring cup and add the vanilla; set aside.

3. In a food processor, process 185 grams (2 cups) of the almonds until finely ground, 20 to 30 seconds. Add the chocolate and pulse until the chocolate is finely ground, 10 to 15 pulses. Add the sugar and salt, then process until well combined, about 30 seconds, scraping the bowl as needed. With the machine running, gradually pour in the egg mixture. Continue processing until the batter is smooth and homogeneous, about another 15 to 20 seconds. Remove the blade and scrape the bowl.

4. Pour the batter into the prepared pan, then sprinkle evenly with the remaining 48 grams (⅓ cup) almonds. Bake until the center feels firm when gently pressed and a toothpick inserted at the center comes out with moist, fudgey crumbs attached, 30 to 35 minutes.

5. Let cool in the pan on a wire rack for 30 minutes. Run a knife around the sides of the cake, then invert onto a rack. Peel off the parchment and reinvert the cake onto a platter. Serve warm or at room temperature.

Lemon-Buttermilk Pound Cake

Start to finish: 1½ hours (30 minutes active) / Servings: 8

___

13 tablespoons (1½ sticks plus 1 tablespoon) salted butter, room temperature, divided

467 grams (2 cups plus 3 tablespoons) white sugar, plus extra, divided

330 grams (2¾ cups) cake flour

½ teaspoon baking soda

¼ teaspoon table salt

¾ cup buttermilk

2 tablespoons grated lemon zest, plus 3 tablespoons lemon juice

5 large eggs, separated

Pound cake historically has had a propensity to density. So thick was the batter of equal parts butter, sugar, flour and eggs that 18th-century cookbook author Hannah Glasse recommended beating it for an hour. But despite all that flogging, and even with modern techniques, the cakes remained resolutely heavy. We figured there was a better way. For our pound cake, we separated the eggs, a trick we learned from pastry chef Kathryn King of Atlanta's Aria restaurant. She makes a lemon-buttermilk pound cake she got from her grandmother that is lofty and light. Gently whipping the egg whites, a trick lifted from sponge cakes, built lightness into the cake. King also adds baking soda, unusual in a pound cake, as well as buttermilk and lemon juice, which contribute a slightly tart flavor and add acid. King, like Violet bakery's Claire Ptak, emphasizes under-whipping the whites. Likewise, we took a gentler hand when creaming the butter and sugar. At Aria, the cake is sliced, buttered, toasted and served with fresh fruit and whipped cream. It's also delicious plain with just a spoonful of whipped cream.

Don't overbeat the whites. *They should appear smooth and glossy, with gentle peaks that curl back on themselves. And don't wait until the end of the baking time to check the cake for doneness; pans cook at different rates due to color and composition.*

1. **Heat the oven to 325°F** with a rack in the middle position. Rub 1 tablespoon of the butter evenly over a Bundt pan, then use a pastry brush to ensure it gets into all corners. Sprinkle in a bit of sugar, then turn the pan to evenly coat all surfaces.

2. **In a bowl, whisk** together the flour, baking soda and salt. In a liquid measuring cup, combine the buttermilk and lemon juice; set aside.

3. **In a stand mixer** with a whisk attachment, whip the egg whites on medium-high until light and foamy, about 1 minute. With the mixer running, slowly sprinkle in 39 grams (3 tablespoons) of the sugar and continue to whip until the whites are thick and glossy and hold soft peaks, about 1 minute. Transfer the whites to a bowl and set aside, then add the remaining 2 cups of sugar and the lemon zest to the stand mixer's bowl.

4. Using the paddle attachment, mix 428 grams (2 cups) of the sugar and zest on low until the sugar appears moistened and begins to clump, about 1 minute. Add the remaining 12 tablespoons of butter and mix on medium-low until the mixture is cohesive, then increase the mixer to medium-high and beat until pale and fluffy, about 3 minutes. Reduce the mixer to low and add the yolks, one at a time, mixing until incorporated.

5. Add a third of the flour mixture, then mix on low. Add half of the buttermilk mixture, then mix again. Repeat the process of adding and mixing, ending with the final third of flour. Fold ⅓ of the whipped egg whites into the batter until combined, then gently fold in the remaining whites until barely combined. Transfer the batter to the prepared pan and smooth the top.

6. Bake until the cake is golden brown and bounces back when gently pressed, 50 to 60 minutes, rotating the pan halfway through baking. Cool the cake in the pan on a wire rack for 10 minutes, then remove from the pan and cool completely.

Chocolate-Hazelnut (Gianduja) Crostata

Start to finish: 1 hour 15 minutes (45 minutes active)
Servings: 10

163 grams (1¼ cups) hazelnuts

65 grams (½ cup) all-purpose flour

35 grams (¼ cup) whole-wheat flour

214 grams (1 cup) white sugar, divided

¼ teaspoon baking powder

Table salt

6 tablespoons (¾ stick) salted butter, cut into ½-inch cubes and chilled

1 large egg yolk, plus 3 large egg whites

2½ teaspoons vanilla extract, divided

4 ounces bittersweet chocolate, chopped

1 teaspoon instant espresso powder

The chewy, rich filling for this dessert was inspired by gianduja, a chocolate-hazelnut paste first created in Turin, Italy. The crust, made with whole-wheat flour, is simply pressed into the bottom of a springform pan; its nuttiness pairs perfectly with the intense filling. If you like, dust the baked crostata with powdered sugar before serving, or top wedges with unsweetened whipped cream or crème fraîche. The crostata is best served the same day, but leftovers can be covered in plastic wrap and refrigerated overnight; bring to room temperature before serving.

Don't underprocess the hazelnut and sugar mixture. Grinding it until fine and paste-like is key to the filling's thick, decadent texture.

1. Heat the oven to 375°F with a rack in the lowest position. Evenly mist a 9-inch springform pan with cooking spray. Spread the hazelnuts on a rimmed baking sheet and toast until deep golden brown, about 10 minutes. Wrap the nuts in a kitchen towel and rub vigorously to remove the skins. Set aside.

2. In a food processor, combine both flours, 53 grams (¼ cup) of sugar, the baking powder and ⅛ teaspoon salt. Process until combined, about 5 seconds. Scatter the butter over the mixture and pulse until it resembles coarse sand, 10 to 12 pulses. Add the egg yolk and ½ teaspoon of vanilla extract, then process until evenly moistened and clumping together, 20 to 30 seconds.

3. Transfer the dough to the prepared pan; do not wash the food processor. Press into an even layer covering the bottom of the pan and prick with a fork about every ½ inch. Bake until the crust is golden at the center and slightly darker at the edges, 15 to 20 minutes.

4. Meanwhile, make the filling. In a small microwave-safe bowl, microwave the chocolate on 50 percent power, stopping to stir every 30 seconds, until smooth and melted, about 3 minutes. Set aside.

5. In the food processor, pulse the hazelnuts until roughly chopped, about 8 pulses; measure out ¼ cup and set aside. Add the remaining 161 grams (¾ cup) sugar and process until the mixture resembles wet sand and sticks to the corners of the bowl, about 2 minutes. Scrape the bowl. Add the egg whites, the remaining 2 teaspoons vanilla extract, espresso powder and ¼ teaspoon salt. Process until smooth, about 10 seconds. Add the chocolate and process until incorporated, another 10 seconds, scraping the sides as needed.

6. Spread the chocolate-hazelnut mixture in an even layer on the crust, then sprinkle the reserved chopped nuts around the perimeter. Bake until slightly puffed and the edges begin to crack, 20 to 25 minutes.

7. Let cool on a wire rack until the edges pull away from the sides of the pan, about 15 minutes. Remove the pan sides. Serve the crostata warm or at room temperature.

Senegalese Mango and Coconut Rice Pudding

Start to finish: 1 hour (plus cooling) / Servings: 4

---

2 tablespoons honey

14- to 16-ounce ripe mango, peeled, pitted and cut into ½-inch chunks

Table salt

1 tablespoon lime juice

45 grams (½ cup) unsweetened shredded coconut

14-ounce can coconut milk

2 tablespoons white sugar

2 teaspoons vanilla extract

2 cups cooked and cooled long-grain white rice (see headnote)

Senegalese coconut rice pudding—called sombi—usually has a porridge-like consistency and is eaten as a snack or for breakfast. We preferred it a little thicker and enjoyed it as dessert, so after learning the recipe from Pierre Thiam in Dakar, we adapted the version in his book "Yolele!" and paired it with diced mango that is gently cooked in caramelized honey. This recipe calls for 2 cups of cooked long-grain rice. Rinse and drain ¾ cup long-grain white rice, then combine it with 1 cup water in a small saucepan. Bring to a boil over medium-high, then cover, reduce to low and cook until the water has been absorbed, about 15 minutes. Transfer the rice to a kitchen parchment–lined baking sheet or large plate and cool to room temperature.

Don't stir the mango too often as it cooks; each time the lid is removed, steam escapes. This can dry out the mango too quickly and cause it to scorch.

---

1. **In a 10-inch nonstick skillet** over medium-high, cook the honey without stirring for 2 minutes; it will bubble vigorously and smell lightly caramelized. Stir in the mango, ¾ cup water and ⅛ teaspoon salt, then bring to a simmer. Cover, reduce to medium-low and cook, stirring only occasionally, until very tender and the moisture has completely evaporated, 25 to 30 minutes. (If most of the liquid has evaporated after about only 15 minutes but the mango is still firm, reduce to low to prevent scorching.) Off heat, stir in the lime juice.

2. **Meanwhile, in a medium saucepan** over medium-high, toast the coconut, stirring occasionally, until golden brown, 1½ to 2 minutes. Stir in the coconut milk, sugar, vanilla and ¼ teaspoon salt, then bring to a simmer. Reduce to medium-low and cook, stirring occasionally, until slightly thickened, about 5 minutes.

3. **Remove ¼ cup of the coconut mixture** and set aside. Add the rice and 1 cup water to the saucepan and stir to combine. Cook over medium, stirring frequently, until the liquid is absorbed and the rice is creamy, 15 to 20 minutes. Remove from the heat and let cool for 15 minutes.

4. **Spoon the rice pudding** into serving bowls, top with the mango and drizzle with the reserved coconut mixture. Serve warm.

French Apple Cake

Start to finish: 1 hour (25 minutes active), plus cooling
Servings: 8

---

8 tablespoons (1 stick) salted butter, plus more for pan

¼ teaspoon ground allspice

1½ pounds Granny Smith apples, peeled, cored, cut into ¼-inch slices

1 pound Braeburn or Golden Delicious apples, peeled, cored cut into ¼-inch slices

156 grams (12 tablespoons) white sugar, divided

¼ teaspoon table salt

2 tablespoons brandy or Calvados

86 grams (⅔ cup) all-purpose flour, plus more for pan

1 teaspoon baking powder

2 large eggs

2 teaspoons vanilla extract

This simple dessert is less cake than sautéed apples set in a thick, custardy crumb under a golden, sugary crust. We liked using two varieties of apples, one tart and one sweet—the variation in the apples' sweetness gave the cake a full, complex flavor. The cake is delicious served plain, but we also loved it with crème fraîche or ice cream.

Don't use a spatula to scrape the browned butter out of the skillet—simply pour it into the bowl. A skim coat of butter in the pan is needed to cook the apples. And don't slice the cake until it has fully cooled; if it is at all warm, the texture at the center will be too soft.

1. **Heat the oven to 375°F** with a rack in the middle position. Coat a 9-inch springform pan with butter, dust with flour, then tap out the excess.

2. **In a 12-inch skillet** over medium-high, melt the butter. Cook, swirling the pan frequently, until the milk solids are golden brown and the butter has a nutty aroma, 1 to 3 minutes. Pour into a small heat-safe bowl; don't scrape the skillet. Stir the allspice into the butter. Set aside.

3. **Add all the apples,** 26 grams (2 tablespoons) of sugar and the salt to the still-hot skillet and set over medium-high. Cook, stirring occasionally, until the moisture released by the apples has evaporated and the slices are beginning to brown, 12 to 15 minutes. Add the brandy and cook until evaporated, 30 to 60 seconds. Transfer to a large plate, spread in an even layer and refrigerate uncovered until cool to the touch, 15 to 20 minutes.

4. **In a small bowl,** whisk together the flour and baking powder. In a large bowl, whisk together the eggs, vanilla and 117 grams (9 tablespoons) of the sugar; gradually whisk in the butter. Add the flour mixture and stir until smooth; the batter will be very thick. Add the cooled apples and fold until evenly coated. Transfer to the prepared pan, spread in an even layer and sprinkle with the remaining 1 tablespoon sugar.

5. **Bake until the cake is deeply browned,** 35 to 40 minutes. Let cool completely in the pan on a wire rack, about 2 hours. Run a knife around the inside of the pan and remove the sides before slicing.

Maple-Whiskey Pudding Cakes

Start to finish: 45 minutes (20 minutes active) / Servings: 4

___

6 tablespoons maple syrup

1 teaspoon cider vinegar

6 tablespoons whiskey, divided

8 tablespoons (1 stick) salted butter, cut into 1-tablespoon pieces, divided

Table salt

107 grams (½ cup) white sugar

¼ cup whole milk

1 large egg

1 teaspoon vanilla extract

90 grams (¾ cup) pecans, toasted

65 grams (½ cup) all-purpose flour

1 teaspoon baking powder

These individual desserts bake up with a gooey sauce beneath a layer of rich, tender cake. We tried a few different types of whiskey. Our favorites were Jameson for its clean, bright flavor and Rittenhouse rye for its spicy depth. This recipe can easily be doubled to serve eight. Serve the pudding cakes warm, with vanilla ice cream or lightly sweetened whipped cream.

Don't stir the maple-whiskey syrup into the batter after dividing it among the batter-filled ramekins. With baking, the syrup will form a sauce at the bottom.

___

1. In a small saucepan over medium, combine ½ cup water, the maple syrup, vinegar, 4 tablespoons of whiskey, 2 tablespoons of butter and ⅛ teaspoon of salt. Bring to a boil, stirring occasionally. Reduce to low and simmer for 5 minutes. Remove from the heat and set aside.

2. In another small saucepan over medium, melt the remaining 6 tablespoons butter. Cook, swirling the pan, until the milk solids at the bottom are deep golden brown and the butter has the aroma of toasted nuts, about 5 minutes. Transfer to a medium bowl and cool to room temperature.

3. Meanwhile, heat the oven to 325°F with a rack in the middle position. Mist four 6-ounce ramekins with cooking spray and place on a rimmed baking sheet. When the butter is cool, whisk in the sugar, milk, egg, vanilla and remaining 2 tablespoons whiskey. Set aside.

4. In a food processor, process the pecans until finely ground and beginning to clump, 30 to 40 seconds. Add the flour, baking powder and ¼ teaspoon salt, then pulse until combined, about 5 pulses. Add the butter mixture and pulse until a smooth, thick batter forms, about 5 pulses, scraping down the bowl once.

5. Divide the batter evenly among the prepared ramekins. Gently pour the maple mixture over the batter in each ramekin. Do not stir. Bake until the cakes are puffed and the centers jiggle only slightly, 25 to 30 minutes. Let cool on the baking sheet for 10 minutes before serving; the cakes will fall slightly as they cool.

French Walnut Tart

Start to finish: 2¼ hours (20 minutes active) / Servings: 10

For the tart shell:

87 grams (⅔ cup) all-purpose flour

46 grams (⅓ cup) whole-wheat flour

40 grams (3 tablespoons) white sugar

¼ teaspoon table salt

6 tablespoons (¾ stick) salted butter, cut into ½-inch cubes and chilled

1 large egg yolk

1 teaspoon vanilla extract

For the filling:

107 grams (½ cup) white sugar

¼ cup honey

⅓ cup crème fraîche

4 tablespoons (½ stick) salted butter

1 tablespoon cider vinegar

⅛ teaspoon table salt

2 large egg yolks

230 grams (2½ cups) walnuts, roughly chopped and lightly toasted (see note)

This simple tart comes from the Périgord region of France, an area known for its walnuts. A cookie-like pastry shell is filled with the rich, subtly bitter nuts and buttery caramel. Our version tones down what often is cloying sweetness with a small measure of crème fraîche and a dose of cider vinegar (you won't detect it in the finished dessert). Whole-wheat flour in the crust plays up the earthiness of the walnuts. To toast the walnuts, spread them in an even layer on a rimmed baking sheet and bake at 325°F until fragrant and just starting to brown, about 8 minutes, stirring just once or twice; do not overtoast them or they will taste acrid. The dough-lined tart pan can be prepared in advance; after the dough is firm, wrap tightly in plastic and freeze for up to two weeks. The tart is superb lightly sprinkled with flaky sea salt and accompanied by crème fraîche or unsweetened whipped cream.

Don't overcook the caramel. *Aim for an amber hue; if it gets much darker than that, the finished tart will taste bitter.*

1. **Heat the oven to 325°F** with a rack in the lower-middle position. Mist a 9-inch tart pan with removable bottom with cooking spray. Line a rimmed baking sheet with kitchen parchment.

2. **To make the tart shell,** in a food processor, combine both flours, the sugar and salt, then process until combined, about 5 seconds. Scatter the butter over the mixture and pulse until it resembles coarse sand, 10 to 12 pulses. Add the egg yolk and vanilla, then process until the mixture is evenly moistened and cohesive, 20 to 30 seconds; the mixture may not form a single mass.

3. **Crumble the dough** into the prepared tart pan, evenly covering the surface. Using the bottom of a dry measuring cup, press into an even layer over the bottom and up the sides; the edge of the dough should be flush with the rim. Use a fork to prick all over the bottom, then freeze until the dough is firm, 15 to 30 minutes.

4. **While the dough chills,** to make the filling, pour ¼ cup water into a medium saucepan. Add the sugar and honey into the center, avoiding contact with the sides. Cook over medium, swirling the pan frequently, until the mixture is amber in color, about 8 minutes. Off heat, add the crème fraîche, butter, vinegar and salt, then whisk until the butter is melted and the mixture is well combined. Let cool until just warm, about 30 minutes.

5. While the caramel cools, set the dough-lined tart pan on the prepared baking sheet. Bake until lightly browned, about 30 minutes. Cool on the baking sheet on a wire rack for about 5 minutes.

6. Whisk the yolks into the warm honey filling, then add the nuts and stir until evenly coated. Pour the filling into the warm tart shell, then gently spread in an even layer. Bake until the edges of the filling begin to puff and the center jiggles only slightly when gently shaken, 25 to 35 minutes.

7. Let the tart cool on the baking sheet on a wire rack for about 1 hour. Remove the pan sides. Serve warm or at room temperature.

Pistachio-Cardamom Cake

Start to finish: 1 hour 10 minutes (15 minutes active), plus cooling / Makes one 9-inch loaf

---

214 grams (1 cup) white sugar

2 teaspoons grated orange zest, plus ¼ cup orange juice (about 1 orange)

185 grams (1⅓ cups) shelled, unsalted pistachios, toasted and cooled

130 grams (1 cup) all-purpose flour, plus more for pan

2 teaspoons baking powder

1½ teaspoons ground cardamom

½ teaspoon table salt

4 large eggs

½ cup plus 2 tablespoons plain whole-milk Greek-style yogurt

¼ cup olive oil, plus more for pan

2 teaspoons vanilla extract

93 grams (¾ cup) powdered sugar

Baking a cake can be daunting. Enter the loaf cake, as easy as a quick bread but with more polish. Rose Bakery in Paris, created by Briton Rose Carrarini and her French husband, Jean-Charles, has elevated the style to an art form, producing tempting loaf cakes in all manner of flavors. We were particularly taken by a green-tinged, nut-topped pistachio cake. For our version, we paired toasted pistachios with cardamom and ground orange zest, giving it a distinctly Middle Eastern flavor. Combining ground nuts with rich Greek-style yogurt, olive oil and plenty of eggs ensured a moist, appealingly coarse crumb. We got the best results from grinding the nuts until they were nearly as fine as flour, but still had some texture. If you can't find unsalted pistachios, reduce the salt in the recipe by half. Cooling the cake was essential to maintain the thick consistency of the glaze.

Don't skip toasting the pistachios. The differences in flavor and texture were significant between raw and toasted. Toast the nuts at 300°F until they're quite fragrant and begin to darken, 10 to 15 minutes.

1. Heat the oven to 325°F with a rack in the middle position. Lightly coat a 9-by-5-inch loaf pan with olive oil and dust with flour. In a food processor, combine the white sugar and orange zest; process until the sugar is damp and fragrant, 5 to 10 seconds. Transfer to a large bowl.

2. Add the pistachios to the processor and pulse until coarse, 8 to 10 pulses. Set aside 2 tablespoons of the nuts for topping. Add the flour, baking powder, cardamom and salt to the processor with the nuts. Process until the nuts are finely ground, about 45 seconds.

3. To the sugar mixture, whisk in the eggs, ½ cup of the yogurt, the oil, orange juice and vanilla. Add the nut-flour mixture and fold until mixed. Transfer the batter to the prepared pan, and smooth the top. Bake until golden brown, firm to the touch and a toothpick inserted at the center comes out with moist crumbs, 50 to 55 minutes. Cool in the pan on a wire rack for 15 minutes. Remove from the pan and let cool completely, about 2 hours.

4. In a small bowl, whisk the remaining 2 tablespoons of yogurt with the powdered sugar until thick and smooth. Spread over the top of the cake. Sprinkle with the reserved nuts. Let set for 10 minutes before serving.

Salted Peanut and Caramel Tart

Start to finish: 2½ hours (1 hour active)
Makes one 9-inch tart

For the tart shell:

130 grams (1 cup) all-purpose flour

50 grams (½ cup) almond flour

66 grams (⅓ cup) white sugar

¼ teaspoon table salt

6 tablespoons (¾ stick) salted butter, cut into ½-inch cubes and softened

1 large egg yolk

1 teaspoon vanilla extract

For the peanut butter–meringue filling:

188 grams (¾ cup) creamy (smooth) peanut butter (see headnote)

2 large egg whites

1 teaspoon vanilla extract

Pinch table salt

164 grams (½ cup) corn syrup

107 grams (½ cup) white sugar

For the peanut-caramel topping:

54 grams (¼ cup) white sugar

3 tablespoons heavy cream

2 tablespoons salted butter, cut into 2 pieces

68 grams (½ cup) dry-roasted, salted peanuts, roughly chopped

Flaky sea salt, such as Maldon (optional)

The peanut butter and marshmallow sandwich—also known as the Fluffernutter—is inarguably all-American. And Le Petit Grain, a Parisian boulangerie headed by Edward Delling-Williams, created a delicious riff on that childhood favorite with their elegant individual tartlets called tartes cacahuètes (literally, peanut tarts). A buttery, cookie-like pastry is filled with an airy peanut butter meringue that is topped with caramel-coated roasted peanuts. For ease, our version makes a single 9-inch tart. Pay attention to the timing in the recipe, which can be tricky. To make the meringue filling, the whipped egg whites and sugar syrup need to be ready at the same time. If your egg whites reach soft peaks before the syrup is ready, reduce the mixer speed to low while you wait for the syrup to finish; this prevents the whites from turning dry and stiff. You'll need a candy or digital thermometer for gauging the doneness of the sugar syrup. The finished tart will keep at room temperature for up to 12 hours. If you're storing it longer than an hour or so before serving, wait to add the flaky salt garnish until just before serving and cover the tart with plastic wrap or foil.

Don't use natural peanut butter (the variety that requires stirring to mix in the oil on the surface); even the creamy variety of natural peanut butter has a slight grittiness that's detectable in the tart filling. Make sure the mixer bowl and whisk attachment for whipping the meringue are perfectly clean; a trace of fat will prevent the egg whites from attaining the proper volume.

---

1. To make the tart shell, mist a 9-inch tart pan with removable bottom with cooking spray and set on a rimmed baking sheet. In a stand mixer fitted with the paddle attachment, combine both flours, the sugar and salt, then mix on low until combined, about 5 seconds. With the mixer on low, add the butter one piece at a time. When all the butter has been added, continue mixing on low until the mixture resembles coarse sand, about 2 minutes. Add the yolk and vanilla, then mix on low until the dough is evenly moistened and cohesive, 2 to 3 minutes; the dough may not form a single mass.

2. Crumble the dough into the prepared tart pan, covering the bottom as evenly as possible. Using the bottom of a dry measuring cup, press the dough into an even layer over the bottom and up the sides of the pan. Prick the bottom and sides about every ½ inch with a fork. Set in the freezer on the baking sheet to chill until firm, at least 15 minutes or up to 1 hour.

3. Meanwhile, heat the oven to 300°F with a rack in the middle position. When the tart shell is firm, bake it on the baking sheet until deep golden brown, 1 to 1¼ hours. Let cool on the baking sheet set on a wire rack for at least 15 minutes.

4. To make the peanut butter–meringue filling, put the peanut butter in a small microwave-safe bowl; set aside. In a clean, dry mixer bowl, combine the egg whites, vanilla and salt, then attach to the mixer along with the whisk attachment. In a small saucepan, combine the corn syrup, sugar and ¼ cup water. Bring to a boil over medium-high and cook until the syrup reaches 238°F, 3 to 4 minutes; swirl the pan once or twice before the syrup reaches a boil. When the syrup has boiled for 2 minutes, begin whipping the whites on medium and whip until they hold very soft peaks when the whisk is lifted, about 1 minute. When the syrup reaches 238°F, remove the pan from the heat and let stand just until the bubbling slows, no more than 15 seconds. Then with the mixer running on medium-high, slowly pour the hot syrup into the egg whites, aiming for the area between the whisk and the sides of the bowl. After all the syrup has been added, continue whipping on medium-high until the bowl is just warm to the touch, about 3 minutes; do not overbeat.

5. Meanwhile, microwave the peanut butter on high until pourable, 30 to 60 seconds, stirring once about halfway through. When the egg whites are ready, reduce the mixer to low and pour in the peanut butter. Once all the peanut butter is added, stop the mixer, then fold with a silicone spatula until homogeneous, taking care not to deflate the whites. Gently pour the filling into the tart shell and spread in an even layer; set aside.

6. For the peanut-caramel topping: Place 2 tablespoons water in a small saucepan. Carefully pour the sugar into the center of the pan, and stir gently with a clean spoon just until the sugar is evenly moistened. Bring to a boil over medium and cook, gently swirling the pan (do not stir) until the syrup is deep amber-colored and lightly smoking, 5 to 6 minutes. Carefully pour in the cream (the mixture will bubble and steam vigorously), then stir to combine. Add the butter, remove from the heat and continue stirring until the butter is melted and incorporated. Stir the peanuts into the caramel.

7. Working quickly, pour the caramel mixture evenly over the filling, then use a small spatula to gently spread it to the edges; be careful not to push the peanuts into the filling. Let cool for at least 15 minutes. Remove the outer ring from the tart pan, then sprinkle lightly with flaky salt (if using). Serve at room temperature.

Toasted Bread Pudding with Cream and Pistachios

Start to finish: 30 minutes, plus chilling / Servings: 10

5 ounces melba toast

268 grams (1¼ cups) white sugar

1 teaspoon lemon juice

2 tablespoons salted butter, cut into 2 pieces

1 tablespoon plus 1 teaspoon orange blossom water, divided

8-ounce container mascarpone cheese

½ cup heavy cream

135 grams (1 cup) raw unsalted shelled pistachios, chopped

Pomegranate seeds, raspberries or strawberries, to serve (optional)

In her book "The Palestinian Table," Reem Kassis explains that the name of this dessert, aish el saraya, translates as "bread of the royal palaces." Made from syrup-soaked toasted bread (we call for melba toast) topped with creamy whipped mascarpone and finished with pistachios and pomegranate seeds, it is simple to make, but offers elegant and rich flavors and textures. If you are not a fan of orange blossom water, which has an intensely floral aroma, instead use three or four strips of orange zest in the syrup (remove the zest before pouring the syrup over the bread) and 1 teaspoon vanilla extract in the mascarpone mixture.

Don't overwhip the mascarpone mixture or it will turn too stiff and have a curdled appearance.

1. **Mist a 9-inch round springform pan** with cooking spray and set aside. In a food processor, process the melba toast until the largest pieces are pea-sized, 30 to 45 seconds. Transfer to a large bowl and set aside.

2. **In a small saucepan** over medium-high, combine 1¼ cups water, the sugar and lemon juice. Bring to a boil, stirring to dissolve the sugar. Reduce to medium and cook until the syrup is slightly thickened, 3 to 4 minutes. Remove from heat, add the butter and 1 tablespoon orange blossom water, then stir until the butter is melted.

3. **Pour the hot syrup** over the melba toast and set aside until all of the liquid has been absorbed, about 10 minutes, stirring occasionally. Transfer to the prepared springform pan and press into an even layer. Cool to room temperature.

4. **In a stand mixer** with the whisk attachment, whip the mascarpone, cream and remaining 1 teaspoon orange blossom water on medium-high until smooth and the mixture holds stiff peaks when the whisk is lifted, about 1 minute; do not overbeat.

5. **Spread the mascarpone mixture** over the bread, smoothing it with the back of a spoon or a small spatula. Sprinkle the pistachios over the top. Cover and refrigerate for at least 2 hours or up to 24 hours. To serve, remove the sides of the pan. Top with pomegranate seeds or berries (if using), then cut into wedges.

Tangerine-Almond Cake with Bay-Infused Syrup

Start to finish: 1 hour 10 minutes (20 minutes active), plus cooling / Servings: 8

For the cake:

12 tablespoons (1½ sticks) salted butter, room temperature, plus more for pan

225 grams (2¼ cups) blanched almond flour

87 grams (⅔ cup) all-purpose flour

½ teaspoon baking powder

214 grams (1 cup) white sugar

1½ tablespoons finely grated tangerine zest

2 teaspoons finely grated lemon zest

¼ teaspoon table salt

4 large eggs, room temperature

3 tablespoons sliced almonds

For the syrup:

71 grams (⅓ cup) white sugar

3 tablespoons tangerine juice

2 tablespoons lemon juice

3 small bay leaves

Syrup-soaked cakes are common throughout eastern Mediterranean countries. Easy to make, the cakes also keep well because of the hygroscopic (water retaining) nature of the syrup. Our tangerine-almond cake has a moist, pleasantly dense texture thanks in part to almond meal. (Use blanched almond flour; unblanched almond meal makes for a drier and less appealing cake.) We infuse our citrus syrup with bay leaves, adding an herbal note. We loved the unique flavor of tangerines in this cake, but if you can't find them, substitute orange zest and juice. If you don't have an 8-inch round cake pan, use a 9-inch pan and reduce the baking time to about 45 minutes.

Don't invert the cake without the buttered parchment. The cake's exterior is tacky and will easily stick to other surfaces, peeling off the crust and the almonds.

1. Heat the oven to 325°F with a rack in the middle position. Butter the bottom and sides of an 8-inch round cake pan. Line the bottom with a round of kitchen parchment, then butter the parchment. In a medium bowl, whisk together the almond flour, all-purpose flour and baking powder.

2. In the bowl of a stand mixer with a paddle attachment, mix the sugar, both zests and the salt on low until the sugar appears moistened and clumps, about 1 minute. Add the butter and mix on medium-low until the mixture is cohesive. Increase the mixer to medium-high and beat until pale and fluffy, about 3 minutes. Reduce the mixer to low and add the eggs, one at a time, scraping down the bowl after each addition.

3. Add the dry ingredients and mix on low just until combined, 10 to 15 seconds. Use a silicone spatula to fold the batter until no streaks of flour remain. The batter will be very thick. Scrape the batter into the prepared pan. Spread into an even layer, then sprinkle the almonds on top. Bake until the cake is golden brown and the center feels firm when lightly pressed, about 55 minutes, rotating the pan halfway through.

4. Meanwhile, make the syrup. In a small saucepan over medium, combine all ingredients. Bring to a simmer, stirring until the sugar dissolves. Remove from heat and let the syrup steep until needed.

5. When the cake is done, return the syrup to a simmer over medium. Use a toothpick or skewer to poke holes all over the cake's surface. Brush all of the hot syrup evenly onto the hot cake. Cool the cake in the pan until barely warm to the touch, about 30 minutes.

6. Lightly butter a sheet of kitchen parchment, then place it on the cake, buttered side down. Invert a large plate on top of the parchment, then invert the plate and cake pan together. Lift off the pan and remove the parchment round. Re-invert the cake onto a serving platter and let cool completely.

Chocolate-Orange Tart

Start to finish: 2 hours (45 minutes active), plus cooling
Servings: 8

___

For the tart shell:

130 grams (1 cup) all-purpose flour

50 grams (½ cup) almond flour

71 grams (⅓ cup) white sugar

¼ teaspoon table salt

6 tablespoons salted butter, cut into ½-inch cubes and chilled

1 large egg yolk

1 teaspoon vanilla extract

For the filling:

78 grams (6 tablespoons) white sugar

2 teaspoons grated orange zest plus 2 tablespoons orange juice

¼ teaspoon table salt

¼ teaspoon ground cinnamon

1½ cups (12 ounces) whole-milk ricotta cheese

1 large egg plus 1 large egg yolk

1 teaspoon vanilla extract

1½ ounces semisweet chocolate, chopped

The filling of this tart was inspired by the chocolate, orange and ricotta tart served at Rose Bakery in Paris, but we found the crust in the pastry case of Vancouver's Beaucoup Bakery—a crisp, slightly crunchy almond meal affair that had us at first bite. Rose Carrarini's decadent cheesecake-style filling is made with ricotta, cream, orange zest and dark chocolate, all bound together with a little flour. We added cinnamon and lightened our take, leaving out cream and flour and reducing the amount of chocolate so the ricotta and orange came through more clearly. For the crust, we used all-purpose and almond flours and pressed the dough right into the tart pan (no rolling). The result had great flavor and texture, and it didn't shrink or slump when blind baked. For do-ahead ease, the tart shell can be prepped, pressed into the pan, pricked all over, then frozen for up to two weeks; do not thaw before baking.

Don't use skim-milk ricotta; whole-milk is needed for a rich, creamy consistency. Some ricottas with more lactose will brown more deeply than others. We liked Calabro, which is low in lactose.

___

1. Heat the oven to 300°F with a rack in the middle position. Mist a 9-inch tart pan with a removable bottom with cooking spray. Set on a baking sheet and set aside.

2. To make the tart shell, in a food processor, combine both flours, the sugar and salt; process until combined, about 5 seconds. Scatter the butter over the dry ingredients and pulse until the mixture resembles coarse sand, 10 to 12 pulses. Add the yolk and vanilla, then process until the mixture is evenly moistened and cohesive, 20 to 30 seconds; the mixture may not form a single mass.

3. Crumble the dough into the tart pan, evenly covering the surface; do not wash the food processor. Using the bottom of a dry measuring cup, press the dough into an even layer over the bottom and up the sides of the pan. Use a fork to prick the dough all over the bottom and sides, then freeze until firm, at least 15 minutes or up to 1 hour.

4. Bake on the baking sheet until the tart shell is deep golden brown, 1 to 1¼ hours. Let cool on the sheet on a wire rack for 15 minutes. Increase the oven to 350°F.

5. Meanwhile, prepare the filling. In the food processor, combine the sugar, orange zest, salt and cinnamon; process until the sugar is moistened and fragrant, about 15 seconds. Add the ricotta and process until smooth, about 30 seconds, scraping the bowl as needed. Add the egg, egg yolk, orange juice and vanilla, then process until combined, another 10 to 15 seconds.

6. Pour the filling into the still-warm crust, then sprinkle evenly with the chocolate. Carefully slide the baking sheet into the oven and bake until the filling is slightly puffed at the edges but the center still jiggles slightly, 25 to 35 minutes. Let cool completely on the wire rack, about 2 hours.

7. If serving the tart at room temperature, remove the outer ring from the tart pan. If serving the tart chilled, keep the outer ring in place and refrigerate uncovered for 1 hour, or until the chocolate is set, then loosely cover with plastic wrap. Refrigerate for up to 2 days; remove the outer ring from the pan before serving.

Lemon-Almond Pound Cake

Start to finish: 1½ hours (20 minutes active), plus cooling
Makes one 9-inch loaf

---

195 grams (1½ cups) all-purpose flour, plus more for the pan

4 large eggs, room temperature

2 teaspoons vanilla extract

241 grams (1 cup plus 2 tablespoons) plus 54 grams (¼ cup) white sugar

2 tablespoons grated lemon zest, plus 3 tablespoons lemon juice, divided

100 grams (1 cup) almond flour

1½ teaspoons baking powder

½ teaspoon table salt

14 tablespoons (1¾ sticks) salted butter, cut into 14 pieces, room temperature

3 tablespoons sliced almonds

For this plush, velvety pound cake, we took a cue from Rose Carrarini of Rose's Bakery in Paris and replaced some of the wheat flour with almond flour. Almond flour makes the cake's crumb extra tender and moist and gives it a more interesting texture than wheat flour alone. Grating the lemon zest directly into the mixer bowl allows you to capture the maximum amount of flavorful essential oils; rather than fish out the zest to then measure it, we usually just eyeball it. We finish the cake with a tangy-sweet lemon glaze, brushing it on while the loaf is still hot so the syrup is readily absorbed. Thanks to generous amounts of eggs and butter, this cake keeps well. Store it in an airtight container at room temperature for up to three days.

Don't use cold butter or cold eggs. The butter must be softened to room temperature so it integrates into the sugar-flour mixture. And the eggs must be at room temperature, too, not chilled, so they don't cause the butter to stiffen up when added to the mixer. Lastly, don't rotate the cake as it bakes. Jostling the pan increases the chance the batter will deflate, resulting in a dense, underrisen cake.

1. Heat the oven to 325°F with a rack in the middle position. Coat a 9-by-5-inch loaf pan with cooking spray, dust evenly with flour, then tap out the excess. In a 2-cup liquid measuring cup or small bowl, beat the eggs and vanilla until combined; set aside.

2. In a stand mixer fitted with the paddle attachment, mix the 241 grams (1 cup plus 2 tablespoons) sugar and the lemon zest on low until fragrant, about 1 minute. Add both flours, the baking powder and salt and mix until combined, about 10 seconds. With the mixer on low, add the butter a piece at a time. Once all the butter has been added, continue mixing on low until the mixture is crumbly and no powdery bits remain, 1 to 2 minutes.

3. With the mixer still running, add the egg mixture in a slow, steady stream and mix for about 10 seconds. Increase to medium-high and beat until the batter is light and fluffy, 1 to 1½ minutes, scraping the bowl once or twice. The batter will be thick.

4. Transfer the batter to the prepared pan and smooth the surface, then sprinkle evenly with the sliced almonds. Bake for 45 minutes, then reduce the oven to 300°F. Continue to bake until the top is deep golden brown and a toothpick inserted at the center of the cake comes out clean, another 30 to 35 minutes.

5. While the cake bakes, in a small sauce-pan over medium-low, heat the remaining 54 grams (¼ cup) sugar and 2 tablespoons of lemon juice, stirring often, until the sugar dissolves and the mixture reaches a simmer. Immediately remove from the heat and stir in the remaining 1 tablespoon lemon juice. Set aside to cool.

6. When the cake is done, cool in the pan on a wire rack for 10 minutes. Invert the cake onto the rack, then turn it upright. Using a toothpick, poke small holes in the surface at 1-inch intervals. Brush all of the lemon-sugar syrup onto the cake, allowing it to soak in. Cool completely before slicing, about 2 hours.

MAKING LEMON-ALMOND POUND CAKE

1. In a stand mixer with the paddle attachment, mix the 241 grams (1 cup plus 2 tablespoons) sugar and lemon zest on low until fragrant, about 1 minute.

2. After adding both flours, the baking powder and salt, keep the mixer on low and add the 14 tablespoons room-temperature butter one piece at a time.

3. After all the butter has been added to the bowl, continue mixing on low until the mixture is crumbly and no powdery bits remain, 1 to 2 minutes.

4. With the mixer still running on low, pour in the egg and vanilla mixture in a slow, steady stream, then continue to mix for about 10 seconds.

5. Increase the speed to medium-high and beat until light and fluffy, 1 to 1½ minutes, scraping down the bowl once or twice. The batter will be thick.

6. Transfer to a loaf pan; smooth the surface. Sprinkle with almonds, then bake at 325°F for 45 minutes. Reduce to 300°F and bake for another 30 to 35 minutes.

7. Cool the cake in the pan for 10 minutes. After inverting the cake onto the rack, use a toothpick to poke small holes in the surface at 1-inch intervals.

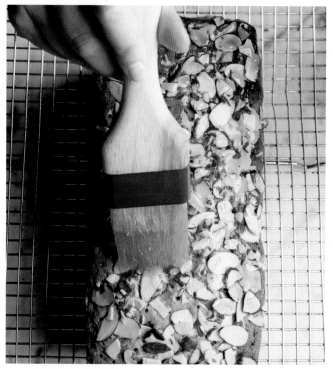

8. Brush the lemon syrup onto the surface of the cake, allowing it to soak in. Cool the cake completely before slicing, about 2 hours.

Ricotta-Semolina Cheesecake

Start to finish: 1 hour (20 minutes active), plus cooling and chilling / Servings: 10

43 grams (¼ cup) semolina flour, plus more for the pan

161 grams (¾ cup) white sugar, divided

2 teaspoons grated lemon zest, plus 1 tablespoon lemon juice

16-ounce container (2 cups) whole-milk ricotta

8-ounce container (1 cup) mascarpone

43 grams (¼ cup) semolina flour, plus more for the pan

4 large eggs, separated

2 tablespoons dry Marsala wine

¼ teaspoon table salt

This is a delicate dessert that mimics the texture of a New York–style cheesecake without the heft. It takes inspiration from a style of cake prepared in Germany and Italy. Instead of cream cheese, whole-milk ricotta kept it light; our favorite supermarket brand is Calabro. Mascarpone added plenty of flavor and a rich, creamy texture. Whipped egg whites also helped keep things light, and semolina flour gave structure to the cheese mixture and created a "crust" on the exterior. Lemon zest and juice brightened the flavors, and Marsala added an Italian touch while also cutting through the richness. If you don't have Marsala, dry sherry is a good substitute. A citrus curd or fruit compote made a great topping for this barely sweet cheesecake. Try our flavorful fruit compotes (see recipe p. 647).

Don't be surprised if the cake cracks as it cools. The whipped egg whites give it a light, fluffy texture, but also make it delicate enough that cracks are inevitable.

1. **Heat the oven to 350°F** with a rack in the middle position. Coat the bottom and sides of a 9-inch springform pan with cooking spray, then dust evenly with semolina, tapping out the excess.

2. **In a food processor,** combine ½ cup of the sugar and the lemon zest. Process until moist and fragrant, about 15 seconds. Add the ricotta and mascarpone and process until smooth, about 30 seconds, scraping the sides as needed. Add the semolina, egg yolks, Marsala, lemon juice and salt, then process until combined, about 10 seconds. Transfer to a large bowl.

3. **In a stand mixer** with a whisk attachment, whip the egg whites on medium-high until light and foamy, about 1 minute. With the mixer running, slowly add the remaining ¼ cup of sugar and continue to whip until the whites hold soft peaks, 1 to 2 minutes. Add a third of the egg whites to the cheese mixture and fold until combined. Add the remaining whites and fold until just incorporated. Transfer to the prepared pan, spreading in an even layer and tapping on the counter to release air bubbles.

4. **Bake until the top is lightly browned** and the cake is just set but still jiggles when shaken, 40 to 45 minutes. Let cool completely in the pan on a wire rack, about 2 hours. Cover and refrigerate for at least 2 hours. Run a knife around the inside of the pan and remove the pan sides before slicing.

Coconut-Cashew Cake

Start to finish: 1 hour / Makes one 9-inch cake

---

170 grams (1 cup)
semolina flour

30 grams (⅓ cup) plus
2 tablespoons unsweetened
shredded coconut, divided

14-ounce can coconut milk

218 grams (1 cup packed)
light brown sugar

4 tablespoons (½ stick) salted
butter, melted and slightly
cooled

3 large eggs

1½ teaspoons baking powder

½ teaspoon ground
cardamom

¼ teaspoon table salt

32 grams (¼ cup) unsalted
roasted cashews, chopped

Rich with the flavor of coconut, traditional Burmese semolina cake, called sanwin makin, is made by cooking the semolina into a thick, dense porridge before baking. We lightened the cake's texture by using a straightforward cake-mixing method and added ground cardamom for fragrance and flavor. Toasting the semolina and shredded coconut first brings out their nuttiness, and soaking them in coconut milk softens their texture so the cake bakes up with a soft crumb. Roasted cashews added texture and visual appeal to the golden-brown cake. Though sanwin makin is usually served chilled, we liked it better at room temperature and even slightly warm, with lightly sweetened whipped cream on the side.

Don't use light coconut milk, which lacks the richness of full-fat coconut milk. And don't forget to stir the coconut milk before using. Avoid cream of coconut and sweetened coconut flakes, both of which contain added sugar. They will make the cake too sweet.

---

1. Heat the oven to 350°F with a rack in the middle position. Mist the bottom and sides of a 9-inch round cake pan with cooking spray. Line the bottom with a round of kitchen parchment, then mist the parchment.

2. On a rimmed baking sheet, combine the semolina and the 30 grams (⅓ cup) of shredded coconut in an even layer. Toast until fragrant and golden at the edges, 10 to 12 minutes, stirring halfway through. Transfer to a large bowl, immediately add the coconut milk and whisk to combine. Set aside until the liquid is absorbed, 15 minutes.

3. Increase the oven to 375°F. To the semolina mixture, add the brown sugar, butter, eggs, baking powder, cardamom and salt. Whisk until well combined; the batter will be very thin. Pour the batter into the prepared pan and sprinkle with the cashews and remaining 2 tablespoons shredded coconut.

4. Bake until a toothpick inserted at the center comes out clean, 28 to 33 minutes. Let cool on a wire rack for 20 minutes. Run a knife around the edges, then invert the cake onto the rack and remove the pan and parchment. Re-invert onto a serving plate. Serve warm or at room temperature.

Lime-Glazed Sweet Potato and Coconut Cake

Start to finish: 3 hours (20 minutes active) / Servings: 12

100 grams (½ cup) coconut oil, melted and slightly cooled, plus more for pan

12 ounces orange-fleshed sweet potatoes, peeled and cut into 1-inch chunks

195 grams (1½ cups) all-purpose flour

60 grams (⅔ cup) unsweetened shredded coconut

2 teaspoons ground ginger

2 teaspoons baking powder

½ teaspoon baking soda

½ teaspoon table salt

199 grams (1 cup) packed dark brown sugar

1 tablespoon grated lime zest, plus 2 tablespoons juice

3 large eggs

¾ cup whole milk

1 tablespoon vanilla extract

93 grams (¾ cup) powdered sugar

In this cake inspired by the Macanese dessert called batatada, sweet potatoes give the crumb a plush, moist yet light texture. Yellow sweet potatoes are the traditional choice, but we preferred the color of orange-fleshed sweet potatoes. Both unrefined and refined coconut oil worked; the former has a fuller, more intense flavor and aroma that accentuate the shredded coconut in the cake. You'll need a food processor with at least an 11-cup capacity to accommodate the sweet potato puree.

Don't use sweetened shredded coconut. It will make the cake much too sweet.

1. **Heat the oven to 350°F** with a rack in the middle position. Coat a 13-by-9-inch metal baking pan with coconut oil. Place the sweet potatoes in a microwave-safe medium bowl, cover and microwave on high for about 5 minutes, stirring once halfway though, until the potatoes are completely tender. Carefully uncover and set aside to cool slightly.

2. **In a food processor,** combine the flour, coconut, ginger, baking powder, baking soda and salt. Process until the coconut is finely ground, 1 to 2 minutes. Transfer to a large bowl. In the processor, combine the brown sugar and lime zest, then process until fragrant, about 30 seconds. Add the sweet potatoes and process until completely smooth, 60 to 90 seconds, scraping the bowl as needed.

3. **Add the eggs, milk and vanilla,** then process until combined, about 10 seconds. With the machine running, add the melted coconut oil through the feed tube, then process until fully incorporated. Pour the sweet potato mixture into the dry ingredients and gently whisk to combine. Transfer the batter to the prepared pan and spread evenly.

4. **Bake until the cake is golden brown** and a toothpick inserted at the center comes out clean, 30 to 35 minutes. Let cool in the pan on a wire rack for 15 minutes.

5. **Meanwhile, in a small bowl,** whisk the powdered sugar and the lime juice until smooth. Brush the glaze evenly onto the warm cake. Let the cake cool completely in the pan, about 2 hours.

Stovetop Chocolate Cake

Start to finish: 35 minutes (10 minutes active), plus cooling
Servings: 8

Steaming a standard chocolate cake batter produced a light, moist cake, and let us avoid having to turn on the oven. To elevate the cake above the water that steams it, we fashioned a ring from foil. Brown sugar and espresso powder gave the cake complexity, while sour cream added richness and a welcome tang. We liked serving this cake dusted with powdered sugar or topped with whipped cream. If your Dutch oven has a self-basting lid—bumps or spikes on the underside—lay a sheet of parchment or foil over the top of the pot before putting the lid in place to prevent water from dripping onto the surface.

Don't open the Dutch oven too often while steaming, but do check that the water is at a very gentle simmer. You should see steam emerging from the pot. If the heat is too high, the water will boil away before the cake is cooked.

130 grams (1 cup)
all-purpose flour

29 grams (⅓ cup)
unsweetened cocoa powder

1 teaspoon baking soda

¼ teaspoon table salt

218 grams (1 cup packed)
light brown sugar

2 large eggs

1 teaspoon instant
espresso powder

½ cup sour cream

6 tablespoons (¾ stick)
salted butter, melted and
slightly cooled

1½ teaspoons vanilla extract

1. Cut an 18-inch length of foil and gently scrunch together to form a snake about 1 inch thick. Shape into a circle and set on the bottom of a large Dutch oven. Add enough water to reach three-quarters up the coil. Mist the bottom and sides of a 9-inch round cake pan with cooking spray. Line the bottom with a round of kitchen parchment, then mist the parchment. Place the prepared pan in the pot on top of the foil coil.

2. Sift the flour, cocoa powder and baking soda into a medium bowl, then whisk in the salt. In a large bowl, whisk the sugar and eggs until slightly lightened, about 30 seconds. Whisk in ½ cup water, the espresso powder, sour cream, butter and vanilla. Add the flour mixture and whisk gently until just combined.

3. Pour the batter into the prepared pan. Cover and heat on high until the water boils. Reduce to low and steam, covered, until the center of the cake is just firm to the touch, about 23 minutes.

4. Turn off the heat and remove the lid. Let stand until the cake pan is cool enough to handle. Transfer the pan to a wire rack, then run a paring knife around the edges. Let cool completely, then invert the cake onto a plate and remove the pan and parchment. Re-invert onto a serving plate.

Spanish Almond Cake (Tarta de Santiago)

Start to finish: 1 hour 10 minutes, plus cooling
(10 minutes active) / Servings: 8

This flourless cake from Galicia, Spain, traditionally is made with separated eggs and flavored with citrus and/or cinnamon. We liked it made more simply, with whole eggs and just a small measure of vanilla and almond extracts. A sprinkling of chopped almonds and coarse raw sugar on top gives the surface a chewy-crisp crust that contrasts wonderfully with the dense, plush crumb of the cake's interior. Crème fraîche and fresh berries are perfect accompaniments. Allow the cake to cool to room temperature before serving.

Don't underbake the cake. *Rather than use a skewer or tooth-pick to test the center for doneness, check the browning and crust development. The cake is ready when the surface is deeply browned and the crust feels firm when gently pressed with a finger.*

240 grams (1 cup plus
2 tablespoons) white sugar

3 large eggs, plus
3 large egg whites

¼ teaspoon table salt

¼ teaspoon almond extract

¼ teaspoon vanilla extract

250 grams (2½ cups)
blanched almond flour

35 grams (3 tablespoons)
turbinado or demerara sugar

37 grams (⅓ cup) sliced
almonds, roughly chopped

1. Heat the oven to 350°F with a rack in the middle position. Mist the bottom and sides of a 9-inch round cake pan with cooking spray, line the bottom with a round of kitchen parchment, then mist the parchment.

2. In a large bowl, combine the white sugar, whole eggs and egg whites, salt and both extracts. Whisk vigorously until well combined, 30 to 45 seconds; the mixture will be slightly frothy but the sugar won't be fully dissolved. Add the almond flour and whisk until incorporated. Pour the batter into the prepared pan, then sprinkle evenly with the turbinado sugar and chopped almonds. Bake until deeply browned and the crust feels firm when gently pressed with a finger, 45 to 55 minutes. Let cool in the pan on a wire rack for 10 minutes.

3. Run a knife around the edges of the cake, then invert onto a plate. Remove the pan and parchment then re-invert the cake onto a serving plate. Let cool completely before serving.

Maple–Browned Butter Pie

Start to finish: 3 hours (45 minutes active), plus cooling
Makes one 9-inch pie

For the crust:

98 grams (¾ cup) all-purpose flour, plus more for dusting

70 grams (½ cup) whole-wheat flour

13 grams (1 tablespoon) white sugar

¼ teaspoon table salt

7 tablespoons salted butter, cut into ½-inch pieces and chilled

6 to 8 tablespoons ice water

For the filling:

8 tablespoons (1 stick) salted butter, cut into 4 pieces

107 grams (½ cup) white sugar

111 grams (⅓ cup) honey

18 grams (2 tablespoons) fine cornmeal

½ teaspoon table salt

3 large eggs, plus 1 large egg yolk, well beaten

½ cup maple syrup (see headnote)

½ cup heavy cream

2 teaspoons vanilla extract

2 teaspoons cider vinegar

Maldon sea salt flakes, to serve (optional)

This dessert is the creation of Briana Holt of Tandem Coffee + Bakery in Portland, Maine. The nutty flavor and flaky yet sturdy texture of the whole-wheat pastry perfectly complement the buttery, silky custard filling. We recommend using the darkest maple syrup you can find so the smoky maple notes hold their own with the butter, eggs and cream. A sprinkle of flaky sea salt just before serving balances the filling's sweetness and adds a pleasing crunchy contrast, but this flourish is optional. The pie can be covered with plastic wrap and refrigerated for up to two days; bring to room temperature before serving.

Don't skip or skimp on the pie weights when prebaking the crust; they're essential for preventing the dough from shrinking, slipping and bubbling. We highly recommend using metal or ceramic pie weights. These materials conduct heat well, unlike dried beans and rice—common pantry-staple pie weights—so they aid with browning, and their hefty weight holds the dough in place as it bakes. Also, don't forget to lower the oven temperature to 325°F after placing the prebaked crust on a wire rack.

1. To make the crust, in a food processor, combine both flours, the sugar and salt; process until combined, about 5 seconds. Scatter the butter over the flour mixture, then pulse until the pieces are the size of small peas, 10 to 14 pulses. Transfer the mixture to a medium bowl. Sprinkle with 1 tablespoon ice water, then toss with a silicone spatula, making sure to scrape along the bottom of the bowl until the water has been absorbed. Repeat with the remaining ice water, adding it 1 tablespoon at a time, until the mixture forms pebbly clumps; you may not need all the water. Using your hands, press the clumps together firmly into a rough ball, then form the ball into a 4-inch disk. Wrap tightly in plastic wrap and refrigerate for 1 hour.

2. Heat the oven to 375°F with a rack in the middle position. On a well-floured counter and using a rolling pin, roll the dough into a 12-inch circle. Drape the dough over the rolling pin and transfer to a 9-inch pie plate. Gently ease the dough into the plate by lifting the edges while pressing down into the corners. Trim the edges, leaving a ½-inch overhang, then tuck the overhang under itself so the dough is flush with the rim of the pan. Using your fingers, crimp and flute the edge of the dough. Refrigerate uncovered until firm, about 30 minutes, or cover with plastic wrap and refrigerate for up to 8 hours.

3. Line the chilled dough with a large piece of heavy-duty foil, pressing the foil into the corners and up the sides of the pie plate, then fill evenly with 2 cups pie weights; loosely fold the foil to cover the fluted edge. Bake until the edges of the crust are light golden brown, about 35 minutes. Transfer to a wire rack and remove the foil and weights. Reduce the oven to 325°F.

4. While the crust is baking, make the filling. In a 10-inch skillet over medium-high, melt the butter. Cook, swirling the pan frequently, until the milk solids at the bottom are golden brown and the butter has a nutty aroma, 1 to 3 minutes. Scrape the butter into a medium heatproof bowl and let cool until warm, about 15 minutes.

5. To the browned butter, whisk in the sugar, honey, cornmeal and salt. Add the eggs and yolk, then whisk slowly and gently until well combined. Add the maple syrup, cream, vanilla and vinegar, then whisk gently until homogeneous. Pour the filling into the crust (it's fine if the crust is still warm).

6. Bake until the edges of the filling are puffed and the center jiggles when the pie plate is gently shaken, 40 to 45 minutes. Transfer to the wire rack and let stand until the filling is fully cooled and set, 3 to 4 hours. Sprinkle with Maldon salt (if using).

Pineapple-Cornmeal Upside-Down Cake

Start to finish: 1¼ hours, plus cooling / Servings: 12

---

162 grams (1¼ cups) all-purpose flour

Table salt

¾ teaspoon baking powder

½ teaspoon baking soda

½ teaspoon ground allspice

45 grams (5 tablespoons) fine yellow cornmeal

¾ cup buttermilk

140 grams (½ cup) whole-milk ricotta cheese

8 tablespoons (1 stick) salted butter, cut into 1-tablespoon pieces, room temperature, divided

3 tablespoons packed dark brown sugar

Eight ¼-inch-thick fresh pineapple rings (about 1 pound), cut into quarters

214 grams (1 cup) white sugar

2 large eggs, room temperature

Briana Holt, of Tandem Coffee + Bakery in Portland, Maine, makes a rich, sturdy buttermilk cake with cornmeal for texture and flavor, as well as ricotta cheese to keep the crumb tender and moist. We adapted her winning formula and paired the cake with fresh fruit to update the classic all-American pineapple upside-down cake. To avoid a soggy layer where cake and fruit meet—a common problem with upside-down cakes—we first cook the pineapple to remove excess moisture, and we make sure the fruit is hot when the batter is poured on top so it begins to bake upon contact. To get the timing right, begin mixing the batter after placing the pan with the pineapple in the oven. This gives you 5 to 10 minutes to finish the batter; if it's ready sooner, it can wait a few minutes. A nonstick cake pan works best because the dark finish speeds the bake time; if your pan is not nonstick, increase the oven temperature to 350°F and give the cake an extra 5 minutes or so to finish baking.

Don't use canned pineapple, as the fruit is thickly sliced and may not fully cook through. Its flavor also is dull and "cooked" compared to fresh. For convenience, however, you can use store-bought peeled and cored fresh pineapple sold in the produce section of the supermarket. Don't use part-skim ricotta cheese; the cake needs the richness of whole-milk ricotta.

1. **Heat the oven to 325°F** with a rack in the middle position. Mist a 9-by-2-inch round nonstick cake pan with cooking spray. In a medium bowl, whisk together the flour, ½ teaspoon salt, the baking powder, baking soda and allspice. In a small bowl, whisk together the cornmeal, buttermilk and ricotta.

2. **In a nonstick 12-inch skillet** over medium-high, combine 2 tablespoons of the butter, the brown sugar and a pinch of salt. Cook, stirring occasionally, until bubbling. Add the pineapple and cook, stirring often, until softened and caramelized and the liquid has nearly evaporated, 8 to 10 minutes.

3. **Transfer the pineapple and butter** mixture to the prepared cake pan, distributing the fruit in a single layer. Bake for 5 to 10 minutes while you prepare the batter.

4. **In a stand mixer** with the paddle attachment, beat the remaining 6 tablespoons butter and the white sugar on medium-high until light and fluffy, about 3 minutes. Reduce to medium and add the eggs one at a time, scraping the bowl with a spatula between additions, then beat until well combined, about 1 minute. With the mixer on low, add the cornmeal-buttermilk mixture, then beat until just combined, about 30 seconds; the mixture will look curdled. Scrape down the bowl.

5. With the mixer running on low, add the dry ingredients and mix just until the batter is evenly moistened, about 20 seconds; the batter will be thick. Using the spatula, scrape the bottom and sides of the bowl and give the batter a few folds to ensure no pockets of flour remain.

6. Remove the cake pan from the oven (close the oven door) and carefully scrape the batter onto the hot pineapple, then spread in an even layer and smooth the surface with the spatula. Bake until golden brown and a toothpick inserted at the center of the cake comes out clean, 40 to 45 to minutes.

7. Cool on a wire rack for 20 minutes. Run a paring knife around the pan to loosen the cake, then invert it onto a serving platter. Cool to room temperature.

Bête Noire

Start to finish: 1 hour 40 minutes, plus cooling and chilling
Servings: 12

___

8 tablespoons (1 stick) salted
butter, cut into 16 pieces, plus
more for the pan

12 ounces bittersweet
chocolate, finely chopped

4 ounces semisweet
chocolate, finely chopped

1 large navel orange

½ cup bourbon

160 grams (¾ cup) plus
70 grams (⅓ cup) white sugar

3 tablespoons black
peppercorns

2 tablespoons Angostura
bitters

6 large eggs, beaten

Whole-milk Greek yogurt,
to serve

Bête noire is a flourless chocolate cake that gets its silky, ultrasmooth, almost custard-like texture from the sugar syrup in the base, as well as from gentle baking. We bring a uniquely complex flavor to our version by caramelizing sugar with black peppercorns before dissolving the caramel with orange juice and bourbon. A combination of bittersweet and semisweet chocolate yields a rounder, richer finish than just one type of chocolate, while Angostura bitters lend a spiciness and depth that balance the sweetness of the dessert. We forgo the classic ganache coating and opt to use quickly candied orange zest for a garnish that adds contrasting color and texture. Though the cake requires at least 4 hours of chilling to fully set, it's best served at room temperature, so be sure to remove the cake from the refrigerator at least two hours before serving. For neat slices, dip the knife in hot water, then wipe it dry before each cut.

Don't use a whisk to combine the ingredients for the batter; a large silicone spatula is better. A whisk incorporates air, which leads to bubbles rising to the surface during baking and marring the smooth, shiny surface. Also, don't forget to run a knife around the edges of the cake the moment it comes out of the oven; loosening the edges from the sides of the pan prevents the cake from cracking as it cools. Finally, don't cover the cake before refrigerating, as a cover may trap condensation that can drip onto the cake.

___

1. Heat the oven to 275°F with a rack in the middle position. Coat the bottom and sides of a 9-inch springform pan with butter. Line the bottom of the pan with kitchen parchment, then butter the parchment. Set a wire rack in a rimmed baking sheet. In a large bowl, combine the bittersweet and semisweet chocolates and the butter; set a fine-mesh strainer across the bowl, then set aside.

2. Using a vegetable peeler, remove just the outer zest of the orange, not the white pith beneath, in long strips; set the strips aside. Halve the orange and juice it into a liquid measuring cup. Measure 3 tablespoons of the juice into a medium saucepan. Add the bourbon to the remaining juice in the measuring cup, then add enough water to equal 1 cup total liquid; set aside.

3. Add the 160 grams (¾ cup) sugar to the juice in the saucepan, then add the zest strips and peppercorns. Set over medium-high and cook, without stirring but occasionally swirling the pan, until the sugar dissolves, 1 to 2 minutes. Continue cooking, swirling the pan often, until the sugar caramelizes to deep mahogany brown and the peppercorns begin to pop, 4 to 5 minutes. Remove the pan from the heat and carefully pour in the orange juice-bourbon mixture; the caramel will bubble up and harden. Set the pan over medium, bring to a simmer and cook, stirring, until the caramel has dissolved and the peppercorns no longer stick together, 1 to 2 minutes. Remove from the heat and stir in the bitters.

4. Immediately pour the hot sugar syrup through the strainer into the chocolate-butter mixture; reserve the strained solids. Jostle the bowl to ensure the chocolate and butter are fully covered with syrup, then let stand for 2 to 3 minutes. Using a silicone spatula, gently stir until the mixture is well combined and completely smooth; it should be barely warm.

5. Add the beaten eggs to the chocolate mixture and stir with the spatula until homogeneous and glossy, 2 to 3 minutes. Pour into the prepared springform pan. Gently tap the sides of the pan to remove any air bubbles, then use the back of a spoon to smooth the surface. Set the pan on the prepared baking sheet and bake until the cake barely jiggles when the pan is gently shaken, about 45 minutes.

6. While the cake is baking, transfer the zest strips from the strainer to a small, shallow bowl, removing and discarding any peppercorns stuck to them. Sprinkle the strips with the 70 grams (⅓ cup) sugar, then toss until the strips are completely coated. Cover loosely and store at room temperature until ready to serve.

7. Remove the cake from the oven and immediately run a thin, sharp knife around the edges to loosen the sides of the cake from the pan. Cool to room temperature in the pan, then refrigerate uncovered for at least 4 hours or up to 24 hours.

8. About 2 hours before serving, remove the cake from the refrigerator. Remove the zest strips from the sugar and shake off excess sugar; reserve the sugar for another use. Cut the strips lengthwise into thin strips. Remove the sides of the spring-form pan. Arrange the zest slivers on the cake around the edges. Slice the cake and serve with small spoonfuls of yogurt.

French Almond-Rum Cake (Gâteau Nantais)

Start to finish: 3¼ hours (25 minutes active) / Servings: 12

For the cake:

16 tablespoons (2 sticks) salted butter, room temperature, plus more for the pan

6 large eggs

300 grams (1⅓ cups) white sugar

2 tablespoons grated lemon zest

250 grams (2½ cups) almond flour

¼ teaspoon table salt

80 grams (½ cup plus 2 tablespoons) all-purpose flour

6 tablespoons dark rum

For the rum syrup:

38 grams (3 tablespoons) white sugar

1 tablespoon whole allspice

1 teaspoon black peppercorns

½ cup dark rum

For the lemon glaze and garnish:

186 grams (1½ cups) powdered sugar

¼ teaspoon table salt

3 tablespoons lemon juice, plus more if needed

47 grams (½ cup) sliced almonds, toasted

Gâteau Nantais originated in Nantes in western France. Made with generous amounts of butter, eggs and almond flour, the cake's crumb is rich, moist and pleasantly dense, and becomes even more so after it's brushed with a rum syrup. The classic finish is a rum icing, but we opted instead for a bracing lemon glaze that brings out the lemon zest in the cake. You can serve the cake as soon as the glaze sets, but its flavor and texture improve if allowed to rest overnight at room temperature. If storing for longer, cover and refrigerate (up to three days), but bring to room temperature before serving. If you have a dark, nonstick cake pan (which transfers heat more quickly than lighter aluminum) reduce the temperature to 325°F and bake for the same time.

Don't use a small saucepan to make the syrup, and don't forget to remove the pan from the burner before pouring in the rum. These steps help ensure that the alcohol won't ignite. After removing the cake from the pan, don't re-invert it—leave it bottom side up, as the perfectly flat surface is easy to glaze. Finally, don't allow the cake to cool before brushing on the syrup; absorption is better if the cake is still hot.

1. To make the cake, heat the oven to 350°F with a rack in the middle position. Generously butter the bottom and sides of a 9-inch round cake pan. In a small bowl or liquid measuring cup, beat the eggs.

2. In a stand mixer with the paddle attachment, beat the butter, white sugar and lemon zest on medium until light and fluffy, 2 to 3 minutes, scraping the bowl as needed. Add the almond flour and salt, then beat on medium just until incorporated. With the mixer running, gradually add the eggs and beat until homogeneous, scraping the bowl as needed. Increase to medium-high and continue to beat until the mixture is light and fluffy, about 3 minutes, scraping the bowl once or twice. With the mixer running on low, gradually add the all-purpose flour and mix until incorporated, then slowly add the rum and beat just until combined. Scrape the bowl to ensure no pockets of flour or rum remain. The batter will be thick.

3. Scrape the batter into the prepared pan, then spread in an even layer and smooth the surface. Bake until deep golden brown and the center of the cake springs back when gently pressed, 50 to 55 minutes.

4. Meanwhile, to make the rum syrup, in a large saucepan combine the white sugar, ⅓ cup water, allspice and peppercorns. Bring to a boil over medium-high, stirring to dissolve the sugar, then boil for 3 minutes. Remove the pan from the heat and stir in the rum. Bring to a simmer over medium and cook for 2 minutes. Pour the mixture through a fine-mesh strainer set over a small bowl; discard the solids and set the syrup aside.

5. When the cake is done, let cool in the pan on a wire rack for 5 minutes. Invert the cake onto another wire rack; do not re-invert. Immediately brush the top and sides of the cake with all of the rum syrup. Cool to room temperature, about 1 hour. Transfer the cooled cake to a platter.

6. To make the lemon glaze, in a medium bowl, whisk together the powdered sugar and salt, then gradually whisk in the lemon juice; the glaze should be smooth, with the consistency of yogurt. If it is too thick, whisk in additional lemon juice ½ teaspoon at a time to attain the proper consistency.

7. Pour the glaze onto the center of the cake, then use an offset spatula or the back of a spoon to spread the glaze toward the edges, allowing just a small amount to drip down the sides. Sprinkle with the toasted almonds. Let stand at room temperature to set the glaze, about 1 hour.

Danish Dream Cake

Start to finish: 50 minutes, plus cooling / Servings: 12

210 grams (1¾ cups) cake
flour, plus more for the pan

1½ teaspoons baking powder

4 large eggs

214 grams (1 cup) white sugar

2 teaspoons vanilla extract

¼ teaspoon table salt

1¾ cups whole milk, divided

299 grams (1½ cups) dark
brown sugar

12 tablespoons (1½ sticks)
salted butter

340 grams (3¼ cups)
unsweetened shredded
coconut

In our version of drømmekage (dream cake), a light, fluffy vanilla cake meets a buttery coconut-brown sugar topping. The topping is spread onto the still-warm cake, then a brief stint under the broiler caramelizes the surface. When applying the topping, spoon it onto the cake's edges, which are sturdier than its center, then spread inward to cover the entire cake. You will need a broiler-safe 9-by-13-inch baking pan for this recipe (note that neither nonstick nor Pyrex is considered broiler-safe). For slicing, use a serrated knife to make clean cuts. Wrapped well and stored at room temperature, leftovers will keep two days.

Don't underwhip the eggs and sugar. The mixture should be beaten with the whisk attachment until pale and thick. The air incorporated during whipping is in part what makes the cake light. Also, don't forget to tent the finished cake with foil after broiling. It's an unusual step, but the foil traps a little moisture and prevents the topping from forming a brittle crust so the cake is easier to cut for serving.

1. Heat the oven to 350°F with a rack in the middle position. Mist a broiler-safe 9-by-13-inch baking pan with cooking spray, dust evenly with flour, then tap out the excess. In a small bowl, whisk together the flour and baking powder, then sift into a medium bowl or onto a large sheet of kitchen parchment.

2. In the bowl of a stand mixer with the whisk attachment, beat the eggs, white sugar, vanilla and salt on low until the sugar dissolves, about 20 seconds. Increase to medium-high and whip until the mixture is pale and thick, 5 to 6 minutes. Reduce to low, add about one-third of the flour mixture and mix until almost incorporated, about 10 seconds. With the mixer running, slowly pour in ½ cup of milk. Repeat with half of the remaining flour mixture and another ½ cup of the remaining milk. With the mixer still running, add the remaining flour mixture and mix just until no flour clumps remain, about 20 seconds. Using a silicone spatula, fold the batter, scraping along the bottom of the bowl, to ensure the ingredients are well combined. The batter will be very thin.

3. Pour the batter into the prepared pan. Bake until just beginning to brown and a toothpick inserted into the center of the cake comes out clean, about 22 minutes. Set the pan on a wire rack and heat the broiler.

4. In a medium saucepan, combine the remaining ¾ cup milk, the brown sugar and butter. Bring to a boil over medium-high, stirring to dissolve the sugar, then boil for 4 minutes. Remove from the heat, add the coconut and stir until evenly moistened. Spoon the topping onto the outer edges of the warm cake, then gently spread into an even layer over the surface. Broil until the top is bubbling and deep golden brown, 2 to 3 minutes, rotating the pan if needed for even browning.

5. Set the pan on a wire rack and tent with foil. Let cool for at least 30 minutes. Cut into pieces and serve warm or at room temperature.

German Apple Cake (Apfelkuchen)

Start to finish: 1½ hours, plus cooling / Servings: 8

---

130 grams (1 cup) all-purpose flour, plus more for the pan

1½ teaspoons baking powder

214 grams (1 cup) white sugar, plus 2 tablespoons for sprinkling

4 ounces almond paste, broken into rough ½-inch pieces

¼ teaspoon table salt

8 tablespoons (1 stick) salted butter, cool room temperature

3 large eggs, room temperature

2 teaspoons vanilla extract

2 small Granny Smith apples (about 12 ounces total), peeled, cored and halved lengthwise

Powdered sugar, to serve

Apfelkuchen, or apple cake, is a classic German sweet of which there are numerous versions. We were particularly fond of Luisa Weiss' recipe in "Classic German Baking," which is her adaptation of a recipe she found on a package of almond paste. Almond paste gives the cake's crumb a custardy richness, a moist, tender texture and a pleasant—but not overpowering—almond fragrance and flavor. Tangy-sweet sliced apples are fanned on top of the batter and baked into the surface to elegant effect. You will need an apple corer to punch out the cores from the apples before halving them. If you don't own one, halve the apples, then notch out the cores with a paring knife. This recipe was developed with a conventional—not nonstick—springform pan. If yours is nonstick or otherwise has a dark finish, to prevent overbaking, heat the oven to 350°F and begin checking for doneness on the low end of the time range.

Don't use marzipan in place of the almond paste. Marzipan is sweeter than almond paste. Also, make sure the almond paste is fresh and pliable, not dried out and hard, or it won't break down properly during mixing. The apples can be peeled, cored and halved before you make the cake batter, but don't slice the apple halves until the batter is in the pan. If sliced sooner, the apples may discolor.

1. Heat the oven to 375°F with a rack in the middle position. Mist a 9-inch spring-form pan with cooking spray, then dust with flour; tap out the excess. In a small bowl, whisk together the flour and baking powder.

2. In a stand mixer with the paddle attachment, mix the 214 grams (1 cup) sugar, almond paste and salt on low until the paste has broken into crumbly bits, 2 to 3 minutes. Add the butter and mix until combined, about 30 seconds. Increase to medium-high and beat until the mixture is pale and fluffy, about 3 minutes, scraping the bowl as needed. Reduce to medium, then add the eggs, one at a time, beating for about 20 seconds after each addition.

3. Scrape down the bowl, then add the vanilla and continue mixing on medium until well-combined, about 2 minutes. Reduce to low, add the flour mixture and mix just until the batter is evenly moistened, about 10 seconds; it will be thick. Using the spatula, scrape the bottom and sides of the bowl and give the batter a few folds to ensure no pockets of butter or flour remain. Transfer to the prepared pan and spread in an even layer, smoothing the surface.

4. Slice each apple half into ⅛-inch-thick half circles; do not separate the slices. With your hand, gently press down on each half to fan the slices. Divide the fanned apples into 8 equal portions without undoing the fanned effect. Slide a thin spatula or butter knife under the apples, then slide the slices off the spatula near the outer edge of the cake with the slices fanning outward from the center. One at a time, position another 6 sets of slices on the cake, creating an evenly spaced spoke pattern. Place the last set of apple slices in the center. Sprinkle the remaining 2 tablespoons sugar evenly over the top.

5. Bake until the edges of the cake are deep golden brown and a toothpick inserted at the center comes out clean, 50 to 60 minutes. Cool in the pan on a wire rack for 30 minutes. Run a paring knife around the inside of the pan to loosen, then remove the pan sides. Serve warm or at room temperature; dust with powdered sugar just before serving.

Cranberry and Candied Ginger Buckle

Start to finish: 1 hour 10 minutes (30 minutes active), plus cooling / Servings: 12

---

390 grams (3 cups) all-purpose flour, plus more for pan

214 grams (1 cup) white sugar

1 tablespoon baking powder

1 teaspoon ground cinnamon

¼ teaspoon table salt

12 tablespoons (1½ sticks), plus 2 tablespoons salted butter, cut into ½-inch cubes and chilled, reserved separately

42 grams (3 tablespoons) packed dark brown sugar

40 grams (⅓ cup) sliced almonds

3 large eggs

1 cup sour cream

1 tablespoon vanilla extract

12-ounce bag fresh or thawed frozen cranberries (3 cups)

85 grams (½ cup) finely chopped candied ginger

Powdered sugar, to serve (optional)

A buckle is a fruit-studded cake with a buttery crumb topping; it's a great breakfast treat, an excellent midday sweet alongside tea or coffee, or a not-too-heavy after-dinner dessert. Our version is loosely based on a recipe in "Rustic Fruit Desserts" by Cory Schreiber and Julie Richardson. Instead of making an entirely separate crumb topping, we remove a portion of the flour-sugar-butter mixture that is the base of the cake, then mix in a few additional ingredients to create a mixture that bakes up with just the right crumbly texture. Covered tightly, leftovers keep for up to three days at room temperature

Don't forget to thaw the cranberries if using frozen. *If the fruits are freezer-cold, they will cause the batter to stiffen, which will make mixing difficult.*

1. **Heat the oven to 375°F** with a rack in the middle position. Mist a 9-by-13-inch baking pan with cooking spray, dust evenly with flour, then tap out the excess.

2. **In a food processor,** combine the flour, white sugar, baking powder, cinnamon and salt. Pulse until well combined, 6 to 8 pulses. Scatter the 12 tablespoons butter over the dry ingredients and pulse until the mixture resembles coarse crumbs, about 20 pulses. Transfer to a large bowl, then measure out 165 grams (1 cup) of the mixture and return it to the food processor. To the food processor, add the brown sugar, almonds and remaining 2 tablespoons butter, then pulse until the mixture begins to clump and resembles wet sand, about 20 pulses; transfer to a medium bowl and set aside.

3. **In another medium bowl,** whisk together the eggs, sour cream and vanilla. Pour into the large bowl of flour-butter mixture and fold the batter with a silicone spatula until only a few streaks of flour remain. Add the cranberries and candied ginger, then fold until evenly distributed; the batter will be thick. Transfer to the prepared pan and spread in an even layer.

4. **Using your hands,** squeeze the almond-flour mixture into rough ½-inch clumps, then scatter evenly over the batter in the pan. Bake until the topping is golden brown and a toothpick inserted at the center comes out clean, 40 to 45 minutes. Cool in the pan on a wire rack for at least 30 minutes before slicing. Dust with powdered sugar just before serving, if desired.

Sweet Fresh Corn Pudding

Start to finish: 1 hour (40 minutes active) / Servings: 6

___

8 tablespoons (1 stick) salted butter, cut into 8 pieces, plus more for ramekins

135 grams (½ cup plus 2 tablespoons) white sugar, divided, plus more for ramekins

4 teaspoons grated lemon zest, divided

65 grams (½ cup) all-purpose flour

2 cups corn kernels

1 cup heavy cream

⅛ teaspoon table salt

2 large eggs, separated, plus 2 large egg whites, room temperature

2 teaspoons vanilla extract

Powdered sugar, to serve (optional)

This is our adaptation of a recipe from Vivian Howard's "Deep Run Roots" that transforms sweet summer corn into a light, elegant dessert. Fresh corn is best, as the kernels are tender and succulent; you'll need three ears to yield the 2 cups kernels. Frozen corn kernels work, too, but make sure to fully thaw them, then pat dry with paper towels to remove excess moisture. For convenience, the unbaked, sugar-sprinkled soufflés can be covered with plastic wrap and refrigerated up to two hours before baking. Or if you don't plan to serve all six, extras can be covered tightly with plastic wrap then foil and frozen for up to a week. To bake from frozen; simply uncover (do not thaw), set on a baking sheet and bake for 25 to 30 minutes; they may rise slightly less than when baked fresh, but still will be delicious. Serve hot from the oven with fresh blackberries, raspberries and/or blueberries.

Don't forget to thoroughly clean the bowl and beaters you use to whip the egg whites. Any residual oils will prevent the whites from attaining the proper airiness. Don't open the oven during baking; this will cause the soufflés to deflate.

___

1. Heat the oven to 400°F with a rack in the middle position. Generously butter six 6-ounce ramekins. Sprinkle each with 1 teaspoon sugar and turn to coat, then tap out the excess. Place the ramekins on a rimmed baking sheet; set aside.

2. In a small bowl, combine 27 grams (2 tablespoons) white sugar with 1 teaspoon of lemon zest. Using your fingers, work the zest and the sugar together, then set aside.

3. In a large saucepan, whisk together the flour and 54 grams (¼ cup) of the white sugar. In a blender, combine the corn, cream and salt, then puree just until smooth, about 15 seconds. Whisk the puree into the flour mixture, then set the pan over medium and cook, stirring constantly with a silicone spatula, until the mixture reaches a boil and forms a thick, shiny paste, 5 to 7 minutes. Remove from the heat, then stir in the butter 2 tablespoons at a time until fully incorporated. Transfer to a large bowl and cool to room temperature, about 5 minutes. Whisk in the egg yolks, the remaining 3 teaspoons zest and the vanilla.

4. In a stand mixer with the whisk attachment, whip the egg whites on medium-high until light and foamy. With the mixer running, slowly add the remaining 54 grams (¼ cup) white sugar, then continue to whip until the whites hold soft peaks when the whisk is lifted, 1 to 2 minutes; do not overwhip. Using a silicone spatula, fold about a quarter of the whites into the corn mixture until just a few streaks remain. Gently fold in the remaining whites, taking care not to deflate them.

5. Divide the mixture evenly among the prepared ramekins. Run the tip of your thumb along the inside edge of each ramekin to create a small channel; this gives the soufflés better rise. Sprinkle with the lemon sugar, dividing it evenly.

6. Bake the soufflés until golden brown and well risen, 20 to 22 minutes; they should jiggle slightly when the baking sheet is gently shaken. Do not open the oven door during baking. Transfer the baking sheet to a wire rack. Dust the soufflés with powdered sugar (if using) and serve right away.

Yogurt Panna Cotta with Sumac Syrup

Start to finish: 3¾ hours (45 minutes active) / Servings: 6

1½ teaspoons unflavored powdered gelatin

2 cups plain whole-milk yogurt

2 lemons

1 cup heavy cream

72 grams (⅓ cup) plus 54 grams (¼ cup) white sugar, divided

2 large thyme sprigs

Table salt

1 tablespoon ground sumac

This panna cotta is more nuanced than standard all-cream panna cotta. Just the right amount of yogurt adds a creamy suppleness and a subtle tang, and lemon zest and thyme lend their perfume. Panna cotta is made in individual portions that often are unmolded for serving, but we simply bring the ramekins to the table, each topped with a spoonful of sweet-tart sumac- and lemon-infused syrup. Sumac is a Middle Eastern spice with a brick-red hue and tangy, citrusy flavor; look for it in well-stocked supermarkets and Middle Eastern grocery stores.

Don't use nonfat or low-fat yogurt. Whole-milk yogurt is essential for smooth, lush richness. And don't use Greek yogurt, which is too thick.

1. In a small bowl, sprinkle the gelatin over 2 tablespoons water; set aside. Place the yogurt in a medium heatproof bowl or 1-quart liquid measuring cup, then place a fine-mesh strainer across the top; set aside. Using a vegetable peeler, remove eight 4-inch-long strips of zest from 1 lemon; grate the zest from the second lemon and reserve separately from the zest strips. Squeeze ¼ cup juice from the lemons.

2. In a small saucepan, combine the cream, 4 strips lemon zest, the 72 grams (⅓ cup) sugar, thyme and a pinch of salt. Cook over medium, stirring, until the mixture begins to simmer at the edges. Remove from the heat, add the gelatin mixture and stir until fully dissolved. Cover and let stand for 5 minutes.

3. Strain the cream mixture into the yogurt; discard the solids in the strainer. Whisk in the grated lemon zest. Divide the mixture evenly among six 6-ounce ramekins. Refrigerate, uncovered, until cold and set, at least 3 hours. If storing for longer than 3 hours, cover with plastic wrap and refrigerate for up to 3 days.

4. Meanwhile, in a small saucepan, combine the lemon juice, the remaining 4 zest strips, the 54 grams (¼ cup) sugar, ½ cup water and a pinch of salt. Simmer over medium and cook, stirring occasionally, until reduced to ⅓ cup, 5 to 7 minutes. Remove from the heat, stir in the sumac and cool to room temperature.

5. Pour the syrup into a fine mesh strainer set over a small bowl; discard the solids. Cover and refrigerate until cold or for up to 3 days. To serve, uncover the ramekins and spoon chilled sumac syrup onto each panna cotta, dividing it evenly.

Glazed Maple–Whole Wheat Muffins

Start to finish: 1½ hours, plus cooling and drying
Makes 12 muffins

For the muffins:

32 grams (¼ cup) all-purpose flour, plus more for the pan

251 grams (1¾ cups) whole-wheat flour

72 grams (½ cup) fine yellow cornmeal

2 large eggs, plus 2 large egg yolks

342 grams (1½ cups) plain whole-milk yogurt

¼ cup maple syrup

1 tablespoon vanilla extract

1 tablespoon grated lemon zest

107 grams (½ cup) white sugar

1 tablespoon ground cinnamon

1 tablespoon baking powder

½ teaspoon baking soda

1 teaspoon table salt

8 tablespoons (1 stick) salted butter, melted and cooled

For the glaze:

248 grams (2 cups) powdered sugar

½ cup maple syrup, room temperature

4 tablespoons (½ stick) salted butter, melted and cooled

1 tablespoon lemon juice

⅛ teaspoon table salt

These two-grain, maple-sweetened breakfast treats were inspired by muffins baked by Briana Holt at Tandem Bakery + Coffee in Portland, Maine. The smoky, caramel notes of pure maple syrup accentuate the nuttiness of whole-wheat flour, and a modest amount of cornmeal in the batter adds pleasing texture. Be sure to use fine cornmeal, not coarse stoneground, so the granules hydrate and soften properly. And for the richest maple flavor, use the darkest syrup you can find. These muffins like to stick to the pan, so be sure to generously oil both the cups and the flat surface of the muffin pan, then dust the cups with flour, even if your pan is nonstick. An easier alternative is to use baking spray such as Baker's Joy or Pam Baking; these formulations include flour for simple one-step pan prep.

Don't use Greek yogurt, as its moisture content is too low to properly hydrate the cornmeal and whole-wheat flour. Don't make the glaze in advance—mix the ingredients just before you're ready to glaze the muffins so it won't begin to dry and harden. Finally, don't glaze the muffins until they're fully cooled to room temperature or the glaze won't cling.

1. To make the muffins, heat the oven to 375°F with a rack in the middle position. Generously mist a standard 12-cup muffin pan with cooking spray, dust with all-purpose flour and tap out the excess. In a small bowl, whisk together the whole-wheat flour and cornmeal. In a large bowl, whisk together the eggs and yolks. Add the yogurt, maple syrup, vanilla and lemon zest; whisk until thoroughly combined. Add the whole wheat flour–cornmeal mixture (reserve the bowl), then stir with a silicone spatula until evenly moistened; let stand for 15 minutes to hydrate.

2. Meanwhile, in the now-empty small bowl, whisk together the all-purpose flour, white sugar, cinnamon, baking powder, baking soda and salt. After the whole-wheat flour mixture has hydrated for 15 minutes, add the sugar mixture and stir with the spatula until just incorporated, then add the melted butter and fold until homogeneous. Cover and refrigerate for 15 minutes.

3. Scoop the batter (it will have become lighter and fluffier) into the cups of the prepared muffin pan, dividing it evenly; the cups will be full. Bake until light golden brown and a toothpick inserted at the centers comes out with a few crumbs attached, 15 to 17 minutes. Cool in the pan on a wire rack for 15 minutes, then remove the muffins from the pan (if needed, rap it against the counter to loosen the muffins), setting them right side up directly on the rack. Cool completely.

4. To make the glaze, in a medium bowl, whisk together the powdered sugar, maple syrup, melted butter, lemon juice and salt. Set the wire rack with the muffins in a rimmed baking sheet. One at a time, hold the base of a muffin and dip the top into the glaze to fully and evenly coat. Turn the muffin upright while allowing excess glaze to drip back into the bowl, then set right side up on the rack. Let the glaze dry for about 30 minutes before serving.

Double Chocolate Cake with Honey-Rosemary Syrup

Start to finish: 1 hour 40 minutes (40 minutes active), plus cooling / Servings: 12

For the cake:

130 grams (1 cup) all-purpose flour, plus more for the pan

1 teaspoon baking powder

½ teaspoon baking soda

¼ teaspoon table salt

113 grams (4 ounces) bittersweet chocolate, finely chopped

40 grams (½ cup) unsweetened cocoa powder

¾ cup boiling water

10 tablespoons (1¼ sticks) salted butter, room temperature

214 grams (1 cup) white sugar, plus 2 tablespoons for sprinkling

4 large eggs, room temperature

2 teaspoons vanilla extract

½ cup buttermilk

For the syrup:

71 grams (⅓ cup) white sugar

113 grams (⅓ cup) honey

3 sprigs rosemary

Pinch of table salt

This unique syrup-soaked chocolate cake is our adaptation of a dessert by Briana Holt, who flavors her cake with piney, peppery juniper berries. We opted for herbal, resinous (and more readily available) fresh rosemary. Either is a delicious match for chocolate. If you'd like to try juniper, in a small skillet over medium, toast 2 teaspoons dried juniper berries until fragrant; let cool, then pulverize in a spice grinder to a fine powder. Whisk 1 teaspoon of the ground juniper into the dry ingredients for the cake; use the remainder in place of the rosemary to make the syrup, but when transferring the syrup from the saucepan to a liquid measuring cup, pour it through a fine-mesh strainer. However you choose to flavor it, make the cake a day ahead if you can; its texture improves as the syrup slowly soaks in. Store leftovers in an airtight container at room temperature for up to two days.

Don't measure the ¾ cup water and then bring it to a boil or too much will steam off as it heats. Instead, boil a larger quantity of water in a kettle or saucepan, then measure the ¾ cup. Don't underbake the cake or it will sink as it cools. When testing doneness, make sure the toothpick comes out clean and dry from the cake's center. Finally, to ensure even absorption, drizzle on the syrup in four applications, with a brief rest between each. If applied all at once, the syrup will pool on the surface and turn the top soggy.

1. To make the cake, heat the oven to 350°F with a rack in the middle position. Mist a 9-inch springform pan with cooking spray, then dust with flour; tap out the excess. In a small bowl, whisk together the flour, baking powder, baking soda and salt.

2. In a medium bowl, combine the chocolate and cocoa. Pour the boiling water over the top, jiggling the bowl to ensure all the chocolate is submerged. Let stand for 1 to 2 minutes, then whisk until smooth; set aside.

3. In a stand mixer with the paddle attachment, beat the butter and 214 grams (1 cup) sugar on low until just combined. Increase to medium-high and beat until light and fluffy, 2 to 3 minutes. Reduce to medium and add the eggs one at a time, scraping the bowl once halfway through. Reduce to low, then add the chocolate mixture and vanilla; scrape the bowl. With the mixer running on low, add about a third of the flour mixture, followed by half of the buttermilk, then scrape the bowl. With the mixer running, add half of the remaining flour mixture, followed by the remaining buttermilk, then finish with the remaining flour mixture. Fold the batter by hand to ensure it is homogeneous. The batter will be thick but pourable.

4. Transfer the batter to the prepared pan and spread in an even layer. Sprinkle evenly with the remaining 2 tablespoons sugar. Bake until the cake forms a thin, crisp center crust and a toothpick inserted at the center comes out clean, 40 to 50 minutes.

5. Meanwhile, make the syrup. In a small saucepan, combine the sugar, honey, rosemary, salt and ⅓ cup water. Bring to a boil over medium, stirring occasionally to dissolve the sugar. Transfer to a liquid measuring cup and cool to room temperature.

6. When the cake is done, cool in the pan on a wire rack for 15 minutes. Remove and discard the rosemary from the cooled syrup, then drizzle about a quarter of the syrup onto the warm cake. The syrup will not be immediately absorbed; let stand for about 5 minutes to allow it to soak in. Drizzle on the remaining syrup in 3 more applications, allowing a 5-minute rest between each.

7. Cool the cake completely in the pan, at least 1 hour, but preferably overnight (if storing overnight, wrap the pan in plastic and store at room temperature). To serve, run a paring knife around the pan to loosen the cake, remove the sides of the pan and cut the cake into wedges.

Semolina-Sesame Cake

Start to finish: 4¼ hours (30 minutes active)
Servings: 16 to 18

___

6 tablespoons (¾ stick) salted butter, cut into 6 pieces, plus more for the pan

170 grams (1 cup) semolina flour

68 grams (¾ cup) unsweetened shredded coconut

72 grams (½ cup) fine yellow cornmeal

321 grams (1½ cups) white sugar, divided

84 grams (¼ cup) honey

Four 3-inch strips lemon zest, plus 2 tablespoons lemon juice

¾ teaspoon table salt, divided

454 grams (2 cups) plain whole-milk yogurt

30 grams (2 tablespoons) tahini

½ teaspoon baking soda

1 tablespoon baking powder

35 grams (¼ cup) raw sesame seeds

2 teaspoons orange flower water (optional)

The start-to-finish time is long, but this tender-crumbed, syrup-soaked cake, very loosely based on Lebanese sfouf, is simple to make and requires little hands-on effort. We toast the semolina, coconut and cornmeal to heighten the flavors and aromas, then after cooling, we allow them to hydrate in a mixture of yogurt, tahini and water. This results in a uniformly moist, evenly textured crumb. Because it is soaked with syrup, the cake keeps well, so it can be made in advance. Tightly covered, it will keep for a day at room temperature; after that, store it in the refrigerator for up to two additional days, but bring to room temperature before serving.

Don't add the yogurt to the toasted semolina-coconut mixture until the mixture has cooled for about 30 minutes. If added when hot, the semolina quickly absorbs the yogurt and the cake bakes up with a crumbly texture. .

___

1. In a 12-inch skillet over medium, melt the butter. Add the semolina, coconut and cornmeal, then cook, stirring often, until the mixture begins to brown, 4 to 5 minutes. Transfer to a large bowl and cool until barely warm to the touch, about 30 minutes.

2. Meanwhile, in a medium saucepan, combine 214 grams (1 cup) of the sugar, the honey, lemon zest, ¼ teaspoon salt and ½ cup water. Bring to a boil over medium, stirring to dissolve the sugar, then cook until slightly more viscous, about 5 minutes. Transfer to a 2-cup liquid measuring cup or small bowl; you should have about 1¼ cups. Cover and set aside until ready to use.

3. Heat the oven to 350°F with a rack in the middle position. Butter the bottom and sides of a 9-inch square baking pan. Into the cooled semolina mixture, whisk the yogurt, tahini and ½ cup water. Let stand at room temperature for another 30 minutes to hydrate.

4. In a small bowl, whisk together the remaining 107 grams (½ cup) sugar, the remaining ½ teaspoon salt, the baking soda and baking powder. Whisk the mixture into the semolina-yogurt mixture. Transfer to the prepared pan and spread into an even layer. Sprinkle the sesame seeds evenly over the surface and bake until golden brown, 35 to 40 minutes. Cool on a wire rack for 10 minutes.

5. Remove and discard the lemon zest from the syrup, then stir in the lemon juice and orange flower water (if using). With a toothpick, poke holes in the warm cake at 1-inch intervals. Slowly and evenly pour on the syrup. Let stand for 2 hours. To serve, cut into pieces directly in the pan.

Mexican Sweet Corn Cake

Start to finish: 1¼ hours (25 minutes active), plus cooling
Servings: 10 to 12

___

3 medium ears fresh corn, preferably yellow, husked

36 grams (¼ cup) fine yellow cornmeal

14-ounce can sweetened condensed milk

57 grams (¼ cup) plain whole-milk yogurt

165 grams (1¼ cups plus 2 tablespoons) all-purpose flour

2 tablespoons cornstarch

2 teaspoons baking powder

¼ teaspoon table salt

2 large eggs, plus 2 large egg yolks

½ cup grapeseed or other neutral oil

Powdered sugar, to serve

This simple baked treat is ubiquitous in Mexican food markets, street stalls and restaurants. Called panqué de elote, pan de elote or pastel de elote, its texture lands somewhere between cake and cornbread while hinting at custard. At La Cocina de Mi Mamá in Mexico City, we had it for breakfast, as it's commonly served. But finished with a dusting of powdered sugar, we think it also makes a casual, homey dessert. Cornmeal is not a typical ingredient in panqué de elote; we add a small amount to account for the fact that fresh Mexican corn used for making this type of cake is starchier and drier than the fresh corn available in the U.S. If you have more than 250 grams (1½ cups) corn after cutting the kernels from the ears, it's best to save the extra for another use rather than use it in this recipe; the additional moisture may make the cake too wet. Yellow corn yields a cake with a warm golden hue, but white corn also works.

Don't use frozen corn kernels—it results in a dense, gummy texture. Made with fresh corn, the cake's crumb is much lighter and softer. After adding the flour mixture to the corn puree, don't whisk vigorously. Gentle mixing, just until no pockets of flour remain, will minimize gluten development so the cake bakes up tender.

___

1. **Heat the oven to 350°F** with a rack in the middle position. Mist a 9-inch round cake pan with cooking spray. Using a chef's knife, cut the kernels from the ears of corn. Measure 250 grams (1½ cups) kernels and add to a blender; if you have extra corn, reserve it for another use. To the blender, add the cornmeal, condensed milk and yogurt, then puree until smooth, 15 to 20 seconds, scraping down the blender as needed. Let stand for 10 minutes. Meanwhile, in a small bowl, whisk together the flour, cornstarch, baking powder and salt.

2. **To the blender,** add the whole eggs and yolks, and the oil; blend on low until smooth, 5 to 10 seconds. Pour the puree into a large bowl. Add the flour mixture and whisk just until evenly moistened and no lumps of flour remain. Transfer to the prepared cake pan and bake until golden and a toothpick inserted into the center of the cake comes out clean, 40 to 45 minutes.

3. **Cool in the pan on a wire rack** for 30 minutes. Run a paring knife around the pan to loosen the cake, then invert directly onto the rack and lift off the pan. Re-invert the cake onto a serving platter and cool completely, about 1 hour. Serve dusted with powdered sugar.

French Spice Bread
(Pain d'Épices)

Start to finish: **1 hour 25 minutes (10 minutes active),** plus cooling / Makes **one 9-inch loaf**

Honey-based spice breads and cakes have been produced in one form or another throughout Europe since the Middle Ages. For good reason: The hygroscopic honey retains moisture, ensuring the breads remain moist during storage. Its antibacterial properties also act as a preservative. Meanwhile, the spices—and therefore the flavor—only improve with time. We wanted a lighter, less sweet alternative to the more common gingerbread, something that tasted as good straight up as it did toasted and topped with butter and marmalade for a quick breakfast or afternoon-coffee accompaniment. This French version is just that. For a fruitier version, add 1 cup golden raisins, chopped dates, figs or dried apricots. Melting the butter in a liquid measuring cup in the microwave, then using the same cup for the honey, made it easy to measure out and add the honey; it slid right out. For maximum spice flavor, we used pepper and three kinds of ginger. If you can't find crystallized (candied) ginger, just skip it; the cake still will be delicious. And if you can't find ground mace, substitute ¼ teaspoon each of ground nutmeg and allspice.

Don't use baking spray in place of butter. While spray is fine in many situations, butter helps create the dark crust that sets pain d'épices apart from other quick breads. Use melted butter and a pastry brush to liberally coat the inside of the pan.

8 tablespoons (1 stick) salted butter, melted, plus more for the pan

228 grams (1¾ cups) all-purpose flour

100 grams (1 cup) almond flour

1½ teaspoons ground cinnamon

1 teaspoon baking soda

1 teaspoon ground ginger

½ teaspoon ground mace

Table salt and ground black pepper

334 grams (1 cup) honey

½ cup whole milk

2 large eggs

2 tablespoons minced crystallized ginger

1 tablespoon finely grated fresh ginger

2 teaspoons grated orange zest

1. Heat the oven to 325°F with a rack in the upper-middle position. Coat the bottom and sides of a 9-by-5-inch loaf pan with butter. In a medium bowl, whisk together both flours, the cinnamon, baking soda, ground ginger, mace, ¼ teaspoon salt and ½ teaspoon pepper. In a large bowl, whisk together the butter and honey until smooth. Add the milk, eggs, crystallized ginger, fresh ginger and orange zest; whisk until thoroughly combined.

2. Add the flour mixture to the wet ingredients and fold only until no dry flour remains. Transfer the batter to the prepared pan. Bake until firm to the touch and a toothpick inserted at the center comes out with a few moist crumbs, 65 to 70 minutes. Let cool in the pan on a wire rack for 10 minutes. Remove from the pan and let cool completely, about 2 hours.

Brown Butter–Cardamom Banana Bread

Start to finish: 1 hour 15 minutes (25 minutes active)
Makes one 9-inch loaf

For flavorful banana bread without additional effort, we paired one of banana's most complementary spices, cardamom, with nutty browned butter. Toasting the cardamom briefly in the hot butter intensified the flavor. For just the right texture, we found we needed two leaveners. Baking powder gave the bread lift; baking soda resulted in a well-browned top and a dense crumb. Measuring the bananas in a 1-cup dry measuring cup was important; the difference in moisture between four small and four large bananas could throw off the balance of the ingredients. While we preferred the deeper flavor of dark brown sugar here, light brown works just as well. Sprinkling granulated sugar over the top of the loaf just before baking created a crisp, brown crust that we loved.

8 tablespoons (1 stick) salted butter, plus more for the pan

260 grams (2 cups) all-purpose flour

1 teaspoon baking powder

1 teaspoon baking soda

½ teaspoon table salt

1¼ teaspoons ground cardamom

2 cups mashed bananas (about 4 very ripe bananas)

149 grams (¾ cup packed) dark brown sugar

2 large eggs

2 teaspoons vanilla extract

1 tablespoon white sugar

1. Heat the oven to 350°F with a rack in the upper-middle position. Lightly coat a 9-by-5-inch loaf pan with butter. In a large bowl, whisk together the flour, baking powder, baking soda and salt.

2. In a medium saucepan over medium, melt the butter. Once melted, continue to cook, swirling the pan often, until the butter is fragrant and deep brown, 2 to 5 minutes. Remove the pan from the heat and immediately whisk in the cardamom. Carefully add the bananas (the butter will sizzle and bubble up) and whisk until combined. Add the brown sugar, eggs and vanilla, then whisk until smooth. Add the banana mixture to the flour mixture and, using a silicone spatula, fold until just combined and no dry flour remains.

3. Transfer the batter to the prepared pan and sprinkle evenly with the white sugar. Bake until the loaf is well browned, the top is cracked and a toothpick inserted at the center comes out clean, 50 to 55 minutes, rotating the pan halfway through. Cool the bread in the pan on a wire rack for 10 minutes, then turn out the loaf and cool completely before serving. Cooled bread can be wrapped tightly and stored at room temperature for up to 4 days or refrigerated for a week.

Broken Phyllo Cake with Orange and Bay

Start to finish: 2 hours (30 minutes active), plus cooling
Servings: 10 to 12

For the syrup:

214 grams (1 cup) white sugar

Four 3-inch strips orange zest, plus ½ cup orange juice

3-inch cinnamon stick

2 cardamom pods, lightly smashed

3 bay leaves

For the cake:

227 grams (8 ounces) phyllo, thawed

214 grams (1 cup) white sugar

1 tablespoon grated orange zest

240 grams (1 cup) whole-milk Greek yogurt

1 cup grapeseed or other neutral oil

5 large eggs

1 tablespoon baking powder

¼ teaspoon table salt

In "Aegean," chef Marianna Leivaditaki tells of her attempts at portokalopita, a cake made with dry, broken-up bits of phyllo dough in place of flour. Like many Mediterranean sweets, the cake is doused with syrup after emerging from the oven, which partly explains the tendency toward a heavy, sodden texture. She recounts that it was a friend's mother who baked the best, lightest version of portokalopita she'd ever had, and she obtained the recipe. The phyllo, cut into strips and dried in the oven, creates a layered structure in the cake that, when soaked with syrup, takes on a moist, pudding-like consistency. Greek yogurt and oil add richness while eggs bind and lift, with an assist from baking powder. The cake is citrusy with grated orange zest, and the soaking syrup is infused with cinnamon, cardamom and bay for added flavor and fragrance. (Leivaditaki suggests dusting the cake with bay dust, but we put the bay into the syrup.) If you like, serve slices of the cake topped with a spoonful of lightly sweetened cream whipped with a little Greek yogurt. Leftovers keep well wrapped in the refrigerator for up to four days; serve slices slightly chilled or at room temperature.

Don't forget to zest the orange *before juicing it. To remove the zest in strips, a Y-style peeler is the best tool. You will need two large oranges for this recipe—one to provide the zest strips and juice for the syrup and one to supply the grated zest for the cake. Also, don't use a cake pan that's less than 2 inches deep. In a shallower pan, the syrup may overflow the rim. Lastly, don't allow the cake to cool before pouring on the syrup. And after the second half of the syrup is poured on, don't be alarmed if the syrup floods the pan. As the cake cools, it will absorb the syrup.*

1. To make the syrup, in a small saucepan, combine the sugar, orange zest strips and juice, cinnamon, cardamom, bay and ½ cup water. Bring to a simmer over medium-high, stirring to dissolve the sugar, then transfer to a 2-cup liquid measuring cup or small bowl; you should have about 1⅔ cups. Cool to room temperature.

2. Meanwhile, to make the cake, heat the oven to 350°F with a rack in the middle position. Mist a 9-by-2-inch round cake pan with cooking spray, line the bottom with a round of kitchen parchment, then mist the parchment.

3. Roll the thawed phyllo lengthwise, then slice the roll crosswise ½ inch thick. Transfer to a rimmed baking sheet, using your hands to unfurl and separate the strips. Distribute in an even layer and bake until brittle and light golden brown, 15 to 18 minutes, scraping up and flipping the phyllo once about halfway through; it's fine if many of the pieces break as they're turning. Cool to room temperature on the baking sheet.

4. In a stand mixer with the paddle attachment, beat the sugar and grated orange zest on medium until fragrant, about 30 seconds. With the mixer running on low, add the yogurt, oil, eggs, baking powder and salt. Increase to medium and beat until the mixture is well combined, about 1 minute, scraping the bowl as needed. Remove the bowl from the mixer and, if needed, scrape any zest that is stuck to the paddle attachment back into the bowl.

5. Add half of the phyllo to the batter base and, using a silicone spatula, fold until the phyllo is reduced in volume and almost evenly moistened. Add the remaining phyllo and fold until well combined and no dry patches of phyllo remain. Pour the batter into the prepared pan and spread in an even layer without compressing the phyllo. Bake until deep golden brown and a toothpick inserted at the center of the cake comes out clean, 45 to 50 minutes. When the cake is almost done, remove and discard the zest strips, cinnamon, cardamom and bay from the syrup.

6. Set the cake on a wire rack. Using a toothpick, immediately poke holes through the cake's thickness every ½ inch or so. Slowly pour half the syrup evenly onto the warm cake, then let stand for about 5 minutes to allow the syrup to soak in. Slowly pour on the remaining syrup. The cake will not immediately take in all of the syrup, so liquid will flood the pan; this is normal. Cool until room temperature and all the syrup has been absorbed, at least 2 hours.

7. Run a paring knife around the inside edge of the pan to loosen the cake, then invert onto a platter. Lift off the pan and peel off the parchment. Re-invert the cake onto a serving plate.

Banana Custard Pie with Caramelized Sugar

Start to finish: 2¼ hours (40 minutes active), plus cooling
Servings: 8 to 10

___

195 grams (1½ cups) all-purpose flour

½ teaspoon table salt, divided

57 grams (4 tablespoons) salted butter, cut into pieces

57 grams (¼ cup) vegetable shortening, cut into pieces

1 pound ripe but firm bananas

2 large eggs, plus 1 large egg yolk

¼ cup whole milk

14-ounce can sweetened condensed milk

1 teaspoon vanilla extract

23 grams (3 tablespoons) white sugar (optional, for caramelizing the surface)

___

Handmade, freshly baked pies sold by the slice are a specialty of the beach town of Yelapa in Jalisco state on Mexico's west coast. Inspired by those Yelapa delights, recipe writer Paola Briseño González created a simple, rustic banana custard pie with a sturdy, sandy-textured crust. We adapted her recipe, blending a banana into the custard mixture instead of only studding it with slices, for a creamy filling suffused with tropical flavor. As with most custard pies, this crust must be prebaked, so you will need pie weights for this recipe (about 2 cups works best to prevent shrinking and slipping during prebaking). And if you own a kitchen torch, this pie is a good reason to dig it out. It's an optional step, but sprinkling the baked, cooled pie with sugar and brûléeing it until caramelized elevates the dessert, giving it a crackly-crisp surface and a lovely dappled look. Serve slices with lightly sweetened, softly whipped cream. Covered well, leftovers will keep in the refrigerator for up to three days (though if you caramelized the surface, the sugar crust will gradually soften).

Don't use underripe bananas, but don't use overripe ones, either. The bananas should be ripe so they're sweet and creamy but not so ripe that they're brown and mushy in texture. Don't make the dough in advance. It's easiest to work with when just made. Also, don't roll it too thin; aim for ¼-inch thickness. If the dough tears when putting it into the pie plate, simply patch it; it's very forgiving that way.

___

1. Heat the oven to 375°F with a rack in the middle position. In a medium bowl, whisk together the flour and ¼ teaspoon salt. Make a well in the center; set aside.

2. In a small saucepan, combine the butter, shortening and ¼ cup water. Bring to a simmer over medium-high, stirring to melt the solids. As soon as they're melted and the mixture is simmering, pour it into the well of the dry ingredients. Working quickly, stir with a silicone spatula until the dry ingredients are evenly moistened and without any dry patches; the dough will be very soft and resemble wet mashed potatoes. Turn it out onto a large sheet of plastic wrap and, using your hands, form it into a 6- to 8-inch disk.

3. Cover the dough disk with another large sheet of plastic wrap and roll it into a 12-inch round of even thickness. Peel off the top sheet of plastic. Using the bottom sheet of plastic, carefully flip the round into a 9-inch pie plate, centering it as best you can. Ease the dough, still on the plastic wrap, into the corners and up the sides of the pie plate. Carefully peel off the plastic. If needed, patch any tears in the dough. Trim the excess dough and flute or crimp the edge. Carefully line the dough with a large sheet of foil, gently pressing it into the corners and up the sides, then fill with about 2 cups pie weights.

4. Bake until the dough is set, about 20 minutes. Carefully lift out the foil with weights, then prick the shell all over with a fork to deflate any air bubbles and prevent additional ones from forming. Bake until the pie shell is lightly browned, another 12 to 15 minutes. Transfer to a wire rack to cool until barely warm to the touch. Reduce the oven to 325°F.

5. Peel the bananas and slice them into ¼-inch rounds. Lay as many slices in the pie shell as will fit in a single, tightly packed layer, then set the pie plate on a rimmed baking sheet. Add the remaining banana slices to a blender along with the whole eggs plus yolk, milk, condensed milk, vanilla and the remaining ¼ teaspoon salt. Blend until smooth, 15 to 30 seconds.

6. Pour the mixture into the pie shell, taking care not to overfill it (some of the banana slices will rise to the surface); the pie shell may not hold all of the filling, depending on how much it shrank during prebaking. Carefully transfer the baking sheet to the oven and bake until the filling is puffed, lightly browned at the edges and the filling jiggles only slightly when the pie plate is gently shaken, 55 to 65 minutes. Transfer to a wire rack and cool to room temperature.

7. If caramelizing the surface, sprinkle the sugar evenly onto the cooled pie. Using a kitchen torch, caramelize the sugar until spotty brown. Serve within an hour, before the sugar crust softens. (The pie also is good served chilled, but if caramelizing the sugar, do so just before serving, as refrigeration will soften the sugar crust.)

Ricotta-Semolina Cake with Caramelized Apples

Start to finish: 1¼ hours, plus cooling / Servings: 8 to 10

28 grams (2 tablespoons) salted butter, plus 170 grams (12 tablespoons) salted butter, softened, divided

2 medium crisp, sweet apples (about 8 ounces each), peeled, cored and sliced into ¼-inch-thick wedges

26 grams (2 tablespoons) packed dark brown sugar

3 large eggs, separated, room temperature

Pinch of table salt

214 grams (1 cup) white sugar, divided

15-ounce container whole-milk ricotta cheese (see headnote), room temperature

1 teaspoon vanilla extract

150 grams (¾ cup) semolina flour

Adapted from "Summer Kitchens" by Olia Hercules, this cake-cheesecake hybrid is inverted out of the baking pan to reveal a layer of silky, buttery, golden-hued apples. The ricotta-based cake is deliciously rich but whipped egg whites folded into the batter give the crumb a little lightness, while semolina lends both structure and texture. We suggest using firm, sweet apples that won't easily break down with cooking; Honeycrisp, Fuji and Gala are good varieties. So that the egg whites achieve the proper amount of lift, be sure the mixer bowl and whisk attachment are perfectly clean, as any trace of fat will prevent full aeration. If you happen to have two bowls for your mixer, use one to whip the whites and one to mix the batter—no need to transfer the whites after whipping them. Store leftovers in the refrigerator tightly wrapped or in an airtight container for up to three days; bring to room temperature or gently rewarm in a 300°F oven for a few minutes before serving.

Don't use artisanal or homemade ricotta. Regular supermarket ricotta works best in the recipe because it's softer, moister and more finely curded than many high-end types. And be sure the ricotta is at room temperature before use. If it's cold, it will cause the butter to stiffen and make mixing more difficult.

1. **Heat the oven to 400°F** with a rack in the middle position. Mist an 8-inch square baking pan with cooking spray; line the bottom with a square of kitchen parchment and mist the parchment.

2. **In a 12-inch nonstick skillet** over medium-high, cook the 28 grams (2 tablespoons) butter, stirring, until the butter begins to brown, about 30 seconds. Add the apples, stir to coat, then distribute in an even layer. Cook without stirring until beginning to brown, about 2 minutes. Using a silicone spatula, stir and flip the apples, then redistribute in an even layer. Cook, stirring occasionally, until the apples are tender and translucent, about another 2 minutes. Off heat, add the brown sugar and stir gently until melted and combined with the apples. Transfer the mixture to the prepared pan and gently press into an even layer that covers the entire bottom; set aside.

3. **In a stand mixer** with the whisk attachment, beat the egg whites on medium-high until frothy, about 20 seconds. With the mixer running, add the salt, then gradually add 54 grams (¼ cup) of white sugar. Continue to beat until the whites hold soft peaks, about 2 minutes. Transfer the whites to a medium bowl; reserve the mixer bowl and attachment (no need to wash them).

4. In the now-empty mixer bowl, combine the remaining 170 grams (12 tablespoons) butter and the remaining 160 grams (¾ cup) white sugar. Using the whisk attachment, beat on medium-high until lightened and fluffy, about 3 minutes, scraping the bowl once or twice. With the mixer running on medium-low, add the yolks one at a time, beating until incorporated, about 20 seconds, after each addition. Stop the mixer and scrape the bowl. Add the ricotta and vanilla, then beat on medium-low just until incorporated, 25 to 30 seconds; do not overmix (the mixture will not be smooth). Remove the bowl from the mixer and fold by hand with the spatula, scraping the bottom and sides of the bowl, to ensure the mixture is well combined.

5. Sprinkle the semolina over the ricotta mixture and fold with the spatula until incorporated. Scoop about ½ cup of the whipped egg whites onto the mixture and fold them in to lighten and loosen the base. Scrape on the remaining whites, then gently fold until no white streaks remain. Scrape the batter on top of the apples and, using a small offset spatula, gently spread into a smooth, even layer. Bake until golden brown and the center is just slightly wobbly when the pan is gently jiggled, 30 to 35 minutes.

6. Cool in the pan on a wire rack to room temperature, 1½ to 2 hours. Run a paring knife around the inside edge of the pan to loosen the cake, then invert onto a platter. Lift off the pan and peel off the parchment.

Italian Flourless Chocolate Torta

Start to finish: 1 hour (30 minutes active), plus cooling
Servings: 8 to 10

___

141 grams (10 tablespoons) salted butter, cut into 10 pieces, plus more for the pan

6 ounces bittersweet chocolate, chopped

20 grams (¼ cup) Dutch-processed unsweetened cocoa powder, plus more for dusting

1 tablespoon instant espresso powder

4 large eggs, separated, room temperature

160 grams (¾ cup) white sugar, divided

100 grams (1 cup) almond flour

½ teaspoon table salt

3 tablespoons dark rum

Pasticceria Gollini in Vignola, Italy, not far from Modena, is home to the sumptuous flourless chocolate cake known as torta Barozzi. Created in 1886 by pastry chef Eugenio Gollini and named for Jacopo Barozzi da Vignola, a 16th century architect, the much-loved sweet continues today to be produced according to a closely guarded secret recipe. Impostor recipes abound, as professional and home bakers alike have attempted to re-create the dessert, and we ourselves set out to devise a formula. It's well known that torta Barozzi is made without wheat flour (and is therefore gluten free). Instead, a combination of ground peanuts and almonds—along with whipped egg whites—deliver a structure that's somehow rich and dense yet remarkably light. We found that we could skip the peanuts, as almond flour alone worked well. To achieve a complex chocolatiness, we use both cocoa powder and bittersweet chocolate (ideally, chocolate with about 70 percent cocoa solids). Instant espresso powder accentuates the deep, roasty, bitter notes and a dose of dark rum lifts the flavors with its fieriness. Serve with lightly sweetened mascarpone or whipped cream, or with vanilla gelato.

Don't use natural cocoa. The recipe will still work, but the cake will be lighter in color and not quite as deep in flavor as when made with Dutch-processed cocoa. Take care not to overbake the cake. Remove it from the oven when a toothpick inserted at the center comes out with a few sticky crumbs clinging to it. After 30 to 45 minutes of cooling, the cake is inverted out of the pan; don't worry about re-inverting it. True torta Barozzi is left upside-down for cutting and serving; we do the same with ours.

___

1. **Heat the oven to 350°F** with a rack in the middle position. Butter an 8-inch square pan, line the bottom with a parchment square and butter the parchment.

2. **In a medium saucepan over medium,** melt the butter. Remove from the heat and add the chocolate, cocoa and espresso powder. Let stand for a few minutes to allow the chocolate to soften, then whisk until the mixture is smooth; cool until barely warm to the touch.

3. **In a large bowl,** vigorously whisk the egg yolks and 107 grams (½ cup) of the sugar until lightened and creamy, about 30 seconds. Add the chocolate mixture and whisk until homogeneous. Add the almond flour and salt, then whisk until fully incorporated. Whisk in the rum; set aside.

4. **In a stand mixer** with the whisk attachment or in a large bowl with a hand mixer, whip the egg whites on medium-high until frothy, 1 to 2 minutes. With the mixer running, gradually add the remaining 53 grams (¼ cup) sugar, then beat until the whites hold soft peaks, about 2 minutes. Add about a third of the whipped whites to the yolk-chocolate mixture and fold with a silicone spatula to lighten and loosen the base. Scrape on the remaining whites and gently fold in until no streaks remain. Transfer to the prepared pan and gently shake or tilt the pan to level the batter.

5. **Bake until the cake** is slightly domed and a toothpick inserted at the center comes out with a few crumbs attached, 30 to 35 minutes. Cool in the pan on a wire rack for 30 to 45 minutes; the cake will deflate slightly as it cools.

6. **Run a paring knife around** the inside edge of the pan to loosen the cake, then invert onto a platter; if needed, peel off and discard the parchment. Cool completely. Dust with cocoa before serving.

Chèvre Cheesecake with Black Pepper–Graham Crust

Start to finish: 2½ hours (40 minutes active), plus cooling and refrigerating / Servings: 12 to 16

---

7 tablespoons salted butter, melted and cooled slightly, divided

195 grams (1¾ cups) graham cracker crumbs

1 teaspoon ground black pepper

1 teaspoon plus 156 grams (¾ cup) white sugar, divided

½ teaspoon table salt, divided

454 grams (1 pound) fresh goat cheese (chèvre), cool room temperature

Two 8-ounce (226-gram) packages cream cheese, cool room temperature

Two 8-ounce (226-gram) containers crème fraîche, cool room temperature

112 grams (⅓ cup) honey

4 large eggs, plus 2 large egg yolks, cool room temperature

1 tablespoon grated lemon zest

Angie Mar, chef/owner of Beatrice Inn in New York City, may be best known for her artistry with all things meat, but we're smitten with her chèvre cheesecake, the recipe for which is found in her book "Butcher + Beast." Made with equal parts chèvre (fresh goat cheese) and cream cheese plus a generous measure of crème fraîche, the cake has the perfect amount of savoriness and tanginess—and a surprisingly light texture despite its richness. In addition to scaling Mar's recipe to fit into a standard 9-inch springform, we mixed lemon zest into the filling to lift the flavor and add citrusy notes that play off the black pepper in the crust. The best way to gauge doneness of the cake is with an instant thermometer inserted through the side (in the area where the filling has risen above the pan), with the probe angled slightly down and to the center; 145°F to 150°F is the finished temperature. To cut clean slices, warm the knife blade by dipping it into a pitcher of hot water; wipe the blade dry before and after each cut, and rewarm it as needed. Covered tightly with foil and refrigerated, the cheesecake keeps well for up to four days, though the crust softens over time.

Don't forget to allow the cheeses to warm to cool room temperature before mixing. If they're refrigerator-cold, the filling is more likely to wind up with lumps. Note that this recipe involves multiple oven settings: 300°F, 450°F, off (with the cake still inside and the door propped open) and 250°F. Don't forget to run a knife around the cheesecake after the cake has cooled for 10 minutes—this helps prevent cracking.

1. **Heat the oven to 300°F** with a rack in the lower-middle position. Brush the bottom of a 9-inch round springform pan with 1½ teaspoons of melted butter; reserve the brush. In a large bowl, stir together the cracker crumbs, pepper, 1 teaspoon sugar and ¼ teaspoon salt. Add 6 tablespoons of the remaining melted butter and stir until evenly moistened. Transfer to the prepared pan and use the bottom of a ramekin or dry measuring cup to firmly press into an even layer. Bake until the crust is fragrant and golden, 15 to 17 minutes. Let cool on a wire rack until barely warm, 15 to 20 minutes.

2. **Brush the inside walls of the pan** with the remaining 1½ teaspoons of melted butter, then set on a rimmed baking sheet. Increase the oven temperature to 450°F. In a stand mixer with the paddle attachment, beat the goat cheese and cream cheese on medium until creamy, airy and well combined, about 3 minutes, scraping the bowl and paddle once or twice. Add the remaining 156 grams (¾ cup) sugar and the remaining ¼ teaspoon salt, then

beat on medium-high until the mixture is smooth and fluffy, about 1 minute, scraping the bowl and paddle halfway through.

3. With the mixer on medium-low, gradually add the crème fraîche, followed by the honey. Scrape the bowl and paddle. With the mixer on low, add the whole eggs one at a time, beating until combined after each addition and scraping the bowl and paddle after the first 2 eggs. Add the yolks and beat until fully incorporated.

4. Detach the bowl from the mixer, and use a spatula to stir in the lemon zest, scraping the bottom of the bowl, until evenly distributed. Pour into the springform pan; the pan may be filled to the rim. If necessary, smooth the surface with the spatula.

5. Bake the cheesecake on the baking sheet for 20 minutes; the filling will have risen above the rim of the pan and the surface will be golden. Turn off the oven and prop open the door with the handle of a wooden spoon for 10 minutes; the surface of the cake will darken slightly during this time.

6. Close the oven door and heat the oven to 250°F. Continue to bake until the center reaches 145°F to 150°F (insert an instant-read thermometer through the side of cake, in the area where it has risen above the pan, with the probe slightly angled down so the tip is at the center of the cake), 35 to 40 minutes.

7. Set the baking sheet with the cheesecake on a wire rack and cool for 10 minutes. Run a narrow-bladed knife around the edge of the cheesecake to loosen the sides, then cool for 1½ to 2 hours; the cake will deflate slightly as it cools. Refrigerate uncovered until cold, at least 6 hours or up to overnight (if refrigerating for longer than 3 hours, cover tightly with foil after the cheesecake is fully chilled). Remove the pan sides before slicing.

Yogurt Loaf Cake with Coriander and Orange

Start to finish: 1 hour (15 minutes active), plus cooling
Makes one 8½-inch loaf cake

228 grams (1¾ cups) all-purpose flour, plus more for the pan

1 tablespoon ground coriander, toasted (see headnote)

2 teaspoons baking powder

¼ teaspoon table salt

3 large eggs

214 grams (1 cup) white sugar, plus 2 teaspoons for sprinkling

2 tablespoons grated orange zest

120 grams (½ cup) plain whole-milk yogurt

2 teaspoons vanilla extract

½ cup grapeseed or other neutral oil

In France, gâteau au yaourt is a dead-simple anytime cake that uses an entire container of yogurt, then employs the empty container as the measuring device for the flour, sugar and oil. The crumb is fine and moist, similar to a pound cake, but not nearly as rich. Since there is no standardized sizing for yogurt in the U.S., we devised a recipe with conventional measurements. Toasting the coriander softens its flavor and brings out its aroma; in a small skillet over medium, toast the spice, stirring often, until fragrant, 3 to 5 minutes, then transfer to a small bowl or plate to cool. Macerated fresh berries are the perfect accompaniment to the cake. Toss sliced fresh strawberries, raspberries and blueberries with a little sugar and let stand until juicy. Tightly wrapped and stored at room temperature, the cake will keep for up to three days.

Don't forget to flour the loaf pan after misting it with cooking spray to ensure the cake doesn't stick. Make sure to invert the baked cake out of the pan after about 10 minutes of cooling. This also will help prevent sticking as well as prevent the sides from becoming too moist. And the cake will cool faster, too.

1. **Heat the oven to 350°F** with a rack in the middle position. Mist a 8½-by-4½-inch loaf pan with cooking spray, dust evenly with flour, then tap out the excess.

2. **In a medium bowl,** whisk together the flour, coriander, baking powder and salt. In a large bowl, whisk the eggs, 214 grams (1 cup) sugar and orange zest until well combined and lightened in color, about 1 minute. Add the yogurt and vanilla, then whisk until well combined. Add the oil and whisk until homogeneous. Add the flour mixture and whisk just until no streaks remain. The batter will be very fluid.

3. **Pour the batter** into the prepared pan and sprinkle evenly with the remaining 2 teaspoons sugar. Bake until a toothpick inserted at the center of the cake comes out with few crumbs attached, 40 to 45 minutes.

4. **Let the cake cool in the pan on a wire rack** for 10 minutes. Invert the cake onto the rack, lift off the pan and turn the loaf upright. Cool completely, about 1½ hours, before slicing and serving.

Almond-Coconut Cake with Cherries and Pistachios

Start to finish: 1¼ hours (20 minutes active), plus cooling
Servings: 10 to 12

141 grams (10 tablespoons) salted butter, melted and cooled, plus more for the pan

100 grams (1 cup) almond flour

86 grams (⅔ cup) all-purpose flour

40 grams (½ cup) shredded unsweetened coconut

1 teaspoon baking powder

½ teaspoon table salt

3 large eggs, room temperature

106 grams (½ cup) plus 1 tablespoon white sugar

73 grams (⅓ cup) packed light brown sugar

½ teaspoon almond extract

255 grams (9 ounces) fresh sweet cherries, stemmed and pitted, or 225 grams (1½ cups) frozen pitted sweet cherries, thawed and patted dry

48 grams (⅓ cup) unsalted roasted pistachios, chopped

Powdered sugar, to serve (optional)

In 2012 in London, Itamar Srulovich and Sarit Packer opened Honey & Co., a tiny restaurant that serves up thoughtfully prepared Middle Eastern comfort food. The couple has since opened Honey & Smoke and Honey & Spice and have authored multiple books. This rustic cake is our adaptation of a recipe from their first title, "Honey & Co.: The Cookbook." Dense, moist and filled from top to bottom with fruity, nutty flavor and texture, the cake is great as dessert, brunch or with coffee or tea any time of the day. Honey & Co. flavors it with mahleb, a baking spice made from the seeds from a variety of cherry; we use easier-to-source almond extract. Store leftovers in an airtight container at room temperature for up to three days.

Don't use sweetened shredded coconut, as it will make the cake too sugary. Unsweetened shredded coconut—not wide shavings—is the right variety. If fresh cherries are out of season, don't hesitate to use thawed frozen cherries—they're equally tasty on the cake. Lastly, don't worry that inverting the cake out of the pan will cause the toppings to fall off. The fruit and nuts are baked in, so only a few small pieces may come loose, if any.

1. Heat the oven to 350°F with a rack in the middle position. Butter a 9-inch round cake pan, line the bottom with a round of kitchen parchment, then butter the parchment.

2. In a medium bowl, whisk together both flours, the coconut, baking powder and salt. In a large bowl, combine the eggs, the 106 grams (½ cup) white sugar, brown sugar and almond extract, then whisk until well combined. Whisk in the melted and cooled butter. Whisk in the dry ingredients until homogeneous; the batter will be thick but pourable.

3. Pour the batter into the prepared pan. Using your hands, tear the cherries in half over the batter, allowing the juice to fall onto the surface, then drop the pieces onto the surface in an even layer. Sprinkle with the pistachios and the remaining 1 tablespoon white sugar.

4. Bake until a toothpick inserted at the center of the cake comes out clean, 50 to 55 minutes. Cool on a wire rack until barely warm to the touch, about 1 hour. Run a paring knife around the inside edge of the pan to loosen the cake, then invert onto a platter. Lift off the pan and peel off the parchment. Re-invert the cake onto a platter. If desired, dust with powdered sugar just before serving.

Amalfi-Style Lemon Cake

Start to finish: 1 hour (25 minutes active), plus cooling
Servings: 10 to 12

---

428 grams (2 cups) white
sugar, divided

2 tablespoons grated lemon
zest, plus ¾ cup lemon juice

260 grams (2 cups) all-
purpose flour

2 teaspoons baking powder

½ teaspoon table salt

198 grams (14 tablespoons)
salted butter, room
temperature

3 large eggs, room
temperature

½ cup whole milk, room
temperature

Giovanna Aceto, whose family owns a generations-old lemon farm on the Amalfi Coast of Italy, showed us how to make torta al limone, a simple lemon cake popular throughout the region. Naturally, Aceto used farm-grown lemons, a variety called sfusato amalfitano that mature to the size of softballs; the fruits are wonderfully fragrant and have a subtle sweetness. Lucky for us, in recipes such as torta al limone, regular supermarket lemons work perfectly well, as their tartness can be offset by adding a little more sugar. Lemon zest perfumes the cake, then a lemon syrup is poured on after baking to keep the crumb moist and add a layer of tangy-sweet flavor. We use a Bundt pan as a substitute for the conical fluted pan that Aceto uses for her torta. The fastest, simplest way to prep the Bundt pan is with baking spray, which is similar to cooking spray, but with added flour. Alternatively, mix 2 tablespoons melted butter and 1½ tablespoons flour, then brush the mixture onto the pan, making sure to coat all the peaks and valleys.

Don't forget to grate the zest before juicing the lemons; grating is much easier when the fruits are whole. Also, don't allow the cake to cool for more than about 10 minutes before the first application of syrup. Absorption is better and more even when the crumb is warm. But after pouring on the second half of the syrup, don't let the cake cool for longer than 30 minutes or it may be difficult to remove from the pan.

1. Heat the oven to 350°F with a rack in the middle position. Mist a 12-cup nonstick Bundt pan with baking spray. In a small sauce-pan, combine 214 grams (1 cup) of sugar and the lemon juice. Cook over medium-high, stirring, until the sugar dissolves, 4 to 5 minutes. Pour into a 2-cup glass measuring cup or small bowl; you should have about 1¼ cups syrup. Cool while you make and bake the cake.

2. In a medium bowl, whisk together the flour, baking powder and salt. In a stand mixer with the paddle attachment, beat the remaining 214 grams (1 cup) sugar and the lemon zest on medium until fragrant, 1 to 2 minutes, scraping the bowl once or twice. Add the butter and beat on medium-high until the mixture is light and fluffy, scraping the bowl as needed, 3 to 5 minutes.

3. With the mixer running on low, add the eggs one at a time, beating until combined after each addition and scraping down the bowl as needed. Increase to medium and beat until well aerated, about 3 minutes. With the mixer running on low, add about one-third of the flour mixture followed by about half of the milk. Next, add about half of the remaining flour mixture, then the remaining milk and finally the remaining flour mixture. Mix on low until just combined, about 1 minute. Fold the batter a few times with the spatula to ensure no pockets of flour remain; the batter will be thick.

4. Scoop the batter into the prepared pan and spread in an even layer. Bake until golden brown and a toothpick inserted into the cake about 2 inches from the edge comes out clean, 35 to 40 minutes.

5. Cool in the pan on a wire rack for 10 minutes. Poke the cake with a toothpick every ½ inch or so, inserting the toothpick as deeply as possible into the cake. Slowly pour half of the syrup evenly over the cake, then let stand for about 5 minutes to allow the syrup to soak in.

6. Slowly pour the remaining syrup onto the cake, then cool for 30 minutes. If the cake looks stuck to the sides in any spots, including the center tube, carefully loosen those areas by insert-ing a thin-bladed knife between the cake and the pan. Invert the cake onto a platter, lift off the pan and cool to room temperature.

Chocolate-Hazelnut Cream Cake

Start to finish: 1¾ hours, plus cooling and chilling
Servings: 12

___

For the whipped ganache:

170 grams (6 ounces) white chocolate, finely chopped

1 packet (7 grams) unflavored gelatin

2 cups heavy cream

8-ounce container mascarpone cheese

2 tablespoons honey

For the cake:

40 grams (½ cup) unsweetened Dutch-processed cocoa powder (see headnote), plus more for the pan

216 grams (1⅔ cups) all-purpose flour

321 grams (1½ cups) white sugar

½ teaspoon baking powder

½ teaspoon baking soda

¼ teaspoon table salt

2 large eggs

1 cup buttermilk, preferably low-fat

⅔ cup grapeseed or other neutral oil

2 teaspoons vanilla extract

For the soaking syrup:

71 grams (⅓ cup) white sugar

1 teaspoon instant espresso powder

For assembly:

95 grams (⅓ cup) chocolate-hazelnut spread, such as Nutella

35 grams (¼ cup) toasted skinned hazelnuts, half roughly chopped, half very finely chopped, reserved separately

This impressive and sumptuous special-occasion dessert, composed of two "go-to" recipes from Dominique Ansel's book "Everyone Can Bake," is easier to make than you might think. We did modify both his chocolate cake and the mascarpone whipped ganache, and we also added a coffee syrup for moistening the cake before assembly. We fold a chocolate-hazelnut spread (such as Nutella) into half of the whipped ganache to sandwich between the cake layers; the remaining whipped ganache is spread on top, creating a unique striped effect. The cake itself has the deepest, richest flavor and color when made with a good-quality dark Dutch-processed cocoa powder—we had the best results with Valrhona. Part of the beauty of this dessert is that the cake and filling can be made ahead; even after assembly, the dessert will hold nicely for up to 24 hours. We recommend making the ganache base and the cake a day in advance and refrigerating them separately. The following day, whip the ganache, assemble the dessert and refrigerate for at least two hours or for up to an entire day. For neat slices, cut the cake with a serrated knife that's been warmed in hot water and wiped dry. To store leftovers, press plastic wrap directly against the cakes' cut sides and refrigerate for up to two days.

Don't whip the ganache before the mixture is completely cold and set. If whipped too soon, it won't attain the proper light, fluffy volume. When spreading the whipped ganache on the top layer of cake, the less you manipulate it, the better. Overworking may cause the ganache to become grainy and lose its velvety smoothness. Finally, don't allow the cake to stand for more than about 30 minutes before serving; if it loses too much of its chill, the filling softens and the layers may begin to slide apart.

___

1. To make the ganache, put the white chocolate in a medium bowl; set aside. In a small bowl, stir together the gelatin and 2 tablespoons water; set aside. In a medium saucepan over medium, combine the cream, mascarpone and honey. Cook, stirring often, until the mascarpone is fully melted and the mixture begins to bubble at the edges, 6 to 8 minutes. Remove from the heat, add the gelatin mixture and whisk until completely dissolved. Immediately pour the cream mixture over the white chocolate, then let stand for about 1 minute.

2. Whisk the chocolate mixture until completely smooth. Press plastic wrap directly against the surface and cool to room temperature, then refrigerate until well chilled and fully set, at least 4 hours or up to 24 hours.

5. Pour the batter into the prepared pan, then rap the pan 4 or 5 times against the counter to release any large air bubbles. Bake until a toothpick inserted at the center of the cake comes out clean, about 45 minutes. Cool in the pan on a wire rack for about 20 minutes. Run a paring knife around the edge of the cake to loosen, then invert it onto the rack and lift off the pan. Remove and discard the parchment, then carefully re-invert the cake and let cool completely. Wrap the cake in plastic wrap and set on a large, flat plate. Refrigerate for at least 4 hours or up to 24 hours.

6. When ready to assemble, make the soaking syrup. In a 1-cup liquid measuring cup or small microwave-safe bowl, stir together the sugar and ¼ cup water. Microwave on high for 30 seconds, then stir until the sugar is fully melted and the syrup is clear. Add the instant espresso and whisk until dissolved. Cool to room temperature.

7. Unwrap the chilled cake and set it on a cutting board or other flat surface. Using a pastry brush, brush the sides of the cake evenly with 1½ tablespoons of the syrup. Using a serrated knife and a gentle sawing motion, carefully slice off and remove the domed surface of the cake, creating a level top. Now slice the cake horizontally into 2 even layers. Carefully lift off the top layer and set aside; transfer the bottom layer to a cake platter. Brush the surface of both cake layers with all of the remaining syrup, dividing it evenly; the layers should be well moistened but not soggy.

8. Transfer the chilled ganache to the bowl of a stand mixer. Using the whisk attachment, whip on high until lightened and fluffy, about 5 minutes, scraping the bowl once. Meanwhile, put the chocolate-hazelnut spread in a large bowl and stir to smooth and soften. Scoop half (about 440 grams/3 cups) of the whipped ganache into the bowl containing the chocolate-hazelnut spread, and, using a silicone spatula, gently fold until homogeneous. Scoop the chocolate-hazelnut ganache onto the center of the bottom cake layer, then use an offset icing spatula to spread it in an even layer, all the way to the edges of the cake.

9. Using a wide metal spatula, lift the top cake layer and gently center it on the chocolate-hazelnut ganache layer; do not press on the cake. Using the whisk attachment, re-whip the remaining ganache on high until smooth, about 30 seconds. Scoop it onto the center of the top layer of the cake and spread it in an even layer or, if desired, create swirls in the surface. Scatter the finely chopped nuts over the top, followed by the roughly chopped nuts. Refrigerate uncovered for at least 2 hours or for up to 24 hours. Before serving, let the cake stand at room temperature for 20 to 30 minutes.

3. To make the cake, heat the oven to 350°F with a rack in the middle position. Mist the bottom and sides of a 9-by-2-inch round cake pan with cooking spray, line the bottom with a round of kitchen parchment, then mist the parchment. Using a paper towel, evenly spread the oil. Dust the pan evenly with cocoa and knock out any excess.

4. In a large bowl, whisk together the cocoa, flour, sugar, baking powder, baking soda and salt. In a medium bowl, whisk the eggs, buttermilk, oil and vanilla until homogeneous. Add the liquid ingredients to the dry ingredients, and, using a large silicone spatula, fold until the batter is completely smooth.

Swedish "Sticky" Chocolate Cake

Start to finish: 45 minutes (20 minutes active), plus cooling
Servings: 10 to 12

12 tablespoons (1½ sticks) salted butter, cut into 2 pieces

40 grams (½ cup) unsweetened cocoa powder, plus more to serve

249 grams (1¼ cups) packed dark brown sugar

4 large eggs

¼ teaspoon table salt

98 grams (¾ cup) all-purpose flour

75 grams (½ cup) semisweet chocolate chips

This gooey-centered chocolate cake, a popular sweet in Sweden, is called kladdkaka, which translates as "sticky cake." It's a snap to make, with only seven ingredients and an easy dump-and-stir mixing method. For our version, we brown the butter to add a subtle nuttiness, and we use brown sugar for its molasses notes. The cake can be served warm or at room temperature. Top slices with whipped cream, ice cream or gelato.

Don't whisk the eggs into the cocoa-sugar mixture while the mixture is still hot or the eggs may begin to cook on contact.

1. **Heat the oven to 325°F** with a rack in the middle position. Mist a 9-inch springform pan with cooking spray and line the bottom with a round of kitchen parchment.

2. **In a medium saucepan** over medium-high, cook the butter, stirring, until the milk solids at the bottom of the pan are browned and the butter has a nutty aroma, 1 to 3 minutes. Whisk in the cocoa and sugar; transfer the mixture to a medium bowl and let cool until barely warm to the touch.

3. **One at a time,** whisk the eggs into the cocoa-sugar mixture, followed by the salt. Whisk in the flour, add the chocolate chips and stir until evenly distributed. Spread the batter evenly in the prepared pan. Bake until the edges of the cake spring back when lightly pressed, 30 to 35 minutes. Cool in the pan for 30 minutes, then remove the pan sides. Serve dusted with cocoa powder.

FLAVORED WHIPPED CREAMS
Plain whipped cream is fine, but a cake this rich begs for a topping spiked with bright balancing flavors. And making those tweaks to your typical whipped topping is easy.

TANGY DAIRY: Mix **1 cup heavy cream, ¼ cup Greek yogurt or sour cream** and **1½ tablespoons powdered sugar** until uniform and frothy, then whip until soft peaks form.

ALTERNATIVE SUGARS: Mix **1 cup heavy cream** and **1 table-spoon light brown sugar** until uniform and frothy, then whip until soft peaks form.

BOOZY: Mix **1 cup heavy cream, 1½ tablespoons powdered sugar** and **1 teaspoon kirsch or triple sec** until uniform, then as usual.

Portuguese Sponge Cake
(Pão de Ló)

Start to finish: 45 minutes (25 minutes active), plus cooling
Servings: 8 to 10

___

120 grams (1 cup) cake flour

1 teaspoon baking powder

⅜ teaspoon table salt

4 large eggs, plus
4 large egg yolks

2 teaspoons vanilla extract

214 grams (1 cup) white sugar

¼ cup extra-virgin olive oil

Outside Lisbon, home cook Lourdes Varelia baked us a classic Portuguese sponge cake called pão de ló. Its outward appearance was, to us, unusual—deeply browned, wrinkly and sunken, and the dessert was brought to the table in the parchment in which it was baked. And another surprise was in store: slicing revealed a layer of gooey, barely baked batter between the upper crust and the airy, golden-hued crumb. Sweet, eggy and tender, the un-adorned cake was simple yet supremely satisfying. When attempting to re-create pão de ló at Milk Street, we turned to a recipe from "My Lisbon" by Nuno Mendes, who, in an uncommon twist, adds olive oil, giving the cake subtle fruity notes along with a little more richness. We adjusted ingredient amounts and added some baking powder as insurance for a lofty rise. The cake is delicious with Mendes' suggested garnishes—a drizzle of additional olive oil and a sprinkle of flaky sea salt—but it also is excellent with fresh berries and lightly sweetened whipped cream. Leftovers will keep in an airtight container at room temperature for up to three days.

Don't overbake the cake. The best way to test for doneness is to insert a toothpick 2 inches from the edge, not into the center of the cake; the toothpick should come out clean. The type of cake pan—dark-colored nonstick or conventional light-toned metal—affects how quickly the cake bakes, so the recipe includes two different baking times, one for dark pans and one for light. Don't be alarmed if the cake sinks and shrinks dramatically and forms folds and creases as it cools; this is normal.

___

1. Heat the oven to 375° with a rack in the middle position. Cut a 12- to 14-inch round of kitchen parchment. Mist a 9-inch spring-form pan with cooking spray and line the pan with the parchment round, pushing the paper into the edge and against the sides of the pan, allowing it to form folds and pleats. In a small bowl, whisk together the flour, baking powder and salt.

2. In a stand mixer with the whisk attachment, beat the whole eggs, egg yolks and vanilla on medium until frothy, about 2 minutes. With the mixer running, gradually stream in the sugar. Increase to medium-high and beat until very thick, pale and tripled in volume, about 6 minutes.

3. Reduce to medium-low and, with the mixer running, add the flour mixture 1 spoonful at a time, then slowly drizzle in the oil. Immediately stop the mixer (the oil will not be fully incorporated), detach the bowl and fold with a silicone spatula just until the batter is homogeneous; it will be light, airy and pourable.

4. Pour the batter into the prepared pan and bake until the cake is domed and well-browned, the center jiggles slightly when the pan is gently shaken and a toothpick inserted 2 inches in from the edge comes out clean, 22 to 25 minutes if using a dark-colored pan or 30 to 33 minutes if using a light-colored pan.

5. Cool in the pan on a wire rack until barely warm, about 1 hour; the cake will deflate as it cools. If areas of the cake's circumference stick to the sides of the pan, run a knife around the inside of the pan to loosen. Lift the cake out of the pan using the edges of the parchment or remove the sides of the springform pan. When ready to serve, carefully pull the parchment away from the sides of the cake, then cut into wedges.

Sweet Potato Cupcakes with Cream Cheese–Caramel Frosting

Start to finish: 1½ hours / Makes 12 cupcakes

For the cupcakes:

336 grams (12 ounces) orange-flesh sweet potato, peeled and cut into ½-cubes

130 grams (1 cup) all-purpose flour

1 teaspoon baking powder

½ teaspoon baking soda

½ teaspoon table salt

½ teaspoon ground cinnamon

¼ teaspoon ground ginger

¼ teaspoon ground cloves

¼ teaspoon ground cardamom

2 large eggs, room temperature

143 grams (½ cup) packed light brown sugar

½ cup grapeseed or other neutral oil

1 teaspoon grated orange zest

¼ cup whole milk, room temperature

For the frosting:

107 grams (½ cup) white sugar

112 grams (8 tablespoons) salted butter, cut into 1-tablespoon pieces, room temperature, divided

2 tablespoons heavy cream

8-ounce package cream cheese, cut into rough ½-inch chunks, room temperature

1 teaspoon vanilla extract

124 grams (1 cup) powdered sugar

These ochre-toned, spiced cupcakes with a light orange scent are an adaptation of a recipe from "The Back in the Day Bakery Cookbook" by Cheryl Day and Griffith Day, owners of Back in the Day Bakery in Savannah, Georgia. The frosting here is no ordinary cream cheese frosting. It's flavored with a buttery, bittersweet caramel that brings out the earthiness of the sweet potato and the warm notes of the spices in the cupcakes. Store extras, if you have any, in the refrigerator in an airtight container for up to three days; bring to room temperature before serving.

Don't add the caramel to the cream cheese base if the caramel is still warm; it will make the frosting too soft for spreading onto the cupcakes. And as soon as the caramel is incorporated into the frosting, stop the mixer, as overbeating will also result in a goopy consistency. (If the frosting does end up too soft, refrigerate it for 10 to 15 minutes, or until it firms up enough to be spreadable.)

1. To make the cupcakes, in a medium microwave-safe bowl, combine the sweet potato and ¼ cup water. Cover and microwave on high until completely tender, about 8 minutes, stirring once about halfway through. Pour off and discard the liquid in the bowl, then mash the potato with a fork until smooth. Measure out 186 grams (¾ cup) of the sweet potato and set aside; discard the remainder or reserve for another use.

2. Heat the oven to 350°F with a rack in the middle position. Line a 12-cup muffin pan with muffin liners. In a medium bowl, whisk together the flour, baking powder, baking soda, salt, cinnamon, ginger, cloves and cardamom; set aside.

3. In a stand mixer with the paddle attachment, beat the eggs and brown sugar on medium until well combined and lightened, 2 to 3 minutes. With the mixer running on low, add the oil, orange zest and the mashed sweet potato, then beat until homogeneous, about 1 minute. Scrape down the bowl.

4. With the mixer running on low, add about one-third of the flour mixture followed by about half of the milk. Next, add about half of the remaining flour mixture, then the remaining milk and finally the remaining flour mixture. Mix on low until just combined, about 30 seconds. Fold the batter a few times with the spatula to ensure no pockets of flour remain.

5. Divide the batter evenly among the cups of the prepared muffin pan; each should be about two-thirds full. Bake until a toothpick inserted at the center of a cupcake comes out clean, 20 to 25 minutes. Cool in the pan on a wire rack for 15 minutes, then transfer the cupcakes directly to the rack. Cool while you make the frosting.

6. To make the frosting, in a medium saucepan, combine the white sugar and ¼ cup water. Cook over medium, occasionally swirling the pan, until the sugar dissolves, 2 to 3 minutes. Increase to medium-high and cook, gently swirling the pan, until the caramel is medium-dark amber in color and smokes lightly, 6 to 8 minutes. Remove the pan from the heat and immediately add 84 grams (6 tablespoons) of the butter and the cream; the mixture will bubble vigorously. Whisk until the caramel is smooth, transfer to a small bowl and cool to room temperature.

7. In the stand mixer with the whisk attachment, beat the cream cheese, vanilla and the remaining 28 grams (2 tablespoons) butter until smooth, 2 to 3 minutes, scraping the bowl as needed. With the mixer running on low, gradually add the powdered sugar, then beat on medium until light and fluffy, about 1 minute. Stop the mixer, add the caramel and beat on low until well combined, about 1 minute, scraping the bowl as needed.

8. Top the cooled cupcakes with the frosting, either spreading it with a small icing spatula or piping it on with a pastry bag fitted with a tip.

Glazed Sour Cream and Brown Sugar Bundt Cake

Start to finish: 1½ hours (30 minutes active), plus cooling
Servings: 12 to 14

For the cake:

293 grams (2¼ cups) all-purpose flour

½ teaspoon baking soda

½ teaspoon table salt

½ teaspoon ground cardamom

226 grams (16 tablespoons) salted butter, room temperature

436 grams (2 cups) packed light brown sugar

1 teaspoon vanilla extract

1 teaspoon grated lemon zest

3 large eggs, room temperature

270 grams (1 cup) sour cream, room temperature

For the glaze:

42 grams (3 tablespoons) salted butter

109 grams (½ cup) packed light brown sugar

½ cup heavy cream

Sour cream and brown sugar have an affinity for each other, and the combination gives this nostalgic cake, adapted from "The Back in the Day Bakery Cookbook" by Cheryl Day and Griffith Day, a plush, moist crumb and a rich, caramel sweetness. A little ground cardamom adds a whisper of fragrance and flavor. Finished with a shiny butter and brown sugar glaze, the cake finds great company in a cup of coffee or tea. To ensure the cake doesn't stick, pan prep is important, but the flutes, ridges and center tube of a Bundt pan make oiling and flouring a challenge. For that reason, we prefer to use nonstick baking spray, which is similar to regular cooking spray but includes flour—mist the pan and it's ready to go. If you don't have baking spray, mix 2 tablespoons melted butter and 1½ tablespoons flour, then brush the mixture onto the pan, making sure all interior surfaces are coated. Store leftover cake in an airtight container for up to three days.

Don't boil the glaze mixture, but also don't cook it at a lazy simmer. It should simmer vigorously in order to reach the correct consistency for coating the cake, so adjust the heat as needed. Be sure to cool the glaze for 10 to 15 minutes before spooning it onto the cake; during this time it will thicken slightly.

1. To make the cake, heat the oven to 325°F with a rack in the middle position. Mist a 12-cup nonstick Bundt pan with baking spray. In a medium bowl, whisk together the flour, baking soda, salt and cardamom; set aside.

2. In a stand mixer with the paddle attachment, beat the butter and brown sugar on medium until light and fluffy, 3 to 5 minutes. Add the vanilla and lemon zest; continue to beat on medium until combined, about 30 seconds. Scrape down the bowl. With the mixer running on medium-low, add the eggs one at a time, beating until combined after each addition and scraping down the bowl as needed.

3. With the mixer running on low, add about one-third of the flour mixture followed by about half of the sour cream. Next, add about half of the remaining flour mixture, then the remaining sour cream and finally the remaining flour mixture. Mix on low until just combined, about 1 minute. Fold the batter a few times with the spatula to ensure no pockets of flour remain. Scoop the batter into the prepared pan and spread it in an even layer, then rap the pan against the counter to remove any air bubbles and smooth the top.

4. Bake until the cake is golden brown and a toothpick inserted about 2 inches from the edge comes out clean, 60 to 65 minutes. Cool in the pan for about 15 minutes, then invert onto a wire rack and cool to room temperature.

5. To make the glaze, in a medium saucepan, combine the butter, brown sugar and cream. Bring to a simmer over medium, stirring with a silicone spatula to dissolve the sugar, then cook, stirring often and adjusting the heat as needed to maintain a vigorous simmer (but not a boil), until the spatula drawn through the mixture leaves a wide trail, about 5 minutes. Remove the pan from the heat and cool until the glaze clings heavily to a spoon, about 10 minutes. Meanwhile, transfer the cake to a platter.

6. Spoon the glaze onto the cooled cake, letting it slowly drip down the sides. If the glaze is too thin and quickly runs down the cake, let it cool until thickened to the correct consistency; if it is too thick and simply sits in place, gently rewarm it. Let the glaze set for 5 to 10 minutes before slicing and serving.

Chocolate-on-Chocolate Three-Layer Cake

Start to finish: 2 hours (1 hour active), plus cooling
Servings: 16 to 20

___

For the cake:

360 grams (3 cups) cake flour, plus more for the pans

255 grams (9 ounces) unsweetened chocolate, finely chopped

1 tablespoon vanilla extract

2 cups hot coffee

4 large eggs, room temperature

1 cup grapeseed or other neutral oil

270 grams (1 cup) sour cream, room temperature

642 grams (3 cups) white sugar

1½ teaspoons baking soda

1 teaspoon table salt

For the frosting:

255 grams (9 ounces) semisweet chocolate, chopped

339 grams (24 tablespoons) salted butter, room temperature

2 tablespoons whole milk

1 teaspoon vanilla extract

310 grams (2½ cups) powdered sugar, sifted

This grand, triple-layer, old-fashioned chocolate cake comes from "The Back in the Day Bakery Cookbook" by Cheryl Day and Griffith Day, proprietors of Back in the Day Bakery in Savannah, Georgia. Cheryl Day learned the recipe from her grandmother, but put her own stamp on it with a few tweaks, including the addition of coffee, which adds complexity and intensifies the roasty, bittersweet notes of the chocolate. The cake is made with unsweetened chocolate and the frosting calls for semisweet; for the best flavor, search out good-quality chocolate for both. You will need three 9-by-2-inch round cake pans. Some ovens cannot comfortably fit three pans on the same rack; if this is the case with yours, the recipe includes instructions for baking on two different racks. Leftovers will keep in the refrigerator well covered or under a cake dome for a few days, but bring to room temperature before serving.

Don't leave the unsweetened chocolate for the cake in large pieces. Finely chopping it helps ensure that it fully melts with the heat of the coffee. When making the frosting, be sure the melted chocolate is cool to the touch before beating it into the butter. Finally, don't trim the cake layers while they're still warm. The cake will cut more cleanly and with less "crumbing" when cooled to room temperature.

---

1. To make the cake, heat the oven to 350°F with a rack in the middle position (if your oven cannot comfortably fit 3 cake pans on a single rack, position the racks in the upper- and lower-middle positions). Mist three 9-inch round cake pans with cooking spray. Line the bottoms with rounds of kitchen parchment, then mist the parchment. Dust the pans with flour, then knock out the excess.

2. In a medium bowl, combine the unsweetened chocolate and vanilla. Pour the hot coffee over the mixture, then let stand for 2 to 3 minutes to soften the chocolate. Whisk until completely smooth, then cool until barely warm to the touch. In a large bowl, whisk the eggs and oil until well combined. Whisk in the sour cream, then add the cooled melted chocolate mixture, then whisk until homogeneous.

3. In a stand mixer with the paddle attachment, mix the flour, sugar, baking soda and salt on low until well combined and aerated, 2 to 3 minutes. With the mixer running on low, add the chocolate-sour cream mixture to the dry ingredients in 3 additions, beating for 45 to 60 seconds after the first 2 additions and scraping the bowl as needed. After the final addition, increase to medium and beat until well combined, about 1 minute. Fold the

5. Run a paring knife around the inside edge of each pan to loosen the cakes. One at a time, invert the cakes onto the racks, lift off the pans and peel off and discard the parchment. Carefully turn the cakes upright and cool to room temperature.

6. To make the frosting, in a medium saucepan over medium, bring about an inch of water to a simmer. Put the semisweet chocolate into a heatproof medium bowl and set the bowl on top of the saucepan; make sure the bottom does not touch the water. Stir occasionally until the chocolate is completely melted. Remove the bowl from the pan and set aside until cool to the touch, stirring occasionally.

7. In a stand mixer with the paddle attachment, beat the butter on medium until smooth and creamy. With the mixer running on low, add the cooled chocolate and mix until fully incorporated, 2 to 3 minutes, scraping down the bowl as needed. Add the milk and vanilla; beat on low until combined, about 30 seconds. With the mixer running on low, gradually add the powdered sugar, then continue beating until fully incorporated and the frosting is smooth, about 1 minute, scraping the bowl as needed. Increase to medium and beat for 1 minute to slightly aerate.

8. To assemble the cake, using a serrated knife and a gentle sawing motion, carefully slice off the domed surface from each of the 3 cake layers, creating level tops. Set 1 layer cut side down on a cake plate. (If you like, to keep the plate clean as you frost the cake, cut 5 kitchen parchment strips, each measuring roughly 6 by 3 inches, and tuck them under the edges of the bottom cake layer so they cover the plate). Scoop about ¾ cup frosting onto the center of the cake and, using an icing spatula, spread in an even layer to the edges of the cake. Place a second cake layer cut side down on top, aligning it with the bottom layer, then frost it in the same way. Place the final cake layer cut side down on top. Spread the remaining frosting onto the top and sides of the cake. (Remove and discard the parchment strips, if used.)

batter with the spatula, scraping along the bottom and sides of the bowl to ensure no pockets of flour or chocolate mixture remain; the batter will be thin.

4. Divide the batter evenly among the prepared pans. Rap each pan against the counter to remove any air bubbles. Place the pans in the oven, spacing them evenly on the rack (if baking on 2 racks, place 2 pans on the upper rack and 1 on the lower). Bake until a toothpick inserted into the center of the cakes comes out clean, 35 to 40 minutes (if using 2 oven racks, 25 minutes into baking, quickly move the 2 pans on the upper rack to the lower rack and the pan on the lower rack to the upper rack, then continue to bake). Let the cakes cool in the pans on wire racks for about 15 minutes.

Small Sweets

14

Chocolate Meringue Cookies

Start to finish: 1 hour 10 minutes (40 minutes active)
Makes 24 cookies

---

8 ounces bittersweet
chocolate, finely chopped,
divided

4 tablespoons (½ stick) salted
butter, cut into 4 pieces

20 grams (¼ cup)
unsweetened cocoa powder

½ teaspoon instant
espresso powder

3 large egg whites

145 grams (⅔ cup) packed
light brown sugar

1 teaspoon vanilla extract

¼ teaspoon table salt

These rich, yet airy flourless chocolate cookies have crisp edges and chewy interiors. They rely on whipped egg whites for their structure. To ensure your whites attain the proper volume with beating, make sure the mixer bowl, whisk and whisk attachment are perfectly clean and without any trace of oil or fat. Either Dutch-processed or natural cocoa works well in this recipe. Leftover cookies can be stored in an airtight container for up to three days; the edges will lose their crispness but the cookies will still taste good.

Don't omit the step of heating the egg whites and sugar over the saucepan of simmering water. This ensures the sugar fully dissolves so the cookies bake up with shiny, crisp exteriors. But also make sure you don't overheat the mixture (100°F is the ideal temperature), which can cause the whites to cook. Also, the melted chocolate mixture should still be warm when you fold in the whipped egg whites. If it has cooled and thickened, it will be impossible to fold in the whites without deflating them. If needed, before folding in the whites, return the bowl of chocolate to the saucepan and re-melt the mixture.

1. **Heat the oven to 350°F** with racks in the upper- and lower-middle positions. Line 2 baking sheets with kitchen parchment. Measure out 2½ ounces (½ cup) of the chopped chocolate and set aside.

2. **In a medium saucepan over high,** bring 1 inch of water to a boil, then reduce heat to maintain a simmer. In a medium bowl, combine the remaining 5½ ounces chopped chocolate, the butter, cocoa and espresso powder. Set the bowl on the saucepan over the simmering water (the bottom of the bowl should not touch the water) and let the mixture melt until completely smooth, stirring often with a silicone spatula. Set aside to cool slightly; keep the saucepan and water over the heat.

3. **In the bowl of a stand mixer,** whisk together the egg whites, sugar, vanilla and salt. Set the bowl on the saucepan over the simmering water and, while whisking constantly, heat the mixture to 100°F. Attach the bowl to the mixer fitted with the whisk attachment and whip on medium-high until the mixture holds soft peaks when the whisk is lifted, 3 to 4 minutes.

4. **Using a silicone spatula,** fold ⅓ of the egg white mixture into the chocolate mixture until almost completely combined. Add the remaining egg whites and fold until a few streaks of white remain. Add the reserved chopped chocolate and fold gently until no white streaks remain.

5. **Drop the batter in** 2-tablespoon mounds spaced 1½ inches apart on the prepared sheets. Bake until the tops have cracked but the interiors still look moist, 12 to 14 minutes, switching and rotating the sheets halfway through. Cool on the baking sheets for 10 minutes, then transfer the cookies to a wire rack to cool completely, about 30 minutes.

Lamingtons

Start to finish: 4½ hours (50 minutes active)
Makes 16 individual cakes

For the cake:

150 grams (1¼ cups) cake flour, plus more for pan

3 large egg whites, room temperature

½ cup whole milk, room temperature

½ teaspoon vanilla extract

214 grams (1 cup) white sugar

1 teaspoon baking powder

¼ teaspoon table salt

6 tablespoons (¾ stick) salted butter, cut into 6 pieces, room temperature

For the glaze:

¾ cup whole milk, room temperature

4 ounces unsweetened chocolate, chopped

¼ cup refined coconut oil

124 grams (1 cup) powdered sugar

Pinch table salt

225 grams (2½ cups) unsweetened shredded coconut

The inspiration for these Lamingtons—small chocolate-coated, coconut-covered cakes from Australia—came from Le Petit Grain boulangerie in Paris. We skipped the customary jam filling, but these treats are so delicious we don't think you'll notice. We bake a simple butter cake in a square pan, then cut the cooled cake into two-bite cubes. Freezing the cubes before coating them with the chocolate glaze allows for easy handling, and helps the coating firm up quickly. The cake can be cut and frozen up to two days in advance, but if you freeze it for more than just an hour or so, be sure to wrap it well to protect it from drying out. Finished Lamingtons will keep in an airtight container in the refrigerator for one day or in the freezer for several days (if frozen, let stand at room temperature for about 30 minutes before serving).

Don't cut the cake while it's warm. *Allow it to cool completely, about two hours, so it cuts cleanly and neatly. And make sure to use a serrated knife; a regular knife will crush the cake's delicate crumb.*

1. To make the cake, heat the oven to 325°F with a rack in the middle position. Mist the interior of an 8-inch square baking pan with cooking spray, dust with flour, then tap out the excess. Line the bottom with kitchen parchment. In a 2-cup liquid measuring cup or small bowl, whisk together the egg whites, milk and vanilla; set aside.

2. In a stand mixer fitted with the paddle attachment, combine the flour, sugar, baking powder and salt, then mix on low until combined, about 10 seconds. With the mixer running, add the butter one piece at a time. Once all the butter has been added, continue mixing until sandy and no large butter pieces remain, 2 to 3 minutes. With the mixer still running, pour in all but ¼ cup of the egg-milk mixture and mix until combined. Increase to medium-high and beat until the mixture is light and fluffy, about 1 minute. Reduce to medium, then slowly add the remaining egg mixture, scraping the bowl once or twice.

3. Transfer the batter to the prepared pan and spread evenly. Bake until light golden brown and a toothpick inserted at the center comes out clean, 30 to 35 minutes. Cool in the pan on a wire rack for 10 minutes, then run a paring knife around the edges to loosen. Invert the cake onto a large plate, lift off the pan and remove and discard the parchment. Re-invert the cake onto the rack to be right side up and cool completely, about 2 hours.

4. Line a rimmed baking sheet with kitchen parchment. Using a serrated knife, trim off the edges of the cake, then cut the cake into 16 even squares. Place the squares on the prepared baking sheet, cover with plastic wrap and freeze until firm, at least 1 hour or up to 2 days.

5. To make the glaze, in a medium saucepan over high, bring 1 inch of water to a boil, then reduce to medium-low. In a medium heat-proof bowl that fits on top of the saucepan, combine the milk, chocolate and coconut oil. Set the bowl on the saucepan, over the simmering water, and warm the mixture, whisking gently and occasionally, until melted and smooth. Remove the bowl from the pan, then whisk in the powdered sugar and salt; reserve the saucepan and warm water. Place the coconut in a small bowl.

6. Remove the cake squares from the freezer. Using your fingers, dip 1 cake square into the chocolate and turn to coat each side, then scrape off any excess against the edge of the bowl. Toss in the coconut to coat on all sides, then return to the baking sheet. Repeat with the remaining cake squares, chocolate glaze and coconut. If the glaze cools and becomes too thick, return the bowl to the saucepan and gently rewarm the glaze. Let the coated cakes stand until the glaze sets slightly, about 30 minutes.

Chocolate-Almond Spice Cookies

Start to finish: 1¼ hours (30 minutes active), plus cooling
Makes about 24 cookies

¾ teaspoon ground cinnamon

½ teaspoon ground cardamom

½ teaspoon ground ginger

339 grams (1⅓ cups plus ¼ cup white sugar)

250 grams (2½ cups) blanched almond flour

26 grams (¼ cup) unsweetened cocoa powder

½ teaspoon table salt

4 large egg whites, lightly beaten

1½ teaspoons vanilla extract

5 ounces bittersweet chocolate, finely chopped

This recipe is a loose interpretation of the Swiss chocolate-almond holiday cookie known as Basler brunsli. Traditionally, the dough is rolled and cut into shapes before baking, but we opted for an easier drop cookie studded with bits of chocolate. Even without butter, these cookies are intensely rich—and they happen to be gluten-free, too. Both Dutch-processed cocoa and natural cocoa work. If you have a 2-tablespoon spring-loaded scoop, use it for portioning the dough; otherwise, two soup spoons get the job done. The dough can be made ahead and refrigerated in an airtight container for up to 24 hours; bring to room temperature before shaping and baking. The baked and cooled cookies keep well in a well-sealed container at room temperature for up to two days.

Don't skip toasting the almond flour; it gives the cookies a fuller, deeper flavor. But don't forget to allow the almond flour to cool after toasting; if the flour is too hot when the egg whites are added, the whites will cook. Take care not to overbake the cookies or they will become tough.

1. Heat the oven to 375°F with racks in the upper- and lower-middle positions. Line 2 baking sheets with kitchen parchment. In a small bowl, stir together the cinnamon, cardamom and ginger. Measure ¼ teaspoon of the spice mixture into another small bowl, stir in the 54 grams (¼ cup) sugar and set aside.

2. In a 12-inch skillet over medium, combine the almond flour and remaining spice mixture. Cook, stirring frequently and breaking up any lumps, until fragrant and lightly browned, 5 to 7 minutes. Transfer to a large bowl and let cool until barely warm to the touch, 15 to 20 minutes.

3. Into the almond flour mixture, whisk in the remaining 285 grams (1⅓ cups) sugar, the cocoa and salt. Use a spatula to stir in the egg whites and vanilla until evenly moistened. Stir in the chocolate. The dough will be sticky.

4. Using two soup spoons, drop a few 2-tablespoon portions of dough into the spiced sugar, then gently roll to coat evenly. Arrange the sugar-coated balls on the prepared baking sheets about 2 inches apart. Repeat with the remaining dough.

5. Bake until the cookies have cracks in their surfaces and a toothpick inserted into a cookie at the center of the baking sheets comes out with few crumbs attached, 12 to 15 minutes, switching and rotating the sheets halfway through. Let the cookies cool on the baking sheets for 5 minutes, then transfer to a rack to cool completely.

Triple Ginger Scones with Chocolate Chunks

Start to finish: 1¼ hours (40 minutes active)
Makes 12 scones

---

455 grams (3½ cups) all-purpose flour, plus more for dusting

67 grams (5 tablespoons) white sugar

4 teaspoons baking powder

½ teaspoon baking soda

2 tablespoons ground ginger

1½ teaspoons grated nutmeg

1 teaspoon table salt

1½ teaspoons ground black pepper

1¼ cups cold buttermilk

2 tablespoons finely grated fresh ginger

1 tablespoon grated orange zest

18 tablespoons (2 sticks plus 2 tablespoons) salted butter, cut into ½-inch pieces and chilled

150 grams (1 cup) roughly chopped bittersweet chocolate

154 grams (1 cup) finely chopped crystallized ginger

1 large egg, beaten

These rich, flavor-packed oversized scones are the creation of Briana Holt of Tandem Coffee + Bakery in Portland, Maine. Ginger in three different forms—ground, fresh and crystallized—gives these breakfast pastries plenty of kick, as does ground black pepper. Keep both the butter and buttermilk in the refrigerator until you're ready to use them so they stay as cold as possible, which makes the dough easier to handle. Holt recommends serving the scones after they've cooled to room temperature, but we also loved them warm, while the chocolate is soft and melty.

Don't worry if the flour-butter mixture doesn't form a cohesive dough immediately after all the buttermilk has been added. In fact, it will be very crumbly, but a brief kneading and the act of shaping and pressing the mixture into disks will bring it together. When kneading, though, take care not to overwork the dough, which will result in tough, not tender, scones.

1. **Heat the oven to 375°F** with racks in the upper- and lower-middle positions. Line 2 rimmed baking sheets with kitchen parchment. In a large bowl, whisk together the flour, sugar, baking powder, baking soda, ground ginger, nutmeg, salt and pepper. In a 2-cup liquid measuring cup or a small bowl, stir together the buttermilk, grated ginger and orange zest.

2. **To a food processor,** add about ½ of the flour mixture and scatter the butter over the top. Pulse until the butter is in large pea-sized pieces, 10 to 12 pulses. Transfer to the bowl with the remaining flour mixture. Add the chocolate and crystallized ginger, then toss with your hands until evenly combined. Pour in about ⅓ of the buttermilk mixture and toss just a few times with your hands, making sure to scrape along the bottom of the bowl, until the liquid is absorbed. Add the remaining buttermilk in 2 more additions, tossing after each. After the final addition of buttermilk, toss until no dry, floury bits remain. The mixture will be quite crumbly and will not form a cohesive dough.

3. **Lightly dust the counter with flour,** turn the mixture out onto it, then give it a final toss. Divide it into 2 even piles, gathering each into a mound, then very briefly knead each mound; it's fine if the mixture is still somewhat crumbly. Gather each mound into a ball, then press firmly into a cohesive 5-inch disk about 1½ inches thick. Brush the tops of each disk lightly with beaten egg. Using a chef's knife, cut each disk in half, then cut each half into 3 wedges. Place 6 wedges on each prepared baking sheet, spaced evenly apart.

4. **Bake until the scones** are deep golden brown, 27 to 30 minutes, switching and rotating the baking sheets halfway through. Cool on the baking sheets on wire racks for 5 minutes, then transfer directly to a rack and cool for at least another 5 minutes. Serve warm or at room temperature.

Tahini Swirl Brownies

Start to finish: 40 minutes / Makes 16 brownies

4 tablespoons (½ stick) salted
butter, plus more for pan

4 ounces bittersweet
chocolate, finely chopped

16 grams (3 tablespoons)
unsweetened cocoa powder

3 large eggs

240 grams (1 cup plus
2 tablespoons) white sugar

1 tablespoon vanilla extract

½ teaspoon table salt

180 grams (¾ cup) tahini

43 grams (⅓ cup)
all-purpose flour

Tired of one-note brownies, we looked to the Middle East for a grown-up version of this American standard. We loved the halvah brownie from Tatte Bakery & Cafe in Cambridge, Massachusetts. Halvah is fudge-like candy from the Middle East made from tahini, a rich sesame seed paste. At Milk Street, we fiddled with how much tahini to use—its fat content was the major problem. To start, we reduced the tahini and the amount of butter, substituted cocoa powder for some of the chocolate and added an egg to cut through the rich brownie base. Then, we reversed our thinking and instead of trying to add tahini to a classic brownie batter, we added chocolate to a tahini base. For a final touch, we swirled reserved tahini batter into the chocolate to create a visual and textural contrast and let the tahini flavor shine. The best way to marble the brownies was to run the tip of a paring knife through the dollops of batter. Be sure to fully bake these brownies—they are extremely tender, even wet, if not baked through. The tahini's flavor and color will intensify over time, so make a day ahead for a more pronounced sesame taste.

Don't skip stirring the tahini before measuring; the solids often sink to the bottom.

1. Heat the oven to 350°F with a rack in the middle position. Line an 8-inch square baking pan with 2 pieces of foil with excess hanging over the edges on all sides. Lightly coat with butter.

2. In a medium saucepan over medium, melt the butter. Off heat add the chocolate and cocoa, whisking until smooth.

3. In a large bowl, whisk the eggs, sugar, vanilla and salt until slightly thickened, about 1 minute. Whisk in the tahini. Fold in the flour until just incorporated. Transfer ½ cup of the mixture to a small bowl. Add the chocolate mixture to the remaining tahini mixture and fold until fully combined.

4. Pour the batter into the prepared pan, spreading evenly. Dollop the reserved tahini mixture over the top, then swirl the batters together. Bake until the edges are set but the center remains moist, 28 to 32 minutes. Cool in the pan on a wire rack for 30 minutes. Use the foil to lift the brownies out of the pan and cool on the rack for at least another 30 minutes; the longer they cool, the better they cut. Cut into 2-inch squares.

Rosemary–Pine Nut Cornmeal Cookies

Start to finish: 1½ hours (30 minutes active), plus cooling
Makes 24 cookies

This cookie is sweet enough to track as a treat, but pairs as well with Parmesan as it does a glass of milk. Our inspiration was a hazelnut-rosemary biscotti by Claudia Fleming, the former pastry chef of New York's Gramercy Tavern who famously blended savory flavorings into classically sweet dishes. We reimagined Fleming's biscotti as crisp, pat-in-the-pan shortbread. The dough got sticky in a warm kitchen, but 10 minutes in the refrigerator fixed that. Letting the cookies cool completely before cutting produced uneven shards; 15 minutes was the sweet spot for a sturdy but sliceable texture.

Don't use dried rosemary. *Fresh has a better flavor and softer texture.*

195 grams (1½ cups) all-purpose flour

72 grams (½ cup) fine cornmeal

107 grams (½ cup) white sugar

1 tablespoon minced fresh rosemary

2 teaspoons grated orange zest

16 tablespoons (2 sticks) salted butter, softened, divided

1 cup pine nuts

63 grams (3 tablespoons) honey

1. Heat the oven to 325°F with a rack in the lower-middle position. Line a 9-by-13-inch baking pan with foil, letting the edges hang over the long sides of the pan. In a bowl, combine the flour and cornmeal; set aside.

2. In the bowl of a stand mixer fitted with the paddle attachment, combine the sugar, rosemary and orange zest. Mix on low until the sugar is moistened and begins to clump, 1 to 2 minutes. Add 14 tablespoons of the butter, increase to medium-high and beat until light and fluffy, 3 to 5 minutes, scraping down the bowl twice. Reduce to low and gradually add the flour mixture (this should take about 30 seconds). Scrape down the bowl and mix on low until the dough forms around the paddle, about 1 minute.

3. Crumble the dough evenly over the bottom of the prepared pan. Coat the bottom of a dry measuring cup with oil, then use it to press the dough into an even layer. Sprinkle the pine nuts over the dough in a single layer and press down firmly.

4. In a small bowl, microwave the remaining 2 tablespoons of butter until melted. Add the honey and stir until combined. Brush the mixture over the bars, then bake until the top is deep golden brown, 40 to 45 minutes.

5. Let the bars cool in the pan for 15 minutes. Using the foil, lift the bars and transfer to a cutting board. Cut into 24 pieces. Let the bars cool completely on a wire rack before serving. The cooled cookies can be stored in an airtight container at room temperature for up to 1 week.

Swedish Gingersnaps (Pepparkakor)

Start to finish: 3½ hours (30 minutes active), plus cooling
Makes about 24 cookies

In search of a cookie that would deliver grown-up ginger-bread flavor, we came across Swedish gingersnaps, a cookie that goes as well with wine as coffee. For these cookies, we needed to balance dark brown and white sugars to get a workable dough that crisped properly. Baking soda helped with browning and gave the cookies lift, making them crunchy but not hard. The pepparkakor's distinctive spice came from ground and fresh ginger, black pepper and cayenne, and we pumped up all of them. The dough can be made up to two days in advance. The cookies keep for up to a week in an airtight container.

Don't portion the dough right after mixing; it will be too soft and sticky. Because it is made with melted butter (to avoid using a stand mixer), the dough must chill first.

217 grams (1⅔ cups) all-purpose flour

¼ teaspoon baking soda

8 tablespoons (1 stick) salted butter

100 grams (½ cup packed) dark brown sugar

78 grams (6 tablespoons) white sugar

¼ cup dark corn syrup

2½ tablespoons ground ginger

1 tablespoon finely grated fresh ginger

1 teaspoon ground cinnamon

¾ teaspoon finely grated orange zest

¼ teaspoon table salt

½ teaspoon ground cloves

¼ teaspoon ground black pepper

⅛ teaspoon cayenne pepper

1 large egg

Turbinado sugar, for sprinkling

1. In a large bowl, whisk together the flour and baking soda; set aside. In a medium saucepan over medium, combine the butter, both sugars, the corn syrup, both gingers, the cinnamon, orange zest, salt, cloves, black pepper and cayenne. As the butter melts, whisk until the sugar dissolves and the mixture begins to simmer. Remove from the heat. Cool until just warm to the touch, about 30 minutes.

2. Whisk the egg into the cooled mixture until smooth. Add to the dry ingredients and fold until no dry flour remains. Refrigerate for at least 2 hours or up to 2 days.

3. Heat the oven to 350°F with racks in the upper- and lower-middle positions. Line 2 baking sheets with kitchen parchment. Working with a tablespoon of dough at a time, use dampened hands to roll into balls. Arrange 12 dough balls on each baking sheet, spacing evenly.

4. Lay a sheet of plastic wrap over the balls on each sheet and use the bottom of a dry measuring cup to flatten each to about ¼ inch thick. Remove the plastic and sprinkle each cookie with a generous pinch of turbinado sugar. Bake until richly browned, 14 to 16 minutes, switching and rotating the baking sheets halfway through. Cool on the sheet for 10 minutes, then transfer to a wire rack and cool completely.

Semolina Polvorones

Start to finish: 3 hours (45 minutes active), plus cooling time
Makes 24 cookies

54 grams (¼ cup) white sugar

1½ teaspoons grated
orange zest

57 grams (½ cup) coarsely
chopped walnuts

128 grams (¾ cup)
semolina flour

½ teaspoon ground cinnamon

2 large egg yolks

½ teaspoon vanilla extract

Pinch table salt

87 grams (⅔ cup)
all-purpose flour

10 tablespoons (1¼ sticks)
salted butter, cut into ½-inch
pieces and chilled

Powdered sugar, to coat

Polvorones are Spanish cookies popular across Latin America, Spain and the Phillipines. They're basically a simple shortbread—and sadly can be simply bland. Our inspiration was a lesser-known Basque variation made with semolina and spiced with orange zest and cinnamon. We also borrowed a Filipino technique of toasting the flour first. In fact, we toasted both our walnuts and semolina to give the cookies deep, complex flavor. Adding the ground cinnamon to the hot semolina bloomed it, bringing out its aroma. Flattening the cookies too much made them delicate; ½-inch-thick discs held up best when tossed in powdered sugar. Likewise, the cookies are fragile when hot out of the oven, so let them cool several minutes before transferring to a wire rack. You can bake both sheets of cookies at once on the upper and lower-middle racks, but we got more even browning baking one sheet at a time.

Don't be alarmed if the semolina smokes slightly during toasting. And don't coat the cookies with powdered sugar until you're ready to serve them; they look best immediately after they're sugared.

1. In a food processor, pulse together the white sugar and orange zest. In a 10-inch skillet over medium, toast the walnuts, stirring, until lightly browned and fragrant, 3 to 5 minutes. Transfer to the food processor. Wipe the skillet clean, then add the semolina and toast, stirring, until beginning to brown, 2 to 3 minutes. Reduce heat to medium-low and toast, stirring constantly, until speckled, golden brown and fragrant, another 2 to 3 minutes. Off the heat, stir in the cinnamon, then transfer to a plate and cool to room temperature.

2. In a small bowl, use a fork to beat the yolks and vanilla. Add the salt to the walnuts and sugar, then process until coarsely ground, about 10 seconds. Add the flour and semolina mixture, then process until combined, about 5 seconds. Add the butter and pulse until the mixture resembles damp sand, 10 to 12 pulses. Drizzle in the yolk mixture and pulse until large clumps gather around the blade. Transfer the dough to the counter and knead briefly, then wrap in plastic wrap and refrigerate for at least 1 hour and up to 2 days.

3. Heat the oven to 325°F with a rack in the middle position. Line 2 baking sheets with kitchen parchment. Roll the dough into 24 balls (1 tablespoon each) and arrange evenly on the baking sheets. Press the balls gently into discs about ½ inch thick.

4. One at a time, bake each sheet until well browned, 23 to 28 minutes, rotating halfway through. Let the cookies cool on the sheet for 10 minutes, then transfer to a wire rack and cool completely. Just before serving, gently drop each cookie into powdered sugar to coat.

Date-Stuffed Semolina Cookies (Ma'amoul)

Start to finish: 1 hour (30 minutes active), plus cooling
Makes 36 cookies

For the dough:

170 grams (1 cup) semolina flour

130 grams (1 cup) all-purpose flour

71 grams (⅓ cup) white sugar

¼ teaspoon table salt

10 tablespoons (1¼ sticks) salted butter, cut into 10 pieces and chilled

2 tablespoons plain whole-milk yogurt

2 teaspoons rose water

1 teaspoon vanilla extract

Powdered sugar, for dusting (optional)

For the filling:

5 ounces (1 cup) medjool dates, pitted

4 ounces (1 cup) walnut pieces, lightly toasted and cooled

1 tablespoon honey

2 teaspoons grated orange zest

½ teaspoon ground cardamom

⅛ teaspoon table salt

These semolina-based cookies stuffed with dates, nuts or other fillings are a popular Middle Eastern treat often served on holidays. Though they are often made using a complex molding technique, we simplified and came up with a rolling method anyone could do. A combination of semolina and all-purpose flours gave our cookies a rich, crumbly texture and complex flavor. Chilled butter prevented the dough from getting overly sticky, but if your kitchen is particularly warm and the dough is soft and shiny after mixing, refrigerate it for 30 minutes before proceeding. Covering the dough with plastic wrap while making the filling and rolling it out between sheets of kitchen parchment further prevented the dough from drying out. If the dough begins to crack while shaping the cookies, gently pinch the cracks back together. You can substitute pistachios for the walnuts, but the filling will take an extra minute or so to form into a paste. While rose water is traditional, a good substitute is 2 teaspoons each of orange juice and orange zest, plus ¼ teaspoon almond extract. These cookies keep for up to three days in an airtight container at room temperature.

Don't use deglet dates. Soft, plump medjool dates were essential to producing the proper consistency of the paste, and they made for a moister, more flavorful filling.

1. Heat the oven to 325°F with racks in the upper- and lower-middle positions. Line 2 baking sheets with kitchen parchment.

2. For the dough, in a food processor combine both flours, the white sugar and salt. Process until combined, about 5 seconds. Add the butter and process until the butter is completely incorporated, 15 to 20 seconds. Add the yogurt, rose water and vanilla, then process until the dough comes together, about 1 minute. Transfer to the counter and knead until the dough is smooth, then cover with plastic wrap and set aside.

3. For the filling, in the processor, combine all filling ingredients and process until a smooth paste forms, 45 to 60 seconds.

4. To assemble the cookies, set the dough between 2 sheets of kitchen parchment and roll into a 12-by-9-inch rectangle, cutting and patching the dough together as needed. Cut the dough into thirds lengthwise to form three 12-by-3-inch strips. Divide the filling into thirds and roll each portion into a 12-inch rope. Place one rope down the middle of each strip of dough, then wrap the dough completely around the filling. Pinch the seam to seal. Place each roll seam side down and cut each crosswise into 12 rounds, gently reshaping if necessary. Evenly space the cookies seam side down on the prepared baking sheets.

5. Bake until the bottoms are golden but the tops are still pale, 25 to 30 minutes, switching and rotating the sheets half-way through. Cool the cookies on the sheets for 5 minutes, then transfer to a wire rack and cool completely, about 30 minutes. Dust with powdered sugar, if desired.

Australian Oat-Coconut Cookies (Anzac Biscuits)

Start to finish: 30 minutes / Makes 24 cookies

125 grams (1¼ cups) old-fashioned rolled oats

112 grams (1¼ cups) unsweetened shredded coconut

158 grams (1 cup plus 2 tablespoons) whole-wheat flour

10 tablespoons (1¼ sticks) salted butter

100 grams (½ cup packed) dark brown sugar

¼ cup brewed coffee

63 grams (3 tablespoons) honey

2 teaspoons vanilla extract

1 teaspoon grated orange zest

1 teaspoon baking soda

In Australia and New Zealand, Anzac Day (April 25) honors servicemen and women past and present. The date marks the day the Australian and New Zealand Army Corps (ANZAC) landed at Gallipoli in Turkey during World War I. There are a number of traditions associated with the day, including the Dawn Service marking the pre-dawn landing on Gallipoli. And there are more lighthearted rituals, such as the drinking of "gunfire coffee"—black coffee with a splash of rum—and the eating of Anzac biscuits, an oat and coconut cookie that is both simple and delicious. We wanted a bolder more modern rendition. Though golden syrup is traditional, we found honey and dark brown sugar were good stand-ins. And toasting the coconut and the oats deepened the flavor of the biscuits. Be sure to have all ingredients measured beforehand; it's important to combine everything as soon as possible after the baking soda has been incorporated into the wet ingredients. Underbaking the cookies gave them chewy centers. An oiled 1 tablespoon measuring spoon helped portion out the cookies.

Don't roll these cookies into balls. *It will compress them and result in dense cookies.*

1. **Heat the oven to 350°F** with racks in the upper- and lower-middle positions. Line 2 baking sheets with kitchen parchment. In a large skillet over medium-high, toast the oats, stirring often, until fragrant and beginning to brown, about 5 minutes. Reduce the heat to medium-low and add the coconut. Toast until golden, stirring constantly, 1 to 2 minutes. Transfer to a large bowl. Stir in the flour. Wipe out the skillet.

2. **Return the skillet to medium-low** and add the butter, sugar, coffee, honey, vanilla and orange zest. Cook, whisking, until the butter melts and the mixture boils. Off heat, add the baking soda and stir until completely mixed, pale and foamy. Add to the oatmeal mixture and stir until just combined.

3. **Scoop or drop heaping tablespoons** of dough, spaced about 2 inches apart, onto the prepared baking sheets. Bake until the cookies have risen and are deep golden brown but still soft at the center, 8 to 10 minutes, switching and rotating the pans halfway through. Cool on the pans for 5 minutes, then transfer to a wire rack to cool completely.

Rye Chocolate Chip Cookies

Start to finish: 1 hour (20 minutes active), plus cooling
Makes 24 cookies

---

130 grams (1 cup)
all-purpose flour

½ teaspoon baking soda

¼ teaspoon table salt

140 grams (1 cup) finely
ground rye flour (see note)

12 tablespoons (1½ sticks)
salted butter, cut into pieces
and chilled

268 grams (1¼ cups)
white sugar

2 large eggs

1 tablespoon molasses,
preferably blackstrap

1 tablespoon vanilla extract

1¼ cups good-quality dark
chocolate chips or 7½ ounces
bittersweet chocolate,
roughly chopped

113 grams (1 cup) pecans,
toasted and chopped
(optional)

We've eaten plenty of Toll House chocolate chip cookies. And while they're good, we wanted something different— a more complex cookie with a robust flavor that could balance the sugar and chocolate. We found inspiration on a visit to Claire Ptak's Violet bakery in London, where she's a fan of switching things up. Think rye flour for an apricot upside-down cake. Rye is a little bitter, a little savory, and it makes the perfect counterpoint for the sugary high notes of a chocolate chip cookie. First, though, we had to make a few adjustments. Rye has less gluten than all-purpose flour so it bakes differently and requires more liquid. We decided to go almost equal parts rye and all-purpose flours and recommend that you weigh for best results. Toasting the rye flour added complex, nutty flavor that balanced the sweetness of the cookies. Rye flour texture and flavor varies from brand to brand; we preferred the cookies' spread and chew when made with Arrowhead Mills Organic Rye, with Bob's Red Mill Dark Rye as a close second. A touch of molasses deepened the flavor and added slight bitterness. These cookies continue to firm up after they come out of the oven; it is best to check them early and err on the side of under-baking.

Don't use coarsely ground rye flour, as it absorbs moisture differently than finely ground, causing these cookies to spread too much during baking. Unfortunately, labels usually do not specify, but if the flour is visible in its packaging, coarsely ground has a granularity similar to cornmeal; finely ground rye has a powderiness much like all-purpose flour. We found Hodgson Mills rye flour, which is widely available, to be too coarse.

---

1. Heat the oven to 350°F with a rack in the upper-middle and lower-middle positions. Line 2 baking sheets with kitchen parchment. In a medium bowl, whisk together the all-purpose flour, baking soda and salt. In a 12-inch skillet over medium-high, toast the rye flour, stirring constantly, until fragrant and darkened by several shades, 3 to 5 minutes. Remove the skillet from the heat, add the butter and stir until melted, then transfer to a small bowl. Let cool for 10 minutes, stirring once or twice. The mixture will still be warm.

2. In a large bowl, whisk together the sugar, eggs, molasses and vanilla until smooth, about 30 seconds. Gradually stir in the rye mixture. Add the flour mixture and stir until combined. Stir in the chocolate chips and nuts, if using. Let rest until a finger pressed into the dough comes away cleanly, about 5 minutes.

3. Drop 2-tablespoon mounds of dough about 2 inches apart on the prepared baking sheets. Bake until the edges feel set when gently pressed but the centers are still soft, 13 to 15 minutes, switching and rotating the baking sheets halfway through. Let cool on the sheets for 5 minutes, then transfer to a wire rack and cool for 10 minutes.

Belgian Spice Cookies (Speculoos)

Start to finish: 1 hour, plus cooling
Makes about 6 dozen cookies

___

¾ teaspoon ground cinnamon

¾ teaspoon ground coriander

¾ teaspoon ground allspice

2 tablespoons white sugar

320 grams (2⅔ cups) cake flour, plus more for dusting

1½ teaspoons baking soda

⅛ teaspoon ground cloves

12 tablespoons (1½ sticks) salted butter, cool room temperature

218 grams (1 cup) packed light brown sugar

¼ teaspoon table salt

2 tablespoons dark corn syrup

Speculoos are Belgian spice cookies with a light, airy crispness. Creaming the butter and sugar until light and fluffy is important, so make sure the butter is softened to cool room temperature, then beat in the stand mixer for the full 5 minutes. The dough can be cut in any shape, but the baking time may need to be adjusted if the cookies are much smaller or larger than 2 inches.

Don't use light corn syrup in place of dark; light corn syrup lacks the caramel notes that mimics the flavor of the type of brown sugar (made from beets) traditionally used to make speculoos.

___

1. Heat the oven to 350°F with a rack in the middle position. Line 2 baking sheets with kitchen parchment. In a small bowl, stir together the cinnamon, coriander and allspice. Measure 1 teaspoon of the mixture into another small bowl, whisk the white sugar into it and set aside. In a medium bowl, whisk together the cake flour, baking soda, cloves and remaining spice mixture.

2. In a stand mixer with the paddle attachment, beat the butter, brown sugar and salt on low until combined, about 30 seconds. Increase to medium-high and beat until fluffy and pale, about 5 minutes. With the mixer running, gradually add the corn syrup and 2 tablespoons water. Using a silicone spatula, scrape the sides of the bowl, then mix for another 30 seconds. Reduce to low, add the flour mixture and mix until the ingredients just begin to form an evenly moistened dough, about 15 seconds.

3. Dust the counter liberally with flour and scrape the dough onto it. Gently knead the dough, giving it 2 or 3 turns, until smooth; it should feel moist and supple but should not be sticky. Divide the dough in half; wrap 1 piece in plastic and set aside. With your hands, pat the second piece into a rough 8-by-6-inch rectangle.

4. Using a well-floured rolling pin, roll the dough rectangle to an even ⅛-inch thickness. With a 2-inch rectangular or round cookie cutter (ideally with a fluted edge), cut out cookies as close together as possible. Use an offset spatula to carefully transfer the cutouts to one of the prepared baking sheets, spacing them about ½ inch apart.

5. Gently pat the dough scraps together, then re-roll and cut out additional cookies; transfer the cutouts to the baking sheet. If desired, use a slightly smaller cutter of the same shape to imprint a decorative border (do not cut all the way through the dough) and use a toothpick to poke a few holes in the centers. Sprinkle the cookies evenly with half of the spiced sugar, then refrigerate uncovered for 15 minutes.

6. While the first sheet of cookies chills, repeat with the remaining dough and second baking sheet. Place the first sheet of cookies in the oven, then immediately refrigerate the second sheet. Bake until the cookies are firm and beginning to brown, 16 to 18 minutes, rotating once halfway through. Cool on the baking sheet for 10 minutes, then use a wide metal spatula to transfer them to a wire rack. Repeat with the second sheet of cookies. Cool completely before serving.

Whipped Cream Biscuits

Start to finish: 30 minutes, plus cooling / Makes 8 biscuits

---

260 grams (2 cups)
all-purpose flour

1½ tablespoons white
sugar, divided

2½ teaspoons baking powder

¼ teaspoon table salt

¼ teaspoon baking soda

⅔ cup heavy cream, plus
more as needed

½ cup sour cream

4 tablespoons (½ stick)
salted butter, chilled and
cut into ¼-inch cubes, plus
1 tablespoon, melted

We first heard of whipped cream biscuits from a central Pennsylvanian cook, then later found recipes for them in a handful of Southern cookbooks. We think they fall in the same category as whipped cream cake, which gets some of its lift from the cream. Instead of relying exclusively on baking powder or baking soda for leavening, these biscuits benefit from the air trapped in stiffly beaten cream. The result is a particularly fluffy texture that doesn't have the heavy-handed richness of an all-butter biscuit. This recipe is designed to work as a dessert, not a breakfast biscuit, and that makes it an ideal candidate for strawberry shortcake. We wanted a bolder filling than one finds in the average shortcake. To avoid waste—as well as the need to reroll scraps—we cut our biscuits into squares. For a savory variation, decrease the sugar to 2 teaspoons and skip the final sprinkle.

Don't forget to decrease the temperature when you put the biscuits in the oven. Starting the biscuits in a very hot oven helped them rise and brown better, but keeping them at that temperature will overcook them.

1. **Heat the oven to 475°F** with a rack in the middle position. Line a baking sheet with kitchen parchment. In a large bowl, whisk together the flour, 1 tablespoon of the sugar, the baking powder, salt and baking soda. In a second large bowl, use a whisk or electric mixer to beat the cream and sour cream to soft peaks; set aside. Scatter the butter cubes over the flour. With your fingertips, rub together until the butter is thoroughly and evenly dispersed in the flour.

2. **Add the whipped cream mixture** to the flour mixture. Use a large silicone spatula to fold and press until large clumps form and no dry flour remains. Use your hand to knead the dough in the bowl until it forms a shaggy mass, adding additional cream 1 tablespoon at a time, if needed.

3. **Turn the dough out** onto a lightly floured counter and divide in half. Form each piece into a rough 5-inch square about ¾ inch thick. With a bench scraper or chef's knife, cut each square into 4 pieces. Evenly space the biscuits on the prepared baking sheet. Brush the tops with the melted butter and sprinkle with the remaining ½ tablespoon sugar.

4. **Place the baking sheet** in the oven and immediately reduce the temperature to 425°F. Bake until golden brown on top and bottom, 15 to 18 minutes, rotating the pan halfway through. Let cool on the baking sheet for 10 minutes.

MACERATED STRAWBERRIES WITH LIME

We favored small to medium strawberries for this recipe. If your berries are quite large, cut them into 1-inch pieces instead of quartering them.

Don't hull your strawberries before washing them; they may get water-logged and lose flavor.

Start to finish: 20 minutes
Makes about 4 cups

2 pounds strawberries, washed, dried, hulled and quartered

¼ cup white sugar

4 teaspoons grated lime zest

⅛ teaspoon table salt

In a large bowl, use a potato masher or fork to mash 2 cups of the strawberries until few chunks remain. Stir in the sugar, lime zest and salt. Fold in the remaining strawberries. Cover and let sit until syrupy, at least 15 minutes or up to 2 hours.

TANGY WHIPPED CREAM

Adding a dollop of sour cream to heavy cream can balance the sweetness of a cake and help define the flavor of mediocre fruit. We also add brown sugar and vanilla, lending a depth and complexity to a treat that typically is one note.

Start to finish: 5 minutes
Makes about 2 cups

1 cup heavy cream

¼ cup sour cream

2 tablespoons packed brown sugar

½ teaspoon vanilla extract

Pinch table salt

In the bowl of a stand mixer, combine all ingredients. Using the whisk attachment, mix on low until uniform and frothy, about 30 seconds. Increase speed to medium-high and whip until soft peaks form, 1 to 2 minutes.

Venetian Cornmeal and Currant Cookies (Zaletti)

Start to finish: 30 minutes (10 minutes active), plus cooling
Makes about 40 cookies

---

75 grams (½ cup) dried
currants

3 tablespoons orange liqueur,
such as Cointreau

12 tablespoons (1½ sticks)
salted butter, softened

107 grams (½ cup)
white sugar

1 tablespoon grated
orange zest

73 grams (½ cup) fine
yellow cornmeal

¼ teaspoon table salt

1 large egg yolk

1 teaspoon vanilla extract

195 grams (1½ cups)
all-purpose flour

Zaletti are buttery, crisp Italian cornmeal cookies studded with raisins or currants. The dried fruit usually is first plumped in grappa, a fiery Italian brandy, but we opted instead to use orange liqueur for its more nuanced flavor. We then upped the citrus notes with grated orange zest. The cooled cookies will keep in an airtight container for up to one week.

Don't use coarsely ground cornmeal or polenta. Their rough texture will result in crumbly, rather than crisp, cookies.

---

1. Heat the oven to 350°F with racks in the upper- and lower-middle positions. Line 2 baking sheets with kitchen parchment. In a small saucepan over medium, bring the currants and orange liqueur to a simmer. Cover, remove from the heat and set aside.

2. Meanwhile, in a stand mixer with the paddle attachment, beat the butter and sugar on medium until light and fluffy, 1 to 2 minutes, scraping the bowl as needed. Beat in the zest for about 30 seconds. Mix in the cornmeal, salt, egg yolk and vanilla until combined, about 30 seconds. Add the flour and mix on low until incorporated, another 30 seconds, then mix in the currants and their liquid.

3. Form the dough into 1-tablespoon balls (each about 1 inch in diameter) and space evenly on the prepared baking sheets. Using your hand, flatten each to a 2-inch round about ¼ inch thick. Bake until golden brown at the edges, 15 to 20 minutes, switching and rotating the sheets halfway through. Cool on the sheets for 5 minutes, then transfer to a wire rack and cool completely.

Sauces, Pickles and Relishes

15

Pickled Chilies (Nam Prik)

Start to finish: **35 minutes (5 minutes active)** / Makes **1 cup**

These jalapeño chilies pickled in fish sauce, lime juice and a little sugar are a milder variation of the often fiery Thai dressing called nam prik. The chilies, and their sauce, add a balanced hit of heat, sweet and acid. We find them a delicious way to add bright flavor to our Thai fried rice (see recipe p. 160), or any Thai or Vietnamese dish. Whisk in a little peanut oil for a quick salad, vegetable or slaw dressing. Add a spoonful to stews, or even scrambled eggs or roasted or sautéed vegetables.

In a bowl, stir together all ingredients. Refrigerate for at least 30 minutes or up to 1 week.

4 jalapeño chilies, stemmed, seeded (if desired) and thinly sliced crosswise

¼ cup fish sauce

¼ cup lime juice

1 teaspoon white sugar

Tamarind Dipping Sauce

Start to finish: **20 minutes** / Makes **about 2 cups**

We developed this sauce to go alongside our Chiang Mai chicken (see recipe, p. 254), but it's also great with sticky Asian spareribs, stirred into Asian soups, drizzled over steamed or sticky rice, as a base for steaming mussels, or tossed with sliced cucumber and torn mint leaves for a quick salad. And it's good with grilled meats, poultry and fish, especially salmon. Tamarind is a brown pod containing seeds and a sticky, sour pulp. Tamarind pulp is most commonly available as blocks and will keep for several weeks in the refrigerator. A blender gave the sauce its smooth consistency. For a milder flavor, remove the seeds and ribs from the chili. If you can find palm sugar, it would be an authentic substitute for the brown sugar.

1. In a medium saucepan over medium, combine the lemon grass, shallot, oil and chili. Cook, stirring, until just beginning to brown, 3 to 5 minutes. Add the tomato paste and ginger and cook, stirring constantly, until fragrant, about 30 seconds. Add 2½ cups water, the tamarind and sugar. Bring to a boil, then reduce heat to medium-low and simmer until the tamarind has softened, about 15 minutes. Off heat, stir in the fish sauce and soy sauce.

2. Let the mixture cool slightly, then transfer to a blender. Blend until smooth, about 1 minute. Strain through a fine-mesh strainer, pressing on the solids; discard the solids. Stir in the lime juice, then taste and season with pepper. Use immediately or refrigerate for up to 2 weeks.

2 lemon grass stalks, trimmed to the lower 6 inches, dry outer layers discarded, chopped

1 large shallot, chopped

3 tablespoons grapeseed or other neutral oil

1 serrano chili, stemmed and chopped

1 tablespoon tomato paste

1 tablespoon finely grated fresh ginger

2 ounces tamarind pulp, seeds removed

5 tablespoons packed light brown sugar

¼ cup fish sauce

1 tablespoon soy sauce

3 tablespoons lime juice

Ground black pepper

Sweet-and-Sour Mint Dressing (Sekanjabin)

Start to finish: **10 minutes active, plus 1 hour cooling**
Makes **about ½ cup**

French vinaigrette may be the dressing we know best, but step out of Europe and the choices multiply. In many cultures, sauces—not just vinegar and oil—dress vegetables, grains or greens. The range of acids and fats expands, as does the potential for sweeteners and wild cards such as tamarind paste, miso or a bold splash of fish, soy or oyster sauce. We were introduced to one of the simplest, most appealing dressings by Yasmin Khan, author of "The Saffron Tales." The Iranian dressing sekanjabin is an ancient blend of cider vinegar, honey or sugar, and mint concentrated into a syrup to use straight as a dressing or diluted in a drink. We preferred unfiltered cider vinegars. And we loved the dressing on cold roasted vegetables.

Don't use a distinctively flavored honey, such as orange blossom or buckwheat. The flavor will overpower the delicate mint.

½ cup plus 2 tablespoons
cider vinegar, divided

167 grams (½ cup)
clover honey

½ teaspoon kosher salt

1½ cups lightly packed
fresh mint

In a small saucepan over medium, combine ½ cup of the vinegar, the honey and salt. Simmer until large bubbles appear and the mixture reduces to about ½ cup, about 7 minutes. Off the heat, add the mint, pushing it into the syrup. Let cool to room temperature. Strain into a bowl, pressing the solids. Stir in the remaining 2 tablespoons of vinegar. Cool. Refrigerate for up to 1 month.

Three ways to use sekanjabin:

BROILED EGGPLANT WITH CHILIES AND CILANTRO

Start to finish: 20 minutes
(10 minutes active) / Servings: 4

2 pounds eggplant, cut
crosswise into 1-inch slices

½ cup olive oil

Kosher salt and ground black pepper

½ cup chopped fresh cilantro

2 tablespoons chili-garlic sauce

2 tablespoons sweet-and-sour
mint dressing

Heat the broiler and set an oven rack
6 inches from it. Line a rimmed baking
sheet with foil. Arrange the eggplant
on the foil and brush both sides with
the olive oil. Season with salt and
pepper. Broil until well browned, about
10 minutes. Flip each slice and broil
again until well browned, another 5 to
10 minutes. Let cool. In a large bowl,
combine the cilantro, chili-garlic sauce
and dressing. Cut each eggplant slice
into 6 pieces and toss with the dressing.

ROASTED CAULIFLOWER WITH CURRY AND MINT

Start to finish: 45 minutes
(10 minutes active) / Servings: 4

½ cup olive oil

1 teaspoon curry powder

1 teaspoon ground cumin

1 teaspoon kosher salt

½ teaspoon ground black pepper

2 medium heads cauliflower (about
4 pounds total), cored and cut into
2-inch pieces

3 tablespoons minced fresh mint

2 tablespoons sweet-and-sour
mint dressing

Heat the oven to 475°F with an oven
rack in the middle position. Line a
rimmed baking sheet with foil. In
a large bowl, combine the oil, curry
powder, cumin, salt and pepper. Add
the cauliflower and toss. Transfer to
the prepared baking sheet, reserving
the bowl. Arrange the pieces cut side
down. Roast until well browned, about
30 minutes. Let cool. In the reserved
bowl, combine the mint with the
dressing. Add the cauliflower and
toss to coat.

ROASTED BROCCOLI RABE WITH FENNEL AND CHILI FLAKES

Start to finish: 30 minutes
(10 minutes active) / Servings: 4

1 pound broccoli rabe,
ends trimmed, well dried

½ cup olive oil

1 tablespoon ground fennel

1 teaspoon kosher salt

1 teaspoon ground black pepper

1 teaspoon red pepper flakes

2 tablespoons sweet-and-sour
mint dressing

Heat the oven to 500°F with an oven
rack in the middle position. Line a
rimmed baking sheet with foil. In a
large bowl, toss the broccoli rabe with
the oil, fennel, salt, black pepper and
red pepper flakes. Transfer to the
baking sheet, reserving the bowl.
Roast, stirring halfway through, until
just beginning to brown, 12 to 15
minutes. Let cool. Return to the bowl
and toss with the dressing.

Cilantro-Jalapeño Adobo Sauce

Start to finish: **20 minutes** / Makes **about 1 cup**

Spanish for marinade, adobo can be many things, but it began as a blend of olive oil, vinegar and spices that was slathered over meat and other foods to keep them from spoiling. We wanted a sauce that could go with just about anything and were inspired by a Mexican-style adobo from Rick Bayless, who blends together garlic, serrano chilies, cilantro, parsley and oil. We wanted to cut back on the oil and heat, so we chose jalapeño peppers over serrano chilies; the latter can vary widely in heat level. We dropped the parsley and went all in on cilantro; its fresh, clean flavor was even bolder when it didn't need to compete with another herb. Our sauce packs moderate heat; if you prefer a milder version, replace two of the jalapeños with one large Anaheim or poblano chili. Since it's blended with oil, the herb sauce can be refrigerated for up to three weeks.

Don't forget to wash and dry your herbs. *Cilantro can be quite sandy. A salad spinner is the easiest way to wash and dry it.*

1. Heat the broiler with an oven rack 6 inches from the element. Arrange the jalapeños and garlic on a rimmed baking sheet and broil, turning as necessary, until the chilies are evenly blistered and the garlic skins are spotted brown, 8 to 10 minutes. If the garlic blackens too quickly, remove it first. Cover with foil and let sit until cool enough to handle, about 10 minutes. Peel, stem and seed the chilies and peel the garlic, trimming away any scorched bits.

2. In a food processor, combine the chilies, garlic and all remaining ingredients. Process until smooth, 1 to 2 minutes, scraping the bowl as needed. Taste and season with salt and lime juice as desired.

4 large jalapeño chilies

6 medium garlic cloves, unpeeled

5 cups (about 4 ounces) lightly packed fresh cilantro leaves and tender stems

6 tablespoons extra-virgin olive oil

1 tablespoon lime juice, plus more as needed

¾ teaspoon kosher salt

½ teaspoon sugar

Central Mexican Guacamole

Start to finish: **10 minutes** / Servings: 4

Many guacamole recipes are a muddle of flavors. We prefer the simplicity of Central Mexican guacamole, which is seasoned with just three things—serrano chilies, white onion and cilantro. No garlic. No lime juice. Whether you use a mortar and pestle or a mixing bowl and the back of a fork, the onions, chilies and cilantro get mashed to a paste that permeates the avocados. Though acid is needed to balance the fat of the avocados and slow down oxidation (that ugly browning), lime juice can overpower guacamole. In Central Mexico, tomato provides the acid. Chopped fresh tomatoes offer a gentler acidity and flavor that—unlike limes—complement rather than compete with the other ingredients. Guacamole hinges on the ripeness of the avocados; they should be soft but slightly firm.

Don't discard the seeds from the chilies. *This recipe relies on them for a pleasant heat.*

In a bowl, combine 2 tablespoons of the cilantro, the chilies, onion and ½ teaspoon salt. Mash with the bottom of a dry measuring cup until a rough paste forms, about 1 minute. Scoop the avocado flesh into the bowl and coarsely mash with a potato masher or fork. Stir in half of the tomatoes until combined. Taste and season with salt. Transfer to a serving bowl and sprinkle with the remaining cilantro and tomatoes.

4 tablespoons finely chopped fresh cilantro, divided

1 or 2 serrano chilies, stemmed and finely chopped

2 tablespoons finely chopped white onion

Kosher salt

3 ripe avocados, halved and pitted

1 pint grape tomatoes, finely chopped

Harissa

Start to finish: **15 minutes** / Makes **about 1½ cups**

Our version of harissa, the spicy condiment that originated in North Africa, adds delicious punch to dips, soups, sauces and vinaigrettes. New Mexico chilies did the best job of matching harder-to-find North African chilies, bringing balanced heat. For more fire, a bit of cayenne can be added. Plenty of recipes call for either sun-dried tomatoes or roasted red peppers; we found a combination gave our harissa the sweet, ketchup-like profile Americans love and helped make it more of an all-purpose sauce, rather than simply a hot sauce. Frying the chilies, whole spices and garlic in oil is easier and works better than the traditional method of toasting in a dry skillet. And while most recipes call for rehydrating the dried chilies, we found the hot oil softened them adequately, giving the harissa a pleasant, slightly coarse texture. Adding garlic to the mix mellowed its bite, and leaving the cloves whole ensured they wouldn't burn (and meant less prep work). We favored white balsamic vinegar for its mild acidity and slight sweetness. Lemon juice or white wine vinegar sweetened with a pinch of sugar are good substitutes.

4 dried New Mexico chilies, stemmed, seeded and torn into rough pieces

½ cup grapeseed or other neutral oil

6 medium garlic cloves, peeled

1 teaspoon caraway seeds

1 teaspoon cumin seeds

1 cup drained roasted red peppers, patted dry

½ cup drained oil-packed sun-dried tomatoes

1 tablespoon white balsamic vinegar

Kosher salt

Cayenne pepper

In a small saucepan over medium, combine the chilies, oil, garlic, caraway and cumin. Cook, stirring often, until the garlic is light golden brown and the chilies are fragrant, about 5 minutes. Carefully transfer the mixture to a food processor and add the red peppers, tomatoes, vinegar and ¾ teaspoon of salt. Process until smooth, about 3 minutes, scraping the bowl once or twice. Taste and season with salt and cayenne. Serve immediately or refrigerate in an airtight container for up to 3 weeks.

HARISSA HISTORY

Harissa (pronounced ha-REE-sah) may well be one of the original hot sauces, and it has enjoyed a bit of piggyback popularity as Sriracha and other spicy condiments have attracted near cultish followings. Chilies didn't land in Africa until the mid-16th century via conquerors, colonialists and traders returning from Central America. The easy-to-grow ingredient found a warm reception in arid African climates, adding an affordable kick to previously bland grain-based diets. Tunisia is credited with the birth of harissa, but it is popular across the region. Tunisians have a stronger predilection for spice than their neighbors, so their harissa emphasizes heat over nuance. In Morocco, where the cuisine is more complex, tomato paste, rose water and preserved lemon might play into the condiment's flavor. Our recipe is honest to its origins but suited to the foods and flavors of the American palate. We use our harissa sauce in all kinds of ways, including adding some kick to roasted potatoes (p. 135).

SPICY HARISSA DIPPING SAUCE

Start to finish: **5 minutes**
Makes **1 cup**

Use this sauce anytime you'd reach for ketchup.

¾ cup mayonnaise

2 tablespoons harissa

2 tablespoons ketchup

Hot sauce

In a bowl, stir together the mayonnaise, harissa and ketchup. Season with hot sauce, to taste.

GREEK YOGURT-HARISSA DIP

Start to finish: **5 minutes**
Makes about **2 cups**

This works well as an appetizer with crudités and crackers or as a sandwich spread with cold cuts, leftover chicken or grilled lamb.

2 cups plain whole-milk Greek-style yogurt

3 tablespoons harissa

2 tablespoons chopped fresh parsley, mint or a combination

1 teaspoon white sugar

Kosher salt and ground black pepper

In a bowl, stir together the yogurt, harissa, herbs and sugar. Taste and season with salt and pepper.

HARISSA-CILANTRO VINAIGRETTE

Start to finish: **5 minutes**
Makes about **½ cup**

This dressing pairs well with assertive greens or can be drizzled over roasted beets, cauliflower or broccoli. It's also a terrific sauce for salmon.

2 tablespoons lemon juice

1 tablespoon harissa

1 tablespoon water

2 teaspoons honey

Kosher salt

5 tablespoons extra-virgin olive oil

Ground black pepper

2 tablespoons chopped fresh cilantro

In a bowl, whisk together the lemon juice, harissa, water, honey and ¼ teaspoon of salt. Add the oil and whisk until emulsified. Taste and season with additional salt and pepper, then stir in the cilantro.

Japanese-Style Salt-Pickled Radish and Red Onion (Yasai no Sokuseki-zuke)

Start to finish: 45 minutes (10 minutes active)
Makes about 2 cups

These simple pickles are made with salt to draw out the vegetables' water, and the salty liquid that results serves as a brine for curing. Lemon zest pairs well with the peppery radishes and onion, and a small piece of kombu seaweed adds savoriness. After draining and rinsing, the pickles can be refrigerated for up to two days. Serve them as a crunchy condiment to round out a meal.

Don't be afraid to firmly massage *the radishes with the salt. But after adding the onion, massage gently and briefly, just until the onion wilts.*

1. In a 1-quart zip-close bag, combine the radishes and 1 teaspoon salt. Seal the bag, removing as much air as possible, then massage the salt into the radishes. When liquid begins to collect and the radishes are wilted, after about 1 minute, add the onion. Reseal the bag, again removing as much air as possible, and gently massage until the onion is just wilted, another 30 seconds.

2. Add the zest and kombu, reseal the bag, removing as much air as possible, then massage to evenly distribute and soften the kombu. Lay the bag flat in a baking dish or rimmed baking sheet. Top with a second baking dish or baking sheet and weigh down with about 4 pounds of cans or filled bottles. Let stand at room temperature for 30 minutes, or refrigerate for up to 1 day.

3. Drain in a colander and discard the kombu. Rinse under cold water. Drain well, squeezing gently to remove as much moisture as possible.

10 ounces small red radishes, thinly sliced, or 10 ounces daikon, peeled, halved lengthwise and thinly sliced

Kosher salt

½ small red onion, thinly sliced

1 tablespoon grated lemon zest

2-inch square kombu seaweed, cut or broken into 5 pieces

Colombian Avocado Salsa (Ají de Aguacate)

Start to finish: **15 minutes** / Makes 3½ cups

Colombian food does not tend to be spicy, so we seeded the chilies for this salsa. The Anaheims gave the sauce deep pepper flavor, while the habanero added fruitiness and heat.

Don't use fully ripe avocados, *which made thin salsa. They should give only slightly when pressed.*

1. In a food processor, process the scallions and all 3 chilies until finely chopped, about 20 seconds. Add the cilantro, vinegar and 1½ teaspoons salt. Process until the cilantro is finely chopped, about 10 seconds, scraping the sides as needed.

2. In a medium bowl, mash the flesh from 2 avocado halves and ⅓ of the chopped eggs with a fork until mostly smooth but with some lumps. Roughly chop the remaining 4 avocado halves and transfer to the bowl. Add the lime juice and fold with a silicone spatula to combine.

3. Reserve 2 tablespoons of the chopped tomato and 2 tablespoons of the remaining chopped eggs for garnish. Mix the remaining tomato and eggs into the avocado mixture, then gently fold in the chili-cilantro mixture. Taste and season with salt.

4. Transfer the salsa to a serving bowl and top with the reserved tomato and chopped eggs.

4 scallions, cut into 1-inch lengths

2 Anaheim chilies, stemmed, seeded and cut into rough 1-inch pieces

1 habanero chili, stemmed and seeded

1¼ cups lightly packed fresh cilantro

2 tablespoons white vinegar

Kosher salt

3 ripe avocados (see note), halved and pitted

3 hard-cooked large eggs, peeled and chopped

2 tablespoons lime juice

1 plum tomato, cored, seeded and finely chopped

Greek Dips

TZATZIKI

Start to finish: **15 minutes** / Makes about 3½ **cups**

The cucumber-yogurt dip known as tzatziki is often seasoned with lemon juice in the U.S. But in Greece cooks prefer red wine vinegar because it adds sharp acidity without the citrus notes to compete with the other ingredients. Thick and cooling, tzatziki can be served as a dip, but it's also an ideal condiment or accompaniment for grilled meats and seafood and fried foods.

Don't use nonfat Greek yogurt. Without any fat, the flavor of the tzatziki is weak and thin. Also, when shredding the cucumbers, don't shred the cores, as the seeds are watery and have a slight bitterness and unappealing texture.

2 English cucumbers, halved crosswise

Kosher salt

1¾ cups plain whole-milk or low-fat Greek yogurt

½ cup extra-virgin olive oil

3 medium garlic cloves, finely grated

3 tablespoons chopped fresh mint, plus more to serve

3 tablespoons chopped fresh dill, plus more to serve

4 teaspoons red wine vinegar

1. Set a colander in a medium bowl, then set a box grater in the colander. Grate the cucumber halves on the grater's large holes, rotating and grating only down to the seedy core. Discard the cores. Sprinkle the shredded cucumber with 2 teaspoons salt and toss. Set aside to drain for 10 minutes.

2. Meanwhile, in a medium bowl, whisk the yogurt, oil, garlic, mint, dill and vinegar.

3. A handful at a time, squeeze the shredded cucumber to remove as much liquid as possible, then set on a cutting board; reserve 2 teaspoons of the cucumber liquid. Finely chop the squeezed cucumber, then stir into the yogurt mixture. Stir in the reserved cucumber liquid and ½ teaspoon salt. Transfer to a serving bowl and sprinkle with additional mint and dill.

SPICY FETA DIP (TIROKAFTERI)

Start to finish: **10 minutes** / Makes about 3½ cups

Tirokafteri is a Greek cheese-based dip or spread that can be flavored numerous ways. In our version, we build complexity by combining two cheeses with different characteristics: creamy, tangy chèvre (fresh goat cheese) and firm, briny feta. Roasted red peppers give the dip sweetness and color; the Anaheim chili and hot smoked paprika lend some heat. If you don't have hot smoked paprika, you can substitute with ½ teaspoon sweet smoked paprika plus ¼ teaspoon cayenne pepper.

Don't add more Anaheim chili if you're looking to increase the spiciness. Instead, up the hot paprika or toss a Fresno chili into the food processor before pureeing.

8 ounces chèvre (fresh goat cheese)

½ cup drained roasted red peppers, patted dry

1 Anaheim chili, stemmed, seeded and chopped

3 tablespoons extra-virgin olive oil,
plus more to serve

¾ teaspoon hot smoked paprika

½ teaspoon honey

Kosher salt and ground black pepper

6 ounces feta cheese, crumbled (1½ cups)

½ cup fresh dill, chopped, plus more to serve

1. In a food processor, combine the goat cheese, roasted peppers, Anaheim chili, oil, paprika, honey, ½ teaspoon salt and ¼ teaspoon black pepper. Process until smooth, about 1 minute, scraping the bowl as needed.

2. Transfer to a medium bowl. Fold in the feta and dill, then taste and season with salt and pepper. Transfer to a serving bowl and top with additional oil, dill and black pepper.

Tomatillo-Avocado Salsa

Start to finish: **15 minutes** / Makes 1½ cups

___

This smooth, herbal salsa is a nice alternative to toma-
to-based versions. The tartness of the tomatillos balances
the creamy richness of the avocado. We greatly preferred
serrano chilies over jalapeños here, as they provided more
fruitiness and flavor. Serve with tortilla chips, tacos,
quesadillas, enchiladas and fried or scrambled eggs.

Don't forget to seed the serrano chilies. *This salsa is meant
to be creamy and cooling, not sharp and spicy. Also, be sure to
roughly chop the chilies before adding them to the processor
so they break down easily.*

___

In a food processor, combine the tomatillos, cilantro, scallions,
chilies, garlic, oil and 1¼ teaspoons salt. Process until finely
chopped, about 1 minute. Add the avocado and lime juice, then
process until smooth and creamy, about 1 minute, scraping the
bowl as needed. Taste and season with salt.

3 medium tomatillos (about
6 ounces), husked, cored and
halved

¼ cup lightly packed fresh
cilantro

3 scallions, roughly chopped

2 serrano chilies, stemmed,
seeded and roughly chopped

1 medium garlic clove,
smashed and peeled

1 tablespoon grapeseed
or other neutral oil

Kosher salt

1 ripe avocado, halved, pitted,
peeled and roughly chopped

2 teaspoons lime juice

Ancho Chili Salsa Roja

Start to finish: **15 minutes** / Makes **about 1½ cups**

In this salsa, fresh tomato, garlic and shallot complement the earthy, smoky notes of ancho chilies. Use it as a dip for tortilla chips, spooned onto tacos or in a marinade for beef, pork or chicken.

1. In a 12-inch skillet over medium, toast the chilies, pressing with a wide metal spatula and flipping once or twice, until fragrant and a shade darker in color, 2 to 4 minutes. Transfer to a medium bowl and pour in enough boiling water to cover. Let stand until softened, about 10 minutes.

2. Drain the chilies and discard the soaking liquid. Transfer to a food processor or blender. Add the garlic, shallot, tomato, sugar, 1 teaspoon salt and ½ cup water. Process until finely chopped and well combined, about 20 seconds, scraping the sides as needed.

3 medium ancho chilies, stemmed, seeded and torn into pieces

Boiling water

1 large garlic clove, smashed and peeled

1 medium shallot, roughly chopped

1 medium vine-ripened tomato, cored and roughly chopped

2 teaspoons white sugar

Kosher salt

Miso-Ginger Dressing

Start to finish: **10 minutes** / Makes **about 1 cup**

Miso and ginger are mainstays of the Japanese kitchen. This recipe combines them with items common to the Western pantry—Dijon mustard and honey—to create a zesty dressing. The creamy texture and mild, sweet-salty flavor of white miso, also called shiro miso, worked best. Walnuts gave the dressing richness and body. If the dressing becomes too thick after being refrigerated, gradually whisk in water to thin it. Because of its creamy, thick texture, this dressing goes well with heartier salad greens, as well as vegetables, grains, beans, chicken and fish.

Don't toast the walnuts. *They provide texture, but their flavor should be subtle. Toasting them makes them too assertive.*

In a blender, combine all ingredients except the oil. Blend until the walnuts are finely ground and the dressing is smooth, about 1 minute. Add the oil and blend until emulsified, about 30 seconds.

USE THIS DRESSING:

- On a chopped salad of romaine, cucumbers, cherry tomatoes, radishes, red onion and mint

- On a radicchio, endive and arugula salad with roasted beets and toasted chopped walnuts

- Tossed with or drizzled over blanched vegetables, especially green beans, asparagus, broccoli, cauliflower and carrots

- As a sauce for poached whitefish or salmon

- As a dressing for cabbage slaws—thinly sliced red, white or napa cabbage with grated carrots, sliced scallions, diced jalapeño and herbs, such as fresh parsley, cilantro, basil or mint

- As a dressing for a shredded chicken salad with blanched sugar snap peas, thinly sliced red pepper and celery and fresh herbs

- As a dressing for a rice salad with diced celery, cucumber, toasted chopped almonds, raisins, sliced scallions and chopped parsley or mint

- Drizzled on grilled vegetables, especially eggplant, zucchini, yellow squash, asparagus and onions

⅓ cup walnuts

⅓ cup white miso

1 teaspoon grated lemon zest, plus ¼ cup lemon juice (1 to 2 lemons)

¼ cup water

1-ounce piece fresh ginger, peeled and thinly sliced

1 teaspoon Dijon mustard

1 teaspoon honey

½ teaspoon ground white pepper

½ cup grapeseed or other neutral oil

Muhammara

Start to finish: 20 minutes / Makes 2 cups

Muhammara is a spicy-tart dip for flatbread made from walnuts and roasted red peppers. The name comes from the Arabic word for reddened, and the dish originated in Syria, where it often is served alongside hummus and baba ganoush. Aleppo pepper is made from ground dried Halaby chilies; it tastes subtly of cumin and fruit, with only mild heat. Look for it in well-stocked markets and spice shops, but if you cannot find it, simply leave it out—the muhammara still will be delicious. Serve with flatbread or vegetables for dipping or use as a sandwich spread.

Don't forget to pat the roasted peppers dry after draining them. Excess moisture will make the muhammara watery in both flavor and consistency.

1. In a small skillet over medium, toast the cumin, stirring, until fragrant, about 30 seconds. Remove from the heat and set aside.

2. In a food processor, process the pita bread and walnuts until finely ground, about 45 seconds. Add the cumin, roasted peppers, Aleppo pepper (if using), pepper flakes, 2 teaspoons salt and 1 teaspoon black pepper. Process until smooth, about 45 seconds, scraping the bowl as needed.

3. Add the pomegranate molasses and lemon juice and process until combined, about 10 seconds. With the machine running, drizzle in the oil. Taste and season with salt and pepper, then transfer to a serving bowl. Drizzle with additional pomegranate molasses and oil, then sprinkle with parsley.

4 teaspoons ground cumin

7-inch pita bread, torn into rough pieces

1 cup walnuts

Two 12-ounce jars roasted red peppers, drained and patted dry (2 cups)

1 teaspoon Aleppo pepper (optional; see headnote)

½ teaspoon red pepper flakes

Kosher salt and ground black pepper

3 tablespoons pomegranate molasses, plus more to serve

2 tablespoons lemon juice

6 tablespoons extra-virgin olive oil, plus more to serve

Chopped fresh flat-leaf parsley, to serve

Vietnamese Scallion Sauce

Start to finish: 20 minutes / Makes about ½ cup

Vietnamese scallion oil, called mõ hành, is used as a garnish or condiment on a number of different foods, from grilled clams on the half shell to steamed rice. It adds fresh allium notes as well as bright green color to any dish it's drizzled onto. And since fat carries flavor, it also acts as a flavor booster. At its most basic, mõ hành is made by pouring hot oil over sliced scallions to release their flavor and tenderize them. Our version includes savory fish sauce (or soy sauce), pungent ginger and a little sugar to build complexity. It's delicious spooned onto simply cooked asparagus, shrimp or skirt steak (recipes p. 629). Or try it on grilled pork chops, corn on the cob or steamed dumplings. Leftover scallion oil can be refrigerated in an airtight container for up to three days; return it to room temperature before serving.

Don't just slice the scallions. For proper texture and flavor, the scallions should be chopped. Slice them first, then run the knife blade over them a few times to further break them down.

1. **In a medium heatproof bowl,** combine the scallions, ¼ teaspoon salt and 1 teaspoon pepper. Using your fingers, gently rub the salt and pepper into the scallions until the scallions begin to wilt.

2. **In a small saucepan** over medium-high, heat the oil until shimmering, then pour the hot oil over the scallions; the scallions will sizzle. Stir, then stir in the fish sauce, ginger and sugar. Cool to room temperature.

½ cup chopped scallions
(5 or 6 scallions; see headnote)

Kosher salt and ground black pepper

¼ cup peanut or other neutral oil

1½ tablespoons fish sauce or soy sauce

1½ tablespoons finely grated fresh ginger

1 teaspoon white sugar

PAN-SEARED SKIRT STEAK

In a 12-inch skillet over medium-high, heat **1 tablespoon neutral oil** until barely smoking. Add **1 pound beef skirt steak** (trimmed and cut into 3- to 4-inch sections) and cook, until well browned on both sides, 5 to 7 minutes total, flipping once about halfway through. Transfer to a plate and let rest for 10 minutes. Cut the steak against the grain into thin slices. Drizzle with scallion oil.

PAN-SEARED SHRIMP

In a 12-inch skillet over medium-high, heat **1 tablespoon neutral oil** until barely smoking. Add 1½ **pounds extra-large (21/25 per pound) shrimp** (peeled and deveined) in an even layer and cook without stirring until well browned, about 3 minutes. Stir the shrimp, then remove the pan from the heat and stir constantly, allowing the skillet's residual heat to finish the cooking, until the shrimp are opaque throughout, another 20 to 30 seconds. Serve over steamed white rice and topped with scallion oil.

SEARED AND STEAMED ASPARAGUS

In a 12-inch skillet over medium-high, heat **1 tablespoon neutral oil** until barely smoking. Add 1½ **pounds asparagus** (trimmed and halved on the diagonal) and cook, stirring only a few times, until charred. Add 3 tablespoons water, then immediately cover. Reduce to low and cook, stirring just once or twice, until the asparagus is crisp-tender, 2 to 3 minutes. Serve with scallion oil spooned over.

Salsa Macha Costeña

Start to finish: 30 minutes / Makes about 3 cups

---

2 cups olive oil (see headnote) or neutral oil

4 medium garlic cloves, smashed and peeled

½ cup blanched slivered almonds

½ cup peanuts (see headnote)

3 tablespoons raw cocoa nibs

2 tablespoons sesame seeds

5 medium (1½ ounces) guajillo chilies, stemmed, seeded and torn into rough 2-inch pieces

2 (¼ ounce) chipotle or morita chilies, stemmed, seeded and torn into rough 2-inch pieces (see headnote)

2 (1¼ ounces) ancho chilies, stemmed, seeded and torn into rough 2-inch pieces

1 teaspoon dried oregano

2 teaspoons cider vinegar

Kosher salt

Salsa macha is a dark, thick, rich and nutty condiment. The base of the salsa is always oil, but the combination of nuts, spices and dried chilies that give it character varies cook to cook. This version from Puerto Vallarta native Paola Briseño González is earthy, complex and mildly spicy—and delicious on just about anything, including scrambled eggs, quesadillas and grilled seafood. Cocoa nibs, an unusual addition, lend texture along with pleasantly bitter notes that perfectly complement the chilies and nuts. The salsa's smokiness comes from chipotle or morita chilies. Both are dried smoked jalapeños, but beyond that, there seems to be little agreement about the exact differences between the two. Either will work in this recipe, but steer clear of chipotle chilies in adobo sauce. Feel free to use whatever type of unflavored peanuts you have on hand, whether they're roasted or raw, salted or unsalted. The salsa can be refrigerated in an airtight container for up to several months; bring to room temperature before serving.

Don't use extra-virgin olive oil, as its flavor is too assertive. Rather, use regular olive oil or light olive oil, or even a neutral oil such as grapeseed. And don't rush cooking the garlic, nuts and seeds. The goal is to coax all the oils, and flavors, from the nuts, seeds and chilies by slowly frying them in the oil.

1. In a medium saucepan over medium, combine the oil and garlic and cook, stirring, until the oil starts to bubble, about 4 minutes. Add the almonds, peanuts, cacao nibs and sesame seeds. Cook, stirring occasionally, until the garlic and nuts are fragrant and lightly golden, 8 to 10 minutes. Add all three chili varieties and cook, stirring, until they soften and brighten in color, about 2 minutes. Remove from the heat, stir in the oregano and cool for 10 minutes.

2. Using a slotted spoon, transfer the solids to a food processor (it's fine if tiny bits remain in the oil) and add the vinegar and 1 teaspoon salt; reserve the oil. Process until the mixture is chopped, 30 to 60 seconds, scraping down the bowl as needed. Add the oil and pulse until the solids are evenly and finely chopped, about 4 pulses. Taste and season with salt. Transfer to a container and use right away or cover and refrigerate for up to several months (bring to room temperature before serving).

Honey-Chili Sauce

Start to finish: **5 minutes** / Makes **about ¾ cup**

You can pay big money for spicy honey these days, or you can make your own. Our version skews Asian by spiking mild honey with chili-garlic sauce, and it takes honey to some unexpected places. Any mild honey, such as clover, will work. It's great drizzled over sweet potatoes, grilled or roasted vegetables, corn on the cob, or chicken or pork. And don't stop there. Consider a drizzle over pepperoni pizza, or on a soppresatta and mozzarella sandwich. Or use it to jazz up a grilled cheese.

In a small bowl, stir together all ingredients.

167 grams (½ cup) honey

3 tablespoons unseasoned rice vinegar

1 tablespoon chili-garlic sauce

Jalapeño-Mint Sauce

Start to finish: **5 minutes** / Makes about 1¼ cups

This light, bright sauce takes moments to prepare and pairs particularly well with grilled or roasted fish, especially meaty swordfish, halibut and salmon. We also like it as a sauce alongside grilled vegetables and roasted cauliflower. Or use it as a sauce for tacos or lettuce wraps, or as a dressing for room-temperature pasta salads. Three-inch jalapeños—ribs and seeds removed—worked best for balanced heat. If you prefer a spicier sauce, incorporate a few seeds.

Don't let this sauce sit for more than an hour or two; it's best served soon after it is made. If it begins to separate, stir to recombine.

In a food processor, combine all ingredients. Process until smooth, about 1 minute, scraping the bowl as necessary. Taste and season with salt. Serve immediately.

1 cup lightly packed fresh
mint leaves

⅔ cup extra-virgin olive oil

3 medium jalapeño chilies,
stemmed, seeded and
roughly chopped

2 tablespoons lime juice

1 tablespoon honey

2 teaspoons finely grated
fresh ginger

1 garlic clove,
smashed and peeled

¾ teaspoon kosher salt, plus
more as needed

Slow-Roasted Tomatoes

Start to finish: 3½ hours (15 minutes active)
Makes about 32 halves

We love what a burst of bright tomato flavor can do for a recipe. But supermarket tomatoes are a disappointment, especially during winter. So we looked for a way to improve year-round tomatoes and found it by way of a slow roast to concentrate flavor. We began by coating halved plum tomatoes with a mix of tomato paste and vinegar, then roasting them on kitchen parchment–lined baking sheets along with garlic. We tried several variations of vinegar, including white and regular balsamic; we found white balsamic worked best. Mixing olive oil into the coating mixture made the vinegar and tomatoes burn and stick to the parchment. Drizzling the olive oil over the tomatoes separately worked better. Medium plum tomatoes, roughly 4 ounces each, were ideal. If your tomatoes are smaller, start checking them after three hours in the oven.

¼ cup white balsamic vinegar

¼ cup tomato paste

2 teaspoons kosher salt

1 teaspoon ground
black pepper

4 pounds plum tomatoes
(about 16 medium), halved
lengthwise

¼ cup extra-virgin olive oil

1. Heat the oven to 325°F with a rack in the middle position. Line a rimmed baking sheet with kitchen parchment. In a large bowl, whisk together the vinegar, tomato paste, salt and pepper. Add the tomatoes and toss to coat. Arrange the tomatoes cut side up on the prepared baking sheet. Drizzle evenly with the oil.

2. Roast until the tomatoes are shriveled, caramelized and lightly charred at the edges, about 3½ hours, rotating the pan halfway through. Serve immediately, or let cool, transfer to a lidded container and refrigerate for up to 1 week.

Homemade Chipotles in Adobo Sauce

Start to finish: 45 minutes (5 minutes active)
Makes **16 chipotles with sauce**

Canned chipotles in adobo are a great pantry staple. The chilies (or even just a spoonful of the sauce) are an easy way to add moderate heat and deep, smoky flavor to sauces, soups, meats and sandwiches. They are made by drying and smoking jalapeño peppers, then packing them in a rich sauce made from tomatoes and even more chilies. We love homemade even more; the texture of the chilies is firmer and the sauce is thicker and more robustly flavored. Be sure to use dried morita chipotles, which are shiny and dark. They are smaller, sweeter and smokier than tan-colored meco chipotles, which tend to be leathery and nutty.

In a medium saucepan, combine the chipotles and 3 cups water. Bring to a boil, then simmer for 20 minutes. Remove all but 4 of the chilies from the pan and set aside. In a blender, combine the cooking water and the remaining 4 chipotles. Add the remaining ingredients. Blend until mostly smooth, then return to the pan. Add the reserved chilies, then simmer, stirring occasionally, until thickened, about 20 minutes. Cool, then refrigerate. The chipotles keep for up to 1 month.

20 dried morita chipotle chilies (about 1¼ ounces), stems removed

1 medium yellow onion, roughly chopped

6 medium garlic cloves

⅓ cup cider vinegar

¼ cup ketchup

¼ cup packed light brown sugar

1 teaspoon ground cumin

1 teaspoon ground coriander

1 teaspoon kosher salt

½ teaspoon dried thyme

Pickled Vegetables (Escabeche)

Start to finish: 45 minutes (30 minutes active), plus cooling
Makes about 4 cups

Escabeche translates as marinade, or pickle, and refers to a variety of pickled dishes popular in Spanish and Latin American cooking. Here, we pickle vegetables for a piquant side dish. Salting the vegetables before pickling them enhanced their crispness and intensified their final flavor. That's because salting removes water, allowing them to better absorb the brine. Once cooled, the pickled vegetables can be eaten immediately, but their flavor improves with time. We left the whole spices in the brine to infuse even more during storage.

Don't slice the onions crosswise. We preferred the texture and appearance of onions sliced from pole to pole. And the thinner the slices the better; aim for about ⅛-inch thickness.

1. In a bowl, toss together the onions, carrots, jalapeños and salt. Let sit for 30 to 60 minutes. Transfer the vegetables to a colander and rinse well, then set aside to drain.

2. Meanwhile, in a medium saucepan over high, combine the vinegar, 1 cup water, sugar, peppercorns, coriander, pepper flakes, if using, allspice and bay leaf. Bring to a boil, then reduce to medium and simmer for 5 minutes.

3. Transfer the vegetables to a canning jar or heatproof, lidded container. Pour the hot brine over them, ensuring they are fully submerged. Cool to room temperature, about 2 hours, then cover and refrigerate for up to 1 month.

1 large red onion (¾ pound), halved and thinly sliced lengthwise

½ pound carrots, peeled, halved lengthwise and thinly sliced on the diagonal

2 jalapeño chilies, thinly sliced crosswise

5 teaspoons kosher salt

1 cup distilled white vinegar

½ cup white sugar

½ teaspoon black peppercorns

½ teaspoon coriander seeds

¼ teaspoon red pepper flakes (optional)

6 allspice berries

1 bay leaf

Other uses for pickling brine:

GET INTO A PICKLE

The pickling brine for our escabeche can be used:

- To poach fish or boneless chicken breasts (use equal parts water and brine)

- In place of citrus juice in salsa or ceviche

- In vinaigrettes, store-bought barbecue sauces and bloody mary cocktails

- To deglaze a pan

- To braise chicken or pork (use pickling brine for 20 percent of the liquid)

- To brighten the flavor of cooked beans (stir in brine immediately after cooking)

- To glaze vegetables (combine brine, butter and a sweetener, such as maple syrup, honey or sugar)

MUSTARD VINAIGRETTE

Start to finish: 5 minutes
Makes about 1 cup

To vary this recipe, add minced garlic, shallot or fresh thyme and/or a squeeze of honey.

1 tablespoon Dijon mustard

3 tablespoons pickling brine

¾ cup extra-virgin olive oil

Kosher salt and ground black pepper

In a bowl, whisk together the mustard and brine until smooth. Continue to whisk and add the oil slowly until the dressing is emulsified, about 15 seconds. Season with salt and pepper.

VINEGAR-BASED BARBECUE SAUCE

Start to finish: 10 minutes
Makes about 1⅓ cups

1 cup pickling brine

¼ cup ketchup

2 tablespoons packed brown sugar

1 tablespoon red pepper flakes

1 teaspoon ground black pepper

Kosher salt

In a medium bowl, whisk together all ingredients except the salt. Season to taste.

SPICY PEANUT SAUCE

Start to finish: 10 minutes
Makes about 1 cup

This recipe works equally well with creamy or chunky peanut butter.

½ cup natural peanut butter

¼ cup pickling brine

1 tablespoon soy sauce

1 tablespoon white sugar

1 garlic clove, minced

½ teaspoon red pepper flakes

2 tablespoons water, plus more as needed

In a blender, combine all ingredients. Blend until smooth, adding water 1 tablespoon at a time to achieve desired consistency.

Spicy Garlic-and-Herb Oil

Start to finish: **10 minutes** / Makes **about 1 cup**

This herb-rich oil is great brushed on to warm piadine (see recipe p. 434). It also can be served as a dip for bread. If you like, substitute fresh oregano, marjoram or mint for the dill. Other uses: Drizzle over pasta, polenta and fried eggs, or use as a base for vinaigrettes with lemon juice or white balsamic vinegar.

In a food processor, combine all ingredients and process until smooth, about 20 seconds, scraping the bowl as needed.

2 cups lightly packed fresh flat-leaf parsley leaves

½ cup plus 2 tablespoons extra-virgin olive oil

½ cup roughly chopped fresh chives

¼ cup roughly chopped fresh dill

1 tablespoon red pepper flakes

1 large garlic clove, smashed and peeled

1 teaspoon kosher salt

½ teaspoon ground black pepper

Spiced Yogurt Dressing

Start to finish: **5 minutes** / Makes **about 1½ cups**

Our spiced yogurt dressing was inspired by Madhur Jaffrey, the Delhi-born actress, cookbook author and television chef who has spent decades exploring the food of her homeland and beyond. We loved the yogurt dressing in her book, "Vegetarian India." The warm spices in this thick dressing work with everything from simple salads of romaine or spinach to poached salmon, herbed chickpeas and roasted vegetables, such as beets, cauliflower and broccoli. Use it to dress farro or barley salads, as a dipping sauce for whole artichokes, over warm or room-temperature potatoes or with grilled or roasted lamb. For a thinner consistency, add water, a tablespoon at a time, whisking until smooth after each addition. Because it is made without herbs or much garlic, it refrigerates well for up to five days.

Don't overdo the garlic. *More than ⅛ teaspoon of finely grated raw garlic—use a wand-style grater—easily overpowered the dressing.*

In a medium bowl, whisk together the yogurt, coriander, cumin, turmeric, salt, pepper, cayenne and garlic. Add the oil, vinegar and honey, then whisk until smooth. Add water, 1 tablespoon at a time, to reach desired consistency.

1 cup plain whole-milk
Greek-style yogurt

2 teaspoons ground
coriander

¾ teaspoon ground cumin

½ teaspoon ground turmeric

½ teaspoon kosher salt

¼ teaspoon ground
black pepper

⅛ to ¼ teaspoon
cayenne pepper

⅛ teaspoon finely
grated garlic

3 tablespoons
extra-virgin olive oil

3½ teaspoons
red wine vinegar

1 teaspoon honey

Fig-Olive Tapenade

Start to finish: 20 minutes / Makes about 2 cups

A paste made of figs and olives may sound like an oddball pairing, but the two work well together. The sweetness of the figs mitigates the brine and bitterness of the olives. A combination of Kalamata and more pungent oil-cured olives provided the best balance of flavor and creamy texture. To easily pit the olives, whack them with the side of a chef's knife to flatten, then simply use your fingers to pull out the pits. Soaking the figs made up for any difference in moisture content and ensured they ground easily to a smooth paste. We love this tapenade smeared on crostini, either alone or with fresh cheese or caramelized onions, as a dip for crudités, tossed with steamed vegetables or potatoes, as a topping for beef, chicken or fish, combined with olive oil and vinegar for a quick vinaigrette, or stirred into pasta.

***Don't forget to check your olives for pits**, even if they're labeled "pitted." We prefer to buy olives with pits and prep them ourselves, but pitted olives will work.*

5 ounces (1 cup) dried black mission figs, stemmed

1 cup Kalamata olives, pitted, rinsed and patted dry

½ cup oil-cured olives, pitted

¼ cup capers, rinsed and squeezed dry

2 oil-packed anchovy fillets, patted dry

1 teaspoon minced fresh rosemary

½ teaspoon grated orange zest

½ teaspoon red pepper flakes

¼ cup extra-virgin olive oil

1. In a small saucepan, bring 1 cup water to a boil. Add the figs, remove from the heat, then cover and let sit for 15 minutes. Drain the figs, reserving the soaking liquid. In a food processor, combine the figs, both olives, capers, anchovies, rosemary, zest, pepper flakes and 2 tablespoons of the fig soaking liquid. Process until a smooth paste forms, 1 to 2 minutes, scraping the bowl halfway through.

2. With the processor running, add the oil in a steady stream and process until incorporated, about 30 seconds. Transfer to a bowl or lidded container and let sit for 1 hour before serving. Tapenade can be refrigerated for up to 3 weeks.

Green Goddess Tofu Dressing

Start to finish: 20 minutes, plus chilling
Makes about 1½ cups

Green goddess salad dressing is one of those enchantingly retro recipes most of us have heard of even if we haven't actually tried it. The original recipe went heavy on the mayonnaise and later versions included sour cream and even avocado. We took the dressing to a lighter place with silken tofu, which provided a creamy base. From there we piled on the herbs. We liked parsley's clean, herbaceous flavor combined with the mellow onion note of chives and tarragon's distinctive licorice flavor. Lemon zest added a hit of citrus, but the juice was too sharp. Instead, we opted for sweet-tart white balsamic vinegar. We preferred the more neutral flavor of shelf-stable tofu—found in the Asian foods aisle—over its refrigerated counterpart. While the dressing can be served right away, we preferred to let the flavors meld for at least an hour. It keeps for up to four days refrigerated.

Don't use dried tarragon. *If fresh tarragon isn't available, substitute 3 tablespoons of chopped fresh dill or basil.*

---

2 tablespoons white balsamic vinegar

1 small garlic clove, smashed and peeled

8 ounces drained silken tofu (1 cup)

¾ cup lightly packed fresh flat-leaf parsley

⅓ cup roughly chopped fresh chives

¼ cup grapeseed or other neutral oil

2 tablespoons chopped fresh tarragon

1½ teaspoons grated lemon zest

1 oil-packed anchovy fillet

½ teaspoon kosher salt

¼ teaspoon ground black pepper

In a blender, combine all ingredients. Blend until smooth and uniformly pale green, 1 to 2 minutes. Transfer to a jar and refrigerate for at least 1 hour.

USE THIS DRESSING:

- Rice salad with chopped toasted almonds, diced celery and peas
- Chopped chicken salad with bacon, avocado and tomatoes
- Shredded chicken salad with spinach, sliced cucumbers, grated carrots and sliced red cabbage
- Fusilli pasta salad with grilled zucchini, summer squash, olives and cherry tomatoes
- Broiled or grilled fish
- Shrimp or seafood salad with diced celery, red pepper and lemon zest on frisee
- Romaine and watercress salad with chopped hard-cooked eggs and avocado

Whipped Feta

Start to finish: 15 minutes / Makes about 1½ cups

---

8 ounces feta cheese

2 tablespoons lemon juice

1 medium garlic clove, smashed and peeled

3 ounces cream cheese, room temperature

⅓ cup extra-virgin olive oil

½ teaspoon smoked paprika

½ teaspoon red pepper flakes

¼ teaspoon ground black pepper

2 tablespoons chopped fresh mint, plus more to garnish

2 tablespoons chopped mild Peppadew peppers

This easy, whipped feta cheese spread is based on the traditional Greek dip, htipiti (pronounced h'tee-pee-tee). There are many variations, some as simple as feta, red pepper flakes and extra-virgin olive oil, others with herbs and roasted red peppers. We shifted to Peppadew peppers, which added a sweet-tart kick to balance the creaminess of the cheese. A brief soak in water removed some of the salt from the cheese and made it easier to control the dish's seasoning. Raw garlic tasted harsh and bitter; infusing lemon juice with a smashed clove provided gentler flavor. Processing the feta and cream cheese before adding the remaining ingredients was the key to a light, whipped texture. To increase the heat, use cayenne pepper or hot Peppadews, or add more red pepper flakes. The whipped feta can be refrigerated for up to a week. This makes the perfect dip for crudités or pita points, or use as garnish on pasta or grilled meats and vegetables. It's terrific as a sandwich spread, too, especially when topped with sautéed greens—spinach, kale or chard—and a fried egg. Try serving it alongside lamb chops or even slices of seared steak.

Don't use pre-crumbled feta. It can be dry and chalky. Look for block feta packed in brine, ideally made with sheep's or goat's milk.

1. **In a medium bowl,** cover the feta with fresh tap water and let sit for 10 minutes. In a small bowl, combine the lemon juice and garlic and let sit for 10 minutes. Discard the garlic clove. Drain the feta and pat dry, then crumble.

2. **In a food processor,** combine the feta and cream cheese. Process until smooth, about 30 seconds. Add the oil, lemon juice, paprika, pepper flakes and black pepper. Process until well mixed, about 30 seconds. Scrape the bowl, add the mint and Peppadews, then pulse until combined.

3. **Taste and season** with pepper flakes and black pepper. Refrigerate for at least 30 minutes before serving. Garnish with mint.

Fruit Chutney

Start to finish: 25 minutes, plus cooling
Makes about 2½ cups

---

1 large red onion, diced
(about 1½ cups)

2 tablespoons salted butter

1 tablespoon grapeseed
or other neutral oil

Kosher salt

2 teaspoons coriander
seeds, crushed

1 teaspoon yellow mustard
seeds, crushed

2 Granny Smith apples,
peeled, cored and chopped

¼ cup white sugar

⅓ cup dried apricots, diced

⅓ cup dried cherries,
roughly chopped

⅓ cup dried currants

⅓ cup cider vinegar

⅓ cup water

In India, chutney, or chatni, refers to a variety of sauces made from numerous ingredients. Elsewhere in the world, it is considered mostly a sweet-savory jam-like condiment. In our version—which was inspired by a chutney by London baker Claire Ptak—red onion lent a slight, pleasant bite. A combination of salted butter and neutral oil worked best for sauteing. Sulfured and unsulfured dried apricots fared equally well in this recipe. The cooled chutney can be refrigerated for up to two weeks. Our favorite way to use this chutney was in a gooey grilled cheese (see sidebar), but it also is great as a topping for grilled pork chops, in a turkey sandwich or simply as a component on a cheese board.

Don't grind the mustard and coriander seeds. Crush them with a mortar and pestle, or use the side of a wide chef's knife to crush them against the cutting board.

In a medium saucepan over medium, combine the onion, butter, oil and ⅛ teaspoon salt. Cook, stirring occasionally, until the onion is softened, 9 to 11 minutes. Add the coriander and mustard seeds and cook for 1 minute. Stir in the apples, sugar and ¼ teaspoon salt. Cook until the sugar is dissolved, about 1 minute. Add the apricots, cherries, currants, vinegar and water, then stir to combine. Bring to a simmer and cook until the chutney is thickened but the apples still hold their shape, 10 to 12 minutes. Remove from the heat and cool.

GRILLED CHEESE WITH FRUIT CHUTNEY

Start to finish: 10 minutes
Makes 1 sandwich

Homemade chutney is the highlight of this sandwich, but if you use store-bought, look for Stonewall Kitchen Apple Cranberry Chutney or another high-quality variety with a thick texture. This recipe is easily doubled using a 12-inch skillet.

3 to 4 tablespoons chutney

Two ½-inch-thick slices
sourdough or seeded rye bread

2 to 3 ounces Gruyere, Comte, Gouda
or raclette cheese, thinly sliced

1 tablespoon salted butter, softened

Kosher salt

1. Evenly spread the chutney over 1 slice of bread, then top with the cheese in an even layer, followed by the second slice of bread. Spread half the butter over the top of the sandwich, then sprinkle with a pinch of salt.

2. Heat a 10-inch stainless steel or cast-iron skillet over medium-high for 2 minutes. Reduce heat to low and add the sandwich, buttered side down. Spread the remaining butter over the top of the sandwich, then cover the pan and cook until the bottom is golden brown, 3 to 5 minutes.

3. Flip the sandwich and cook, covered, until the second side is golden brown and the cheese is melted, 2 to 3 minutes. If the bread toasts faster than the cheese melts, remove from the heat and let sit, covered, for 1 to 2 minutes, or until the cheese is fully melted.

Fruit Compotes

Compote is French for "mixture" and generally refers to fruit that's been slowly stewed in syrup long enough to soften, but not lose its shape. Unlike preserves and conserves, it's usually made fresh for consumption with a particular meal. Just what that meal should be is up to you. Our fruit compotes play well with yogurt, oatmeal and granola in the morning, but also can help elevate a bowl of ice cream or slice of pound cake later in the afternoon. These compotes are perfect served over cakes—we particularly like the blueberry-lavender with our lemon-buttermilk pound cake (p. 492) and ricotta cheesecake (p. 519).

SPICED APRICOT COMPOTE

Start to finish: 15 minutes, plus cooling / Makes about 2 cups

We liked the texture and tartness pomegranate seeds gave this compote, but they can be omitted. Both sulfured and unsulfured apricots worked.

12 ounces dried apricots (about 2 cups), roughly chopped

1¼ cups water

2 tablespoons packed light brown sugar

Two 3½-inch cinnamon sticks

2 star anise pods

Two 3-inch strips lemon zest, plus ½ teaspoon lemon juice

Pinch of kosher salt

⅓ cup pomegranate seeds

In a medium saucepan over medium-high, combine the apricots, water, sugar, cinnamon, star anise, lemon zest and salt, then bring to a boil. Reduce to medium-low and simmer, stirring occasionally, until the apricots are plump and softened, and the liquid is thick and syrupy, 10 to 12 minutes. Off heat, stir in the lemon juice and pomegranate seeds. Discard the cinnamon sticks, star anise and zest. Cool to room temperature.

BLUEBERRY-LAVENDER COMPOTE

Start to finish: 10 minutes, plus cooling / Makes about 2 cups

Frozen blueberries can be substituted for fresh, but be sure to thaw and drain them first.

15 ounces blueberries (about 3 cups)

54 grams (¼ cup) white sugar

Two 2-inch strips lemon zest, plus ¼ teaspoon lemon juice

¼ teaspoon dried lavender

Pinch of kosher salt

In a medium saucepan, use a potato masher or fork to mash half of the berries. Stir in the sugar, lemon zest, lavender and salt. Bring to a boil over medium-high, stirring frequently. Add the remaining blueberries and return to a boil. Reduce heat to medium-low and simmer, stirring occasionally, until the juices thicken and most of the berries have popped, 6 to 8 minutes. Off heat, stir in the lemon juice. Discard the zest. Cool to room temperature.

APPLE-PEAR COMPOTE

Start to finish: 25 minutes, plus cooling / Makes about 2 cups

Gala, Golden Delicious, Cortland or Jonagold apples all worked well; Bartlett and Anjou pears were our favorite. Calvados or apple brandy also was delicious in place of the bourbon. To make it easier to fish out the cloves at the end, stick them through the lemon zest before adding them to the pan.

2 apples (12 to 16 ounces), peeled, cored and cut into ½-inch chunks

2 firm, ripe pears (12 to 16 ounces), peeled, cored and cut into ½-inch chunks

½ cup bourbon

109 grams (½ cup) packed light brown sugar

Two 3-inch strips lemon zest, plus 1 teaspoon lemon juice

5 whole cloves

Pinch of kosher salt

In a medium saucepan over medium-high, combine all ingredients but the lemon juice, then bring to a boil. Reduce to medium-low, cover and cook, stirring occasionally, until the fruit is soft but still intact, about 15 minutes. Uncover, increase heat to medium-high and cook until the liquid is thick and syrupy, 5 to 7 minutes. Off heat, stir in the lemon juice. Discard the zest and cloves. Cool to room temperature.

Drinks

16

Chili-Pineapple Margarita

Start to finish: **1 hour 30 minutes** (20 minutes active)
Servings: **2**

The smooth, round flavor of reposado tequila worked best with the chilies in this cocktail.

---

1. In a small saucepan, combine 1 cup of the sugar, the water, both zests and both chilies. Bring the mixture to a boil, stirring occasionally, then remove from the heat and steep for 15 minutes. Strain into a jar, discarding the solids. Let cool.

2. While the syrup cools, in a small bowl, stir together the salt, chili powder and the remaining 1½ teaspoons of sugar. Spread the mixture on a small plate. Use the orange wedge to moisten the rims of 2 rocks glasses, then dip in the chili salt, turning to coat.

3. In a cocktail shaker, combine the tequila, pineapple juice, lime juice and 1½ ounces (3 tablespoons) of the chili syrup. Add 2 cups of ice and shake vigorously until chilled, 10 to 15 seconds. Strain into the prepared glasses.

1 cup plus 1½ teaspoons white sugar, divided

1 cup water

Four 1-inch strips lime zest

Four 1-inch strips orange zest, plus 1 orange wedge

1 jalapeño chili, halved

1 habanero chili, halved

1 tablespoon kosher salt

¾ teaspoon chili powder

4 ounces (½ cup) reposado tequila

2 ounces (¼ cup) pineapple juice

1½ ounces (3 tablespoons) lime juice (1 to 2 limes)

Pisco Sour

Start to finish: **5 minutes** / Servings: **2**

This Peruvian staple is traditionally made with lime juice, but we preferred a brighter blend of lemon and lime. "Dry shaking" the cocktail with one ice cube helps create the sour's signature foam.

In a cocktail shaker, combine the pisco, egg white, both juices and the syrup. Add 1 ice cube and shake vigorously for 15 seconds. Fill the shaker with ice, then shake vigorously for 15 seconds. Strain into chilled glasses and sprinkle 3 to 4 dashes of bitters over each.

3½ ounces pisco

1 egg white

½ ounce lemon juice

½ ounce lime juice

½ ounce simple syrup

Angostura bitters

Singapore Sling

Start to finish: **5 minutes** / Servings **1**

At Smoke & Mirrors bar in Singapore, this lightly fruity update to the original Singapore sling is topped with pineapple juice bubbles. We found a strip of orange zest was similarly tropical and more practical.

In a cocktail shaker, combine the rye, orange juice, cassis, simple syrup and bitters. Add 1 cup ice, then shake for 15 to 20 seconds, or until the sides of the shaker are quite cold. Strain into a chilled coupe glass. Top with a splash of prosecco and the orange zest.

1½ ounces rye whiskey

¾ ounce orange juice

⅓ ounce cassis liqueur

⅓ ounce simple syrup

3 dashes angostura bitters

Prosecco

2-inch strip orange zest

French 75

Start to finish: **5 minutes** / Servings: **1**

A half-teaspoon of a saltwater solution—and Angostura bitters—give exceptional balance to this slight tweak on the classic French 75. We liked the clean flavors that resulted from almost-equal proportions of gin and sparkling wine. To prepare the saltwater solution, combine ¼ teaspoon Morton kosher salt and 6 tablespoons plus 1 teaspoon water.

In a cocktail shaker, combine the lemon juice, simple syrup, saltwater solution, gin and bitters. Fill the shaker with ice, then shake vigorously for 15 seconds. Pour into a coupe or flute glass and top with the sparkling wine.

¾ ounce lemon juice

¾ ounce simple syrup

½ teaspoon 4-percent saltwater solution (see headnote)

1½ ounces gin

2 dashes Angostura bitters

2 ounces sparkling wine

Vieux Carré

Start to finish: **5 minutes** / Servings: 1

---

1 ounce cognac

1 ounce rye

1 ounce sweet vermouth

¾ ounce Bénédictine

Dash Angostura bitters

Dash orange bitters

Ice cubes

This New Orleans' classic straddles the delicious space between an Old Fashioned and a Manhattan: rich and bold, yet not heavy. Typically, this drink is made with a combination of Angostura and Peychaud's Bitters, the latter of which adds anise-minty notes. That's a delicious choice, but we've come to favor the brightness orange bitters add.

In a stirring glass, combine the cognac, rye, vermouth, Bénédictine and both bitters. Stir with ice cubes. Strain into a coupe.

Tequila at High Noon

Start to finish: **5 minutes** / Servings: 2

For our take on the classic tequila sunrise, we substituted the mildly bittersweet Italian spirit Aperol for the typical (and often too sweet) grenadine. And we loved the way a dose of chocolate bitters—½ teaspoon's worth—complemented the orange juice.

In a cocktail shaker, combine all ingredients. Fill the shaker with ice, then shake vigorously for 15 seconds. Strain into chilled rocks glasses.

4 ounces tequila blanco

4 ounces orange juice

1 ounce lemon juice

1 ounce Aperol

½ teaspoon chocolate bitters

Lemon Grass Martini

Start to finish: **5 minutes** / Servings: **1**

This classic vodka martini—inspired by a similar cocktail served at Bully Boy Distillers in Boston—gets gentle layers of herbal, lemony flavor from lemon grass-infused vodka. When infusing, we prefer mid-shelf vodkas—nothing so cheap as to be harsh, but nothing so pricey that we mind flavoring it.

1. To make the infusion, trim 2 stalks of lemon grass to 8 inches each (about 55 grams), peeling away any dry outer layers. Cut each stalk into 3 or 4 pieces, then combine with 1 cup vodka in a blender. Pulse for 3 to 5 seconds, just long enough to roughly chop the lemon grass. Let sit for 5 minutes, then pour through a mesh strainer, pressing on the solids. The infusion makes 1 cup of vodka, enough for 4 cocktails. Extra can be refrigerated indefinitely; stir before using.

2. In a large glass, combine the vodka and vermouth. Add the ice, then stir for about 15 seconds, or just until the sides of the glass feel chilled. Strain into a cocktail glass. Gently squeeze the lemon zest, then rub it around the rim of the glass before dropping it in.

2 ounces lemon grass-
infused vodka

½ ounce dry vermouth

1 cup ice

2-inch strip lemon zest

Batch-Muddled Mojitos

Start to finish: **10 minutes** / Servings: **8**

A stand mixer makes muddling mojitos for a crowd a breeze. The syrup and rum can be combined, covered and refrigerated for up to 24 hours; any longer than that and the flavors mellow too much. We especially enjoy the slight salinity of San Pellegrino with these mojitos, but any carbonated water works. If you prefer to mix individual servings, don't combine the rum and syrup. Instead, fill highball glasses with ice, pour 1½ ounces syrup and 2 ounces rum into each, stir, then top with carbonated water, if using.

Don't forget to wash the limes *to remove any wax or residue that may be on them. Warm water works best.*

1. **In a stand mixer** with the paddle attachment, mix the limes, mint, sugar and salt on low until the limes release their juice, the mixture is fragrant and a syrup has formed, 1 to 1½ minutes.

2. **Strain the syrup** into a medium bowl, pressing on the solids to extract as much liquid as possible, then discard the solids. Transfer the syrup to a pitcher and stir in the rum.

3. **Fill 8 highball glasses with ice,** then pour in the cocktail, dividing it evenly. Top each with carbonated water, to taste, then garnish with a mint sprig.

7 limes, roughly chopped

4 cups lightly packed fresh mint, plus sprigs to garnish

¾ cup white sugar

Pinch of kosher salt

16 ounces white rum

Ice, to serve

Carbonated water, to serve

Index

maple-whole wheat muffins with, 544

Mexican corn cake with, 551

pineapple upside-down cake with, 528–29

polenta of, 168, 172

semolina-sesame cake with, 548

cornstarch

Japanese fried chicken with, 257

Sichuan-chili chicken with, 270

couscous

with chicken and chickpeas, 303

herb-and-pistachio, 176

North African chicken and, 262–63

"risotto," 210–11

toasted pearl, 208, 209

cranberries

buckle with ginger and, 539

Persian herb omelet with, 17

Persian jeweled rice with, 169

cream

biscuits with, 606

bread pudding with, 509

brown sugar tart with, 479

caramel chocolate mousse with, 485

chocolate-hazelnut cake with, 570–71

corn pudding with, 540

lemon tart with, 481

maple-browned butter pie with, 526

mashed potatoes with, 111

Parmesan besciamella with, 202, 203

pasta with, 200, 217

pizza with fontina-Parmesan, 438, 439

quiche with, 6–7

sweet potato gratin with, 134

whipped, 483, 573, 607

yogurt panna cotta with, 543

See also sour cream

cream cheese

caramel frosting with, 576–77

chèvre cheesecake with, 562

whipped feta with, 642

crème fraîche

chèvre cheesecake with, 562

chicken with garlic-herb, 316–17

pastel azteca casserole with, 314

quiche with, 6

tarts with, 482, 502

See also sour cream

Crisponi, Luigi, 97

crostata, chocolate-hazelnut, 494

cucumbers

fattoush with, 22

German salad with, 36

Japanese potato salad with, 21

Persian salad with, 33

quick-pickled, 238, 239

salad of smashed, 49

Sichuan chicken salad with, 25

tzatziki (dip) with, 374–75, 622

cumin

chickpea and harissa soup with, 64

lomo saltado with, 397

Mexican chicken soup with, 67

potatoes with, 117

stir-fried beef with, 393

currants

couscous with, 176

fruit chutney with, 644

kale and cheese scones with, 454

Venetian cornmeal cookies with, 609

curry

Cape Malay chicken, 267

cauliflower with, 615

chicken vindaloo, 311

eggs braised with, 10

fish braised with, 243

Japanese chicken and vegetable, 312–13

potato and green pea, 106

Vietnamese chicken, 307

D

da Scalo, Nunzia, 207

dates

quinoa pilaf with, 171

semolina cookies with, 598–99

toffee pudding with, 486

Day, Cheryl, 576, 578, 580

Day, Griffith, 576, 578, 580

Delling-Williams, Edward, 506

De Waal, Nimco, 68

dill

chicken roasted with, 316–17

Egyptian eggplant with, 116

garlic-and-herb oil with, 638

Georgian chicken soup with, 54

German cucumber salad with, 36

Middle Eastern rice with, 165

Persian herb omelet with, 17

salmon with, 238, 247

Turkish tomato and onion salad with, 39

di Noto, Guiseppe, 220

di Noto, Piera, 220

dip and dipping sauces

chili-lime, 254, 255

garlic-and-herb oil, 638

for Japanese fried chicken, 257

muhammara, 627

spicy feta, 623

spicy harissa, 619

tamarind, 613

tzatziki, 374–75, 622

whipped feta, 642

yogurt-harissa, 619

doro wat (chicken stew), 95

dressings

ginger-soy, 252

green goddess tofu, 641

herbed (savory), 328

lemon, 23

miso-ginger, 626

spiced yogurt, 639

sweet-and-sour mint, 614–15

See also vinaigrettes

drinks. See cocktails

duck, borsch with, 90–91

Duguid, Naomi, 329

dukkah (nut-and-seed seasoning), 132, 133

dumplings, soup with passatelli, 82–83

Dunlop, Fuchsia, 104, 226

E

eetch (bulgur-tomato salad), 164

eggplant
    chicken and rice with, 296
    with chilies and cilantro, 615
    Spanish ratatouille with, 110
    spicy Egyptian, 116
eggs
    caramel chocolate mousse with, 485
    cheesecakes with, 519, 562
    chickpea and harissa soup with, 64
    Chinese stir-fried, 15
    chocolate cakes with, 473, 491, 530
    chocolate tart with, 480
    Colombian avocado salsa with, 621
    corn pudding with, 540
    curry braised, 10
    fluffy olive oil scrambled, 3
    French almond-rum cake with, 532
    French toast with, 484
    garlic and cilantro soup with, 89
    lemon tart with, 481
    maple-browned butter pie with, 526
    Mexican meatballs stuffed with, 412
    passatelli in brodo with, 82
    Persian herb omelet of, 17
    pork loin stuffed with, 352, 355
    Portuguese sponge cake with, 575
    potato salads with, 21, 31
    pound cakes with, 492, 514
    quiche with, 6–9
    soba noodles with, 183
    soft-cooked, 89, 341
    spaghetti carbonara with, 229
    Spanish almond cake with, 525
    Spanish-style, 13
    sunny-side up fried, 3
    Thai braised pork with, 358–59
    Thai fried rice with, 160
    toffee pudding with, 486
    Turkish scrambled, 5
egg whites
    chocolate cookies with, 585, 589
    peanut and caramel tart with, 506
    ricotta-semolina cake with, 558
egg yolks

brown sugar tart with, 479
    Georgian chicken soup with, 54
    Spanish garlic soup with, 55
enchiladas verdes (green enchiladas), 286
Erdäpfelsalat (Austrian potato salad), 31
escabeche (pickled vegetables), 636

F

fasolada (white bean soup), 76
fatteh (pita and chickpea salad), 27
fattoush (pita bread salad), 22
fennel (bulb)
    mussels with, 245
    porchetta with, 342, 343
    Provençal braised chicken with, 321
    quiche with, 8
    Roman braised beef with, 414
    salads with, 48, 414, 415
fennel (seeds)
    broccoli rabe with, 615
    cracked potatoes with, 105
    porchetta with, 342–43
    pork roasted with, 368
    shrimp with feta cheese and, 236
    Venetian rice and peas with, 175
Fernandez, Diego, 35
Ferruzza, Piera, 193
feta cheese
    cauliflower with, 129
    flatbreads filled with, 462
    Greek white bean soup with, 76
    shrimp with, 236
    tomato rice with, 170
    Turkish scrambled eggs with, 5
    whipped, 642
figs
    braised beef with, 429
    tapenade with, 640
fish
    curry-coconut braised white, 243
    ginger-scallion steamed cod, 235
    See also anchovies; salmon
fish sauce
    beef salads with, 394, 409

pickled chilies with, 612
    Thai fried rice with, 160
    Thai-style coleslaw with, 41
    turkey basted with, 326
    Vietnamese chicken curry with, 307
    Vietnamese scallion sauce with, 628
flatbreads, 446–47
    focaccia, 450–51, 466–67
    Italian, 434
    lahmajoun, 452–53
    pork, green olive, and feta, 462
    prosciutto, arugula, and ricotta, 435
    spiced beef, 435, 449
    spinach and cheese, 463
    Taiwanese scallion pancakes, 442–43
    Turkish, 460–61
    yogurt and olive oil, 374, 377
    za'atar, 448, 458–59
    See also pizza; tortillas
Fleming, Claudia, 594
flour
    bread, 440
    corn, 441
    spelt, 488
    See also almond flour; cornmeal;
        rye flour; semolina flour
focaccia
    potato-and-herb, 466–67
    tomato-olive, 450–51
foil-parchment packet, 382, 384–85
Franklin, Peter, 304
French 75, 653
French toast, sherry-soaked, 484
frosting
    chocolate, 580–81
    cream cheese–caramel, 576–77
Fuensanta, Doña, 146

G

gai yang (Chiang Mai chicken), 254
garam masala (seasoning), 10, 154
García, Eduardo, XVI, 150
garides saganaki (shrimp with feta
    cheese), 236

garlic
- Brussels sprouts with, 109
- carnitas with, 346
- cauliflower with, 113
- chicken roasted with, 316–17
- chicken traybake with, 279
- chicken vindaloo with, 311
- chimichurri with, 352
- Colima-style pork with, 372
- Cuban-style pork with, 382
- Filipino chicken adobo with, 285
- Georgian chicken soup with, 54
- harissa with, 618
- lamb and chickpeas stew with, 57
- lemon-saffron chicken with, 289
- lentil salad with, 145
- Madeiran pork with, 381
- Oaxacan refried beans with, 146
- porchetta with, 342
- pork in Veracruz sauce with, 371
- soup with cilantro, chickpeas, and, 89
- spaghetti with, 215, 220
- Spanish soup with, 55
- Spanish-style eggs with, 13
- spicy oil with herbs and, 434, 638
- Taiwanese five-spice pork with, 341
- Thai rice soup with, 62
- three-cup chicken with, 258
- Tuscan beef stew with, 402
- za'atar-roasted chicken with, 260
- *See also* chili-garlic sauce

gâteau Nantais (French almond-rum cake), 532–33

Gesualdi, Doriana, 195

ghee
- Ethiopian chicken stew with, 95
- Ethiopian collard greens with, 125
- pork schnitzel with, 378

gianduja (chocolate-hazelnut paste), 494

gin, French 75 cocktail with, 653

ginger
- buckle with cranberries and, 539
- carrots pickled with, 361
- cod steamed with, 235

- Colima-style pork with, 372
- dressings with, 252, 626
- Ethiopian collard greens with, 125
- French spice bread with, 552
- green beans with, 108
- jalapeño-mint sauce with, 633
- Japanese fried chicken with, 257
- rice with coconut and, 163
- scones with triple, 591
- Swedish gingersnaps with, 595
- Swiss chard with, 104
- Thai rice soup with, 62
- Vietnamese scallion sauce with, 628
- yakiudon with pickled, 188, 189

Glasse, Hannah, 492

gnocchi, potato, 198–99

gochujang (Korean chili paste)
- pork and kimchi stew with, 101
- pulled pork with, 360
- sour cream with, 361

Goldstein, Darra, 54

Gollini, Eugenio, 561

gomen wat (stewed collard greens), 125

Gonzàlez, Paola Briseño, 372, 426, 556, 630

gozleme (stuffed flatbread), 460
- spinach and cheese, 463

graham crackers, cheesecake with, 562–63

grapes, fattoush with pickled, 22

greens
- Ethiopian stewed collard, 125
- Eventide salad with spring, 28
- fattoush with romaine, 22
- salad of bitter, 29
- *See also* arugula; kale; spinach; Swiss chard; watercress

guacamole, Central Mexican, 617

Gurkensalat (cucumber-dill salad), 36

Gutenbrunner, Kurt, 407

Guzmán, Gonzalo, 81

H

halvah (fudge-like candy), 593

ham, Japanese potato salad with, 21

Hanna, Yousef (Zuzu), 458

harissa (condiment), 618–19
- chicken couscous with, 262–63
- chickpea soup with, 64
- Egyptian eggplant with, 116
- potatoes roasted with, 135

Hazan, Marcella, 182

hazelnuts
- chocolate cake with, 570–71
- crostata with, 494
- salads with, 23, 48

herbs. *See* specific herb

Hercules, Olia, 90, 316, 368, 558

Holt, Briana, 454, 488, 526, 528, 544, 546, 591

hominy
- Mexican chicken soup with, 67
- pozole rojo (stew) with, 81

honey
- chèvre cheesecake with, 562
- chocolate cake with syrup of, 546–47
- dressings with, 614, 626
- French spice bread with, 552
- French walnut tart with, 502
- Ikarian braised pork with, 367
- maple-browned butter pie with, 526
- pork tenderloin bites with, 337
- sauce with chilies and, 632
- semolina-sesame cake with, 548
- Senegalese pudding with, 497
- whipped cream with, 483

horseradish
- mashed potatoes with, 111
- salad with, 48
- sauce of fresh, 390, 391

hot sauce
- cauliflower with, 123
- chili and tomatillo, 286, 348, 349
- Somali chicken soup with, 68
- *See also* chilies; harissa

Howard, Vivian, 540

hummus
- with black beans and salsa, 152–53
- Israeli, with beef topping, 138–39

pork in Veracruz sauce with, 371

pork loin stuffed with, 352, 355

shrimp with feta cheese and, 236

spaghetti puttanesca with, 216

tapenade with and, 640

onions

Cape Malay chicken curry with, 267

Central Mexican guacamole with, 617

chicken couscous with, 262–63

chicken traybake with, 279

Croatian mashed potatoes with, 119

Ethiopian chicken stew with, 95

fruit chutney with, 644

Georgian chicken soup with, 54

Lebanese lentils and rice with, 143

lomo saltado with, 397

Mexican stewed beans with, 150

Persian jeweled rice with, 169

Peruvian pesto with, 185

pickled red, 43, 319, 346, 347, 348, 620, 636

Punjabi chickpeas with, 154

salad with tomatoes and, 374–75

Senegalese braised chicken with, 277

sumac-spiced chicken with, 259

Turkish salad with, 39

See also scallions; shallots

orange

beef stew with, 410

bête noire with, 530

braised beef and, 429

bread pudding with, 509

caramelized pork with, 365

caramel oranges, 470–71

cocktails with, 650, 652, 654–55

cornmeal cookies with, 609

Cuban-style pork with, 382

French toast with, 484

Ikarian braised pork with, 367

phyllo cake with, 554–55

pistachio-cardamom cake with, 505

Provençal braised chicken with, 321

pulled chicken with, 288

tarts with, 481, 512–13

toffee pudding with, 486

vinaigrette with, 121

whipped cream with, 483

yogurt loaf cake with, 565

oregano

chicken tinga with Mexican, 298

chimichurri with, 352, 419

porchetta with, 342

pork tenderloin with, 364

tomato rice with, 170

za'atar-roasted chicken with, 260

Oropeza, Olga Cabrera, 293

Orr, Peter, 198

Ottolenghi, Yotam, 23, 40, 176, 201

ouzo

shrimp, orzo, and zucchini with, 240

tomato rice with, 170

Oxaal, Stephen, 47

P

Packer, Sarit, 567

paella, chicken and bean, 294–95

pain d'épices (spice bread), 552

panade technique, 388

pancakes, Taiwanese scallion, 442–43

pancetta

pasta with zucchini, saffron, and, 200

porchetta with, 342

ragù Bolognese with, 205

Roman braised beef with, 414

salad with vinaigrette of, 29

Sardinian herb soup with, 97

spaghetti with, 191, 228, 229

Thai fried rice with, 160

Venetian rice and peas with, 175

Panizza, Roberto, 196

panna cotta, yogurt, 543

pão de ló (sponge cake), 575

paprika

Austrian beef stew with, 407

berbere seasoning with, 95

bucatini with, 201

Cuban-style pork with, 382

cumin-coriander potatoes with, 117

feta dip with, 623

piri piri chicken with, 264

pork tenderloin with, 337, 364

red chimichurri with, 419

shrimp and chickpea stew with, 98

Spanish garlic soup with, 55

Parmeggiani, Paolo, XV, 82

Parmesan cheese

bitter green salad with, 29

cauliflower steaks with, 127

focaccia with, 466

garlic and cilantro soup with, 89

Italian bean soup with, 87

lasagna Bolognese with, 202, 203

passatelli in brodo with, 82

pasta with, 200, 217

pizza sauce with fontina and, 438, 439

pork cutlets with, 362

risotto with, 166, 210

skirt steak salad with, 431

spaghetti with, 216, 219, 221

vegetable broth with, 167

Venetian rice and peas with, 175

zucchini and herb salad with, 23

parsley

cauliflower with, 113

chermoula sauce with, 249

chicken roasted with, 316–17

chimichurri with, 352

couscous with, 176, 210, 303

flatbread topping with, 435

French carrot salad with, 50

garlic-and-herb oil with, 638

green goddess dressing with, 641

herbed dressing with, 328

Middle Eastern rice with, 165

panzanella with, 43

pea and sweet potato stew with, 70

Persian herb omelet with, 17

pork in Veracruz sauce with, 371

risotto with, 166

salad of lemon and, 324–25

Sardinian herb soup with, 97

Senegalese salad with, 26

The following recipes were added to Milk Street Television Season 5 episodes after this cookbook was printed. These recipes can be accessed at
177milkstreet.com/season5recipes

Tahini Toffee Pudding
Za'atar Schnitzel

ACKNOWLEDGMENTS

Milk Street is aptly named for its address, 177 Milk Street in Boston. But we also are a group of people who work all over the world, from Australia to Los Angeles, from San Francisco to Barcelona. This global community of like-minded cooks, editors and designers has brought you the book that you are holding in your hands and they deserve a kindly mention.

In particular, I want to acknowledge J.M. Hirsch, our tireless editorial director, Matthew Card, food editor, Michelle Locke, books editor, Dawn Yanagihara, recipe editor, Bianca Borges, contributing food editor, and Shaula Clark, managing editor, for leading the charge on conceiving, developing and editing all of this. Also, Jennifer Baldino Cox, our art director, and the entire design team who deftly captured the look, feel and energy of the recipes. Special thanks to Brianna Coleman, art director of photography, Connie Miller, photographer, Christine Tobin, stylist, and Gary Tooth, designer.

Our team of production cooks who have been showing up at Milk Street for most of the last year did yeoman's work including Diane Unger, Courtney Hill, Rebecca Richmond, Calvin Cox, Rose Hattabaugh and Elizabeth Mindreau. Deborah Broide, Milk Street director of media relations, has done a spectacular job of sharing with the world all we do at Milk Street. Wes Martin, who runs our kitchen, deserves a special mention; he shopped and personally delivered ingredients to our cooks who were safe at home during the height of the pandemic.

We also have a couple of folks to thank who work outside of 177 Milk Street. Michael Szczerban, editor, and everyone at Little, Brown and Company have been superb and inspired partners in this project. And my long-standing book agent, David Black, has been instrumental in bringing this project to life both with his knowledge of publishing and his friendship and support. Thank you, David!

Finally, a sincere thank you to my business partner and wife, Melissa, who manages our media department, from television to radio. Melissa has nurtured the Milk Street brand from the beginning so that we ended up where we thought we were going in the first place.

And, last but not least, to all of you who have supported the Milk Street project. Each and every one of you has a seat at the Milk Street table.

Christopher Kimball

Christopher Kimball is founder of Christopher Kimball's Milk Street, a food media company dedicated to learning and sharing bold, easy cooking from around the world. It produces the bimonthly *Christopher Kimball's Milk Street Magazine*, as well as *Christopher Kimball's Milk Street Radio*, a weekly public radio show and podcast heard on more than 220 stations nationwide, and the public television show *Christopher Kimball's Milk Street*. He founded *Cook's Magazine* in 1980 and served as publisher and editorial director through 1989. He re-launched it as *Cook's Illustrated* in 1993. Through 2016, Kimball was host and executive producer of *America's Test Kitchen* and *Cook's Country*. He also hosted *America's Test Kitchen* radio show on public radio. Kimball is the author of several books, including *Fannie's Last Supper*.

Christopher Kimball's Milk Street is changing how we cook by searching the world for bold, simple recipes and techniques. Adapted and tested for home cooks everywhere, these lessons are the backbone of what we call the new home cooking. We are located at 177 Milk Street in downtown Boston, site of our editorial offices and cooking school. It also is where we record *Christopher Kimball's Milk Street* television and radio shows and is home to our online store, which curates craft food and cookware products from around the world. Visit 177milkstreet.com to shop and for more information.